THE WAR OF THE REVOLUTION

THE MACMILLAN COMPANY
NEW YORK · CHICAGO
DALLAS · ATLANTA · SAN FRANCISCO
LONDON · MANILA
In Canada
BRETT-MACMILLAN LTD.
GALT, ONTARIO

THE WAR OF
THE REVOLUTION

By *CHRISTOPHER WARD*

Edited by *JOHN RICHARD ALDEN*

IN TWO VOLUMES

VOLUME ONE

THE MACMILLAN COMPANY : NEW YORK

1952

The maps on pages 217, 299, 345, 367, 583, 601, 607, 727, 759, 789, 805, 819, and 829 also appear in *The Delaware Continentals, 1776–1783*, by Christopher L. Ward, copyright, 1941, by the Historical Society of Delaware.

Editor's Preface

The origins of *The War of the Revolution* are to be found in part in the late Mr. Ward's studies of the history of the Delaware Line. His volume on *The Delaware Continentals, 1776–1783*, published in 1941, contains much more than the story of one of the best units in the Continental army. Approximately one half of Mr. Ward's last work is to be found in his earlier monograph, which was put forth in a limited edition and which deserved a much wider circulation. This material, which deals with land operations in the middle and southern states after 1776, was revised by the author. To it Mr. Ward added about forty new chapters on the campaign of 1775; operations in New England, northern New York, and Canada; border conflicts; and the Yorktown campaign.

The author intended to write a history of the campaigns on land rather than a complete history of the war. He largely accomplished his purpose, although his manuscript, as submitted to the editor, contained no account of the war beyond the Alleghenies. The editor has supplied a brief description of that portion of the conflict in one chapter, emphasizing the role of George Rogers Clark.

A few words about the labors of the editor. *The War of the Revolution*, with the exception of the chapter mentioned in the preceding paragraph, has been little altered by the editor. Additions to the citations and bibliography have been inserted in order to present a few of the more important scholarly contributions concerning the War of Independence not available to the author. Some obvious errors in the text which Mr. Ward would surely have removed had they been brought to his attention have been corrected.

In so large a work, other mistakes undoubtedly remain, despite the efforts of both author and editor. The editor has also tried to perform the last minute tasks of completing citations and bibliographical entries, and similar duties. *The War of the Revolution* remains, however, the work of Mr. Ward in point of view, interpretation, emphasis, and all fundamental matters.

Relying largely upon more or less standard secondary authorities and printed source material, the author has written a detailed and accurate account of the military operations on land of the War of Independence. He has contributed a most useful work of reference. He has also added to the great store of splendid writing upon the Revolutionary period. His account of the day of Lexington and Concord thrilled even an editor who was not unfamiliar with the events of April 19, 1775.

It is not possible for the editor to express the gratitude of the author to all the persons who assisted him. Mr. Kenneth Roberts and Mr. Carl Van Doren gave him helpful advice. The editor must declare his appreciation of services performed by three assistant instructors attached to the Department of History of the University of Nebraska, Miss Lois Christensen, Mr. Carl Bader, Jr., and Mr. Philip Holmgren. Dr. John Powell, Professor G. W. Gray, and Mr. Rodman Ward gave him advice, encouragement, and help in various ways.

JOHN RICHARD ALDEN

Preface

This book is not a history of the American Revolution. It is a history of the war that was caused by the Revolution. As John Adams well said: "A history of the first war of the United States is a very different thing from a history of the American Revolution. . . . The revolution was in the minds of the people and in the union of the colonies, both of which were accomplished before hostilities commenced. This revolution and union were gradually forming from the years 1760 to 1776."

With the Revolution as thus properly described, this book is not concerned, except in the brief résumé of the causes of the war in the first chapter. Its aim is to tell the story of the war on land, the campaigns, battles, sieges, marches, encampments, bivouacs, the strategy and tactics, the hardships, and the endurance of hardship. It is purely military in its intention and scope.

The war, from the first shot at Lexington in 1775 to the cessation of hostilities in 1782, lasted nearly eight years. It was fought in a territory extending from Quebec southward to Georgia and from the Atlantic seaboard westward to the frontier settlements. Many of its campaigns, in the various regions in which they were fought, were simultaneous.

In the spring of 1776, while the American army under Arnold was still struggling to keep a foothold in Canada, a British army under Henry Clinton was on its way south to attack Charleston in South Carolina. On September 11, 1777, while Washington was fighting the Battle of the Brandywine, Burgoyne was on his way down the Hudson to Saratoga.

It will be seen, then, that an attempt to tell the tale of the various campaigns and battles in strict chronological order would involve leaping, chapter by chapter, from one campaign to another, from the North to the South and from the East to the West, and would result in hopeless confusion. Fortunately for the sake of clarity in this chronicle, the whole territory involved was fought over, by different armies, in well defined sections, in the North from Canada down to the Mason and Dixon line, in the South from Virginia down to Georgia, with practically no overlapping. It has therefore been thought best to treat the campaigns separately in the two sections, thus enabling the reader to follow the movements of the armies and the progress of the various campaigns with a minimum of confusion.

While making no pretensions to the role of a military expert, the author has ventured to express opinions as to the strategy and tactics employed in some of the operations herein recorded. In doing so, he relies upon the dictum of Baron Jomini in that eminently authoritative military treatise, *Précis de l'art de la guerre*, "The theory of the great speculative combinations of war is simple enough in itself; it only requires intelligence and attentive reflection," and upon von Moltke's statement that "strategy is the application of common sense to the conduct of war."

CHRISTOPHER WARD

Contents

VOLUME TWO

The War in the South

xii   *Contents*

Maps

VOLUME ONE

VOLUME TWO

The War in the North

CHAPTER 1

The Causes of the War

Tuesday, the 17th of May, 1774, was an unpleasant day in Boston. A pelting rain, driven by a strong east wind, poured upon the town. Gutters ran full; hollows in the cobbled streets became puddles. The few of its citizens who owned umbrellas found some shelter under those newfangled, cumbrous contrivances of oiled silk or linen spread on clumsy ribs of whalebone.[1] The thousands of others who were abroad that day could only turn the brims of their hats down, the collars of their coats up, wrap their cloaks around them, and take the storm as it came, with a philosophical endurance born of habit.

But the provincial troop of horse, the Ancient and Honourable Artillery Company, the Boston Grenadier Corps, fine, tall fellows in notably handsome uniforms, and more companies of militia, drawn up in line along King Street, could not even flap their hats or turn up their collars. They had to stand stiffly at attention in their ordered ranks, while the rain beat upon their faces and dripped from their noses and chins.

The Boston Cadets, the "Governor's Own," were equally defenseless as they marched against the blast down King Street. So were "a number of His Majesty's Council, several Members of the Commons House of Assembly [and] many principal Gentlemen of the town" who followed the soldiers, in dripping discomfort.

At the Long Wharf the procession halted. The military formed its ranks, and the gentlemen following grouped themselves in proper disposition as a reception committee. All eyes, not only those of the official party but those also of the thronging multitude of common people gathered around and behind them, were turned upon one of His Britannic Majesty's ships of war lying at the wharf.

There was a ruffle of drums aboard the ship; the guns on the other war vessels in the harbor and in the batteries in the town began a thunderous salute and the bells in all the steeples rang out as the expected guests, brave in scarlet coats and white breeches that glittered with gold braid, descended the gangplank and were welcomed with all due form and ceremony and with more or less sincerity according to the political principles of the individual greeters. Whether Boston liked it or not, it was indeed an occasion of moment, for these impressively arrayed military personages were none other than Lieutenant General the Honorable Thomas Gage, commander in chief of all His Majesty's forces in the American colonies and Governor of the Province of Massachusetts Bay, and his staff—his "family," in the language of the period.

The official greetings over, a procession was formed. Led by the guard of honor, the great man with his entourage and the official civilians, followed by thousands of unofficial sight-seers, proceeded up King Street. The rain, on their backs now, was no doubt less discomforting.

The troop of horse, the artillerymen, the grenadiers, and the embodied militia, all amateur soldier boys, stood stiffly at attention while their officers gave these awe-inspiring professionals their very best in the way of a military salute, which the general politely returned. They then fell in behind the procession in its march up King Street to the Town House.

In the Council Chamber, His Excellency presented his commission and was sworn in by the President of the Council. From the balcony of the State House, the High Sheriff read the new Governor's proclamation "continuing all Officers &c in their places till further orders." It was answered by "three huzzas from the concourse of the people," three volleys of musketry from the soldiers of Boston, and the discharge of the Ancient and Honourables' three three-pounder brass fieldpieces.[2]

After the Governor had "received the compliments of civil and military officers and other gentry" and reviewed the militia he was escorted to Faneuil Hall, "where an elegant entertainment was provided at the expence of the province. . . . Many loyal toasts were drank, and the strictest harmony and decorum observed." He then rode in a carriage to the Province House, his official residence.[3]

From all these sights and sounds one might have supposed that it was a day of rejoicing in Boston, that the coming of the new governor was hailed by the people as a fortunate event. But no, the flapping flags, the pealing bells, the saluting guns, all the parade and circumstance of welcome were mere matters of form; the huzzas of the populace were no more than throat-deep. The people of Boston knew what his coming meant and what his orders were; they dreaded what he had come to do. Against him and what he represented, Boston harbored strong feelings of antagonism.

Gage was no stranger in America. After about seventeen years of military service in Britain and on the continent of Europe, he had come to America in 1755 and had taken part in Braddock's disastrous expedition against the French and Indians. He had fought bravely under Braddock, and also under Abercromby in the ill-fated British attack upon Ticonderoga in 1758. Serving as governor of Montreal after the conquest of Canada, he had become commander in chief of the British army in America late in 1763, succeeding his good friend Sir Jeffrey Amherst. His wife, born Margaret Kemble, was an American and a member of a prominent New Jersey family, a cousin of Philip Schuyler and a relative of colonial Van Cortlandts and Bayards. He was a good soldier and was devoted to his duty. He was handsome and dignified, his manners were pleasing; and he was described by the historian William Smith as "a good-natured, peaceable, sociable man." With these qualities, and replacing at least temporarily the hated Governor Thomas Hutchinson, he might have been received with pleasure—would have been so received ten years earlier.

On the other hand, Bostonians had known of him as the commander of the British forces in America who had directed the activities of the four regiments sent to town in 1768, and they had not forgotten the consequent bloody affair in their streets in 1770. To be sure, the regulars had been ordered to Boston by the British cabinet, and Gage had merely executed its orders; but the memory of the "Boston Massacre" would have diminished his welcome now, even if he had come with the most amicable intentions. But he had, in fact, come under orders from his government to deprive the town and the whole province of much of their liberty, and also to close the port of Boston to commerce, which could paralyze the town's chief industries, impoverish its substantial citizens, beggar its working people, and bring them near to starvation. The whole affair of his reception, although many Bostonians sincerely welcomed him, was a triumph of good manners over deep-seated, implacable, and not unjustified resentment.[4]

To appreciate the situation, to understand the causes that gradually developed from mere muttered discontent an animosity that led to violent resistance and finally to the War which it is the purpose of this book to chronicle, one must go back a matter of a decade, to the year 1763.

For a much longer time than that the American colonies had been subject to certain restrictions imposed by the government of Great Britain. The

Navigation Acts, which restrained or rather canalized their sea-borne commerce for the benefit of the shipping interests of the mother country, the Molasses Act, which penalized the importation of molasses and sugar from other than British sources, the various acts which forbade the development of manufactures in the colonies, might seem to have been sufficient to arouse rebellious sentiments in the minds of the colonists long before the year 1763. But in fact there were certain advantages to the Americans in their operation. There were also certain extralegal methods of evasion, which served to lighten their burdensome features. So that, on the whole, there was little opposition to them on the part of the inhabitants of the colonies, and their relations with the home government were not strained. Indeed, the era preceding 1763 came in after days to be regarded by them as a golden age to which they would fain return.

In that year the Peace of Paris ended the Seven Years' War in Europe, a part of which was the French and Indian War in America. That war and three other great conflicts in the preceding seventy years had drained Great Britain's treasury and piled up a public debt of £136,000,000. To sustain this burden and to meet heavy current expenses—heavy in part because it had been decided to keep a regular army of about 6,000 men in America after 1763—she felt obliged to find new sources of income outside the kingdom; and the prosperous American colonies seemed to be the best available source. The consequence was a series of British financial measures to which the Americans strongly objected. Additional causes for American discontent lay in new restrictions placed upon their paper currency, upon westward migration, and upon their trade, and in demands that the colonists give quarters and supplies to the regular army upon certain occasions. Indeed, the very presence of the regulars in America caused great dissatisfaction when the army was stationed in the settled areas.

The Sugar Act of 1764, a successor to the Molasses Act, which had lapsed, clearly displayed the intention of the British government to secure substantial revenue from the mainland American colonies. It cut the duty on molasses in half, while raising that on sugar; and it imposed other new, though less important, duties. It did not differ greatly in form from the old act, except for one startling assertion. While the Molasses Act had been regarded as only a regulation of commerce, such small revenue as it provided being merely incidental, this new law baldly stated in its preamble that one of its purposes was to raise a revenue; in other words, it was in great part a taxing measure.[5] The British government proposed to collect threepence upon every gallon of molasses entering the colonies from the foreign West Indian islands, and shook up its collecting agencies to make certain that the colonists would pay. They had rather effectively avoided paying the duties set up in 1733.

No one had objected on principle to the Molasses Act, although the colonial merchants had flouted it. However, to the relatively new principle of the Sugar Act there was immediate and, in the minds of the Americans, well founded objection; and nowhere in the colonies was it stronger or more vocal than in this same town of Boston, where Samuel Adams became the leader of resistance. The Americans were all the more unhappy because Britain was determined not only to pass the act but to enforce it, and also to enforce the long disobeyed Acts of Navigation.

Adams declared that taxes imposed on the colonists, "without their having a legal representative where they are laid," reduced them "from the character of free subjects to the miserable condition of tributary slaves." [6] This was the answer in principle. The practical answer was a development of the technique of smuggling to such a degree that the new measures were partly nullified.

But the mother country had another rod in pickle for her refractory children, guaranteed to be proof against the tricks of the wiliest smuggler. This was the famous Stamp Act of 1765 requiring that revenue stamps be affixed to all papers in lawsuits, all commercial paper, bills of lading, ship charters, probates of wills, surveys and conveyances of land, leases, bills of sale, and a host of other legal documents, as well as newspapers, pamphlets, playing cards, and so on. The cost of the stamps ranged from a halfpenny on a small newspaper to £6 on a grant of franchise. Heavy penalties were imposed on violators of the act, and, worst of all, unstamped documents were declared void in law.[7]

As a taxing measure it was fair enough, the taxes being widely and rather equally distributed and easily collected. Nor was it a novel method of taxation, for such stamps had long been in use in England. But it could not in any sense be regarded as a regulation of commerce; it was a taxing act pure and simple, without disguise, palliation, or apology. Against it the colonists reacted even more strongly than against the Sugar Act.

In Virginia, Patrick Henry is said to have suggested to George III that he should profit by the examples of Tarquin, Caesar, and Charles I, and the House of Burgesses declared against tax laws not emanating from its own legislature. Pennsylvania and the other middle colonies passed similar resolutions. Massachusetts called for a congress of colonial representatives to take steps in the matter. The Stamp Act Congress met in New York in October, 1765, with members from nine of the thirteen colonies present.

The Congress proceeded to declare, in substance, the colonies' loyalty to the Crown and "all due subordination" to the Parliament, but asserted that it was essential to the freedom of a people that no taxes should be imposed without its consent; that the colonists were not and could not be represented in Parliament; that only their own legislatures could tax them. The Congress added the practical argument that the stamp taxes were so heavy as to prevent them from buying English goods and so were inimical to the prosperity of England, as well as of the colonies. An address to the King, a Memorial to the House of Lords, and a Petition to the Commons all expressed the unhappiness of the colonists.

Meanwhile, intense excitement prevailed throughout the colonies. The Virginia resolutions were broadcast. Associations called Sons of Liberty were formed in the northern provinces to resist the execution of the law. They acted with vigor, indeed with violence. In Boston they hanged Oliver, the stamp officer, in effigy and smashed the windows of his house. He resigned his office, but the Sons of Liberty were not appeased. They burned the records of the vice-admiralty courts, newly empowered to enforce the customs laws; they sacked the office of the Comptroller of Customs, and they climaxed their vandalism by wrecking the fine mansion of Governor Hutchinson, destroying his furniture, defacing his paintings, and casting into the street and burning his books, historical documents and manuscripts, the finest collection of the sort in America. Terrified stamp officers almost universally resigned their posts or refused to do their duty. When the stamps arrived there was hardly anyone willing to receive and issue them. And when they arrived the colonists destroyed them or secured promises from officials that they would not be sold.

November 1, 1765, the day the act was to go into effect, was observed throughout the colonies as a day of mourning; muffled bells were tolled, minute guns were fired, and flags were set at half-staff. How could business go on? How could the courts function, newspapers be issued, ships chartered or cleared, land conveyed, goods sold, without stamps? The solution was simple. Unstamped newspapers appeared, and though for a time business was suspended it was soon largely resumed. The law was simply disregarded, and the act nullified.

But it still stood on the statute books, a menace to every American interest. To enforce its repeal, a general boycott of English goods was organized, and a movement to encourage manufactures despite their unlawfulness was inaugurated. The effect of these measures was impressive. Factories in England were closed; thousands were thrown out of work; and manufacturers and merchants faced bankruptcy. When Parliament met in December, it had to reconsider its action. The addresses of the Stamp Act Congress might have been disregarded, but not the flood of petitions for repeal of the act that came from the commercial classes of Englishmen. William Pitt, the idol of the English people, declared that Parliament had no right to levy the stamp tax, and after a long and heated debate the obnoxious act was repealed.

The news of the repeal was received in America "in a transport of mingled surprise, exultation, and gratitude." Fireworks, festivities, resolutions, and addresses of thanks were evidences of the joy of the people. Moreover, there was a great outburst of loyalty to England. Statues of the King were voted in New York and Virginia. Pitt, Barré, and Conway, leaders of the movement for repeal, were honored by effigies or portraits displayed in public places. The Sons of Liberty faded away. John Adams said that the repeal "hushed into silence almost every popular clamor." Yet this was in fact but an armistice, a temporary truce and not a permanent peace between the government of Great Britain and the self-assertive colonists.

In July, 1766, there was a change in the ministry. Pitt, though disabled by physical and perhaps even mental infirmities, accepted the responsibility of leading it and then betook himself to the House of Lords as Earl of Chatham. The Duke of Grafton became prime minister in form, but exercised little influence. Leadership of the Commons was assumed by Charles Townshend, no friend of America. Unfortunately for the empire, no doubt, Pitt was too sick to control affairs, and Townshend had an opportunity to shine.

Townshend was a brash young man, whose "wonderful endowments [were] dashed with follies and indiscretions." [8] Early in 1767 he boasted that he knew the mode by which a revenue could be drawn from America without offense to the Americans.[9] His scheme was based on a distinction which had been suggested or implied by some colonists and by some Englishmen between "external taxes," that is, duties on imports, to which they did not object, and "internal taxes" such as those imposed by the Stamp Act, which they denounced. He brought in a bill to impose duties on colonial importations from Britain of glass, certain painters' materals, and tea. The proceeds were to be used to pay the salaries of the colonial governors and judges, thus freeing crown officers in America from dependence upon colonial legislatures. He coupled with this a bill to legalize writs of assistance—general search warrants to be used by the revenue officers in enforcing the new revenue law; a bill establishing new courts of vice-admiralty; and a bill creating a special Board of Commissioners of the Customs in Boston, responsible directly to the British Treasury and controlling completely a reorganized American customs service.

But, in relying on the external-internal tax distinction to procure the acquiescence of the Americans, he failed to realize that most Americans were actually opposed to external as well as internal taxes for revenue. The colonists had tasted blood in their fight against the Stamp Act. They considered that they themselves had in effect repealed that law before Parliament did. What they had once done, they felt able to do again. Moreover, there was a growing discontent with the older statutes, the Navigation Acts and those forbidding manufactures. Though long accepted without objection and, in practice, to a considerable degree nullified by simple disobedience of their provisions, these were now felt to be oppressive.

In this state of mind, the colonists cheerfully threw overboard whatever distinction between the two kinds of taxes they had formerly offered. All taxes for revenue, of whatever sort, were now equally hateful. Since 1765 they had been objecting to the standing army as an instrument of tyranny. Now they denounced the new Board of Customs, which would inconveniently interfere with the custom of smuggling. Also they wanted to pay their own governors and judges, basing the desire upon the feeling that their hold on the purse strings was a safeguard against oppression by these officers.

On more justifiable grounds, they were opposed to the writs of assistance, which would enable any customs officer to search not only any ship, but also "any House Shop Cellar Warehouse or Room or other place," [10] without showing cause for such intrusion.

With the passage of the Townshend acts, the short-lived era of good feeling among the colonists toward the mother country came to a sudden end. Massachusetts made the first move toward effective opposition to the new laws by sending a Circular Letter to the other colonies urging concerted action. The British ministry ordered the colonial governors to compel the various colonial legislatures to rescind all resolutions directed against those laws, and to dissolve the assemblies if they refused. Such steps were taken in half a dozen of the colonies, but they only poured oil on the flames of discontent.

Practical measures were taken by the Americans. The general boycott of English goods was gradually revived by new Nonimportation Agreements. The Sons of Liberty became active in their enforcement. When John Hancock's sloop *Liberty* was seized by royal officials at a wharf in Boston in June, 1768, on a charge of smuggling, a mob attacked them. The Commissioners of Customs fled in terror to Castle William, a fortress on an island in Boston harbor.

These and other acts of violent resistance could not be overlooked by the British government. General Gage was instructed to move two regiments of foot to Boston for police duty. When these regulars landed at the beginning of October, 1768, Boston declined to furnish free quarters in town and certain supplies for them, as seemingly required by an act of Parliament. Colonel Dalrymple, commander of the troops, had to rent any available lodgings for his men and for two more regiments of infantry that joined them in following months. Instead of being concentrated in barracks under firm control of their officers, the soldiers were scattered throughout the town, with unfortunate results.

Bostonians regarded them as foreign troops and accordingly hated them, ostracized them, insulted them in the streets and called them opprobrious names. They responded by swaggering, insolent, contemptuous conduct. The natural result was frequent brawls and rough encounters between the citizens and the soldiers.

On March 5, 1770, this mutual ill-feeling culminated in a serious affair. A mob of citizens pelted some of the intruders with snowballs and stones and reviled them with scurrilous language. There was a close encounter, so close that some of the mob struck at their opponents' muskets with clubs, daring them to fire, and knocked one of them down. The soldiers fired into the crowd. Eleven of the citizens fell, three of them dead, two mortally wounded. This was the famous "Boston Massacre."

Quite naturally, it caused great excitement throughout the town. Bells were rung to summon the populace. The whole town poured out into the streets. Drums were beaten to call out the militia. Several companies formed around the Town House. It looked as if the war was to begin then and there. But Governor Hutchinson succeeding in quieting the people and in obtaining Dalrymple's promise to withdraw the troops to Castle William in Boston harbor.

Meanwhile the continued boycott of British goods was seriously affecting the English economy. Exports to America shrank to half their former value, and there was nothing that the army could do about it. Confronted with this situation, several members of the ministry urged a policy of conciliation and proposed entire repeal of the Townshend taxes; but the King was firm in his demand that "there must always be one tax to keep up the right" to tax. When the others were abolished, in April, 1770, the tax on tea was retained.

At the time of the "massacre" war, at least a local civil war, had been a very near thing; but after the alteration in the tax law and after the excitement in Boston had subsided, there ensued a long period of quiet throughout the colonies. The Americans were back in the golden age of 1763, except for the tea tax. This fact, coupled with a growing weariness of the prolonged conflict, induced a spirit of nonresistance, which degenerated into apathy. The Nonimportation Agreements were violated with increasing frequency. Complaints of such violations by this colony were made by that. Such charges were met by countercharges of the same sort. Intercolonial enmities arose out of these recriminations. The partly built, ill cemented union of the colonies was falling apart. Another shock was needed to revive the fainting spirit of liberty. It came in June, 1772.

The British armed schooner *Gaspée*, while pursuing a suspected smuggling vessel, ran aground in the waters of Rhode Island. Drums beat in Providence. Eight boats full of volunteers put off, surrounded the schooner, seized it, and burned it. In the fracas the British commander was wounded. America hailed the deed as a blow against oppression; England was outraged. British investigators could not discover the names of the culprits, known to many citizens. Finally, the British authorities, perhaps loath to excite renewed animosity in the presently quiescent colonies, dropped the matter.

Distrust of the colonial courts as impartial tribunals now impelled the ministry to revive the project of paying the judges out of the royal treasury, beginning in Massachusetts. That colony astutely countered the move by offering the judges higher salaries than were to be paid by Britain, and the judges accepted the offer. Samuel Adams, who had been almost in despair over the decline of the spirit of resistance and the relaxation of the bonds of unity, saw his chance. In April, 1773, he proposed the organization of Committees of Correspondence to act as connecting links between the various Massachusetts towns. Within a few months, many such bodies appeared, some of them acting for towns, others for colonies. Soon they formed a network throughout the colonies.

Still quietude prevailed throughout America. Only a general abstention from English tea indicated the underlying spirit of opposition to Parliamentary taxation. With characteristic ineptitude the British government seized on that minor element in the contest and erected it into a major dispute.

The East India Company had been hit by the refusal of the Americans to import its tea. In the port of Philadelphia, for example, only one chest of English tea had been entered in the customhouse in five years, while an ample supply had been smuggled in from other sources. Seventeen million pounds had accumulated in the Company's English warehouses, and it was nearing bankruptcy. Government officials were largely interested in the Company. To relieve its embarrassment, an arrangement was made to reimburse the Company for the import duties it paid in England, and to allow it to export directly to its own agents in America instead of through English merchants to American merchants as theretofore. It could then sell tea in the colonies at prices less than those at which smuggled tea was sold, even though its agents paid the threepence a pound American duty to the English government; and the cantankerous colonials would get their tea, tax and all, cheaper than ever before, and even cheaper than it was being sold in England. So why should they worry about the tax? They would surely buy the Company's tea.

But they did worry. News of the scheme was like a bellows blast to the smoldering embers of resistance to "tyranny." After years of quiescence, "the whole country was in a blaze from Maine to Georgia." [11] It is said that "the transition from apathy to agitation was sudden" [12] and widespread. It was an amazing phenomenon. The duties had been legally in force for six years, and for half of that time they had been either quietly paid or tranquilly disregarded. No one was now to be forced to buy the Company's tea. So why should the colonials excite themselves about it?

It has been said that they were aroused by an attempt, at once injurious and insulting, to bribe them to surrender their rights "not to be taxed, by offering them cheaper tea." [13] A more cynical, probably less truthful, statement is that the blaze was not sudden; that it took two full months to work it up; that it was, in fact, ignited by certain Philadelphia merchants who had profited by dealing in the smuggled tea and now saw their business in peril. Be the truth as to this what it may, Philadelphia did take the lead in arousing enmity to the scheme by a series of resolutions denouncing it as "a violent attack upon the liberties of America." Committees pressed the Company's agents, consignees of the expected tea, to resign. Boston followed suit, and so did New York and Charleston. "The cry of endangered liberty once more excited an alarm from New Hampshire to Georgia." [14] Boston was "as furious as it was in the time of the Stamp Act." [15] Whatever the incitement, the resulting conflagration was genuine enough.

The announced intention of the Americans was to prevent the landing of the tea, and it was carried out. At Charleston, no consignee having appeared to pay the duty, a cargo was seized by the customs officers, stored in damp cellars, and left to rot. The captains of the tea ships bound to Philadelphia and New York saw that they could not land their cargoes and carried them back to England. But it was reserved for Boston to climax the opposition in the most spectacular manner. In December, 1773, it held a "tea party," in which an organized mob tossed overboard tea valued at £15,000.

George III, who for a long time had had Boston "on the brain," now saw red. A message from the cabinet to Parliament resulted in quick and drastic action. Four new measures to punish that hotbed of treason were enacted.

The first, known as the Boston Port Act, closed the port of Boston to all commerce and ordered it blockaded. Marblehead and Salem were to be the only Massachusetts ports. The second annulled several parts of the province's charter. Its Assembly was left to function, but the upper chamber, the Council, was to be appointed by the King. The inferior judges, the sheriffs, and other executive officers were to be appointed by the Governor. Juries were to be chosen by the sheriffs, who owed their appointments to the royal chief executive. Town meetings, the very core of self-government in Massachusetts, were to be held only with the Governor's permission, except one each year to choose assemblymen, selectmen, and constables. The third act provided for the removal to England or to another colony for trial of anyone indicted for a capital offense committed in the course of a riot or of enforcement of the revenue laws. The fourth legalized the quartering of troops on the town.

To enforce these laws, General Gage was appointed governor of the province. Which brings us around, at last, to the point where this introductory chapter began.

CHAPTER 2

Boston Port Closed

Boston's population numbered about 20,000, almost all of English origin, there having been but little immigration from the European continent or even from Ireland. It was, of all the colonial ports, the most active in ship-building, codfishery, whaling, and sea-borne commerce in general. It contained important American rum distilleries, which were dependent on a supply of molasses from the West Indies. As elsewhere in the colonies, so in Boston the repressive acts of Parliament had prevented the development of manufactures. The town lived on its ships, its wharves, its shipyards, rope-walks, and sail lofts. To survive, it had to have free passage for its vessels. For its food, in some part, it needed access by water to the grazing grounds on the small islands in its outer harbor, where beef cattle and sheep were pastured.

At the stroke of noon on June 1, the Port Act went into effect. From that moment, Boston harbor was sealed against the rest of the world by a tight blockade. General Gage had been instructed to compel "a full and absolute submission" to the new law. The terms of the act made it unlawful to load or receive at any wharf in the port, at any "island, creek, landing-place, bank or other place" within Massachusetts Bay, any goods whatsoever, in any vessel whatsoever, coming from or going to "any other country, province or place whatsoever." Gage construed his mandate as covering every possible movement of goods, even within the harbor. An adjacent island was a "place"; Charlestown, separated from Boston only by the Charles River, was a "place"; therefore the town was cut off not only from the sea by the blockading ships, but also from such "places." "Did a lighter attempt to

15

land hay from the islands, or a boat to bring in sand from the neighboring hills, or a scow to freight to it lumber or iron, or a float to land sheep, or a farmer to carry marketing over in the ferry-boats, the argus-eyed fleet was ready to see it, and prompt to capture or destroy." [1]

The effect upon the town was immediate, universal, and disastrous. Although church bells had tolled, days of fasting and prayer had been observed, and badges of mourning had been displayed, nothing had availed to avert the coming catastrophe. When it came, the town was stopped dead in its tracks. The great warehouses were closed; the wharves were deserted, and the porters and stevedores were thrown out of work. The shipyards suspended operations, and the carpenters were idle. Ships were tied up at the piers, and the sailors walked the streets. Mercantile houses had no more business, and their clerks no more employment. The town was paralyzed and was like to starve. It might have starved, indeed, but for the alms bestowed upon it by other towns and the other colonies. Connecticut sent it hundreds of sheep. From elsewhere in New England came flour, cattle, fish, and other foods. The Carolinas sent stores of rice and considerable sums of money. Delaware sent money and promised more. Contributions of food and money came from all the other colonies and even from Canada; Quebec sent more than a thousand bushels of wheat. For a full year Boston lived in part on these supplies. And with them came messages of encouragement and adjurations to the Bostonians to stand by their refusal to ransom their town by paying £15,000 for the tea that had been destroyed.[2]

Gage, in accordance with instructions from the King, established the capital of the province in Salem and took up his official residence there, leaving Earl Percy, son and heir of the Duke of Northumberland, in command of several regiments of troops who were brought to Boston to support British authority in the summer of 1774.

At Salem, on June 17, the General Assembly met, under protest against the removal of the capital to that place. Gage sent his secretary with an order dissolving the session. The door was locked against him so that he could only read the order to the crowd on the stairs. The Assembly proposed a continental congress and elected five delegates to represent Massachusetts.

Thirty-six members of the Governor's Council were appointed by Gage a few weeks later. Eleven of them immediately declined to serve. The rest were so insulted, ostracized, and in every way harassed by the people that, finally, no more than sixteen remained in office, and these were forced to seek refuge in Boston under protection of its garrison.

In late August a session of the Supreme Court was to be held in Boston.

Gage came over from Salem to give it his personal support. The judges took their seats; but not a single man in the jury panel would consent to be sworn. The judges told the Governor that it was not possible to hold court even in Boston. Nor was it possible anywhere else in the province. Judges, even justices of the peace, sheriffs, and other executive officers, either voluntarily or through coercion, declined to perform their duties. In Boston the King's law, as far as it was pronounced by Parliament in the obnoxious statutes, was enforced by the military. But not even in Boston was enforcement of any other law possible. "Three hundred thousand people continued their usual avocations without a legislature or executive officers, without sheriffs, judges or justices of the peace." [3] Yet order prevailed generally. The habits of a law-abiding people prevailed, even though the machinery for law enforcement had ceased to exist. "Though the tribunals were void and silent, crime was repressed and private rights were secure, because the people were a law to themselves." [4]

In September, Gage incautiously called the General Court, consisting of the Council and the Assembly, to meet in Salem on October 5. But, realizing that his appointees to the Council would not be allowed to take their seats, he withdrew the summons. The members of the lower house, nevertheless, gathered in Salem. After two days of intentional neglect by the Governor they adjourned to Concord and organized as a Provincial Congress—a body entirely outside the law and unknown to it—which acted thereafter as the only effective government of the province outside Boston.

In the meantime Gage had taken up residence in Boston and was steadily accumulating troops. To provide quarters for them, other than the tents on the Common and such empty warehouses as he had been able to rent, he called for workmen to build barracks. Though thousands in the town were unemployed, no one would or dared work for him. He had to send to New York and to Halifax for the necessary artificers. The people of the town countered this move by widespread sabotage. Barges transporting bricks for the barracks were sunk, wagons loaded with bricks were upset, straw for the soldiers' beds was burned. November had come and nearly gone before the soldiers could be removed from their chilly quarters on the Common to more adequate shelter.

The Continental Congress, which the Bostonians had suggested, met in Philadelphia on September 5. Twelve of the thirteen colonies sent delegates to make up the most substantial, mentally vigorous, politically powerful, and determined body of colonial representatives that had ever assembled in America. An address to the King, couched in respectful words, an address to the People of England, and a Declaration of Rights again stated the grievances of the colonies and recited thirteen Acts of Parliament to which Americans could not submit.

The addresses and the declaration made no demand for independence, nor suggestion of a resort to force to uphold the rights claimed. They were only petitions for relief from oppression, which, however, the delegates had little expectation of receiving without more pressure than such petitions alone would exert. To give them practical force, reliance was placed upon a renewal of such a boycott of English goods as had theretofore been so effective. It was therefore voted that an Association of the colonies be formed, agreeing not to import any goods from Great Britain or Ireland, nor any East India tea, nor any of certain products from the British West Indies. In addition it was agreed that consumption of British goods and exportation of goods to Britain be curtailed.

The American petitions availed nothing; neither the King nor the Parliament gave them the slightest heed. The only substantial results of the Congress were the Association and the bringing together for the first time of the leading men of the colonies to act in unison, which paved the way for the next meeting of Congress in 1775 and for united action.

Across the river from Boston, on Quarry Hill in Charlestown there was a magazine, "the powder-house," in which was kept a store of gunpowder belonging to the province and to several of the near-by towns. The towns, during August, had been removing their stocks and storing them within their own precincts, as if in readiness for use. To Gage these proceedings seemed ominous of coming trouble; he decided to take steps accordingly.

On the first of September, at dawn, a force of 260 soldiers embarked at the Long Wharf, crossed over to Charlestown and carried off 250 half-barrels, the entire remaining stock of the precious explosive. While this was going on, a detachment marched to Cambridge and confiscated two field-pieces lately procured by the militia regiment of that town. These guns and the powder were removed to Castle William. This unexpected little operation was effected peaceably, without opposition and therefore without bloodshed; but its results were far more disastrous than the withdrawal of powder by the towns had been.

News of the seizure spread swiftly throughout the province, and, as it spread, it grew in importance. By afternoon it was widely reported that the people of Charlestown had resisted the seizure, and that the troops had fired on them and killed six. By midnight this was known forty miles away in Shrewsbury. Everywhere, the rumor was received as a call to arms, and the people responded. By the next day 4,000 armed men, from all the country within thirty miles of Boston, had crowded into Cambridge; Worcester

County and Hampshire were on the march. On the 3rd, Israel Putnam, down in Pomfret, Connecticut, heard not only that the King's soldiers had shot down six of the people of Charlestown and wounded many more, but also that the King's men-of-war had bombarded Boston. By that time thousands —twenty, thirty thousand, it was said—were moving on foot toward Cambridge.[5]

On the 4th, the Committee of Correspondence of Connecticut sent the dreadful news to New York. Within a week, the Continental Congress in Philadelphia had heard of that "dreadful catastrophe." "The effect of the news we have," wrote John Adams to his wife, "both upon the Congress and the inhabitants of this city, was very great. Great indeed! Every gentleman seems to regard the bombardment of Boston as the bombardment of the capital of his own province. Our deliberations are grave and serious indeed." [6] It was, of course, an absurd idea that Gage would bombard his own town, the only place he held in the colonies. The effect upon the Congress, in unifying its members and hastening their action, was, nevertheless, decided and effective.

Many of the thousands on the march to Cambridge were turned back by word that the rumor was false; those already there were dispersed, and the excitement died down. The incident had been, however, an impressive demonstration of the inflammatory nature of the situation and of the insufficiency of the British forces in Boston to contend successfully with all New England in arms. Gage recognized his weakness and called on the home government for reinforcements: to reduce New England, a very respectable force must take the field. He recognized, also, the insecurity of his position, even in merely defensive operations, and set about strengthening it.

Boston was almost an island, being connected with the mainland by a very slim isthmus known as the Neck, at its narrowest part no wider than the causeway built across a depression that was submerged at high tide. From old times, there had been a slight fortification at the town end of this causeway. The excitement about the powder had hardly died when, on September 5, Gage ordered the erection of substantial defensive works on the mainland beyond the Neck and thereby again alarmed the people.

The selectmen of Boston protested; they apprehended an intention of shutting the town off from the rest of the province, of reducing it to the condition of a garrisoned stronghold. Gage replied that the works were merely to protect the troops and the people of Boston from attack, and that he had no intention of interrupting ordinary traffic. Although strikes and all forms of sabotage delayed the work, he succeeded in erecting a rather elaborate fortification. mounting two 24-pound cannon and eight 9-

pounders, which did nothing to allay the inflammation in the minds of the people.

The Americans did what they could to redress the balance of arms inside and outside Boston. One night they stripped a battery at Charlestown of its guns and delivered them outside the lines. Another night they brought off four cannon from the gun-house near the Common. Countrymen, returning from selling their products in the town, day after day concealed muskets, ammunition, and military gear in their wagons and carried them past the guard at the Neck. Gun running became a popular avocation. Admiral Graves, in command of the harbor blockade, could think of no way to preserve the guns in the North Battery other than spiking them, which he did.

The Provincial Congress, sitting in Concord and later in Cambridge during the latter part of 1774, appropriated what was to them the huge sums of £15,627 sterling for the purchase of twenty fieldpieces, four mortars, twenty tons of grape and round shot, ten tons of bombshells, five tons of bullets, one thousand barrels of powder, five thousand muskets and bayonets, and seventy-five thousand flints, to which the Committee of Supplies, in charge of such purchases, added three hundred fifty spades and pickaxes, one thousand wooden mess bowls, and a supply of pork, flour, dried peas, and rice. These military stores were to be deposited in Concord and Worcester. Provision was later made for securing tentage and various other kinds of munitions and supplies.

The Congress provided for the organization of regiments of "minutemen" (of whom more hereinafter) by drawing one-fourth of the men in the regular militia for that purpose. It also named Jedediah Preble, Artemas Ward, and Seth Pomeroy as general officers in command of all the forces of the province, divided into three corps: one at Charlestown, one at Roxbury, the third at Cambridge. A Committee of Safety was appointed to take charge of all the colony's affairs after the dissolution of the Congress. On December 10 it dissolved itself, having first appointed committees to notify the neighboring provinces, Connecticut, Rhode Island, and New Hampshire, of its acts and to request them to provide men to make up an army of 20,000 in all.

Gage issued a proclamation declaring the acts of the Provincial Congress to be treasonable, which, indeed, they were, and prohibiting the people from complying with its requisitions or recommendations. It had no effect whatever upon the colonials; they were busy all through the winter collecting and storing munitions of war. On every village green throughout New England, the militia were drilling more often than ever before and with more serious intent. The cannon at Fort Island in Rhode Island, six 24-pounders, eighteen 18-pounders, fourteen 6-pounders, and six 4-pounders, were seized and carried to Providence, "to prevent their falling into the hands of the King, or any of his servants." Four hundred Portsmouth, New Hampshire, men demanded the powder of that province, which was stored in the fort at New Castle. The British commander refused to give it up and fired upon them with three 4-pounders and his musketry. They "stormed" the fort, secured the captain and his garrison of five "invalid" soldiers and carried off ninety-seven barrels of powder, fifteen hundred muskets, and several pieces of artillery.[7]

On February 26, 1775, to counter the activities of the Americans in seizing powder and arms, Gage sent Colonel Leslie with 240 men to Salem to seize a few brass fieldpieces deposited there. He sailed on a transport to Marblehead, whence he had to march five miles to his destination. Salem had timely news of his approach. A large crowd, including the militia colonel, Timothy Pickering, and 40 armed men, assembled in a shipyard where carriages for the guns were being made and hoisted the drawbridge spanning a small stream that the British force would have to cross.

Leslie arrived and demanded that the bridge be replaced. He was informed that this was a private road and that no trespassing would be permitted. He turned his attention to two "gundalows," which lay in the stream. But their owners jumped into them and began to scuttle them. There was a scuffle, in which a few of the Salemites were "pricked with bayonets" but no one was seriously wounded.

Leslie had his orders, which included crossing that bridge, but he was at his wit's end as to how to execute them. At length, a Salem clergyman intervened. He told Leslie that if he crossed the stream in opposition to the Salemites he would certainly be overwhelmed by the population, but if he would pledge his word to advance no farther than thirty rods beyond the bridge to a point where the unfinished gun-carriages were, and then, if he found no guns, to return, the bridge would be let down. Leslie agreed, crossed the stream, marched the agreed distance, found no guns, faced about, and returned to Marblehead and so to Boston. In the telling, the proceeding seems farcical, but if he had not yielded Salem might have won the honors later conferred on Lexington by Major Pitcairn and his men, for the alarm had gone forth, the minutemen were responding to it, and a company from Danvers arrived on the scene just as Leslie's detachment was marching away.[8]

The news of violent opposition by the Americans did not shock the King nor, indeed, particularly displease him. "I am not sorry," he wrote, "that the line of conduct seems now chalked out. . . . The New England Gov-

ernments are in a state of rebellion. Blows must decide whether they are
subject to this country or independent." "He was prepared to fight and was
in a hurry to begin." [9]

When the Parliament met, on November 29, the address from the throne
began with notice of "a most daring spirit of resistance and disobedience to
the law . . . fresh violences of a very criminal nature" in Massachusetts,
and of the measures the crown had taken to restore "peace, order and
good Government" there. Lords and Commons answered that "a rebellion
at this time actually exists within said Province," which was not an over-
statement, and besought His Majesty to "take the most effectual measures
to enforce due obedience to the laws and authority of the supreme Legislature." They also assured him that it was "our fixed resolution, at the hazard
of our lives and properties," to stand by him—a gallant assurance, indeed,
which seemed to contemplate that the coming war was to be fought against
hordes of invading Yankees in the towns, villages, and fields of old England,
with the King himself in the battle-front and the lords and gentlemen of the
Commons in the firing line.

To avoid such an untoward event, an addition of 6,000 men to the
military and naval forces was provided for, with an increase of the force
in Boston to 10,000 soldiers. But this Parliament struck a still shrewder
blow against the offending Americans with a statute, commonly called the
Fishery Act, which restrained the New England colonies from all trade with
Great Britain, Ireland, and the West Indies, and excluded them from the
Newfoundland fisheries, under penalty of forfeiture of vessels engaged. The
scope of the act was soon enlarged to include the other American colonies,
except New York and Georgia, neither of which had yet joined in the Continental Association of the colonies boycotting English goods. During the
consideration of these measures the Parliament had been bombarded with
petitions from the London merchants and from the mercantile and manufacturing interest of all the other great towns, as well as with remonstrances
from the colonies, urging the great importance of the American trade and
the vast sums already due from the colonial merchants for goods shipped to
them (estimated, for the City of London alone, at £2,000,000), which
these restrictions would render impossible of payment, and praying that
"healing remedies" be applied to restore the normal commerce between
Great Britain and the colonies. But the "King's friends" ignored these petitions and voted for the new oppressive acts by such majorities as 260 to 90
in the Commons.

The restraints on ordinary commerce were felt by all the colonies, but
the exclusion from the fisheries dealt a dreadful blow to New England, the

prosperity of which had been built up and was still largely dependent on the capture of codfish and whales. Nantucket, for instance, had a whaling fleet of 140 vessels, which was the principal support of its 5,000 inhabitants.

At the same time that the Parliament was in session in St. Stephen's Hall, partly warmed, no doubt by good sea-coal fires, the Provincial Congress of Massachusetts was sitting in Cambridge "in a house without a fire," so cold that it was resolved "That all those Members who incline thereto may sit with their Hats on" [10] which seems in a way to symbolize the contrast in resources between the two countries at that time.

The Massachusetts Congress had met on February 1 to take steps to meet those "most speedy and effectual measures for supporting the just rights of his Crown and the two Houses of Parliament" which the King proposed to take, and for which he had asked from the Commons an augmentation of his forces. The steps taken certainly justified His Majesty's accusation of rebellion. Two additional general officers were appointed by the rebels in the persons of John Thomas and William Heath; provision was made for a commissary to receive all "Stores, Ordnance, Arms and Provisions . . . until the Constitutional Army shall take the field"; there were many other arrangements looking toward armed conflict with the King's troops, including an address to the Stockbridge Indians, welcoming and promising "a Blanket and a Red Ribbon" to each one that "enlisted in the service" of the colony; a code of rules to govern the army—usually called "Articles of War" —was adopted; delegates were chosen to visit the other New England colonies and ask them to add their quotas to the forces of Massachusetts. The Congress finally adjourned on April 15—four days before the fatal day of Lexington and Concord.

CHAPTER 3

The Two Armies

While all these events were occurring, Gage had been adding to his forces. By the beginning of 1775, he had in Boston nine regiments of British infantry and parts of two others, the 4th or King's Own, the 5th, the 10th, the 23rd or Royal Welch Fusiliers, the 38th, the 43rd, the 47th, the 52nd, the 59th, three companies of the 18th or Royal Irish, and six companies of the 65th; also five companies of the Royal Artillery. The 64th was quartered in Castle William.

The strength of each regiment was supposed to be 477 of all ranks; but there was always a considerable actual shortage, and it has been estimated that the average effective number of rank and file was about 292. The total number, including the artillery, may therefore be computed at about 4,000. In the harbor lay four ships of the line, the *Scarborough*, the *Boyne*, the *Somerset*, and the *Asia,* each carrying sixty guns or more, "besides frigates and sloops and a great number of transports," from which Gage had drawn 460 marines.[1]

These soldiers were fair samples of the personnel of the British army that was to fight in the war. Their characteristics as soldiers, their equipment, leadership, and organization, were typical of the military power against which America was to contend.

In the eighteenth century, the British army had been built up by the crown contracting with this or that distinguished soldier or gentleman of position to raise a regiment. To him as its colonel was paid so much for each man enlisted, and thereafter an annual sum sufficient to pay and clothe his men. Sometimes, instead of receiving pay for enlistments, the colonel was permitted to nominate the officers, to whom he sold their commissions. A commission so acquired became the property of the holder and entitled him to receive the pay and allowances appropriate to his rank for the rest of his life, subject, however, to a reduction to half-pay if his regiment were disestablished in time of peace.[2]

As a species of property, such a commission could be sold if the holder desired to withdraw from the service; and it was by this means that promotion in the army was commonly obtained. Otherwise advancement was possible only when a vacancy in a superior rank occurred through death; and even then the hope was faint because as many as ten captains, for example, might be candidates for the commission of a dead major. The system of purchase practically restricted commissions to possessors of means.[3] The officers were almost all "men of family," that is to say, technically gentlemen. There were no military schools, except for the artillery. Raw lads of the officer class generally entered the army at the age of sixteen by favor or by purchase, learning their profession thereafter in actual service.

The common soldiers were far removed from the officers in the social scale. They were obtained by voluntary or by compulsory enlistment. The weekly pay of four shillings and sixpence was so reduced by charges for clothing, medicine, and many other impositions that they often got practically nothing in coin. Their food was "notoriously poor," their hardships severe. As a consequence, voluntary enlistment was largely confined to silly lads befooled by the glamour of the scarlet coat or to men and boys who were either desperate or drunk. Debtors released from imprisonment, criminals pardoned on the condition that they enlist, boys and men made drunk by the recruiting sergeant and persuaded to take "the King's shilling" while hardly aware of what they were doing made up a considerable part of the army.[4] "By lies they lured them, by liquor they tempted them, and when they were dead drunk they forced a shilling into their fists." [5]

Compulsory enlistment was made possible by the "Act against vagabonds," a statute authorizing impressment of "any sturdy beggar, any fortune teller, any idle, unknown or suspected fellow in a parish, that cannot give an account of himself . . . anyone who had been in gaol," or was "known as an incorrigible rogue"; poachers were fair game. But, though the recruiting officers interpreted these provisions broadly, enlistments, voluntary and involuntary taken together, were not enough to keep the ranks of the army up to the standard of strength, a condition that compelled the British government, within a short time after the war began, to employ foreign mercenaries.[6]

It would seem that the British army, so made up, would have been lacking in all the elements that go to building a force reliable in camp and on the march and effective in action; but its record in the war is all to the contrary. In the first place, it must be remembered that in conditions of economic hardship criminals are often made out of men not naturally vicious, and that under the extraordinarily severe code of criminal law then obtaining minor offenders were speedily converted into long-term felons or sentenced to death. It must also be observed that desperate men often make the best soldiers. In the second place, the effects of drill and discipline must not be overlooked. At all events, the British soldier in this war unquestionably displayed qualities of hardihood, courage, persistence, and military effectiveness that did honor to his nation.

Each regiment was composed of eight companies of ordinary foot soldiers, a company of light infantry, and one of grenadiers. These last two groups were the élite, the flower of the army, selected from the ranks for special qualities.

The light infantry were chosen for physical ability, vigor, audacity, alertness, and general fighting qualities outside ordinary service in the line of battle. Their chief duties were reconnaissance, skirmishing, outpost work and surprises, and flanking the army on the march.

The grenadiers were likewise selected troops; but they were chosen for qualities additional to those of the light infantry. They were first organized in the British army in 1678 to use a new weapon, a small iron bomb with an ignited fuse that was thrown by hand. As presumably able to throw such missiles a greater distance, the tallest and strongest men in each regiment were picked to be grenadiers. To permit slinging their muskets on either shoulder while they were engaged in such bombing, they wore brimless caps, instead of the usual broad-brimmed hats. These caps in time developed into the tall miterlike headpieces familiar in pictures of grenadiers, which added to their apparent height and gave them a more formidable appearance. The hand grenade had become practically obsolete in 1774, when the grenadiers were armed like the rest of the infantry. They were, nevertheless, retained in the army as a picked corps.

Both the light infantry and the grenadier companies remained in the regimental organization except when detached for special duty. They were known as "flank companies" because, in line of battle, they held the posts of honor at the flanks of their own regiments; they also led or flanked their regiments when in column of march. However, both the light companies and the grenadiers were frequently assembled in battalions of their own class for special operations or even as fighting units in a general battle. Some military critics deplored this practice because it skimmed the cream of the infantry and deprived the regular regiments of their best fighting men, who would have stiffened the line in defense and given it greater élan in attack. Nevertheless, it continued even to the extent of forming permanent regiments, such as the well known Grenadier Guards.

Gage had no cavalry at the beginning of 1775; but in June he did have a mounted force, a contingent of 400 men of the 17th Light Dragoons. These are to be distinguished from cavalry, whose arms were properly a heavy saber and a pair of horse pistols, and whose principal duties were to scout, to protect the flanks of the line or column, to circumvent the enemy's line, to cut communications, to pursue retreating enemies, and to act as shock troops, striking at the opposing force when it showed signs of weakness or disorder. Unlike the cavalryman, the dragoon, who was properly armed with a short musket or a carbine, a sword, and pistols, traveled on horseback but fought on foot; he was simply a mounted infantryman, and his horse, not being intended for shock tactics, was a light, wiry animal. When not engaged in battle he was usually employed for vedette work (as a mounted sentinel in advance of outposts), for orderly duty, and foraging. The distinction between the two arms (indicated in the phrase "horse, foot, and dragoons"), however, tended to diminish; dragoons were sometimes used as shock troops, as in the Battle of Monmouth in 1778 and at Camden in 1780, and the name came to be applied to pure cavalrymen,[7] as in the case of Tarleton's and William Washington's cavalry, often called dragoons.

The uniforms of the British infantrymen were modeled after those in use in Germany. They were highly ornamental, very fine for parade, but as impractical for active service as could well be imagined. The scarlet coat was lavishly decorated with colored linings, facings, and pipings, lace, and brass buttons; the waistcoat was either scarlet or white. The white breeches and the coat sleeves, also the long buttoned gaiters of some regiments, coming well above the knee, were all as tight as possible. The waist belt was broad and tight; it carried the bayonet scabbard. There was also a belt from the left shoulder to the opposite hip, carrying the cartridge box. The standing coat collars were stiff, and the movements of the head were further hampered by a high, stiff leather stock under the chin. The hats were of various types, some with broad brims cocked in the familiar, triangular form, others tall and pointed grenadier-fashion. These were often made of bearskin. None of them had a visor or brim to shield the eyes from the sun.

The hair was generally worn in a queue or club stiffened with grease and white powder, as were the tight curls in front of the ears.

Keeping all this apparatus in order—shining the brass, pipe-claying the leather, cleaning the cloth, blacking the shoes, braiding and dressing the queue, as well as polishing the arms—took from two to three hours a day. In active service, of course, much of this elaborate toilet was necessarily neglected; but the uniform and equipment were the same, so awkward, cumbersome, stiff, and constricting as greatly to hamper the movements of the soldier and to reduce his efficiency.[8]

The infantry officer was armed either with a spontoon—a sort of pike or spear with an ornamental head, which was both a badge of office and a weapon—or with a fusil, a short musket. He also wore a light dress sword.

The standard weapon of the infantry private was the musket, commonly called the brown Bess, after the first matchlock guns introduced into the British army by Queen Elizabeth, their barrels and metal fittings having been browned. By this time, however, the barrels were steel-bright. Any musket that had been inspected in the Tower of London was especially stamped, and was called a Tower musket.[9]

The brown Bess was a smoothbore gun; rifles were not yet in use in the British army. It weighed about ten pounds, was about four and a half feet long, and carried a twenty-one-inch bayonet. It had no rear sight. Its caliber was three-quarters of an inch. Because its bullet weighed more than an ounce, it had great stopping power, but the range was short: a ball fired with a regulation charge from such a gun, held horizontally at a height of five feet, fell harmlessly to the ground at about 125 yards. It was also very inaccurate, because its bore was usually untrue; but that mattered little, for the British soldier was no marksman. He had not been trained to take aim at a single object, nor even at the mass of the enemy. His instructions were to throw his gun to his shoulder in a horizontal position "point it—not sight it—toward the enemy and, at the word of command, pull the trigger."[10] As an English historian, Trevelyan, puts it: "He was taught to point his weapon horizontally, brace himself for a vicious recoil and pull a ten pound trigger till his gun went off: if, indeed, it did go off when the hammer fell." [11]

Loading involved biting the end off a cylindrical paper cartridge that contained powder and ball, shaking a little powder into the pan, closing its lid, dropping the butt of the gun on the ground, pouring the rest of the powder into the barrel, striking the gun to jar some powder into the touchhole, dropping in the ball, cramming the paper into the muzzle, and ramming it down to act as a wad. The process of firing was almost equally involved: when the trigger was pulled the cock fell, striking its flint against a piece of steel called the frizzen; from this contact, a shower of sparks (perhaps) fell on the powder in the pan; the powder flashed; there was a spurt of flame outward from the touchhole and inward into the charge, by whose explosion the bullet was projected. There was an appreciable interval of time between the pulling of the trigger and the explosion of the charge. Often, indeed, there was no explosion. The flint might be so worn as to fail to spark; the powder in the pan might be damp and so fail to ignite; the touchhole might be stopped up.[12]

In the British army the steps in loading and firing were taken in response to a series of orders by an officer. Up to a few years before the Revolution, the manual required sixteen distinct orders to put the soldier through forty-nine motions. By 1764 this had been simplified so that eight orders sufficed to effect priming and loading (but not presenting and firing) in twelve movements. The Americans reduced this to ten motions in response to a single order, "Prime and load!" It was also a part of their instructions to sight, not merely point, the musket. Two or three shots in a minute were reckoned a good rate of fire.[13]

Such delays and uncertainties and such a lack of precision made the brown Bess less useful as a gun than as a stock for a bayonet. Indeed, the "white weapon" was much the most effective British arm throughout the war. The usual practice was to advance the line to within a hundred yards or so of the enemy before firing one or more hit-or-miss volleys, and then to charge with the bayonet. Such attacks were the most dreaded by the Americans and the most often successful.

To oppose the regularly organized, fully equipped and trained British troops, Massachusetts had only its militia. That term must be understood in its true meaning. The militia included the entire potential fighting strength of the province. Every man between the ages of sixteen and sixty years was required by law to possess a gun and its proper equipment of ammunition and accessories, and to be enrolled in the company of his own township. He was supposed to turn out at certain intervals, perhaps four times a year or oftener, with the rest of his company for training; hence the common appellation, "trainbands."

The primary purpose in instituting this system in the early days of the colony had been to provide for defense against attacks by the Indians; there was no intention of sending the militia out of the province. But when, on the outbreak of the French and Indian War in 1754, it became necessary to furnish a force to operate in French territory, a new arrangement was authorized.

Service in several new regiments raised at that time was made voluntary. The officers were appointed by the governor, and each was authorized "to beat his Drums anywhere within the Province for enlisting Volunteers for His Majesty's Service in a Regiment of Foot to be forthwith raised for the Service and Defence of His Majesty's Colonies in North America." [14] This force served until the conclusion of the war in 1763, when it was disbanded, its members returning to the ranks of the militia. By their experience in the trainbands, but more especially by their service in actual war, many Massachusetts men had become familiar with the duties of a soldier. Not all of them, however, were to be useful in the coming struggle with Great Britain. Many were strong in their allegiance to the crown, in whose support they had fought.

When Gage came to Boston, the colonels of perhaps a full half of the thirty Massachusetts militia regiments were stanch Loyalists, who would in no event call out their men for action against the King's troops. The major general, the head of the entire force of militia, was a Tory. To remedy this condition, the Worcester Convention prevailed upon all the officers of that colony's three regiments to resign. It then provided for the organization of its militia in seven regiments, the towns to elect the company officers, who should choose the field officers. It went beyond this by directing the officers of each company to enlist a third of their men to be ready to act "at a minute's notice," these new companies to be made up into regiments. This was the origin of the famous minutemen.

The Worcester idea spread through the colony. Patriot officers willingly resigned, and Tories were so intimidated that they also gave up their commissions. The Provincial Congress, when assembled at Concord in October, 1774, approved the plan and directed that it be followed throughout the colony. Thus the militia of the province was rid of its Tory officers, and, as the minutemen were chosen with regard to the soundness of their political principles, the patriotism of their regiments was assured.

The minutemen have bulked large in the romance of the Revolution; but they had, in fact, a brief existence and were of little importance in the war. The formation of their regiments proceeded slowly; Woburn, for example, voted the establishment of its regiment as late as April 17, 1775, only two days before the Lexington-Concord engagements. In that same month, the Provincial Congress decided to abandon the scheme, to rely no longer upon the militia and the minutemen and to enlist, for a term of eight months, an army of 13,600 volunteers, thus reverting to the system used in the French and Indian War. It recognized the existence of the minutemen regiments by providing that their officers be given preference for commissions in the new army. Thus the minuteman passed out of existence after a career of no more than six months in the earliest companies and of a few days in the latest.[15]

There was a third class of soldiers in the Massachusetts militia scheme, the "alarm companies." These were not, as might be supposed, to be called out on the first alarm. They were, in fact, a last resort, an ultimate reserve, being composed of boys, old men, magistrates, and clergymen. Naturally, they were of little importance in the conflict.[16]

But few of these Massachusetts troops, of any class, were uniformed. The great majority came to their training days and turned out on alarms in their civilian clothes. Their guns were of any sort: brown Bess muskets surviving the French and Indian War; muskets issued in King George's War thirty years before; even perhaps a few Queen's arms, twice as old, dating from Queen Anne's War; American-made muskets of all dates; fowling pieces, blunderbusses, any kind of gun that would fire bullets or buckshot, except rifles. The rifled gun was unknown in New England, so that John Adams in Philadelphia attending the First Continental Congress wrote to his wife of "a peculiar kind of musket, called a rifle," used by "riflemen . . . from Pennsylvania, Maryland and Virginia . . . the most accurate marksmen in the world." [17]

The accouterments of the American militia were few and simple; a powder horn and a bullet pouch or a cartridge box, a bullet mold, and a bag of extra flints were the essentials. There might be added a haversack and a rolled blanket. Some of them, not many, had bayonets.[18]

CHAPTER 4

Lexington

During all the months from Gage's arrival in May of 1774 through the summer, fall, and winter, the British army lay inactive in Boston. No hostile move into the surrounding country was made, except Leslie's fruitless expedition to Salem. There were, however, a few peaceful excursions to exercise the troops, which were viewed with suspicion by the Provincial Congress. One day in February it interrupted its morning session at Concord to appoint a committee "to observe the motions of the troops said to be on their way to this town." [1] These expeditions, though harmless in themselves, did forebode more purposeful forays; Gage had not forgotten the stores of provincial munitions at Concord and Worcester. Also they put the Americans on the alert.

Late in February, Gage sent Captain Brown and Ensign De Berniere with one private to sketch the roads and test the political situation in Suffolk and Worcester counties. They were disguised, in "brown cloathes and reddish handkerchiefs" around their necks, so carefully that a Negro serving maid in the first tavern they stopped at recognized them at once as British soldiers and told their man that if they went much further "they would meet with very bad usage." At the next tavern the landlord, contrary to Yankee custom, asked them no questions at all, because "he had seen all he wanted without needing to ask." Farther on, they were overtaken by a horseman who looked them over carefully "and then rode off pretty hard." Later certain other equestrians asked them point-blank whether they were British soldiers, and at Marlborough they found the town "alive and buzzing." If they had not precipitately departed in the darkness of night from a certain Loyalist's house there, they would have been seized by the Committee of Correspondence for the town, which a few minutes later searched the house from garret to cellar. They got back to Boston thoroughly convinced that the political situation west of Boston might be very much better indeed without being too good, and that to surprise Concord invisible troops would be needed.[2]

By March, the tension in the people's minds was so great that a simple exercise march aroused the countryside; "expresses were sent to every town near," a couple of cannon were posted on the Watertown bridge, the planks were removed from the bridge at Cambridge, and the Provincial Congress voted that whenever troops of the number of 500 marched out of Boston "the Military Force of the Province ought to be assembled." [3] This nervous apprehension was nowhere more intense than among the patriots in Boston itself.

Thousands of men in that town were out of work, with nothing to do but loaf on street corners, loiter near the fortifications on the Neck, linger about the wharves, watch what was going on, and talk about what they saw. Paul Revere, silversmith, engraver, and ingenious craftsman, as well as express rider when important news was to be carried to New York or Philadelphia, had a group of watchmen "chiefly mechanics." They patrolled the streets, met secretly, exchanged the results of their observations, and reported them to Dr. Joseph Warren, who conveyed them to the Committee of Safety at Concord. Several other secret societies were similarly engaged. There was not much done in Boston that was not observed.[4]

When on April 15 the grenadiers and light infantry were ordered "off all duties 'till further orders" to learn "new evolutions," Lieutenant John Barker of the King's Own was not alone in suspecting this was "by way of a blind" and there was "something for them to do." [5] Revere's patrolmen were equally suspicious. They had an eye on the waterfront, and they had already seen the boats belonging to the transport vessels, which had been hauled up for repairs, "launched and carried under the sterns of the men of War." They too "expected something serious was to be transacted." [6] And, Yankee-fashion, they guessed, and guessed right, that an expedition was being prepared to go by boat across Back Bay to East Cambridge and so by road to Concord. Next morning Warren sent Revere to Lexington to warn John Hancock and Samuel Adams.

Returning to Boston that night, Revere arranged with "a Col. Conant & some other Gentlemen" in Charlestown "that if the British went out by water, we would shew two lanthorns in the North Church Steeple, and if by land [across the Neck] one, as a signal." This arrangement was made, not to inform Revere himself awaiting it in Charlestown booted and spurred and "impatient to mount and ride," as in Longfellow's poem, but to notify Conant and the "other Gentlemen" so that they might send word to Concord and elsewhere, Revere being "apprehensive" it would be difficult for him to cross the Charles River, "or git over Boston neck." [7]

Gage had planned a secret expedition to surprise Concord. To intercept wayfarers and prevent news of the foray from anticipating it, he sent mounted officers on the afternoon of April 18 to patrol the roads. The soldiers to be engaged in the enterprise were not to be notified until just before the time to march, when they were to be awakened "by the sergeants putting their hands on them and whispering gently to them" and "conducted by a back way out of the barracks without the knowledge of their comrades." The strictest silence was to be observed by everyone concerned.[8] But Boston's ears were cocked, and not all the British soldiers were muzzled.

One Jasper, a gunsmith, is said to have heard about the intended move in the afternoon from a British sergeant. John Ballard, a stableman, is reported to have overheard someone in the Province House say that there would be "hell to pay to-morrow." Earl Percy had been taken into Gage's confidence that evening; while crossing the Common immediately afterward, he heard one man say to another, "The British troops have marched, but they will miss their aim." "What aim?" inquired his lordship. "Why, the cannon at Concord." [9] Solomon Brown, a young man of Lexington, met the interception committee on his way home from Boston. He carried the news to William Munroe, sergeant of the Lexington minutemen, who collected eight of his company and posted them as a guard over the house where Hancock and Samuel Adams were lodging, to prevent their being kidnaped, and sent three others back toward Boston to watch the British patrol.[10]

Joseph Warren had the news before the British expedition had more than started from the barracks. He sent for Revere and William Dawes, another experienced express rider. Dawes was the first to come and was immediately dispatched to Lexington, to warn Hancock and Samuel Adams, and then to Concord. Revere arrived at Warren's house soon after Dawes. There were two main roads leading to Concord. One was by way of the Neck towards Roxbury, then around to Cambridge and Menotomy—now Arlington— and on through Lexington; it was much the longer. The other went from Charlestown to Medford and then to Menotomy, where it joined the other. Dawes managed to elude the guard at the Neck by mingling in the darkness with some soldiers passing that way, and took the first road. Revere stayed long enough to get his boots and surtout and to bid Captain John

Pulling, Jr., set the two lanterns in the Old North Church steeple. Two friends then rowed him with muffled oars across the river to Charlestown. Conant and some others, having seen the lights in the steeple, were at the wharf to meet him. A horse was furnished, and about eleven o'clock he was on his way.[11]

For this expedition, Gage had detached the grenadier and light infantry companies from his regiments, under general command of Lieutenant Colonel Francis Smith of the 10th foot. Major John Pitcairn of the marines led the light infantry, which marched in advance.[12] The number of men in the detachment is variously stated, from 600 to 800.[13]

They assembled at the foot of Boston Common at about half past ten in the evening of the 18th of April, embarked in boats on the Back Bay, and crossed to Lechmere Point, opposite the north end of the town. Because the water was too shallow to allow the boats to touch dry land, the men had to wade ashore. Lieutenant John Barker of the 4th (King's Own) regiment has described the subsequent proceedings: "After getting over the Marsh where we were wet up to the knees, we were halted in a dirty road and stood there 'till two o'clock in the morning waiting for provisions to be brought up from the boats and to be divided, and which most of the Men threw away, having carried some with 'em. At 2 oclock we began our March by wading through a very long ford up to our Middles." Thus inauspiciously began the journey to Concord.[14]

In the meantime, Dawes and Revere were speeding on their errands of alarm. Dawes met with no obstacles or interruptions, but Revere encountered a number of difficulties. He had intended to cut across from the road through Medford to Cambridge and so on to Menotomy, but he had hardly entered the crossroad before he saw two horsemen waiting in his path, British officers. "I was near enough to see their Holsters & cockades." One started toward him; but he wheeled about and "rid at full Gallop" back to the main road and so through Medford, alarming the dwellers of roadside houses as he went. At Medford he called on Captain Hull to turn out his company of minutemen. He woke up Menotomy and the houses beyond it and at last came to Lexington about midnight. At Parson Clarke's house he called on the guard to let him in. The sergeant asked him not to make so much noise, the family were asleep. "Noise!" Revere is reported to have said. "You'll have noise enough before long. The regulars are coming out!" That was enough. Hancock and Adams prepared for a hasty escape.[15]

Revere waited at Clarke's house half an hour for Dawes to come up by the longer road, and together they set out again for Concord. They were overtaken by young Dr. Samuel Prescott, who was returning home from a long evening with his sweetheart in Lexington. The three went on, alarming the houses they passed. About halfway between the two towns, they met two British officers, and two more emerged from a field beside the road. Dawes wheeled his horse about and rode hard back to Lexington. Revere and Prescott were ordered, at pistol point, to turn off the road into a pasture lot. Doing this, they immediately put spurs on their horses to escape in different directions. Prescott jumped his over a stone wall and got away. Revere struck out for a wood, but was met and taken by six other officers who had been concealed there. With them appeared three other prisoners, the men who had been sent out by Sergeant Munroe from Lexington to observe the enemy. That was the end of the Ride of Paul Revere.

He was dismounted and questioned. He told his captors that the country had been alarmed and that five hundred men were assembling at Lexington. They heard "a voley of [alarm] Guns, which appeared to alarm them very much." They took Revere's horse for one of their sergeants, gave him the small nag the sergeant had ridden, marched them all back toward Lexington, cut the bridles and girths of their captives' horses, drove them away, and rode off. Revere walked back to Clarke's house, found Hancock and Adams ready to leave, and went with them to Burlington in a chaise driven by the parson's son.[16]

Colonel Smith was so determined to preserve the secrecy of the foray that, on leaving the "dirty road" at Lechmere Point, he avoided the bridge across Willis Creek, for fear that the tramping of his men upon its planks might give the alarm, and led them through the ford mentioned by Barker. So, wet to the waist, they marched on through the cold night. Sometime after two o'clock, they halted in Somerville to let the men drink at a well. Then they went on, picking up prisoners here and there to prevent an alarm. Cambridge was next; then, at three o'clock, Menotomy, where three members of the Provincial Congress heard their tramp-tramp, fled from their beds in their nightgear, and hid in a field of corn stubble. Here six companies of light infantry, under Pitcairn, were detached and sent ahead. Now they were drawing near to Lexington.[17]

All through the night, as they passed through town after town, men awoke, dressed, took to horse, and rode away to call out the thousands who were finally to overwhelm these redcoats.

At Lexington, Revere's alarm at midnight had called out Captain Jonas Parker and his company of minutemen. One hundred and thirty of them gathered on the village green; but no more news came and the night was cold. After they had stood around cheerlessly and, as it seemed, pointlessly for an hour or so, Parker dismissed them with orders to respond again at the beating of the drum. Many went back to their near-by homes; the rest waited in Buckman's tavern close to the green.[18]

At half past four came the expected news. Riding at full gallop, Thaddeus Bowman brought it. The British were coming! They were close at hand, less than half a mile behind him! Alarm guns were fired. The minutemen in the tavern came on the run; others came from their houses. But some had no ammunition. They hurried to the meetinghouse, where the town's supply was kept. Men without guns gathered to look on. There was confusion all about the green. Finally, seventy armed men at the most were drawn up in two lines spaced somewhat apart.[19]

Lexington Green was a triangle bordered by roads. The road from Boston to Concord ran along its base.[20] Parker's men were drawn up not more than a hundred yards from this road, by which the British must march. What Parker expected to do with his three score men against Smith's six or eight hundred no one knows. He would protect the town, someone has suggested. But such an effort was hopeless, and besides Lexington was in no danger from the British. Their object, as everyone knew, was the stores at Concord. None of the towns on the way had been molested. Gallant as Parker's stand may have been, it was in effect nothing more than a challenge to the enemy which, if accepted, could only result, as it did, in futile bloodshed.[21]

It was a cold day for the season of the year, with a strong east wind; but the sky was blue, and the sun shone clear. The polished steel of ordered ranks of gun barrels and bayonets glittered brightly as Pitcairn's column came in sight, and one of the Americans saw the situation in its true proportions. "There are so few of us," he said, "it is folly to stand here." "The first man who offers to run shall be shot down," replied Parker. So there they stood, an offering for a sacrifice.[22]

Pitcairn's six light companies came on in column of march and saw the minutemen in form to oppose them. The Marine Major ordered his men into line of battle. As was customary, the rear ranks came forward at the double to line up with those in front, shouting and huzzaing as they ran. To the militia it appeared that they "rushed furiously," as if with bloody intent; but they only formed a line three deep in two sections or platoons, a little apart from each other.

Parker gave an order to his men: "Stand your ground! Don't fire unless fired upon! But if they want to have a war, let it begin here!" Some of the men, nevertheless, did drift away.

Pitcairn, with two other officers, rode to the front, within a hundred feet of Parker's lines. "Lay down your arms, you damned rebels, and disperse!"

Parker at last saw the hopelessness of the situation and ordered his men to disband and not to fire. They began to melt away, taking their muskets.

"Lay down your arms! Damn you! Why don't you lay down your arms?" shouted Pitcairn.

"Damn them! We will have them!" cried one of the officers, meaning the rebels' muskets.

Then there was a single shot, and from some one of the British officers, not Pitcairn, a command: "Fire, by God! Fire!" A volley from one platoon rang out—"They did not take sight," says a witness; the bullets went high over the Americans' heads. Pitcairn "struck his staff or Sword downward with all Earnestness as a signal to forbear or cease firing," but without avail. "The Soldiery and young Officers wanted to have at the damned Dogs, & in their impetuosity burst out into firing & continued it contrary to the Command of Pitcairn." [23] There was another volley that tore through the already retreating American ranks, answered by the feeble discharge of a scattered few, and then the Redcoats charged. Jonas Parker had fired once and had been wounded by a bullet; yet he stood his ground and was reloading his gun when he was cut down—his is a name worthy of remembrance. The rest fled, the British firing at them as long as they were within range. Eight dead men lay on the ground; ten wounded got away. Of the British, one private was slightly wounded in the leg, and Pitcairn's horse was grazed in a couple of places. The British officers had great difficulty in re-forming their men, who "were so wild they cou'd hear no orders." [24] When they were formed at last and when Smith with the main body came up, they fired a volley, gave a great cheer for their victory, "the musick struck up"—there was no hope of secrecy now—and they started off toward Concord, just as the sun rose.

That was the famous Battle of Lexington, which of course was no battle at all, not even a skirmish, for there was no contest. But who fired the first shot is a question unanswered after 165 years. The older American historians patriotically say Pitcairn. George Bancroft, for example, says so baldly and asserts further that he gave the order to fire; and so does John Fiske. For many years Pitcairn has been held in odium as a murderer of unresisting men, a "bloody butcher." But he denied it; he "insisted upon it to the day of his Death" at Bunker Hill "that the Colonists fired first: & that he commanded not to fire & endeavored to stay & stop the firing after it begun." Ezra Stiles, President of Yale College, recording this denial, believed that he was innocent, that he fired no shot and gave his men no order to fire, but that he was deceived as to the origin of the first shots. Stiles suggested, most reasonably, that these came from some of the British soldiers behind Pitcairn "as he turned to give Orders" not to fire, and regarded him as "a Man of Integrity & Honor" which, indeed, he was.[25] Pitcairn has been characterized truly as "a man whose humanity and tact had won him the love of his command, and the respect of people of all shades of opinion in the town . . . a brave and humane man." [26] His fall in battle two months later so grieved his command that their firing "slackened for some minutes, many of his men echoing these words—'We have lost a father!' " [27] A certificate of character not lightly to be disregarded.

CHAPTER 5

Concord

The alarm had gone forth, not only by Revere and Dawes to Lexington, but far and wide throughout eastern Massachusetts. Conant and his friends at Charlestown took care of the country roundabout; and from town to town, as the news came, riders carried it on posthaste. Lynn, ten miles to the north, was awakened in the early morning. Billerica, seventeen miles northwest, was aroused by two in the morning, and Acton, five miles farther, soon after. So it spread by an interlacing of expresses. Woburn was out before break of day. Reading at sunrise heard the alarm guns. At Danvers bells rang and drums beat at nine o'clock. At Tewksbury, twenty miles from Boston, a hard-riding messenger awoke Captain John Trull about two o'clock, and Trull fired his gun to awaken General Varnum at Dracut across the Merrimack. Andover, twenty-five miles away, heard the alarm at sunrise; Pepperell, thirty-five miles, at nine o'clock. Before noon, a white horse, dripping with sweat and bloody from the spur, galloped into Worcester, its rider crying: "To arms! To arms! the war has begun!" and it reached the church before it fell exhausted. So the news spread. Everywhere in the counties of Middlesex, Essex, Norfolk, and Worcester bells, guns, and drums called out the minutemen. Everywhere they were afoot and on the march.[1]

To Concord young Dr. Prescott, who had escaped when Revere was captured, brought the evil tidings between one and two o'clock in the morning. The alarm bell was rung, and the first to respond, gun in hand, was the Reverend William Emerson, minister of that town. Then came the minutemen, Captain David Brown's company, Captain Charles Miles's, and Cap-

40

tain Nathan Barrett's. Captain George Minot's alarm company of old men and boys gathered with the rest at Wright's tavern on the town square. Uncertain as to the truth of the news, they sent a messenger back to Lexington to confirm it. Meanwhile, they set about removing and hiding the military stores.[2]

The chief depository was at Colonel James Barrett's house. After the first alarm he hurried home, and the work of concealment and removal went on. Much of the stores had been sent away the day before. Now musket balls, flints, and cartridges were put into barrels in the attic and covered with feathers. Powder was hauled into the woods and hidden. A plow was got out, furrows were struck in a near-by field; light cannon and muskets were laid in them, and other furrows covered them up. By this and that means, the movable articles were put away.[3]

The road from Lexington, as it approached Concord, swung in a curve along the base of a long, narrow ridge which rose abruptly from the plain to a height of sixty feet. Near the end of this ridge lay the principal buildings of the village, the meetinghouse, courthouse, two or three taverns, and perhaps twenty-five dwelling houses. Passing these, it swung to the right beside a similar elevation at right angles to the first, turned squarely to the left, crossed the so-called North Bridge over the Concord River, beyond which was a third eminence two hundred feet high, called Punkatasset Hill, and so went on to Colonel Barrett's place, the chief objective of the British expedition.[4]

The first reinforcements of the little Concord companies came from nearby Lincoln, Captain William Smith's company. The force assembled now made up "150 of us or more." It seemed proper to make a reconnaissance. "We thought," wrote Corporal Amos Barrett of Brown's company, "we wood go and meet the Britsch . . . We marched Down to wards L[exington] about a mild or a mild [and a] half and we see them acomming. we halted and stay[d] till they got within about 100 Rods then we was orded to the about face and march[d] before them with our Droms and fifes agoing and also the B[ritish]. we had grand musick." [5] So, with rattle of drum and squeal of fife came the war to Concord.

Captain Minot's alarm company, the Reverend William Emerson wrote in his diary, had taken post on the first ridge above the meetinghouse, where stood the Liberty Pole, as the most advantageous situation—that is to say, at the end of the first ridge overlooking the town. But, with the news that the enemy "were just upon us & that we must retreat, as their N°
[number] was more than thribble ours," the old men and boys withdrew to the second ridge overlooking the bridge. The able-bodied minutemen, how-

ever, held their station on the first ridge.[6] It was now about seven o'clock in the morning.

The British came on, the light infantry in advance, followed by the grenadiers. Seeing the provincials on the height above the road, Colonel Smith threw out the light troops as flankers to clear the ridge, while the grenadiers kept to the road. Pitcairn's men "ascended the height in one line, upon which the Yankees quitted it without firing," [7] and retired to the second ridge already occupied by the alarm company.

"Scarcely had we form'd," says the clergyman's diary, "before we saw ye brittish Troops, at the Distance of a ¼ of a Mile, glittering in Arms, advancing toward [us] with ye greatest celerity. . . . Some were for making a Stand notw[ithstanding] ye Super[iority] of y^r [their] N° but others more prudent tho't best to retreat till our Strenth sh'd be equal to ye Enemy's by Recruits from neigh^g [neighboring] towns y^t were contin[ually] coming into our Assistance." [8] Colonel James Barrett, in general command of the militia of the district, had now returned from his work of concealing the stores. He ordered all the Americans to withdraw across the bridge, take post on Punkatasset Hill, and await reinforcements.[9]

Without hindrance the British came on into the village. Three of the light companies, under Captain Laurie, were stationed to guard the North Bridge: one at its eastern end, the two others on two near-by hills. Three others, led by Captain Parsons, crossed the bridge and marched up the road to Colonel Barrett's place; and the rest, under Captain Pole, were posted about the South Bridge.

While the British superior officers refreshed themselves in the taverns, carefully paying for what they had, the grenadiers began to search the houses.[10]

The search was not very successful, nor was the loss to the Americans very severe. Two 24-pound iron cannon were found in the town and their trunnions broken off—but they were later repaired. A hundred barrels of flour were found, and some were broken open; the others were rolled into the millpond—but the outer flour swelled and waterproofed the rest, so that much of it was salvaged. Five hundred pounds of musket bullets were thrown into the millpond, but most of them were afterwards dredged up.[11] A number of gun carriages were destroyed by fire, together with a lot of trenching tools and some wooden spoons and trenchers; and the British set fire to the courthouse and a blacksmith shop, but soon extinguished the flames themselves. All in all, the rewards of this laborious and, as it proved to be, fatal expedition, were small indeed.[12]

Meanwhile, the men on Punkatasset Hill had moved down to a smaller elevation nearer the bridge. On that little mound clouds had been gathering that were soon to break into a storm. From Acton, minutemen, 38 of them under Captain Isaac Davis, and two companies of militia of unknown numbers, Simon Hunt and Joseph Robin commanding, were the first to arrive. Bedford answered the call with John Moore's and Jonathan Willson's minutemen, 79 strong. William Smith had brought 62 from Lincoln. Unattached volunteers made up a force of three or four hundred. They watched the grenadiers at work in the town, and saw smoke rising from they knew not what fires. Colonel Barrett consulted with his officers. Joseph Hosmer, adjutant, came to them with a question: "Will you let them burn the town down?" They answered with a decision "to march into the middle of the town for its defence or die in the attempt." [13] Barrett gave the order. They were to march, but not to fire until fired upon. So down the hill they marched to do battle with the flower of the King's army.

Major John Buttrick with Lieutenant Colonel John Robinson of Westford at his side led the procession. Isaac Davis's little Acton company in double column, two fifers shrilling the notes of "The White Cockade," two drums beating time to the tune followed. Miles's Concord company fell in next, and then Brown's and Barrett's. Hunt followed with his Acton militia. Bedford and Lincoln and the unattached volunteers closed the column.[14]

Captain Laurie, in command at the bridge, saw them coming and sent to Colonel Smith for reinforcements. Smith ordered two or three companies forward, "but put himself at their head by which means he stopt 'em from being [in] time enough, for being a very fat heavy Man he wou'd not have reached the Bridge in half an hour tho' it was not half a mile to it." [15]

Laurie withdrew his men to the east end of the bridge, leaving a few to take up the planks. Buttrick shouted to the men at work to stop and quickened the pace of his militia. For some unknown reason, the men lifting the planks stopped and went back to their own ranks. Laurie tried to dispose his men to resist the Americans, but "the Rebels got so near him that his people were obliged to form the best way They cou'd . . . the three companies got one behind the other so that only the front one cou'd fire: the Rebels when they got near the bridge halted and fronted, filling the road from top to bottom." [16]

The first fire came from the British, two or three "dropping shots" that splashed harmlessly in the water. But one bullet whistled by the ear of one of the captains. In utter astonishment, "God damn it! They're firing ball!" exclaimed Captain Timothy Brown. Then came a single shot from the British. The bullet struck Luther Blanchard, one of the fifers who had played them down the hill, in the side. making a slight wound. Then a volley rang out. Captain Isaac Davis, at the head of the Acton company, sprang high in the air and fell dead; Abner Hosmer, also of Acton, collapsed on the ground with a bullet through his head. Two others were wounded. Buttrick turned to his men and shouted, "Fire, fellow soldiers! For God's sake, fire!" And they did. Three British privates fell dead; four out of the eight British officers at the bridge, a sergeant and four men were wounded.[17]

The fight at the bridge was all over in two or three minutes. The British retreated in disorder towards the village, leaving their dead and one wounded man, met Smith's reinforcement of grenadiers, re-formed their ranks, and withdrew into the village. The Americans crossed the bridge and pursued the enemy, but only for a few rods. Then, undisciplined as they were, they broke ranks. A number of them went back across the bridge, picked up the bodies of Davis and Hosmer, and carried them off. About two hundred went a little farther, to the near end of the ridge on which they had taken their second position earlier in the day. Strung along behind a stone wall, they waited; but the enemy never came within range. Because of this disruption of the American force, the British light companies under Captain Parsons that had gone to Barrett's place were able to return, cross the bridge, and rejoin their comrades unscathed.[18]

Smith's grenadiers and the light companies from the bridge got back to the village about ten o'clock. An hour later, Parsons's men joined them. Another hour elapsed before they were ready for the return march. At noon they set out, having commandeered two chaises to carry their wounded.[19]

For the first mile, they marched unmolested. But then followed one of the strangest battles of the war, nearly sixteen miles long and a few hundred yards wide. It began at Meriam's Corner on the road to Lexington.

Only three to four hundred men had been in the fight at the bridge; but others had been on the way. Chelmsford sent 60 under Captain Oliver Barron and 43 under Moses Parker. Oliver Crosby, Edward Farmer, and Jonathan Stickney brought a hundred from Billerica. Framingham turned out 147 under Simon Edgett, Jesse Emes, and Micajah Gleason. The roads were black with hurrying men. Reading outnumbered the other towns with 290 men in four companies, Captains John Bacheller, Thomas Eaton, John Flint, and John Walton commanding. Woburn "turned out extraordinary" and rivaled Reading with 256 led by Samuel Belknap, Jonathan Fox, and Joshua Walker; and Sudbury's six companies, numbering 249, under Nathaniel Endworth, Aaron Haynes, Isaac Locker, John Nixon, Joseph Smith, and Moses Stone, were a good third. William Whitcomb led 81 from

Stow, while Westford added 113 under Oliver Bates, Jonathan Minot, and Joshua Parker.[20]

The men who had fought at the bridge had hurried northward across the Great Meadow to Meriam's Corner. The rest had followed or came up with them there. A few companies were gathered about the Meriam house. Smith had thrown out flanking parties parallel to the highway and at some distance from it on either side. As those on the side of the road nearer the house passed by, they wheeled suddenly and fired a harmless volley. The Americans replied, and two of the enemy fell; others were wounded. So this second battle began.[21]

Nearing a small stream, the flankers went down to the road to cross a bridge with the others. Dense groves of trees lined the road at this point: they were full of Americans, who had hurried ahead. Into the crowd pressing across the bridge, they poured a deadly fire. "A grait many Lay dead and the Road was bloddy." [22]

The British column went on. The Americans hurried to get ahead, take cover, and fire again. Parker's company from Lexington, now with full ranks, 120 strong and hot with anger, joined the hunters in Lincoln township. From Cambridge came Captain Thatcher's company, 77 men. Others from the near-by countryside flocked to them. "It seemed as if men came down from the clouds." [23] From houses and barns, from behind walls, rocks, and trees came flashes of flame and puffs of smoke, and redcoats dropped, the dead to lie where they fell, the wounded to keep on as best they could and as long as they could. To some of the British, it was a new sort of warfare, not the kind they had been drilled for, where men faced each other and shot it out, where a bayonet charge might prove decisive. It was dishonorable, this hiding and shooting at men who could not even see you. It was downright savagery. Their anger was fierce, the more bitter because it had so little vent in reprisal. "They were so concealed," said Lieutenant Barker, "there was hardly any seeing them." [24]

But it was not all one-sided. The flanking parties, well back from the road, were sometimes forgotten by the too eager Americans, who were between them and the main column. Many were shot in the back as they were drawing trigger from behind a wall or tree. The flankers took a heavy toll of their adversaries.

The British force was no longer a marching column. It was a disorderly mass of men crowding the road. Soldiers were leaving what had been ordered ranks, ransacking roadside houses and taverns for meat and drink. As they entered Lexington township, Smith halted his men and posted a rear guard to hold back the Americans while he re-formed his ranks. But there was no pursuing force to hold back. Their enemies were all around them on every side. From behind a pile of rails came a blast of fire. Smith was wounded in the leg. Pitcairn's horse plunged, threw its rider, leaped a wall, and ran directly toward the ambuscade. It was captured, and Pitcairn's pistols are now preserved in an American museum.[25]

The attempt to reorganize was not successful. The rearguard was driven in, and the rout continued. Barker reports of this time that the Americans were "increasing from all parts," while the British were "reducing from deaths, wounds and fatigue, and we were totally surrounded with such an incessant fire as it's impossible to conceive, our ammunition was likewise near expended." [26] De Berniere likewise describes the confusion of the British: "When we arrived within a mile of Lexington, our ammunition began to fail, and the light companies were so fatigued with flanking they were scarce able to act, and a great number of wounded scarce able to get forward made a great confusion . . . so that we began to run rather than retreat in order—the whole behaved with amazing bravery, but little order; we attempted to stop the men, but to no purpose, the confusion increased rather than lessened." [27]

So they passed through the village, along the edge of the green, where the conflict had begun that morning. With the least bit of organization among the Americans, Smith's force might have been stopped there, surrounded, and either taken or destroyed. But it was not an American army that so pursued and hemmed them in; it was simply a horde of angry, revengeful, individual men, each on his own, with no coherence, no concert of action. So the invaders were permitted to stumble on, fatigued to the last degree, but still able to go a little farther before they fell utterly exhausted.

There was one more effort to reduce the confusion in the British ranks. Near Lexington village "the officers got to the front and presented their bayonets, and told the men that if they advanced they should die: Upon this they began to form under a very heavy fire." [28] It was the last gasp of British discipline, before those beaten men fell on their faces under the protection of a rescue party.

When Smith had first got to Menotomy, between two and three o'clock in the morning, he had been alarmed by the increasing and seemingly hostile curiosity of the countryside about the movement of his force and had sent an express back to Boston asking for reinforcements. But Gage had already anticipated the need of relief for his Concord expedition and had given orders in the evening of the 18th for the 1st brigade and a battalion of the Royal Marines to parade at four o'clock the next morning—a reason-able precaution which was largely nullified by a series of errors.[29]

First, the brigade major was not at home when the orders were delivered to his servant. He came in late, and his man forgot to tell him about them. There was no parade at four o'clock. At five, Smith's express arrived, and the matter was looked into. At six, part of the brigade was on parade, but no marines. That stirred inquiry again, and it was found that the orders had been addressed to Pitcairn, and left at his quarters, he being then on the way to Concord. It was nine o'clock when the relief started, a delay nearly fatal to Smith's force.[30]

The relief consisted of the 4th or King's Own Regiment, the 23rd, Royal Welch Fusiliers, the 47th, less their flank companies who were with Smith, and the 1st battalion of marines with two 6-pound fieldpieces. The whole force numbered about 1,000, and was under the command of Brigadier General Earl Percy. With all their fifes and drums derisively playing "Yankee Doodle," they marched across the Neck.[31]

Percy was the son and heir of the Duke of Northumberland. There is a legend that as his force passed through Roxbury a schoolboy laughed so heartily at the tune the fifers were playing that Percy asked him the reason. He answered, "To think how you will dance by and by to Chevy Chase," the reference being to the ballad in which appears this verse:

> To drive the deer with hound and horne
> Erle Percy took his way.
> The child may rue that is unborne
> The hunting of that day! [32]

At Cambridge the planks of the bridge across the Charles had been lifted, but piled on the far side. Soldiers crossed on the stringpieces and replaced them; but the supply train of two wagons with its guard of twelve men had to wait until they could be well secured, and then proceeded far in the rear of the column. It soon fell easy prey to a dozen "old men of Menotomy," led by a half-breed Indian, who took both wagons and supplies after two of the guard had been killed and several wounded by a discharge of musketry from behind a stone wall.[33]

Percy was beyond Menotomy village when he first heard the sounds of warfare.[34] "As we advanced," Lieutenant Frederick Mackenzie of the Royal Welch Fusiliers wrote in his diary, "we heard the firing plainer and more frequent, and at half after 2, being near the Church at Lexington, and the fire encreasing, we were ordered to form the Line, which was immediately done by extending on each side of the road. The Grenadiers & Light Infantry were at this time retiring towards Lexington, fired upon by the Rebels, who took every advantage the face of the Country afforded them." But as soon as they "perceived the 1st Brigade drawn up for their support, they shouted repeatedly, and the firing ceased for a short time." [35]

It was high time for a rescue. "We had been flatter'd ever since the morning," says Barker, "with expectations of the Brigade coming out, but at this time had given up all hopes of it." [36] The wasted remnants of Smith's command hurried to the protection of Percy's line, "so much exhausted with fatigue, that they were obliged to lie down for rest on the ground, their tongues hanging out of their mouths, like those of dogs after a chase." [37]

"We could observe a Considerable number of the Rebels, but they were much scattered and not above 50 of them to be seen in a body in any place. Many lay concealed behind the Stone walls and fences. They appeared most numerous in the road near the Church and in a wood in the front and on the left flank of the line." [38] On these Percy trained his guns, harming only the church, through which he sent one ball, while the provincials retired behind a swamp. Some of his men, seeing the Americans retire, broke from their ranks in pursuit, but the swamp stopped them. They then entered the village, looted some houses, and burned one large group of farm buildings and several dwellings.[39]

All this while, the Americans were dodging here and there, creeping around the enemy's flanks, appearing and disappearing as they took cover behind trees, walls, and houses, sniping or firing small volleys, and inflicting much injury upon the massed British troops.

Percy gave the exhausted men an hour's rest. At half past three he resumed the retreat, with Smith's men in front covered by the fresh troops and strong parties on the flanks. The more impressive array of the combined forces and the vigilance of the flankers somewhat daunted the Americans, and, for a time, the British marched in comparative safety. Of necessity they proceeded slowly, and there was a fine chance to loot the roadside houses. Percy exercised no restraint on such depredations. He evidently wished to terrorize the countryside. Many of his men carried heavy burdens of household goods of all sorts. But as he neared Menotomy the aspect of affairs began to change again. The Americans were pressing more closely on his rear guard and against his passing column, and the firing from cover grew stronger and stronger, for his enemies were rapidly increasing in numbers. New companies of minutemen and militia had been hurrying to the battle from the eastern towns and now were arriving.

Brookline brought 95 men into play; Watertown, 134; Medford, 59;

Malden, 76; Roxbury, 140. Needham sent 185; Beverly, 122. Menotomy turned out 52, and Danvers, 331. Dedham was left "almost literally without a male inhabitant before the age of seventy and above that of sixteen"; its 337 topped all the rest.[40] There were 2,000 or more men to resume the attack. General William Heath and Dr. Joseph Warren urged them on against the British rear guard. Percy halted his column and turned his two 6-pounders on them, but with no effect, except to scatter his pursuers temporarily. So they went on again. The flankers kept the Americans back from the roadside or shot down those who were too reckless in making a near approach. They entered the houses, looted them, tried to burn them. At one point a group of minutemen, too few to stand openly against the enemy, had retreated into a house. Twelve were bayoneted, and the house was plundered. "We were now," says Lieutenant Barker, "obliged to force almost every house in the road, for the Rebels had taken possession of them and galled us exceedingly . . . all that were found in the houses were put to death." [41] The fury of the fight was at its height. Forty Americans fell in Menotomy, and forty British. Many of these were killed in close personal encounter, clubbed muskets against bayonets.

In Cambridge there was a mile and a half of continuous battle. The sight of the burning houses and of the British soldiers loaded down with plunder had inspired the Americans with a fierce rage. If it had been possible to organize them into a single body, get ahead of the column, obstruct the road with felled trees, send out detachments to waylay and destroy the flanking troops, which were not numerically too strong, and, from the stone walls beside the road, concentrate their fire on the main column, Percy's troops might have been held up and destroyed. But there was no central control over the various elements of the American forces, these township companies. Heath at Menotomy tried to form them into regiments; but he had no staff to carry his orders, and, if there had been one, it could not have brought together and reduced to order those half-trained men scattered over the country who did not even preserve their companies as units.[42]

At Cambridge, Percy, to avoid the bridge over the Charles, shrewdly and unexpectedly changed his course from that on which he had come from Boston and took the road to Charlestown. It was shorter as well as safer. But in what is now Somerville he was forced to renew the fight. His field-pieces were again in action, with no more substantial result than before. Fire from a grove of trees cut down a number of his men. The rest hurried on faster. At Prospect Hill there was a considerable gathering of Americans, and many of the invaders fell. Once more Percy halted his column and made play with the guns, and these were unlimbered again a little farther on. In spite of the harassment of the retreating troops, the looting and destruction of property continued.[43]

The weary, almost exhausted soldiers at the head of the column, Smith's men, had expended almost all their ammunition when, after sunset, they at last crossed the little isthmus that connects Charlestown with the mainland and were free from their pursuers. In the twenty hours that they had been afoot they had marched thirty-five miles, had fought continuously for half that distance, had had little to eat, and many of them had been wounded.

The British losses that day were 73 killed, 174 wounded, 26 missing, a total of 273 casualties out of about 1,800. The Americans lost 49 killed, 41 wounded, and 5 missing, a total of 95. It has been computed that 3,763 Americans were engaged in the day's fighting at one time or another, though perhaps not much more than half that number at any one time.[44]

The fact that in so long a battle, subjected to the fire of so numerous a force, the British lost no more than 15 per cent of their men is noteworthy. If each American, in his whole day's work, had hit his mark only once, the British force would have been destroyed twice over. The militia and minutemen were supposed to carry thirty-six cartridges, or the equivalent in loose powder and bullets. If the average man fired only twenty charges (and we hear of many who fired nearly twice that number) no fewer than 75,000 shots must have been discharged at the enemy, with a total of hardly more than 247 hits. Only one bullet out of 300 found its mark. In all his day's work, only one man out of 15 hit anybody.

It is of course true that the flankers kept the roadside walls and other close cover fairly free of the Americans, compelling them to use the second line of walls at more than point-blank distance from the marching column. It is also true that those same roadside walls protected the British, in some places "almost to the height of their shoulders." [45] Nevertheless, there were many times when a heavy fire was poured upon them at short range, and the results of the entire proceeding should prove the fallaciousness of the belief so often expressed that the Yankees were superior marksmen, dead shots in fact. They were not. They could not be when armed only with the musket or fowling piece of the period. Their inaccuracy and short range have been previously noted, and the Yankees had had little practice in shooting, because of the infrequency of training days and the scarcity and expense of gunpowder.

The comments of the English officers engaged are interesting. That of Percy is noteworthy as showing a change in his opinion that the Americans were "cowards" and "timid creatures." He noted that "many of them concealed themselves in houses & advanced within 10 yds. to fire at me and

other officers, tho' they were morally certain of being put to death themselves in an instant . . . nor will the insurrection here turn out so despicable as it is perhaps imagined at home. For my part, I never believed, I
confess, that they wd have attacked the King's troops, or have had the
perseverance I found in them yesterday." [46]

Lieutenant Barker thought the whole affair was "as ill plan'd and ill
executed as it was possible to be." Especially, he complained of the "three
hours on Cambridge marsh waiting for provisions that were not wanted."
That delay, he thought, allowed the country people to get intelligence of the
movement and gave them time to assemble. But for it, there would have
been "no interruption at Lexington" and a surprise at Concord.[47]

Captain Evelyn, however, still called "the Yankeys . . . the most absolute cowards on the face of the earth," and attributed their conduct to
"enthusiasm and madness." [48]

CHAPTER 6

The Siege of Boston

At ten o'clock in the morning of April 19, Israel Bissel, postrider, mounted his horse at Watertown. In his pocket was a letter:

To all Friends of AMERICAN Liberty let it be known: That this morning before break of day, a Brigade consisting of about one thousand or twelve hundred men . . . Marched to *Lexington* where they . . . Killed 6 Men and wounded 4 Others . . . another Brigade are now upon their March from Boston supposed to be about 1000. The bearer Israel Bissel is charged to alarm the Country quite to Connecticutt and all persons are desired to furnish him with fresh Horses as they may be needed. . . .

J. Palmer—one of the Com^y of S^y

At noon Bissel's horse fell dead at Worcester, thirty-six miles away. No fresh horse was immediately forthcoming, so he spent the night there; but by seven the next evening he was at New London, Connecticut, having given the tidings to Israel Putnam at Pomfret on the way. In the night he went on. Lyme had the news at one o'clock in the morning, Saybrook at four, Guildford at seven, Branford at noon, New Haven in the evening. A night there and on again. Fairfield saw him at four in the afternoon. Connecticut had been alarmed, but Israel Bissel did not stop. He was in New York on the 23rd. There the "faction," as the Loyalists called the Rebels, immediately "paraded the town with drums beating and colours flying." A sloop, loaded with provisions for the British in Boston, was unloaded. The arsenal was entered, and a thousand stand of arms were seized. "The whole city became one continued scene of riot, tumult and confusion. Troops enlisted for the service of the rebellion." So New York, hesitating and doubtful before, was aroused and began to swing into line with the other colonies.

But the furore he had excited did not stay Bissel. He was off again southwards, riding night and day through New Jersey, New Brunswick at two in the morning, Princeton at six, Trenton at nine, then Philadelphia. A feat of endurance was that ride of Israel Bissel's.

A second dispatch, with fuller details, came to New York on the 25th and went on by relays of express riders, again riding night and day. Baltimore had it on the 27th at ten in the evening; Annapolis, at half past nine the next morning; Edenton, North Carolina, on May 4th; and finally, having been given out at every town and village the whole way, it reached Charleston, South Carolina, on the 10th.[1]

From every point on the road the "momentous intelligence" spread to the outlying districts and, by letters and word of mouth, reached the farthest corners of the colonies, the towns on the seaboard, the villages and farms, the backwoods settlements. Everywhere the response was a call to arms.

The veteran Colonel Israel Putnam, who was now retired to his Connecticut farm after having seen hard service in the French and Indian War, was "in leathern frock and apron . . . assisting hired men to build a stone wall' when Bissel brought him the news. He instantly answered the call, in his working clothes. Rousing the militia officers as he rode through the towns, "he reached Cambridge at sunrise the next morning," a hundred miles in eighteen hours on the same horse.[2]

Massachusetts men were flocking to Cambridge even before Putnam had the news. By one o'clock of the 20th, New Hampshire was afoot. Sixty men from Nottingham, joined by others on the way, made the distance to Haverhill, twenty-seven miles, by dusk, "having run rather than marched," and were in Cambridge, fifty-five miles, within twenty hours. Colonel John Stark, hardy backwoodsman, was in command of 300 of his fellow colonists at Chelsea by the morning of the 22nd. Two thousand of them were ready to come the next day.[3]

Connecticut's action was swift; thousands were on the way by the 24th. Rhode Island was on the march before Percy got back to Charlestown. Within the shortest possible time Boston was surrounded from Roxbury to Chelsea by an unorganized, undisciplined mass of men.

The minutemen had never been really organized; their officers had not even been commissioned. As separate bodies they soon ceased to exist. The militia was composed of boys and men varying in age from sixteen years to sixty. The responsibilities of many of them would prevent them from entering upon a continuous campaign. It was no army that surrounded Boston, and what force was there was soon melting away. Within four days after Concord the Massachusetts men, many of whom had departed immediately after the fighting was over, were greatly reduced in numbers, and hundreds from New Hampshire had gone home. General Artemas Ward wrote to the Congress that he was in danger of being "left all alone." [4]

The Massachusetts Provincial Congress, sitting on Sunday April 23, voted that an army of 30,000 men be "immediately raised and established," of which 13,600 were to be "raised immediately by this Province." The thousands needed to make up the full number were not provided for; but committees were sent to the other New England colonies to "request their concurrence." [5]

Rhode Island's assembly promptly voted a brigade of three regiments, 1,500 men, and appointed as brigadier general Nathanael Greene, who was "worth a thousand men" and more.[6] New Hampshire fixed 2,000 as its quota, with Nathaniel Folsom as the major general, but Colonel John Stark "the most trusty officer" in command.[7] Connecticut ordered the enlistment of 6,000, with David Wooster as the major general and Joseph Spencer and Israel Putnam as brigadiers. Of the Massachusetts forces, Artemas Ward, John Thomas, William Heath, John Whitcomb, and Joseph Warren were appointed major generals.[8] Not all the promised thousands materialized; Connecticut never sent more than half her quota; both New Hampshire and Rhode Island fell short of theirs. But, by June, there were perhaps 15,000 men encamped before Boston.

They stretched in a half-circle around Boston, from Roxbury to Chelsea. The center, at Cambridge, was held by Ward with fifteen Massachusetts regiments, Major Samuel Gridley's battalion of four companies of artillery, Putnam's own regiment and other Connecticut troops, 9,000 in all. The right wing, at Roxbury, Dorchester, and Jamaica Plains, was commanded by General Thomas. He had 4,000 Massachusetts men, Greene's Rhode Island regiments, and the greater part of General Spencer's Connecticut troops, three or four artillery companies, a total of about 5,000. On the left, there were three companies of Colonel Samuel Gerrish's Massachusetts regiment at Chelsea; Colonel John Stark's New Hampshire regiment, the largest in the army, at Medford; and the much smaller regiment under Colonel James Reed, also from New Hampshire, near Charlestown Neck, about 1,000 in all from that state.[9]

General Artemas Ward was in supreme command of the Massachusetts troops; and the New Hampshire troops had been directed to place themselves under his orders.[10] The other colonies' forces were at this time amenable only to their own commanders, though Connecticut also submitted her men to Ward's orders after Bunker Hill. Yet from the first they all seem to have cooperated in obedience to Ward.

This hastily assembled force was short of supplies of every kind—arms, ammunition, tents, blankets, provisions, and camp utensils. Of ordnance fit for siege operations, it had practically none—no more than a few large iron cannon, two or three mortars and howitzers. Sixteen fieldpieces, of which perhaps only six were fit for service, constituted their mobile artillery. Late in June, New Hampshire offered "some" 24- and 32-pounders, and the Massachusetts Committee of Safety asked for three of the smaller size.[11]

The supply of small arms was better, for generally each man brought his own firelock; yet more than a thousand men were deficient in this respect in the middle of June. Bayonets were conspicuously lacking, and uniforms almost altogether absent. The greatest shortage was in the most essential element, gunpowder. Much of Massachusetts' small stock had been seized by Gage. Late in April there were but 82 half-barrels available; on May 25 the Committee of Safety drafted 68¼ barrels from five of the eastern counties.[12]

Massachusetts had only 1,100 tents, but set about making more out of ships' sails. As many of the troops as possible were crowded into dwellings, which had been vacated by their owners removing from the combat zone. The buildings of Harvard College gave shelter to many.[13]

How to feed such an army was a problem, as it continued to be throughout the war—often, indeed, almost insoluble. In the morning after the battle "all the eatables in the town of Cambridge, which could be spared, were collected for breakfast, and the college kitchen and utensils procured the cooking." Some beef intended for the Boston market was secured, and "a large quantity of ship-bread at Roxbury, said to belong to the British army, was taken." After that the Commissary General was directed to "supply the troops with provisions, in the best manner he can, without spending time on exactness"; and somehow he managed to do it.[14]

All communication between the town and the rest of the province was now cut off. But in the town there were thousands of patriots who wished to leave it, and outside it were many Loyalists who longed for the protection the British troops could afford them. After a complicated negotiation an agreement was made allowing an exchange. Gage stipulated that all the inhabitants should first deposit all their arms in Faneuil Hall, which they did to the extent of 1,778 firelocks, 634 pistols, 973 bayonets, and 38 blunderbusses. Those coming in and going out were allowed to carry their personal effects except arms and ammunition, and the exception was soon extended to include salable merchandise, provisions, and medicines.

Thousands took advantage of this arrangement. It has been estimated that "near half" of the patriots went out. Wagons from outside were allowed to enter the town, to bring in and carry out the effects of those coming and going. Plans were made to distribute an estimated 5,000 poor refugees from Boston in various other towns. But after a while the Tories in Boston protested against the Whigs' being allowed to go out, wishing to hold them as hostages against an attack and, perhaps, a burning of the town. Various obstacles and delays developed, and the system broke down.[15]

The condition of the British army, shut up in the town with no access to the country, unable to procure fresh meat or vegetables, was unenviable. Captain George Harris of the 5th Regiment wrote home about it: "However we block up their port, the rebels certainly block up our town, and have cut off our good beef and mutton. . . . At present we are completely blockaded, and subsisting almost on salt provision." He was cultivating his own little garden of salads and greens. Lieutenant Barker wrote, "We can get no fresh provision, but must live on our allowance of salt meat." [16]

From a military point of view, the situation was a stalemate. Boston was blockaded on the land side, but it was not properly besieged. As long as the fleet kept open communication by water, the Americans could not hope to starve it out. Unless there was some definitely active move on one side or the other, the condition might last until doomsday. But the Americans dared not attempt to take the town. For one thing, they could not concentrate all the available force of the four provinces against it; the seacoast towns, in fear of attacks by the fleet, were holding their own men at home and calling for more. There were no siege guns to batter the defenses, and the men were not sufficiently disciplined and coordinated for storming operations. As for the British, they had had their lesson on April 19; they knew they had not nearly enough to try offensive operations outside the town.

There were, however, some little excursions from both sides. Gage needed hay for his horses and the few beef cattle he had. On May 21 he sent four sloops, with a subaltern and thirty men, to bring off a supply from Grape Island in the harbor. General Thomas sent three companies in a lighter and a sloop to oppose them. There was a harmless exchange of fire before the British were driven off, with only seven or eight tons of hay; the Americans burned all the rest, eighty tons.[17]

The Americans countered, on May 27, with an expedition against two other harbor islands, Hog and Noddle's, on which a considerable number of horses, cattle. and sheep were at pasture. Wading through a narrow

MAP OF THE SIEGE
OF BOSTON

SCALE

0   1/2   1 MILE

shallow channel to Hog Island, they drove off all its livestock, but on Noddle's the British admiral, Samuel Graves, had landed a considerable quantity of stores. Having observed the hostile operations, he sent an armed schooner, the *Diana*, with forty marines, to protect his property.

The Americans had already taken off three or four hundred head of sheep, cattle, and horses, killed what other stock they could not remove and burned all the hay, when the enemy began to fire on them. They then retired to Hog Island, where a handful of them "squated Down in a Ditch on the marsh" and there was "a hot fiar untill the Regulars retreeted." Though "the Bauls Sung like Bees" around their heads, no one was hurt. But that was not all.[18]

The *Diana* got in trouble with adverse wind and tide and could not get away. Graves sent ten or twelve barges from the fleet to tow her, and after them the armed sloop *Britannia*. Putnam marched a thousand men with two fieldpieces to attack this little flotilla from Chelsea Neck. Graves answered by mounting three guns from his ship on Noddle's Island. Gage sent eighty marines and two 12-pounders to assist him. As the *Diana* approached the shore where the Americans stood, there was a heavy fire from all the guns on both sides and from the American musketry. Putnam led his men into the water waist-deep to get in closer range. It was growing dark, and the aim of both sides was blind. The towing barges cut loose and rowed away; the *Diana* went aground. She fell on her beam ends, and her men were taken off by the *Britannia* without waiting to save anything. The Americans swarmed aboard, looted her, and set her on fire. There were few casualties in those twelve hours of fighting; four Americans were slightly wounded, two British killed and several wounded. The Americans were pleased with their capture of four 4-pounders and twelve swivels from the *Diana* and the salvage of her ironwork. They went back to the islands three days later and carried off several hundred sheep and some cattle and horses. Other such forays stripped Pettick's Island of five hundred sheep and thirty horned cattle, and Deer Island of eight hundred sheep and more cattle. The American commissariat was greatly refreshed by these exploits.[19]

Gage anticipated a possible attack on his defenses on Boston Neck by adding to their strength. An abatis—that is to say, a row of felled trees, their butts embedded in the ground, their sharpened major limbs pointed outward—was constructed in front of one of the outer bastions, and a triple row of *chevaux-de-frise*—timbers fitted with iron spikes—was built across the road. Mortars and guns were mounted there, and batteries were erected at various points of vantage in the town. The troops were removed from their barracks to a camp on the Common, and heavy details, as many as a fifth of the whole force, were constantly on guard duty.[20] But all this was defensive, calculated merely to hold the town; there was no sign of any intention to go beyond that. The British government, however, had awakened to the fact that Gage's force was inadequate to achieve more than such a negative success; reinforcements were on the way.

Six regiments, or parts of regiments, the 35th, 49th, 63rd, 64th, 65th, and 67th, had landed in Boston in April, May, or early June, or were on the way across the ocean, also the 17th Light Dragoons, a detachment of 600 marines, and some drafts to recruit the regiments already there. With such additions Gage had, by the middle of June, a force of about 6,500 rank and file.[21]

On May 25 the frigate *Cerberus* arrived. She had on board three very distinguished gentlemen and members of Parliament: Major General William Howe, Major General Henry Clinton, and Major General John Burgoyne. They were entering upon a service from which two of them were to emerge with blasted reputations, the third with but little credit.

William Howe, not yet a knight, was in his forty-fifth year, a tall, soldierly-looking man, although his figure had been overextended and his naturally heavy features coarsened by excessive indulgence in food and drink. He was of a very dark complexion, like his brother the admiral, whose nickname was "Black Dick." He was a man of easy manners and easy morals, an inveterate gambler, a hearty drinker; his intimate relations with Mrs. Joshua Loring during his stay in America were notorious. In politics he was a Whig, and he had been opposed to coercing the Americans. When he stood for Parliament in the Whig interest at Nottingham, he promised his constituents that he would decline any command against the Americans that might be offered to him. When the King, less than a year later, assigned him to such a command, he asked whether he was to consider it as a request or as an order. He was told that it was an order and accepted it, excusing his compliance to his constituents by saying he "could not refuse without incurring the odious name of backwardness to serve my country in distress."

He had started his career as a soldier at the age of seventeen, with a cornet's commission in the Light Dragoons. After considerable military experience on the European continent, he first saw service in America as a major of infantry at the capture of Louisburg in 1758. In the next year he gained distinction for gallantry in leading the advance, a "forlorn hope" of twenty-four men, up the Heights of Abraham in Wolfe's attack on Quebec. He was always foremost in battle and conspicuously cool under fire. He became a major general in 1772.

He was a clever strategist, an able tactician; his plans were excellently

conceived and well carried out, but he was too often content with victory
in the battle itself, failing to follow up his successes as he might have done.
The fault was marked at Long Island, in the succeeding operations on Manhattan Island, and, indeed, in all his campaigns, as will be seen hereafter.
These repeated failures have been attributed by some to his Whiggish pro-
clivities, which were favorable to the Americans; by others to his naturally
sluggish temperament, which was aggravated by his dissipation; by others
again, especially when he found the Americans intrenched against him, to
memories of the slaughter of his troops at Bunker Hill. On the whole, though
he outmaneuvered Washington repeatedly and won battle after battle, his
conduct of the war in America was a failure; and he returned to England
to face a Parliamentary inquiry, which might have condemned him had it
been pushed to a conclusion.[22]

Henry Clinton, the only son of a British admiral and colonial governor
of New York, was but thirty-seven years old when he came to Boston. He
was not a man of colorful personality and, in contrast to his companion
generals, he seems rather a negative character in the drama of the Revolution. He had obtained a commission as a lieutenant in the 2nd Foot Guards
at the age of thirteen years; he was a lieutenant colonel at twenty, a major
general at thirty-four. He had seen some service in Germany between 1760
and 1763.

In his American career Clinton showed no indubitable evidence of military ability, certainly none of brilliance in his profession. He commanded
the first unsuccessful attack on Charleston, in 1776, and the second, which
resulted in its capture in 1780; and in neither did he display unusual talents.
His most able exploit was the conduct of his army in its removal from Philadelphia across New Jersey in 1778, when he reached New York without
serious losses, in spite of attacks by Washington's pursuing forces. He cannot be blamed for his failure to relieve Burgoyne at Saratoga in the circumstances then existing. His successful attacks on Forts Clinton and Montgomery in 1777 were planned with soldierly skill and carried out with
sufficient audacity; but on the whole his career in America was far from
brilliant. After his return to England, he was the object of adverse criticism
by Lord Cornwallis, with whom he engaged in a bitter controversy.[23]

In John Burgoyne we meet with a character of conspicuous interest, who
aspired to renown in such diverse fields as war, statesmanship, and literature.
It is ironical that he was defeated in that field in which he showed most
ability.

He was a scion of an ancient Lancashire family of repute and substance;
at this time he was in his fifty-third year. He was handsome in the full-fed

British style of the period, and was a wit, a playwright, a man of fashion, and a member of Parliament. He was also a good soldier, and in certain military respects was much in advance of his time. His treatise on the duties of officers urged that soldiers be treated like thinking human beings; they should not be subjected to frequent and brutal corporal punishment, and there should be no "training men like spaniels by the stick," as he called it. He insisted that the officers should read books, learn how to write accurately, know something of mathematics, and acquire a practical knowledge of the equipment of their calling; in all these points there was vast room for improvement among the British officers of the day, whose ignorance was generally of "Stygian density." Practicing his own precepts, he was popular with his men, who nicknamed him "Gentleman Johnny." "On every occasion he was the soldiers' friend."

He had entered the army in 1744 at the rather advanced age of twenty-two years, but sold out in 1747 and did not rejoin until 1756, being merely a captain at the age of thirty-four. He served on the European continent as a brigadier with considerable credit for seven years. His capitulation at Saratoga finished his military career.[24]

The arrival of the three generals produced no improvement in the situation of the British army. If any one of them had displaced Gage in supreme command, he would undoubtedly have seen, like Gage, that the pressing need was for still more troops. The army could not take the aggressive until the large forces which Gage had consistently demanded since the fall of 1774 reached America.

Burgoyne, indeed, was of no help to Gage; he was, on the contrary, a menace. He began a voluminous correspondence with some of the home authorities in which he dilated upon Gage's errors and thus injured him in the judgment of the ministry.

In a different and well meant endeavor, he gave his chief a push down the declining path of reputation. Gage, instructed by the cabinet to proclaim martial law in Massachusetts, decided to use the proclamation as a "last effort . . . to spare the effusion of blood." Burgoyne wrote it for him, and "no manifesto was ever worse adapted to the taste of its intended readers." Its flamboyant, inflated, and verbose style widened the eyes of the simple New Englanders in sheer amazement; its accusatory and threatening substance aroused bitter resentment where it did not excite derision.

It called the people an "infatuated multitude . . . conducted by certain well known incendiaries and traitors." It warned that "those who are invested with supreme rule . . . do not bear the sword in vain," and threatened "the fulness of chastisement." It asserted that the leaders of the Americans imposed on the credulity of their followers with "the grossest forgeries, calumnies, and absurdities that ever insulted human understanding," and used "the animated language of ancient and virtuous times . . . to countenance the most abandoned violations . . . of the just rights and interests of mankind." It noted that the rebels "with a preposterous parade of military arrangement have effected to hold the Army besieged."

Proceeding to a generous offer of pardon to all persons who would lay down their arms and return to the ways of peace, except "Samuel Adams and John Hancock, whose offences are of too flagitious a nature to admit of any other consideration than that of condign punishment," it announced, of course, martial law throughout the province.[25] That from a general who dared not set his foot outside the town of Boston and could no more enforce martial law throughout the province of Massachusetts than he could throughout the empire of the Khan of Tartary.

Even in London the preposterous character of this manifesto was appreciated; its style was recognized as Burgoyne's, and much fun was made of it: "They *affect* to hold the army besieged . . . the next time you write to your friends, say in plain English that the Americans have *effected* the siege." [26]

That proclamation was issued on the 12th of June. Five days later much was to happen, but previous events in another part of the colonies must be given attention before the story of the siege of Boston is continued.

CHAPTER 7

Ticonderoga

Fort Ticonderoga was called "the Key to the gateway to the continent," by which was meant the way from Canada to the English colonies. In a wilderness the best route is by water; from Canada southward this was furnished by the St. Lawrence River, the Richelieu, Lake Champlain, and the Hudson. At the point where Lake George discharges its waters into Champlain, the larger lake narrows to a width of half a mile, and at one point two opposite headlands leave a passage between them of less than a quarter of a mile. There on the western side, on an eminence rising a hundred feet above the water, stood the fort.[1]

The French first occupied this position in 1755. After plans by Vauban, the great military engineer, they built a fort with stone bastions surrounded by a star-shaped outer wall, the whole complete with glacis, counterscarps, covered ways, and demilunes. They called it Fort Carillon. In 1758 with a garrison of 4,000, under Montcalm, they held it against 6,000 British regulars and 10,000 provincial troops under Lieutenant General James Abercromby. In the next year, Sir Jeffrey Amherst invested it with 11,000 men; the French commander, Bourlamaque, had but 3,500. He blew up the works and retreated. The British rebuilt it in less substantial fashion and named it Ticonderoga. After the Peace of Paris in 1763, ending the French and Indian War, there was no frontier between Canada and the colonies to be guarded; the fort was manned by a skeleton garrison, used only as a supply post on the route, and allowed to fall into decay.[2]

When the relations between Britain and her American colonies became strained to the point of breaking, the New Englanders had cause to fear that

Guy Carleton, in command at Montreal, might enlarge his small force of regulars with French Canadians and Indians and attack them in the rear. To discover the inclinations of the Canadians in the contest with Britain, the Massachusetts Provincial Congress in February, 1775, sent John Brown of Pittsfield to Montreal and Quebec. His report was discouraging, and to it he added: "One thing I must mention to be kept as a profound Secret, the Fort at Tyconderogo must be seised as soon as possible should hostilities be committed by the King's Troops. The people on N. Hampshire Grants have ingaged to do this business and in my opinion they are the most proper Persons for the Jobb." Brown's information as to the New Hampshire Grants people taking on the job had been derived from one Ethan Allen whom he had met in Pittsfield.[3]

Ethan Allen was a true son of the backwoods, born in a log cabin in Litchfield, Connecticut, the eldest son of a substantial farmer. He had begun his schooling under a clergyman with a view to entering Yale College; but on his father's death he had to care for a family of a widow and seven other orphans. After a short tour of duty with a Connecticut regiment in the French and Indian War, he set up an iron furnace, tried lead mining, and, in 1768, removed to the New Hampshire Grants, now Vermont.

In the conflict between the settlers there and the government of New York, which claimed ownership of the Grants, Allen was a colonel of the Green Mountain Boys, defenders of their rights to land under grant of the Governor of New Hampshire. The contest was violent and tumultuous, just the sort of fight to suit such a man as he.

In 1775 he was thirty-seven years old. He was tall (he is often described as "gigantic"), broad-shouldered, lean, and straight; his bodily strength was enormous. He has been credited with "boldness, adroitness, toughness, pride, fortitude, cheerfulness and a terrific volubility in invective . . . an amplitude and appalling humor of profane swearing," also with "rough and ready humor, boundless self-confidence and a shrewdness in thought and action equal to almost any emergency." Although his schooling was brief and scanty, he was a great reader and was later to produce several pamphlets on the rights of the Green Mountain Boys, as well as a narrative of his captivity by the British, composed of "staunch, blunt, boastful, blundering, fearless words," and, rather surprisingly, a tract entitled *Reason the Only Oracle of Man,* a very cogent deistic argument.[4]

Another man had thought about Ticonderoga. When the news of Lexington and Concord came to New Haven on the 20th of April, Captain Benedict Arnold summoned his company of militia to march to Cambridge and applied to the authorities of the town for ammunition; he was thought too hasty, and his request was refused. His answer to that was that he would break in the magazine and take what he wanted. "None but Almighty God shall prevent my marching," said he. They gave him the ammunition.[5]

Arnold was familiar with the Lake Champlain and St. Lawrence country. Happening to meet Colonel Samuel Holden Parsons on the way to Cambridge and hearing him lament the lack of cannon in Ward's army, he told him that a plentiful supply could be had at Ticonderoga. Parsons went on to Hartford with this suggestion in mind.[6]

At Cambridge, Arnold broached the matter to the Committee of Safety, giving it "certain information" that there were eighty pieces of heavy cannon, twenty brass pieces, and a dozen large mortars, besides small arms and stores, at Ticonderoga, three or four more brass guns at Skenesboro near by, and that the fort was "in a ruinous condition and has not more than fifty men at the most." [7] The committeemen were interested indeed. On May 3 they gave him a colonel's commission and authorized him to enlist "not exceeding 400" men, to march to Ticonderoga and "reduce the same," taking possession of "the cannon, mortars, stores &ca." This was to be a special commission for a "secret service," and the committee reserved the right to dismiss the force to be raised "whenever they shall think proper." [8]

Benedict Arnold was at this time thirty-four years old. Though only of middle height, his appearance was commanding. He was well formed, muscular, capable of great endurance, active, graceful in his movements, and exceptionally adept in athletic exercises, such as running, fencing, boxing and skating; he was also an expert marksman with gun and pistol, and an accomplished horseman. His salient facial features were clear cut and handsome; his hair was black, his skin swarthy, his clear, bright eyes light in color.

He came of a substantial family; a collateral ancestor of the same name had been governor of Rhode Island. He had a fair common-school education, which included some Latin. As an apprenticeship to a druggist he ran away at the age of seventeen to fight in the French and Indian War. He was advertised in the newspapers in 1759 as a deserter. In any case, he returned to finish out his term. At twenty-one he set up his own drugstore and bookshop in New Haven. His business flourished, and he branched out into the West Indies, sometimes sailing his own ships. He is also said to have shipped horses between Canada and the West Indies, which gave the British a chance to belittle him as a mere "horse-jockey." By the year 1775 he was a well-to-do merchant, the "possessor of an elegant house, storehouses, wharves, and vessels."

In the Revolutionary War he had an adventurous and, as was inevitable with his disposition, a stormy career, but proved himself to be a soldier of outstanding merit. He was original in his ideas, audacious in action, quick to form his plans, and swift to execute them. Though imperious of will, arrogant, restive under orders, and possessed of a passionate belief in his own judgment and in his own superior ability as a soldier, he was a most capable commander of men. He did not merely order his troops forward, he led them; he was a fighting man, and he had, as he deserved to have, the devotion of his troops. An old soldier of his command at Saratoga said of him: "He was our fighting general, and a bloody fellow he was. He didn't care for nothing, he'd ride right on. It was 'Come on boys!' 'twarn't 'Go, boys!' He was as brave a man as ever lived."

His treason has become almost the only popularly known element of his career, overshadowing and blotting out the memory of his expedition against Quebec, his exploits on Lake Champlain, his relief of Fort Stanwix, and his services in the fighting which led to Saratoga. But for his betrayal of his charge at West Point, he would have stood out in American history as one of the great soldiers in the Revolution.[9]

Parsons, arriving at Hartford after his roadside conversation with Arnold, "undertook and projected" with four or five others the taking of Ticonderoga. They sent an express to Ethan Allen at Bennington, asking him to gather a force of Green Mountain Boys and hold them in readiness for the proposed adventure; they appointed Major Halsted, Captain Edward Mott, Captain Noah Phelps, and Bernard Romans as a committee to conduct their part of the affair, and provided them with a war chest of £300. Phelps and Romans went on in advance on the 28th, and were followed by Epaphras Bull, Captain Mott and sixteen associates the next day. At Pittsfield, Massachusetts, they met James Easton and John Brown. Easton raised between forty and fifty men, and the whole party set out for Bennington, where they met Allen with about a hundred of his Boys.[10]

A Committee of War was chosen, consisting of Easton, Phelps, and Bull, with Mott as chairman; Allen was given command by a "universal" vote, with Easton and Seth Warner as his first and second lieutenants. It was decided to send Samuel Herrick with thirty men to surprise and capture Major Philip Skene at his settlement, Skenesboro—now Whitehall—and take his boats.[11] Captain Asa Douglass was sent to Panton, also to procure boats. Other small parties were directed to secure the roads to the north, to prevent warning of the attack from reaching the fort. Gershom Beach, a backwoods blacksmith, was detailed to rouse more Green Mountain Boys; he is said to have covered sixty miles of wilderness in twenty-four hours.[12]

These proceedings in the evening of May 9 were hardly over when a very impressive gentleman in a brave uniform with a scarlet coat arrived and informed the gathering that he had come to take command of them by virtue of a commission and orders from the Massachusetts Committee of Safety. It was Benedict Arnold, who, having heard of the expedition from Pittsfield, had left recruiting officers at Stockbridge and, with one manservant, had hurried on to Castleton.[13]

The men of the little army were "extremely rejoiced" to learn that the Committee of Safety endorsed the project, but "shockingly surprised when Colonel Arnold presumed to contend for the command of those forces that we had raised, who we had assured should go under the command of their own officers." Although the leaders "generously told him our whole plan, he strenuously contended and insisted that he had a right to command them and all their officers."

But Arnold had met more than his match. His demand had "bred such a mutiny among the soldiers which had nearly frustrated our whole design, as our men were for clubbing their fire-locks and marching home." [14]

Allen was not present at this discussion; he had gone forward to Shoreham —now Orwell—two miles below the fort, where, in Hand's Cove, the forces were to assemble. The next morning, all those at Castleton followed him. Arnold renewed his contention as to the command and finally got, as he says, joint command with Allen, until he could "raise a sufficient number of men to relieve his [Allen's] people." It is doubtful, however, that he got more than the right to march beside Allen at the head of the men in the attack on the fort.[15]

Early in the morning of May 10, about two hundred men had assembled at Hand's Cove—Easton's and Allen's forces, augmented by others from the country roundabout. Between them and the fort stretched two miles of water. The moon had set, the sun not yet risen; it was dark, and squalls of wind and rain were blowing up to make the crossing more hazardous. There were no boats; those expected from Skenesboro had not come. It was near dawn when a scow appeared; it had been commandeered by two boys who had heard of the proposed attack. Soon after, Asa Douglass brought another, with a few recruits.[16]

Allen and Arnold, with eighty-three men, crowded into the two boats and landed about half a mile below the fort at daybreak. The boats were sent back for the rest, but there was no time to wait if there was to be a surprise. Allen drew the men up in three ranks and addressed them. He reminded them that, for a long time past, they had been "a scourge and a terror to arbitrary power," and that their "valor has been famed abroad." He now proposed to lead them upon "a desperate attempt, which none but the bravest of men dare undertake. . . . You that will undertake voluntarily, poise your firelocks!" Every firelock was poised.[17]

Allen and Arnold, side by side, led the advance, Arnold in his fine uniform, Allen in one of his own devising—a green coat, with large gold epaulets, and yellow breeches. Behind them went a straggling column of men in every sort of garb—buckskin, linsey-woolsey, or what not, beaver hats, felt hats, coonskin caps, buckled shoes or moccasins—armed with firelocks, pistols, swords, knives, or simple clubs, not a bayonet among them all.[18]

The main entrance in the south wall of the fort was in a ruinous condition. The leaders and their men swarmed through and over the ruins and came upon a single sentry, guarding a wicket in the curtain of the main fort. He pointed his musket at the intruders and pulled the trigger; it flashed in the pan. He turned and fled through a covered way into the middle of the fort, shouting an alarm, the attackers close behind him, yelling like Indians. Another sentry slightly wounded one of the officers with a bayonet. Allen hit him on the head with the flat of his sword and ordered him to show the way to the officers' quarters. Leaving their men drawn up in two lines, back to back, Allen and Arnold followed the sentry to a staircase in the west barracks.[19]

A door at the head of the stairs opened and disclosed an officer, Lieutenant Jocelyn Feltham, wearing coat and waistcoat, but carrying his breeches in his hand. Allen shouted at him, "Come out of there, you damned old rat," (or "skunk," or "bastard," according to different accounts), and dashed up the stairs along with Arnold and followed by others. The astonished officer asked by what authority they intruded. Allen, according to his own later account, rose to the occasion with a deathless utterance:

"In the name of the Great Jehovah and the Continental Congress!" he shouted.

It has been remarked that the officer had about as much respect for the Continental Congress as Allen had for the Great Jehovah.[20] But this astounding speech and the demands that followed for immediate surrender of "the Fort and all the effects of George the Third," with the alternative of a massacre of every man, woman, and child in the place, brought the commander, Captain William Delaplace, to terms; he handed his sword to Allen and ordered the garrison paraded without arms.

The entire force consisted of the two officers, two artillerymen, a couple of sergeants, and forty-four privates, many of them invalids; but there were also twenty-four women and children. In fact Ticonderoga, with its ruined walls, its meager garrison, its flock of women and children, was more like a backwoods village than a fort. Allen's report to the Continental Congress characteristically tells of the taking of "the Fortress of Ticonderoga by storm" and of "the resistless fury . . . of the Soldiery [who] behaved with uncommon ranker when they Leaped Into the fourt." [21]

They certainly did behave with "uncommon ranker" after the surrender. "There is here at present," Arnold reported the next day, "near one hundred men, who are in the greatest confusion and anarchy, destroying and plundering private property, committing every enormity and paying no attention to publick service." He had forbidden them to behave so riotously, but Allen had "positively insisted" that he should have no command, and he was powerless to control them.[22]

It was necessary now to dispose of the prisoners. Allen wrote to Governor Jonathan Trumbull of Connecticut of the 12th, "I make you a present of a Major, a Captain and two Lieutenants of the regular Establishment of George the Third." The major was Skene, whom, with his daughter and various dependents, Herrick had captured at Skenesboro. These prisoners were dispatched to Hartford. Lieutenant Colonel Seth Warner took a party to Crown Point, another disabled British post, and, without resistance, captured the garrison, one sergeant, eight privates, and ten women and children, also a number of cannon.[23]

Arnold's discontent with his anomalous position in the fort, where he had no recognized command and very little good-fellowship, was relieved on the 13th, when Captain John Brown and Captain Eleazer Oswald arrived in a small schooner and several bateaux, captured at Skenesboro, with fifty recruits "enlisted on the road." Arnold was a sailor; Allen was not. So there was no objection to Arnold's having command of a naval expedition against St. Johns, a frontier Canadian post on the Richelieu River, some miles beyond Lake Champlain. When he had yet thirty miles to go, the schooner was becalmed. Arnold and thirty-five men in two bateaux rowed all night and, early in the morning of the 17th, surprised the unresisting garrison, a sergeant and fourteen men, and took the post, along with a 70-ton sloop, armed with two brass 6-pounders, and its crew of seven. There were others of the King's forces at Chambly, twelve miles away, and reinforcements for St. Johns, to the number of two hundred, were hourly expected. Arnold's men took all the more valuable stores, destroyed five bateaux, and set sail with four others, the sloop, and the schooner, for Crown Point.[24]

But Allen had his ambitions for further conquest, too. He had embarked with ninety men in four bateaux and followed Arnold. The two expeditions, Allen's going, Arnold's returning, met about six miles south of St. Johns and saluted each other with three volleys apiece. Allen boarded Arnold's sloop and learned that he was too late, that St. Johns had been taken, and that its garrison was now in irons in the hold. But, though it had been taken, it had been abandoned. That did not suit Allen; he would occupy it and hold it. However, at the moment, he was in straits, "his men being in a starving condition," as Arnold put it. In fact, Allen, in his enthusiasm for conquest, had neglected the purely incidental matter of feeding his men *en route*. Arnold supplied him, and he went on in spite of warnings as to the impracticability of his venture. At St. Johns, Allen learned that the expected reinforcements were near at hand. He first decided to ambush them, placed his men accordingly, and sent out scouts. But cooler thoughts supervened; his men were tired after three days and nights with little sleep and little food. When the new forces were within two miles of him, he withdrew across the river, where his wornout men lay down to sleep. They were surprised by a volley of grapeshot from six fieldpieces ranged on the other side; the relief for the garrison had come up. They swarmed into their boats with such celerity as to leave three of their number behind, and rowed lustily away, exchanging harmless shots with the enemy as they pulled out of range.[25]

Arnold, now at Crown Point, reported to the Massachusetts Committee of Safety that he had one hundred fifty men of his own—"Colonel Allen's men are in general gone home"—and that he had determined to hold the fort at the Point until the arrival of wheels and of draught animals should enable him to remove the cannon.[26] He had armed his sloop and his schooner with "carriage guns" and swivels in anticipation of an attempt by the British to recapture the place. But the ambitions of the two leaders were not yet satisfied. They decided to send a force to Pointe au Fer and fortify it. Allen's designs went far beyond that; he was going to conquer all Canada. "I will lay my life on it," he wrote to the New York Congress, "that, with 1500 men and a proper train of artillery, I will take Montreal . . . it would be no insuperable difficulty to take Quebeck." [27] But they were stopped in their tracks by word from the Continental Congress.

The Congress had news of the taking of Ticonderoga on May 18. It at once resolved that the fort should be abandoned and all the guns and stores removed to the south end of Lake George, with a provision that an exact inventory of them be taken, "in order that they may be safely returned when the restoration of the former harmony between Great Britain and these colonies so ardently wished for by the latter shall render it prudent." [28]

But Arnold, even if he could not go any farther, had no intention of giving up the ground he had gained. On May 29 he wrote to the Continental Congress and to the Massachusetts Provincial Congress stating his surprise and alarm at the proposal, which would leave "our very extensive frontiers open to the ravages of the enemy." The same day he wrote to the Provincial Congress of New York, giving full details as to the number of men and the amount of supplies needed to hold the posts on the lake. Allen was equally averse to giving them up and even more eloquent in expressing his views to the New York Congress.[29]

These two were not alone; New England wanted the forts held; so did northern New York. Alarmed by reports that an expedition to retake the Champlain posts was contemplated in Canada, and that Guy Carleton was soliciting the Six Nations of Indians to join in such an effort, the northern colonies protested against the abandonment of Ticonderoga, the strongest position on the lake, and persuaded the Continental Congress to change its mind. On May 31 it resolved that Connecticut be requested to send strong reinforcements to Crown Point and "Ticonderogo" and that New York be requested to furnish supplies. Connecticut had already ordered four hundred men to march to the forts, with 500 pounds of its "pittance of powder," followed by a thousand more men under Colonel Benjamin Hinman. The forts were to be retained, but not with Colonel Benedict Arnold in command.[30]

A committee from Massachusetts, sent up to ascertain the needs of the forts, brought Arnold the news that he was to be second in command under Hinman. To the colonel, who had been signing his name as "Commander-in-Chief," and had just sent a long letter to the Continental Congress outlining an elaborate plan for the conquest of Canada which he was willing to undertake, and in which Hinman's regiment was to play a subordinate part, this demotion was displeasing. It was more than that, it was humiliating and altogether disgusting; "he would not be second in command to any person whomsoever." He immediately left the service under a double impulsion, his discharge by the committee and his own resignation.[31]

No exercise of military genius was involved in the taking of the Champlain posts, nor was there needed any display of valor. They fell like ripe apples from a shaken limb. Nevertheless, their capture was of vast importance to the colonies. Leaving out of consideration their subsequent value in the operations in that territory, the guns which they yielded were of inestimable value to the Americans. Many of them were found to be in such bad condition as to be useless, but no fewer than seventy-eight were serviceable, ranging from 4-pounders to 24-pounders. There were also six mortars, three howitzers, thousands of cannon balls of various sizes, nine tons of musket bullets, thirty thousand flints, and a large quantity of miscellaneous apparatus. The guns were what the army besieging Boston most needed. They were not at once removed, for lack of transport, but in the coming winter a way was found to carry them to the army.[32]

Bunker Hill

When the frigate *Cerberus* with the three major generals was entering Boston harbor, General Burgoyne was told that "10,000 country people" surrounding the town were holding its garrison in check. "What?" he is said to have exclaimed. "Ten thousand peasants keep five thousand of the King's troops shut up? Well, let us get in, and we'll soon find elbow-room." [1] It may have been at his suggestion that Gage and his three colleagues, not long after their arrival, decided to seize and fortify Dorchester Heights on the Charles River, which, though a commanding position overlooking the town of Boston, had been neglected by both sides. This operation was to have been effected on June 18. [2]

Five days before that date, news of the intended movement was conveyed to the American command; and on June 15 the Committee of Safety decided on countermovements: that "Bunker's Hill in Charlestown be securely kept and defended, and also some one hill or hills on Dorchester Neck be likewise secured." Bunker's Hill was to be cared for at once, Dorchester being left to further consideration. [3]

Charlestown was a peninsula, roughly triangular in shape, opposite the north side of Boston. Its base was separated from Boston by the half-mile width of the Charles River. Its peak terminated in a narrow isthmus, the Neck, so low as to be often overflowed at high tide. The Mystic River washed its northeasterly side; the Charles widened into a large bay on the northwest. Its length was about a mile from north to south; its greatest width was about half a mile.

It had a rolling surface culminating at three points in low hills. The first,

Bunker's Hill, began at the Neck and rose gradually for 300 yards to a rounded top 110 feet high, sloping on its east and west sides to the water. This was connected by a low ridge with Breed's Hill, the second eminence, the top of which was about 600 yards distant; its height was 75 feet. The easterly and westerly slopes of this hill were steep. At the water side on the west was the village of Charlestown. Near the base of Breed's Hill, on its easterly side, the approach was broken by brick kilns, clay pits, and an area of swampy land. The third and smallest hill, Moulton's, only 35 feet high, lay at the southeast corner of the peninsula near the meeting of the Mystic and the Charles. Outside the little town the whole surface of the peninsula was divided into different holdings, separated by rail fences or stone walls and used chiefly for hay and pasture, with orchards and gardens here and there. In the middle of June, 1775, some parts had been mowed, the hay left on the ground to cure; in other places, and particularly on the sloping approach to Breed's Hill from the southeast, the grass, fully knee-high, was still standing. A narrow road ran from the Neck, passed Bunker's Hill, and encircled Breed's.[4]

At the recommendation of the Committee of Safety and on the day that it was made, General Artemas Ward assembled a council of war. The names of all the officers attending have not been ascertained; but it appears that General Putnam, Joseph Warren, lately appointed a major general but not yet commissioned, Brigadier General Seth Pomeroy, and Colonel William Prescott were there. The matter was discussed. Ward and Warren had been opposed to fortifying Bunker's Hill when it had been proposed at earlier meetings, and seem to have been reluctant now. The lack of powder—there were only eleven barrels in the whole camp—rendered rather more than doubtful the ability of the Americans to hold it, even if it should be successfully fortified. But Putnam was strong for the adventure. "The Americans," he is supposed to have said, "are not at all afraid of their heads, though very much afraid of their legs; if you cover these, they will fight forever." Pomeroy seconded him, and Prescott agreed, whereupon the others consented and the order was made, without deciding how the defenders were going to "fight forever" after their ammunition gave out.[5]

Artemas Ward, on whom the major responsibilities of American leadership were descending, was a descendant of William Ward, one of the early Puritan settlers of New England. His father was a well-to-do farmer of Worcester County. His education was that of the average country boy of the period in the short terms that "school kept" in Shrewsbury, supplemented by some home study under the supervision of the local preacher.

which led to his entry into Harvard and his graduation there, followed by a later degree of A.M.

In 1755, at the age of twenty-eight, he was a major of militia, and three years later he marched with Abercromby's army against Ticonderoga. In the course of a year's service he attained a lieutenant colonelcy; but had little experience in that grade. He came home with his health impaired, and never again was a robust man. He was politically active in the civil disturbances following the Stamp Act, and was a delegate to the First and Second Provincial Congresses.

Ward was a man of medium height, "too stout for his forty-seven years," and at this time was afflicted with bladder stone, but not physically incapacitated thereby. He was precise, even elegent, in his dress. His long, sharp nose, pointed chin, and bright, knowing eyes indicated intelligence, but did not reveal his really dominant mental characteristics—slowness of thought, extreme caution, taciturnity, and inflexibility of opinion. These elements of his character were displayed in his measured speech and his habit of using biblical terms and phrases in conversation. As undistinguished as his appearance was his character, except for honesty, firm patriotism, and devotion to the American cause.

Ward was, in fact, better fitted for the council chamber or the judicial bench than for military leadership, especially in enterprises demanding forthright boldness of plan and unhesitating speed in execution.[6]

General Israel Putnam is a colorful character about whom legends have clustered so thickly as to conceal the man within. His name is still universally known, while much greater men have faded from memory since the Revolution, showing how effectively romantic adventures create reputations and embalm them.

He was a farmer, fifty-seven years of age, widely known throughout New England by the affectionate title of "Old Put." He had led the first Connecticut company sent out in 1755 in the French and Indian War, in which he saw long and hard service and was engaged in many sensational exploits. He was captured by Indians, tied to the stake to be burned, and rescued at the very last moment by a French officer. He was a prisoner at Montreal for a long time until exchanged. He led a regiment to attack Havana and was shipwrecked on the coast of Cuba. He fought the Indians again in 1764. This record, strengthened by the tradition of his victorious battle with a veritable werewolf, and by the later story of his escape from capture by the British, by riding his horse at a headlong gallop down a flight of rocky steps, has made his name a household word throughout New England. In

1775 he was believed to be not only a good soldier, but a great soldier, fit to be a major general, which he was not.

He was a rather short, broad-shouldered, burly man, with a big round head crowned by an unruly shock of gray hair. His round, open face gave evidence of the frank, generous, outspoken, jovial disposition that made him universally popular. He was courageous, enterprising, energetic, active, and persevering. As colonel of a fighting regiment, he would have been admirably placed; he would have led his men against the enemy, and they would have followed him with a cheer. Of the conduct and care of an army, of strategy in major operations, of shrewd planning of a campaign or even of a single battle, of careful preparation for the execution of plans, of the management of large bodies of men in the field, of resourcefulness in taking advantage of unexpected opportunities in battle on a large scale, or making unexpectedly necessary changes in plan, he knew nothing and should not have been expected to know anything. *Colonel* Israel Putnam he should have remained throughout the war.[7]

Colonel William Prescott, who was to lead the detachment to Bunker's Hill, was born in 1726 to a Massachusetts family of wealth and position. His early education was limited in scope, but he made up for that by his devotion to books. In person he was tall, over six feet, well set up and muscular; his features were strong and clear-cut. His disposition was kindly, his manners simple but courteous; yet he had the habit of command and the power to exact obedience from his men, whose respect he deservedly enjoyed. His customary movements were unhurried, and his coolness and self-possession in moments of danger were notable.[8]

Another important participant in the enterprise was Joseph Warren, who was but thirty-four years of age. His family dated from 1659 in Massachusetts. He was well educated with the degree of A.M. from Harvard. He had studied medicine and had acquired a large practice in Boston; his wife was Mercy Otis, the brilliant sister of James Otis. After the passage of the Stamp Act he undertook "a serious examination of the right of Parliament to tax the colonies" and, as a result, allied himself with those who resisted British measures.

His natural enthusiasm and strong impulses led him to take an active part in politics, in which he became an associate of Hancock, the Adamses, and the rest of the patriot malcontents; he was in especially close relationship with Samuel Adams. He soon became one of the leaders of the movement, to which he lent his abilities as a writer and an orator. He was the author of the Suffolk Resolves, one of the earliest and boldest declarations of refusal of obedience to the oppressive acts of Parliament. He frequently acted as presiding officer of the Provincial Congress, and was chairman of the Committee of Safety.

Though Warren had had no military experience, he was chosen to be major general, and is said to have intended to pursue a career in arms.

He was of middle height, well built, graceful in figure, active in movement, scrupulously neat in attire, and elegant in address. His fine, open countenance was indicative of his integrity, his modesty, and his gentle, friendly, and courteous disposition; yet he was courageous morally and physically, swift of thought and action, high-spirited, enthusiastic, capable of quick resentments and fiery impulses, and hot of speech in support of the cause which he had adopted. To that cause he unreservedly devoted his fine talents; indeed it had become the ruling passion of his short life. His too early death in the coming battle was universally and most feelingly lamented as an irreparable loss to his friends and to his country.[9]

Ward ordered the Massachusetts regiments of Prescott, Colonel James Frye, and Colonel Ebenezer Bridge, with a fatigue party of two hundred men drafted from Putnam's Connecticut regiment and commanded by Captain Thomas Knowlton, as well as Captain Samuel Gridley's Massachusetts artillery company, forty-nine men and two fieldpieces, to parade in the camp at Cambridge at six o'clock in the evening of June 16. They were to be equipped with packs, blankets, a day's rations, and the necessary entrenching tools. They would have made up a party of about fourteen hundred all told; but Prescott's regiment turned out only two-thirds of its paper strength, and the other two were short of their full number, so that there were between a thousand and twelve hundred actually assembled. Frye being ill with the gout, his men were led by Lieutenant Colonel James Brickett.[10]

When they were properly drawn up on the Cambridge Common, the Reverend Samuel Langdon, President of Harvard College, offered a prayer for the success of their undertaking. At about nine o'clock a column was formed, and they set out for a destination of which they were ignorant, not even the company officers having been informed of the purpose of the expedition. Colonel Prescott, preceded by two sergeants carrying dark lanterns "open in the rear," led the way; by his side marched Colonel Richard Gridley, a veteran who had seen service at Louisburg thirty years before and in many other campaigns. He was now chief engineer of the American army. Prescott wore military costume, a blue coat, "lapped and faced," and a three-cornered hat. Some of the other officers may have worn uniforms, but not the common soldiers. They were "mostly husbandmen," and they wore their ordinary clothes.[11] An eyewitness of their assemblage has left an engaging description of them:

To a man, they wore small-clothes, coming down and fastening just below the knee, and long stockings with cowhide shoes ornamented by large buckles, while not a pair of boots graced the company. The coats and waistcoats were loose and of huge dimensions, with colors as various as the barks of oak, sumach and other trees of our hills and swamps, could make them and their shirts were all made of flax, and like every other part of the dress, were home-spun. On their heads was worn a large round top and broad brimmed hat. Their arms were as various as their costume; here an old soldier carried a heavy Queen's arm, with which he had done service at the Conquest of Canada twenty years previous, while by his side walked a stripling boy with a Spanish fusee not half its weight or calibre, which his grandfather may have taken at the Havana, while not a few had old French pieces, that dated back to the reduction of Louisburg. Instead of the cartridge box, a large powder horn was slung under the arm, and occasionally a bayonet might be seen bristling in the ranks. Some of the swords of the officers had been made by our Province blacksmiths, perhaps from some farming utensil; they looked serviceable, but heavy and uncouth.[12]

At Charlestown Neck they were met by General Putnam, Major John Brooks, and some wagons loaded with fascines, gabions, empty hogsheads, and entrenching tools. Here Captain John Nutting of Prescott's regiment was detached, with his company and ten of Knowlton's men, and sent into Charlestown to watch for movements of the enemy, while the main body marched on over Bunker's Hill and to the foot of Breed's. Prescott then called the officers together, told them for the first time the purpose of the expedition, and consulted with them as to the position of the proposed entrenchment.[13]

His orders were explicit, to fortify Bunker's Hill, but there seemed to be reasons for choosing Breed's instead. It was nearer Boston. On the other hand, Bunker's was higher and nearer the Neck, their only avenue of escape if driven from their works. The matter was debated. Putnam and another general officer, whose name does not appear, were for Breed's but Putnam urged that they should first fortify Bunker's to cover a retreat, if that became necessary. The debate was prolonged; Gridley became impatient at the delay, urging a quick decision, as much valuable time was being wasted. At last it was decided first to erect the main works on Breed's, and then the auxiliary defenses on the other hill.[14]

Gridley marked out the lines of a redoubt about eight rods square. The south side, facing Charlestown, was the strongest, having near its middle a redan, or angular projection. The north side, towards Bunker's Hill, had an open entrance. There was a sally port at the southeast corner, protected by a blind.[15]

It was about midnight when the pick-and-shovel work was begun. Thoroughly used to those tools, the farmers worked steadily and swiftly to make up for the delay. They had but four hours before dawn would discover them to the enemy and expose them to attack.

Prescott detached Captain Hugh Maxwell's company of his own regiment and sent it down to patrol the shore on the Boston side of the peninsula. More than once he and Major Brooks also went down to see that there was no alarm in the enemy's camp. It was a warm, still night, dimly lit by the stars in a cloudless sky. They could see the dark outlines of the ships lying at anchor in the narrow channel of the Charles and, very near to the shore on which they stood, the *Lively* with her twenty guns, the *Falcon* sloop with sixteen, the *Symmetry,* armed transport with eighteen, the *Glasgow* with twenty-four, and the great sixty-eight-gun *Somerset*. They could hear their bells marking the half-hour and the reassuring cry of "All's well" from the British sentries. Finding everything quiet, Prescott recalled Maxwell's men a little before dawn.[16]

Soon the faint light of the coming day discovered to the watch on the *Lively* the walls of the redoubt, now six feet high. Without delay, her captain put a spring on her cable, swung her about so as to bring her guns to bear, and opened fire. The sound of her cannon aroused the British camp and the whole town of Boston. Admiral Graves signaled the *Lively* to cease firing; but about nine o'clock it was resumed by his order, and began from the other ships and the battery on Copp's Hill as well.[17]

When Prescott looked about him in the light of day, he saw his little redoubt, perched all alone on that hilltop, with no outworks, no support whatever, except the houses in Charlestown, the fences and walls on that side, and a swamp at some distance on the other. There was really nothing to prevent its being outflanked by troops marching out of musket range on either side. He prepared at once to extend his defenses on the east by runing a straight line of breastworks about twenty rods long from near the southeast corner of the redoubt and parallel with its eastern face, down the slope of the hill to the swamp. The Charlestown houses, walls, and fences would have to be relied on for protection of his other flank.[18]

The ships, chiefly the *Lively, Falcon,* and *Spitfire,* and the Copp's Hill battery kept up their bombardment of the redoubt. The fire from the vessels was ineffective; their guns were too light, and they could not be elevated sufficiently to bear on their target. The battery was too far away to do much damage. The roar of the guns was terrifying to the inexperienced American soldiers; but the round shot bounced about without doing any harm, and the work on the defenses went on without interruption. At last one of the men, working on the outside of the redoubt, was hit and killed. That was a shock to them all. One of the subalterns announced the casualty to Prescott, and asked what should be done. "Bury him," said the colonel. The brusqueness of the reply shocked the questioner. "What?" said he. "Without prayers?" A clergyman present volunteered to perform a burial service. Many of the men laid down their tools and gathered about the body. Prescott ordered them back to their work, "but religious enthusiasm prevailing, the chaplain again collected his congregation," and the corpse was interred in due form.[19]

This incident worked upon the fears of some of the men. A number of them left the ground and never returned. To reassure the rest, Prescott mounted the parapet, and, thus exposed to the fire of the enemy, walked along it, encouraging his men and directing their labors. But more than fear of the big guns was working on the minds of the weary men, more than mere fatigue was exhausting their bodies.

As the sun rose in a cloudless sky, the temperature also rose; the day became one of the hottest of that summer. There was little movement of the air outside the redoubt; inside, there was none. Dust from the disturbed, dry earth hung about them in clouds; they breathed it; their lips were caked with it; their faces were grimy with sweat and dirt. Inexperienced in warfare and inefficiently organized, many of them had neglected the order to bring a day's food; now they were faint with hunger. A cannon ball smashed the two hogsheads that had held their supply of water; no more could be had except when carried in buckets from the wells in the village. "We began to be almost beat out," Peter Brown wrote to his mother after the battle, "being tired by our Labour and having no sleep the night before, but little victuals, no Drink but Rum," which though undeniably stimulating does not, when taken straight, quench thirst.[20]

All that was bad enough, but there had begun to creep into their minds doubts as to the capacity and good faith of their leaders, a suspicion that they were deserted by their comrades in Cambridge. They had been promised relief in the morning; none had come, no new men, nor any food. "The Danger we were in," wrote Brown, "made us think there was Treachery & that we were brot there to be all slain, and I must & will say that there was Treachery, Oversight & Presumption in the Conduct of our Officers." [21] It is a wonder that there was not a wholesale desertion, that the whole enterprise did not break down before any British soldier appeared in the field.

That would have been the outcome, one is forced to think, but for one man, Colonel William Prescott.

He never swerved from obedience to his orders, never faltered in the prosecution of his task. When some of his officers urged him to send to headquarters to ask for relief, for his tired men to be replaced by others, he refused. "The men who have raised these works are the best able to defend them," said he. "They have learned to despise the fire of the enemy; they have the merit of the labor, and shall have the honor of the victory." He did, however, send for supplies and reinforcements.[22]

Because of the heat he had discarded his uniform coat and put on a banian, a light linen coat. His hat and wig were laid aside; his bald head glistened with sweat, as he went about inside and outside the redoubt, encouraging his men or driving them to their labor with sharp commands, keeping them at it by the sheer power of his will, until by eleven o'clock they had finished the works, made the banquettes (or fire steps), and could rest. One veteran of the day said long afterward, "I tell ye that if it had not been for Colonel Prescott, there would have been no fight." [23]

The Neck was so raked by shot from the armed transport *Symmetry* and two gunboats that Captain Samuel Gridley refused to risk one of his artillery horses across it when Major Brooks, bearing Prescott's request to Ward for reinforcements, asked for a mount; Brooks had to go on foot. He reached headquarters in Cambridge at ten o'clock. Ward had already refused an earlier request from Putnam; he still hesitated. At the very time when courage and resolution to take risks and to dare possible dangers were most needed at headquarters, they were wanting. Ward doubted that the British would attack Prescott; he feared they would rather take this opportunity to seize his own stores of munitions and supplies at Cambridge and Watertown; and he did not wish to weaken his forces there. He referred Prescott's request to the Committee of Safety, then in session in his house. Richard Devens of Charlestown, one of its members, was so "impassioned and vehement" in urging that troops be sent that the Committee recommended their dispatch, and Ward yielded. The New Hampshire regiments of Colonel John Stark and Colonel James Reed, then at Medford, were ordered to go.[24]

All this while Putnam was not idle. His particular post was on Bunker's Hill, where he had planned to erect defenses to cover a possibly necessary retreat from Breed's. But while waiting for the completion of the redoubt, so as to get the intrenching tools, he was never idle; "burning with zeal and intrepidity," he was riding about here, there, and everywhere. He was a general and a whole general's staff at once. Twice he had ridden to Cambridge, crossing the Neck through the ships' fire there, fearless and unhurt, to demand reinforcements, which Ward refused. He was now at Breed's, now at Bunker's, now at the Neck or at any other place on the peninsula; he was seen "in so many places that he would appear to have been ubiquitous." When the works on Breed's were complete, he called on Prescott to send the tools to him at Bunker's. Prescott had only about three hundred of his Massachusetts men and Knowlton's fatigue detachment in the redoubt; he feared that any that were sent with the tools would not come back. "They shall every man return," said Putnam. Prescott yielded. "An order was never obeyed with more readiness. From every part of the line within hearing volunteers ran, and some picked up one, some two shovels, mattocks &c., and hurried over the hill." Not one of them came back.[25]

Gage had called a council of war as soon as possible after the first alarm. It was plain to all its members that the American position was bad, since it was nearly surrounded by water that was completely dominated by the King's ships. Its only communication with the other American forces for supplies and reinforcements was by way of the narrow Neck, which was exposed to the fire of the guns of some of the British ships. The only question discussed was how best to capture or destroy the provincials. Clinton, it is said, favored an immediate landing, with a force of five hundred men, on the peninsula south of the Neck and in the rear of the redoubt. Some of the ships or gondolas could then blast the Neck itself with such a concentration of fire that no aid could reach the redoubt. Cut off from either supports or retreat, the Americans must starve in their fort or come out and fight in the open between two fires, for another force could be landed at the other end of the peninsula to cooperate with the first.[26]

Gage and the majority of the council objected to this plan. It was argued that it was not good military practice to interpose a force between two bodies of the enemy—in this case, the men on the peninsula and the rest of the American army. However sound the maxim, it was not so sound as to overrule all other considerations in a particular case. A different plan was proposed and adopted. As matters then stood, it was not a bad plan. The British would land a strong force below Moulton's Point on the southeast corner of the peninsula, march it up the east side along the Mystic, out of musket shot of the redoubt, flank it, and attack it in the rear. It must be remembered that at that early hour, when the extended breastwork had not even been begun and the redoubt stood all alone, there was ample clear space for this maneuver; it might easily have succeeded, had it been promptly executed. But it was fatally delayed.[27]

"As the shore where it was judged most proper to land was very flat, the

MYSTIC RIVER

BUNKER HILL

RAIL FENCE

BRICK KILN

MOULTON'S HILL

MOULTON POINT

BREED'S HILL

BREASTWORKS

THE REDOUBT

FIRST BRITISH LANDING

Gunboats

Symmetry

Falcon

SECOND BRITISH LANDING

Lively

CHARLESTOWN

Glasgow

Somerset

Lively
(second position)

THE BATTLE OF
BUNKER HILL
JUNE 17, 1775

0 200 400 600 800 1000 1200 1400

SCALE OF FEET

COPP'S HILL

landing could not be made with facility after the tide of ebb was much run off," and it was necessary to wait for "High Water at two o'clock in the afternoon." So Howe wrote to his brother in England.[28] Thus, instead of landing on the other side at the Charlestown wharves, where only a weak force of skirmishers would have had to be beaten off, and flanking the re-doubt on that side, or subjecting the British soldiers to the inconvenience of wading ashore at Moulton's Point, full six hours were wasted, and the Battle of Bunker's Hill had to be fought out to its bloody conclusion.

The British orders were given accordingly. Ten companies of light in-fantry, ten of grenadiers, and the 5th and 38th Regiments were to embark at the Long Wharf, the 43rd, 52nd, and the light infantry and grenadiers of the 35th at the North Battery, about fifteen hundred rank and file in all. At the Battery, the 47th, 1st Battalion of Marines, and the light infantry and grenadiers of the 2nd Battalion of Marines and of the 63rd Regiment, were to be held in reserve, about seven hundred rank and file. Howe, as senior major general under Gage, commanded the expedition, with Brigadier Gen-eral Sir Robert Pigot as his second. The men carried their full kit, blankets, and cooked provisions for three days.[29]

The embarkation began about midday, and the bombardment of the peninsula was simultaneously increased to a terrible intensity. The great *Somerset* and two floating batteries at the ferry and the batteries on Copp's Hill, to which Gage had added three 24-pounders, concentrated their fire on the redoubt. The *Glasgow* frigate, the *Symmetry* armed transport, and two gunboats moored in the Charles poured their fire on the Neck, while the sloops *Falcon* and *Lively* swept the low ground in front of Breed's Hill to clear a space for the landing. The ships engaged in this bombardment could fire eighty guns in a single broadside.[30]

The scene on the water was brilliant almost beyond description. Twenty-eight barges, in two parallel lines of single file, loaded with scarlet-coated men, were rowed precisely in line around the end of the peninsula. In each of the two leading boats were six brass fieldpieces. The noonday sun, shin-ing down upon glistening steel and polished brass, was reflected in a thou-sand points of light, while, all about, the guns of the fleet belched flame and smoke in a thunderous roar. It was such a sight as the tired, hungry, thirsty, dirty, shirt-sleeved farmers, peering over the walls of their little fort, had never before seen, war in all its pride and glory, before it dissolved into blood and horror.[31]

The landing was made about one o'clock without resistance, and the troops were at once formed in three lines on Moulton's Hill, while Howe was examining the American works. He saw at once that the situation had changed since the early morning. Whereas then the redoubt had stood alone, with no supporting defenses, leaving a broad way around it on the east, now the breastwork extended eastward and dangerously narrowed that way. Yet it was not entirely cut off; there was still room for a flanking movement. There was, however, another matter to be considered. On Bunker's Hill there was a considerable crowd of men who had left the redoubt at various times, or who had crossed the Neck and stopped there. Putnam held them to erect his proposed covering works. But to Howe they doubtless looked like a reserve force. There was a danger that his flanking movement might land him between two American forces. Also he saw a column emerge from that formless mass of men and march toward the redoubt. The Americans there were being reinforced. He was going to need more men than he had brought. He ordered his men to break ranks and refresh themselves with the food they had brought, while he obtained his reserves and part of his main force for which there had not been room in the first embarkation.[32]

The reinforcements that Howe saw marching to the redoubt from Bunker's Hill were the New Hampshire troops under John Stark and James Reed. When they received their orders to march from Cambridge, there were no cartridges on hand. To each man were issued two flints, a gill of powder, and about a pound of lead, cut from the organ pipes of a Cambridge church. They were directed to march to their quarters and make up fifteen cartridges each. Those that had bullet molds used them; the others pounded bits of lead into slugs to fit their muskets. Few of them had cartridge boxes; the rest carried loose powder in their horns and the bullets in bags. They then started on a four-mile march to Charlestown. Stark's regiment, consisting of thirteen companies, was the largest in the army. Reed's was small.[33]

Meanwhile, the news of the landing of the British had thrown Cambridge into confusion. Bells were rung, drums were beaten, and officers ran hither and thither calling out their men to do they knew not what. Orders arrived from Putnam for the Connecticut troops to come on. Ward, with the stubbornness of his natural disposition, would not be convinced that this was the real attack; he still feared that it was a feint, and that his stores were in danger. Exactly what orders he gave is not known. It appears that some provisions, including barrels of beer, were to be sent to the peninsula; but the supply that reached the troops was tantalizingly scanty. It also appears that he reserved his own regiment, John Paterson's, Thomas Gardner's, and a part of Ebenezer Bridge's, and ordered the rest of the Massachusetts troops to Charlestown. But no one knew clearly what he was to do. Jonathan

Brewer's regiment, John Nixon's, Moses Little's, James Scammon's and Samuel Gerrish's, all Massachusetts troops, were under arms and marching about, with vague notions of what was expected of them. When Colonel Stark, leading his regiment and Reed's, approached the Neck, he found two regiments halted in the road, fearing to cross through the barrage thrown by the *Symmetry* and her attendant gunboats. Stark asked them, if they did not intend to cross, to let his men through, which they gladly did. He marched his men across the Neck at a very deliberate pace. Captain Henry Dearborn of the front company suggested "quickening the march of the regiment," that it might sooner be relieved of the cross fire. "With a look peculiar to himself," says Dearborn, "he fixed his eyes on me and observed with great composure—'Dearborn, one fresh man in action is worth ten fatigued men.'" At the top of Bunker's Hill, Stark halted to survey the scene.[34]

When Prescott saw the British forces landed at Moulton's Point and deployed as if for immediate action, against his left, he realized that the gap between the far end of the breastwork and the edge of the peninsula offered an avenue for flanking and even encircling his main position. He at once ordered Knowlton to move his Connecticut troops from the entrenchments and, with two guns, to oppose the enemy's right wing in its approach on that side.

Near the base of Bunker's Hill and about six hundred feet behind the line of the breastwork, there was a fence "half of stone and two rayles of wood." It was about two hundred yards long, running parallel with the breastwork to the river bank, and, if held, it would prevent Howe's flanking movement. Knowlton took post there. To strengthen this frail barrier, his men tore down a near-by rail fence, set it up in front of the other, with a little distance between, and stuffed this space with newly cut grass which lay all about. It seems to have been, as one of his men said, "a slight defence against musquet-ball," but it had a sufficient appearance of strength to deceive the enemy.[35]

From his place on Bunker's Hill, Stark saw that this fence was thinly held by Knowlton's men, fewer than two hundred on a two-hundred-yard length. He "harangued his regiment in a short but animated address," to which they responded with three cheers, and then led them at the double down the slope of Bunker's Hill to the fence to reinforce Knowlton. It was fortunate for the Americans that Stark came to that point, for he saw at once that, while the fence extended to the river bank, there was still a way around it. The edge of the hard ground was a bluff eight or nine feet high. Below it was a strip of beach, narrow at the near high tide then prevailing, but wide enough to permit a column to pass along it. With stones from adjacent walls, he built a breastwork across the beach clear to the water's edge. He lined this with a triple row of his best men, posting the rest and Reed's men along the fence with Knowlton.[36] One other minor element of the American defenses has been generally overlooked by historians of the battle. To cover the ground between the east end of the breastwork and the west end of the rail fence, three small flèches, V-shaped entrenchments, had been built.[37]

There were, then, four distinct elements in the fortifications: the redoubt, the breastwork, the rail fence, and the wall on the beach. When the battle began they were manned as follows: the redoubt and the breastwork by Prescott's and parts of Brewer's, Nixon's, Woodbridge's, Little's, and Ephraim Doolittle's Massachusetts regiments, the last named under Major Willard Moore; the fence by Knowlton's Connecticut troops, Reed's New Hampshire, and part of Stark's; the wall on the beach by Stark himself and part of his men.[38]

Two other unfortified positions were held by the Americans to guard Prescott's right flank on the side of the redoubt toward Charlestown. In a cartway along a fence, near the right of the redoubt a company of Little's regiment and a few other troops, including Nutting's company, which had been guarding the shore in the village, were posted. Three companies—Wheeler's of Doolittle's regiment, Crosby's of Reed's, and one from Woodbridge's—were stationed in the main street of Charlestown at the foot of Breed's Hill; these constituted the extreme American right.[39]

Before the battle began two notable volunteers appeared on the field and were greeted with cheers. One was Joseph Warren. As he had been appointed a major general, Putnam offered him command at the rail fence; he declined it. He asked only where he could be of most service as a volunteer. Putnam indicated the redoubt, where he would be under cover. Warren said he did not seek a place of safety. "Where will the attack be the hottest?" he asked. Putnam still pointed to the redoubt. "That is the enemy's object. If that can be maintained, the day is ours." At the redoubt Prescott offered to yield his command. Warren again declined, and fought in the battle as a simple soldier.[40]

The other newcomer was General Seth Pomeroy—old Seth Pomeroy, carrying his nearly seventy years as lightly as he bore the musket which he himself had made and had carried at the siege of Louisburg thirty years before. He had ridden to the Neck on a borrowed horse. As it was not his own, he would not submit it to the raking fire there, but dismounted, crossed on foot, and trudged all the way to the rail fence, where he took his place with the others amid an enthusiastic welcome.[41]

Soon after his first landing Howe had pushed forward two outposts: one of four companies of light infantry in front of his main body in a depression which sheltered it from the fire of the redoubt; the other, two battalions under Pigot, to a position farther west and just below the southern foot of Breed's Hill. This detachment became the nucleus of Pigot's wing in the attack.[42]

Pigot, in his position on the British left, was annoyed by the fire of the Americans from Charlestown on his left. Admiral Samuel Graves had come ashore to see what help the fleet could give. Pigot spoke to him about "the mischief his left wing sustained by the fire from Charlestown." Graves sent orders to burn the place. Under a shower of red-hot cannon balls and of carcasses (hollow iron balls pierced with holes and containing lighted combustibles) from the ships and the batteries on Copp's Hill, it was "instantly set on fire in many places." It had been practically deserted, except for the few American troops, who were soon driven out by this bombardment. No effort was made to extinguish the fires, and soon the entire town was in flames.[43]

The reserve ordered up by Howe landed between one and two o'clock west of Moulton's Hill below the western foot of Breed's, and near Pigot's outpost. Howe then disposed his troops for the attack. His own right wing was drawn up in three lines, the classic British battle order, the light infantry in front, the grenadiers in the second line, the 5th and 52nd Regiments in the third. Pigot had three companies of light infantry, three of grenadiers, the 38th, 43rd, and 57th Regiments, and the 1st Battalion of marines. The two divisions were about equal in number, thirty-seven companies in Pigot's, thirty-eight in Howe's; but Howe's was stronger, because he had the greater number of flank companies, picked men.[44]

Howe is said to have addressed his troops in the usual eighteenth century manner. He was happy to have the honor of commanding so fine a body of men, who, he was sure, would "behave like Englishmen, and as becometh good soldiers." He would not desire one of them "to go a step further than where I go myself at your head"—a promise he kept, for, in the good old fashion, he fought in the front ranks.[45]

Before advancing his infantry, he sent his artillery forward and opened fire on the redoubt, the breastwork, and the rail fence. Three ships, three floating batteries, and the battery on Copp's Hill, from six different directions, centered their fire on the works. Howe's fieldpieces were, however, soon silenced, not by the feeble fire from the American artillery posted in the gap between the breastwork and the rail fence, but by the discovery that their side boxes contained twelve-pound balls, instead of six-pound. Howe sent off for the proper balls, ordering the substitution of grape in the meanwhile; but the distance was too great for grape to be effective. There was a further difficulty when the guns, supported by the grenadiers of the 35th, were pushed forward to support the attack. They got into boggy ground and could not be moved. Altogether, Howe's fieldpieces were of little avail at that time, except to scare the Americans, who had an exaggerated idea of the deadliness of artillery.[46]

From the formation of Howe's line, it would have seemed that he intended to advance in the conventional three-line formation directly upon the American works, with no other plan than to make a dogged frontal attack. This, indeed, has been the story of the battle in most of the histories and pictures of the combat; but such was not the case. Howe was too able a strategist to employ such a wasteful method if a flanking movement were possible, as was to be proven more than once in this war. He still had in mind his original plan flanking and encircling the American left. Although the defenses had been so greatly extended since that plan was formed, it still seemed possible to carry it out by smashing the extreme left while appearing to lead his men to a direct attack on the works, and this he proceeded to attempt.[47]

He drew off his front line of light infantry to the right and formed them, eleven companies, in column on the beach. This left his battle line in two ranks, grenadiers in front. With these his advance began. In heavy marching order, carrying knapsacks, blankets, and all their accouterments—with their ammunition, food, and firelocks, an estimated weight of a hundred pounds for each man—the main body of redcoats marched down from Moulton's Hill, across the lowland, and up the lower slopes of Breed's toward the breastwork and rail fence. At the same time Pigot's division breasted Breed's Hill against the redoubt, which he intended to envelop.[48]

The day was hot. The unmown grass, through which they had to march, was thick and long, reaching to their knees. There were walls and fences, which they had to throw down or climb over. The brick kiln and its adjacent ponds in the hard ground between two swamps broke their ranks, which had to be re-formed. They stopped from time to time to let the artillery come up and resume its fire. Altogether, the march against the American works was as painful as it was slow. As seen from Boston, across the Charles, it was, however, a brilliant and awe-inspiring spectacle. The people thronged the river shore; they crowded the hills; they perched on rooftops and gazed at "one of the greatest scenes of war that can be conceived," as General Burgoyne wrote to a friend in England.[49]

There were those two scarlet-clad lines of men pushing forward slowly, so slowly that the suspense was heavy to bear, their gun barrels and bayonets flashing back the rays of the sun. There were the guns, the fieldpieces, the great guns on the ships and on Copp's Hill, flashing with flame, emitting clouds of white smoke in a continuous rolling of thunder. In the foreground was Charlestown, scores of houses in one great blaze, its tall church steeples flaming high in the air, ships upon the stocks burning, the crash of buildings, whole streets of buildings, falling together. From it vast, billowing clouds of smoke arose, drifted toward the central scene, now obscuring this or that element, now lifting and disclosing it again. And, in the midst of it all, that little redoubt anxiously yet grimly silent, as it awaited the shock of battle. It was, said John Burgoyne, "a picture and a complication of horror and importance beyond anything that ever came to my lot to be witness to." [50]

The plan for the attack seems to have consisted of three parts. Pigot's division was to march against the redoubt and the breastwork, not to attack them, but to engage the attention of their defenders and hold them in check. The light infantry were to storm the little position on the beach, break through, and come onto the field behind the rail fence. Then Howe's grenadiers and regulars would fall on the rail fence, which would be under the fire of the light infantry in their rear. Thus the whole American left would be shattered, and the redoubt and breastwork isolated and surrounded.

As soon, therefore, as the whole line started its slow advance, "frequently halting to give time for the artillery to fire," [51] the 11 light infantry companies formed in column of fours on the narrow beach, those from the 23rd Regiment, the famous Royal Welch Fusiliers, in the lead, followed by those from the 4th, the King's Own Regiment. They were ordered not to fire, but to take their objective with the bayonet. The beach was level and unobstructed by grass, walls, or fences. Their advance could therefore be more rapid than that of the main forces, and, as theirs was to be the first attack, they doubtless made good time.

The familiar story has it that the Americans were told not to fire until they could see the whites of the enemies' eyes, nor until the order was given, and then to aim low. Stark's men from behind their roughly piled stone wall on the beach could see the scarlet-clad column advancing steadily and swiftly upon them, coming nearer and nearer until it was almost close enough to deploy and charge. It was only 150 feet away when the order came. A blast of fire struck the Fusiliers and tore the leading ranks apart.

The column halted, recoiled, but came on again, the King's Own pushing through the broken Fusiliers. Again the Yankee muskets spoke, again men fell in heaps. The officers shouted at the men, urged them forward. Though they did re-form and try once more, it was like pushing a wax candle against a red-hot plate—the head of the column simply melted away. Ninety-six lay dead on the beach; they "lay as thick as sheep in a fold." The rest turned and ran. That part of Howe's plan had failed.[52]

But with his grenadiers and his regulars Howe had to go on. His pretty plan was wrecked. There would be no turning movement of his enemy's extreme left, no confusion and dismay behind the rail fence caused by fire on its flank and rear. He had to make a direct, frontal attack on the fence, whether he would or no. He did go on. His men marched steadily forward. They were checked and obstructed by fences and walls at the point where their bayonet charge should have begun, and there the fire from the fence broke upon them in a withering blast that shattered their lines. Every man in Howe's personal staff was either killed or wounded.

The grenadiers in front stopped, began to fire instead of charging; but they aimed too high, most of their bullets passing over the heads of the Americans, while the renewed fire from the fence still fell heavily upon them. The second line came up and "mixt with them" in disorder, and at last the whole force fell back in confusion, out of range. Meanwhile Pigot had made his attempt against the redoubt, hardly more than a feint, and had also fallen back. So ended the first attack.[53]

In the American lines there was joy and exultation. These farmers had met the famous British regulars and beaten them. At but little cost, they had strewn the ground with their enemy's dead. But Prescott knew that the battle was not yet won. The British would not give over their attack after one repulse. He mingled with his men, praising their valor, reminding them that there was yet work to be done, and encouraging them to stand to it. There were pitifully few in the redoubt now, no more than one hundred and fifty. Putnam, who had been at the fence, rode back over Bunker's Hill, where there were hundreds of men, calling on them to reinforce Prescott. He rode down to the Neck. Ward had sent men from Cambridge; but they had halted, fearing to penetrate the feeble barrage still being laid down upon that isthmus. Putnam rode through it, called on them to follow him, and rode back again, entreating them to come on. A few did, but only a few. Nor did he get many more from Bunker's Hill.[54]

Howe soon re-formed his shattered ranks. Within a quarter of an hour the second attack began, but not on the same plan. The American left, the

rail fence, had proved to be too strong. His light infantry, rallied from their
defeat on the beach, had rejoined his force. They were now to march against
the fence to engage American attention, while Howe and Pigot threw their
whole force against the redoubt and the breastwork. The artillery left behind, columns were formed and marched forward until they were within a
hundred yards, where they deployed in line of battle and opened fire. The
American lines were silent, until the enemy were within a hundred feet.
Then came from them a blast of fire, more devastating than before. It was
not merely a single volley. The Americans loaded and fired again and again,
not only from the redoubt, breastwork, and fence, but also from the three
little flèches, "from whence the Grenadiers received a very heavy fire," and
from some buildings on Pigot's left.

Though mown down like grass under the scythe, the British struggled to
advance. A bayonet charge was intended, but, against that fire, it was
sheerly impossible. "An incessant stream of fire poured from the rebel lines;
it seemed a continued sheet of fire for nearly thirty minutes. Our Light-infantry were served up in Companies against the grass fence, without being
able to penetrate—indeed, how could we penetrate? Most of our Grenadiers
and Light-infantry, the moment of presenting themselves, lost three-fourths,
and many nine-tenths of their men. Some had only eight or nine men a
company left; some only three, four and five. On the left Pigot was staggered
and actually retreated. Observe, our men were not driven back; they actually
retreated by orders." [55] Whether they retreated by order or by the instinct
of self-preservation, they did retreat, down the slope of the hill, far out of
range of the American muskets, and there was a long cessation in the fighting, so long that the Americans began to think they saw a victory.[56]

Putnam had been incessant and indefatigable in his efforts to reinforce the
lines from the crowd on Bunker's Hill, but with little success. Captain John
Chester, who with his company had been called by Putnam from Cambridge
to the scene of action about noon, describes what he found on his arrival.
He had marched at the same time as three regiments. When he got to the
hill "there was not a company with us in any kind of order. They were
scattered, some behind rocks and hay-cocks, and thirty men, perhaps, behind an apple-tree." British bullets, flying high over the American lines, had
landed among the men on the hill, and the guns on the ships had been
pouring their fire on it. Some of the men there were wounded. Their solici-
tous comrades carried them to safety, "frequently twenty men round a
wounded man, retreating, when not more than three or four could touch
him with advantage. Others were retreating, seemingly without any excuse,

and some said they had left the fort with leave of their officers, because they had been all night and day on fatigue, without sleep, victuals, or drink." [57]

Putnam found one of these reinforcing regiments scattered about on the safe side of Bunker's Hill. Its colonel, Samuel Gerrish, who was "unwieldy from excessive corpulence . . . prostrate on the ground," declaring that he was "completely exhausted . . . Putnam ordered them on to the lines; he entreated them, threatened them, and some of the most cowardly he knocked down with his sword, but all in vain." The adjutant, Christian Febiger, who was to distinguish himself by more than one act of valor, did rally a detachment and led it to the lines.[58] Gerrish was afterward cashiered. Two other Connecticut companies, under James Clark and William Coit, arrived in time to have some part in the battle. Colonel James Scammons marched his regiment to Lechmere Point. He was ordered to "march to the hill." He marched to Cobble Hill, about a mile from Bunker's. After a while, he went on to Bunker's, "where the shot flew very thick." "Before we got to the top of the hill, Colonel Scammons ordered a retreat," and retreat they did. Scammons was later tried by court-martial; but, on his plea that he had misunderstood his orders, was acquitted.[59]

Four hundred fresh men, the 63rd Regiment and the 2nd Battalion of marines, sent for after the first attack, had now joined Howe, and he began his preparations for another assault, in spite, it is said, of the remonstrances of some of his officers, who urged that it would be downright butchery of his men to send them again into that deadly fire. He ordered all knapsacks and other superfluous equipment laid aside. The troops were to advance in columns, without firing a shot, and take the works with the bayonet. The artillery was to be pushed forward into the gap between the east end of the breastwork and the west end of the rail fence, so as to enfilade the breastwork and drive out its defenders. Preparations were made accordingly.

Clinton, watching the scene from Copp's Hill, was not restrained by lack of orders from Gage. He crossed and, when he landed, "collected all the guards and such wounded men as could follow, which to their honour were many, and advanced in column with as much parade as possible to impress the enemy," a heroic picture. He joined Pigot's division in the attack.[60]

Within the American lines there had been little loss of men, but there was a depressing scarcity of powder; not much was left in the powder horns. The few remaining cannon cartridges were broken open, and their contents distributed. The defenses were manned with as much resolution as before, but with little hope.[61]

The British guns were brought up. Their columns were on the march again. There was to be only a slight demonstration against the rail fence, while Howe threw his division upon the breastwork, and Pigot and Clinton concentrated on the redoubt. The artillery secured its desired position and opened a raking fire on the breastwork's defenders. They were swept away, either off the field or into the redoubt. The infantry plunged forward with their bayonets advanced, and once more met a deadly fire. The Americans "rose up," wrote young Lord Rawdon, "and poured in so heavy a fire upon us that the oldest officers say they never saw a sharper action. They kept up this fire until we were within ten yards of them, nay, they even knocked down my captain . . . after we had got into the ditch of the entrenchment. . . . There are few instances of regular troops defending a redoubt till the enemy were in the very ditch of it." [62]

On Pigot's extreme left, which had curved around to the west side of the redoubt, the marines had a hard time. They were checked by that desperate fusillade, fell into confusion, and began to shoot instead of charging. Major Pitcairn, their commander, was killed, along with many others. The 47th came up and formed beside them. Under the urgent commands of their adjutant, they ceased firing, "rushed on, leaped the ditch and climbed the parapet, under a most sore and deadly fire." [63]

But that was the end. Those last volleys faded out into a sputtering finish, "like an old candle," for there was no more powder. Nor were there bayonets to meet bayonets. The British swarmed over the parapet, leaped down into the redoubt. Its defenders met them with clubbed muskets and stones. The bayonet work of the British, said Adjutant Waller of the marines, was shocking. Yet there were only thirty of the Americans killed in the redoubt. Prescott ordered a retreat. Some of his men clambered over the parapet and got away. The rest crowded toward the gateway in the rear wall, where there might have been a ghastly massacre; but the dust hung so thick in the air that the British could hardly tell friend from foe, and did not fire into the mass at the gateway. Prescott had to fight his way to it, his sword against a British bayonet.[64]

When the beaten men emerged from their fort, they found themselves between the two bodies of their enemy, which had come around opposite sides of the work. Each was afraid to fire for fear of hitting the other. But when the retreating men were clear of those two forces they were heavily fired upon. Joseph Warren, one of the last to leave the redoubt, was shot through the head; and many others fell.[65]

The defenders of the rail fence had suffered little in this last attack, which on their part of the works was but a feint. They withdrew with some degree of regularity, taking their only fieldpiece with them. Old Seth Pomeroy, grasping his veteran musket, its stock shattered by a bullet, walked away backward, still facing the foe. Chester's company, lately arrived with some others, hurried down from Bunker's Hill, posted themselves behind a stone wall, and, "by a brisk fire from our small-arms," covered the retreat as best they could.[66]

But there were others who might have helped and did not. The men behind the rail fence, Knowlton's and Stark's, might have attacked the British right wing in its rear, while it was busy with the redoubt. Unfortunately, there was no concert of effort between them and Prescott; the two wings of the Americans fought as if they had been engaged in different battles. There were many hundred, perhaps a thousand, fresh men with Putnam on Bunker's Hill no more than six hundred yards away—enough, with Stark's and Knowlton's men, to turn the tide of battle if they had come up and attacked the disorganized enemy; but they themselves were a mere mass of men without organization or unified command and they did not even fire a shot to cover the retreat. Prescott, going off the field, came upon Putnam, and asked him why he had given the fighting men no support. "I could not *drive* the dogs," Putnam answered. To which Prescott is said to have replied, "If you could not *drive* them up, you might have *led* them up." [67] The Americans had two things yet to learn, how to organize a real army, and how to stand up and fight in the open.

But the retreat was not a rout. The American rear guard kept up "a running fight from one fence or wall to another, till we entirely drove them off the peninsula." So Rawdon wrote. And Burgoyne testified that "the retreat was no flight; it was even covered with bravery and military skill." Yet it was in the retreat that the Americans suffered the heaviest losses. While the greater part of them were passing over the slopes and the top of Bunker's Hill and across the Neck, they were under continuous fire from the ships and batteries as well as from the muskets of their pursuers. More men were struck down then than in the battle itself.[68]

The defeated men withdrew to Winter Hill and Prospect Hill on the road to Cambridge, and immediately began to fortify. They worked all night under the indefatigable Putnam, and by morning had built an entrenchment on Prospect Hill a hundred feet square. Putnam's son came to him the next morning and found him "dashing about among the workmen. . . . He wore the same clothes he had on when I left him on the 16th, and said he had neither put them off, nor washed himself since, and we might well believe him." [69]

The "almost exhausted" British did not cross the Neck. With the aid of fresh troops from Boston, they threw up a line of breastworks on the northern side of Bunker's Hill, content to hold the ground they had so hardly won. This line was afterward elaborated until it became a strong fortress, well ditched, palisaded, fraised, and protected by outlying entrenchments, making such a strong post that no attack upon it was ever seriously proposed by the Americans.[70]

The losses of the British in this battle were exceedingly heavy. Out of about 2,400 engaged, including the late arrived 400, who had taken part in only the last attack, 1,054, including 92 officers, had been shot; 226 of them were killed. Howe had twelve officers in his staff on the field; every one of them was shot down. Among the light infantry and the grenadiers, who bore the brunt of the battle, the losses were staggering. Every man but four of the grenadiers of the 4th, the King's Own Regiment, was killed or wounded. Of the grenadiers of the 23rd, the Royal Welch Fusiliers, only three remained unhurt. Lord Percy wrote to his father: "My Reg^t, being one of the first that entered the redoubt, is almost entirely cut to pieces: there are but 9 men left in my co, & not above 5 in one of the others." [71]

The losses of the Americans have never been accurately ascertained. Besides the original 1,200, there may have been 2,000 more on the peninsula, but it is doubtful that more than 1,500 were actually engaged in the battle at any one time. Of these, perhaps 140 were killed, 271 wounded, and 30 captured, though the figures from various sources vary somewhat. The greatest loss was in Joseph Warren's death. His devotion to the cause, his energy, ability, and personal charm were not equaled by any of the other New England leaders at that time.[72]

To the courage, energy, and unbending will of Colonel Prescott it was undoubtedly due that the redoubt and the breastwork were held after the first assault. He inspired his men in the redoubt with his own tenacity and, by force of personal example and unalterable purpose, held them to their task. Their persistence made it possible for the defenders of the rail fence to hold out.

The stories of the part played by the American artillery are as confused (even on the number of guns in action) as its service was ineffective. There were three companies led by Major Scarborough Gridley and Captains Samuel Trevett and John Callender, having two guns each. Two of them were in disgrace after the battle. Gridley led his men a short way on the road from Cambridge, halted on Cobble Hill, and opened a futile fire against the *Glasgow*. Being urged to go forward, he took his guns to the redoubt and fired a few ineffectual shots at the British batteries on Copp's Hill. Burgoyne reported that two of these cannon balls "went one hundred yards over our heads." Gridley "swang his Hat round three Times to the

Enemy and then ceased to fire." He moved to the space between the breastwork and the rail fence, where he was joined by Callender. They seem to have been with Knowlton at the fence for a time, where "Gridley's guns were soon disabled and he drew them to the rear." Callender said his cartridges were too large for his pieces, and withdrew them to Bunker's Hill. Putnam ordered him back; he went, but "soon left his post and was soon deserted by his men." Captain Ford of Bridge's regiment took the guns back to the rail fence. Trevett, against the orders of his superior, Gridley, who was then firing on the *Glasgow*, took his two guns to Bunker's Hill, where one of them was disabled. He took the other to the fence. After the battle, his one gun was the only one carried safely off. Callender and Gridley were tried by court-martial, and both were dismissed from the service. Callender, however, remained with the army as a volunteer in the ranks and at the Battle of Long Island fought "with such signal bravery" that Washington erased his sentence from the orderly book and restored his commission.[73]

The effect of this battle on the minds of the British leaders appears in a letter from Gage to Dartmouth. It was shown that the Americans were "not the despicable rabble too many have supposed them to be." He recognized in them "a military spirit . . . joined with uncommon zeal and enthusiasm. . . . The conquest of this country is not easy." [74] It has often been held by American historians, probably without good cause, that the memory of his enormous loss in this battle intimidated Howe and deterred him from future frontal attacks on fortified positions, particularly on the day after the Battle of Long Island.

By the American people in general, the battle was at first regarded as a defeat, which, of course, it technically was. The whole enterprise was denounced as rash in its conception and discreditable in its execution. "No one, for years, came forward to claim the honor of having directed it; no notice was taken of its returning anniversary." [75] With the passage of time, emphasis began to be laid on the fact that the defenders of the redoubt gave in only when their ammunition was exhausted; their bravery and their effectiveness as long as their powder held out was recognized. At last, it was held to be a virtual victory, and was so celebrated. Its final effect was, in the minds of Americans, to exalt the American raw recruit to a degree of efficiency equal to that of trained and disciplined regular soldiers—a most unfortunate result.

From a military point of view, this conflict was unnecessary, inadvisable. and without justification. There was no good reason for the Americans attempting to hold the Charlestown peninsula against the British. It could give them no advantage in the siege of Boston, unless they were able to mount there such big guns as would dominate the water route to the town and prevent ships from reaching it. They had no such guns. Again, to hold it they would have had to divide their forces, with no means of communication between them and no means of supplying the force on the peninsula except by the Neck, which would always be under fire from the ships. Success in the Americans' effort was impossible by the very nature of the situation.

As for the British attack, enough has already been said in describing their divided counsels to show that the dreadful wastage of their men was probably unnecessary. Seizure of the Neck was feasible, and the consequent surrender of the garrison would have been inevitable.

CHAPTER 9

Washington Takes Command

The Continental Congress sitting in Philadelphia did not formally, by recorded vote, accept responsibility for the army besieging Boston, or, in the phrase commonly current at the time, "adopt it," until July 25, 1775; but it had ordered powder to be bought for it as early as June 3, and practically committed itself to some degree of responsibility early in that month by other resolutions touching on "the Continental Army." The Congress had even gone so far, on the 15th, as to appoint a general "to command all the continental forces, raised or to be raised, for the defense of American liberty," George Washington.[1]

The selection of a Virginian to command an army composed exclusively of Yankees may seem strange, yet there were cogent reasons for it. The most obvious was the fact of his experience in warfare. That experience did not include large and important commands; nevertheless, his reputation as a military man was more widespread throughout the colonies than that of any other colonial. He was a rich man, an aristocrat, and therefore influential among men of his own class, too few of whom were in sympathy with the American cause. He was a southerner, and the support of the southern colonies was needed in a contest hitherto waged by New England alone. He was a moderate man, still hoping for reconciliation with England; putting him at the head of the army would be notice to other moderate men that the radicals were not to have full sway. He was a sound man in his judgments and his decisions, as everyone who came in contact with him quickly realized. He had taken little part in the debates, and so had not aroused ill feeling in the minds of any of his colleagues. Tall, of commanding appearance, reserved in manner, yet plainly capable of energetic action, he looked like a leader. He was the only one of the delegates in the Congress who wore military garb, the blue and buff uniform of a Virginia militia colonel.

Perhaps as accurate a description of Washington's appearance as may be had is that given in 1760 by Captain George Mercer, his aide-de-camp in the Braddock campaign:

He may be described as being as straight as an Indian, measuring six feet two inches in his stockings and weighing 175 pounds. . . . His frame is well padded with well-developed muscles, indicating his great strength. His bones and joints are large, as are his feet and hands.

He is wide-shouldered, but has not a deep or round chest; is neat waisted, but is broad across the hips, and has rather long legs and arms. His head is well shaped though not large, but is gracefully poised on a superb neck. A large and straight rather than prominent nose; blue-gray penetrating eyes, which are widely separated and overhung by a heavy brow. His face is long rather than broad, with high round cheek bones, and terminates in a good firm chin. He has a clear though rather a colorless pale skin, which burns with the sun. A pleasing, benevolent, though a commanding countenance, dark brown hair, which he wears in a cue.

His mouth is large and generally firmly closed, but which from time to time discloses some defective teeth. His features are regular and placid, with all the muscles of his face under perfect control, though flexible and expressive of deep feeling when moved by emotions. In conversation he looks you full in the face, is deliberate, deferential and engaging. His voice is agreeable rather than strong. His demeanor at all times composed and dignified. His movements and gestures are graceful, his walk majestic, and he is a splendid horseman.

Captain Mercer neglected to mention that his "colorless pale skin" was pitted with the scars of smallpox, as were the skins of so many of his contemporaries.

John Adams and Samuel Adams were astute enough to recognize the reasons in favor of selecting Washington to be the commanding general. John made the motion. He noted that "Mr. Washington, who happened to sit near the door, as soon as he heard me allude to him, from his usual modesty, darted into the library room." Hancock, who wanted the job, or at least the refusal of it, showed "a sudden and striking change of countenance. Mortification and resentment were expressed as forcibly as his face could exhibit them." The motion was unanimously approved, and thus, as John Adams wrote to his wife, "the modest and virtuous, the amiable, generous and brave George Washington Esquire" was made "General of the American Army." [2]

Washington's acceptance of the appointment was admirably modest and sincere. He was distressed by a consciousness that his abilities and military experience might not be equal to the task, but he yielded to the desires of the Congress and promised to exert every power he possessed in the cause. He declined payment for his services, asking only for reimbursement of his expenses.[3]

Artemas Ward, Charles Lee, Philip Schuyler, and Israel Putnam were chosen by the Congress as major generals, ranking in that order. Eight brigadier generals were elected: Seth Pomeroy, Richard Montgomery, David Wooster, William Heath, Joseph Spencer, John Thomas, John Sullivan, and Nathanael Greene. Horatio Gates was appointed adjutant, with the rank of brigadier general. Pomeroy, presumably because of his age, did not accept the offered commission. Washington appointed Thomas Mifflin his first aide-de-camp, and Joseph Reed his secretary.[4]

The commander in chief received his orders on June 20. They were in general terms suitable to the occasion, but contained one parenthetical clause which had a far-reaching and seldom salutary effect. He was authorized in all unforeseen contingencies, "or any occasions that may happen, to use your best circumspection and (advising with your council of war) to order and dispose of the said Army as may be most advantageous."[5] It soon became evident and for a long time remained evident that he took that to mean that he must not merely listen to the advice of his generals, but have their express authority before acting in any particular case. The result was that the activities of the army were sometimes dictated and directed by a majority vote of the subordinate generals rather than by the judgment of the commander in chief. This interpretation of his instructions was a consequence of his faithful adherence to the idea that he was merely an instrument of the Congress and not an independent executive. His native modesty and his distrust of his own abilities as a soldier also conduced to this subordination of himself.

Washington left Philadelphia on June 23 in a cavalcade which included Philip Schuyler, Charles Lee, and Thomas Mifflin. They were escorted with much ceremony by a number of the congressional delegates in carriages, accompanied by mounted servants, "a large troop of light horse in their uniforms; many officers of militia besides, in theirs; music playing, etc. etc.," as John Adams wrote to his wife.[6] Little John, plump as a partridge, unquestionably an indoor man, a desk man, envied the gallant soldiers, as all little men envy tall men, all civilians envy the man in uniform, all riders of ambling pads envy the man on a tall horse. "Such is the pride and pomp of war," Adams moralized. "I, poor creature, worn out with scribbling for my bread and my liberty, low in spirits and weak in health, must leave others to wear the laurels which I have sown." No doubt there recurred to his mind what he had lately written: "Oh, that I were a soldier! I will be. I am reading military books." But he never was.

New York, divided in counsel about the conflict, hesitating to take its stand definitely in one camp or the other, was embarrassed when it had to receive the rebel generals on the same day that it must welcome back from a visit to England its royal governor, William Tryon. Fortunately, they landed there several hours apart, so that "the volunteer companies raised for the express purpose of rebellion," as the loyalist judge, Thomas Jones, put it, "the members of the Provincial Congress . . . the parsons of the dissenting meetinghouses, with all the leaders and partisans of faction and rebellion," could meet the generals at four in the afternoon, and conduct them to Leonard Lispenard's house, "amidst repeated shouts and huzzas," and, at nine o'clock, "the members of his Majesty's Council, the Judges of the Supreme Court, the Attorney General . . . the Clergymen of the Church of England," and so on, all the dignified, respectable, and highly placed officials, "with a numerous train of his Majesty's loyal and well affected subjects," could meet the Governor and conduct him, "with universal shouts of applause," to the residence of Hugh Wallace, Esq. "But strange to relate . . . those very people who attended the rebel Generals in the morning . . . now, one and all, joined in the Governor's train and with the loudest acclamations . . . welcomed him back to the colony. . . . What a farce! What cursed hypocrisy!" exclaims the loyal judge.[7]

In New York, Washington detached Major General Philip Schuyler, who was to take command of all the troops in New York colony, and to occupy the posts on Lake George and Lake Champlain. Incidentally, he was to "keep a watchful eye upon Governour Tryon" and, if he attempted "directly or indirectly, any measures inimical to the common cause, [to] use every means in your power to frustrate his designs . . . if forcible measures are judged necessary." While the Continental Congress was not in session, Washington would order such measures; if it were sitting, Schuyler must get his orders from it, because "the seizing of a Governour [was] quite a new thing, and of exceeding great importance." [8]

The rest of the party went on to Cambridge, delayed somewhat on the way "by necessary attentions to the successive Civilities which accompanied me in my whole route," as Washington wrote to the Congress,[9] yet reaching their destination on July 2, only ten days from Philadelphia. He immediately assumed command of the army. Tradition has it that this was done while he stood under a tree on Cambridge Common, known thereafter as the Washington Elm, the troops being paraded before him. But there seems to be no historical basis for the legend. The army was spread over ten miles of defenses, and all trustworthy indications point to his having immediately inspected them piecemeal, without any central ceremony.[10]

At Watertown, on his way, Washington had been received by the Massachusetts Provincial Congress. Its address of welcome apologized for the character of the army he was to command: "The greatest part of them have not before seen service; and although naturally brave and of good understanding, yet, for want of experience in military life have but little knowledge of divers things most essential to the preservation of health, and even life. The youth of America are not possessed of the absolute necessity of cleanliness in their dress and lodging, continual exercise and strict temperance to preserve them from diseases frequently prevailing in camps," [11] all of which Washington soon learned was true enough. "I found," he says, "a mixed multitude of People here, under very little discipline, order, or Government. . . . Confusion and Disorder reigned in every Department." But he did not despair. Within three weeks of his arrival he was able to say, "We mend every day and I flatter myself that in a little Time, we shall work up these raw Materials into good Stuff." [12]

The army lay sprawling about Boston in a great crescent of installations. The Reverend William Emerson, who had been so active in the Concord fight, wrote at this time:

'Tis also very diverting to walk among yᵉ camps. They are as different in their form as yᵉ owners are in their dress; and every tent is a portraiture of yᵉ temper and taste of yᵉ persons that incamp in it. Some are made of boards, some of sailcloth, and some partly of one and partly of yᵉ other. Others are made of stone and turf, and others again of Birch and other brush. Some are thrown up in a hurry and look as if they could not help it—mere necessity—others are curiously wrought with doors and windows done with wreaths and withes in yᵉ manner of a basket. Some are your proper tents and marquees and look like yᵉ regular camp of yᵉ enemy. These are yᵉ Rhode-islanders, who are furnished with tent equipage from among ourselves and every thing in yᵉ most exact English taste. However, I think that yᵉ great variety of yᵉ American camp is upon yᵉ whole rather a beauty than a blemish to yᵉ army.[13]

One particular phase of the reformation of the army, the enforcement of proper distinction between officer and private, was fundamental in Washington's idea of an army. The "leveling spirit," the opinion that every man was just as good as any other man and a little better, was rife in New England, and was utterly subversive of discipline in the army. The officers could not maintain proper dignity and superiority to their men, could not give an order and exact obedience. Instead, they must truckle to them, conduct themselves with humility, and persuade their men to do their duty. This spirit of equality and lack of dignity was prevalent among the officers themselves.

Joseph Reed saw one of them "shaving one of his men on the parade." [14]
Another officer, a colonel and the army's chief engineer, was seen carrying
a large piece of beef, his rations, to his tent. He cheerfully explained that he
did it "to set the officers a good example." [15]

In an army without uniforms, there was no apparent distinction between
officer and private. The first step toward curing the evils of the leveling spirit
would naturally be the introduction of distinctive dress. It was not possible
to supply uniforms, but it was possible to distinguish the different grades
by simpler methods. In one of the earliest of Washington's general orders
provision was made to effect this purpose. The Commander in Chief was to
wear "a light blue Ribband . . . across his breast, between his Coat and
Waistcoat." Washington entered, in his expense account, an item of three
shillings and fourpence, the cost of this decoration. Major generals were to
wear purple; brigadiers, pink; aides-de-camp, green. The field officers were
to have red or pink cockades in their hats; the captains, yellow or buff; the
subalterns, green. The sergeants were to wear a shoulder knot of red cloth
on the right shoulder; the corporals, a green knot.[16] These arrangements,
coupled with the close attention given even to details, soon produced the
desired effect. An observer noted "a great overturning in the camp as to
order and regularity. New lords, new laws. The Generals Washington and
Lee are upon ye lines every day. . . . The strictest government is taking
place, and great distinction is made between officers and soldiers. Everyone
is made to know his place and keep in it." [17]

Washington felt the need of uniformity of dress among all his men. "I
know of nothing," he wrote, "in a speculative view more trivial, yet which
. . . would have a happier tendency to unite the men, and abolish those
provincial distinctions, that lead to jealousy and dissatisfaction." He proposed to the Congress the procurement of 10,000 hunting-shirts. These were
long, loose shirts, of tow cloth, either of its natural color or tanned to "the
shade of a dry or fading leaf," belted at the waist and having double shoulder
capes. They were worn outside the breeches like a frock. Being in common
use among the American backwoodsmen, they came to be regarded, especially by the British, as the distinctive garb of the riflemen. But, though
the Congress approved, and Washington canvassed several of the colonies
for the necessary material, he had to give up the project, because of the
scarcity of tow cloth. Except in the case of a few militia companies, such as
Benedict Arnold's and Joseph Chester's, which wore blue coats faced with
red, the army continued to display its motley dress.[18]

One of the first things that Washington did was to call on the adjutant of
each regiment for an exact return of its men, equipment, and supplies. These,

which should have been completed in half a day, owing to "the imperfect obedience which had been paid to . . . [orders] of a like nature from General Ward," were not forthcoming until after a week had elapsed. They showed a total of 16,770 men on the rolls, of which number 1,598 were on the sick list, 1,429 were absent for one reason or another, leaving 13,743 present and fit for duty.[19]

There was a prompt reorganization of the army into six brigades of six regiments each, and three divisions of two brigades each. Ward was given command of one division to constitute the right wing of the army, posted at Roxbury. Lee commanded another at Prospect Hill, the left wing; Putnam the third, in and about Cambridge, the center.[20] The need for improvement in the fortifications was apparent, and the men were put to work all along the lines. "Thousands are at work every day from four to eleven o'clock in the morning. It is surprising how much work has been done," wrote William Emerson as early as July 17.[21]

The problem of feeding thousands of men, in such a hastily assembled and completely unorganized mass as had swarmed around Boston after the day of Lexington and Concord, had been solved in a haphazard fashion during the two months before Washington took command. The first summons to arms had been sudden and unexpected. The men who hurried from their farms and homes, having no expectation of entering into a protracted service, had brought along pocketfuls of food, those from a distance relying on the inns and taverns to supply them on their march. Each Massachusetts town was, by custom, responsible for supplying its own militia in active service until the province could take over the job. Massachusetts had made provision for the collection of food, and considerable stores had been collected, which were sufficient to feed its men. Each of the other colonies had to care for its own.

Connecticut, having a patriot governor, Jonathan Trumbull, was prompt. An embargo was laid on the export of food. Joseph Trumbull was appointed commissary to collect provisions and supply them to the Connecticut forces; he did the work efficiently. Rhode Island was handicapped at first by its Loyalist governor, Joseph Wanton. But he was soon displaced, and a member of the Committee of Safety was made Chief Commissary with good results. The New Hampshire towns carried the burden for a while, each for its own men, until the province relieved them in May. Being, however, the poorest of them all in the production of foodstuffs, it was obliged to buy from the others, especially from more fertile Connecticut. On the whole, these hastily contrived measures were effective in furnishing the men a sufficient, indeed a comfortable, sustenance.[22]

When the army was adopted by the Congress, Washington was ordered "to victual at the continental expense all such volunteers as have joined or shall join the united army." [23] He appointed Joseph Trumbull commissary general. The daily ration comprised fresh beef or pork or salt fish, bread, peas, beans, or other vegetables, and milk, with a weekly addition of rice or Indian meal. Spruce beer was to be a daily drink, with molasses as a substitute. Candles and soap were also to be provided.[24]

In spite of many difficulties, particularly in the procurement of sufficient wheat flour and in recurring shortages of funds, Trumbull succeeded in his arduous tack of feeding the army during its stay before Boston. In June, 1776, Washington wrote to the Congress, "Few Armies, if any, have been better and more plentifully supplied than the Troops under Mr. Trumbull's care." [25]

In July and August there were brought into the army the first soldiers drawn from outside New England, and remarkable men they were. The Congress on June 14 had voted "That six companies of expert rifflemen, be immediately raised in Pennsylvania, two in Maryland and two in Virginia," each to consist of sixty-eight privates and the usual officers. Recruiting was promptly effected. In Pennsylvania there were so many candidates that three additional companies were authorized, and the whole nine were organized as a battalion, with William Thompson as colonel and Edward Hand second in command. Virginia turned out its share, Daniel Morgan raising his company, ninety-six men, within ten days. Maryland's first company was commanded by Michael Cresap, a veteran Indian fighter; its second, by Thomas Price.[26]

These men were drawn chiefly from the wilder, western parts of their respective colonies—Scotch-Irish many of them. They were backwoodsmen, "remarkably stout and hardy men; many of them exceeding six feet in height." Their garb was simple: round wool hats, hunting shirts, breeches, stockings, and shoes or leather leggings and moccasins, Indian style. "On the breast [of their shirts] in capital letters, is their motto 'Liberty or Death.' " They had to march from four hundred to seven hundred miles to reach the camp, bivouacking in their blankets at night. Morgan mounted his men and rode with them six hundred miles in twenty-one days. So fit were they, and so inured to exposure and physical exertion, that not a man was lost by sickness on the way. All these added 1,430 men to the army.[27]

They also added a new weapon, before that practically unknown in New England. Rifling the barrel of a gun, that is to say cutting spiral grooves inside the barrel so as to make the bullet rotate in its flight and thus increase its accuracy, was not an American invention. It was practiced in Central

Europe as early as 1500. But the so-called Kentucky rifle was evolved in the American colonies and differed greatly from the European rifled guns, which were short, heavy, clumsy, perhaps an inch in bore, and terrific in recoil. The necessities of American frontier life demanded economy in powder and lead, and therefore a small-calibered weapon of great accuracy. By immigrant expert gunsmiths, chiefly German or Swiss settled in Pennsylvania, such a gun was produced.

The rifle was slender and graceful in appearance and as much as five feet long, sometimes more, the greater length of the barrel being supposed to increase its precision. It carried a ball weighing only a half-ounce. Its range and its accuracy in the hands of an expert were extraordinary. While a musket ball dropped harmlessly to the ground at 125 yards and had little certainty of hitting a target less than man-size at half that distance, expert riflemen put ball after ball into a mark seven inches in diameter at 250 yards. Exhibitions of marksmanship and trick shooting by these men amazed and delighted the Yankees around Boston.[28]

The rifle had, however, its disadvantages. The loading was slower than with the musket. In order that the ball might have close contact with the grooves in the barrel, getting its twist and at the same time the full propulsive effect of the powder, a small disk of greased linen or buckskin was placed on the muzzle, the ball laid upon it and the whole rammed home. This took twice the time necessary to load a musket, and, besides, with its small bore and the grooves in the barrel, the rifle soon fouled and had to be swabbed out. Then, too, the lighter bullet had less stopping power against a charge. For sharpshooting and bush fighting it was a superior weapon; but in such a battle as that on Breed's Hill the musket was more useful.

These backswoodsmen proved to be difficult to deal with in the camp. They were accustomed to acting entirely on their own, and their stubborn individualism was slow to yield to army discipline and routine. The inactivity of the siege chafed them. For a while they found satisfaction in sniping sentries or other exposed men in the British lines, where their reputation for deadly accuracy was great and universal. "They are grown so terrible to the regulars," wrote Joseph Reed, "that nothing is to be seen over the breastwork but a hat." But such practices were regarded by Washington as merely a waste of the scanty supply of powder, and had to be stopped. Washington's orders irked the freeborn riflemen, and, although they were at first pampered by exemption from entrenching and general camp duties, they became unruly and troublesome.[29]

If a rifleman was confined in the guardhouse for some disdemeanor, his comrades broke open his prison and released him. On one occasion such a

culprit was removed to the main guardhouse in Cambridge for safer keeping, whereupon some of Captain James Ross's Pennsylvania company,
armed with loaded rifles, swore by God they would release him or lose their
lives, and "set off as hard as they could run." Washington strengthened the
guard to the number of five hundred men, and ordered several regiments
under arms. He, with Lee and Greene, pursued the mutineers and overtook
them. When he ordered them to ground their arms, they, "beginning to be
frighted at their proceedings," obeyed. They were then surrounded by
another Pennsylvania company and marched back to camp, where they were
tried, convicted of mutiny, and fined 20 shillings each.[30]

On the whole, the riflemen were of little use in the siege. "Gen. Washington said he wished they had never come; Gen. Lee has damned them and
wished them all in Boston." General Thomas wrote that the generality of
them were "as Indifferent men as ever I served with, their Privates mutinous
and often Deserting to the Enemy, unwilling for Duty of any kind, exceedingly vitious and I think the army here would be as well without them as
with them." The whole trouble was that they were, by nature and by experience, totally unfitted for inactive life in camp. Many of them served excellently in the expedition against Quebec, and later in the war when they were
in active service.[31]

Washington thought he had not enough men in his army; but, from the
first, he knew he had not enough ammunition, either powder or lead. On
August 4 he had but 9,940 pounds of powder, "not more than 9 Cartridges
a Man." He repeatedly called on the Congress for more, on all the New
England colonies, and on New York. By the 24th, with help from Philadelphia, he had built up his store to 184 barrels, equal to twenty-five rounds,
and in September he got 7,000 pounds from Rhode Island. But he never
had enough to allow his men to have more than twelve or fifteen rounds at
a time while the British kept their soldiers always supplied with sixty cartridges apiece.[32]

To supplement their weapons during the shortage of ammunition, and
particularly to make up for the lack of bayonets, several thousand iron-
pointed pikes with twelve-foot shafts were procured. As missile weapons,
Benjamin Franklin suggested the use of bows and arrows, supporting his
recommendation with excellent philosophic reasons, which, however, did
not sufficiently commend themselves to the military mind; none was employed.[33]

The shortage of ammunition alone would have prevented any major
hostile movement by the Americans; but there were also other dissuasive

reasons. The British losses on Breed's Hill had been more than made up by the arrival in June and July of reinforcements, so that their number of effectives was over 6,000, with 1,400 sick or wounded in hospitals.[34] Their defenses at Boston Neck had been built up and greatly strengthened, and on Bunker's Hill they had built an elaborate fortress, with a thick parapet, well ditched, fraised, and abatised, of which Washington said "Twenty thousand men could not have carried it against one thousand had that work been well defended." A large part of their army was in barracks in that fort or encamped about it. Except for the dragoons and a few of the infantry, the rest was in the defenses on Boston Neck.[35] An attempt to storm either of these two main positions, especially with an undisciplined amateur army, would have been suicidal.

On the other hand, the Bunker's Hill battle had convinced the British command of the folly of a major attempt against the fortified positions of the Americans, which stretched from Roxbury on the southeast around to Winter Hill and Prospect Hill on the northwest, and which were constantly being strengthened. The British generals knew that even a successful attack would bring no worth-while results. The two forces were therefore in an equilibrium which neither cared to disturb, and a long cessation of major hostile operations on both sides followed Bunker's Hill. There were, however, minor clashes.

In the early morning of July 8 a party of volunteers under Major Benjamin Tupper and Captain John Crane, with two fieldpieces, attacked a British advance post on Boston Neck, drove off the guard, and burnt its house. A similar attack on another post was made three days later and brought forth a harmless cannonade from the works on the Neck. Other little flurries of the same sort helped to enliven the month of July, in one of which the restless riflemen were given a chance against a post on Charlestown Neck. They crept, in true Indian style, on their hands and knees around the post, but, just as they were about to surround it, a relief for the guard arrived. There was an exchange of fire, five of the guard were killed, and two captured. There were no casualties among the Americans, except the loss of one man taken prisoner. The British retaliated by cannonading the American works on Sewall's Point, at the same time attacking and burning a tavern near Roxbury, held as an American outpost, and driving in an American advance guard of sixty men near Boston Neck. The guard was reinforced, and there was a little fight in which several of the British fell, but no Americans. Each of these affairs was noisy, and greatly alarmed the civilians in Boston, who thought a general battle was on.[36]

On the 21st an American party under Major Joseph Vose set off in whaleboats for Nantasket Point. There they drove back a British guard and destroyed the lighthouse on Great Brewster Island, a mile or so offshore. Ten days later, while the British were rebuilding it, Major Benjamin Tupper landed with three hundred Americans and killed or captured all the work party, demolishing their work. Boats from the warships were driven off after a hot little fight. In all, the British lost fifty-three men; the Americans, one killed and two or three wounded.[37]

For nearly a month after that there was little activity on either side. Then came a more important affair. Ploughed Hill was a low eminence on the road connecting Charlestown Neck with Medford, to the west of Winter Hill and Prospect Hill, the two strong points on the American left. It was of value because it was close to and commanded the Mystic River, and because it was within point-blank shot of Bunker's Hill. Washington decided to seize and fortify it.

In the night of August 26 General John Sullivan led out a fatigue party of 1,200 and a guard of 2,400, including 400 of the Pennsylvania riflemen. Work went on all night, and by daylight there was "an Intrenchment in such forwardness as to bid defiance to their Cannon." [38] Bunker's Hill, a ship, and two floating batteries bombarded it all that day. Sullivan had one nine-pounder in place, which he used so skillfully that he sank one floating battery, injured the other, and put a sloop out of commission. The next morning, a column was seen to be forming on Bunker's Hill. It seemed that a battle was imminent. A general alarm was sounded along the American lines, and 5,000 men were marched to the new post. But the enemy did not advance. For several days they continued to fire on the works. Four Americans were killed, two of them by their own folly in attempting to catch cannon balls bouncing along on the ground.[39]

Two other minor incidents occurred before the year ended. A party of 300 British light infantry raided Lechmere Point on November 9 and carried off a dozen head of cattle, despite the efforts of Thompson's Pennsylvania riflemen and parts of two other regiments to stop them. Both sides claimed a victory: the British because they got the beeves; the Americans because the raiding party left hurriedly under fire. Two weeks later a detachment under Putnam, working at night, fortified Cobble Hill, a mound south of the works on Prospect Hill, without physical objection.[40]

These little affairs accomplished nothing toward a final decision in the contest between the two armies. It was desirable for the Americans that a decisive action should be brought on under favorable conditions; but Gage showed no disposition to enter into a general engagement, nor was the condition of the American army such as to promise it a victory. There was still a deficiency in ammunition, and the army was still too uncertain a force to rely upon in an all-out attack on strongly entrenched regulars. Yet it seemed that something must be done; the existing stalemate could not last much longer.

Inactivity was demoralizing the besieging force; desertions, always a major problem among the Americans throughout the war, were much too frequent now to be ignored. The army was further weakened in September by the detachment of 1,000 men, including Morgan's riflemen, to go on the expedition against Quebec under command of Benedict Arnold. There was also to be considered the approaching dissolution of the whole army by expiration of its terms of enlistment; the Connecticut troops were engaged only to December 10, the rest to January 1. There was, also, in the army and among the people generally a growing feeling of dissatisfaction with a merely defensive policy. It was vocal "in Congress, in the newspapers and above all in the taverns." [41] "Murmurs began to be audible that the army was inactive; and that a superiority of numbers might justify an attempt against the town." [42]

Washington was harassed by the conflict among these various considerations. He could not answer the critics of his defensive policy by disclosing the condition of his powder magazines, which was known to few, and thus expose his weakness to his enemies. In this state of mind, he took refuge in the admonition of the Congress to advise with his officers. On September 8 he addressed a circular letter to the general officers, proposing the question "whether in your judgment, we cannot make a successful attack upon the Troops in Boston, by means of Boats, cooperated by an attempt upon their Lines at Roxbury." He pointed out that the coming winter would require better quarters for the men, supplies of clothing, fuel, and blankets, which could not be had. The daily wasting of the stock of powder, the coming dissolution of the army, and, "to sum up the whole . . . the expence of supporting the army will so far exceed any Idea that was form'd in Congress of it, that I do not know what will be the consequence." Yet "to avoid these evils we are not to loose sight of the difficulties, the hazard, and the loss that may accompany the attempt, nor what will be the consequences of a failure." [43]

It can hardly be said that these reasons for an attack were either cogent or compelling, nor that they indicated a conviction in the mind of the commander in chief that the suggested action should be taken. The council of war evidently did not think so; they voted, on September 11, "unanimously that it was not expedient to make the attempt at present, at least."

This result was communicated to the Congress.[44] That august body entertained the idea that it was perfectly competent to direct the operations of the army in the field. On October 3 it voted that "General Washington may, if he thinks proper, for the encouragement of an attack on Boston, promise, in case of success, a month's pay to the army and to the representatives of such of our brave countrymen as may chance to fall, and in case success should not attend the attempt, a month's pay to the representatives of the deceased." [45]—a half-hearted nudge to action, backed by the inducement of a niggling, cheese-paring promise of reward. Another council met and again disapproved the attempt.[46]

Washington had written a very long letter to the Congress on September 21, describing the condition of the army, indicating its needs for the coming winter and especially calling attention to its approching dissolution.[47] The Congress appointed a committee, consisting of Benjamin Franklin, Thomas Lynch, Sr., and Benjamin Harrison, to confer with the commander in chief and with representatives of the New England colonies "touching the most effectual method of continuing, supporting, and regulating a continental army." [48] They were in conference in the camp for five days. Their report resulted in congressional resolutions calling for an army of "30,732 men, officers included," divided into twenty-six regiments (exclusive of riflemen and artillery) of 728 men each, of all ranks. It fixed their pay and rations and the color of their uniforms, brown with distinctive facings for the different colonies.[49]

Although this narrative concerns itself with the fortunes and misfortunes of the American land forces only, and will not attempt to tell the story of the naval operations, some notice must be taken of the exploits of American seamen at this time, and the beginnings of the navy of the United States, because these early maritime exploits were but an extension of the emerging military power of the colonies.

They began in an effort to protect the coasts and ports of the colonies against attacks by British vessels carried on chiefly for the purpose of foraging and seizing supplies. Rhode Island was the first of the colonies to take steps, by chartering, in June, two armed vessels to oppose the British frigate *Rose,* which had been annoying its coast. Massachusetts was next, taking over a schooner and a sloop which the town of Machias in the district of Maine had armed to protect itself against attack. Connecticut followed by arming two similar vessels against a threatened British raid on Gardiner's and Fisher's Islands. So far the Congress had not assumed any responsibility for the protection of the coasts against naval aggression. On July 18 it resolved that each colony, at its own expense, should provide for the protection of its harbors and coastal towns.[50]

All such preparations contemplated merely defensive measures; but offensive operations might greatly profit the American cause. The British army, cooped up in Boston, had to draw all its supplies from sources outside that town: fresh meats and vegetables, for instance, from the West Indies or the more southern American posts; and its other provisions, its munitions of war, clothing, and every such necessary from England. Confident of no interruption of this traffic, because there was no American naval force, the British had armed their coasting vessels lightly, with no more than small arms, while the transocean merchantmen carried no armament at all and sailed without naval convoy. It seemed to be possible, as Governor Nicholas Cooke of Rhode Island pointed out to the Massachusetts Provincial Congress on June 27, for a swift American vessel, even a small one, carrying a suitable armament, to intercept any of these ships and take her, cargo and all. Although the Massachusetts Congress took no action Washington saw the point, and after some hesitation decided to make the experiment with one vessel.[51]

His commission was in the military line only; no authority had been given him in naval matters. However, he found a way. He appointed the shipmaster Nicholson Broughton a captain in the army and ordered him to take command of a detachment of soldiers "and proceed on Board the Schooner *Hannah* . . . lately fitted out & equipp'd with Arms, Ammunition and Provisions at the Continental Expence." His orders were to cruise "against such Vessels as may be found on the High Seas or elsewhere . . . in the Service of the ministerial Army, and to take and seize all such Vessels, laden with Soldiers, Arms, Ammunition, or Provisions for or from Sd. Army." [52]

Broughton soon captured the *Unity*, a vessel laden with provisions and naval stores. Encouraged by this success, Washington sent out other ships, and the Congress took notice. Having information of the sailing from England of two unarmed brigs, "loaded with arms, powder and other stores," it authorized the General on October 5 to apply to Massachusetts for two armed vessels to go after the unprotected brigs and any other such transports. Also, it asked Connecticut and Rhode Island to send out their vessels, all to be "on the continental risque and pay." [53]

By the end of October six schooners were ready for sea, the *Lynch* commanded by Broughton, the *Franklin* by John Selman, the *Lee* by John Manley, the *Warren* by Daniel Adams, the *Washington* by Sion Martindale, and the *Harrison* by William Coit. This was the first continental fleet. It sailed under the pine-tree flag. The *Washington* was captured by the British warship *Fowey* in November, but the others had better luck; many prizes variously laden were brought in. Manley in the *Lee* was conspicuously successful. His capital prize was the ordnance brig *Nancy*, in the entrance to Boston harbor. Her cargo of 2,000 muskets, 100,000 flints, 30,000 round shot, and 30 tons of musket bullets was of immense value to the army. That was something to crow over. "Such universal joy ran through the whole camp as if each grasped victory in his hand." What chiefly excited them was a 13-inch brass mortar. "Old Put mounted on the large mortar . . . with a bottle of rum in his hand, standing parson to christen" it *Congress*. Manley made other captures: an armed ship loaded with provisions, another vessel full of military stores. "His praise was in every mouth." The little navy gave the army sorely needed supplies and equipment.[54]

During that winter "it was a miserable life inside Boston for troops who had sailed from England in the belief that they were to take part in a triumphant and leisurely progress through a series of rich and repentant provinces." [55] It was indeed, and for more reasons than one.

Everything that the British army ate, wore, or used in any way, except small supplies obtained from the West Indies and the other parts of America, had to be brought from England in slow-sailing ships, exposed to the perils of the sea and to the danger of capture by the small but active American fleet. In the cargoes of food there was a heavy loss by mildew and rot on the way. Of eighteen hundred barrels of flour in one cargo, more than eight hundred were spoiled; of six hundred in another ship, only five were edible.[56]

There was generally enough salt meat and dried peas to eat, and occasionally fish. Flour was always scarce; of potatoes, fresh vegetables, and fruits there were practically none. Most of the available milch cows had been slaughtered for beef, and milk was an extreme rarity. There were no longer any cattle or sheep on the islands in the harbor, and but a handful in any of the fields on the near-by coasts. The rejoicing over the dozen head that were taken by three hundred soldiers in the raid on Lechmere Point is an indication of the extreme need of fresh meat. Even when raids on Fisher's and Gardiner's Island in Connecticut yielded two thousand sheep and some oxen, most of them had to be devoted to their "poor sick and wounded people with whom their hospitals were crowded." [57] Scurvy, induced by the lack of vegetable food, appeared among the troops already infected with smallpox, which "raged in the streets and cantonments." [58]

Even fuel was lacking. When cold weather set in, this became serious.

The main force in the works on the Charlestown peninsula suffered severely from the cold, accentuated by the cutting winds and driving snows of an unusually severe winter. On December 12 all except a guard of six hundred were drawn in to winter quarters in Boston. Fire for warmth and for cooking was needed, but there was no store of fuel. Coal and wood were shipped from England, but many vessels with such cargoes were taken by the American cruisers. To meet this want, the unconsumed wooden buildings in Charlestown were torn down. The Old North Church, the steeple of the West Church, wharves, old ships, trees, and a hundred old houses were condemned to be broken up. The Liberty Tree, a great elm under whose shade many patriotic meetings had been held, yielded fourteen cords of wood. Still there was not enough. The soldiers demolished houses and fences indiscriminately. So frequent were such offenses that the provost was ordered to go his rounds, "attended by an executioner," and "to hang up on the spot the first man he should detect" in such depredations.[59]

To the officers, accustomed to various amusements, their stay in Boston was excessively dull and boring. There were no diversions of any sort beyond those they themselves could contrive; they did their best. To make a riding school, the pulpit and pews of the Old South Church were ripped out, and the floor was covered with tanbark. The gallery became a refreshment room, and the church library was fed into the stoves. Faneuil Hall was turned into a playhouse. An original burlesque, "The Blockade of Boston," was presented, in which Mr. Washington, an uncouth figure wearing a huge wig and a long, rusty sword, was attended by a rustic orderly armed with an absurdly long musket. Mr. Washington with an army of rustics was actually and efficiently blockading Boston at the time, so that the jest had a strong tincture of bitter irony.[60]

For the enlisted men there were no such amusements; nor was there any military activity to engage their interest and keep their spirits up except digging for new fortifications, which was not very enlivening. Idleness and boredom bred indiscipline and slovenliness, and the British regulars lost their characteristic smart appearance. Unpowdered hair, dirty linen, unbuttoned gaiters, unpolished arms were surface indications of the deterioration of the rank and file. They were even so degraded "as to borrow from the enemy that habit which was the least worthy of imitation, and chewed tobacco." [61]

And it was all so useless and so hopeless. Gage and his thousands of troops had been in possession of Boston for a year and a half, yet all he had accomplished was to ruin the business of the town and capture one hill with the loss of nearly half of his best troops, while the rest of the province and the rest of America remained in the hands of his enemies. All he could hope to do from Boston was to take more hills, without any more valuable results. There were plenty of hills: Cobble Hill and Ploughed Hill and Winter and Prospect, any one or all of which the Americans would have been glad to sell him at the price of Breed's. The occupation of Boston was entirely barren of advantage at the time, and gave no promise whatever of advantage in the future.

Gage's three colleagues, the major generals, had realized this and had "presumed . . . to offer their advice" to their chief to remove to New York. Clinton elaborated on the advantages of that town and the disadvantages of their present situation. Let victory here be "ever so compleat, it leads to nothing." [62] Burgoyne wrote home about it shortly after Bunker's Hill: "Look, my Lord, upon the country near Boston—it is all fortification. Driven from one hill, you will see the enemy continually retrenched upon the next; and every step we move must be the slow step of a siege." [63] Gage himself had long been of the same opinion. On October 1 he wrote to Dartmouth that "no offensive operations can be carried on to advantage from Boston." Even if he did drive the rebels from their entrenchments, "no advantage would be gained but reputation." It would be "more advisable to make Hudson's River the seat of war," taking New York and leaving only a defensive garrison in Boston.[64]

On August 2 Dartmouth wrote to Gage, communicating the King's order that he return to England "in order to give His Majesty exact information of everything necessary to prepare . . . for the operations of the next year," a polite way of recalling an officer in whom the British government had lost faith. Simultaneously, Howe was given command of the army in the Thirteen Colonies.[65] A month later, Dartmouth wrote to Howe that it seemed "not only advisable, but necessary, to abandon Boston before the winter, to dismantle Castle William and . . . to remove with the Troops either to New York or some other place to the Southward," affording means to "the well-disposed" Bostonians of "getting safely away with their families and effects." [66] Howe assumed the command on October 10.

Howe received Dartmouth's letter on November 9. So, by that time, all the commanding officers in Boston and the authorities at home were in agreement as to the uselessness of holding on to Boston, and orders had been issued and received directing the move to New York. But there were not enough ships. To carry away the army with its equipment and stores and the fugitives with their effects, Howe calculated, 35,172 tons of shipping would be necessary; and he had, of every sort of craft, only 23,570 tons. The army had to stay where it was until spring.[67]

To cheer up the besieged troops, great quantities of supplies were dispatched from England: 5,000 oxen, 14,000 sheep, vast numbers of hogs,
10,000 butts of strong beer, 180,000 bushels of coal, quantities of faggots,
oats, beans, and hay for the horses, dried vegetables, "cured by a new process," and near half a million pounds "in Spanish and Portuguese coinage."
But the transports sailed too late in the fall. Contrary winds held them
back. The preserved vegetables rotted. More than half of the animals died,
"and the tides carried their carcasses in thousands up and down the
Channel." Nearing America, the supply ships met adverse winds. Some
were driven to the West Indies. Others went ashore on the American coasts
and were boarded and plundered. Not a few were picked up by the American cruisers. It was a sorry remnant that reached Boston; but what did
arrive, supplemented by supplies from the more southern colonies, Nova
Scotia, and the West Indies, much improved the condition of the British
army.[68]

In the American camp, in November, all was going well on the surface.
The 17,000 men were well fed, well housed; "the army in great order and
very healthy." [69] True, there was a shortage of blankets and of fuel, but on
the whole the appearance of things was promising. That it was deceitfully
promising was soon to be made evident.

Underlying difficulties that were to threaten the very existence of the
whole army arose out of the impending termination of its period of enlistment. By December 31 the engagement of every man in the camp would
expire; the whole army would fade away. Unless the province of Massachusetts and the whole of New England were to be given over to the enemy,
a new army had to be enlisted and organized before the new year.

A plan for the organization of the new army had been laid down by the
Congress, as described in detail later in this book. In certain respects it
differed from the system in vogue in the New England colonies. For instance,
in some of them the generals were colonels as well, the colonels also captains. This was not permitted by the congressional plan; and the proposed
new order, in this respect, bred dissatisfaction.[70]

The old army was composed of thirty-eight regiments varying in size,
those of Massachusetts, New Hampshire, and Rhode Island numbering 590
enlisted men each, while some of Connecticut numbered 1,000, others 600.
The plan of the Congress called for only twenty-eight regiments of 728
men each, including officers. To rebuild the army according to the new plan,
not only would ten regiments be eliminated, with a corresponding reduction
of their officers in number or in rank, but the companies in them must be

either increased or diminished in size. All sorts of jealousies and objections were generated by this proposal. The custom in New England was to pay the soldiers by the lunar month, four weeks. The pay was now to be by the calendar month, thus cutting out one month's pay in a year. This was naturally displeasing to the men.[71]

Also, Washington had to contend with the ingrained localism of the New Englanders. A national spirit had not yet developed; these men were citizens of their own respective colonies, of their own respective counties and townships, not of the United Colonies as a whole. Washington wrote to Joseph Reed: "Connecticut wants no Massachusetts man in her corps; Massachusetts thinks there is no necessity for a Rhode-Islander to be introduced into hers; and New Hampshire says, it is very hard, that her valuable and experienced officers . . . should be discarded, because her own regiments, under the new establishment, cannot provide for them." John Adams upheld this contention of the colonies: "Can it be supposed that the private men will be easy to be commanded by strangers, to the exclusion of gentlemen whom they know, being their neighbors? It is, moreover, a reflection, and would be a disgrace upon that Province [Massachusetts] to send abroad [to another colony] for commanders of their own men. It would suppose that it had not men fit for officers." It was absurd, of course, but nothing could change this spirit; Washington strove against it, but had to yield to it.[72]

New Englanders had been accustomed to receiving bounties from their own provinces on enlistment. The Congress had been asked to provide for such payments, and had refused to do so. There was discontent on that account. Another thing that displeased the troops was the increase in pay of the company officers; the captains were to receive $26⅔ a month instead of $20 as before, the lieutenants $18 instead of $13⅓, and the ensigns $13⅓ instead of 10, while the privates' pay remained at $6⅔. That emphasized the distinction between officer and man, violated the new England principle of equality, and "chilled the spirits of the commonalty." [73]

Then, too, as the winter drew on, there was increasing hardship. The men's clothing, fit for summer, was now too thin and worn to keep them warm. Blankets were lacking; fuel was worse than scarce. Nathanael Greene, on the last day of the year, wrote: "We have suffered prodigiously for want of wood. Many regiments have been obliged to eat their provision raw, for want of fuel to cook it; and notwithstanding we have burnt up all the fences; and cut down all the trees for a mile round the camp, our sufferings have been inconceivable." [74] Washington told the Massachusetts Assembly that "different Regiments were upon the Point of cutting each others throats for

a few Standing Locusts . . . to dress their food with." Ten thousand cords
of wood were needed, he said.[75]

Underneath all these causes of discontent was plain and simple home-
sickness. The men were not professional soldiers, detached from civilian
life. They were farmers for the most part. They had homes and families from
which they had now been separated for many months. They were tired of
the dreary routine of camp life, the endless round of uninteresting duties
as well as the hardships. They had agreed to serve for a certain period. They
had a very clear notion of the meaning of the terms of a contract. They
would meet those terms, but would not go beyond them. " 'Tis the cast of
the New Englanders to enlist for a certain time and, when the time is expired, to quit the service and return home, let the call for their continuance
be ever so urgent." As John Adams remarked, on another aspect of the
situation: "We cannot suddenly alter the temper, principles, opinions or
prejudices of men." [76]

In spite of all these difficulties and discontents, it was Washington's task
to disband his old army and create a new one, as far as possible out of those
experienced though reluctant men, and at the same time to hold the British
army where it was. "It is not in the pages of History perhaps to furnish a
case like ours," he wrote to the Congress on January 4, 1776. "To maintain
a post within musket shot of the Enemy for six months together, without
powder, and at the same time to disband one Army and recruit another
within that distance of twenty odd British regiments is more than probably
ever was attempted." [77]

He could look for little assistance from his major generals. Schuyler was
at Albany, in command of the troops in northern New York. Artemas Ward
was ineffectual. Putnam was hopeless in matters of administration, and the
eccentric Charles Lee, English by birth, could not handle such a situation.
The job had to be done by Washington alone.

On November 12 the enlistment papers for an army to serve until December 31, 1776, were issued. The first week after that would test the willing-
ness of the men to renew their engagements. It did. Out of 6,000 to 7,000
men who made up the eleven old regiments, 966 enlisted. The general officers issued an address to the troops. The struggle was not hopeless, they
said. Victory was assured. The southern colonies would help. New England
must not fail. And, as to the more immediate, personal considerations, they
urged that never had soldiers' "pay and provision . . . been so abundant
and ample." [78]

Another week passed, and the returns showed that no more than 3,500 had agreed to stay. The Connecticut troops brought the trouble to a head. Their enlistment was to end on December 10, and, in the confusion of the records, many of them believed, as Washington at one time also did, that it ended on December 1. Their officers had fancied they could be persuaded to stay at the end of the month, and had so assured Washington. Now it appeared that most of them would refuse even so short an extension of their term of service; they were going home when their time was up. Such a defection in the face of the enemy might prove fatal. The vacancies caused by their departure must be filled, temporarily at any rate. Washington called on Massachusetts for 5,000 militia and on New Hampshire for 2,000 to fill the gap until January 15, and besought the Connecticut men to stay until these should arrive. But most of them decided to leave the camp on December 1, and many did go. Charles Lee undertook to stop their premature departure.[79]

They were paraded on December 1. The men that were disinclined to stay even for four days after their enlistments expired were formed in a hollow square, and Lee addressed them. "Men," said he, "I do not know what to call you. You are the worst of all creatures." Then he "flung and curst and swore at us and said if we would not stay he would order us to go to Bunker Hill [i.e., to attack the British stronghold] and if we would not go he would order the riflemen to fire at us." They agreed to stay the four days. They got a drink of rum, and were promised another on the morrow.[80]

But they would not remain any longer than that. Washington was disgusted with them. "Such a dirty, mercenary spirit pervades the whole, that I should not be at all surprised at any disaster that may happen," he wrote to Joseph Reed. Indeed, he was almost disheartened. "I have often thought," he wrote on January 14, "how much happier I should have been, if instead of accepting a command under such circumstances, I had taken my musket on my shoulder and entered the ranks, or, if I could have justified the measure to posterity and my own conscience, had retired to the back country, and lived in a wigwam." [81]

General Sullivan wrote to the New Hampshire Committee of Safety denouncing the Connecticut troops, who "to their Eternal Infamy Demand a Bounty to Induce them to Tarry only the three weeks. This is Such an Insult to Every American that we are Determined to Release them at the Expiration of their Term at all hazards." He asked New Hampshire for 2,000 militia to serve only until January 15, 1776.[82]

New Hampshire responded nobly, as did Massachusetts. On December 11 Washington could write: "The Militia are coming fast, I am much pleased with the Alacrity which the good People of this province, as well as those of New Hampshire, have shewn upon this occasion: I expect the whole will be in this day and to Morrow, when what remains of the Connecticut Gentry, who have not inlisted, will have liberty to go to their Firesides." They left amid the jeers and hoots of their more steadfast companions; "they were horribly hissed, groaned at and pelted." [83]

On December 31, when the terms of enlistment of the rest of the army expired, "the same desire of retiring into a chimney-corner seized the troops of New Hampshire, Rhode Island and Massachusetts . . . as had worked upon those of Connecticut." Though many of them offered to stay until the new enlistments had sufficiently made up the strength of the army, they left "by hundreds and by thousands." [84]

General Orders of January 1 began thus: "This day giving commencement to the new army, which, in every point of View, is Continental, The General flatters himself, that a laudable Spirit of emulation will now take place and pervade the whole of it." [85] Then was first "hoisted the union flag in compliment to the United Colonies." There are various accounts of this flag. One describes it as the ensign of Great Britain, but with thirteen stripes, alternately red and white, instead of the superimposed crosses of St. George and St. Andrew, in the canton where are now the stars. [86] Another says that "the combined crosses of England and Scotland, which cover the British flag, on the new ensign shrank to occupy but one corner, while the larger field was crossed by thirteen alternate stripes of red and white." [87]

So the army was now the Continental Army; but a strange army it was, a medley of those old soldiers who had reenlisted, of raw recruits, and of Massachusetts and New Hampshire short-term militia. With such an uncoordinated mass of men as his only force, Washington regarded the situation as "truly Alarming and of this General Howe is well apprized . . . no doubt when he is reinforced he will avail himself of the Information." [88]

There was not only a shortage and a confusion of men; there was also a lack of arms. Few of the new men had brought muskets. Washington had tried to retain the guns of those who departed, valuing and paying for them. But so many of them were in bad condition, and so many were carried off by stealth, that, by the middle of January, he had no more than a hundred muskets with which to arm incoming recruits. [89]

Enlistments continued to lag during January. In the first two weeks no more than a thousand new men were added to the rolls. Washington wrote that the "discontented officers," displaced by the reduction of the number of regiments, "have thrown such difficulties and stumbling blocks in the way of recruiting that I no longer entertain a hope of completing the army by voluntary enlistments, and I see no move or likelihood of one, to do it by other means. . . . Our total number upon paper amounts to about ten thousand five hundred." But many of those on the lists had not come to the camp in spite of orders to do so, and there was little hope of their early coming.[90] They did, however, finally arrive in almost the full number.

January, 1776, was a quiet month. Although Howe's army had been somewhat reinforced and more men were expected, he wrote Dartmouth, "I am under the necessity of repeating to your Lordship, that the apparent strength of this army for the Spring does not flatter me with Hopes of bringing the Rebels to a decisive action." [91] It was, in fact, well settled in his mind that he would evacuate Boston as soon as sufficient transport could be gathered. Meanwhile, he had but to hold on.

The Americans were also inactive. Obviously they were in no condition to attempt the capture of the town. Their energies were sufficiently engaged in re-forming and increasing their army. One little diversion occurred on the 8th, when Major Knowlton with two hundred men crossed at night on the mill-dam to Charlestown, killed one resisting guard, captured the rest, five men, and burned eight out of fourteen still standing houses, which the enemy were daily pulling down for fuel. The flames alarmed the British, and there was much cannonading, with no harmful result to anyone, except to the audience in the Faneuil Hall playhouse, who were then enjoying the burlesque of Washington previously mentioned. They dispersed, "everyone endeavouring to get out as fast as possible, amidst fainting and shrieking among the females." [92]

Continued successes of the American attacks on British shipping cheered the army. Colonel Lord Stirling, soon to rise to the rank of brigadier general, having heard of a transport in distress off Sandy Hook, seized a pilot boat at Amboy, embarked forty men, and, with the assistance of three smaller vessels, took the prize without opposition. She was laden with coal and provisions.[93] Of greater importance, indeed of very great importance to the American cause, was a service rendered by General Knox.

Henry Knox was destined to play so great a part in the war that some special notice of him at this point is desirable. He was born in 1750, the son of a shipmaster who, meeting with financial reverses, was obliged to retire to the West Indies. Henry therefore had to leave school and go to work in a bookshop. Being a studious lad, he took the opportunity the shop provided to continue his education by reading. He became familiar with the classics in English translations and especially with Plutarch's Lives, which turned his taste toward military studies.

At the age of twenty-one he set up his own "London Book-Store" in

Cornhill, Boston, stocked with a miscellaneous shipment from London. It became "a fashionable morning lounge" and prospered. His military studies continued, and he became a member of the Ancient and Honourable Artillery Company, which gave his interest in military science a special character and determined his role in the war.

He had gained some acquaintance with engineering and his services were employed at the outbreak of the war in planning the American fortifications around Boston. After Washington took command he recommended Knox's appointment as colonel of artillery, and he was so commissioned. His subsequent services are a part of the history of the war.

Knox was a young man of large proportions, tall, broad, and thick. In spite of the hardships of the military service during the war, at its end he had attained a weight of 280 pounds. His face was large, full-cheeked, and florid; his gray eyes, rather small but brilliant. His expression was frank and kindly; he was fond of society, gayety, and laughter. His voice was noted for strength, volume, and resonance. His ability as an artillerist has not been questioned, and his integrity as a man, in addition to his technical achievements as a soldier, lent strength to the Revolutionary cause.[94]

Short as the army was of small arms, the lack of artillery was even greater. No offensive operation against Boston could be undertaken without heavy cannon. There were plenty of them at Ticonderoga and Crown Point. Because of bad roads or no roads, and no means of transport, they had lain entirely useless for six months when Washington in mid-November decided to try for them. On the 16th he ordered Knox to go after them: "The want of them is so great that no Trouble or Expence must be spared to obtain them." [95]

Knox reached Ticonderoga on December 5. There he selected for removal eight brass and six iron mortars, thirty iron and thirteen brass guns, and a howitzer. Only one of the cannon was a 24-pounder, the rest ranging from 12 to 18 pounds. Three of the iron mortars were great 13-inchers, weighing a ton each. To these he added a quantity of lead and a barrel of flints. No available wheeled vehicle being strong enough to carry such prodigious weights, they had to be transported on sledges; and Knox constructed forty-three of these. Eighty yoke of oxen to haul them were secured. He drew them to Lake George, loaded them on gondolas, flat-bottomed scows, floated them down to the head of the lake. Snow had fallen but lightly, and a thaw held him up. At last he brought them on sledges to Albany, having crossed the Hudson four times.

At Albany, one of his largest guns broke through the ice at a ferry and sank. He fished it up and went on, down to Claverack and up over the Berkshires. There the snow lay thick, and the grades were heavy; his oxen and horses had hard work. At Framingham the heavier pieces were temporarily deposited; the smaller, he brought on to the camp, where he had the pleasure of presenting to his chief what he justly called "a noble train of artillery." It soon permitted Washington to make a move that hurried the British out of Boston.[96]

CHAPTER 10

Dorchester and Falmouth

As time drew on, and inactivity continued to prevail in both camps, Washington became restive. He felt that throughout the colonies there was a growing demand that his army, now much larger than that of his opponent, should force matters to a conclusion. "To have the Eyes of the whole Continent fixed, with anxious expectation of hearing of some great event, and to be restrain'd in Every Military Operation for want of the necessary means of carrying it on is not very pleasing," he wrote.[1] The lack of necessary means included both small arms and powder. Among his nearly 9,000 men 2,000 were without muskets, and powder was as always dangerously scarce. On February 8 there were no more than nine musket cartridges per man in the camp, and fewer than one hundred fifty barrels of powder in the magazines.[2] Powder from abroad, however, began to come in at New York and Philadelphia, and the promise of a supply encouraged Washington to plan an attack.[3]

On February 16 he called a council of war. The harbor was frozen over, "affording a more expanded and consequently less dangerous Approach to the Town." About half of the 7,200 militia who had been called for had come in. With the 8,797 fit for duty already in camp and 1,405 absent "on command," who might be recalled, the army would number over 13,500. There were believed to be no more than 5,000 British in Boston, which was an error. Therefore, although not much help could be expected from heavy artillery because of shortage of powder, and the principal reliance must be on small arms, yet, he thought, "a stroke, well aimed, at this critical juncture" before the British received expected reinforcements "might put a final end to the war."[4]

But the council, very wisely, demurred. They thought the King's forces in the town were much more numerous than 5,000, as indeed they were: there were about twice that many. Even if not so many, the officers said, they were well furnished with artillery and were backed by their fleet; and an assault should be preceded by a heavy and continued bombardment, which could not be had. There was, however, a practical move to be made, the seizure and fortification of Dorchester Heights "with a view of drawing out the enemy" to an attack.[5] This verdict did not please Washington. "Behold!" he wrote to Reed, "though we had been waiting all the year for this favorite event, the enterprise was thought too dangerous!" But, magnanimously he admitted, "perhaps, the irksomeness of my situation led me to undertake more than could be warranted by prudence . . . it is now at an end, and I am preparing to take post on Dorchester, to try if the enemy will be so kind as to come out to us." [6]

The extreme right of the curving American lines was somewhat beyond Roxbury, near the village of Dorchester. Beyond that a peninsula, about a mile long and half a mile wide, stretched toward the southeast, its extreme end being three-quarters of a mile from the island on which was Castle William. Dorchester Heights were two small hills in the middle of the peninsula and within 250 yards of the water. In front of them, close to the water, was another little hill. From the northern shoulder of the peninsula a sharp spur of land pointed directly at the town, with a space of water not much more than a quarter-mile wide between it and the Neck. At its extremity was another elevation, Nook's Hill.[7] It will be seen that possession of the Heights would threaten the town, the shipping, and Castle William, while heavy guns on Nook's Hill could blast the defenses on Boston Neck with a plunging fire and devastate the greater part of the town.

The fortification of Lechmere Point, close to the water at the left of the American lines, which had been under way for some time, was now complete, and some of the heavy ordnance from Ticonderoga had been mounted there. Several mortars were emplaced at Roxbury, and active preparations for the attempt on the Heights were begun.

The plan was to duplicate the surprise at Breed's Hill by completing the proposed entrenchments in a single night. But the ground was now frozen hard to a depth of eighteen inches, so that quick pick-and-shovel work as at Breed's was not possible. It had taken more than two months to complete the Lechmere's Point works. Therefore, some different method had to be adopted at Dorchester. Colonel Rufus Putnam suggested building the breastwork on the ground, instead of digging it out of the ground. His plan was to use chandeliers, heavy timber frames in which gabions, fascines, and bales of hay could be fitted, thus creating quickly a breastwork which could afterward be strengthened with earth. It was to be faced with an abatis made out of neighboring orchard trees. In front of all, there were to be placed barrels full of earth—a novel form of offensive defense, for they were to add an appearance of strength to the works but, if the British assaulted, could be rolled down the hill to break their ranks and their bones as well.[8]

This novel plan was accepted. The camp was busy in the last days of February and the first of March making chandeliers, gabions, and fascines, and baling hay. It was also busy in other preparations. Washington planned, in case the British should embark for an attack on the Heights, to send 4,000 picked men in two divisions—one under Sullivan, the other under Greene—with General Israel Putnam in general command, across the Back Bay against the undefended west side of Boston, to attack the British works on the Neck in the rear and open a way into the town for other troops. For this purpose, two floating batteries and forty-five bateaux, each to hold eighty men, were secretly collected in the Charles River. All the militia of the neighboring towns were ordered to be in readiness to join the army before the day of the attempt.[9]

To divert the enemy's attention from the real purpose, a heavy bombardment from Lechmere Point, Cobble Hill, and Roxbury was begun on the night of March 2. With a prodigal disregard of the consumption of powder, the artillery "continued in throwing in Shot and Shells 'till daylight." [10] The British replied with a heavy fire. Little harm was done to either army, except by the bursting of three 10-inch and two 13-inch mortars of the Americans, one of which was that big brass 13-incher captured by Manley on the *Nancy* and christened "Congress" with such gusto by Old Put. The cannonade was resumed on the next night and the next after that. As soon as the firing began on the third night, March 4, General Thomas, with a fatigue party of 1,200 men, led by a covering party of 800 under arms and followed by 360 oxcarts loaded with entrenching materials, marched to Dorchester Heights. To conceal from the enemy the necessary passage back and forth during the night, a screen of hay bales was placed along Dorchester Neck.[11]

The covering party was divided, one half going to Nook's Hill, the other to the extreme point toward Castle William. On the two Dorchester hills the chandeliers were placed on the lines of two small redoubts already marked out, and the fascines and bales of hay put in place. Picks and shovels were soon at work on the frozen ground, first to fill the gabions and the barrels and then to strengthen the breastwork, while axmen felled the

orchard trees and made the abatis. The carts went back again and again
for more materials. At three o'clock in the morning the fatigue party was
relieved by a fresh force. So the work went on all through the mild night,
lighted by a bright moon, but concealed from the enemy by a haze that
hung over the lowland in front. The noise of the big guns drowned the
sound of pick and shovel. When the Americans got below the frost line and
the digging became easier, the parapets were thickened with earth piled
against them. More men, including five companies of riflemen, came over
to man the works. By daylight, the two little forts were ready. "Perhaps,"
said General Heath, "never was so much work done in so short a space of
time." [12]

In the British camp the activity did not go unnoticed. At ten o'clock the
night before, Lieutenant Colonel Campbell had somehow discovered and
reported to Brigadier General Francis Smith "that the Rebels were at work
on Dorchester heights." But this was the same General Smith that had led
the march against Lexington and Concord, that "very fat and heavy man"
who was so slow in coming up to the fight at the Bridge. This time he did
nothing at all. The first positive news the British army had of the works was
the sight of them at daybreak. It was a complete and astounding surprise.
Howe viewed them through his glass, and is said to have remarked, "The
rebels have done more in one night, than my whole army could do in
months." [13] In a dispatch to Dartmouth he wrote that it "must have been
the employment of at least twelve thousand men." [14] Lieutenant General
Archibald Robertson of the Royal Engineers wrote in his diary, "A most
astonishing night's work [it] must have Employ'd from 15 to 20,000 men." [15]
Another officer said the works were "raised with an expedition equal to that
of the Genii belonging to Aladdin's Wonderful Lamp." [16]

Surprise speedily gave place to serious consideration of a new problem.
Rear Admiral Molyneux Shuldham, commanding the fleet since the recall
of Graves in December, told Howe that he could not keep his ships in the
harbor under the guns on the Heights, and the army in Boston was in equal
danger. Either the British must evacuate the town, or they must drive the
Americans from their new stronghold. Although Howe fully intended to
evacuate very soon, he could not stomach an expulsion by the colonists. He
tried first a bombardment, but the guns could not be elevated enough to
throw their shot to the hilltops. Then he decided to attack, and immediately
made his preparations. [17]

Brigadier General Jones, with 2,200 men, was to make the attempt.
Five regiments were ordered to embark at the Long Wharf and proceed to
Castle William. From Castle William they were to land on the extreme

point of Dorchester peninsula and attack the nearer redoubt, being sheltered by it from the guns in the other. Two more regiments, with the light infantry and grenadiers, were to embark in flatboats, land on the north side of the peninsula, and join in the assault on that side. In case of success at Dorchester, these troops and certain reinforcements were to attack the lines at Roxbury. The men were to carry their blankets, a day's supply of food, and canteens filled with rum and water. No musket was to be loaded. The bayonet was to be the only weapon.[18] It is said, perhaps untruly, that the men, drawn up before embarking, looked "in general, pale and dejected" and told each other, "It will be another Bunker's-hill affair or worse." [19] So thought the inhabitants of Boston. Again they crowded the hilltops and other high places to watch the show, while the American troops continued all day long to labor at strengthening their works, and Putnam's division, ready for the attack on the town, was paraded on Cambridge common.[20]

The British attack on the Heights was to be delivered that night; but a storm arose, "A Hurrycane or terrible sudden storm," as Timothy Newell wrote in his diary.[21] Heath described it: "About midnight the wind blew almost a hurricane from the south; many windows were forced in, sheds and fences blown down and some vessels drove on shore." [22] The surf was so high on Dorchester beach that no flatboat could land. There was no attack that night, nor on the next day, for the wind continued to blow, and there was a torrential downpour of rain.[23]

That storm has been credited with preventing the planned attack. Howe, in his general orders the next morning, March 5, wrote, "The General desires the Troops may know that the intended Expedition last night was unavoidably put off by the badness of the Weather." But that was not exactly the truth. In fact, the decision to withhold the attack and to evacuate the town had been made five hours before the storm arose. There was a council of war in which some of the officers "advised the going off altogether . . . the General said it was his own Sentiments from the first, but thought the honour of the Troops Concerned." It was "agreed immediately to Embark everything." Howe's statement in the general orders was merely a face-saving device.[24]

While preparations for the evacuation of the town were afoot, the inhabitants who were to remain there became fearful that it might be destroyed, either by bombardment from the American works or by the incendiary torch of the departing army. A delegation of citizens obtained from Howe a promise that he would not burn the town unless the Americans molested his troops during their embarkation. A paper stating this promise, signed by four of the selectmen of the town, was brought to the

American lines. As it was "an unauthenticated paper . . . not obligatory upon General Howe," Washington refused to take any official notice of it. He made no agreement with Howe, but the town was nevertheless tacitly spared by both sides.[25]

While the British in Boston were hurrying their preparations to leave, the Americans went on with their Dorchester works. A party was sent in the night of the 9th to fortify Nook's Hill, the place most dangerous to Boston. Discovering it, the British bombarded the hill, and the American batteries in all the posts from Cobble Hill around to Roxbury responded. The continued thunder of the cannonade terrified all the good folk within hearing distance but, as usual, although more than eight hundred shot were fired, this long-range cannonading had little effect on either side; only five Americans were killed. But Nook's Hill was abandoned by them.[26]

In August, 1775, Dartmouth had written to Gage that if he were driven out of Boston "care must be taken that the officers and friends of the government be not left exposed to the rage and insult of the rebels, who set no bounds to their barbarity." [27] The preparations for the evacuation therefore included their transshipment to whatever destination was chosen for the army. They were to be rescued from "rage and insult," but they were forced to pay a fearful price for that rescue.

The Tories in Boston, both those whose proper residence was in that town and those who had come seeking the protection of the British troops, included many of the personally or politically outstanding people of the province, the wealthiest people, the greater landholders, the more substantial men of business, the best educated, in short the aristocrats. These had looked down on the Adamses, Warren, Otis, and the other agitators for their resistance to the crown, accusing them of various base or petty personal motives. To John Hancock, the only one of the rebel leaders who had a claim to rank in wealth and fashion with themselves, they ascribed wounded vanity as the cause of his recalcitrancy. As a class these Tory leaders were hearty free livers, free spenders, fine dressers, arrogant in their regard for social distinction, scornful of the mob. "Caste-feeling, intense, aggressive and almost universal, beyond any doubt, prevailed in the Tory society of America." [28]

The Tories very generally ridiculed the provincial military leaders raised suddenly from obscurity in the lower walks of life—Knox from his bookshop, Greene from his blacksmithing, Putnam from his tavern and his plow, Pomeroy from his gunsmith shop—to become officers pretending to rank with the gentlemen of His Majesty's army. And now, suddenly, these superior people were to be driven from their offices, their countinghouses, their houses and lands, and their churches (eighteen of them were clergymen). They must abandon their homes, their own country. They who were as firmly wedded to their native land as any other Americans, who loved it as dearly as any of those upstart rebels, they whose patriotism was indeed as strong and as pure, according to their lights, as that of any of the so-called patriots, were now to be forced to flee to the foul, ill-smelling transports and to be carried God knew where, to an exile wherever it would be, with no certainty of ever returning. It is not strange that, in Washington's words, "No Electric Shock, no sudden Clap of thunder, in a word the last trump could not have struck them with greater consternation" [29] than did Howe's order to abandon the town.

The last days of the British army in Boston were days of confusion and distress, of haste and waste, of crooked dealing and actual plundering. The first move was to bring the transports to the wharves and load them with all the ordnance, arms, and stores that could be stowed in them. The lines were stripped of their brass cannon and mortars; iron pieces replaced them. But three great brass mortars broke their lifting tackle and sank in the water; a fourth, the British tried unsuccessfully to burst and had to leave behind. There was no room for the dragoon and artillery horses. There was "a vast deal of Confusion in every Department and no settled plan of operations." [30] Great quantities of stores had to be abandoned, much of them being as nearly destroyed as was possible in the hurry of departure.[31] The soldiers misbehaved, "acting Licentiously and breaking up some stores." It was suggested by one of the officers that "it would be prudent to seize All Cloth, linnen, Shoes, Stockings, etc. in the Different stores in Town . . . which the Rebel Army were very much in need of." [32] Howe directed one Crean Brush, a New York Irish adventurer, to do this. He broke open stores and storehouses and looted their contents indiscriminately to the value of many thousands of pounds, giving worthless receipts. Dwelling houses were not exempt from this thievery. His loot made a full cargo for the brigantine *Elizabeth*. Brush's labors were in vain, however, for he and his vessel, with all the stolen goods, were soon after captured by the Americans.[33]

The poor Tories had pretty much to shift for themselves. They had received vessels, but had been told they must find the sailors to man them.[34] By a liberal use of money they managed to get such portable goods as they most valued aboard and to hire enough seamen to navigate their craft; but they embarked in sad condition. One of them, Benjamin Hallowell, former Commissioner of Customs, had to take into his cabin thirty-six others, "men, women and children; parents, masters and mistresses, obliged to pig together on the floor, there being no berths." [35]

Meanwhile, Washington was becoming impatient. He had no desire to bombard the town, but he wished to hurry the evacuation; and to that end he made more threatening approaches. He threw up a redoubt on the point of the Dorchester peninsula nearest to Castle William. As a final move, "a notice to quit," he again seized Nook's Hill and in spite of a bombardment, ineffectual because only "a few old Iron Guns were left" [36] to be brought to bear on it, he fortified it. With his guns in that position, he could fire on the ships at the wharves at close range and cannonade the rear of the works on Boston Neck.

But it was now the last day of the lingering evacuation, the 17th of March. At nine o'clock in the morning all were on board, except two engineer officers and a few men, left "to fire some houses if there had appeared any Enemy in our rear, but none appeared and we went all off in the greatest order." [37] Yet there were a few minor hostilities. Castle William had not been abandoned; the 64th Regiment posted there was engaged in mining it for its destruction. Some Americans, working on fortifications on Dorchester Point, were fired upon from the Castle, and there were a few shots in reply. At nine in the evening, the fuses of the mines were lighted, and the remaining British boarded their transports, the last ever to set hostile foot on the soil of present-day Massachusetts.[38]

But Charlestown seemed yet to be held. Sentinels could be seen at their posts on Bunker Hill. Two men went over to investigate, and "found the Centinels to be Images dressed in the Soldiers Habit with Laced Hats and for a Gorget an Horse Shoe with Paper Ruffles, their Pieces Shouldered [with] fixed Bayonets, with this Inscription wrote on their Breast (viz.) Welcome Brother Jonathan." [39]

The American troops at Cambridge and Roxbury had been paraded. When the last of the enemy had left, General Ward with five hundred men crossed the Neck and entered the town. Others occupied Charlestown peninsula. On the 20th the main force was in full possession of Boston.

Still there was some apprehension as to the intentions of the enemy. The fleet had anchored in Nantasket Roads about five miles below the town—for what purpose, no one in Boston knew. Washington wrote to Trumbull on the 21st, "I cannot but suspect they are waiting for some opportunity to give us a Stroke, at a moment when they conceive us to be off guard." Three days later, he said, "It surpasses my comprehension and awakens all my suspicions." He complained that "the enemy have the best knack at puzzling people I ever met with in my life." [40] His apprehensions were groundless.

The British were only preparing for their voyage in the leisurely eighteenth century fashion, adjusting their cargoes, which had been so hurriedly shipped, taking in water, and so on. On the 27th they put out to sea, bound not for New York, as Washington thought, but for Halifax.[41]

Howe carried off 11,000 soldiers and sailors and nearly a thousand refugees, among whom were a hundred civil officials. Many of these settled in Nova Scotia, suffering the privations and hardships of pioneers. Others went to England. Few ever returned to their old homes.[42]

Although during the fall and winter of 1775–1776 the British army had lain inactive in Boston, there had been one hostile enterprise on the part of its fleet of which notice should be taken.

Vice Admiral Samuel Graves had been appointed in March, 1774, to command the British naval forces in America; he arrived in Boston harbor on July 1 to undertake the thankless job of enforcing the blockade. He had in his charge from twenty-five to thirty war vessels, ranging from the great ships of fifty to seventy guns down to sloops and cutters. The *Asia*, sixty-four guns, was stationed at New York, the *Rose,* twenty guns, and the *Scarborough*, twenty guns, were part of the time at Newport and Portsmouth respectively. Another ship was held at Halifax. Some of the smaller vessels were engaged in cruising off the coast, or from time to time stationed here and there. The rest lay in Boston harbor.[43]

Although the whole British navy at that time was in a scandalously run-down condition, Graves's fleet was of overwhelming strength as compared with the puny vessels of the Americans. But Graves himself was utterly inefficient. The Americans raided the islands in the harbor almost at will, and he could not prevent them. They gathered a fleet of three hundred whaleboats, hid them by day, and by night went about their nefarious business of burning lighthouses, foraging or whatever they would, in spite of the Admiral. He actually stood in fear that they might, by concerted action, take from him one of his capital ships.[44] Burgoyne wrote to Lord George Germain in August, 1775: "It may be asked in England, 'What is the Admiral doing?' . . . I can only say what he is *not* doing." And he went on to catalogue Graves's inactivities; he was not supplying the camp with fresh meat, not protecting the flocks and herds on the islands, not doing anything that he should do.[45]

Graves was probably nettled by the criticism in the camp and angered by his inability to find and capture, on the high seas, the American cruisers that were intercepting the supply ships. He decided to go after them in the ports and harbors where they hived. On October 6 the *Canceaux* with eight guns and forty-five men, and the schooner *Halifax* with six guns and thirty men, to which were added one hundred soldiers, sailed under command of Captain Henry Mowat. His orders were to "burn, destroy and lay waste" the seaport towns all along the northeast coast as far as Machias, and to destroy all their shipping.[46]

Mowat viewed Gloucester, and decided that the houses were so widely scattered that it would be difficult to burn the town. On the 16th he anchored at Falmouth, now Portland. He warned the people to remove "the human species within two hours, when the punishment would begin"; but, at the supplication of a committee of the townsfolk, he agreed to give them until the next day. Indeed, if they would deliver to him four cannon supposed to be there, all other arms and ammunition, and certain hostages, he would ask further instructions from headquarters. The next morning they refused to deal with him. Mowat then opened fire on the town with cannon balls and incendiary carcasses, and a landing party set additional fires among the buildings. By evening the whole town was ablaze. Two hundred houses, the church, the courthouse, the town house, the public library, the wharves and warehouses, and eleven vessels were "all laid into ashes." Four other vessels were taken. There were no casualties among the British, except two men wounded by the feeble resistance offered them. Graves was satisfied by this one outrage, and sent out no more such expeditions.[47]

CHAPTER 11

The Question of Canada

Canada had long been a word of ill omen to the American colonists, particularly to those of Massachusetts, New Hampshire, and northern New York. Time and again, the Canadian French and their Indian allies had ravaged and devastated the settlements of those colonies. Deerfield and Northampton, Saratoga and Schenectady, Keene, Exeter, Brunswick, and many another village, and countless isolated settlers' homes had succumbed to the bullet, the tomahawk, the scalping knife, and the incendiary torch. In one year alone, 1746, thirty-five bands of these marauders had ravaged the borders of the northern American provinces. When Montreal capitulated in 1760, and Canada fell into the hands of the English by the treaty of 1763, the dread of their northern neighbors departed from the minds of the colonists, only to be revived in a different form fourteen years later, when Parliament passed the Quebec Act.

To an understanding of that act in its effects upon Canada and upon the American colonies, a brief review of the character and conditions of the Canadian people may be helpful.

The inhabitants of Canada fell into four well defined classes. The habitants, who formed the first class, were the basic population. They were descendants of the first settlers, and were French in origin, Roman Catholic in religion, tenant-farmers in occupation, numbering perhaps 60,000 or more. These tractable, hard-working agriculturists held their farms under a sort of feudal tenure from the great landholders, who constituted another class, the aristocrats, seigneurs, and had been well-to-do, largely through the emoluments of office, civil or military, until the English conquest deprived them of official employment and ended the various feudal obligations due from the habitants except the payment of rents, which were of small value. Most of them, including practically all the civil and military officers, had gone back to France after the conquest; no more than 130 heads of families remained. Reduced in wealth even to comparative poverty, their political and social influence lost, these few seigneurs were of little importance in the affairs of the province.

Few in numbers, not more than 2,000, but having, as they thought, great potential political importance, were the people of British origin, many of them immigrants from the American colonies. They were commonly called "Old Subjects" to distinguish them from the lately acquired French subjects. The majority of them were in Montreal, engaged in the fur trade. They were a troublesome lot. They quarreled with the military, were at odds with the seigneurs, and contemned the habitants. As the only true-born British subjects, they claimed privileges above the other classes, even to the extent of demanding self-government by elective bodies of which only they would be electors and members. They would even deny the right of the Catholic French to sit on grand juries, an exclusion based on the then prevailing English law, which excluded Catholics from the elective franchise and from all political offices. James Murray, the first British governor of the province, described them as "chiefly adventurers of mean education," all having "their Fortunes to make and little Sollicitous ab^t the means." [1] Guy Carleton, his successor, had much the same opinion of them.

The fourth class was composed of the Catholic priests. Formerly of great importance in the government, wielding an almost unlimited and almost unrestrained power, even over the French governors and their councils, the English conquest had brought them so low that they asked only for tolerance in their priestly offices. They had been used to requiring the habitants to pay legal dues to the Church. But there was no longer any basis of legality for such requirement, and the habitants paid or did not pay, as they pleased. The clergy, therefore, existed on sufferance only.

Thus Canada was split into incompatible parties: the seigneurs despised both the habitants and the Old Subjects; the habitants disliked the British, no longer respected the seigneurs, and refused to be subservient to the clergy; the Old Subjects held the seigneurs in contempt, scorned the habitants, and were at odds with the government; the poor priests were in good repute with none of the others. Besides all that, the historic ill feeling between Catholics and Protestants was in full force and vigor.

In 1763 a royal proclamation had made Canada a crown colony without an elective assembly, promising one "as soon as the state and circumstances of the said Colonies will admit thereof." Political power had been placed in the hands of a governor and a royally appointed council. It was the promise of an assembly in the future that gave the Old Subjects their hope of political domination, for surely, as in England, the Catholics would be excluded from voting and from sitting in the assembly.

But they were disappointed. Guy Carleton, who succeeded Murray in 1766, was an English aristocrat, a military man with all the qualities of the professional soldier of high rank. He was reserved, stern, remote from civilians, fearless, and inflexible; but he was also high-minded, incorruptible, and, at bottom, magnanimous. He looked upon the humble habitants as the real Canadian people, the solid foundation of the province, and he was emancipated from the English dread of Catholic "Popery." Partly as a result of his efforts the Parliament passed the Quebec Act in 1774.

That act put an end for the time being to any hope of an elective assembly, definitely annulling the vague promise of the proclamation of 1763. It provided for a governor and a council as lawmakers appointed by the crown. It recognized the Catholic Church, with a proper bishop, and restored its right to collect tithes and other dues. It abolished the religious "test oaths," which had disqualified all non-Protestants from holding civil office. It retained the English criminal law, but restored the French law in civil matters. It extended the boundaries of the province to include Labrador on the east and, on the west, all the land north of the Ohio River between the Allegheny Mountains and the Mississippi.

In many of its provisions the Quebec Act was an excellent law and was in advance of the philosophy of its time; but it was not well received by the Old Subjects. They wanted that promised assembly. They also wanted exclusive right to the offices of honor and emolument, and they objected strongly to the "establishment" of the Catholic Church. The Catholic priests objected to the provision requiring them to be licensed by the King only, and the Catholic laity were incensed by the compulsion to pay tithes. The French did not like the retention of English criminal law. The English disliked the restoration of the French civil law. So the cleavages in Canada's population were deepened.[2]

To the Americans the Quebec Act was anathema for several reasons, the first and most objectionable being the extension of the boundaries of Canada. Some of the colonies, notably Connecticut, Massachusetts, and Virginia, had pretensions to some parts of the western lands now given to their northern neighbor. They had seen them taken from the French by the Treaty of Paris in 1763 and, as they thought, reserved for their own settlement. Citizens of the Old Thirteen Colonies had been peering over the crest of the Alleghenies at the new lands beyond. They had even passed over the mountains and had made new settlements in the Ohio valley. They looked forward to unimpeded occupation quite to the Mississippi. This sudden reversal of conditions, by which the conquered territory was restored to Quebec, and perhaps to their old enemies, the French Canadians, was a shock to all the American colonists. Moreover, they saw themselves surrounded on the north and west by an undemocratic government whose legislature was appointed by the crown, not elected by the people, a despotic government whose power might be exerted against them at the will of the King. Also, the American colonists were Protestants in an overwhelming majority and, especially in New England, fiercely jealous of the prevalence of their religion. They had inherited fear and hatred of Catholicism from old England. Now they saw dreaded Popery practically established in all that great territory enclosing them.

There was, too, for those thinking in terms of a war of rebellion, the fact that the St. Lawrence River was a broad waterway by which troops could be carried to Montreal, where they would have access to that other waterway, Lake Champlain, Lake George, and the Hudson, which would, if held by the British, separate the New England colonies from those to the southward.

All these considerations made it desirable that Canada should be joined with the American colonies in the common cause against Britain. The Second Continental Congress in May had, rather ineptly, tried to induce the Canadians to unite "with us in the defence of our common liberty." [3]

In a letter dated May 29, 1775, and addressed "To the oppressed Inhabitants of Canada," the Congress declared that "the fate of the catholic and protestant colonies [was] strongly linked together." It was urged that "the enjoyment of your very religion . . . depends on a legislature in which you have no share and over which you have no control." [4] "The decent manner in which the religious matters were touched" [5] was received with pleasure by the Canadians. But on October 21, 1774, the First Continental Congress had addressed an appeal to the people of Great Britain, setting forth the grievances of the colonies, among which were the Quebec Act establishing in Canada "a religion fraught with sanguinary and impious tenets . . . a religion that has deluged your island in blood and dispersed impiety, bigotry, persecution, murder and rebellion through every part of the world." [6]

Unfortunately the Canadians read that appeal after they had digested the later one addressed to them, and they were not pleased with it. "They could not contain their resentment, nor express it but in broken curses." "Oh! the perfidious, double-faced Congress!" they cried. "Let us bless and obey our benevolent Prince, whose humanity is consistent, and extends to all Religions; let us abhor all who would seduce us from our loyalty, by acts that would dishonour a Jesuit; and whose Addresses, like their Resolves, are destructive of their own objects." [7]

Well then, if Canada would not willingly join, what about compulsion? What about conquest? The Second Continental Congress was at first unwilling to go so far as that. On the 1st day of June, 1775, it resolved "that no expedition or incursion ought to be undertaken or made, by any colony, or body of colonists, against or into Canada." [8]

But that vigorous and ambitious warrior Benedict Arnold was of a different opinion. On June 13 he reported to the Congress that the Indians would not assist the King's troops against the Americans; that Carleton had been unable to raise more than twenty Canadians to help him; that there were only 550 British regulars in all Canada, scattered among five posts. He proposed an attack on Montreal with 1,700 men, through St. John's and Chambly, Quebec being ripe to fall when those places had been taken. He added that "if no person appears who will undertake to carry the plan into execution . . . I will undertake it and . . . answer for the success of it." [9]

And that other vigorous and restless soul Ethan Allen was of the same opinion. When he heard of the resolution of the Congress, adopted on May 18, recommending the removal of the cannon and military stores taken at Ticonderoga to the south end of Lake George and the abandonment of the captured fort,[10] he wrote to the Congress on May 29 a letter of protest, in which he also urged an expedition against Canada: "The more vigorous the Colonies push the war against the King's Troops in Canada, the more friends we shall find in that country. . . . Should the Colonies forthwith send an army of two or three thousand men, and attack Montreal, we . . . would easily make a conquest of that place." [11] On June 2 he even more eloquently adjured the New York Provincial Congress to favor such an attack. "I wish to God," he fervently wrote, "America would, at this critical juncture, exert herself. . . . She might rise on eagles' wings and mount up to glory, freedom and immortal honour, if she did but know and exert her strength. Fame is now hovering over her head. A vast continent must now sink to slavery, poverty, horrour and bondage, or rise to unconquerable freedom, immense wealth, inexpressible felicity and immortal fame." [12]

Allen wanted his Green Mountain Boys enrolled in the Continental service. To that end, he and his lieutenant colonel, Seth Warner, presented themselves on June 23 at the door of the Congress in Philadelphia, and were admitted to the floor of the house. What he said to the Congress, whether he repeated his advice as to Canada, does not appear in the records. He did attain his chief object; his Boys were to be enlisted in a regiment of their own, under officers of their own choice.[13] It may well be that what he told the Congress then influenced it, within the next four days, to reverse its policy as to Canada, and to direct General Schuyler to proceed to Ticonderoga and Crown Point, and "if [he] finds it practicable and that it will not be disagreeable to the Canadians, he do immediately take possession of St. Johns, Montreal and any other parts of the country." [14] At all events, Ethan Allen may be credited with some of the impetus behind that resolution.

Major General Philip Schuyler was a representative of the best Dutch blood in New York, and one of its wealthiest landed proprietors. He was at this time in his forty-third year, slender yet well muscled, erect and commanding in figure, quick and energetic in movement. His face was noticeably florid and unusually expressive of his emotions, its features rather large, but not distinguished. His hair was dark brown, as were his keen, piercing eyes. His voice was clear, inclining to sharpness. His dress was always in accord with the prevailing mode. The manner of life in his mansion in Albany and his country seat at Saratoga was generous and hospitable, elegant indeed, with numerous servants, an ample stable, and a full cellar to care for his guests.

He was not lacking in intelligence, nor in kindliness, nor in courtesy to his equals, though to those of pronounced inferiority of station or of doubtful integrity he was apt to show his sense of his own superiority. In depth and breadth of mind, in stability of intention, in firm decisiveness to plan and to execute, in the ability to meet a confused situation, discern its essentials, and expend his energies upon them only, Schuyler was somewhat deficient. Thus he lacked the executive power needed to make him an effective and successful general officer; nor had his slight martial experience as a captain in the French and Indian War been sufficient to induce a habit of command. Moreover, he had not the physical vigor nor the ruggedness needed to cope with the hardships and deprivations of a wilderness campaign. This want showed itself in the outbursts of temper and exasperation which often succeeded an exhibition of uncomplaining patience on his part. He was a high-minded, public-spirited gentleman and above all a patriot, wholly devoted—rather singularly among the men of his own class in New York—to the American cause. He was wrongly placed as a chief military officer; his proper place was at the council table.[15]

Brigadier General Richard Montgomery was Schuyler's second in command. Born in northern Ireland, the son of a baronet and member of

Parliament, he was well educated, and from his seventeenth year had been a soldier in the British army. He had fought under Amherst at Ticonderoga and Crown Point in 1759. At the age of twenty-six he was a captain. For ten years, he held that rank. In 1772 he resigned from the army and returned to America. In the next year he married one of the Livingstons, a family of wealth and high social position. Two years later he was commissioned a brigadier general in the Continental army. Although of studious habit, preferring the library and domestic life to the camp and the field, he was ardent for the cause of the colonies and responded to the call to arms.

He was tall, slender, of graceful address, yet strong, active, and capable of long endurance of fatigue and hardship. Forceful in command, aggressive in action, patient in adversity, cool in judgment, never negligent of duty, never avoiding danger, he was the complete soldier.[16]

With those two as aide-de-camp was Captain John Macpherson, Jr., the twenty-one-year-old son of a well-to-do Philadelphian. His portrait shows a notably handsome and refined face, and his character was in keeping with it. Bancroft has described him as a "pure-minded, youthful enthusiast for liberty . . . full of promise for war, lovely in temper, dear to the army, honored by the affection and confidence of his chief." [17]

Schuyler's instructions, when he was detached by Washington at New York City on June 25, gave him command of the New York Department. He was to occupy the several posts in the Champlain region, put them "in a fit posture to answer the End designed," and, besides keeping an eye on Governor Tryon, "watch the Movements of the Indian Agent," Colonel Guy Johnson "and prevent, as far as you can, the Effect of his Influence to our Prejudice with the Indians." "The Temper and Disposition" of the Canadians were to be investigated "that a proper line may be mark'd out to conciliate their good Opinion, or facilitate any future Operation." [18]

It will be noted that this was a cautious approach to the possible invasion of Canada, there being no definite orders or directions on the point. The Congress, however, as has been related, gave orders on June 27 for an aggressive movement if Schuyler should find it practicable and not disagreeable to the Canadians.

The Colonel Guy Johnson whom Schuyler was to watch was son-in-law and successor in office to Sir William Johnson, who had been appointed Superintendent of Indian Affairs in the northern department in 1755 and, with a rare talent for dealing with red men reinforced by his "marriage" with the sister of the Mohawk chief, had exercised a strong and generally prevailing influence over the Iroquois League, of Mohawks, Oneidas,

Onondagas, Cayugas, Senecas, and Tuscaroras, or Six Nations.[19] Besides these, there were in Canada the Seven Nations, allies of the League, not so numerous nor in general so warlike, yet including the Abenakis on the St. Francis River—formerly most savage of all and most dreaded by the colonists—and the Caughnawagas, whose chiefs were all "of English extraction Captivated in their infancy." Their superior intelligence made the Caughnawagas important, although the tribe could not muster two hundred braves. Beyond these to the north and west were unnumbered other, unrelated tribes, a great reservoir of potential savagery.[20] Guy Johnson as Superintendent of Indian Affairs since 1774 could cause infinite trouble to the Americans.

There was another influence which prevailed in Canada. Louis St. Luc de La Corne, a Frenchman, had been Superintendent of the Canadian Indians under the French régime, and his son-in-law, Major Campbell, now held a similar office. La Corne was hated and dreaded by the colonists as a "fiend incarnate" and was believed to have been responsible for the massacre of the prisoners taken at the capture of Fort William Henry in 1757.[21] He was now on the side of the British. It was evident to the colonists that the Indian question was one of the most important with which they had to deal in the contemplated invasion of Canada.

Johnson, La Corne and Campbell, Joseph Brant, otherwise called Thayendanegea, a Mohawk chief, and Colonel John Butler, Johnson's assistant, worked assiduously to enlist the Indians under the British standard in 1775. La Corne was especially busy, giving them powder and brandy. At a price of two johannes (about $16) a piece, he got some of the young Caughnawagas to engage; but the older men took the money from them and returned it to him.[22] To help Carleton break down the sales resistance of the Indians, the home government sent a cargo of inducements, "hundreds of proved fowling-pieces, with blue barrels, walnut stocks, trimmings of wrought brass and silver sights . . . neat, bright Indian hatchets," brass kettles, gold laced hats, ruffled shirts, pipes, greatcoats, barrels and barrels of gunpowder and of bullets, pots of paint for facial adornment, blue, rose, yellow, vermilion, all to the value of £2,500.[23] Johnson had the effrontery to deny that he was inciting the red men to fight the Americans. The charge, he said, was manifestly absurd. It was true that he had fortified his house in the Mohawk valley, and that it was guarded by Mohawks; but that was only because he had heard that the New Englanders or the people from Albany were coming in "a considerable number to seize and imprison me." [24] But there were witnesses against him. Samuel Kirkland, missionary among the Iroquois, testified to the contrary. Thirty Indian chiefs, on a mission to the Congress, corroborated Kirkland's testimony. By the middle of July, it was said that Johnson was ready, with 800 or more Indians, to invade Tryon County in the province of New York.[25]

Reports as to the ultimate intentions of the Indians varied. In March, John Brown said he had word from reliable sources that the Caughnawagas, although "repeatedly applied to and requested to join the King's troops," had "peremptorily refused and still intend to refuse." [26] In June, Ethan Allen thought the Indians as a whole were attached "to our interest." He was cynical enough to believe that they acted "upon political principles and consequently are inclined to fall in with the strongest side. At present ours has the appearance of it." [27] This was immediately after Ticonderoga had been taken. But a man who had been in Montreal in the same month reported that the Caughnawagas had actually "taken up the hatchet." [28] In July another, similarly experienced, said they had refused to join Carleton though threatened with dispossession of their lands, and that the Indians were "pretty generally determined to take no part in the quarrel." [29] This was confirmed, also in July, by Captain Remember Baker, a Green Mountain Boy who had been scouting on his own hook. He said the "Seven Nations had agreed not to fight the Yankees." [30] But in August "two persons who have lately come from St. Johns" stated that Johnson had 500 Indians at Montreal "just going to join the English." [31] It was all very confusing and very disconcerting to the Americans, and it was clearly time that something was done about it.

The Continental Congress, in July, had formulated "A Speech to the Six Confederate Nations" telling them at great length about the King's oppression of the colonies and the contest to relieve it. It was couched in the language of parables. "This is a family quarrel between us and Old England," the speech said. "You Indians are not concerned in it. We don't wish you to take up the hatchet against the King's Troops. We desire you to remain at home and not join on either side, but keep the hatchet buried deep." [32]

A "council fire" was held at Albany, commencing August 23 and carried on, with great deliberation, by 700 Indians for more than a week. When they were "weary from having sat long in council," they thought it was "time for a little drink." General Schuyler, Colonel Turbott Francis, and Volkert P. Douw represented the Congress. Samuel Kirkland and James Dean, missionaries among the Indians, were also there to exert their influence. The peace pipe was passed around, which must have been a slow proceeding among 700, and then the Speech was delivered. It was a long speech, and the simple savages took three days to digest it. On the third day Little Abraham, a sachem of the Mohawks. made an elaborate reply. The essential paragraph was heralded by an injunction, "Now, therefore attend and apply your ears closely." It went on to say: "We have fully considered this matter. . . . This, then, is the determination of the Six Nations: Not to take any part, but, as it is a family affair, to sit still and see you fight it out." [33] It should be noted, however, that the Indians at the council fire were chiefly Oneidas and Mohawks of a certain canton of that nation. Most of the Mohawks, with the chief men of the Onondagas, the Cayugas, and the Senecas had gone to Montreal with Brant and Johnson. Therefore this compact was not so reassuring as it seemed on its face to be.[34] In October, however, the Caughnawagas undertook to promise for all the Seven Nations of Canadian Indians that they would not "in the least molest" the colonists.[35]

It must not be supposed that the colonists were averse to having the Indians in the war at all. Massachusetts enlisted the Stockbridge Indians in its forces immediately after the outbreak of the war. There was some excuse for that; they were at least semicivilized.[36] But its Provincial Congress sent a commissioner to the Maine Indians to enlist them and lent a willing ear to a proposal of the Abenakis to take up the hatchet for the colonists, "for which we have no immediate occasion," the Congress said.[37] Ethan Allen had had no compunctions about soliciting four tribes of the Canadian Indians "to help me fight the King's troops," offering them "money, blankets, tomahawks, knives, paint and anything there is in the army, just like brothers." [38] Some seventy or eighty of the red men joined Arnold in Canada; but otherwise very few were, in fact, employed by the colonists early in the war except as scouts, messengers, or guides.[39]

Schuyler and his companions left New York on July 4. After certain necessary delays at Albany and Saratoga, they arrived at Ticonderoga on the 18th and found a sad state of affairs.[40] At the landing place, held by a captain and a hundred men, a sentinel "quitted his post to go and awake the guard, consisting of three men, in which he had no success. I walked up and came to another, a sergeant's guard. Here the sentinel challenged, but suffered me to come up to him, the whole guard, like the first, in profoundest sleep. With a pen-knife only I could have cut off both guards and then have set fire to the block-house, destroyed the stores and starved the people there." So Schuyler reported to Washington on the night of his arrival.

This was his introduction to a post, which he soon found was "in a perfectly defenceless state," not only because "not one earthly thing has been done for offence or defence," but also because the garrison was in a wretched physical and mental condition.[41]

There were about 1,300 men in the posts on the lakes, 600 at Ticonderoga, 400 at Crown Point, 300 at Fort George. They were composed of Colonel Benjamin Hillman's Connecticut regiment, 1,000 men, part of a Massachusetts regiment under Colonel James Easton, numbering a little more than 100, 200 New Yorkers, and a few Green Mountain Boys.[42] At Ti, as the principal post was currently called, the men were "crowded in very bad barracks," insanitary to a degree; many were ill. They were largely without discipline. Those from Connecticut, especially, feeling themselves in Yankee fashion quite the equals of their officers, were insubordinate. Food was scarce: "sometimes we have no flour." The "constant cry for rum" went unappeased.[43] Schuyler found that there had been "a very considerable waste or embezzlement" of the stores.[44] Ammunition was wanting, and when it came to building boats, as the Congress had directed him to do, for an attack on St. John's, he had "not a nail, no pitch, no oakum," and no boards until he could set up a sawmill.[45]

The helpless, defenseless condition of these posts was largely due to the inefficiency of Colonel Hinman. He had come to Ti, as he said, merely to reinforce its garrison and, although he had accepted the chief command of a wilderness post far removed from any superior officer, his idea of his duty was "to wait for orders" and to do nothing until he got them.[46] He had welcomed the news that a superior was on the way to direct him. "I wait, Sir, with impatience for your arrival, as I find myself very unable to steer in this stormy situation," he plaintively wrote to Schuyler, on July 7.[47] He did not last long in the Continental army, not longer than December 20, 1775. After that, he returned to the militia.[48]

Schuyler had recognized the difficulties of his task before he came to Ticonderoga. There were under his command in the whole New York Department, present and fit for duty, no more than 2,500 men.[49] The Congress expected him to add to these the regiment of Green Mountain Boys, 500 in number, which Ethan Allen had been authorized to raise. But Allen had lost favor with the Boys. When some of "the old farmers on the New Hampshire Grants" met at Cephas Kent's tavern in Dorset, on July 27, to nominate the officers of the proposed regiment, they ignored him and elected Seth Warner lieutenant colonel, leaving the colonelcy vacant.[50] Allen came to Ticonderoga alone and solicited a place in Schuyler's force. Schuyler was "apprehensive of disagreeable consequences arising from Mr. Allen's imprudence . . . his impatience of subordination." But after he had made "a solemn promise . . . that he would demean himself properly," he was admitted as a volunteer.[51] The other 499 Boys failed to arrive.

If and when Schuyler attacked Canada with the force then in hand, he would have to use at least 200 of his men to guard the posts he already held, marching with not much more than 1,000 to take Carleton's fortified positions. The British had at least 700 regular troops, to which they might perhaps add as many Indians and a number of whites which he could not even guess at, because Hinman had obtained no information as to the probable attitude of the Canadians toward the proposed invasion.[52] Even without regard for the lack of matériel of every kind, the lack of man power was discouraging. So "with a strange and almost fatal patience," inherent in his Dutch blood perhaps, or resulting from "his patrician habit to order and not to do" or his lack of physical stamina, he lingered at Ti for more than two months, waiting for reinforcements.[53]

Not that he was idle; he got out planks for bateaux and built them, enough finally to carry 1,300 men with twenty days' provisions; he even had, on July 31, "a boat on the stocks (and nearly finished) sixty feet in length," large enough to carry "between two and three hundred men," and had started another. Also he called and called again on New York for more troops, for tents, and for equipment of all sorts from field artillery to bullet molds.[54]

In June, New York had voted to raise four regiments. On July 21 Schuyler asked for them. A week later he did "most earnestly entreat" that they should be sent up to Albany.[55] On August 14 Hinman caustically observed, "The Province of New York abounds with officers, but I have not had my curiosity gratified by the sight of one private." [56] But New York had its reasons for the delay. Its Committee of Safety had written on July 15, "Our troops can be of no service to you; they have no arms, clothes, blankets, or ammunition, the officers no commissions, our treasury no money, ourselves in debt. It is in vain to complain; we will send you soldiers, whenever the men we have raised are entitled to that name." [57]

They started at last. Colonel James Clinton arrived in Albany near the end of August with six companies. Three of these had serviceable muskets, two had guns needing repairs, the sixth had none. Lieutenant Colonel Philip Van Cortlandt got there about the same time, with four companies, "many of the men wanting shirts, shoes, stockings, underclothes," having, that is to say, no uniforms at all except coats and breeches. Three-fourths of them had no blankets, and they had no tents; but thirty men did have muskets. No barracks being available, they were kept penned up in their boats, to their great disgust. "Give us guns, blankets, tents . . . and we will fight the devil himself," they cried. "But don't keep us here in market-boats, as though we were a parcel of sheep or calves." The first of them, four companies under Lieutenant Colonel Rudolphus Ritzema, reached Ticonderoga on August 22.[58]

In his search for more men, Schuyler cast his eyes on Brigadier General Wooster's Connecticut troops sent down to help out in the defense of New York City. On July 17 the Continental Congress directed Wooster to send 1,000 men to Schuyler.[59] Colonel David Waterbury brought his full regiment. New Hampshire offered Schuyler three companies of Rangers, not part of the Continental army, under command of Colonel Timothy Bedel. They were to join him on his march to St. Johns. So, in one way and another, Schuyler gathered a little army.[60]

But, although Schuyler labored to improve the discipline of his men, they were for a long time "much inclined to a seditious and mutinous temper," partly because of their lack of good food, supplies, and equipment, and partly because of intercolonial jealousies. Major John Brown of Massachusetts thought "New York have acted a droll part, and are determined to defeat us, if in their power." [61] A Connecticut man wrote to Governor Trumbull complaining that "all the places of profit" were "filled up with men of the York Government," while Connecticut men were "obliged to do all the drudgery. . . . Commissaries' places are profitable. . . . Why should they have all the places of profit? . . . The advantage of their situation is such that it will make them rich. Are we to be wholly ruled by the Committee of New York?" [62] General Wooster, commanding the Connecticut men sent down to New York, thought it was dishonorable to his province to be subjected to the direction of a body of men—to wit, the New York Congress—when he could have "no faith in their honesty in the cause." "You know not, Sir, half their tricks," he wrote to Trumbull.[63] This distrust of New York permeated the New Englanders, and affected their relationship with their commander, Schuyler, a New Yorker himself.

In July, Schuyler had sent John Brown north to secure information about Carleton's post at St. Johns, the magazines of arms and ammunition in Montreal, and the inclinations of the Indians and Canadians in the contest. This man Brown was one of those remarkable characters that one finds hidden in the crannies of history, almost unknown even to historians. He was an educated man, a graduate of Yale and a lawyer, who had held the office of King's attorney in New York province, whence he had removed to Pittsfield, Massachusetts, to practice his profession. But he was not satisfied with such a sedentary life. He was "a strong, bold, active, fearless man . . . of noble personal appearance, genial air and chivalric manner," the best type of the gentleman adventurer.[64]

We have had a glimpse of him in February, 1775, when the Massachusetts Provincial Congress sent him on a mission to Canada, and have seen that his report recommended the seizure of Ticonderoga, in which he had afterward had a part. That journey was a severe test of his ability as a woodsman, his physical strength, and his pertinacity. It was made in the dead of winter, through deep snows, in intense cold, and over a most difficult country. On Lake Champlain amid broken ice he and his two companions, an old hunter and one who had been an Indian's captive for years, had been frozen in for two days. Thence they had gone on foot through a flooded country. It was a fortnight's journey of "almost inconceivable hardships," he said. At Montreal he talked with all sorts of people while his companions discussed matters of interest with the Caughnawagas. His report did not encourage the hope that the Canadians in general would join the colonists, but he did succeed in establishing friendly relations with some of the Old Subjects, notably one Thomas Waller, and in providing "a channel of correspondence" with them.[65]

He left Crown Point on this second errand, under Schuyler's orders, on July 24, with four companions, a Canadian and three soldiers. The journey could not be made openly as the first had been, for since the taking of Ticonderoga Canada was enemy country. Danger of captivity was now added to the difficulties of travel. After arriving in Canadian territory by boat, they "had a tedious and fatiguing march" of three days "through a vast tract of swamp." In one house where they lodged for the night, they were "surrounded by a large party of the enemy . . . escaping out of a back window,"and on their return trip they were "pursued two days." Nevertheless, they remained in Canada four days, protected by friendly inhabitants, and brought back a full and convincing report, dated August 14.

The French, he said, would not fight against the colonists. The Indians were minded to be neutral, except that they might scout for the British. St. Johns was being fortified. It was supported by two bateaux mounting nine guns each; and two sixty-foot vessels to mount twelve guns each were on the stocks. There were 700 of the King's troops in Canada, 300 of whom were at St. Johns, only 50 at Quebec, and the rest at Montreal, Chambly, and elsewhere. "Now, Sir, is the time to carry Canada. It may be done with great ease and little cost, and I have no doubt but the Canadians will join us. There is a great defection amongst them." [66] By Canadians he meant the Old Subjects.

Information from another source, coming on August 3, confirmed Brown's report except in the disposition of the King's troops, of which there were said to be 470 at St. Johns, 110 at Chambly, 80 at Quebec, and about

20 at Montreal. Samuel Mott, who got this news, urged that "we go forward now with 1500 men [rather] than with 3000 one month hence." [67]

But Schuyler lingered. There were reasons why he did, sufficient in his
mind at least. He had no tents, no carriages for his fieldpieces. Many of his
men were sickly—194 of them on August 14—and his expected reinforcements had not come. He was fully determined to go on, "unless your Excellency or Congress should direct otherwise," he advised Washington on
August 6. As late as August 27 he wrote again to Washington, "To do it has
been my determination, unless prevented by my superiors." [68] It may be
unfair to Schuyler to suggest it, but that recurrent conditional clause seems
to suggest a hope that he might be prevented.

On August 17 he went to Albany to attend the council fire with the
Indians, leaving Montgomery in command on the lakes. That active soldier
had, it seems, been tugging at the leash. On the 19th he wrote that "every
intelligence from Canada evinces the necessity of a vigorous and speedy
effort to crush their naval armament before it gets abroad." Now, in
Schuyler's absence, he slipped the leash.

Montgomery had received a letter from John Brown, whom he had sent
north on another scouting expedition, telling him of the near completion of
Carleton's two vessels: "Their hulls seem to be finished . . . their masts
are preparing . . . they appear of large size." He apologized for "writing
in a dictatorial style," and would not have done so if it were not certain that
the two vessels and their attendant bateaux "can easily sweep the lake. . . .
I therefore humbly beseech that some effectual measures may be immediately entered into to keep the command of this lake." That was enough for
Montgomery.[69]

He at once wrote to Schuyler that he was so much of Brown's opinion
that he thought it "absolutely necessary to move down the lake with the
utmost dispatch." He had therefore, without waiting for Schuyler's approval,
given orders for an advance to Ile aux Noix in the Richelieu River beyond
the foot of the lake, which, with the aid of two 12-pounders and a log boom,
he intended to hold and so prevent Carleton's vessels from entering Champlain. He hoped Schuyler would follow him in a whaleboat, "leaving some-
body to bring on the troops and artillery." He apologized for taking this
step without orders, but felt that to hold back the enemy was of the utmost
importance. "If I must err, let it be on the right side." [70] Schuyler was
usually very touchy about his superiority in command, but he now learned
"with pleasure" that Montgomery had acted in such an important matter
without even consulting him. He seemed, indeed, to be glad that he had
been relieved of responsibility for the venture.[71]

CHAPTER 12

Montreal

Montgomery was now about to begin the attempt against Montreal so long considered. From Ticonderoga his course lay north by way of Lake Champlain to Crown Point. Beyond that the lake widened between shores of almost unbroken wilderness, narrowed again, and emptied at the 45th parallel of latitude into a river, indifferently called the Richelieu or the Sorel, flowing nearly due north. At that point it was almost blocked by an island, the Ile aux Noix. Twenty miles farther north was St. Johns, a small settlement. Ten miles beyond that was Chambly, still smaller. At the mouth of the river, where it emptied into the St. Lawrence, was another little village, Sorel. But, at Chambly, a road led northwest to La Prairie and Longueuil, directly opposite Montreal, the main objective.[1]

In the evening of Monday August 28 the greater part of Waterbury's Connecticut Regiment, four companies of Ritzema's 4th New York, and Mott's small section of artillery, about twelve hundred men in all, embarked in the schooner *Liberty,* the sloop *Enterprise,* and a fleet of gondolas, bateaux, row-galleys, piraguas, and canoes. In the bow of each sailing vessel a 12-pounder was mounted. With a fair wind and a sufficiency of fresh and lusty oarsmen, the excursion began auspiciously, the men evincing "great cheerfulness." [2]

But at ten o'clock it began to rain heavily. They went ashore and bivouacked damply under the trees. On Tuesday they worked their way up to Crown Point. "A barbarous north wind" held them there one day, but the next morning a fair southerly breeze set in. So day by day they went on, going ashore at night to sleep, until, just beyond Isle La Motte, on a "fine, sandy beach" they disembarked to wait for Schuyler.[3]

Returning from the Albany council fire, Schuyler reached Ticonderoga on August 30, "very much indisposed . . . with a bilious fever and violent rheumatick pains"; but the next morning, after ordering forward five hundred of Hinman's regiment, three hundred of Colonel Goose Van Schaick's, and some artillery, he set out in a whaleboat to catch up with his ambitious lieutenant. In the morning of Monday September 4 he found Montgomery awaiting him and at once gave orders to move on. That evening they pitched their tents on Ile aux Noix. Hopefully, they fired three cannon shots, the signal agreed upon with their Canadian friends, who were to gather and join them. There was no response.[4]

The next day found Schuyler in rather worse condition, but he drafted an address to the Canadians telling them that "the Grand Congress" had ordered him to expel the British troops, who wished "to enslave their countrymen." The Congress, he said, "could not conceive that anything but the force of necessity could induce you tamely to bear the insult and ignominy that is daily imposed on you, or that you could calmly sit by and see those chains forging which are intended to bind you, your posterity, and ours, in one common and eternal slavery." Therefore it had ordered him "to cherish every Canadian . . . and sacredly to guard their property." [5] This document he directed Ethan Allen and John Brown to take to James Livingston, a merchant at Chambly who was well affected toward the colonists, and with whom he had been in correspondence.

On September 5 the troops embarked again, with three days' cooked provisions and their arms "in good firing Order"; their tents, baggage, and supplies were left behind under a guard. They were sailing now, all stripped for action, down the broad Richelieu between its heavily wooded shores. At three in the afternoon, they were in sight of the fort at St. Johns, two miles away. As they gazed at it, they saw white puffs of smoke break from its walls, heard the boom of its guns, and realized that they were being "kindly saluted" with round shots and bombs, though none of the missiles reached them.[6]

Half a mile farther on they went ashore "in a close, deep swamp" and started "in grounds marshy and covered with woods" towards the fort. Major Thomas Hobby and Captain Matthew Mead of the 5th Connecticut led a flanking party on the left and a little ahead of the others. They were crossing Bernier's Brook, a deep, muddy, winding stream, when they were met by a surprising blast of close fire. A hundred Indians led by Captain Tice, a New York Tory, had ambushed them. Several of the Americans fell, but the rest fired on the unseen enemy, then wheeled smartly to the left into dense thickets and for half an hour or so there was irregular bush fighting before the Indians retreated. Eight of Schuyler's men were killed or fatally wounded, and eight, including Hobby and Mead, injured less severely.[7]

They advanced no farther. As night fell, they dug "a small intrenchment" where they stood. But the enemy "kept continually throwing their bomb-shells" at this place, so, without tarrying long, they retreated a mile and entrenched again out of reach of the British guns.

That night there came to Schuyler "a gentleman, Mr. ———," whose name he disclosed only to Washington, begging him to erase it from his letter. This person had more effect upon the expedition than all the bombs and Indians. He told the general that the fortification at St. Johns was "complete and strong and plentifully furnished with cannon"; that the vessel there would be ready to sail in three or four days and was to carry sixteen guns; that no Canadians would join the Americans; that they had better not attack St. Johns, but rather return to Ile aux Noix.[8] Such resolution as Schuyler had was not proof against this kind of advice. He told a council of war the next morning that he considered it "absolutely necessary" to retire. The rest of its members agreed "to take measures for preventing her [the ship's] entrance into the lake," measures which, because of "the weak state of our artillery" could be effected only at Ile aux Noix, where an already prepared boom could be thrown across the channel. There they would await "intelligence touching the intentions of the Canadians" and, when reinforced, march by land against Montreal, "should the Canadians favour such a design." [9] So, instead of "expelling" the King's troops from all Canada, or even from the little fort at St. Johns, they all withdrew "without noise." If Major Preston's force at St. Johns had not been so weak that he feared to venture out of his fort, there might have been noise enough at this retirement.[10]

The news was spread abroad in Canada of their fight and flight, in which, so the tale went, 60 Indians had defeated 1,500 Americans in entrenchments, killing 40, wounding 30 more, and sending them back to their refuge at Ile aux Noix; and the victory was celebrated in Montreal by "a grand mass with a *Te Deum*." If anything were needed to ensure the abstention of the Canadians from joining Schuyler, this retreat provided it.[11]

The river was boomed, the island fortified. Now the colonials were in an excellent defensive position, very satisfactory if defense was all that was wanted. And there they received reinforcements, 300 of Hinman's Connecticut troops, 400 of the 2nd New York under Colonel Goose Van Schaick, with three pieces of cannon. Counting certain detachments sent out before that, Schuyler had altogether 1,700 men, more than twice the British regulars in all Canada. And he had five guns and three mortars.[12]

At this juncture (September 9) Schuyler received a reply to the letter he had sent by Ethan Allen and John Brown to James Livingston, the well affected merchant living at Chambly. Livingston urged him to interpose a force between St. Johns and Chambly so as to prevent Preston and his vessel from escaping to the St. Lawrence. If Schuyler would do that, Livingston promised to help him with "a considerable party of Canadians." They might even capture the vessel, loaded with "provisions and warlike supplies" and "slenderly manned." [13]

Schuyler fell in with this suggestion. He made elaborate plans. Two row-galleys, each carrying a 12-pounder, the sloop, the schooner, and ten bateaux "with 350 picked men" were to lie in the river to prevent Preston's vessel, the *Royal Savage*, from going south to the lake; and 700 men were to go again to a point near St. Johns, 200 of them to act as a covering party, protecting the boats, while 500 circumvented the fort and invested it on the north.[14]

On the 10th of September 800 men set out and landed at about ten o'clock in the evening near the first breastwork erected in the former attempt. The covering party of 300, under Montgomery, held that position, while Colonel Ritzema with 500 New Yorkers started along the shore to march around the fort. Flankers were thrown out in the woods on their left. It was dark in that forest, and the flankers, remembering the ambush on the former expedition, were nervous and apprehensive. There might be an Indian behind every tree. They drew toward the right, toward the open beach and, suddenly in the darkness, collided with the head of the main column. An instant and overpowering panic set in. They were ambushed again! They were certain of it, though only one chance shot from one of their own men had been heard. The covering party heard a noise as of many men coming in a hurry. Back they came, the whole 500, scrambling through the woods, through swamps as hard as they could go, for the boats. Ritzema was the last to come, all by himself.[15]

Montgomery took them in hand, rallied them, exhorted them "to act like men," formed them, and started them off again. They had gone a quarter of a mile, when some small shells and grapeshot from one of Preston's bateaux crashed and rattled through the trees. Half of them turned tail and ran again for the boats. But Ritzema, with the rest in a straggling band, went on to the second entrenchment of the previous excursion. A few of the enemy were holding a small house there. Ritzema had only 50 men with him. A few shots were exchanged, and two of the enemy were killed. Though 200 more of his men came up, he decided to retire. It was then three o'clock in the morning. The whole expedition spent the night at the landing place, their only satisfaction being that one of their 12-pounders had gone through that bateau of Preston's from stem to stern, torn it apart, and perhaps destroyed its crew of 35 men, or, at least had given them a ducking.[16]

In the morning another council of war decided to try again. But the officers were uncertain of the obedience of the men. They felt it necessary to call a sort of town meeting and let the privates vote on the question. The men agreed to go on. But just then Lieutenant Samuel Lockwood, who had been scouting down the river, returned and told them that the *Royal Savage* lay a little below "completely equipped." Part of Waterbury's New Yorkers at once ran to the boats, intending to get away as quickly as possible. Faced by such demoralization, fearing, too, that the schooner might come up and destroy their bateaux, the officers gave up the attempt. They embarked again for Ile aux Noix.[17]

Montgomery was not satisfied to retreat so ignominiously. After they had gone a few miles he stopped the fleet, went ashore with his officers, and called on the men to follow him on a march against St. Johns. But one of them called out that the schooner was coming. That finished it. "The Troops were hardly restrained from pushing off without their officers." So back to their haven of safety they all went, an expedition defeated by imagination.[18]

At the main camp the returning heroes were received with such jeers and upbraidings by those who had stayed safe at home, that they were "unable to bear the reproach of their late unbecoming behaviour." Schuyler, who was so ill that he could not leave his tent, concerted with Montgomery to take advantage of this state of mind. On September 13 they ordered the artillery into the boats, with the intention of carrying the whole force down the river again. The main party was to land as before, against St. Johns. The schooner and the row-galleys, manned by "determined volunteer crews and good rowers," were boldly to attack and board the *Royal Savage.* But the next day it rained, and on the next after that Ethan Allen came in to report his findings as to the disposition of the Canadians, which necessitated further consideration. That night Schuyler's "disorder reattacked . . . [him] with double violence." The 15th was again rainy, and Schuyler was so ill that "every prospect of a speedy recovery vanished." On September 16 he "was put into a covered boat and left Isle aux Noix."[19] Montgomery, of course, assumed command.

It would have been useless to call for volunteers in any event. Six hundred of the men were on the sick list, including half of Waterbury's contingent of Connecticut paladins. Sulkiness was prevalent throughout the camp, and mutiny was in the offing. One man cocked his gun and threatened to shoot an officer. Unauthorized parties wandered about the island, plundering its few inhabitants. Frequent false alarms of enemy approaches kept the camp in a turmoil. Courts-martial were of no avail, for no witnesses could be found to testify against the culprits. The officers were about ready to give up the whole expedition as a hopeless job when things took a turn for the better.[20]

Allen had helped by reporting that all the Caughnawagas had deserted Preston at St. Johns, and on the 16th the expected reinforcements began to arrive: Seth Warner and 170 of his Green Mountain Boys, "able bodied, stout, active fellows, used to the woods"; Colonel Timothy Bedel and 100 New Hampshire Rangers; and an Independent Company of Volunteers, including some Dartmouth students. These were soon followed by Captain John Lamb's Independent Company of New York Artillery—in all, something more than 400 men. Montgomery had now about 2,000 in his camp. Besides these, Easton's 200 men and the 1st New York Battalion, 125 strong, were coming from Ti.[21]

At the time Schuyler took over the command of Ticonderoga, the post at St. Johns was but a barracks, some brick buildings, and a stone house; but plans had been made to strengthen it. Two redoubts about a hundred feet square and six hundred feet apart were built of earth. One surrounded the brick buildings; the other, the stone house. A strong stockade, defended by a seven-foot ditch and fraised with pointed pickets in part and in part abatised, was drawn around the redoubts on three sides; and a moat was dug on the fourth, the river side. Cannon were mounted on the redoubts. Altogether, it was a sturdy little fort, offering a chance for a stubborn defense.[22]

Carleton's whole force of regulars was composed of 376 of the 7th Regiment, the Royal Fusiliers, and 263 of the 26th, the Cameronians.[23] Fewer than 200 men drawn from these regiments, with a few artillerymen and Indians, had garrisoned St. Johns fort at the time of Schuyler's first abortive attempt upon it. Carleton might have abandoned it and the whole Richelieu River and concentrated his forces for the defense of Montreal; but the Canadians and the Indians would have interpreted that as evidence of weakness and of fear, and would have been moved to withhold the help he so sorely needed. He had therefore decided to make a strong stand at St. Johns. To its garrison were added enough regulars to make up 500. His dire need for more men and the curiously amphibious character of the river operation appear in his withdrawing, in August, a midshipman and 12 sailors from the newly arrived armed brigantine, *Gaspé,* and sending them to the fort.

Earlier in the year, he had helped Lieutenant Colonel Allan Maclean, an old campaigner, to raise troops among the veteran Scottish soldiers who had emigrated to Canada. Maclean enlisted 70 in a company called the Royal Highland Emigrants. These went to St. Johns, and 100 Canadian volunteers with 40 artillerists and a few artificers increased the garrison to about 725 men all told. But Carleton felt he must have more.[24]

He tried the Canadians. Among the Old Subjects "damn'd rascals of Merchants, [he] met with little or no success." [25] They mostly favored the Americans. The seigneurs and the clergy used their influence among the French Canadians, but the sturdy habitants answered with armed opposition to enlistment, and with oaths on the Cross never to fight the Americans. The Indians had failed him. He had to do with what he had.[26]

On September 16 Montgomery organized his naval force, his schooner and sloop, ten bateaux, and two row-galleys (each with a 12-pounder), and 350 men, and sent them to lie in the river to prevent the *Royal Savage* from running upstream and cutting his communications with his base, Ticonderoga. He then embarked the rest of his troops and landed them at St. Johns.

He had already sent Major John Brown with 100 Americans and 30 or 40 Canadians to Chambly. Brown heard that a British supply train was on the way to the fort. He waylaid it in the night of the 17th about two miles north of its destination and captured the supplies. Expecting prompt aid from Montgomery, he entrenched. But before any help came, 100 British regulars and as many of the volunteers with two fieldpieces sallied out of the fort to attack him. Brown withdrew into the woods with his booty. There was a considerable exchange of fire until Colonel Bedel came up with 500 men and drove the enemy back to their stronghold. This new force was then posted in an entrenched camp about a mile north of St. Johns, while Brown went on with his foraging, which was quite successful. He gathered in twenty wagons laden with clothing, "rum, pork, wine &c." Montgomery sent other parties to take posts at Longueuil and La Prairie and hold those two approaches to Montreal. The rest were encamped about the fort. On the south side entrenchments were erected, and batteries of two guns and some small mortars were put in place. The siege of St. Johns was properly begun.[27]

Montgomery had promptly sent Ethan Allen on to Chambly to gather and take command of a body of Canadian volunteers. John Brown had gone to La Prairie on a similar errand. The very next day after he was dispatched, the energetic Allen wrote to his chief that he was at St. Ours, within twelve miles of Sorel, that he had 250 Canadians under arms, that, "as I march, they gather fast," and that he might be expected at St. Johns with 500 men in about three days. In a week's time, he could raise one or two thousand, he said. "I swear by the Lord I can raise three times the number of our army in Canada, provided you continue the siege; all depends on that. . . . God grant you wisdom, fortitude and every accomplishment of a victorious General . . . to fail of victory will be an eternal disgrace, but to obtain it will elevate us on the wings of fame." So wrote optimistic and eloquent Ethan to the general upon whom he was never to lay eyes again.[28]

At Longueuil, looking across the river at the twinkling lights of Montreal, Allen had a vision. He had told Trumbull in July that, if he had been given command of the Green Mountain Boys regiment, he would have advanced into Canada and invested Montreal. He was in Canada now, and there, just across the river, lay Montreal, practically defenseless. He could see victory before him and hear the rustle of the "wings of fame." Opportunity was knocking at his door.

But his Canadian recruits proved unstable; all but 80 of them drifted away. So he forgot his dream and turned back for St. Johns with his diminished force. He had gone but a little way on the road, when he met Brown, who had about 200 men. These two ambitious and daring souls agreed upon a scheme not merely to invest, but to take Montreal. Allen was to cross below the town, Brown above. Each would, as silently as possible, approach the town gate at his end. Brown's party was to give three huzzas as a signal of his arrival on the Montreal side and his readiness to attack.

Allen, having added 30 "English Americans" to his force, attempted a crossing in the night of October 24. There were so few canoes available that only one-third of his men could go at a time. They were all across before daylight, approached the town, and waited for Brown's signal. It never came. It was too late to retreat and make those three crossings again. At daybreak he would be discovered. Two-thirds of his men, left on the Montreal shore, while the first contingent crossed, would be too weak even to defend themselves. He took a good position two or three miles from the town, and waited for an attack.

News that "Ethan Allen, the Notorious New Hampshire Incendiary," was at hand threw the town "into the utmost Confusion." Carleton ordered the drums beaten. "The better sort of Citizens English & Canadian turned out under Arms." Thirty or forty soldiers, followed by about two hundred volunteers and a few Indians, issued from the Quebec Gate and advanced upon the intruders. Allen had posted his men behind trees and buildings and behind a small stream, and a smart little fight ensued. But two parties of

English and Canadians, constituting Allen's flanks, soon fled into the woods. Allen saw that he was to be surrounded. He retreated, keeping up a running fight, but was so hard pressed that he had to surrender himself and his forty remaining men.[29]

Allen's impetuosity was definitely harmful to the American cause. The complete failure of his attack heartened the loyal Canadians and disheartened those who might have joined Montgomery. The Indians now favored the winning side. "Thank God, that day's Action turned the minds of the Canadians," wrote one of them. Seth Warner wrote, "His defeat hath put the french people in to grate Constarnation." Schuyler, at Ticonderoga, reported to the President of Congress that he was "very apprehensive of disagreeable consequences arising from Mr. *Allen's* imprudence," and recalled for Hancock's benefit that he had "always dreaded" Allen's "impatience of subordination"—which was of course quite true. Carleton seized upon this turn of affairs and sent word through the province that 15 out of every 100 men must take up arms. Though the habitants in general refused to obey, Carleton did gather 900 new men to add to his force, but they began to desert "thirty or forty of a night"; he was approaching "as forlorn a State as before." [30]

The siege of St. Johns was continued, but under great difficulties. It was growing colder, and heavy rains set in. "Whenever we attempt to raise batteries, the water follows in the ditch when only two feet deep." [31] The camp was in low, swampy ground, and nothing could be kept dry. "Our men Sometimes have been Wet near Twenty Days together," said Jonathan Trumbull. "We have been like half-drowned rats crawling through a swamp," wrote Montgomery.[32] There was a vast amount of illness among the troops. Supplies of all kinds were short. Late in September the men were on a half-allowance of pork, and the flour was giving out. Powder, as always, was scanty.[33]

All this sowed seeds of dissatisfaction among the men, and they had favorable ground to grow upon. The Yorkers disliked the Yankees, and the Yankees distrusted the Yorkers. Besides, there was that ineradicable "leveling spirit" among the New Englanders, "such an equality among them, that the officers have no authority. . . . The privates are all generals," said Montgomery. He disliked, too, some of the men from his own province: "The first reg^t of Yorkers is the sweeping of the York streets." [34] The whole army was unruly, frequently near to mutiny. The men had to be coddled, their permission obtained before this or that could be done. At one time, when Montgomery wanted to erect a battery in a certain position, his field officers absolutely refused to do so. "I cannot help observing to how little purpose I am here," he wrote. "Were I not afraid the example would be too generally followed, and that the publick service might suffer, I would not stay an hour at the head of troops whose operations I cannot direct." He complained to Schuyler that it was impossible to command men "who carry the spirit of freedom into the field, and think for themselves." [35]

Schuyler, down at Ticonderoga, had found a similar condition, "a scandalous want of subordination and inattention to my orders," which had been chiefly responsible for the lack of supplies at St. Johns. He took hold, however, and in six days sent as much in the way of provisions as had before been shipped in three weeks. Conditions at the siege were immediately bettered. But he met with that same intercolonial jealousy, that disinclination of the troops from the various provinces to merge their identities so as to make a united army.[36]

It prevailed even among some of the higher officers. General David Wooster's distaste for submission to commands emanating from New York has been already mentioned. When the Continental mustermaster wanted to enroll Wooster's troops in the Continental army, he demurred "not thinking himself a Continental officer," and his men refused to sign.[37] They were sent up to Ticonderoga. Two hundred and fifty arrived in October, in advance, and Schuyler ordered them on to St. Johns. They answered that they did not "choose to move" until Wooster arrived. "Do not Choose to move! Strange language for an Army," the disgusted major general wrote to the Continental Congress. "But the irresistible force of necessity obliges me to put up with it." One of their lieutenant colonels demurred when he was directed to send a small detachment with powder and rum up to St. Johns, fearing he would be blamed by Wooster for obeying Schuyler's order. But Schuyler believed that ultimately they would "condescend to go." [38] When Wooster came, however, Schuyler found him tractable. He agreed not to dispute Montgomery's superior command at St. Johns.[39] So a regiment of the Connecticut men, 335 all told, sailed on October 22 for St. Johns, though "with the greatest reluctance," [40] and arrived on October 26. With them were 225 men of the 4th New York under Major Barnabas Tuthill.

Meanwhile, the siege had continued; and the fact that so many of the King's troops were bottled up had made some impression on the Canadians. St. Luc de La Corne found that the Indians were inclining to the Americans. He sent some Caughnawagas to Montgomery "with a string of wampum" and indefinite "proposals of an accommodation." Montgomery distrusted him but would not overlook any chance for aid. "He is a great villain and as cunning as the devil, but I have sent a *New Englander* to negotiate with him"—a left-handed compliment to the Yankee whom he sent, the ubiquitous Major John Brown. The conference came to nothing.[41]

At Chambly, down the river from St. Johns, there was a fort, an impressive, castlelike stone structure, with walls sixteen feet high and higher bastions at its corners. However, the walls were very thin and were pierced only for muskets. It was held by Major Stopford with a garrison of 88 officers and men. In the nighttime, two American bateaux carrying a few 9-pounders slipped past the guns of St. Johns and of the *Royal Savage* and landed at Chambly. James Livingston brought up 300 Canadians; Brown and Bedel brought down 50 Americans. They established batteries, and opened fire. The guns shot a couple of holes in the thin masonry and knocked down a chimney. Stopford surrendered the fort, with 10 officers, 78 privates of the Royal Fusiliers, 30 women, 51 children, 6 tons of gunpowder, 3 mortars, 150 muskets, 6,500 musket cartridges, 500 hand grenades, 300 swivel-shot, and 138 barrels of edible provisions.[42]

The investment of St. Johns was now tight above and below, but there was one thing left to bother the Americans, that armed schooner of Preston's anchored close to the fort. At last they concentrated their fire on her and on her mate, the floating battery. The *Royal Savage* and her companion both went down.[43]

Carleton had long considered a rescue. Allan Maclean had gathered a force of his countrymen. These, with 60 of the Royal Fusiliers from Montreal and a large number of Caughnawaga Indians, nearly 800 in all, assembled on an island in the St. Lawrence. On October 30, Carleton and La Corne leading part of them, they started across to Longueuil. But Seth Warner with his Green Mountain Boys and the 2nd New York was on the opposite bank. They opened fire with grapeshot from a little 4-pounder and with musketry. The boats were thrown into confusion, and the expedition turned back. Another party, led by Maclean, tried for a landing farther up the river. At the sight of a detachment of Americans posted there, they also retreated.[44]

There was by this time a strong battery on the west side of the Richelieu, with only the river and the moat, no walls, between it and the interior of St. Johns fort. Its bombardment was effective. The stone house was wrecked, the brick houses were shot through and through. There was no safe refuge anywhere in the enclosure, but still the garrison held on. It seemed evident that nothing less than an assault through a breach in its walls would take the fort.

To effect that, the position that Montgomery had before been prevented from taking by "the general dissatisfaction" of his troops, was occupied on the 25th. It was a hill on the northwest side of the fort. A battery of 12-pounders, some lighter guns, and several mortars was erected there. For about six hours all the artillery played on Preston's hold, but even this concentrated fire made no breach in the fort's earthen walls.

Then Montgomery tried other tactics. He sent one of the prisoners taken from Carleton's rescue force to tell Preston his case was hopeless, and Preston saw the point. On November 2, after holding out for fifty-five days, and with only three days' provision left in his magazines, he capitulated.[45]

The next day Montgomery drew up his troops before the fort. A motley array they were. The Yorkers were in uniform, as were Lamb's artillerymen, theirs being blue with buff facings. The Green Mountain Boys wore greatcoats of green turned up with red. But the Connecticut men, though admired for "Strength, Stature, Youth & Agility," wore any sort of clothes they happened to have. There marched out of the fort first the Royal Fusiliers in red coats faced with pale yellow, then the handful of the Royal Artillery in dark blue coats, red facings and sashes, white waistcoats and breeches, gold-laced cocked hats, and jack boots. The marines from the *Gaspé* in their short petticoats followed, with the Royal Highland Emigrants in kilts and the assorted mob of Canadians, artificers and workmen bringing up the rear. They were paraded, and Captain Lamb's artillerymen with a detachment from every regiment of the Americans marched past them and into the fort. Then Preston's men laid down their arms. One of the officers taken that day was the unfortunate John André.[46]

Montgomery treated his captives well. The officers were allowed to retain their side arms and private effects. The men were given the reserve store of clothing.[47] When this became known, "the officers of the First Regiment of Yorkers and [of Lamb's] Artillery Company were very near a mutiny . . . there was no driving it into their noddles, that the clothing was really the property of the soldier, that he had paid for it," wrote Montgomery. "I wish some method could be fallen upon of engaging *gentlemen* to serve."[48] The Canadians were allowed to go home. The regulars were to proceed to some port where they could embark for Great Britain.

Now it was necessary to proceed promptly to Montreal and to possess it. The Connecticut men were unwilling to go farther. Montgomery had "to coax them" by promising their dismissal as soon as Montreal was occupied.[49]

The march was begun on November 5, and it was most difficult. The old corduroy road had disintegrated into a succession of rotten logs and half-frozen mudholes. It snowed and rained. In places the mire was knee-deep.

The men were badly clothed and ill shod, but they pulled through to La Prairie. On the 11th, the first of them crossed to an island in the river and, on the next day, in a gale of wind, landed above Montreal.

Carleton, with something like 150 regulars and a few militia, remained in the town until the 11th; but its walls were so thin that they "could only turn Musketry," and in part had fallen down. The place was not defensible against even light artillery. He therefore put on shipboard the most valuable military stores and destroyed the rest as soon as he heard that the Americans were at La Prairie. He sailed on the 11th under fire from the American shore batteries. Montgomery spoke fairly to a deputation of Montreal citizens, and they surrendered on the 13th. At Sorel another battery threatened Carleton's little fleet. The wind was adverse. The ships turned back a few miles. Then Major Brown boarded one, under a flag, and told its commander that he had two 32-pounders in his "grand battery" at Sorel—a gross exaggeration. The *Gaspé*, two other armed vessels, and eight smaller craft were surrendered, with not only their cargoes and their crews, but also the soldiers formerly garrisoning Montreal.[50]

Carleton himself remained in the *Gaspé* until shortly before its capture. Then, "dressed like a man of the people" and accompanied by one or two of his officers, he was rowed with muffled oars down the river and by an obscure channel through the islands opposite Sorel, escaping finally to Quebec.[51]

Arnold's March to Quebec

If one's antagonist can be forced to fight on two fronts at once, he is always at a disadvantage. While Schuyler's forces were still lingering at Ticonderoga, preparing for the advance toward Montreal, Washington in Cambridge had been pondering this strategic axiom. There was another front which might be developed: Quebec, 150 miles down the St. Lawrence from Montreal. If those two towns were attacked at the same time Carleton would be at a serious disadvantage and would be easy to overcome at one or the other, probably at both. Quebec, then, should be the object of an expedition simultaneous with that against Montreal.

The road seemed to be open—a waterway. The best, often the only possible route through a wilderness was a waterway, which permitted men to travel in boats with their provisions and supplies, escaping the hardship of a struggle through dense forests. This route had been considered in reverse by the French more than once as affording a means of attacking Boston. It had been repeatedly mapped and described, with varying degrees of correctness. It had been discussed during the French and Indian War "as a Rout by which an Army might pass, the best and shortest way, to attack Canada and Quebec." [1] In the spring of 1775 Colonel Jonathan Brewer of Massachusetts had offered to lead 500 volunteers against Quebec by this route, a project which he believed "he Could Execute With all the feility [felicity] Imaginable." [2] It is possible that Washington was made aware of this proposal.

The way led up the Kennebec River to the Great Carrying Place, where the Indians bound to Canada from New England used to leave the Kennebec and take their canoes across a twelve-mile stretch of land to the Dead River. The stretch was broken into four portages by three ponds, across which boats could float, so that they had to be carried only about eight miles. After paddling about thirty miles up the Dead River, the Indians would proceed across the Height of Land about four miles to a stream emptying into Lake Megantic, from which the Chaudière River flows into the St. Lawrence within four miles of Quebec. Various portages were to be expected wherever falls or rapids on the rivers interfered with passage by water. The map of Captain John Montresor, a British army engineer, and his description made this rout seem to be quite feasible. Montresor had not told the whole tale of its difficulties and dangers; Washington, however, accepted at more than its face value the scanty information concerning it which had been conveyed to him.

On August 20, 1775, he wrote to Schuyler: "The Design of this Express is to communicate to you a Plan of an Expedition which has engaged my Thoughts for several Days. It is to penetrate into Canada by Way of Kennebeck River, and so to Quebeck. . . . I can very well spare a Detachment for this Purpose of one Thousand or twelve Hundred men, and the Land Carriage of the Rout proposed is too inconsiderable to make an objection." [3] That last sentence clearly shows how little he knew of the proposed "Rout." His thoughts about such an expedition soon crystallized into a decision to send it, and he looked about for someone to lead it. His choice of a com mander could hardly have been bettered.

After resigning on June 24 his command at Ticonderoga, Arnold went to Cambridge to settle his accounts with the Provincial Congress and secure from it the sums of money due him. He was at loose ends while this business dragged to a long deferred conclusion, because he had no office in the Continental army nor any connection with it. When Washington offered him command, as colonel, of an expedition against Quebec, he offered it to a man who still cherished the desire to invade Canada—a desire which had been frustrated at Ticonderoga. Arnold accepted with avidity.

It appears, indeed, that matters were far advanced before Washington wrote that letter to Schuyler, for on August 21 Arnold was writing to Reuben Colburn, a Kennebec boatbuilder who happened to be in Cambridge, making certain inquiries on behalf of the commander in chief. How soon could 200 light "Battoos" be procured or built at Kennebec, capable of carrying six or seven men each with their provisions, "say 100 wt. to each man," each boat to be furnished with four oars, two paddles, and two setting-poles? What would they cost? Could a quantity of fresh beef be procured at Kennebec? He also wanted information as to "the Difficulty attending an Expedition that way, in particular the Number, & length, of the Carrying Places, wheather Low, Dry land, Hills or Swamp, Also the Depth of Water in the River at this Season, wheather an easy Stream or Rapid." [4] This inquiry discloses Washington's ignorance, and Arnold's, of the nature and condition of the river they proposed to use as a road to Canada.

Colburn's reply was satisfactory as to the boats and their cost—40 shillings each with their equipment—for on September 3 Washington gave him an order for them. He also directed him to engage a company of twenty men, "Artificers, Carpenters and Guides," to go along under Colburn's command, "to bespeak all The Pork and Flour you can from the Inhabitants upon the River Kennebeck," and to notify the public there that the commissary would be in the market for sixty barrels of salted beef.[5] To get the desired information as to the route, Colburn sent Dennis Getchell and Samuel Berry to examine it and report to him.

On September 5 notice of the expedition appeared in General Orders. The detachment was to consist of two battalions of five companies each, comprising in all, with the usual battalion and company officers and musicians, 742 men; also Captain Daniel Morgan's company of Virginia riflemen and two companies of Colonel William Thompson's rifle regiment from Pennsylvania, under Captains Matthew Smith and William Hendricks, about 250 in all. To these should be added the surgeon, his mate and two assistants, two adjutants, two quartermasters, the chaplain, and six unattached volunteers, a total of 1,051. Service in the expedition was to be voluntary, and it was desired that none but "active Woodsmen" "well acquainted with batteaus" should present themselves. They were all to parade on Cambridge Common in the morning of September 6. The desire for woodsmen acquainted with bateaux was, unfortunately, not met in fact; nor does it appear that any effort was made to comply with that suggestion in the order. The men other than the riflemen were drawn chiefly from Massachusetts, Connecticut, Rhode Island, and New Hampshire Regiments, and were mostly farmers, few of them having had any experience in the wild woods or in the management of bateaux.[6]

The unattached volunteers were an interesting lot. Matthias Ogden of New Jersey, Eleazer Oswald of Connecticut, Charles Porterfield and John McGuire of Virginia, and Matthew Duncan of Pennsylvania were five, all of whom afterward became officers in the Continental army. But the sixth deserves more particular notice, because of his subsequent career.

Aaron Burr was a youth of distinguished lineage, the grandson of the great Jonathan Edwards, the son of the Reverend Aaron Burr, second president of the College of New Jersey at Princeton. Young Aaron had been ready to enter the college at the age of eleven, "a strikingly pretty boy, very fair, with beautiful black eyes and such graceful engaging ways as to render him a favorite." For want of age his admission was postponed for two years, and then he entered as a sophomore. After his graduation in 1772 at the age of sixteen he continued his residence in the college and for a while read theology. Skepticism soon undermined his hereditary beliefs, and he turned to the law. Lexington and Concord inflamed his naturally aggressive spirit. After Bunker's Hill, he called a college mate, Matthias Ogden, to the colors, and together they joined the army as independent volunteers immediately after Washington took command. Idleness fretted Burr's restless soul, actually worried him into an intermittent fever. When he heard of the proposed expedition to Quebec he got up from a bed of sickness and, despite the remonstrances of his friends, insisted on being allowed to go along.

He was nineteen years old, no more than five feet six inches tall, of slight figure and boyish countenance, but with a surprising capacity for enduring fatigue and privation. It was his indomitable will rather than his physical strength that sustained him. His intelligence was abnormally keen, his spirit unbreakable, his ambition unbounded. His subsequent career in the army was brilliant. He was in command of a regiment at the age of twenty-one, and in command of a brigade in the Battle of Monmouth at twenty-two.

He had the defects of his qualities. His overleaping ambition, his keen perception of the readiest means of bringing to pass what he desired, and his habit of ignoring conscientious scruples, resulted in the errors of conduct in civil affairs that ruined his life and blotted out the fame he won as a soldier.[7]

In the list of officers one name stands out above all the rest—Daniel Morgan of Morgan's Rifles. Although born in New Jersey to a Welsh immigrant family, Morgan was a true son of the backwoods. He ran away from home at the age of seventeen and went on foot through Pennsylvania into the wilder parts of Virginia, now West Virginia. There his character was formed and he acquired his fame as a backwoodsman.

He was first employed to run a sawmill and then became a teamster. Within two years he had set up in business with his own wagon and horse, hauling supplies to the remoter settlements. In this capacity he was employed in Braddock's expedition against Fort Duquesne. He served with distinction first as a private and then as an officer of the Virginia militia throughout the French and Indian War, in the war against Pontiac, and in "Lord Dunmore's War" with the Indians. That he was commissioned to raise a company of Virginia riflemen to join Washington's army at Cambridge has already been told.

He was a tall man, well over six feet, broad-shouldered, deep-chested, and stout of limb, weighing over two hundred pounds, all bone and muscle, yet active, even graceful, in movement. His physical and mental hardihood in endurance of fatigue under the most severe conditions matched his powerful frame. Although his usual manner of speaking was abrupt and severe and he was prone to swift angers and stern judgments, his open countenance indicated the good-humored, kindly character that lay beneath the surface and was displayed to his friends and to his men when they merited his approval. His schooling had been of the scantiest; he read with difficulty, wrote almost illegibly, and was puzzled by the simplest problems in arithmetic. But his natural genius and acquired knowledge of men and affairs, his keen intelligence, and his sound reasoning served him well in all his enterprises. His courage, daring, and resourcefulness in military affairs, added to his other characteristics, made him a great leader of men in the war upon which he was now entering.[8]

Washington's orders to Arnold were full and comprehensive, impressing upon him the necessity of discovering "the real Sentiments of the Canadians towards our Cause." If they were "averse to it and will not co-operate or at least willingly acquiesce . . . you are by no Means to prosecute the Attempt." Arnold was to restrain his men from the "Imprudence and Folly" of showing "Contempt of the Religion" of the Canadians "by ridiculing any of its Ceremonies or affronting its Ministers or Votaries . . . and to punish every Instance of it." There was to be no plundering of either friend or foe; all provisions and supplies were to be purchased and paid for. Although the expedition was to be pushed with vigor, yet, "if unforeseen Difficulties should arise or if the Weather shou'd become so severe as to render it hazardous to proceed in your own Judgment and that of your principal Officers (whom you are to consult) In that case you are to return." To the last injunction, it would seem Arnold paid little attention.[9]

In the expeditionary force the riflemen made up one corps. The musketmen were in two battalions, the first under Lieutenant Colonel Roger Enos and Major Return Jonathan Meigs, both from Connecticut, with five companies commanded by Captains Thomas Williams of Massachusetts, Henry Dearborn of New Hampshire, Oliver Hanchet of Connecticut, William Goodrich of Massachusetts, and Scott, whose first name and province of origin are unknown. The second battalion was led by Lieutenant Colonel Christopher Greene of Rhode Island and Major Timothy Bigelow of Massachusetts, with five companies under Captains Samuel Ward, Jr., of Rhode Island, Simeon Thayer, John Topham, Jonas Hubbard, and Samuel McCobb, all of Massachusetts. Isaac Senter of Rhode Island was the surgeon, Samuel Spring the chaplain. Christian Febiger was brigade major.

On September 11 the riflemen set out for Newburyport; but the musketmen, when paraded on Cambridge Common, "refused to march till we had a month's pay," says the journal of Ephraim Squier, a private. Whether it was back pay or pay in advance does not appear; but the matter seems to have been promptly adjusted, for by the 13th all had marched.[10]

By the 16th the expeditionary force had arrived in Newbury or the adjacent Newburyport, where a fleet of eleven sloops and schooners had been assembled. Three scouting vessels had been sent out to see if there were any British ships in the way. No news of such dangers having been received by the 19th, the fleet sailed, "drums beating, fifes playing and colours flying," [11] Arnold's topsail schooner in the lead. With no untoward incident on the way, except the extreme seasickness of most of these landsmen—"such a sickness, making me feel so lifeless, so indifferent whether I lived or died!" wrote Simon Fobes in his diary—the fleet made the voyage of a hundred miles to the mouth of the Kennebec in eleven hours. Sailing up the river, it reached Gardinerstown by the 22nd. There Arnold went ashore, a spruce figure in a scarlet coat, with collar, lapels, and cuffs of buff, silver-plated buttons, ruffled shirt, white linen waistcoat, breeches and stockings and black half-garters, the whole topped by a plumed cocked hat.

He inspected the bateaux provided for the expedition and found that there were 200 of them as ordered, but many were "smaller than the directions given and very badly built." [12] It was hardly Colburn's fault that they were not first-class. He had had only eighteen days to go home from Cambridge, assemble the workmen, and put through such a building program as he had never before been called upon to undertake, even with a sufficient time allowance. There was not nearly enough seasoned timber available, and so he had, perforce, used green stuff. It was unfortunate but unavoidable. Arnold could not reject them; he had to content himself with ordering twenty more.

These bateaux were of a type in common use on the Kennebec, with narrow, flat bottoms, widely flaring sides and long, pointed stems and sterns, capable of carrying heavy loads and not easily capsized. They were to be propelled by oars or paddles in still or flowing water and to be poled up rapids. They answered well on the lower Kennebec, but no one had ever tried to take them all the way up, past waterfalls, through the most difficult portages, across high, rough country, all the way to the St. Lawrence. Canoes, yes, but such heavy boats, especially when so ill built, emphatically no.

Besides the bateaux Colburn had to furnish information as to the route. The two men, Getchell and Berry, whom he had sent out had returned. Their report was not reassuring. They had gone as far as the Dead River, had met an Indian, Natanis by name, who told them he was employed by Carleton "to Watch the Motions of an Army or Spies that was daily expected from New England," and that a British officer with six men was posted on the Chaudière to look out for the Americans. Natanis declared that if the two scouts were any farther he would inform Carleton. By another Indian they had been told that a great number of Mohawks in Johnson's pay were at Sartigan, the uppermost settlement on the Chaudière. Otherwise, they said, the way was fair and was marked by blazed trees, the portages "pretty possible," the water shoal. Arnold read this report, but paid little attention to the threats of Natanis: "a noted villain," he called him in a letter to Washington, "and very little credit, I am told, is to be given his information." [13]

More helpful were a map of the route and a description of "the quick water and carrying places to and from Quebeck," furnished him by Samuel Goodwin.

By the 24th Arnold's force had reached Fort Western—now Augusta— thirty miles up the river, some in the sailing vessels, the rest in the bateaux. This "fort" was a couple of blockhouses and a magazine surrounded by a palisade, useful in the French and Indian War but no longer held as a military post. It was the real starting point for the expedition. Here Arnold detached and sent off two advance parties.

Lieutenant Archibald Steele of Smith's company of riflemen, "a man of an active, courageous, sprightly and hardy disposition," with seven men selected from the rifle companies, was ordered to reconnoiter the way to Lake Megantic, the source of the Chaudière. Steele had orders to capture or kill that "noted villain" Natanis.[14] Lieutenant Church, with a similar party and a surveyor, was to note "the exact courses and distances to the Dead River." These parties set out in canoes with guides.

The main force was then split into four divisions. The first was composed of the riflemen under command of Morgan,[15] who were to go forward as quickly as they could to clear the road, especially over the Great Carrying Place between the Kennebec and the Dead River. They departed four or five men in each bateau, the rest marching beside the river and taking turns in the boats.

The second division of three companies of musketmen left the next day, led by Lieutenant Colonel Greene and Major Bigelow. Major Meigs led the third division of four companies on the following day, and Lieutenant Colonel Enos with the fourth, three companies and Colburn's artificers, got away two days later. Arnold then started in a canoe to get to the head of the column. The bateaux of each division carried provisions estimated to be sufficient for forty-five days, although Arnold expected "to perform the march," which he figured at 180 miles, in twenty days.[16]

As the river for half a mile beyond Fort Western came against them in impassable rapids, the boats and supplies were presumably hauled by the neighboring inhabitants in wagons or on sleds to a point whence they could go by water. But even then the water was so swift that it was hard to propel the boats by oar and pole. It took them two days to make the eighteen miles to Fort Halifax, another abandoned military post. Above that, they came to Ticonic Falls, which no boat could ascend; here was their first real portage. The bulk of the cargoes was unloaded and carried to the next point of embarkation, each barrel of flour, pork, and so on being slung on two ropes, through which two poles were thrust, so that four men could take the ends on their shoulders. The bateaux were similarly carried by four men on two poles. The boats weighed 400 pounds each, and there were about 65 tons of provisions, ammunition, and general supplies, say in all 100 tons weight of the most unhandy material, to be carried in this instance a half-mile. It was a case of going back and forth until all was got over.

Not far above they came to Five Mile Falls, a series of tumultuous rapids, "very dangerous and difficult to pass." [17] They had "a scene of trouble to go through." The boatmen had often to leap overboard and struggle with their clumsy craft to keep them straight or drag them over shoals. They would be in the icy cold water to their waists, to their chins, even over their heads when they plunged into an unexpected "deep bason." "After much fatigue and a Bondance of difficulty," [18] they got through, but not without damage.

The rocky river bottom, sunken logs, tree roots had scraped and torn the bottoms of the boats and opened their seams. They "began to leak profusely." Indeed, at least one of them, Dr. Senter's, was "in such a shattered condition" that he had to buy another from a near-by settler [19] the day before they came to Skowhegan Falls.

Even the approach to Skowhegan was difficult. The river made a sharp turn between two ledges no more than twenty-five feet apart, forming a

MAP OF
ARNOLD'S ROUTE
SCALE OF MILES

0   10   20   30   40   50

QUEBEC

L.Megantic

Hurricane Falls

Dead R.

Great Carrying Place

Mt Bigelow

Carritunk Falls

River

Norridgewock Falls

Bombazee Rips

Skowhegan Falls

Rangeley Lakes

NEW HAMPSHIRE

Androscoggin R.

Ticonic Falls

Sebasticook R.

Fort Halifax

Kennebec

Fort Western (Augusta)

Gardiner's Mill

Colburn's

Gardinerstown (Pittston)

Pownalborough (Dresden)

Merrymeeting Bay

MAINE

ARROWSIC I.

Georgetown

Phipsburg

Parker's Flats

SEGUIN I.

Portland

ATLANTIC OCEAN

NEW MASS.

Newburyport

Merrimac R.

MASS.

Cambridge

BOSTON

chute through which the whole force of the water drove against them. There was a half-mile of this and then the falls themselves, divided by a towering mass of rock split in the middle by a narrow cleft. There was no going ashore for a carry on either side; the river banks were not banks but vertical rock walls. The boats and their cargoes had to be carried through that cleft, narrow, steep, and rough underfoot, and pushed through five miles of "small falls and quick water" above it.[20] The men lay that night, as often they did, in wet clothes that froze upon them.

So they went on, through Bombazee Rips, where again the banks closed in and the water came down in a torrent, until they came "face to face with the roar and foam of the great Norridgewock Falls." [21] These were three falls, a half-mile apart, and the carry around them was a mile and a half long. Some settlers appeared with two sleds drawn by oxen, and helped with the supplies, but the bateaux had to be carried by the men.

Those boats were in bad shape now, "nothing but wrecks, some stove to pieces." [22] Colburn's carpenters set to work to repair their bottoms and caulk their seams. But nothing could be done regarding supplies spoiled in the leaky boats. Quantities of dry salted codfish had been loaded loose in them. The water had washed away the salt, and the fish had spoiled. The salt beef had also gone bad. Casks of bread and of dried peas had absorbed water, swelled, and burst. All this provender had to be thrown away. Arnold's men had nothing now but salt pork and flour.

Three days were consumed in getting around Norridgewock and in repairing the boats. On October 9 they were again under way. Eleven of Arnold's estimated twenty days for the whole journey were past, and they had gone but one-third of the distance. Up to this time they had been within reach of civilization of a sort, occasional settlements and isolated farms from which they had sometimes been able to buy beef cattle. Now all that was left behind. The rest was sheer wilderness.

They made fourteen miles in the next two days with one portage around Curritunk Falls. The river was shallower and swifter, harder to work the boats through. The weather grew colder, and continuous, heavy rains fell. On the 11th they came to the Great Carrying Place between the Kennebec and the Dead River. That is, Arnold himself came to it on October 11. It must be understood that the itinerary given here is only approximately correct. The four divisions of the troops had not kept the intervals first allotted to them. This one would get ahead faster than its follower, or that one would overtake the one before it. Arnold himself was backward and forward, now with one division or another, now alone with his own canoemen.

When he reached the Great Carrying Place, Morgan's men and the second division under Greene were already there.

The first portage of the Great Carrying Place was a mere Indian trail, Morgan's men had had little time to do anything with it; the rest of the army was close upon them. It had rained so hard on the 8th that no work could be done. The ground was soaked; there was no dry place to sleep. The army had to sit up all night close to their fires.

The bateau men had to carry their unwieldy burdens, and the rest their cargoes "through a most terrible piece of woods conceivable," [23] through bogs where they sank "half-leg deep," and over rocky ledges, three and a quarter miles to the first pond. Though the pork had been removed from the barrels and strung on poles for easier carriage, seven or eight trips were necessary to get everything across. The weather was exceedingly bad, with heavy winds and snow squalls. "A prodigious number of trout" caught in the pond made a welcome addition to their narrow diet. A moose someone killed also helped out. They were three days on this carry and in crossing the pond, a distance of five miles.

The first pond having been crossed in the crazy boats, the second carry was found to be little more than half a mile, and the footing was fair. But the second pond was disappointing. "The water was quite yellow," and it was all they had to drink. They were greatly worn down by fatigue and hardship. Many of them—"a very formidable number" [24]—were ill, some of them desperately ill. This bad water sickened them so much more that a log blockhouse was built for a hospital. It was "no sooner finished than filled."

The way to the third pond was longer, about a mile and a half. It was "extremely bad, being choaked with roots which we could not clear away." [25] But there were more trout in that pond.

The fourth portage was three miles long, and it was difficult. A mile up and a mile down brought them to what looked like "a beautiful plat of firm ground, covered by an elegant green moss," interspersed with groves of spruce and cedar. In fact, it was a treacherous bog. At nearly every step they sank halfway to their knees and found at the bottom sharp snags and roots that tore their shoes and bruised their feet. There was a mile and a half of this. So, stumbling along, falling now and again, dropping their burdens and recovering them again, they at last emerged, "plastered with mud from neck to heel," [26] at Bog Brook, which led into the Dead River.

While the main body was crossing the Great Carrying Place, it was met by Lieutenant Church's party of pioneers returning to report to Arnold.

Lieutenant Steele also, with two of his men but not the other five, came back to report. Steele's party had reached the Chaudière River without unusual difficulty, but their return march was another matter.

It had started in "a most severe storm of rain," which lasted a day and a night. Their provisions had run out. On the first day of the return trip on the Dead River, John Henry, one of the party, had only "a solitary biscuit and an inch of pork." He ate half his store that day. They shot a duck and divided it. His portion was one leg, another man got the head and feet. The next day Henry ate the other half of his biscuit and pork, and they made fifty miles. The day after that one of the two canoes struck a submerged snag and was ripped through its whole length, its ribs torn from its gun-wales. They sewed them in place with cedar roots and patched the skin with birch bark and pitch made out of turpentine and the grease in their pork bag. They had gone five hundred yards when another snag broke the canoe in two pieces held together only by the gunwales. They mended it as before. They shot a moose, smoked its flesh, and ate it raw. They were so weak that they could not carry their canoes across the Great Carrying Place, so they abandoned them and set out on foot. Steele and two others pushed ahead to get help.

The five remaining lived wretchedly on the moose meat for four days. Half cured and without salt or bread, it sickened them. They "staggered along . . . falling every now and then, if our toes but touched a twig or tuft of grass." [27] On October 17 Morgan's pioneers sighted five scarecrows, gaunt, haggard, ghastly creatures, so weak they could scarcely stumble along. The rest of Steele's party had returned.

After Steele had reported the results of his exploration Arnold sent him and Church forward again, with twenty axmen and a surveyor, "to clear the portages and take a survey of the country." [28] He also wrote a letter to a friend in Quebec, John Mercier, telling of his approach with 2,000 men "to frustrate the arbitrary and unjust measures of the ministry and restore liberty to our brethren of Canada," [29] and dispatched it by two Indians, Eneas and Sabatis, and one John Hall, who could speak French. That letter in some way got into Carleton's hands and resulted in the arrest and imprisonment of Mercier.

Now began the trip up the Dead River, a deceptive stream that belied its name. Its black waters were deep, and so smooth that they seemed to be standing still. "A most gentle and leisurely stream" [30] it was, to all appearances. But, though it flowed like oil, its current was swift beyond all expec-

tations. The few oars and paddles were not enough to make headway against
it. The boatmen had to grasp the bushes on its precipitous banks and pull
themselves along. And it meandered in such great bends and windings that,
after two hours' hard work, they "seemed to have gained nothing in our
course." [31] But they made thirteen miles before they camped that night.
They also made a most discouraging discovery. Their food was on the point
of giving out.

Although Arnold had written only a day or two before to Enos, commander of the fourth division, that the first three had provender enough for
more than three weeks, Greene's division, which had got ahead, now found
itself out of bread and almost out of flour. While it had been passing Morgan's riflemen they had helped themselves to Greene's supply of food without his knowledge.[32] Arnold sent Major Bigelow with three lieutenants and
100 men in twelve bateaux back to get flour from Enos, in whose division
there was supposed to be a surplus. Morgan's and Meigs's divisions, somewhat better supplied, pushed ahead; but Greene had to lie in his camp for
five days, awaiting Bigelow's return.

Bigelow came back with two barrels of flour, all Enos would let him
have. It was a desperate situation for Greene's men. There was nothing to
do but send back the least able men; the rest had to tighten belts and push
on after the other divisions.

Rain began to fall gently on the 19th. It increased in volume on the next
day, and by the 21st it developed into a raging tempest, driven by winds of
hurricane force. Trees crashed into the river, "tumbling on all quarters" [33]
and blocking the way. Floods of water drenched the men and their few supplies. Tents were few. In camp most of the men had no protection except
such as could be had from hemlock boughs. The river rose and flooded the
country. It overflowed its eight- or ten-foot-high banks and poured into the
camp of Morgan's men during the night of the 21st. Where a campfire had
burned at evening, the morning saw a lake four feet deep. Barrels of pork
were swept away, and bateaux filled and sank.

About midnight the rain had ceased and stars had come out; but the
wind still blew, and it grew very cold. Wet through, chilled to the bone,
and hungry, the men looked out upon a strange scene that morning. The
whole country was under water. The river, which had been but sixty yards
wide, was now two hundred, and it was a torrent of "terrifying rapidity"
and overwhelming force. "None but the most strong and active boatmen"
tried to breast it. The rest started on foot, "making large circuits" to avoid
the drowned land. "This was one of the most fatiguing marches we had as

yet performed . . . having no path and being necessitated to climb the steepest hills and that without food." [34] But they had to go on or starve to death.

Those who took to the boats had an almost impossible task. The swift current tossed the clumsy bateaux here and there, upset them, and threw the boatmen and the precious provisions into the ungovernable flood. At last it seemed that the expedition must break down completely. A council of war was held. Arnold's unwavering determination so inspired officers and men that the council voted to go on. The men responded with more than courage. When any of them, exhausted by fatigue and hunger, were told by their comrades that they "would not be able to advance much further, they would raise up their half-bent bodies and force an animated look into their ghastly countenances, observing at the same time that they would soon be well enough." [35] But twenty-six hopeless cases were sent back to the hospital; forty-eight more soon followed them. Captain Hanchet of Meigs's division, with fifty men, undertook to hasten forward to get food in the Chaudière valley. Arnold went ahead of him with a small party. The supply in Greene's division was so low that the men were reduced to boiling some tallow candles in a gruel made of water and a little flour.

The rear division had now, October 25, come up with the second, Meigs having gone on. Arnold had ordered Greene and Enos to send back "as many of the Poorest men of their Detachment as would leave 15 days provision for the remainder." [36] Greene, Enos, and the officers of their respective companies met for a conference. Although not covered by Arnold's orders, the question was put whether the two whole divisions should go on or go back. Greene, his major, Bigelow, his three captains, and Enos voted to go on. Enos's captains, Williams, McCobb, and Scott, his adjutant, Hide, and Lieutenant Peters voted to abandon the expedition. It was six to five in favor of going on. Enos, "though [he] voted for proceeding, yet had undoubtedly pre-engaged" with his officers "to the contrary, as every action demonstrated." [37] He decided to abandon the enterprise. Greene's party then asked for a division of the food. Their "expostulations and entreaties" were in vain. Being "the weakest party," they could not compel the others "to a just division." Enos said that "his men were out of his power" and he could not enforce an order to divide. At last two and a half barrels of flour were given up, and Greene's men went back to the foremost divisions, "with a determined resolution to go through or die." Enos led his party down to Fort Western in eleven days of comparatively easy travel.

So the remains of the little army, now fewer than seven hundred men, struggled on. The boatmen in the few surviving bateaux fought the swift current through rapid after rapid. Those on shore found the country rougher than ever, full of hills and hollows, rocky ledges and bogs, ravines and dense forests. At last the expedition came to a point where it could leave the river and enter on a chain of ponds that extended to the edge of the Height of Land.

Their provisions were now virtually at an end. In all, there were only four or five pounds of flour for each man. "The riflemen were wholly destitute of meat before this for eight days." They took rawhide intended for mending their moccasins, chopped it into bits, and tried to make soup of it; but it remained only rawhide. Some of the officers, on the night of the 27th, had nothing but "the jawbone of a swine destitute of any covering." [38] They boiled it, with a little thickening of flour, and that constituted their "sumptuous eating." On such fare, after so long a period of starvation, they had to try the longest portage yet encountered, four miles and a quarter over the Height of Land, the watershed between the streams flowing north to the St. Lawrence and those flowing south to the Kennebec.

It was not, however, a portage for most of them; they had nothing to carry. The bateaux had been wrecked and lost until few were left. Morgan kept seven, the other companies only one each. The rest were abandoned. There was a trail of sorts, but it was interrupted by blowdowns, tangled heaps of fallen trees acres in extent which no man could penetrate. Several inches of snow had fallen, covering whatever trail should have been visible. There were mountains, ravines, bogs, and trackless woods to be got over or through. A broken leg, even a sprained ankle, meant death, for no man was strong enough to carry another. Perishing for want of food, worn down almost to the breaking point, they stumbled on and at last got over the divide and down into a beautiful meadow by the side of a brook known as Seven Mile Stream, that being its length from the meadow to Lake Megantic. But Seven Mile Stream was more than a hundred miles from Quebec, and it afforded no relief from marching, except to the few in the remaining bateaux. They had divided the rest of the provisions, five pints of flour and two ounces or less of pork to each man.

On they went, following the stream. The land fell away into a swamp, and the stream divided and divided again into false mouths, as the Mississippi divides and redivides in its water-logged delta. The marching men, struggling through the swamp in different companies, strayed from the stream at its first false mouth. They strayed again at its second. They were now deep in the swamps, far off the right track, hopelessly lost, but still floundering onward, desperately trying to reach Lake Megantic. "We went astray over mountains and through swamps, which could scarcely be passed by wild beasts," says one account, "waded a small river up to our waists, then marched on until night in our wet clothes. At night found ourselves within five miles of the place we started from. We marched fifteen miles in vain."

That night each man made himself a thin gruel of a gill of flour in water, or baked a little cake in the ashes, and nibbled a tiny scrap of pork. The country was the same as before, bogs and thickets and forests. At last the rest came on the tracks of the one company that had found Seven Mile Stream, and not long after they saw Lake Megantic, at which sight they gave "three huzzas." [39]

The Chaudière, a swift running stream, drops 1,100 feet in 75 miles and is broken by dangerous rapids and falls. Arnold and Morgan tried it in their bateaux. In one rapid six of them crashed against rocks. The baggage, arms, and food in them were lost, and one man was drowned. There was a piece of good fortune in this disaster, however, for just below that rapid there was a waterfall unknown to them. "Had we been carried over [it, we] must inevitably have been dashed to pieces & all lost." [40] The two boats of Smith's and Goodrich's companies were wrecked and everything in them was lost.

"November the first dawned upon a famishing army," [41] lying in camps stretching over a distance of twenty-one miles. A few had a little food; many, having eaten their shares without care for the morrow, "set out weak and faint having nothing at all to eat; the ground covered with snow." They ate soap and hair grease. They boiled and roasted moccasins, shot pouches and old leather breeches, and chewed on them. "No one," says Morison, "can imagine, who has not experienced it, the sweetness of a roasted shot-pouch to the famished appetite." Goodrich's men "had been out of provisions for two days," without "a mouthful." They killed the captain's Newfoundland dog and ate all but the bones, which they kept for soup.

The next day many were so weak they could hardly get up from their beds. Some of them could not, and lay there waiting for death. The strongest "stumbled on . . . mile after mile," staggering "like drunken men," their heads hanging, eyes half closed, their brains in a stupor, dully wondering whether they could go one step farther. Men were dropping out of the straggling ranks and falling down, unable to get on their feet again.

"Never perhaps was there a more forlorn set of human beings collected together in one place," wrote Morison, "every one of us shivering from head to foot, as hungry as wolves and nothing to eat save the little flour we had left. . . . It was a dispiriting, heart-rending sight to see these men whose weakness was reduced to the lowest degree, struggling among rocks and in swamps and falling over the logs . . . falling down upon one another in the act of mutually assisting each other. . . . We had all along aided our weaker brethren. . . . These friendly offices could no longer be performed. Many of the men began to fall behind. . . . It was impossible to bring them along. . . . It was therefore given out . . . by our officers for every man to shift for himself and save his own life if possible." The "haggard looks" of those left behind, "their ghastly countenances, their emaciated bodies and their struggles to proceed with us . . . we saw with the bitterest anguish."

And then, at the very verge of their endurance, at the very last moment, the foremost party saw what they could not believe they really saw, horned cattle, driven by men on horses, coming to meet them. The glad cry "Provisions ahead!" was passed back from one group to another and so to those that had been left behind in the camps. "Echoes of gladness resounded from front to rear." [42] Two canoeloads of mutton and flour followed the beasts.

There was little ceremony about the slaughter of the first animal, or its division. The men grabbed the first bits they could lay their hands on, the entrails, and tore at them "as a hungry dog would tear a haunch of meat." [43] The rescue party took joints of the beef and rode on to those in the rear, the last stragglers being many miles behind. At the place of slaughter, two hundred of them, "an assembly of spectres rather than of men," [44] built fires, "laid our meat on the embers and for the first time for more than three weeks past were regaled with the incense of a sumptuous banquet." [45] "We sat down, eat up our rations, blessed our stars, and thought it luxury," says Dr. Senter.

On a pound of meat a day and a little oatmeal they pushed on with renewed spirits, although in sad physical condition. On moccasins worn through and broken shoes—Ogden had tied up his bursted shoes in a flour bag—they had yet sixty or seventy miles to march to the St. Lawrence.

But the wilderness was behind them. They were approaching civilization, or at least, Indian settlements, Sartigan the first. Arnold was there and had laid in a stock of provisions. "The men were furious, voracious and insatiable." In spite of the advice of the officers "to insure moderation, the men were outrageous upon the subject. . . . Boiled beef . . . potatoes, boiled and roasted, were gormandized without stint." Many of them fell ill; three of them died "by their imprudence." [46]

At this place they met that "noted villain," Natanis, whom Arnold had directed Steele to capture or kill, and found him to be a rather agreeable person. It appeared that he had hovered about the army all the way from the

Great Carrying Place, afraid to join it for fear he would be killed. Now, after Arnold had made a pacific address to a large group of Indians, Natanis and about fifty others joined the expedition and started with it down the Chaudière in their canoes.

The straggling force was brought together at the village of St. Mary, about halfway between Sartigan and the St. Lawrence. At this point they left the Chaudière and marched through snow, mud, and water knee-deep due north across the plains of Canada toward the great river.

On the 9th of November the habitants on the bank of the St. Lawrence saw, emerging from the woods, a band of scarecrows, their clothing "torn in pieces . . . hung in strings—few had any shoes but moggasons made of raw skins—many without hats, beards long and visages thin and meager. . . . So at last came to Point Levi 600, much resembling the animals which inhabit New Spain called the Ourang-Outang,"—600 out of 1,100 men who had started. Their journey had taken forty-five days, instead of twenty, as Arnold had predicted. They had traveled 350 miles, instead of 180, from Fort Western.[47]

Arnold's journey to Quebec is one of the most famous military marches recorded in history. If it had resulted in the capture of that stronghold it would have been celebrated as a great triumph. That it failed, by so little as it did, should not obscure its fame as a magnificent exploit. For sustained courage, undaunted resolution, and uncomplaining endurance of almost incredible hardships, those men who grimly persisted to the end deserved high honor and unstinted praise.[48]

CHAPTER 14

Quebec

The city of Quebec stands on a bold promontory between the St. Lawrence, which bends around it, and an affluent, the St. Charles. The blunt nose of the promontory points northeast, and its highest point, on the southeastern or St. Lawrence side, is Cape Diamond, a precipitous, rocky cliff that rises more than three hundred feet above the water. Toward the northwest, the St. Charles side, and toward the southwest the ground declines to somewhat lower levels. Along the base of the great cliff and around the point of the promontory a narrow band or fringe of lowland slopes gently to the water's edge and widens on the St. Charles side. Part of this, around the promontory's nose, was built up and was known as the Lower Town. It was defended in 1775 at its southern end by a blockhouse behind a double row of palisades just below the height of Cape Diamond. There were also timber barriers through which one might penetrate to Sault au Matelot, a narrow, crooked street, slanting upward from the base of the cliffs to an equally narrow, ladderlike passage into the Upper Town, the real city.

This Upper Town occupied the whole end of the higher level of the promontory and contained all the important buildings, including the citadel situated on the height of Cape Diamond. It was defended on the landward side by a strong wall thirty feet high and three-quarters of a mile long drawn across from one river to the other, from which six bold bastions projected, whereon were mounted heavy cannon. It was pierced by three gates, St. Louis Gate in the center, St. Johns near the northern part, and Palace Gate at the northerly approach to the Lower Town. Outside the main wall were certain built-up suburbs, the Palais toward the St. Charles River, St.

Roche in front of the north end of the wall, and St. Johns opposite its middle
section. Beyond St. Roche and St. Johns to the west stretched the Plains
of Abraham, where Wolfe had fought the great fight by which he took
Quebec from the French in 1759.

Such was the fortress at which that little band of gaunt, ragged, starved
Americans, shivering in the cold autumn wind, gazed with hope born of determination on the morning of November 9, 1775.[1]

They had come a long way and a hard way. They had reached the end
of their march; yet a mile of water rolled between them and their grand objective. It was not an unguarded river that they had to cross. The frigate
Lizard with twenty-six guns, the sloop-of-war *Hunter* with sixteen guns, four
smaller armed vessels, and two transports lay at anchor, and small boats
were constantly on patrol.

The shore on which Arnold's army stood had been cleared of every sort
of craft by which a crossing might be made. It is not surprising that
Matthias Ogden thought the "situation now seem'd somewhat ticklish. . . .
We determined, however," he wrote in his journal, to "make a bold push
for Quebec at all events." [2]

The first necessity was boats. They scoured the country for them. One
party found twenty birch-bark canoes and carried them on their shoulders
twenty-five miles to the camp. The Indian Natanis and his friends offered
others. A dozen dugouts were discovered elsewhere and brought by night
to the mouth of the Chaudière, where the little fleet was hid. Iron heads for
pikes were forged in a near-by smithy and scaling ladders prepared. A supply of flour was procured from a neighboring mill. By Friday November 10
they were ready to attempt the crossing.[3]

But that night a storm arose, rain and a gale of wind which whipped the
river into waves that would have swamped their canoes. In the evening of
the 13th it blew itself out; and at nine o'clock, in black darkness, Arnold
with as many of his men as could crowd into the boats started across. Midway in the river one of the canoes collapsed. Its crew was picked up by another, except Lieutenant Steele, who could find no room in the rescue boat.
He clung to its stern and was towed the rest of the way, arriving nearly dead
from the cold. They landed in a cove, the one in which Wolfe had landed to
capture the city sixteen years before. In a deserted house a fire was kindled,
and Steele was "restored . . . to his usual animation." The boats went
back and brought another detachment, but when it had landed, at three in
the morning, the tide was running so strong, and the moon was shining so
brightly that it was deemed unsafe for the remaining 150 men to cross.
They stayed on the opposite shore until the next night.[4]

The journal of one of the participants in the expedition asserts that Arnold, even with so few men, might have taken the city by attacking at once, as he had originally planned to do, because the keys of St. Johns Gate had been lost and it was unfastened. Others have denied that the gate was open. At all events, Arnold could not have known of this defect in the defenses that night. With only a part of his force at hand and no scaling ladders (there had not been room for them in the boats), he wisely did not attempt an assault.[5]

When all the men had been brought over they assembled and climbed to the level above, not by the goat-path that Wolfe had found, but by a slanting road since cut. They were now on the Plains of Abraham within a mile and a half of the city, near a large house that belonged to Major Caldwell, commandant of the Quebec militia. At the approach of Arnold's men, its occupants fled. The Americans crowded in and slept there.

The coming of the Americans was neither unexpected nor unobserved. A patrol boat had sighted the fire in the house in Wolfe's Cove and had been fired upon at Arnold's order. News of their actual arrival on the Quebec side of the river had been conveyed into the town, where there was considerable perturbation, with good reason. Carleton's command had originally consisted of two regiments of British regulars, the 7th and 26th. But at Ticonderoga, Crown Point, St. Johns, Chambly, and Sorel nearly all of them had been killed or captured. Remaining to him in Quebec were about seventy men of the 7th and a few artillerists.

During the storm that had delayed Arnold at the river side, the active and energetic Allan Maclean had slipped into the city with a force of Royal Highland Emigrants he had raised—Scottish veterans of former wars, brave in scarlet jackets faced with blue and laced with white, tartan kilts and hose, and blue bonnets edged with checkered white, red, and green; but they were few, not more than 80. Hector Cramahé, the governor of the city, had raised 200 British and 300 French Canadian militia. There were also 37 marines from the warships, 271 sailors from the armed ships in the harbor, and 74 from the transports. Maclean figured the total to be about 1,200.[6] But there were long walls to defend, and some of the militia were thought to be unreliable, inclined to desert. On the whole, Quebec, though well provided with munitions and food, was not strongly held. Cramahé felt that way about it. He wrote to General Howe, "There is too much Reason to apprehend the Affair will be soon over."[7]

But in Arnold's opinion 2,000 men would be needed "to carry the Town,"[8] and he had not much more than a quarter of that number; nor had he cannon to breach the walls. Moreover, he was short of ammunition and even of small arms. So many cartridges had been spoiled by water that there were only five rounds for each man. Over a hundred muskets were found to be unserviceable. He had no artillery and no bayonets. All he could do at the time was to blockade the town on the land side, and that at the respectful distance of a mile and a half from its walls, where his men were quartered in houses.

There were occasional diversions. A small party of the garrison sallied out and captured an incautious rifleman on sentry duty. Arnold immediately paraded his troops and marched them "bravado-like" [9] "within 80 rods of the wall . . . in such a manner that they could not discover of what number we consisted of," [10] which must have been a difficult job of deception. Cannon were fired upon them, with no hurt. They "gave 3 huzzas" and returned to their lodgings.

In the afternoon following their arrival, Arnold had sent Matthias Ogden, with a white flag and a drum, to deliver to Cramahé a demand for surrender. Ogden was within a hundred feet of St. Johns Gate when a gun thundered and an 18-pound shot hit the ground near him. He "retreated in quick time." [11] Assuming a misunderstanding of his intentions, Arnold sent another letter the next day, with a similar result. The only course was to continue the blockade.

It was no hardship. For the first time since they set out from Newburyport, two months before, the troops had clean, warm, comfortable lodgings and plenty of good food. They would doubtless have been glad to fight it out on that line—in that manner—if it took all winter. That was also quite evidently the intention of Maclean, who had taken over the command of the city from Cramahé. He burned a part of the suburb of St. Johns and certain other houses near the walls, to prevent the Americans from using them as cover, and settled down to hold out against the siege.

But the Americans were soon routed out of their comfortable quarters. On the 18th they had news that Maclean was about to make a sortie and to attack them with 800 men. Also it was reported that a ship with 200 men was coming up the river, and that the *Lizard* had taken a station above the camp to cut off their retreat. A council of war decided to withdraw. So, at four o'clock in the morning of the 19th, "a severely dark and cold night," [12] the entire force started on a march to Pointe aux Trembles—now Neuville—twenty miles up the river. "Most of the soldiers were in constant misery during this march, as they were bare footed, and the ground was frozen and very uneven." [13] In a village at the point they were again quartered in houses. There they remained for nearly two weeks, recuperating their wasted bodies and availing themselves of an opportunity to make shoes out of the hides of the beeves they had killed for food.

It was a gloomy time. For all the effort they had made, all the hardships they had endured to get to Quebec, this period of inactivity was their only reward. The coveted city seemed as far away as when they left Fort Western. They were not even blockading it. Provisions and fuel were being smuggled into it without hindrance. On their march up the river, they had seen an armed schooner go past them, and a little later the sound of a salvo of artillery was heard. Carleton had come to take command, as they soon learned. That was bad news.

But at last good news did come. On December 2 a topsail schooner and several other craft were sighted coming down the river. In the evening a boat put off from the schooner, and, in the light of lanterns and flaring torches, there stepped ashore into a foot of snow "a gentle, polite Man, tall and slender . . . resolute, mild and of a fine Temper," [14] "well limbed, tall and handsome, though his face was much pock-marked," with "an air and manner that designated the real soldier." [15] Richard Montgomery had come from Montreal.

He had brought 300 men and, what was even more important, artillery and "a good supply of ammunition, clothing and provisions." [16] To the troops paraded in front of the little church he made an "energetic and elegant speech, the burden of which was an applause for our spirit in passing the wilderness, a hope for perseverance . . . and a promise of warm clothing. . . . A few huzzas from our freezing bodies were returned to this address of the gallant hero. Now new life was infused into the whole of the corps." [17]

The men liked Montgomery, and he liked them. He wrote to Schuyler: "I find Colonel Arnold's corps an exceeding fine one, inured to fatigue. . . . There is a style of discipline among them much superior to what I have been used to see in this campaign. He himself is active, intelligent and enterprising. . . . I must say he has brought with him many pretty young men." [18]

Montgomery had captured a year's supply of clothing of the 7th and 26th British regiments. Their winter uniforms were Canadian capotes, long, white, full-skirted overcoats of a heavy blanket material, trimmed and bound with blue, and with cape-hoods. The underjackets were of similar material, with corduroy sleeves. Leggings of heavy blue cloth, really overalls, were strapped over sealskin moccasins and reached to the waist. The caps were of red cloth, with a band of brown fur around the base, and were ornamented at the back with a fur tail.[19] These garments were now distributed in part.

Supplementary distributions were made later to the whole force. On the 5th, they marched back to Quebec, the artillery and stores following in bateaux.

The two American forces took up positions before the town: Arnold on the left, the northern side, in half-burned St. Roche, taking over the General Hospital in that suburb; Montgomery on the Plains midway between St. Roche and Cape Diamond. Now again Quebec was blockaded, but it was not Montgomery's intention to rely upon siege tactics. He well knew that they would not suffice to fulfill the desires of his superiors and of the American colonies in general. They wanted the town taken, and they expected him to take it. Schuyler wrote on November 18 that "in all probability the entire possession of Canada . . . will be [ours] soon." [20] Knox had "very little doubt" of Montgomery's success.[21] Washington on December 5 wrote to Schuyler, "I flatter myself that it will be effected when General Montgomery joins him [Arnold] and our Conquest of Canada be compleat." [22] Indeed, the commander in chief was relying on the spoils of Canada for his own troops, as he wrote to Montgomery: "I must beg . . . your attention to the Wants of the Army here, which are not few, and if they cannot in some Parts be supplied by you, I do not Know where else I can apply." Powder he wanted and arms, blankets, and clothing, of all which he understood there was "an Abundance in Canada." [23] The Congress was urgent for the possession of the town and vocal in its urgency. Clearly, Quebec must be taken by one means or another.

But a siege, without great battering guns to breach the wall, must needs be a slow, long drawn-out affair, and of time Montgomery had little to spare. He could not dig trenches to approach the town in the classic manner. He had no engineer to plan them, and they could not be dug in frozen soil. The term of enlistment of all Arnold's New England troops would expire with the year, and Montgomery had no hope of retaining them after that. It would be most difficult, if not impossible, to obtain fresh supplies of ammunition, and even of food, for Montgomery had no money except Continental paper, which would not pass in Canada. And by April, when the ice in the river broke up, British reinforcements could certainly come. A siege would not do.

Montgomery had been fully aware of all that even before he came, and had no intention of relying on a siege. He had written to Robert Livingston from Montreal giving his reasons why "to storming the place . . . we must come at last." [24] He wrote to Schuyler on the day of his arrival before Quebec that he meant "to assault the works, I believe towards the lower town, which is the weakest part." Meanwhile, he proposed "amusing Mr.

Carleton with a formal attack, erecting batteries, &c." He was sorry to have to assault, because he knew "the melancholy consequences," but saw no escape from it.[25]

First, however, he must go through the customary formality of summoning the garrison. He wrote a letter to Carleton in the usual terms. Being mindful of the manner in which Arnold's similar letters had been treated, he had recourse to a ruse. A woman carried the summons to the Palace Gate and said to the guard she had an important communication for the General. Being admitted, she told him she had a letter for him from the American General. Carleton called a drummer boy and bade him take the paper with the tongs and thrust it into the fire. He sent her back to tell Montgomery that he would receive no communication from a rebel.

Ten days later Montgomery tried again. He wrote a fierce letter, calling Carleton's attention to the weakness of his situation in the town, the great extent of his works manned only by "a motley crew of sailors, most of them our friends . . . citizens, who wish to see us within the walls, a few of the worst troops, that call themselves soldiers." He boasted of his own men "accustomed to success, confident of the righteousness of the cause they are engaged in, inured to danger and fatigue, and so highly incensed at your inhumanity . . . that it is with difficulty I restrain them, until my batteries are ready, from assaulting your works, which would give them a fair opportunity of ample vengeance and just retaliation." If Carleton persisted "in an unwarrantable defence," the consequences were to be on his head.[26] In a word, he tried to scare Carleton. But Carleton refused to take fright. When another woman smuggled this demand into the city, she was first imprisoned and then drummed out of town. As a last resort and in an effort to alarm the citizens, a flight of arrows, each bearing a copy of the letter, was shot over the walls with as little result.

Meanwhile, Montgomery was at work on those threatened batteries. Arnold's force advanced to within 150 yards of the wall, and planted five small mortars. On the heights, 700 yards from the town, in the fiercely cold night of December 10, in a heavy snowstorm driven by a northeast gale, a more formidable American battery was begun. Night by night after that gabions were set up there, filled with snow, and then drenched with water, which froze them into solid blocks of ice. In this battery five 6- and 12-pounders and a howitzer were emplaced. From these two positions a heavy fire was poured upon the walls and into the town, "with very little effect," as Montgomery admitted.[27] But Carleton's response with 13-inch shells and 32-pound balls was too much of an answer. Several men were killed, the ice-battery was shattered, and the guns were dismounted

One more effort was made to induce Carleton to surrender. Arnold and Macpherson, with flag and drum, approached the walls. To a messenger sent to meet them they announced a desire to speak with Carleton. The reply was decisive. He would not see them. Would he receive a letter, then? He would not. They could make the best of their way off, for he would receive nothing from Mr. Montgomery.

Within the town Carleton had organized his men. The fusiliers of the 7th, the marines and Royal Scottish, 425 in all, were commanded by Maclean. Major Caldwell commanded 330 British militia. Colonel Voyer led 543 French Canadian militiamen, and Captain Hamilton the sailors and artificers from the ships, 570 of them. Thus there were over 1,800 to defend the town against Montgomery's force, no more than 800 in all. But *Audaces fortuna juvat* was Montgomery's motto.[28]

He was preparing for the attack, but he met with obstacles. The town-meeting spirit became prevalent, especially among Arnold's New Englanders —so much so that it was recognized as necessary "to have the approbation of all the officers and soldiers." That was hard to get. Everybody wanted the town taken, but not everybody wanted to take it. Many of them "appeared unwilling to attempt so daring an enterprise." [29]

The trouble seems to have originated in three of Arnold's officers, Captain Oliver Hanchet of Connecticut and Captains William Goodrich and Jonas Hubbard of Massachusetts. Hanchet, who had "incurred Colonel Arnold's displeasure by some misconduct and thereby given room for harsh language, is at the bottom of it," [30] wrote Montgomery to Schuyler on December 26. These three proposed to organize a separate corps under command of Major John Brown, who had disliked and distrusted Arnold from the time of their first meeting. Montgomery would not allow this. The three companies then appeared to be "very averse from" the proposed assault. "This dangerous party threatens the ruin of our officers," said Montgomery. But he met Arnold's officers "to compose some matters, which were happily settled." [31] He then paraded Arnold's troops, and addressed them "in a very sensible Spirited manner, which greatly animated" them.[32] "The fire of patriotism kindled in our breasts," wrote one of the Connecticut recalcitrants, "and we resolved to follow wherever he should lead." [33]

The attack was to be made in a dark and stormy night, "in the first northwester." [34] The Lower Town, the weakest in its defenses, was to be the primary objective. While a third of the troops, with ladders, feinted an escalade of the Cape Diamond bastion, another third was to attack the

THE ATTACK ON
QUEBEC

NOVEMBER 1775 TO MAY 1776

ST. CHARLES RIVER

ST. ROCHE

PALAIS

PALACE GATE

ST. JOHNS

ST. JOHNS GATE

QUEBEC
UPPER TOWN

LOWER TOWN

HEIGHTS OF ABRAHAM

ROAD TO TROIS RIVIÈRES

ST LOUIS GATE

POINT LEVI

THE CITADEL

DIAMOND BASTION

CAPE DIAMOND

ST. LAWRENCE RIVER

←TO WOLFE'S COVE

ARNOLD'S FIRST CAMP

Lower Town. Weather conditions seemed suitable on the night of the 27th. It was cloudy, and snow was falling heavily. The troops were assembled, but "the storm abated—the moon shone and we retired to repose." [35] Then Stephen Singleton, a sergeant from Rhode Island, deserted and carried word of Montgomery's plan to Carleton. So it was abandoned, and another was made.

This time two feints were to distract the attention of the garrison, one "with a shew of firing the gate of St. John," [36] the other against the Cape Diamond bastion. There were also to be two real attacks. Arnold's corps, strengthened by forty men of Captain John Lamb's artillery company, was to descend to the lower level from the suburb of St. Roche and force the barriers at the north end of the Lower Town, with the intention of getting into the Sault au Matelot, the narrow, crooked street that led into the heart of the Lower Town. Montgomery was to lead the 1st New York along the low ground at the foot of Cape Diamond, strike the southern end of the Lower Town, and meet Arnold, the combined forces then to drive into the Upper Town.

The essence of the plan was the selection of the Lower Town for the real assault, it being the least fortified part of Quebec. But, for that very reason, the plan was defective. Carleton well knew that it was his Achilles heel and had taken precautions accordingly. Houses that might afford shelter to the attackers had been torn down; windows and doors of others had been covered with heavy planks. The Sault au Matelot was blocked and covered with guns at every turn. As against an assault by men with small arms only, the Lower Town and the way of access from it to the Upper Town were now the most strongly defended; but it was the only possible road to victory. It was that way, or not at all.

Montgomery and his officers realized the desperate nature of the attack. Macpherson wrote a letter to his father, "the last this hand will ever write you." In preparation for it Captain Jacob Cheesman of the 1st New York "dressed himself . . . extremely neat, and, putting five gold pieces in his pocket, said that would be sufficient to bury him with decency." [37] But there was no flinching from the attempt.

The plan made and all the parts in it assigned, the Americans waited for a dark and stormy night. But the weather on Thursday the 29th and on Friday was "clear and mild." Saturday morning was fair; but in the afternoon the sky was clouded, the wind rose and brought a spit of snow. Heavy darkness came at sunset. As the night wore on the snow fell more and more heavily, "a thick small Snow" driven by an "outrageous" [38] wind into great drifts heaped and piled upon that which had fallen before, and which had already covered the earth to a depth of two to three feet. The time had come.

At two o'clock in the morning the men were assembled at their respective stations. Soon after four o'clock signal rockets were fired, and the advance began. The storm, a terrific blizzard, was at its height. The wind from the northwest drove snow mixed with hail into the faces of the men as they stumbled through six-foot drifts in the blackest darkness.

The rockets were a signal to the Americans, but they were also a signal to the town. Drums beat to arms. The great bell of the cathedral, the lesser bells of the Jesuit College, of the Recollet monastery, and of the Hôtel Dieu clanged the alarm. Officers ran through the streets shouting, "Turn out! Turn out!" The city's troops rushed to their posts. Lanterns on poles were thrust out over the top of the walls. Flaming fire balls were thrown from the ramparts to light up the ground outside. The little American mortar battery at St. Roche went into action, throwing shells into the town to divert the enemy's attention from the real points of attack. The guns on the walls roared in reply.

Amid this tumult the two feinting parties made their way toward the walls. Livingston's corps of Canadians was near St. Johns Gate, when they broke and ran. The other party, a hundred Massachusetts men led by Captain Jacob Brown, John's brother, kept up a rattling fire against the Cape Diamond bastion. Some militia were sent to reinforce the defenders there, but otherwise little attention was paid to Brown's efforts. Carleton's mind was not distracted from the Lower Town.

Meanwhile, Montgomery and Arnold had marched. Montgomery at the head of the 1st New York, about 300 men in single file, set out on the long circuit around the Diamond bastion, down the slanting road to the fringe of lowland along the river. The way down to Wolfe's Cove was a mile long, steep, narrow, and heaped with drifted snow; and the storm still raged. That part was bad almost beyond bearing. The rest was worse. On the narrow strip of land below the heights the high tides had piled "enormous and rugged masses of ice," [39] creating such obstacles that the men had to clamber up the steep slope of the cliff to get around them. They slipped, slid, and fell. Those that carried the unwieldy scaling ladders, which had been brought across the river, could hardly make way at all. There were two miles of this before they reached the first defenses of the Lower Town.

Arnold had formed his own corps of 600 men, with a forlorn hope of twenty-five men in advance led by himself and Eleazer Oswald, a volunteer. A hundred yards behind these Captain John Lamb and his forty artillerists dragged a 6-pounder on a sled. Behind them again came the riflemen, Morgan's company, followed by Smith's under command of Lieutenant Steele, and Hendricks's company. The New Englanders (except Dearborn's men, who had been late in assembling) with about forty Canadians and Indians, brought up the rear. They set out from St. Roche in Indian file and passed a two-gun battery without discovery. Hurrying on through deep snow, "deeper than in the fields" above, the van got by the Palace Gate unassailed. The main body, "covering the locks of our guns with the lappets of our coats, holding down our heads" against the driving storm, had also safely passed the Gate, when it "received a tremendous fire of musketry from the ramparts above." For a third of a mile, men falling here and there, they ran that gantlet without a possibility of a reply. "We could see nothing but the blaze from the muzzles of their muskets." [40]

At the waterside ships were moored with cables stretched to the houses. In the darkness some of the men ran into these and were thrown down violently. At last they came into a narrow street blocked by a barricade, mounting two guns.

Arnold's plan was to separate his force, right and left, and let Lamb's gun batter the barrier, while Morgan went around its end on the river ice and took it in the rear. But the 6-pounder had been abandoned in a snow-drift sometime before this. One of the guns of the barrier was fired at them with little effect. The other failed to go off. Arnold called on his men to rush the barricade. They responded, ran to it, and fired through the portholes. A bullet from one of the near-by houses hit a rock, ricocheted and hit Arnold in the leg below the knee. He still shouted encouragement to his men; but his wound was bleeding freely, and he had to be supported by two men to the rear and so to the hospital.

By general acclaim Morgan was called upon to take command instead of Lieutenant Colonel Greene. A ladder was set against the barrier, and Morgan mounted it, calling on his men to follow. As his head topped the barricade, a blaze of fire met him. Stunned, he fell backward and lay in the snow, with one bullet through his cap, another through his beard, and grains of burnt powder embedded in his face. In a moment he was on his feet. Up the ladder again he went, and over the top of the fence. His knee hit one of the cannon, and he rolled beneath it. Before any of the defenders could get at him, Charles Porterfield was over, and then the rest. The enemy, followed by the riflemen's bullets, fled into a house and out the back way. But Morgan had run around it, and he shouted to them to surrender if they wanted quarter. They all surrendered. The way into the Lower Town was open.

The Sault au Matelot lay ahead. They entered it. Two or three hundred yards up that street there was another barrier. Behind it was a platform with cannon. The gate in the barrier was open. Now was the time to break through, for the garrison was offering no resistance. Some of them, Canadians, seemed ready to welcome the Americans, shouted, *"Vive la liberté!"* and held out welcoming hands. The whole town appeared to be panic-stricken. Morgan urged his officers to push on through the gate. But there were few men with him. The rest of that long straggling line had not yet come up. He actually had more prisoners than he had of his own men. It was pitch-dark. The storm was still raging. None of the men knew the way through the crooked street and its alleyways, and they had no guide. This was the place appointed to meet Montgomery. The officers decided to stay there until their whole force came up and Montgomery joined them.

After a time the rest of the troops began to arrive, Hendricks and his riflemen, Greene, Meigs, and Bigelow with the Yankees. It was about daybreak when the major part of the American force was again assembled and formed for another attack. But the town had recovered its senses. Troops had been sent to meet the Americans. A party of them sallied out through the gate in the barrier. Lieutenant Anderson, leading them, called on Morgan to surrender. Morgan shot him through the head. Anderson's men retreated, and for a while there was a pause. The spirit of fraternization again prevailed. Men from either side called to the others by name. But that was soon over, and the Americans went at the high barrier.

Mounds of snow were heaped up, ladders set on them. Morgan climbed one, Porterfield another. Humphreys, Lamb, Greene, Meigs, and yet more went up, but the houses in the street beyond were filled with fighting men. Muskets blazed from the windows. A little way up the street a double line of fusiliers presented their bayonets. No one could dare that defense. And upon the Americans and among them fell a shower of bullets. Humphreys fell, and Hendricks, and many another. Lamb and Steele, and more and more, were wounded, while their assailants were safe in the houses.

Yet, though their pieces were wet and most of them failed to fire, the Americans fought on. They tried to outflank the barricade, but it stretched from the bluff to the river. They dared the ladders again and again, even thrust one over the fence to climb down on; but to go over the top would have been sheer suicide. There was a stone house at the end of the barricade, whose gable-end windows looked down beyond the barrier. Riflemen there could shoot down on the defenders, perhaps drive them back. The Americans broke in, but the enemy had perceived the threat of the house. The ladder the Americans had left inside the barrier was set against the house, and a party of the defenders climbed it, entered through a window, came down the stairs, bayonets fixed. There was a fierce fight, in the house, but the Americans were driven out.

In the street again they were under fire of a 9-pounder hastily brought up, and of musketry as before. They retreated for a space, and the officers consulted. Some of them still looked for Montgomery and wanted to hold their position until night. The majority saw the hopelessness of the situation. It was decided to give up the attempt and withdraw.

But Carleton had moved to prevent that. He had sent Captain Laws out of the Palace Gate, with 200 men and two fieldpieces to follow the Americans' tracks down to the lower level and take them in the rear. Laws came running up the Sault au Matelot, and shouted to the Americans to surrender. They jeered at him, cried out that he was their prisoner. He looked around and saw that he was quite alone. His men had not followed as fast as he had run. Expecting them to come on at once, the Americans threw themselves into the houses along the street.

Laws's delayed party arrived, and for a while a desultory fire was maintained. But the Americans' situation was desperate. Hemmed in, front and back, the officers hastily consulted again. Morgan proposed cutting through the force in their rear. Others were for holding on until Montgomery came. But their plight was beyond hope. They were, in Carleton's words, "compleatly ruined . . . caught, as it were, in a Trap." They began to throw down their arms.

Morgan had disdained the shelter offered by the houses. He stood in the street facing his enemies. When he saw that surrender was inevitable, he set his back against a wall, and, with tears of rage and disappointment streaming down his face, defied the enemy to take his sword. They threatened to shoot him. His men implored him not to sacrifice his life. He saw a man in clerical dress in the crowd confronting him and called to him, "Are you a priest?" He was. "Then I give my sword to you. But not a scoundrel of these cowards shall take it out of my hands." [41] So ended that fight, three hours long, in the Sault au Matelot.

But where was Montgomery? His tale of disaster is soon told.

He and some of his men, having overcome the obstacles in their way, came to a barricade. Saws went to work on it. Montgomery himself took a hand, tearing down the half-sawed posts. With Macpherson and Captain Cheesman at his side, he led the forlorn hope through and was confronted by a blockhouse. No more than fifty or sixty of his men followed him. The rest were still struggling with the difficulties of their road. Montgomery and his little band advanced against the blockhouse. No shot was fired from it. They passed it, went on for a hundred yards, came to another barrier, cut through it, rounded Point Diamond, entered on a narrow road, and saw another building before them, a dwelling house. It was loopholed, armed with four small guns, 3-pounders, and held by a corporal with eight British militiamen, a captain and thirty French Canadians, a ship captain, Adam Barnsfair, and nine sailors. John Coffin, a Boston Tory, was with them. Montgomery "called to his men to Come on; they did not advance as quick as he thought they might, he Spoke to them again in the following moving Terms, saying Come on my good soldiers, your General calls you to Come on." [42]

Coffin encouraged the men in the house to withhold their fire until the Americans, indistinctly seen in the darkness and snow, should come closer. Barnsfair and his men stood by their guns with lighted matches ready. Montgomery, Macpherson, and Cheesman, with Aaron Burr, Edward Antil, a sergeant, and a dozen men pushed forward. They were within a few paces of the house, when there came from it a burst of gunfire, grapeshot and bullets. Another burst and another raked the narrow street, until not one of that forlorn hope was left standing. In the snow lay a dozen men. Montgomery was dead, shot through the head. Macpherson and Cheesman lay beside him. Burr, Antil, and one or two others got away unhurt.

That was the end of the attack on the Cape Diamond end of the Lower Town. Colonel Donald Campbell took command and ordered a retreat. What was left of Montgomery's corps struggled back through the storm. Dearborn's belated company, trying to come up with Arnold's division, was caught on the road between two fires and surrendered. Carleton sent out a small force which seized the little battery at St. Roche, picking up Lamb's 6-pounder on the way.

Carleton captured 426 men, sound or wounded, including 30 officers and 5 gentlemen volunteers. The number killed or wounded and not captured may have been 60. The British loss was 5 killed and 13 wounded.[43] There were left to Arnold perhaps 600 men, including such Canadians and Indians as had joined him. Of these, more than 100 time-expired men soon left him, and there were other defections.

Arnold withdrew his little force about a mile, erected defences of frozen snow, and sent Edward Antil to Montreal for reinforcements. But General Wooster, in command there, had only five or six hundred men with whom to hold that town, as well as Chambly and St. Johns. No help could be had from him. Antil went on to Schuyler at Albany. But everything there was in confusion and alarm, because of Tory uprisings along the Mohawk and in Tryon County. There were no reinforcements available for Arnold. Antil went on to Philadelphia, to the Congress, bearing a letter from Schuyler. The Congress, on January 19, voted to reinforce the army in Canada "with all possible despatch," called on New Hampshire, Connecticut, New York, Pennsylvania, and New Jersey for troops for that purpose, and asked Washington to detach one battalion and send it north. It also authorized Moses Hazen to raise a regiment in Canada, Antil to be lieutenant colonel.[44]

From Montreal, Wooster sent 120 men near the end of January, and himself followed later with 60 more. In February, 25 came from Massachusetts. Hard money, some $28,000, was sent to encourage Arnold, now a brigadier general by grace of the Congress. Troops were coming from here and there, but slowly. In the middle of March, Arnold had 617 rank and file, besides Livingston's not very trustworthy Canadians. But smallpox had put 400 of Arnold's men in hospital, and every sort of supplies, food as well as military equipment, was lacking in Montreal and in Arnold's camp. Yet, all this while, Carleton made no move to attack those few hundreds who were still, with some success, blockading his town. He may have had in mind the fate of Montcalm's army, when it sallied out to meet Wolfe on those same Plains of Abraham. At all events he made no hostile move, but busied himself with strengthening his defensive works.

At last, on April 2, Wooster came to the camp with troops that made up the American force to 2,000 men. He took command. Arnold, injured by a fall from his horse, withdrew to Montreal. Wooster mounted batteries on the Heights and on Pointe Lévis and bombarded the town, to which it replied vigorously and with heavier metal. He also made an unsuccessful attempt to burn the vessels in the harbor by means of a fireship.

Early in May, Wooster was superseded by General John Thomas, a more capable, more energetic officer. He found the army, which had been built up to 2,500 men, now reduced by discharges, death, and desertions to 1,900, of whom no more than 1,000, including officers, were fit for duty. The time of 300 had already expired, and 200 more were under inoculation. No more than 500 could be relied upon. A mere ghost of an army was besieging a strongly fortified town of 5,000 inhabitants, mounting 148 cannon, with a garrison of 1,600 fit to fight, besides a frigate, a sloop of war, and several smaller armed vessels as auxiliaries. It was an absurd situation, yet Carleton remained within the walls.

More men were on their way to Thomas, the 2nd New Jersey Regiment and six companies of the 2nd Pennsylvania. Some of them had already arrived when, on May 2, there came bad news from the opposite quarter. A

British fleet, fifteen ships, had entered the mouth of the St. Lawrence. On the 7th, their masts and spars could be descried. General John Burgoyne was coming, with seven Irish regiments, one English, and 2,000 hired German mercenaries. That was the end of the siege of Quebec.

A force of 900 of the garrison, with four fieldpieces, issued from the town. Thomas, with difficulty, gathered a force of 250 to oppose it; his stand was but momentary. His whole army began to retreat, and in no orderly fashion. In a panic the gunners abandoned their pieces. The men under inoculation threw away their muskets and fled. The invalids in the hospital left their beds and stumbled and staggered toward the woods. The Canadian teamsters employed in the service of the army threw up their jobs and left. Clothing, provisions, and stores, even the orderly books and records in headquarters, had to be abandoned. Bateaux loaded with invalids and such stores as could be hastily gathered pushed up the St. Lawrence. Two tons of precious gunpowder, a hundred barrels of flour, and all the hospital stores were seized by the enemy, as they were about to be loaded into boats. One of the American regiments, across the river at Pointe Lévis, was intercepted and had to scatter into the woods. The main body marching on the road by the river, deep with mud, was divided for lack of food. Parties went here and there to levy on the inhabitants, took food by force. It was a mob of muddy, hungry, tired men, wounded men, men sick with smallpox, rather than an army, that streamed westward, leaving the dead and dying in its wake. Enemy ships passed them. Marines landed to cut them off, were driven back, and the struggle westward went on.

At Deschambault, forty miles up the river, Thomas halted his shattered forces and held a council of war. A stand at that point was voted down, and the retreat was resumed, to end at last on the 17th at Sorel, at the mouth of the Richelieu, where certain troops on their way to Quebec were met. Colonel William Maxwell's 2nd New Jersey, which had been left at Trois Rivières as a rear guard, was called in. The regiment which had fled from Pointe Lévis had made its way to the main force. So now all that was left of Thomas's army was gathered together in a disorganized mass, with hardly a trace of military system, "without order or regularity, eating up provisions as fast as they were brought in," [45] a mere mob.

Thomas described it: "A retreating army, disheartened by unavoidable misfortunes, destitute of almost every necessary to render their lives comfortable or even tolerable, sick and (as they think) wholly neglected and [with] no prospect of speedy relief." He himself was ill with the smallpox. There was nothing to do except to continue to retreat. On the 2nd of June, while his men were on the march up the Richelieu to Chambly, he died.

Moses Hazen, temporarily in command at Montreal in the absence of Arnold (who had gone down to Sorel and up the Richelieu with Thomas's force) directed Colonel Timothy Bedel, with 400 men, to hold a small, fortified post at the Cedars, about thirty miles above Montreal. With 150 English and Canadians and 500 Indians, Captain Forster marched against it. Bedel, suffering with the smallpox, went back to Montreal, leaving Major Isaac Butterfield in charge. On the arrival of Forster's troops, Butterfield surrendered without any real contest. A reinforcing American regiment under Major Henry Sherburne was waylaid and, after a gallant fight, overpowered and captured. Arnold, indignant at Butterfield's cowardice, took the field, met Forster, demanded and obtained the return of the captives by promising an exchange, and returned to Montreal.

But reinforcements for Thomas's sadly battered troops were on the way. Brigadier General William Thompson, formerly colonel of one of the Pennsylvania rifle regiments at Cambridge, was coming with a brigade of four regiments dispatched by Washington, comprising 2,000 musketmen, a company of riflemen, and one of artificers. Brigadier John Sullivan led a brigade of 3,300 from New York. He had been directed to take over Thomas's command. On June 1 he arrived at St. Johns, where Thompson's troops had been lying for two weeks. With the fresh and full supplies of food, ammunition, small arms, and cannon brought by these new troops, the prospects for a reinstatement of American fortunes in Canada seemed bright. Everybody was on tiptoe for a second march against Quebec.

The primary objective was to be Trois Rivières, about halfway between Montreal and Quebec, and the coveted stronghold. It was supposed to be held by no more than 800 regulars and Canadians under Maclean. Sullivan ordered Thompson to take it with 2,000 of the best of the Americans. On June 6 they embarked in bateaux and dropped down the river to a point ten miles above Trois Rivières. In the evening of the next day they embarked again for a night attack. William Maxwell, Anthony Wayne, Arthur St. Clair, William Irvine, all men of mettle, led their respective regiments. Thompson himself was a notable fighting man.

At three in the morning of June 8 they landed about three miles above the town. Leaving 250 men to guard the boats, they marched in silence, intending to attack at four points with St. Clair, Maxwell, Irvine, and Wayne leading the several detachments. They had for a guide a habitant, one Antoine Gautier. Whether intentionally or not, he misled them. They tried to recover the right road by going across country, got into a great swamp, and were completely mired. They floundered about in the slimy mud. Shoes and even boots were sucked off their feet. It was near daybreak when they got out and found the road along the shore and close to the river.

Two or three armed vessels fired on them as they came up. For three-quarters of a mile they were under a fire that, having no artillery, they could not return. They swung away into the woods, intending to make a circuit and to return to the road. But they got into "the most Horrid swamp that ever man set foot in," [46] sank in it up to their middles.

Warning of their approach had been brought to the town. A surprise was no longer possible. But they had been told by the Congress that it was "of the highest importance that a post be taken at De Chambeaux." [47] Washington had said to Thomas, "The lower down [the river] you can maintain a stand the more advantageous it will be." He had said, too, that the Quebec "misfortune must be repaired," [48] and Trois Rivières was the first step to that end. They kept on.

For two or three hours they fought their way through the swamp and the tangled forest. At eight o'clock they saw a clearing a quarter of a mile ahead, firm ground. They had been divided, even scattered, in the swampy jungle. Wayne, with 200 men, got out first and saw a body of regulars bearing down upon him.

He threw forward a company of light infantry and one of riflemen, formed the rest, and opened fire. The enemy, twice as many as they, gave back, broke, and fled. Thompson and the rest of his force came out and saw the village lying between them and the river. But between it and themselves they also saw a line of entrenchments. Burgoyne with more than 8,000 men was on his way up the St. Lawrence, and perhaps three-quarters of them had arrived at Trois Rivières.

The Americans attacked, probably not aware of the odds they faced. A heavy fire from the ships and from the trenches converged upon them. It was impossible to advance against it. They fell back into the woods. Thompson tried to rally them for another effort, but they were scattered and disorganized. An irregular fire was kept up for a time. Then the inevitable retreat began.

A British force was landed from the ships above them to cut them off. They could not escape by the road, and another column was coming against their rear. Broken up into larger or smaller parties, each acting for itself, now making a stand and now retreating, they left the road, took to the woods. They were stalked by Indians, ambushed by Canadian irregulars. Through endless swamps and a wilderness of forest, they fled northward for two days. Major Grant held against them their only gateway of escape, the bridge across the Rivière du Loup. Carleton might have captured them

all, but he did not want them. What would he do with them? He had no
provisions to spare, nor were there any in Quebec. Let them go and tell of
his mercy to the people at home. He recalled Grant from the bridge, and
on the third day after the battle, the remains of that proud little army, 1,100
men "almost worn out with fatigue, Hunger & Difficulties scarcely to be
paralleled," [49] their faces and hands swollen by the stings of "Musketoes of
a Monstrous size and innumerable numbers" reached Sorel.

Their losses are not ascertainable. In spite of his prudent leniency Carleton found that he had 236 prisoners on his hands, men who had given themselves up rather than attempt a seemingly impossible escape. The guards of
the Americans' bateaux had escaped in their boats. About 400 in all were
killed, captured, or lost in the woods and swamps. The British lost in killed
and wounded about a dozen.

There were supposed to be 8,000 American troops in all the Champlain
and St. Lawrence regions; but, because of the inroads of the smallpox and
the results of fatigue and deprivation, not 5,000 could have been counted
as effectives, even by straining that term to the limit, before the affair at
Trois Rivières. After it, nearly half of that number, six of the freshest regiments, had been routed, cut to pieces, and completely demoralized. Supplies
of every kind, including food, were lacking, as usual. To get them up from
New York would take weeks at best. There was no money to buy provisions
in Canada. And over 8,000 hearty, well furnished British regulars were
gathering at Trois Rivières. They might march around Sorel to Chambly
and bottle up Sullivan's army on the Richelieu below, then cut off Arnold's
force at Chambly. They were, in fact, on June 13, on their way up the river
by land and in transports.

A letter from Sullivan to Schuyler describes the plight of his army. He
wanted to hold Sorel, he said, but he had only 2,500 men there and 1,000
at other posts, "most of the latter being under inoculation, and those regiments, which had not the small-pox, expecting every day to be taken down
with it." The enemy's force was reported to be "exceedingly superior to
ours," which was certainly true. "I found myself at the head of a dispirited
Army, filled with horror at the thought of seeing their enemy. . . . Smallpox, famine and disorder had rendered them almost lifeless. . . . I found
a great panick . . . among both officers and soldiers . . . no less than
40 officers begged leave to resign. . . . However strongly I might fortify
Sorel, my men would in general leave me." [50]

Even the aggressive Arnold thought there was "more honour in making
a safe retreat than in hazarding a battle against such superiority." "The junction of the Canadas is now at an end," he wrote to Schuyler. "Let us quit

them and secure our own country before it is too late." [51] There was no doubt in anyone's mind that the game was up.

It was by a close margin that the Americans got away at all. The British fleet was at Sorel within an hour after the last of Sullivan's bateaux pulled away up the Richelieu. Arnold, back at Montreal, held on to that town to the last moment. Then, with the remains of its garrison, no more than 300 men, he crossed the river to Longueuil and set out for St. Johns, with the enemy close at his heels.[52]

The two forces having been joined, the whole army, if that mob of hungry, ragged, beaten men, discouraged, disorganized, and rotten with smallpox, could still be called an "army," crowded into boats sent up by Schuyler and pushed off for Ile aux Noix. They were hardly out of musket shot when the van of their pursuers arrived on the shore.[53]

Ile aux Noix is a low, flat island, about a mile long and a quarter-mile wide. A single farm occupied a slight elevation in the middle of it. The rest was a brush-covered waste, with swamps here and there. On this unwholesome desert the 8,000 wretched fugitives disembarked. Two thousand of them were hospital cases already, smallpox cases. Within two days after they landed, a quarter of the rest were stricken with malarial fever or dysentery.

There were not tents enough to shelter even the desperately sick men. Frequent thunderstorms drenched those that lay under rude shelters thatched with brush and grass. Mosquitoes and black flies swarmed in millions, tormenting and torturing sick and well alike. There was no food except salt pork and flour, and not enough wood for fires to cook even that. Medicines gave out. The few surgeons were exhausted. The moans and groans of the sick, of the dying men tortured by the itching and burning of that most loathsome disease, smallpox, could be heard everywhere. And they died like flies. Common grave pits were opened and filled day after day with corpses wrapped in their filthy blankets.

The sights and sounds of that pest-ridden camp were unbearable. Officers, unable longer to stand them, gathered in groups and deliberately drank themselves into insensibility. To stay there was to invite complete destruction. The helplessly sick were bundled into the boats. The half-sick took to the oars. Humiliated by defeat, enfeebled by fatigue, hunger, hardship, and disease, utterly demoralized in every respect, the wreck of a once proud little army rowed away from that island of death.

In the first days of July, Crown Point saw them again, what was left of them. So they came back to that place whence Montgomery had set out, just ten months before, to conquer Canada.

CHAPTER 15

Washington in New York

Washington's uncertainty as to the destination of the British fleet and army at the evacuation of Boston on March 17, 1776, did not deter him from promptly moving to defend New York, which he thought might be next attacked by the enemy. On the 18th he dispatched to that city a Pennsylvania rifle regiment, three companies of Virginia riflemen, and General Heath's brigade. Sullivan's brigade followed on the 29th, then Greene's and Spencer's, and Knox's artillery, in quick succession. Putnam was sent down to take general command. Five regiments were left in Boston under General Artemas Ward. On April 13 Washington himself was in New York.[1]

On June 20, 1775, when Washington had been directed by the Continental Congress to take command of "the Army of the united Colonies," it was in fact an army of the four New England colonies only. Except the few hundred riflemen from Pennsylvania, Maryland, and Virginia who joined him in July and August, 1775, no troops from the other colonies came to reinforce him. When the movement against Canada was begun it was evident that additional troops would be needed. On July 25, the Congress resolved that "a body of forces not exceeding five thousand be kept up in the New York department," [2] but no specific plan for raising them was provided. That was left to the New York Provincial Congress. Not before October did the Continental Congress begin to plan for and provide a real Continental army. On the 2nd of that month it authorized a committee to go to Cambridge and consult with Washington on the subject.[3] On November 4 the report of that committee was considered, and it was resolved that "the new army intended to lie before Boston" should consist of 20,372 men, officers included, enlisted "to the last day of December, 1776." [4]

202

It appears that Washington had agreed to a one-year term of enlistment on the advice of a council of his general officers, who thought it would be "impossible to get the men to enlist for the continuance of the War," [5] but it also appears that the one-year term was contrary to his own judgment. In a letter to Joseph Reed dated February 1, 1776, he enlarged upon "the evils arising from short, or even any limited enlistment." It took, he said, two or three months to acquaint new men with their duty, and even a longer time to bring them into "such a subordinate way of thinking as is necessary for a soldier." By that time the end of the enlistment period is in sight, and "you are obliged to relax in your discipline, in order as it were to curry favour with them" so as to induce them to reenlist. And "with every new set you have the same trouble to encounter." The disadvantages of the one-year period were so great that it would be better "to give a bounty of 20, 30 or even 40 Dollars to every man who will Inlist for the whole time." [6]

He rehearsed this argument in a letter to the Congress dated February 9, 1776, pointing out that the apprehension of his troops leaving him on December 31 had driven Montgomery to his fatal attack on Quebec "under disadvantageous circumstances." He also referred to his own experience in having to dissolve his army at the end of 1775, the evils of which he forcefully particularized. Under such a system, he said, "you never can have a well Disciplined army." [7]

Washington's arguments were and are cogent and convincing to one with an open and unprejudiced mind, but the collective mind of the Americans of that period was not unprejudiced. In an overwhelming majority they were of British extraction. Their ancestors had, to a large extent, left England at the time when the Stuart kings were seeking to create a standing army to oppress the people and deprive them of civil and religious liberty. Cromwell had defeated the Stuarts, only to use his own troops as instruments of tyranny. By both sides of the civil conflict in England, the idea of a standing army was hated and dreaded, and that dread and hatred was an inheritance of their descendants in America. An army for the duration of the war was at this time impossible of acceptance by the general run of the colonists.

But the Congress had not awaited the report of its committee before going ahead. On October 9, 1775, it had "recommended to the Convention of New Jersey, that it immediately raise, at the expense of the Continent two Battalions, consisting of eight companies each, and each company of 68 privates." [8] Three days later a similar "recommendation" for one battalion was made to Pennsylvania, and calls were soon after made on North Carolina for six battalions, on Pennsylvania for four more, on Delaware for one, on Virginia for nine, on Rhode Island for two, on Massachusetts for six, on New Hampshire for two, on South Carolina for five, including one regiment of artillery and one of rangers, on Maryland for two, and on Georgia for one regiment of rangers. It also requested a "German battalion" of eight companies, four to be raised in Pennsylvania and four in Maryland.[9]

Slowly and gradually building up the Continental army, the Congress sought in addition to provide temporary additional reinforcements for "the army at New York." On June 3, 1776, Massachusetts, Connecticut, New York, and New Jersey were called upon for 13,800 militiamen. As a defense for "the middle colonies" a Flying Camp was to be established. Ten thousand militia were called for, 6,000 from Pennsylvania, 3,400 from Maryland, and 600 from Delaware. Perth Amboy in New Jersey was chosen as the site of the camp. Without going fully into the history of this attempt, it may be said that it was a failure. There was an insufficient response to the appeal, and the militia that did respond made but a short stay. Two Continental regiments—one from Maryland, the other from Delaware—were called upon to strengthen this force, but they remained only a few days before they were sent on to New York. By the end of the year, the Flying Camp passed out of existence.[10]

The regiments of the Continental army were to consist of eight companies of 76 privates each, with the usual officers, noncommissioned officers, drum, and fife. The pay and provisions were sufficiently generous according to the standards of the time. The pay for the officers ranged from $50 a month for a colonel to $13⅓ for an ensign. Privates were to receive $6⅔; but out of this sum there were stoppages for clothing furnished them at the rate of $1⅔ per month. Their uniforms were "as much as possible" to be brown, with different regimental facings. They were to receive "good firelocks with bayonets," each musket having a ¾ inch bore, the barrel 3 feet, 8 inches long, the bayonet 18 inches. Their rations were prescribed in detail: "1 lb. of beef, or ¾ lb. pork, or 1 lb. of salt fish . . . 1 lb. of bread or flour" daily, also a pint of milk and a quart of spruce beer or cider per day, with a weekly allowance of peas, beans, or other vegetables, rice or Indian meal, candles, and soap.[11] It needed hardly be said that these provisions for uniforms, arms, and rations, made in a hopeful spirit were seldom realized in fact.

In uniforms, there was little uniformity. Many of the regiments were supplied at the time of enlistment according to their own fancy. The soldiers of Delaware's regiment, for instance, were handsomely turned out in blue coats, faced and lined with red, white waistcoats, buckskin breeches, white woolen stockings, and black spatterdashes or gaiters. They wore small, round, blackjacked leather hats without a visor, but with a peaked front, somewhat after the fashion of the taller hats of the British grenadiers. They were armed with fine English muskets "lately imported," complete with bayonets.[12] But that regiment was said to be "the best uniformed and equipped in the army of 1776." [13] Smallwood's Maryland regiment is frequently described as arrayed in scarlet coats faced with buff; but, although that was its dress uniform at home, only the officers wore it in the Long Island battle, the privates appearing in brown hunting shirts. In the rest of the army military uniforms were rather the exception than the rule. The riflemen usually wore the conventional hunting shirt of gray or brown tow cloth, though Miles's men wore black.[14] The standards for muskets fixed by the Congress were not achieved at this time, nor were they ever in the whole course of the war. They differed in caliber, greatly to the disadvantage of the troops, since no standard size of bullets or cartridges could be maintained. Also bayonets were scarce, and continued to be so to the war's end.

Washington was impressed with the importance of holding New York against the British army. "It is the Place that we must use every Endeavour to keep from them," he wrote to Brigadier General Lord Stirling, who had been left in command there on General Charles Lee's departure for the South early in 1776. "For should they get that Town, and the Command of the North River, they can stop the Intercourse between the northern and southern Colonies, upon which depends the Safety of America." It would also give them "an easy pass into Canada." Its retention by the Americans was of "vast importance," of "infinite importance." [15] So, in spite of the great difficulty of fortifying it against "a powerful sea armament," as Lee had pointed out on his first arrival in New York, Washington concentrated most of his forces there, and busied himself exceedingly with its defensive works.

The town was small in extent, occupying about a square mile at the southern tip of Manhattan Island. Lee, who had been sent down to supervise its defenses, had planned to erect in and about it an elaborate system of forts, redoubts, batteries, entrenchments, and barricades. As they played no part in the actual battle for its possession, they need not be described here, except to note that numerous batteries were to be erected on both sides of the North and East rivers to prevent, or at least to hinder, the passage of enemy vessels to the northward of the town. Lee's opinion early in 1776 was that New York could not be indefinitely defended against the British, but that the British could be made to pay for possession of it.

He had had at first only 1,700 men to work on these extensive defenses. But before he left in March others had come in from Connecticut, New

Jersey, and the outlying districts of New York, and Stirling carried on with them. All the men of the town, white and black, were called out, and a prodigious amount of pick-and-shovel work was done by them and by the troops from Boston when they arrived. But, to defend the town, it was necessary to go beyond its limits and the limits of Manhattan Island.

Directly across the East River lay Long Island, and particularly the little village of Brooklyn and its environs. Brooklyn Heights rose a hundred feet above the water. A recollection of the domination of Boston by Dorchester Heights and of the effect of their occupation by the Americans in making that town untenable was not needed to convince Lee of the importance of these others in the scheme of defense. He had proposed to secure them by "a post or retrenched encampment" [16] for 3,000 men. This work was immediately begun.

The ground chosen was a broad, irregularly shaped peninsula facing the East River and lying between Wallabout Bay on the northeast and Gowanus Cove on the southwest. Those two bodies of water indented the sides of the peninsula, making a neck of land about a mile and a half wide. An irregularly curved zigzag line of entrenchments was drawn from the bay to Gowanus Creek. At the upper end Fort Putnam, a redoubt with five guns, was erected. From a point near the fort, the entrenchments turned at a right angle to the main line and ran to the bay. From the fort, at intervals along the main line to Gowanus Creek, there were built redoubts called, in order, Fort Greene, the Oblong Redoubt, and Fort Box. Each of these works was armed with a few guns.

Within the lines and nearer the river was Fort Stirling, armed with eight guns. On Red Hook, the extreme westerly corner of the fortified peninsula, was Fort Defiance, mounting four 18-pounders and intended to prevent the passage of ships between that point and Governor's Island. There were also two other small works of minor importance. In all they mounted twenty-nine guns, most of them of iron, old and honeycombed with rust.

These forts and the main line of earthworks were ditched and fraised with sharpened stakes set into their embankments, crossing each other and projecting outward at an angle, their points breast-high. The main line was also defended by a broad area of abatis, felled trees, their butts embedded in the ground, their pointed limbs thrust outward. The work of constructing all these defenses, in the town as well as on Long Island, was performed under the supervision of Brigadier General Lord Stirling, a vigorous and energetic officer.

William Alexander, "Earl of Stirling," was not an earl, nor was he a nobleman of any degree. His father, James Stirling, had fled to America in

1716 to escape the consequences of his activities in the cause of the Old Pretender in the year before, and had attained some eminence in his new home as a lawyer, politician, and scientist. William, his only son, was born in 1726. He had engaged in business profitably, and had served as a major of colonial forces in the French and Indian War. His father claimed to be heir to the lapsed title of James Alexander, 1st Earl of Stirling, through some degree of cousinship, but had taken no steps to assert his right on the death of that nobleman in 1737.

When his father died, in 1756, William laid legal claim to the earldom. When his case was first tried in Edinburgh, a jury found in his favor, and he was proclaimed earl at the Market Cross. The decision was reversed in the House of Lords, but he continued to assert his right to the title, and was so addressed in America throughout his life.

In person Stirling "showed a burly figure, and a fresh-coloured visage." [17] He was fond of sociability, and his detractors accused him of undue fondness for the bottle; but it does not appear that this ever lessened his efficiency in his military duties, at least not until evening. He was conspicuous for personal bravery in action. The officers on Long Island gave him "the character of as brave a man as ever lived." [18] He prided himself on his acquaintance with the technical side of his profession. Early in the war he was noted for maintaining a harsh and captious discipline. However, he "shook off the martinet, and became a practical soldier of considerable value in the field. . . . there was sure to be plenty of tough and steady fighting in the quarter towards which Stirling and his division had been ordered." [19]

At the time of Washington's arrival in New York, his army there consisted of twenty-five regiments, numbering about 9,000 rank and file. These he divided into five brigades, under Heath, Spencer, Sullivan, Greene, and Stirling. But, before the end of April, Sullivan was ordered to Canada with six regiments as has been mentioned. The rest were rearranged in four brigades, three of them posted on Manhattan Island, one on Long Island. With such of the militia as had responded to the call of the Congress on June 3, with the return of what was left of Sullivan's detachment, and with the arrival of other Continental regiments from the Flying Camp, the army had been increased to a paper strength of about 28,500 of all ranks by the late summer of 1776. Of these, about 19,000 were present and fit for duty, but the larger part of them were raw recruits, undisciplined and inexperienced in warfare, and militia, never to be assuredly relied upon.[20]

A new arrangement divided this force again into five divisions before the Battle of Long Island. James Clinton's brigade of four Massachusetts regiments, John Morin Scott's four regiments from New York, and John

Fellows's four regiments from Massachusetts made up Israel Putnam's division. The second division, under William Heath, contained Thomas Mifflin's brigade of two Pennsylvania regiments, two regiments from Massachusetts, and one from Rhode Island, also George Clinton's brigade of five New York regiments. Joseph Spencer's division included the brigade of Samuel Holden Parsons—four regiments from Connecticut and one from Massachusetts—and James Wadsworth's seven Connecticut regiments. John Sullivan, who had returned from Canada, commanded a division composed of Lord Stirling's brigade—one Maryland regiment, one from Delaware, a Pennsylvania rifle regiment, a Pennsylvania musketry battalion, and three corps of Pennsylvania militia—and Alexander McDougall's brigade, two regiments from New York, one from Connecticut, and one of artificers. Nathanael Greene had in his division John Nixon's brigade of three Massachusetts regiments, two from Rhode Island, and one from Pennsylvania, Nathaniel Heard's brigade of five New Jersey regiments, Oliver Wolcott's brigade of twelve regiments of Connecticut militia, and Nathaniel Woodhull's two regiments of Long Island militia. Colonel Henry Knox commanded the artillery.

Up to a short time before the battle, Putnam's, Spencer's, and Sullivan's divisions, with the Connecticut militiamen, say 20,000 in all, were posted in and about the city. Heath's division was separated into several parts; Mifflin's brigade of 2,400 men was on Manhattan Island at Fort Washington, and George Clinton's 1,800 were at Kingsbridge. Two regiments of Greene's division were on Governor's Island. Greene himself, with the rest, fewer than 4,000, was on Long Island.[21]

Long before Howe evacuated Boston, it became apparent even to the British government that the plans for subduing the American colonies had been conceived on too small a scale; Howe's 7,000 men were not enough to do the job. By October, 1775, the plans had been enlarged to call for a total British army of 55,000 men, and an addition of 12,000 men to the navy. Recruiting was begun in all parts of the British Isles; but, as an English historian says, there was in Britain "hardly any enthusiasm for the war among the classes from which soldiers were drawn." Ireland was combed, but the Irish were enjoying a year of unprecedented agricultural prosperity. Food was plentiful; hunger, the usual incentive to enlistment, was unknown. Scotland showed better results. There were many land-hungry Highlanders who hoped to appease their desires in the vast acres of a conquered America. But on the whole the enlistments were not enough. It was necessary to look elsewhere.[22]

The petty princes of Germany had soldiers for rent. From the Duke of Brunswick, the Landgrave of Hesse-Kassel, and the Prince of Waldeck, England hired at this time 17,775 men to be shipped to America, where they were all called by one hated name, Hessians. Others were added in the course of the war to a total number of 29,875.[23]

On June 25 three warships arrived in lower New York Bay, bringing General Howe from Halifax to the scene of his next conflict—for him, more fortunate. He hoped to use New York as a base for the conquest of the colonies. He had only a small force, but it was the forerunner of a greater soon to come. Four days later its real magnitude began to develop. Forty-five more ships hove in sight, and in another day eighty-two appeared. One hundred and thirty ships of war and transports disembarked 9,300 soldiers on Staten Island. But this was not all. Admiral Lord Howe, brother of the general, followed with a fleet of one hundred fifty sail, full of fighting men fresh from England. On July 12 they joined the others. A little later Admiral Sir Peter Parker, with nine warships and thirty transports bearing 2,500 men under General Henry Clinton and General Lord Cornwallis, came limping northward from their defeat at Charleston. Commodore Hotham brought six men-of-war and twenty-eight transports on August 12, and disembarked 2,600 of the Guards and 8,000 Hessians.[24]

In the British camp on Staten Island, across the Narrows from Long Island, there were twenty-seven regiments of the line, four battalions of light infantry, four of grenadiers, two of the Guards, three brigades of artillery, one regiment of light dragoons, and 8,000 Hessians, with Major General Howe and Generals Clinton, Lord Percy, Lord Cornwallis, and von Heister, all of them skilled in the science of war and the art of command. It was an army of 32,000 trained, disciplined, professional soldiers, completely armed, fully equipped, abundantly supplied—the greatest expeditionary force Great Britain had ever sent out from its shores. It was supported by a fleet of ten ships of the line, twenty frigates armed with 1,200 guns, and hundreds of transports, manned by more than 10,000 seamen. Britain had drawn from her war chest the staggering sum of £850,000.

To oppose this mighty force the Americans had 19,000 largely untrained, undisciplined, untried amateur soldiers, poorly armed, meagerly equipped and supplied, led by an amateur commander in chief, who was supported by amateur officers. They were backed by not a single warship nor a single transport, and their war chest was in large part a printing press in Philadelphia emitting issues of paper dollars, worth whatever one could induce another to give for them and diminishing in value day by day. To be sure they

now had something very specific for which to fight, because independence
had been declared early in July.

To make matters worse for the Americans, their inadequate force was
divided between New York and Long Island with the broad expanse of the
East River separating them, and with no means whatever of keeping open
a line of communication if British warships were interposed.

In their camp the British soldiers were unseen by the Americans; but
their fleet was only too visible. "Onlookers gazed with awe on a pageant
such as America had never seen before—five hundred dark hulls, forests
of masts, a network of spars and ropes and a gay display of flying pennants.
There were ships of the line with frowning sides, three tiers of guns and
high forecastles; there were graceful frigates, alert and speedy . . . tenders
and galleys to land the thousands of men from the unwieldy transports." [25]
It is no wonder that panic fear was in the hearts of half of New York's people, and gleams of joy were in the eyes of the other half, who were opposed
to independence and who supported the British.

The first definitely threatening move was made by two warships, the
Phoenix of forty-four guns and the *Rose* of twenty-eight. On July 12, with
two tenders, they stood in toward the town. In the American camp the
alarm was sounded; the troops took their posts. As the ships swept by the
town on their way up the North River, the batteries there and those on
Paulus Hook—now Jersey City—opened fire. The ships replied with broadsides.[26] Throughout the town there was a mad panic. Washington described
its effect on the women: "When the men-of-war passed up the river, the
shrieks and cries of the poor creatures, running every way with their children, were truly distressing, and I fear they will have an unhappy effect on
the ears and minds of our young and inexperienced soldiery." [27]

Past battery after battery, batteries that were supposed to prevent their
passage, the ships held their course to Tappan Bay, forty miles above the
town. Fireships were sent against them, with no success. Six days later,
they came back, running the same gantlet and anchored again in the Narrows, practically unharmed.[28]

It seems that the whole fleet, or any part of it, might have landed troops
at any time on the north end of Manhattan Island and cut off the whole
American army from any possible retreat, to bag it at leisure. Nothing of
the sort was done, however, and, from the time of the first arrival of the
British, what form the attack would take, whether against New York or
against Long Island, remained an open question, puzzling and harassing to
the American command. It was at last answered.

CHAPTER 16

Long Island: The Preliminaries

At dawn on the 22nd of August three British frigates, *Phoenix, Rose* and *Greyhound,* and two bomb ketches, *Carcass* and *Thunder,* took station in Gravesend Bay, Long Island, about a mile east of the Narrows. Another frigate, *Rainbow,* anchored in the Narrows off Denyse Point, the part of Long Island nearest to Staten Island. Seventy-five flatboats, eleven bateaux, and two row-galleys, built for the occasion and manned by sailors from the fleet, were assembled at Staten Island, and 15,000 soldiers, fully equipped for active service, and forty fieldpieces were drawn up before the British camp.[1]

At eight o'clock in the morning a British advance corps, consisting of four battalions of light infantry and Preston's 17th Light Dragoons, and a reserve, four battalions of grenadiers, the 33rd and the 42nd, or Black Watch Regiment, and Colonel Carl von Donop's corps of Hessian grenadiers and jägers, 4,000 men in all under the command of Clinton and Cornwallis, embarked. In ten well ordered divisions they were rowed across to Denyse Point. Under cover of the guns of the *Rainbow* they went ashore and were drawn up in military formation. The next trip of the boats brought 5,000 more men to a point below the others, which was under the guns of the three frigates and the two bomb ketches. By noon 15,000 men had been landed without opposition, mishap, or delay.[2] Three days later, on the 25th, they were joined by two brigades of Hessian grenadiers under General Philip von Heister, "a tough old soldier of the Seven Years War." [3] These were ferried over standing in the boats, "with muskets sloped and in column of march, preserving the well-considered pomp of German discipline." [4]

211

"The Soldiers & Sailors seemed as merry as in a Holiday, and regaled themselves with the fine apples, which hung everywhere upon the Trees in great abundance." [5]

There was no American opposition whatever to any of these landings. Colonel Edward Hand and 200 men of the 1st Pennsylvania Continental Regiment had been in camp in an outpost near Denyse Point. On the first alarm they marched toward New Utrecht, "to watch the movements of the enemy," who were soon discovered approaching them on the way to Flatbush. Hand turned, and marched parallel with the enemy advance guard, but at a respectful distance from it, "in the edge of the woods." Finding "it impracticable for so small a force to attack them," [6] he sent a detachment ahead to burn all the standing grain and slaughter as many cattle as possible, while his main body returned to its camp, gathered up its baggage, and after some light skirmishing, took up a position on Prospect Hill.

Cornwallis, with the reserve, ten battalions of light infantry and von Donop's Hessians, possessed the village of Flatbush and camped there.[7] The main body encamped nearer the shore, along the road running from near the bay in the vicinity of Gravesend to New Utrecht. Its camp extended from that village on the west to Flatlands village on the east.[8]

The British now occupied a broad, low plain extending from the shore northward from four to six miles and eastward a greater distance. In it lay the four villages named. Looking north from their camp, the invaders faced the most prominent feature of the terrain, which was to be their battleground.

Stretching northeast from near the waterside at Gowanus Cove nearly all the way across the island and forming a barrier between the British army and the Brooklyn defenses, ran a ridge or range of hills, varying in height from one hundred to one hundred fifty feet. It was called the Heights of Guan, or Guian. On the southerly side, fronting the British, the rugged face of the heights rose abruptly forty to eighty feet from the plain, then ascended less precipitously to the full height of the ridge. On the northerly side the ground sloped more gradually to the lower land beyond. The entire surface of the ridge was covered by dense woods and thickets penetrable only with difficulty by men on foot, entirely impassable by horse-drawn artillery or by troops in formation except at four points where roads led through natural depressions or "passes." One of the roads circumvented the westerly end of the main ridge; the others went through at different points toward the east.[9]

The first road, to the left of the British, starting at Gravesend ran westerly through New Utrecht to a point near the shore of the Narrows, then turned north parallel with the shore, finally quite close to the edge of Gowanus Cove, and so around the westerly end of the ridge on its way to Brooklyn. It was called the Gowanus Road. The second ran from Flatbush almost due north, through Flatbush Pass, then split in two, both branches coming finally to Brooklyn. The third road took off from the second just before Flatbush Pass, swung to the east, then to the north, and ran through Bedford Pass to the village of Bedford, whence a straight road ran to Brooklyn. These three roads accounted for more than three miles of the length of the ridge between the westerly and easterly passes. The fourth ran northeast from Flatlands to Jamaica Pass, nearly three miles east of Bedford Pass.[10] These four passes, with their respective roads, were obviously to be defended in force if any attempt was made to hold the ridge against an advance from the south.

After the arrival of the British on Staten Island there were changes in the command of the American troops on Long Island. Major General Nathanael Greene fell ill of a fever and took to his bed in New York. On August 20 Washington turned the command of the troops about Brooklyn over to Major General John Sullivan. This change was unfortunate, because Greene, a much abler general officer, had a thorough knowledge of the Long Island terrain, while Sullivan knew little of the lay of the land. Still more unfortunate was another change, made on the 24th, by which Major General Israel Putnam superseded Sullivan in general command on Long Island, Sullivan being retained there as a subordinate.[11] Putnam, who knew practically nothing of the topography of the island, was for other reasons totally unfit for the controlling position into which he had been put.[12]

There were changes in the forces defending the Brooklyn position as well. Immediately on receiving news in New York of the landing of the British on the 22nd, Washington sent over Miles's Pennsylvania riflemen, Atlee's Pennsylvania musketry battalion, Chester's and Silliman's newly raised Connecticut regiments, Lasher's New York Independent companies, and Drake's New York minutemen, about 1,800 men in all.[13] There were consequently about 5,800 men in and about the Brooklyn lines; but more than two-thirds of these were militia, not dependable even behind entrenchments and totally unreliable in a stand-up fight in an open field. Even the loyalty of the New York and Long Island contingents was seriously suspected.[14]

Although Washington knew of the landing of some of the enemy on Long Island, he was led to think, even as late as the 24th, that they amounted to no more than eight or nine thousand, a minor part of the whole force. Therefore, expecting an attack on "our works on the Island and this city at the same time," [15] he retained three-quarters of his whole army on the New York side, including many of the better regiments. Any respectable intelligence service, of which he had at this time almost none, could have told him that the major part of the British army and all its best general officers were on Long Island, and that without doubt the grand attack, the only immediate attack, was to be made on Brooklyn. Nevertheless he did send over other reinforcements, Parsons's Connecticut Continentals, Lutz's Berks County (Pennsylvania) militia, Hay's militia from Lancaster County, and Kachlein's Berks riflemen, perhaps fewer than 2,000 in all. These Pennsylvania militiamen were about half of Stirling's brigade, and Stirling crossed with them, leaving his best two, his only thoroughly dependable regiments, Smallwood's Maryland and Haslet's Delaware Continentals, in camp on the Manhattan side.[16]

Washington expected an immediate attack after the British had settled themselves on Long Island; but Howe was in no hurry. There was brisk skirmishing in front of Flatbush Pass on the 23rd. At the same time von Donop's Hessians made a move against Bedford Pass, evidently to try it out; but they met a sharp fire from Hand's corps, which advanced to meet the enemy, drove them back, and burned some houses they had held. They returned in force and regained their former position, the Americans retiring to their post on the ridge. From the ridge on the following day the Americans harassed the Flatbush camp with round shot and grape from their field-pieces. But the heavier artillery of the Hessians soon silenced them. There were few casualties on either side.[17]

In the afternoon of the 26th Cornwallis, leaving the Black Watch and the Hessians in the Flatbush camp, moved the rest of his troops to Flatlands village, where the British headquarters had been established. The Hessian General von Heister, who had landed the day before with two brigades, took over the command at Flatbush.[18] This movement to Flatlands might have indicated to an intelligent observer that neither the Flatbush nor the Bedford Pass was to be the scene of the main attack, because it shifted the weight of the British force away from them; but none of the Americans on the ridge seems to have understood its meaning.

By this time, however, Washington had come over from New York. At last he realized that the strength of the British was on Long Island, and that "the grand push" was to be against Brooklyn.[19] He ordered more men over, Lieutenant Colonel Thomas Knowlton with 100 Connecticut Continentals, two or three independent companies from Maryland, and, most important, Smallwood's Maryland and Haslet's Delaware Continental regiments, the best equipped and (the Delawares) the largest in the army. By a singular coincidence the Smallwood and Haslet regiments arrived under command of their majors, Mordecai Gist for Maryland and Thomas McDonough for Delaware; their colonels and lieutenant colonels had been detailed to sit in a court-martial in New York on that day. Now Stirling's brigade was complete in its camp outside the Brooklyn lines. By these additions, Putnam's command on Long Island was built up to about 7,000 men fit for duty.[20] On the evening of the 26th the coast, or Gowanus, road was guarded by Hand's 200 of the 1st Pennsylvania Regiment, half of Atlee's Pennsylvania musketry battalion, some part of Lutz's Pennsylvanians, and certain detachments of New York troops, perhaps 550 in all. On their left, more than a mile and a half distant at the Flatbush Pass, the center of the line, were Daniel Hitchcock's Rhode Island and Moses Little's Massachusetts Continental regiments, commanded, respectively, by their lieutenant colonels, Elias Cornell and William Henshaw, and Knowlton's detachment of Connecticut Continentals, perhaps fewer than 1,000 in all. They held a rude fortification of felled trees, mounting three guns and one howitzer.

At the Bedford Pass about a mile to the east were stationed Colonel Samuel Wyllys and his Connecticut Continentals and Colonel John Chester's Connecticut State Regiment, under command of Lieutenant Colonel Solomon Wills, about 800 men, with three guns and a fortification like that at Flatbush Pass; also Colonel Samuel Miles with about 400 Pennsylvania riflemen. Thus there were probably fewer than 2,800 men in all posted along more than three miles of the densely wooded ridge in separate detachments, with no communication between them except by sentinels stationed at intervals. It was a long line and a thin line; pierced at any point, it must give way. Facing them on the plain below were seven times their number; in military efficiency, man for man, one might say fifteen times their number.

But what about Jamaica Pass, three miles to the east of the Bedford road? It was guarded, too—by a mounted patrol of five young militia officers. While the right of this long line rested on Gowanus Cove, its left was in the air.[21]

CHAPTER 17

Long Island: The Battle

At about midnight on the 26th of August, Hand's Pennsylvanians, who had been on constant duty for four days picketing the American right, were relieved by a detail of Kachlein's and Hay's troops under Major Edward Burd. Hand's men, "not having lain down the whole time and almost dead with fatigue," [1] retired to the fortified lines to rest. Now all was quiet along the American front; but on the British side something was happening.

At the far left of the British positions, near the Narrows, lay Major General James Grant with his two brigades, 5,000 strong.[2] In the center von Heister's Hessians and the Scottish Black Watch still occupied Flatbush. But the main body of the British army had been massed at Flatlands. All these were astir that night.

At nine o'clock in the evening a column of march was formed at the principal post at Flatlands. General Henry Clinton led the van, made up of the 17th Light Dragoons and a brigade of light infantry. General Lord Cornwallis came next with the reserve—that is to say, the 1st Brigade of four battalions of grenadiers, two regiments of foot, and the 71st (Fraser's Highlanders), with fourteen pieces of field artillery. After them fell in General William Howe and General Lord Percy with the main body—the Guards and three brigades of infantry comprising twelve regiments, with ten guns. Bringing up the rear were one regiment and the baggage train with its guard and four guns. In this column were 10,000 soldiers and twenty-eight pieces of artillery.[3]

Led by three Tories from Flatbush, this formidable array set out on the road to the Jamaica Pass. Proceeding with the utmost caution, it left the

216

THE BATTLE OF LONG ISLAND
August 27, 1776
at 8–9 o'clock A.M.

KEY { AMERICAN TROOPS
BRITISH TROOPS
HESSIAN TROOPS }

New York
Ft. George

EAST RIVER

Governors Island

Red Hook
Ft. Defiance

WALLABOUT BAY

Brooklyn Ferry
Ft. Stirling

Redoubt
Ft. Putnam
Redoubt
Ft. Greene
Ft. Box

American
Camp

Brooklyn

PUTNAM

MILL DAM

OLD JAMAICA ROAD

Bedford

HOWE

CLOVE RD.

FLATBUSH ROAD

Cortelyou House

PORTE RD.

SULLIVAN

CHESTER
WILLS
WYLLYS
E. Bedford PASS

FLATBUSH PASS

PARSONS
ATLEE

MD. & DEL.

STIRLING

GRANT
Red Lion Inn

MARTENSE LANE

GOWANUS BAY

NARROWS ROAD

H E I G H T S

Howard's Tavern

MILES

JAMAICA PASS

New Lots

Shoemaker's Bridge

British

To Flatlands

Night march or

Flatbush

von HEISTER

H E I G H T S

straight road to the pass for a minor road to the right, crossed Shoemaker's Bridge along a narrow causeway, and reached Halfway House, very near the entrance to the pass, between two and three o'clock in the morning. Having made this circuitous approach, the van came around into the rear of the patrol of five men posted there. Captain Evelyn of the King's Own infantry, leading the advance, surrounded and captured the hapless five without resistance. From them it was learned that the pass was entirely undefended. Clinton's army marched through this gateway in the ridge and halted at dawn for rest and refreshment.[4]

Some time after the departure of the British flanking force, General Grant and his 5,000 men began an advance up the Gowanus Road toward the American right. Grant's task was largely to occupy the Americans while the main British attack developed on the American left. At the Red Lion Inn, where the road swung to the left to follow the shore line closely, his van came upon Major Burd's picket post. There was an exchange of fire before Burd's men started to fall back toward the ridge; but in the confusion and darkness the major and a number of his men were captured.[5]

The sound of the firing alarmed the detachment guarding that pass, and word was sent to Putnam in the American camp. Grant, in accordance with the general plan, had not continued his advance beyond the point of the first encounter. There was time for a reinforcement of the main position of the Americans on that end of the ridge. It was three o'clock when Putnam got the news. He hurried to Stirling's tent in the camp outside the lines, awakened him, and directed him "to march with the two regiments nearest at hand" to meet the enemy and "to repulse them." [6] As it happened, Smallwood's Marylands and Haslet's Delawares lay nearest. Responding "with alacrity" [7] to Stirling's call, these untried young soldiers less than two weeks with the army, less than a day in their new camp, and fresh from their homes, their farms, and their shops, marched out in the darkness to meet 5,000 British veterans. Three-o'clock-in-the-morning courage is proverbially the rarest kind. Dawn came while they were on their way. It was noted afterward that the sun that morning "rose with a red and angry glare," [8] as if portending coming evils.

About half a mile short of the Red Lion Inn, Stirling came upon Colonel Atlee with 120 of his Pennsylvania Musketry battalion, who had been on guard at that point,[9] and Lieutenant Colonel Joel Clark leading Huntington's regiment of Connecticut Continentals. Grant's van, again in motion, was in sight, marching directly toward them. Stirling ordered Atlee forward to hold the enemy until he could form his troops on the ridge.[10]

Atlee took a position in an orchard beside the road at the foot of the west end of the ridge. Although his men had never before faced an enemy in battle, they held their ground and exchanged fire with Grant's advance until Stirling had selected his ground and drawn up his troops. Then they retired to join him.

The ground chosen was on a slope running up from the Gowanus Road to a wood at the top of that end of the ridge. Because of the lay of the land and the position of the road, Stirling's line was most peculiarly shaped like a V. On the right branch, as viewed from behind, the Marylanders were drawn up; on the left, Haslet's Delaware regiment.[11]

The right wing of the line rested on a marsh at the foot of the hill; the left had no support. The two parts of Atlee's regiment—the men originally on guard there and those now newly arrived—having been joined together, Stirling posted them and Huntington's regiment in the woods on his unprotected left. Kachlein's Pennsylvania riflemen had now come up, and he divided them, placing half behind a hedge in front of his right and the rest in front of the woods near Atlee.[12] This extreme left, somewhat separated from Stirling's own troops, was put under command of Brigadier General Samuel Holden Parsons of Connecticut, who was early on the scene.

The shape of Stirling's line created a singular condition, in that his extreme left was nearer his extreme right than either was to his center. Because of this anomaly, a part of the Delaware battalion, held in reserve on the end of one wing, was called upon in the course of the fighting to meet and repulse the advance of the 2nd British Grenadiers attacking the end of the other wing.

Another remarkable thing about Stirling's formation was that, instead of letting his men break ranks and take cover, he drew them up in the open in formal order, and, in the words of one of them, offered the British "battle in the true English taste." [13] So in line they stood, to quote Haslet, "upwards of four hours, with a firm, determined countenance, in close array, their colors flying, the enemy's artillery playing on them all the time." [14]

Their position was precarious. In their rear was a marsh bordering Gowanus Creek. They had no connecting support on the left except Parson's command at some distance, and beyond that none at all. On their far right was the bay commanded by the British fleet, and in front was Grant's division outnumbering them four to one, for Grant soon brought up the 42nd Highlanders, drawn from von Heister's corps at Flatbush, and two companies of American Loyalists. He had then about 7,000 men facing not more than 1,600 Americans. In reply to the American challenge, he drew up his troops as if for immediate attack. One brigade was extended in a double line in front of the Americans' right, the rest in a single line against their left. The extent of this latter line threatened to overlap the Americans. Stirling accordingly desired Parsons to move Atlee's and Huntington's regiments to a point in the woods farther to the left, leaving Kachlein's riflemen nearer at hand. This shift, though necessary to meet Grant's tactics, separated the two bodies by a considerable distance, and left Stirling, with not much more than a thousand men, to oppose Grant.[15]

Parsons's troops, filing off to the left, saw before them "a hill of clear ground," which seemed to be a desirable position from which to watch the enemy's movements. As they were approaching within forty yards of its top, they were surprised by a volley of musketry from the 23rd and 44th British regiments and a part of the 17th Light Dragoons, who had penetrated the woods. They wavered and fell back in some confusion; but most of them were soon rallied, and they advanced again with somewhat surprising coolness. Their fire was so effective that the enemy retired, leaving twelve dead and five wounded. The American loss in this preliminary encounter included Atlee's lieutenant colonel, Caleb Parry, and a few minor casualties. Parsons's contingent held the hill.[16]

Within half an hour this detachment was again attacked by the same British regiments; but, partly under cover of trees and fences, partly in the open, it delivered such a heavy fire that again the enemy were repulsed. In the engagement the British Lieutenant Colonel Grant was killed. Parsons's men exhausted their ammunition, and would have been obliged to retreat but for the timely arrival of a new supply.[17] A third attack was threatened, but the enemy did not carry it out, contenting themselves with holding the Americans' attention at a safe distance. As a matter of fact the strategy of the whole battle did not call for a full-scale assault upon the American right at this time. These several little engagements, though hot, were intended merely to hold the Americans' attention while the larger plan for the battle was being worked out.

Returning now to Stirling, and going back somewhat in time, we find his men in ordered line of battle as first drawn up, and Stirling addressing them. Recalling that he had chanced to be in the gallery of the House of Commons when General Grant, then a member, had made his famous boast that, with 5,000 men, he could march from one end of the American continent to the other, Stirling told his men: "He may have 5,000 with him now. We are not so many. But I think we are enough to prevent his advancing further on his march over the continent than that mill-pond." [18]

It is noteworthy that this was the first time that American and British forces ever met in formal array in the open field. It may also be remarked that Stirling's formation was the only one on the American side that was preserved throughout the battle.

Grant's next move was to advance a small body of light infantry within 150 yards of Stirling's right. Protected by the trees and hedges of an orchard, they opened fire, to which the Americans briskly replied. This exchange continued about two hours, after which the light infantry withdrew to the main line. A two-gun battery under Captain Benajah Carpenter of Rhode Island had come from the American lines and was posted to command the road. It opened upon the enemy. To answer it, Grant posted one howitzer about 300 yards from Stirling's right, and another 600 yards from his left.[19] There followed sustained and vigorous cannonading from both sides. Except for the body of light infantry while they were in the orchard, it does not appear that any part of the two forces was within musket shot of the enemy. The few American accounts of this stage of the battle dwell on the "heavy fire from their cannon and mortars." "The balls and shells flew very fast," yet did little damage.

The plain fact again was that Grant did not intend to drive Stirling from his position until the proper time according to the plan of the high command. But Stirling's men did not know this. At every moment of the four hours of the cannonading they seemed to face the possibility of attack by the overwhelming number of their opponents. That they, raw recruits as they were, stood firmly in line under the fire of heavy guns—always formidable to untried soldiers—while awaiting that assault, redounds greatly to their credit, especially so since all the time their ears were assailed by the guns of the warship *Roebuck* bombarding the fort at Red Hook, and the fort's batteries replying.

Admiral Lord Howe had tried to bring five other warships up the East River within supporting distance of the land forces. But a strong north wind and a swiftly ebbing tide kept back all save the *Roebuck*, which itself could not sail above Red Hook. Had the attempt succeeded, he could have poured terrible broadsides on Stirling's troops and on the Brooklyn fortifications. Thus bombarded, and at the same time cut off from retreat to New York, the Americans must have been overwhelmed; Washington, Putnam, Stirling, Sullivan, and all the Long Island army would have been killed or captured, and the Revolution might have ended then and there.[20]

At nine o'clock in the morning, after four hours of all this cannon fire, Stirling heard two heavy guns far in his rear—sounds more ominous than the thunder of Grant's guns or the roar of the *Roebuck*'s broadsides. But

no interpretation came to him from headquarters or elsewhere, no orders
to withdraw. He could only surmise some danger behind him, wonder what
it was, and continue to hold his ground.

Up to this time General von Heister's Hessians had contented themselves
with cannonading the American center in the Flatbush Pass, varying it with
a sufficient show of advancing to keep the defenders in constant apprehension of an assault. About nine o'clock, General Sullivan rode out from the
Brooklyn lines and took command of the posts at the two middle passes,
Flatbush and Bedford. He remained at the Flatbush post, with the troops
of Hitchcock, Little, and Knowlton. The post at the Bedford road was about
a mile distant, separated by rugged, broken country.[21]

It may seem impossible that anyone could further stretch and weaken the
already attenuated and feeble American line; but Colonel Miles did just
that. At about seven o'clock, he says, he became convinced that "the main
body of the enemy would take the Jamaica Road." Accordingly he thought
best to get into that position first.[22] It was a good guess, except that it was
made about four hours too late. However, he marched his Pennsylvania
riflemen through the woods toward the Jamaica Pass and away from Wyllys
and Wills, nearly two miles. He was still proceeding at eight o'clock when
he disconcertingly came into contact with the enemy's army—not with its
van, but actually with its baggage and rear guard.

The British, after breakfasting just beyond the Jamaica Pass, had taken
a straight road toward Bedford. Their column of 10,000 men, almost two
miles long, with horse, artillery, and wagons, had been marching five or six
hours over that road in the rear of the American lines, parallel with Miles's
line of march but in an opposite direction and within half a mile of him
without his having observed them.

Their entire movement was a masterpiece of secrecy and silence. Where
it was necessary to cut down young trees to clear the way for the artillery
and wagons, these were sawed instead of chopped for fear that the Americans might hear ax strokes and be alarmed. They had marched nine miles.[23]
Their van had by this time almost reached the village of Bedford, without
any of the Americans even suspecting its presence in the rear of the ridge.

Miles was completely cut off from a retreat to the lines. His 400 men
could do little against the foe. After two or three slight encounters he and
half of his men surrendered. The rest scattered in the woods, found their
way to the American camp, and gave Putnam the first news of the encircling
march of the British.[24] There was still time to send word to Stirling and to
the Flatbush, if not the Bedford, post to withdraw from a position that had

become untenable and concentrate in the fortification. Putnam sent no such word, nor did anyone else. Nothing whatever was done to avert coming disaster.

At nine o'clock, in the village of Bedford, the British fired two heavy guns, the signal for action. Wyllys and Wills at the Bedford Pass heard them. Already alarmed by the firing on their left, between the enemy and Miles's men, they realized their danger and immediately started for the fortified lines.[25] Sullivan, at the Flatbush post, heard the guns, too, and knew the enemy was behind him. Leaving pickets and outposts to delay an attack by the Hessians in front, he fell back, only to meet the British light infantry and dragoons pouring down upon him from Bedford. His men turned their three fieldpieces on these unexpected foemen. But four companies of the Guards overwhelmed the gunners. The Americans recoiled, turned about, and met von Donop's Hessian jägers coming up over the ridge.[26]

In anticipation of the signal von Heister had formed his troops on the plain below the pass, dressing their lines as if on parade, with von Donop's jägers on the right and left flanks, his artillery meanwhile playing on the American position. At the expected sound of the guns he had given von Donop the word. The jägers had dashed forward, reached the top of the wooded ridge, taken cover as they had been trained to do, and advanced from one protected point to another, driving back the American outposts.[27] After them came the Hessian grenadiers. Muskets at shoulder, bayonets gleaming, halting at intervals to re-dress their lines, they advanced "with colors flying, to the music of drums and hautboys, as if they were marching across Friedrich's Platz at Cassel on the Landgrave's birthday. They did not fire a shot, but pressed steadily forward until they could employ their bayonets." [28]

At the top of the ridge the Hessians deployed and fell upon Sullivan's men thrown back by the British. The rifles in the hands of the Americans were good for only a few shots before bayonets were at the breasts of the riflemen, and a clubbed rifle is a weak weapon against half a dozen bayonets. Driven back and forth between the British and the Hessians, the Americans fought as long as they could, and then, along with what was left of Miles's men and Wyllys's and Wills's and the rest, they fled. Through the woods, down the slopes, across the fields, singly, in groups, in companies, they fled. Meeting here and there light infantry, dragoons, and grenadiers who fired at them, they ran for the fortified camp. Many of them reached it, but many were killed and many captured, among them Sullivan. It was in these ragged encounters that most of the American casualties occurred.

The wave of attacks swept westward. Detachments of von Heister's grenadiers, swinging to their left, struck at Parsons's command, Atlee's regiment, Huntington's contingent, and Kachlein's riflemen. There was no possibility of successful resistance; they retreated in broken groups, only to meet the British grenadiers in their rear. Atlee's journal says: "We kept up a close fire until the grenadiers retired. Then not being able, through the weakness of my party, already greatly fatigued and . . . destitute of ammunition, to break through the enemy . . . I filed off to the right [towards the camp] to endeavor, if possible, to escape." He soon fell in with Parsons "and a small number by him." They decided to try to break through the enemy. "I then pushed off," he continues, "with such of the officers and men that were willing to run the hazard."

Almost immediately they came upon a party of Highlanders, from whom they retreated, receiving in their flight "the fire of this party and sundry others, through which we were obliged to run for near two miles." With a handful of men Atlee tried to find a way to the north, toward Hell Gate, but at last had to surrender to a Scottish battalion.[29]

By eleven o'clock the British, as a result of their skillfully planned and perfectly executed strategy, had established themselves within two miles of the American camp, and had swept the ridge clear of their enemy—of all but Stirling's two regiments. These were still holding their ground, "ranks full, their uniforms smart, their weapons the best that money could purchase, their courage high." [30]

Up to this time Grant had made no move against Stirling's position. He had heard the signal guns, but, possibly because he had run short of ammunition, he had not acted as quickly as the other British and Hessian commanders. He had sent to the fleet for more powder and shot. Admiral Howe had sent him not only the desired supply, but also 2,000 marines, a scarcely needed reinforcement of his 7,000 men against Stirling's men. When they arrived, the real attack on Stirling began.

Grant's full force struck at Stirling's center. Unable to withstand the blow, the American line recoiled. The 33rd foot and a detachment of grenadiers swept down from the rear to join Grant. With a party of von Heister's Hessians they attacked the American left. Stirling called up some of Haslet's men, held in reserve, to strengthen his line. They came up and opened fire. The colonel of the 2nd British Grenadiers, whose men were under fire, saw that his assailants, the Delawares, wore uniforms of blue faced with red—the Hessians' colors. They were Hessians, of course, firing on their British comrades in arms by mistake! He sent Lieutenant Wragg of the marines forward with a sergeant, a corporal, and twenty men, to tell them to stop. The unfortunate Wragg was so close to the Delawares when he discovered the mistake that he could not withdraw. He and his entire party were taken by Haslet's men and sent across the Gowanus marsh and creek to the lines.[31]

But this was merely a momentary diversion. Grant's 7,000 and those others that had come to help him would not be denied by Stirling's 950. It was clear that the American position could not be held much longer. Nor was the direct way of retreat to the rear open. Cornwallis was there with the 71st Regiment. The 2nd Grenadiers also overlapped Stirling's left and rear.

Cut off from their natural line of retreat, Stirling's men had only one possible avenue of escape; and that was but barely possible. On their right rear was Gowanus Creek at its widest, and not only that stream, but also the broad marshes lining both its shores. The creek and its swamps were usually considered impassable, but the detachment with the prisoners had crossed them, and there was no other way.

To attempt such a crossing with his whole force in retreat, under the fire of the musketry and cannon of the British before and behind him, was to court and probably to suffer complete disaster. But Stirling met the emergency with characteristic resolution and courage. He detached Major Gist and about 250 men of Smallwood's Maryland regiment. He then ordered Major McDonough with the Delawares and the rest of the Marylands to retreat across the creek. They faced about and, "in perfect order," their shot-torn colors flying, marched away.[32]

Gist's 250 Marylanders, Stirling leading, set out up the Gowanus Road to meet the enemy. If possible, Stirling meant to cut his way through the British. If not, he might be able to engage them and hold them off until the remainder of his command crossed to safety. His plan was born of desperation, a forlorn hope.

Cornwallis in person commanded the British right wing pressing against what had been Stirling's rear. He had established himself in and about the Cortelyou House on the Gowanus Road. Against this position Stirling led his men. When within gunshot, he opened fire and received the enemy's reply which came not only from their musketry, but also from two field-pieces. The British artillery added grape and canister to the rain of bullets.

The little American column halted and fell back, only to advance once more. Again and again and again, five times, the Americans were driven back, and five times returned to the fight. Stirling "encouraged and animated our young soldiers," wrote Major Gist, "with almost invincible resolution."

"General Lord Stirling fought like a wolf," wrote another participant.[33] It seemed at last that they would force Cornwallis to retire and let them through. A sixth time they advanced, but Cornwallis had now been reinforced. For the last time the brave young Marylanders were thrown back, this time "with much precipitation and confusion." They had done all they could, but they could not win through. They broke up, and in small, scattered parties tried to find a way to the American entrenchments; but only Major Gist and nine others succeeded. The rest, all that had not fallen in the fight, were captured, and 256 were either killed or taken prisoner. Stirling alone tried to find a way out, but the enemy, before and behind and on both sides, kept up a "constant firing" on him. He made his way around "the point of a hill" that covered him from their fire, then sought out General von Heister and surrendered his sword.[34]

It was reported at the time that Washington was on a hill within the lines, whence, with a glass, he watched Stirling's fight, and that he displayed great emotion, exclaiming: "Good God! What brave fellows I must this day lose!" [35]

Meanwhile, still in good order, in column of march (so the historians say, though it may be doubted that there was no confusion), McDonough's Delawares and Marylands were retreating. They had made no more than a quarter of a mile when they met a party of the enemy and were fired upon. The artillery in their rear also still played upon them. Apparently with no thought of surrender, they replied to the enemy in front and forced him to give way. Through an opening thus created they got down to the edge of the marsh, and started across the creek.[36]

At that point, Gowanus Creek was eighty yards wide, deep and swift with the inflowing tide. The retreating Americans waded in knee-deep, waist-deep, neck-deep, here and there over their depth; some of them had to swim. Four fieldpieces were firing upon them, and an unknown number of muskets. Fortunately, Smallwood had come over from New York early that morning, too late to join his regiment in the battle. He had foreseen that the retreat must be made at that point if at all. He had secured from Washington "a New England regiment and Captain Thomas's company," and had posted them with two guns to cover the crossing. Their fire dislodged the enemy guns that were firing on the fugitives. Except for half a dozen men either shot down or drowned, the fleeing Americans came safely "out of the water and mud, looking like water-rats." [37]

Howe claimed that the Americans lost 3,200 men in this battle, but the American returns on October 8 showed 1,012 casualties of whom probably

200 were killed, the rest captured. The British casualties were 392 killed, wounded, and taken prisoner.[38]

The Battle of Long Island, as the first in which the American and British forces met in the open field in formal battle array, was of very great importance as an indication of what was to be expected in such encounters thereafter. The disastrous defeat of the Americans boded ill for their future. Consequently, it was extremely desirable to ascertain wherein their army was at fault, and whether the blame for their discomfiture should rest upon the rank and file or upon the leaders. There was much discussion of the question at the time, and it has continued among historians ever since.

Sullivan has been blamed because, being in command of the troops outside the lines, he failed properly to guard the Jamaica Pass; but he denied that he held that command, asserting that it belonged to Stirling and his own function was to command within the lines as subordinate to Putnam.[39] He is credited with having posted the captured patrol at the Jamaica Pass; but, if that be true, it boomerangs upon him because it shows that, in spite of his disclaimer of authority outside the lines, he did in fact exercise such authority. In which case, the pitiful weakness of the post he thus established reflects discredit upon him.

Putnam has been blamed because, having reconnoitered the enemy's positions on the 26th, he should have concluded from the concentration of their forces that they intended to launch their main attack against the Jamaica Pass, and should have arranged for an adequate defense.[40] The fact that Washington, Sullivan, "and others" were with him on that reconnaissance cannot exculpate him, though it may prove them equally blind.

Putnam has been censured also because, having received news, "early in the morning," of the British advance along the road to Bedford, he failed to inform Washington or to order Stirling and the others on the ridge to withdraw while there was yet time.[41] It is true that the news was brought to him first only by one or more fugitives in the rout of Miles's battalion; and doubtless it was long delayed by the distance it had to be brought through the woods. Nevertheless, it does seem that he received it in time to recall Stirling and the others.

George Bancroft blames "the incapacity of Israel Putnam" for "the extent of the disasters of the day," specifically because, "having sent Stirling and the flower of the American army into the most dangerous position," he "neglected to countermand his orders." [42] "The Militia are most indifferent troops." They "will do for the interior Works, whilst your best Men should at all hazards prevent the Enemy's passing the Wood, and approaching your Works." [43] Clearly, if there was error in disposing the American forces, it cannot be ascribed to Putnam alone.

The most all-inclusive charge is made by General Francis V. Greene, who says: "No one exercised general command," although it had been conferred on Putnam. "Putnam did practically nothing as a commanding general." [44] And it is certainly true that, having sent his "best men" out to defend the ridge, he did none of the things proper and necessary to save them from disaster. Even Washington's orders were no warrant to him for leaving them to be surrounded and captured by the British turning movement, which Washington certainly did not expect when he gave the orders.

Washington has been blamed for the defeat, because, though he was familiar with the ground and had arrived within the lines on the 26th, thus certainly putting himself in command superior to Putnam, he did not alter Putnam's dispositions and allowed a manifestly inadequate force, strung out along six miles of the ridge, to attempt to defend it, instead of "keeping his men in the redoubts and repeating the performance of Bunker Hill." [45] He has been censured, too, for not having any cavalry to patrol between the various passes, so that word of the flanking movement could be brought to the camp in time to withdraw the troops from the ridge before they were hopelessly enveloped. Washington Irving says the flanking of the Americans "might have been thwarted had the army been provided with a few troops of light-horse to serve as videttes." [46]

There was no cavalry in the American army. None had been provided by the Congress. Washington had not called for any, nor made a move to organize any on his own. Charles Francis Adams says he "apparently had no conception of the use to be made of cavalry, or mounted men, in warfare," [47] and develops that thesis at length. Yet, strange to say, there was available to him at the time a mounted force which could have provided the patrols so needed. He refused to use it.

There had come over from Connecticut, on the 8th of July, a regiment of four or five hundred volunteers called rather absurdly "Light Dragoons"— mostly farmers mounted on "rough, country horses" and armed with muskets, fowling pieces, or whatever sort of guns they owned. They were not a stylish lot. Dapper, or at least dapper-minded, Captain Alexander Graydon of Philadelphia made great fun of them in his memoirs.[48] Washington received these cavaliers rather cavalierly. He said they could not remain in New York because forage for their horses could not be furnished, "and, if it could be, it would only be at great expense, without a single advantage arising from it." [49] They were discharged, and went home.

Sir George Trevelyan comments that Washington "surveyed that quaint procession too much in the spirit of a country gentleman who rode to hounds. There was plenty of capability and some youth" among them. Two hundred of the best might have been chosen and trained in the next six weeks. "Captain Henry Lee or Captain William Washington would have got a small body of cavalry into shape soon enough. . . . On the 27th of August, 1776, a couple of troops of yeomanry posted and handled by two such officers would have saved many hundred Americans from capture." [50]

One of these horsemen, lingering on the scene, was picked up by the British. Captain Graydon reports, "On being asked what had been his duty in the rebel army, he answered that it was *'to flank a little and carry tidings.'* " No one could have put in fewer or more apt words just what Washington needed on Long Island—someone "to flank a little and carry tidings."

On the whole, it seems impossible to avoid placing the bulk of the responsibility for the mismanagement of affairs on Long Island upon the shoulders of the commander in chief, George Washington. Such has been the verdict of the later and more judicious historians of the war. "There was no excuse for the local dispositions of the defense," says Thomas G. Frothingham.[51] And those dispositions had been made in accordance with Washington's specific orders. Claude H. Van Tyne refers to Washington's "almost fatal errors in both strategy and tactics." [52]

Most of these criticisms of the conduct of the affair on Long Island are directed at the tactics employed there. The fundamental fault lay deeper, in the strategy of the campaign, the attempt to hold New York. That city could not be held without holding Brooklyn Heights. Those Heights could not be held without dividing an army far too weak, even as a whole, successfully to oppose the British. To divide it was to expose the two parts to the danger of being held apart by the British fleet and of being separately and successively overcome by the British army.

Even if Brooklyn Heights had not been there to bring about this unfortunate result, the Americans could not have held New York, for the British armada commanded the waters environing the town. Indeed, New York could easily have been a fatal trap for the American army, since it had only one readily available exit to the mainland: Kingsbridge.

It has been said that the attempt to hold it was based upon political instead of military considerations, that the Congress wanted it held, that the attempt to hold it was necessary to fortify the American spirit of resistance.[53] But if a commanding general sees that a task is impossible of accomplishment, though he may risk and sacrifice an expendable detachment in the attempt, how far is he justified in risking his whole army, the whole army of his country, and with it his country's cause? If on the other hand he fails to perceive the obvious impossibility of the task, how can he be allowed merit as a military leader? And Washington did not perceive the impossibility of holding New York before he attempted it, not even after the defeat on Long Island. As late as September 2 he wrote to the Congress, "Till of late I had no doubt in my mind of defending the place [New York], nor should I have yet, if the men would do their duty." [54]

The truth is, in Van Tyne's words, that Washington had "little genius and not much natural aptitude for war." [55] Or, as the English military historian Sir John Fortescue, a most generous critic of the American commander in chief, puts it, "Though every Englishman must admire him as a very great man and a brave and skilful soldier, it is, I think, doubtful whether he has any claim to be regarded as a really great commander in the field." [56] As Van Tyne says: "It was courage, noble character, the gift of inspiring confidence, and the ability to learn by experience" rather than military genius that were "to place him in the forefront among the leaders of men, safe and competent as a commander-in-chief. Even in the midst of his worst errors, his greatness and his magnanimity surmounts everything." [57] And Fortescue, after commenting on the "very grave flaws in the campaign of 1776 about New York" and in the campaign against Howe about Philadelphia, in 1777, culminating in the Brandywine disaster, recognizes "his constancy, his courage and his inexhaustible patience" as his "finest qualities." [58]

Long Island: The Retreat

By noon of August 27 all the Americans that had escaped death or capture were within the fortified lines on Long Island, expecting with anxiety
a concentrated attack. But it did not come. The British grenadiers and the
33rd Regiment had pursued the fugitives to within musket shot of the lines.
Hot with the ardor of battle, they were eager to storm the entrenchments,
so eager that, in Howe's own words, "it required repeated orders to prevail
on them to desist from this attempt." He "would not risk the loss that might
have been sustained in the assault," it being, as he is reported to have said,
"apparent that the lines must have been ours at a very cheap rate by regular approaches." He therefore withdrew his men to a safe distance.[1]

Astonishingly enough, not recognizing the peril of his position, Washington called for reinforcements from New York; and early the next morning
Colonel John Shee's 3rd Pennsylvania Regiment and Colonel Robert
Magaw's 5th, also Colonel John Glover's Massachusetts Continentals, came
over. There were then within the works perhaps 9,500 men.[2]

For two days following the battle the Americans held their lines, while
within a mile or so and in plain sight lay the British camp. There was
skirmishing throughout the 28th, "pretty smart" skirmishing, Washington
called it.[3] To present a bold face to the enemy, he encouraged the riflemen
to keep up their fire, thus not only maintaining a show of resistance, but
also sustaining the morale of his men.[4]

Pickets and riflemen were thrown out by the Americans about a hundred
rods in front of the lines. About sunset of the 28th the enemy made a push
to drive them in. "The fire was very hot," Colonel Moses Little of Massachu-

setts wrote. "The enemy gave way & our people recovered the ground. The firing ceased, our people retired to the fort." By the next morning the British not only possessed the disputed ground, but had dug trenches and built a breastwork within 150 rods of Fort Putnam. Howe's "approaches" had begun. This first breastwork was a menace of disaster nearing the Americans.[5]

On that same day a northeasterly storm blew up, and a downpour of rain began. It had one immense advantage for the Americans: it prevented Admiral Howe from sending ships up the East River to lie between Brooklyn and New York and thus to cut off their only line of retreat. Otherwise it was exceedingly distressing to them. "We had no tents to screen us from its pitiless pelting," wrote Captain Alexander Graydon of Shee's regiment in his memoirs; "nor, if we had had them, would it have comported with the incessant vigilance required to have availed ourselves of them, as, in fact, it might be said, that we lay upon our arms during our whole stay on the island." [6] In food also they were badly off. They had only hard biscuits and pickled pork, which must be eaten raw, for cook fires were impossible in that downpour.

The rain continued all the next day and the day after that. The camp became a morass and worse. Water lay "ankle deep in the fort"; and in some parts of the trenches the men stood waist-deep in water. Not only was the clothing of the troops soaked, the ammunition of nearly all of them was saturated. But even those who managed to keep a few dry cartridges could not use them, for their muskets were practically valueless, as are all flintlock guns when the flints, the priming pans, and the touchholes become wet.

Howe's reluctance to storm the works immediately after the retreat of the Americans has been attributed to the memory of Bunker's Hill, to the lesson he there learned of the steadfastness and the deadly fire of the Americans, even the militia when behind breastworks. Trevelyan says that the minutemen who defended the redoubt on Breed's Hill saved the American lines on Long Island. But that lesson should have been no deterrent to an assault on the second day or the third day after this battle. No overwhelming fire such as had met him in that former battle could have been delivered against him now. British bayonets would have been met by few American bayonets—the Americans had but few. It is difficult to believe that a determined assault upon those entrenchments would have failed against their tired and hungry defenders, discouraged by defeat and disorganized by the loss of so many officers.[7] Howe may have assumed that his brother's fleet could prevent an American retreat, and that an expensive frontal assault was unnecessary. A veritable Caesar on the battlefield, Howe was commonly sluggish before and after the fighting.

It was an extraordinary situation. "Nine thousand disheartened soldiers, the last hope of their country," says Trevelyan, "were penned up, with the sea behind them and a triumphant enemy in front, shelterless and famished on a square mile of open ground swept by a fierce and cold northeasterly gale. . . . If Howe's infantry had been led to the assault, they would have walked over the intrenchments behind which the beaten army was now gathered." [8] It would have been more than a victory in a battle. Washington was there, with three or four of his ablest generals and the best of his whole army. By their capture the British might have won the war then and there. But Washington *was* there, and he finally saved the day.

On the morning of the 29th he sent orders to General William Heath at Kingsbridge and to Hugh Hughes, Assistant Quartermaster General in New York, to gather every boat of every sort fit for transporting troops and to assemble them on the New York side by dark. Was he planning a retreat? He did not say so. On the contrary his orders to Heath intimated a reinforcement of his lines.[9] But late in that day a council of his general officers agreed that it was "eligible to remove the Army to New York" for eight severally stated reasons, any one of which seemed to be sufficient in itself.[10]

So there was to be a retreat—if it could be accomplished. But the troops were not informed until the last moment. If the truth had been known among the militia and volunteers a panic desire to get out in the first boats might have resulted in riotous confusion. Accordingly general orders were issued in the following terms: "As the sick are an encumbrance to the Army & Troops are expected from the flying camp in New Jersey, under General Mercer, who is himself arrived & cover is wanted for the [new] troops, the commanding Officers of Regt's are immediately to have such sick men removed. . . . As the above Forces under Gen'l Mercer are expected this afternoon, the General [Washington] proposes to relieve a proportionate Number of Regiments & make a change in the situation of them. The Commanding Officers of Regiments are therefore to parade their men with their Arms, Accoutrements and Knapsacks, at 7 o'Clock at the Head of their Encampments & there wait for Orders." [11] Washington could tell a lie when it was needed. He told half a dozen in that one order.

It was obviously necessary that the lines should be manned while the removal of the great body of the troops was in progress, so as to prevent the enemy from discovering the movement and assaulting while the camp was in disorder. To this honorable and dangerous duty Haslet's Delaware regiment was assigned, along with Shee's and Magaw's Pennsylvanians, Chester's

Connecticut battalion, and the remains of Smallwood's Marylanders. This detachment, the pick of the army, was commanded by General Thomas Mifflin.[12] The post of greatest danger, at Fort Putnam, within 250 yards of the enemy's approaches, was taken by Smallwood's and Haslet's men. When Glover's Marbleheaders were withdrawn from their left to help man the boats, the Delaware and Maryland men were exposed to a flank attack which would have been impossible to stem.

At dusk the boats began to arrive. The two amphibious regiments, Glover's from Marblehead and Hutchinson's from Salem, all fishermen or sailors, took them in charge. Between nine and ten o'clock the regiments on parade were drawn off one by one, the volunteers and militia first. With their baggage and equipment on their backs they marched to the ferry landing to embark. Other regiments were marched into their places or extended to right or left to fill the gaps and keep up an appearance of completeness in the line. The utmost quiet and orderliness were preserved; no unusual lights were shown. In fact, the embarkation was begun in almost complete darkness.

The first detachments were ready to embark and the next were on their way to the landing when the elements, which had so far befriended the Americans by preventing Admiral Howe's ships from coming up the river, made trouble. The northeasterly wind so increased in force and the ebb tide began to run so strongly that even the practiced sailors manning the sloops and other sailboats could not make the crossing. There were not enough rowboats to take all the men across in one night. It seemed that the attempt to withdraw must end in disaster. But the wind lessened about eleven o'clock and shifted to the southwest, favoring the sailing craft.

The work went on. Stores of ammunition, supplies, and provisions were brought to the landing. All the artillery was assembled there except five heavy cannon, old and worn and of little value. They were spiked and abandoned.

At two o'clock in the morning, when everything seemed to be going well, an error occurred that might have been fatal. Major Alexander Scammell, acting aide-de-camp to Washington, came to General Mifflin and told him that the boats for the covering party were waiting and he was to march his men to the landing at once. In spite of a protest that there must be some mistake, Scammell insisted that there was none. Accordingly the sentinels and advanced posts were called in. The entire detachment abandoned the lines and marched toward the landing. They were well on their way when they met Washington. He was aghast at this seeming desertion of their duty.

"Good God!" he exclaimed. "General Mifflin, I am afraid you have ruined us by unseasonably withdrawing the troops from the lines." "I did it by your order," Mifflin answered hotly. Washington said that could not be so. "By God, I did!" said Mifflin. Washington replied that it was a dreadful mistake, that there was confusion at the ferry, and that unless the covering party could resume their posts before the enemy discovered their abandonment "the most disagreeable consequences would follow"—surely a masterpiece of understatement. The troops were faced about and their posts, unguarded for nearly an hour, were again occupied.[13] Major General Heath characterizes the immediate return of these men to their posts as "an instance of discipline and true fortitude." "Whoever," he says, "has seen troops in a similar situation, or duly contemplated the human heart in such trials, will know how to appreciate the conduct of these brave men on this occasion." [14]

To the troops holding the lines within sound of the thudding pickaxes and the scraping shovels of the British working on a new and nearer approach, that night must have seemed interminable. Would the hour of their relief come before daylight and certain discovery of the retreat by the enemy? Would they, a few hundreds, be compelled to face an attack by thousands? It was daylight when the order to embark came, and those steadfast battalions marched away.

It was full time they did, for British reconnoitering parties, suspicious of the unnatural silence within the American lines, were already creeping up to spy on the camp. Before daybreak a corporal's guard pushed cautiously through the abatis. At four o'clock the British were peering over the breastworks. Thirty minutes later the British pickets were inside. There was still time to catch the rear guard at the landing, but freakish Nature again favored the Americans. A dense fog settled down. Even at a little distance nothing could be seen. Under its cover the last boats with the last regiments and Washington himself pushed off.

Through six hours of that night, "the hardy, adroit, weather-proof" [15] Marblehead fishermen of Glover's regiment and Hutchinson's skilled Salem fishermen had rowed and sailed from shore to shore. By seven o'clock in the morning 9,500 men and all their baggage, field guns, and horses, equipment, stores, and provisions, "even the biscuits which had not been and the raw pork which could not be eaten," [16] were safe in New York. Howe captured three stragglers, who had stayed behind to plunder.

Both the contemporary and the later historians have praised this successful retreat. Charles Stedman, an officer in the British army at that time, called it "particularly glorious." Alexander Botta wrote, "No military opera-

tion was ever conducted by a great captain with more ability and prudence."
Irving calls it "one of the most signal achievements of the war." Trevelyan
says it was "a master stroke of energy, dexterity and caution, by which
Washington saved his army and his country." Frothingham describes it as
"a feat that seemed impossible." General Francis Vinton Greene, a military
critic of distinction, says, "A more skilful operation of this kind was never
conducted." Any number of others might be quoted in similar terms.[17]

The credit for the achievement must unhesitatingly be accorded to Washington, who not only conceived and planned it but personally supervised its
effective accomplishment throughout the night. Although, as he wrote to the
Congress, he had hardly been off his horse and never had closed his eyes in
the forty-eight hours preceding the retreat, all night long he rode his gray
charger to and fro watching the movements of his men, or stood by the landing to superintend the embarkation. He seemed to be everywhere at once;
and everywhere he cheered, calmed, and encouraged his troops through one
of the most difficult trials a soldier has to endure. He was the last man to
step into the last boat that left the island.

Both Howe's attack and Washington's retreat were masterpieces of planning and execution, and each was successful because of the mistakes of the
other principal. Washington exposed an inadequate force on the ridge and
neglected the Jamaica Pass, thus permitting Howe to encircle his army and
defeat it; Howe failed to follow up his first success by assaulting the American lines, thus giving Washington a chance to withdraw to New York.
Both of them were destined to repeat the same errors in a future battle with
similar results, which throws light upon their respective abilities as military
leaders.

The results of this battle created a great sensation on both sides of the
Atlantic. The surrender of Boston had depressed England, and news of
succeeding events in America was anxiously awaited. Howe's report of the
battle, greatly exaggerating both the number of American troops engaged
and their losses, reached London on October 10. Immediately the court
was "filled with an extravagance of joy." The King conferred the Order of
the Bath on the victorious general. In various towns throughout the kingdom
bells were rung, windows were lighted, cannon were fired, and bonfires
blazed. The English Tories thought the war practically finished. British
stocks rose in Amsterdam. The American agent Silas Deane wrote from
Paris, "The last check on Long Island has sunk our credit to nothing." [18]

In America disappointment and gloom were widespread. General Greene
wrote to Washington, "The country is struck with a panic." [19] Washington
wrote to the Congress that the defeat had "dispirited too great a proportion

of our troops and filled their minds with apprehension and dispair. The militia . . . are dismayed, intractable and impatient to return" to their homes. "Great numbers of them have gone off; in some instances, almost by whole regiments . . . their example has infected another part of the army. I am obliged to confess my want of confidence in the generality of the troops." He urged the Congress to put no dependence "in a militia or other troops than those enlisted and embodied" for longer periods than were then in vogue, and declared his conviction that "our liberties" might be lost "if their defence is left to any but a permanent standing army; I mean, one to exist during the war." [20] The Congress overcame its dread of "standing armies" and resolved on September 16 that eighty-eight battalions be enlisted "as soon as possible to serve during the present war." [21]

Kip's Bay

*

"On this 30th of August, 1776, Washington was probably the most astonished man in America. He had snatched a beaten army from the very jaws of a victorious force, and practically under the nose of the greatest armada ever seen in American waters." [1] He may have been astonished at his successful retreat; he was certainly perplexed as to his next move. He had his army in New York, but what to do with either the army or New York was a puzzle whose solution was far from obvious.

The army was in a deplorable condition, mentally and physically. Dispirited by its recent defeat, dejected by its hardships, dismayed at the prospect of the future, the militia was in the condition described by Washington in his letter to the Congress of September 2. The Continentals were similarly affected, though in a lesser degree. Such discipline as had been achieved in that hastily gathered army of practically raw recruits was greatly relaxed. Their commander in chief took notice of the resultant disorder in general orders on September 4. He expressed his "amazement and concern . . . that the men of every regiment are suffer'd to be continually rambling about, and at such distances from their respective quarters and encampments, as not to be able to oppose the enemy in any sudden approach." He therefore not only commanded but earnestly exhorted "the officers to remedy this fault." Two days later he expressed his purpose "to put a stop to plundering . . . either public, or private property" and threatened to break "with Infamy" any officer who connived at it by inaction. [2]

A more fundamental evil was a growing distrust of Washington himself—not of his character as a man, but of his ability as a general, or at least of the plans for the campaign made by him and his associates in the high command. This feeling was not uncommon among the regimental officers. Colonel John Haslet of the Delaware Regiment, an officer of proven sagacity and sound judgment, expressed it in a letter to Caesar Rodney on September 4 in the words: "The Genl I revere, his Character for Disinterestedness, Patience and fortitude will be had in Everlasting Remembrance, but the Vast Burthen appears to be too much his own. Beardless youth and Inexperience Regimentated are too much about him. . . . W'd to Heaven Genl Lee were here is the Language of officers and men." [3]

Physically, too, everything was in sad condition. The men were tired, soaked to the skin, hungry, and in some part leaderless, by reason of the loss of officers. Their disorganization showed itself in the wet clothing, accouterments, and tents spread about in complete confusion to dry in front of the houses and in the streets.[4]

Desertion was consequently rife, especially among the militia. They went off in whole companies, in whole regiments.[5] Within a few days the Connecticut militia dwindled from 8,000 to 2,000 men. "The impulse for going home," wrote Washington, "was so irrisistable, it answered no purpose to oppose it, tho' I could not discharge, I have been obliged to acquiesce." [6]

The prime necessity, if order was to be restored, was obviously a reorganization of the army. Three grand divisions were made up. Major General Putnam commanded one, composed of Parsons's brigade of Connecticut and Massachusetts regiments, James Clinton's and Fellows's brigades from Massachusetts, Scott's from New York, and Silliman's from Connecticut. Spencer was to command another, until Greene should recover from his illness. It included Nixon's brigade, composed of Hand's Pennsylvania riflemen, Varnum's and Hitchcock's brigades from Rhode Island and Prescott's, Little's, and "Late Nixon's" brigades from Massachusetts. The third division, under Heath, consisted of George Clinton's brigade from New York and Mifflin's brigades comprising Magaw's and Shee's Pennsylvanians, Hutchinson's, Sargent's, and Andrew Ward's brigades from Connecticut, Haslet's Delawares, and Smallwood's remnant from Maryland.[7]

Before these divisions could receive their respective posts, the great question had to be answered: Should New York be held or abandoned? And, if abandoned, should it be left intact and unscathed to the enemy? There were differences of opinion.

Greene's answers were given in a letter to Washington. The city could not be held in the face of an enemy that could land on both sides of the island in its middle section and cut in two the American forces to the north and the south. "The City and Island of New-York are no objects for us . . .

in competition of the general interests of America. Part of the army already has met with a defeat; the country is struck with a panick; any capital loss at this time may ruin the cause. . . . A general and speedy retreat is absolutely necessary. . . . I would burn the city and suburbs" because, "if the enemy gets possession of the city, we can never recover the possession without a superiour naval force. . . . It will deprive the enemy of an opportuny of barracking their whole army together, which, if they could do, would be a very great security. . . . Not one benefit can arise to us from its preservation." Anyhow, "two-thirds of the city of New-York and the suburbs belongs to the Tories," so why worry about its loss by burning? [8] Colonel Joseph Reed, the adjutant general of the army, agreed that it should be burned. Colonel Rufus Putnam, the army's chief engineer, and John Jay, one of the largest propertyholders in the town, likewise urged its destruction.[9]

Washington had already put the question up to the Congress on September 2, before Greene's letter was written: "If we should be obliged to abandon the Town, ought it to stand as Winter Quarters for the Enemy?" And the Congress answered on the 3rd that no damage should be done to it, if abandoned.[10] So that settled that. But the question of evacuation was still open.

Washington himself was in two minds about it. He acknowledged the obvious danger to his whole army, if the enemy should "enclose us . . . by taking post in our rear" and "oblige us to fight them on their own Terms, or surrender at discretion." Yet he still debated whether he should not try to hold the town, because giving it up would "dispirit the Troops and enfeeble our Cause." [11] He put the matter up to a council of war on September 7.

It was generally admitted by the members of the council that the town was untenable, but the majority could not face the logical consequences of their own opinions. The decision was a compromise. Putnam's division, 5,000 men, was to remain in New York. Heath with 9,000 was to hold the ground from Harlem up to Kingsbridge. Greene with five brigades, mostly militia, posted along the East River chiefly in the neighborhood of Turtle Bay and Kip's Bay, at the end of what is now Thirty-fourth Street, was to hold the intervening space.[12] As is the case with most compromises, this one served neither purpose; it was not effective to secure the city, nor to save the army. In fact, as one military historian has said, it was, "of course, fatuous." [13] It strung the army out in three divisions widely spaced over a length of sixteen miles, with its weakest element midway between the two ends, and so invited the enemy to cut it in two and defeat the ends separately—a chance which was not overlooked by the British. Nevertheless, the troops were posted in that manner.

In his letter to the Congress, September 8, telling of the decision of the council of war, Washington said that some of the officers had been not "a little influenced in their Opinion" by their belief that Congress wished the defense of the town "to be maintained at every hazard." [14] To this the Congress replied on the 10th that "it was by no means the sense" of their resolution of the 3rd against destroying the town "that the army, or any part of it, should remain in that city a moment longer than he [Washington] shall think it proper." [15]

Greene was much disturbed in mind by the council's decision disposing the troops in that "so critical and dangerous" manner. Before he heard of this last resolution of the Congress he and five other officers asked Washington to call another council to consider the matter.[16] That council was held on the 12th, and ten of its thirteen members voted "to reconsider" the former decision, that is to say, voted to withdraw from the city.[17] In this decision Washington concurred. "We are now," he wrote to the Congress on September 14, "taking every Method in our Power to remove the Stores &ca. in which we find almost insuperable difficulties; They are so great and so numerous, that I fear we shall not effect the whole before we shall meet with some Interruption." [18]

Lack of transport was the difficulty. Although all the horses and wagons found in the town were impressed and cargoes were shipped up the Hudson in boats, both methods of carriage were too little and too late.

It was not Howe's fault that Washington was pressed for time in reassembling his forces and removing his cannon and stores. The British army lay inactive on Long Island in camps stretching from Brooklyn to Flushing for more than two weeks while Washington was tying and untying the apron strings of the Congress and finally making the proper decision.[19]

There had, indeed, been hostile demonstrations by the navy. On September 3 the thirty-two-gun frigate *Rose* sailed up the East River towing thirty flatboats and anchored in Wallabout Bay above the city. She was fired upon by the batteries on the New York side, and after suffering "a good deal of damage" [20] she retired with her tow to a safer position in the mouth of Newtown Creek. On the 13th, four frigates, the *Phoenix* and the *Roebuck* of 44 guns each, the *Orpheus* of 32, and the *Carysfort* of 28, passed up, and "in supreme Contempt of the Rebels and their Works, did not fire a Gun." The next day, another warship and six transports joined them. The *Renown* of 50 guns, the *Repulse* and the *Pearl*, 32 guns each, with an armed schooner, also went up the Hudson, daring the American batteries, which cannonaded them "as furiously as they could," but with little effect. They anchored above the American works, and thus prevented the further removal of stores from the city by water.[21] The stage was now set for the next act. Howe was ready to attack Manhattan.

The sun rose in a clear, blue sky on Sunday September 15, with a fresh breeze blowing. Early in the morning five warships took stations in the East River, in a line from Kip's Bay towards the south at about two hundred yards from the shore and broadside to it. At ten o'clock eighty-four flat-boats laden with British soldiers put out in four divisions from the Long Island shore. At a little before eleven, the ships opened fire on the entrenchments along the New York side of the river, "such a fire as nothing could withstand." [22] "About 70 large pieces of Cannon were in Play, together with Swivels & small arms," making "so terrible and so incessant a Roar of Guns few even in the Army & Navy had ever heard before." [23] And all this fire was poured upon a line of entrenchments at Kip's Bay held by Captain William Douglas with a brigade of Connecticut militia. "Entrenchments," they were called; but in fact "they were nothing more than a ditch dug along the bank of the river, with the dirt thrown out towards the water." [24]

The boats came up with the line of ships. The fire ceased, but the boats came on, crowded with redcoats and looking like "a clover field in full bloom." They reached the shore at Kip's Bay. The light infantry leaped from them, clambered up "the steep and just accessible rocks" [25]—and found no one to oppose them. Douglas's troops, their frail defensive works already beaten down by the gunfire, had fled "with the utmost precipitation." [26] Wadsworth's brigade, next below them, followed.[27] Parsons's and Scott's militia, farther south, took notice and retreated up the Bowery Road.[28]

Washington, at Harlem when he heard the sound of the bombardment, took horse and rode at full speed to the scene of action. On the Post Road, now Lexington Avenue, about where Forty-second Street crosses it, he met Douglas's men, still retreating precipitately and in confusion. "The demons of fear and disorder seemed to take full possession of all and everything that day," one of them said.[29] Parsons's brigade, also in complete disarray, hurrying north for safety's sake had come up with them.

Washington tried to halt them, to rally them. "Take the walls!" he cried. "Take the cornfield!" Some of them ran to the walls, some into the cornfield. With Putnam and several other officers he tried to form them behind the walls, but there was no controlling them. Washington's anger was spectacular. "He dashed his hat upon the ground in a transport of rage," crying out, "Are these the men with whom I am to defend America?" He snapped a pistol at them. With his riding cane, "he flogged not only private soldiers, but officers as well," a colonel, even a brigadier general.[30] But nothing would do. At the sight of sixty or seventy Hessians coming at them they broke, flung away muskets, knapsacks, even coats and hats, and ran "as if the Devil was in them." "The ground was literally covered" with such discarded encumbrances.[31] And they left Washington almost alone within eighty yards of the oncoming Hessians. Blinded with rage—or with despair—he sat his horse, taking no heed of his imminent danger. He would have been shot or captured had not an aide-de-camp seized his bridle and "absolutely hurried him away." [32]

Putnam, seeing that no stand could be made there, galloped south through Wadsworth's and Scott's brigades coming up in full retreat, to attempt the rescue of Sullivan's brigade, Knox's artillery, and the others still in the town before the British could stretch across the island and hem them in.[33]

He gathered the troops in the city, abandoned the heavy guns and the remaining military stores, and started north. But he knew as little of the geography of Manhattan as he had known of the terrain on Long Island. The Post Road on the easterly side, the main artery leading north and the only one he knew, was held by the enemy. He would have found himself hopelessly entrapped, had not young Aaron Burr, his aide-de-camp, guided him to an unfrequented road along the west side, close to the Hudson.[34]

The day had become intensely hot. Dust hung in stifling clouds over the troops. The water in their canteens was soon exhausted. With dust in their parched throats, sweat streaming from their faces, they slogged along dejectedly. It was hard to keep them going at a reasonable speed. But Putnam now displayed his best native qualities, courage and energy. He rode up and down the two-mile-long column, heartening his men, hurrying them along. They met a detachment of the enemy, beat it off, and at last after dark ended their twelve-mile exhausting march in the main camp at Harlem, where the rest of the army was now collected.[35]

The first division of the British army was led by Howe, Clinton, Cornwallis, Vaughan, Matthews, Leslie, and von Donop. It comprised three battalions of light infantry, four battalions of British grenadiers, three of Hessian grenadiers, the Hessian jägers, and the brigade of British Guards, about 4,000 in all. Immediately on landing, Leslie and the light infantry swung to the right. Von Donop's Hessian grenadiers turned left, met Wadsworth's retreating New York militia, and after a short engagement captured three or four hundred of them. Howe and the rest advanced to Incleberg, otherwise called Murray Hill—a height of land lying between the present Fourth and Sixth avenues and Thirty-fifth and Fortieth streets. There they halted to await the arrival of the second division for which the boats had been sent back.

Repeated trips of the boats brought this division to land about five o'clock. It comprised five brigades and two regiments of British regulars, one brigade of Hessians, and the artillery, about 9,000 men. One brigade was then sent south, and its men were billeted in houses and barns along the Post Road all the way down to the town.

With the main army Howe marched north to McGowan's Pass and rested there for the night.[36] On the way up the Post Road they marched for a time parallel with Putnam's sweating militiamen, separated from them by no greater distance than the width of the present Central Park; but neither force was aware of the other's proximity.[37]

During the afternoon detachments of the British force had ranged about, picking up prisoners here and there, singly or in groups. The Americans lost 17 officers and 350 men that day, nearly all captives; very few were killed. But fifty or sixty cannon and a very considerable amount of ammunition, stores and baggage had been left behind in the town.[38]

That night the British rested, presumably in comfort, in their billets in New York and in the tents of their camp, which stretched across the island from Bloomingdale on the Hudson to Horn's Hook on the East River. Not so the Americans within the hastily entrenched lines on Harlem Heights. "Our soldiers," wrote Colonel David Humphrey, "excessively fatigued by the sultry march of the day, their clothes wet by a severe shower of rain that succeeded towards the evening, their blood chilled by the cold wind . . . and their hearts sunk within them by the loss of baggage, artillery and works in which they had been taught to put great confidence, lay upon their arms, covered only by the clouds of an uncomfortable sky."

That wild flight from Kip's Bay was a sad exhibition. Washington called it "disgraceful and dastardly," but such strong epithets were hardly merited. Douglas's men were not trained, experienced, disciplined soldiers; they were raw militia. With their slight defenses battered down and in the face of an advancing foe of overwhelming numbers, it was natural, indeed it was proper, that this thin line of men should leave their indefensible positions. After that withdrawal they might have rallied, as Washington called on them to do, and annoyed the oncoming enemy for a while. But to what end? They could not possibly have held those stone walls. They would have been enveloped and swallowed up with little delay. A retreat was the only sensible move, though, of course, it ought to have been made in good order.

That is not to say that they reasoned this out. After that withdrawal from their trenches the simple fact is that they were panic-stricken. Panics are often inexplicable in their origin and usually ungovernable in their course. Crowds of people are infected by them without knowing how or where they started. They grow by what they feed upon, ignorance of the reason for their existence. Yielding to them does not prove a lack of personal courage. Habits of discipline, well drilled into men so that they automatically obey orders without questioning the reasons for them, are the only safeguard against such occurrences as this in any army at any time. The militia at Kip's Bay had never had even a chance to acquire such habits.

CHAPTER 20

Harlem Heights

The position to which the Americans retreated from New York was on the narrow neck of land that lies between the Harlem River and the Hudson and is the upper part of Manhattan Island. A plateau called Harlem Heights, occupying the full width of the neck, was bordered on the south and on the two river sides by rocky heights, making it a good defensive position. On this plateau Washington had planned a series of three fortified lines, each extending its full width.

On the first line, about a mile back from the southerly edge of the plateau, three small redoubts had been built at the time of the retreat. The connecting entrenchments were now pushed to completion. The second line with four redoubts, about three-quarters of a mile behind the first, and the third line perhaps a half mile behind the second, were to be built later. The plan, therefore, provided for a defense in depth from the rugged edge of the plateau north for nearly four miles.[1]

The returns of the American army under Washington, dated September 21, show a paper strength of 27,273 infantry rank and file, 104 horse, and 543 artillery. Of this number, 16,124 are listed as "present, fit for duty." [2] But to man the Heights there were probably not more than 10,000, the rest being posted farther north at and about Kingsbridge, where the Harlem River turned west to join the Hudson.

The various elements of the force on the Heights were disposed in depth as follows: Greene's division, comprising Nixon's, Sargent's, and Beall's brigades, 3,300 strong, along the southern edge of the plateau; Putnam's division of James Clinton's, Heard's, and Douglas's brigades, 2,500 men, about halfway between Greene's division and the first fortified line; Spencer's division of Fellows's, Silliman's, Wadsworth's, and Mifflin's brigades, 4,200 men, within the first lines.[3]

Facing this plateau on the south was another, the northern edge of which ran very irregularly across the much broader part of the island. Its nearest approach was on the westerly side, where it extended in a sort of peninsula or tongue of land of about the same width as the northern plateau. At this point the two elevations were separated by a narrow depression, perhaps three-quarters of a mile at its widest, a quarter at its narrowest, called the Hollow Way. At its easterly end it widened to an extensive plain with Harlem village at its eastern side.[4]

The British army encamped on the evening of the 15th on the southerly plateau in lines extending on a two-mile front from Horn's Hook on the East River to Bloomingdale on the Hudson. Its front line was thus two miles or less from the front line of the Americans. Two brigades, including the Guards, lay more than a mile in the rear of the lowest line of the main camp and so about three miles back from the American front line.[5]

In the heights at the northern edge of the southern plateau was a gap called McGowan's Pass, through which ran the only road connecting Harlem Plains and the southern parts of the island. It was held by the British.

Washington had much confidence in the strength of his position, but not in the steadfastness of his troops. In the early morning of the 16th he wrote to the Congress: "We are now Encamped with the Main body of the Army on the Heights of Harlem, where I should hope the Enemy would meet with a defeat in case of an Attack, if the generality of our Troops would behave with tolerable resolution. But, experience, to my Extreme affliction, has convinced me that this is rather to be wished for than expected." [6] His confidence in the strength of his position was justified provided Howe made a frontal attack. His apprehensions as to the behavior of his men, engendered by the rout of the militia at Kip's Bay, were almost immediately dispelled.

The great question in the minds of the American command the night of the 15th was whether Howe would follow up his success by an immediate attack. From the American lines, because of the dense woods on the heights to the south of the Hollow Way, nothing could be seen of the enemy's camp in that quarter. Hence there could be no knowledge of preparations for attack, nor of its launching, until the van of the attacking force emerged from the woods into the Hollow Way. To obtain such information a reconnaissance was necessary.

There was in the army a corps of Rangers, about 120 volunteers chosen chiefly from the Connecticut regiments for detached duty, scouting, and the like. They were commanded by Captain Thomas Knowlton, a figure of note. "Six feet high, erect and elegant in figure and formed more for activity than strength," cool and courageous in battle, "courteous and affable in manners . . . the favorite of superior officers, the idol of his soldiers," he had already achieved reputation at Bunker Hill and on Long Island. To him and his corps Washington looked for information as to Howe's intentions.[7]

Before dawn on the 16th Knowlton led his men down from the American position, across the Hollow Way, and up through the woods on the opposite heights behind which lay the British left. They came at length upon a stone house considerably in advance of the main body of the enemy, and at the same time upon the pickets of two battalions of British light infantry under General Leslie holding an advanced post.

At the alarm the light infantry, about 400 strong, advanced. The Rangers took a position behind a stone wall and opened fire. A brisk skirmish ensued. The Americans had fired eight rounds when they discovered the 42nd Highlanders, the Black Watch, coming up on their left and threatening to flank them. Ten of Knowlton's men having fallen, he gave the order to retreat. The British light infantry pushed forward after them through the woods, but the Rangers got away in good order.[8]

The sound of the firing put both armies on the alert. In the American camp the advancing light infantry could be seen emerging from the woods on the opposite height. It might prove to be the beginning of an attack.

The Americans were ordered under arms, but the enemy halted at the edge of their plateau. Pleased by the sight of the Rangers in retreat, the British "in the most insulting manner sounded their bugle-horns as is usual after a Fox-chase. I never felt such a sensation before—it seemed to crown our disgrace." So Colonel Joseph Reed wrote to his wife.[9] Washington, that old fox hunter, must have recognized the taunting notes of the horns as the customary signal of a fox gone to earth. On top of yesterday's affair at Kip's Bay it was too much. Something must be done to wipe out that disgrace and arouse the spirits of his men.[10] He planned a frontal feint with a small force to draw the British light infantry down to the open ground of the Hollow Way, so that a stronger detachment could encircle their right flank and cut them off. For the feint he ordered out 150 volunteers from Nixon's brigade, led by Lieutenant Colonel Archibald Crary of Rhode Island. Knowlton's Rangers and three companies of riflemen from Weedon's 3rd Virginia Regiment, under command of Major Andrew Leitch, were to be the flanking party, about 230 in number.

THE
WESTCHESTER
CAMPAIGN

Oct. 29

Oct. 28   White Plains
Oct. 28

Dobbs Ferry

Hudson River

American Retreat

Yonkers

Bronx River

British Advance

New Rochelle

Kingsbridge

Fort Lee

Pell's Point

Fort Washington

Throgs Neck

American Lines

British Lines

Hell Gate

MANHATTAN ISLAND

Crary's detachment advanced boldly down into the Hollow Way. Responding to this challenge the British light infantry "immediately ran down the Hill, took possession of some fences and Bushes and a smart fighting began, but at too great distance to do much execution either side." [11] Crary's men fell back a little to draw the enemy on, still maintaining their fire. To support them and give a further appearance of reality to this feigned attack, the rest of Nixon's brigade, about 800 men, was sent down.

While the semblance of a conflict was kept up in front for the better part of an hour, the flanking party, guided by Colonel Joseph Reed, was making its way through the woods and across the valley well to the east of the fighters. Unobserved, it gained a position on the enemy's flank. So far, so good; a few hundred yards more, and it would have mounted the ledge of rocks and swept around in the rear of the foe. But unfortunately some "inferior officers" could not restrain their ardor, or perhaps control their nerves. They gave an order to fire.

The British realized their danger and promptly withdrew to an open field about 200 yards in their rear, where they again formed behind a fence and resumed their fire. Crary's men followed them. The flankers also joined in the battle. The British again fell back, to the top of the ridge, the Americans after them. The fire on both sides was hotly kept up.

On top of the height and within ten minutes of each other, the two commanders of the flanking party, Knowlton and Leitch, fell mortally wounded. Here was a fine chance for the Yankee Rangers and the Virginia riflemen, both now leaderless, to break up in confusion and repeat Kip's Bay. But this time they were the pursuers. They had seen the backs of the redcoats, a stimulating sight. The company commanders took charge. They pressed on "with splendid spirit and animation," and "continued the engagement with the greatest resolution."

Reinforcements were on the way. Washington had seen his little affair, involving a few hundred, grow into a real fight. His men were redeeming themselves from yesterday's disgrace. He ordered forward nine companies of General Reazin Beall's Maryland state troops, Colonel Paul Dudley Sargent's brigade from Connecticut and Massachusetts, the rest of Weedon's Virginians, and, most important for the morale of the army, Douglas's regiment, the one disgraced at Kip's Bay. That old warhorse, Israel Putnam, hurried to the fray, along with General Nathanael Greene, General George Clinton, and two field guns. Meanwhile, the first British contingents had retired into a buckwheat field, the American light artillery having "put them to flight with two discharges." [12] There they were reinforced by additional light infantry and by the Black Watch.

The fighting grew hotter, the Americans firing steadily and the British stubbornly holding their ground. As the American reinforcements came on, Leslie called on the British reserve in that quarter for more troops. From their post three miles in the rear, on the run, "without a halt to draw breath," [13] came British grenadiers, the 33rd Regiment, a battalion of Hessian grenadiers, and a company of jägers, with two fieldpieces hauled by men. This addition brought the number of British engaged up to 5,000.

The jägers and the Highlanders with the two field guns got there first. For two hours, from noon to two o'clock, the combat was spirited. The British guns fired sixty rounds. Then the Hessians and the Scotsmen, their ammunition running low, retreated. The Americans followed them in hot pursuit, back into an orchard, down a slope, and up another hill. The Hessian grenadiers came up to them. The rest of the British reserve was near at hand, when Washington, seeing that the affair was developing into a general engagement in full force, which he by no means desired, sent an aide, Tench Tilghman, with orders to his troops to withdraw. "The pursuit of a flying enemy was so new a scene that it was with difficulty our men could be brought to retire," but they "gave a Hurra! and left the field in good order." [14]

The losses on both sides were, as usual, variously reported, each side minimizing its own and exaggerating the other's casualties. Howe reported for the British 14 killed and about 78 wounded,[15] but Major Baurmeister, a Hessian, said there were 70 dead and 200 wounded.[16] Washington said his loss was "about sixty"; [17] but more probably there were 30 killed and something less than 100 wounded and missing.[18] In the deaths of Knowlton and Leitch the Americans suffered their severest loss. Knowlton was, in Washington's words, "a valuable and gallant officer." [19] Leitch had arrived in camp with Weedon's Virginians but a few days before the battle. He was a brave soldier of great promise.

Though gallantly fought on both sides, it was a small affair. Yet its effects in both camps were immediate and important. Among the Americans the depression engendered by the recent succession of defeats and retreats was dispelled. Many of the soldiers who had fled from Kip's Bay without firing a shot had now helped to drive the British and Hessian regulars back more than a mile, had fought them in the open field at forty yards range for more than an hour, and had withdrawn in good order to their own lines only when commanded to do so, without being pursued. That was good news for the whole army. Caesar Rodney wrote to his brother about it: "That New England men placed to defend the landing-place [Kip's

Bay], behaved in a most dastardly, cowardly, scandalous manner, is most certain; but that courage is not always to be found the same, even in the same person, is equally true, and verified in the very same men; for some of them the day following were in the other engagement and behaved with great bravery." [20]

Moreover the "Southern" and New England troops had fought side by side with equal courage; neither could criticize the other. To be sure, both claimed the honors of the day. Captain John Gooch of Rhode Island gave "the first Lawrells" to the Yankees, while Lieutenant Tench Tilghman of Maryland wrote, "The Virginia and Maryland Troops bear the palm"; [21] but that was only human. As a whole the army had recovered its self-respect and gained greatly in morale. "You can hardly conceive the change it has made in our army," wrote Colonel Joseph Reed. "The men have recovered their spirits and feel a confidence which before they had quite lost." With some suggestion of doubt he added, "I hope the effects will be lasting." [22]

To the British this affair was an eye-opener. The rebels could stand up and fight bravely against the best of the British and Hessian regulars. The campaign was not going to be an easy succession of Kip's Bays. In the light of this discovery, some thought must be given to the next move. So, for nearly four weeks, Howe contented himself with fortifying his lines, forgoing further offensive movements until what he had gained had been secured.

CHAPTER 21

Throg's Neck and Pelham

While the two armies sat facing each other in their respective fortified positions, there was much speculation in the American camp as to Howe's next move. "The General Officers," says Heath in his memoirs, "were divided in opinion." Some of them expected an effort by Howe to make himself master of the whole island, and thought that the reduction of Fort Washington would be first attempted. That stronghold, upon a height overlooking the Hudson, was a mile or more in the rear of the American lines on Harlem Heights, and it is not clear what plan for its conquest was attributed to Howe that did not involve first a frontal attack on Washington's entrenchments. Others looked for a landing at some point on Long Island Sound in a line with or in the rear of the Americans' more northerly defenses, so that they could be flanked.

With this difference of opinion prevailing, it was "determined in council to guard against both." Ten thousand men were to be held on the Manhattan Island "at or near Fort Washington," that is to say, within the existing lines. Heath, with ten thousand, was to hold the Kingsbridge sector at the upper end of the Harlem River, a floating bridge being thrown across that water so that communication with the first body could be maintained. Greene was to command five thousand on the other side of the Hudson at or near Fort Constitution, which was directly opposite Fort Washington.[1]

Washington had 25,000 troops on paper, but only on paper. As has been said, no more than about 16,000 were present and fit for duty, and of these a large proportion were militia, no more to be depended upon than "a broken staff," as Washington put it.[2] The success of this ambitious plan, therefore, would appear more to be desired than expected.

Washington fully realized his difficulties. "It is not in the power of words," he wrote to his brother on September 22, "to describe the task I have to perform. Fifty thousand pounds would not induce me again to undergo what I have done." And to his cousin: "Such is my situation that if I were to wish the bitterest curse to an enemy on this side of the grave, I should put him in my stead with my feelings." [3]

It was not only that he had too few men to defend all the threatened positions, but also that those he did have were not of the best quality. Although the troops engaged in the recent affair at Harlem Heights had proved themselves good soldiers, the American army was not entirely composed of heroes. The present, too long period of inactivity was undermining the army's morale and sapping its discipline. "A spirit of desertion, cowardice, plunder and shrinking from duty, when attended with fatigue or danger, prevailed too generally throughout the whole army," Colonel Joseph Reed wrote of this period.[4]

Courts-martial sat day after day trying cases of insubordination, mutiny, theft, cowardice in the face of the enemy, desertion, and other offenses. Such crimes and misdemeanors are, of course, common in all armies, but in this they were far too prevalent. Washington wrote to the Congress: "Such a spirit has gone forth . . . that neither publick or private property is secure. Every hour brings the most distressing complaints of the Ravages of our own Troops who are become infinitely more formidable to the poor Farmers and Inhabitants than the common Enemy. . . . The Baggage of Officers and the Hospital Stores, even the Quarters of the General Officers are not exempt from Rapine." [5]

Besides these defects in its personnel, the army as a whole was "in want of almost every necessary; Tents, Camp Kettles, Blankets and Clothes of all Kinds." Reinforcements from New England were coming in "without a single Tent nor a necessary of any kind . . . not a pan or a kettle," [6] and winter was on its way. Even now it was cold at night on Harlem Heights.

All this was bad enough, but the prospect for the near future was worse. The entire army could look forward to its dissolution and complete disappearance within the next two or three months, when its term of enlistment would expire. It was true that the Congress had at last, on September 16, overcome its "jealousy of a standing army," [7] and voted for a new army of eighty-eight battalions "to serve during the present war." [8] But who could foretell when that projected force would be an army in being?

Howe remained inactive for twenty-six days while with characteristic deliberation and with equally characteristic sagacity he made his plans. The

American lines were too strong to invite a frontal attack. Nor was that Howe's favored strategy. Circumvention was less costly and more nearly certain of good results.

There was a small peninsula sticking out into the Sound from the mainland almost due east of the American lines, Throg's Neck—originally Throckmorton's, hence Throck's and Throg's, but also Frog's Neck or Point. And there was a road running northwest from that point to Kingsbridge, well in the rear of the main fortified position of the Americans. Howe finally decided to use that road in the hope that he could sweep the American left flank and possibly pin the American army against the Hudson.

Leaving Lord Percy to hold his lines with three brigades, Howe embarked his main army in the evening of October 12 in eighty vessels of all sorts, passed through Hell Gate under cover of a fog and landed an advance force of 4,000 on Throg's Neck. But it was not a neck, a peninsula; it was, in effect, an island, separated from the mainland by a creek with marshy borders. There were but two approaches from it to the main, a causeway and bridge at the lower end, a ford at the upper, and those approaches were not unguarded. Had Howe landed his men farther to the east, his flanking movement would have had much greater chances of success.

General Heath had posted Colonel Edward Hand with a small detachment of his 1st Pennsylvania rifle regiment at the causeway. The riflemen had removed the planks of the bridge and concealed themselves behind a long pile of cordwood beside its western end. When the van of the enemy approached the gap, it was met by a sudden well aimed fire. The surprised troops were thrown into confusion and fell back to the top of the nearest elevation. No further effort was made to pass that way. Twenty-five American riflemen behind a woodpile had stopped the British army. Another British detachment had headed for the ford, but it too was checked, by a guard posted there. Both of these outposts were promptly reinforced. Colonel William Prescott's Massachusetts Continental regiment and Captain-Lieutenant David Bryant with a 6-pounder and its crew went to Hand's aid. Captain John Graham led a New York regiment of Continentals, together with Captain Daniel Jackson and his fieldpiece, to the post at the ford. The defenders then numbered about 1,800 men. Both sides now began to dig in at their respective positions, the riflemen and the jägers keeping up "a scattered popping at each other across the marsh."

The rest of Howe's force arrived in the afternoon, and the bulk of the British army was at the Neck. But Howe saw that the creek and the marshes were not easily to be crossed against such determined opposition. His men went into camp and lay there for six days while their baggage and supplies were brought up from New York.[9]

Howe had got off to a bad start, but his course was not yet run. Throg's Neck was not the only available landing place. There was Pell's Point, only three miles to the east, which was part of the mainland. It offered the Americans no narrow way to defend.

Howe's flanking move placed the American army in great peril, and a council of war assembled at Washington's headquarters on October 16 to consider the situation. General Charles Lee, who had just rejoined the main army after winning laurels by a successful defense of Charleston in South Carolina, vehemently urged a general retreat to safer positions. However, Congress had resolved on October 11 that Washington be "desired, if it be practicable, by every art and whatever expence, to obstruct effectually the navigation of the North River, between Fort Washington and Mount Constitution." [10] That meant that the line of sunken hulks and the "chevaux-de-frise" stretching across the river from Fort Washington to Fort Constitution, which line had already been found to be easily penetrable by British ships, should be maintained, if "practicable." If the chevaux-de-frise was to be maintained, the two forts had to be defended. Since the barrier had already been proved to be useless, the council of war need not have been concerned about this resolution. Accordingly there was no need to hold Fort Washington. However, the generals decided that, as "the enemy's whole force is in our rear at Frog's Point," it was not possible to hold the present positions on the Heights, and at the same time "that Fort Washington be retained as long as possible." [11]

The proposed withdrawal was to go as far as White Plains, leaving Fort Washington, with its garrison of 2,000, fifteen miles away and completely isolated in a country entirely held by the enemy, with no possibility of succor or supplies except from Fort Constitution across the Hudson. Yet it was to be held. A worse military decision has not often been made. The cost incurred was to be frightful.

Stirling's brigade was hurried northward to seize and hold the desired position at White Plains until the main army should arrive. It made the march in about four hours. The movement of the main army northward was begun on the 18th. Over Kingsbridge, which crossed the Harlem River, and along the west bank of the Bronx River, the American column, 13,000 men with artillery, baggage, and supplies, made its slow and toilsome way— slow and toilsome because of the lack of horses and wagons. After a day's journey, the wagons would dump their loads by the wayside and return for more. The artillery was dragged by hand. Thus, by starts and stops and with infinite labor, a day's journey was accomplished in four.[12]

Meanwhile, entrenched posts were established at intervals along the heights on the west side of the Bronx River to protect the movement of the troops on the road farther west and close to the Hudson. Spencer's division held that line until the main American army had reached White Plains.

Howe finally found that more favorable landing place at Pell's Point. On the same day that the Americans started their northward trek, he embarked his army at Throg's Neck and landed it on the Point.

Colonel John Glover, of the amphibious Marblehead regiment, was then commanding a small brigade made up of four skeleton Massachusetts regiments—his own, Colonel Joseph Read's, Colonel William Shepard's, and Colonel Loammi Baldwin's—in all about seven hundred fifty men with three fieldpieces. He had been but lately posted near the little village of Eastchester to guard the roads from Pell's Point towards the American rear. Early in the morning of the 18th he ascended a near-by hill with his glass and discovered in Eastchester Bay, beside the Point, "upwards of two hundred [boats] . . . all manned and formed in four grand divisions." He turned out his men and marched to meet the landing force.

Glover took a position on the road about a mile from the Point. His own regiment was stationed in the rear as a reserve. The others were strung along behind stone walls lining the road, Read's at the front end or left of the line, Shepard's next, and then Baldwin's. A captain and 40 men were detached and sent forward. They met the enemy's advance guard and, at 50 yards distance, received their fire without loss. Their own reply struck down four men. Five rounds were exchanged in which two Americans were killed and several wounded. When the enemy were "not more than thirty yards distant," Glover ordered his little party to fall back, "which was masterly well done." "The enemy gave a shout and advanced." When they were within a hundred feet, Read's men, lying undiscovered behind their stone wall, "rose up and gave them the whole charge; the enemy broke and retreated for the main body to come up."

For an hour and a half there was no further conflict. Then the whole advance unit of the British, 4,000 men with seven guns, came on. At fifty yards distance Read's men again arose and delivered a volley. The British replied with musketry and fieldpieces. Seven rounds were fired by this regiment before it retreated to take a position behind the wall beyond Shepard's battalion. Again the enemy "shouted and pushed on till they came to Shepard, posted behind a fine, double stone-wall." His men fired by platoons seventeen rounds, "causing them to retreat several times."

Another backward movement of the Americans carried Shepard and Read behind Baldwin. Then Glover ordered his brigade off the field, across a creek, and to a position in his rear on a hill. "The enemy halted and played away their artillery at us and we at them, till night, without any damage on our side and but little on theirs," says Glover. After dark the Americans marched away, about three miles, and encamped, "after fighting all day without victuals or drink, laying as a picket all night, the heavens over us and the earth under us." [13]

Glover lost eight killed and thirteen wounded. Howe reported three killed and twenty wounded; but the chief of the attacking force were Hessians, and their losses were not always included in the British official reports. The Americans thought the Hessian losses were very heavy.[14]

Another interesting little affair occurred on October 22. Major Robert Rogers, noted for audacity and ruthlessness in the French and Indian War, commanded a corps of Tories called "The Queen's American Rangers," about five hundred strong. Looked upon as renegades, he and his men were especially detested by the American troops. Moreover they had been aggressively active, attacking and defeating militia companies and capturing quantities of army stores. They were now in a detached camp at Mamaroneck not far from the right wing of the main body of the British. It was decided to try to cut them off.

"The redoubtable Colonel Haslet" was chosen to conduct this enterprise, with his Delaware regiment,[15] "which since the bravery exhibited on Long Island . . . seems to have been chosen for all feats of peculiar danger." [16] Reinforced by certain Virginia and Maryland companies, his force was made up to seven hundred fifty men.

Late in the night of Tuesday the 22nd, Haslet's force set out on the road from White Plains to Mamaroneck, about five miles. It led them so close to the British right that the most profound silence was necessary to avoid discovery. Having accurate knowledge of the usual disposition of Rogers's men, they approached his camp at a point where but a single sentinel was posted. They seized and silenced him. The way seemed open for a surprise attack on the whole camp, but the astute Rogers had that day concluded his encampment was insufficiently guarded and had posted Captain Eagles and sixty men between the lone sentinel and the main position.

Haslet's vanguard came upon their bivouac, fairly stumbling over the sleepers in the darkness. The rest of his force came up on the run, and there ensued a hurly-burly of a fight. To deceive their assailants, the Rangers echoed the Americans' cry: "Surrender, you Tory dogs! Surrender!" In the darkness friend and foe could not be distinguished. There was a hopeless tangle, Rangers and Haslet's men grappling each other indiscriminately. In the turmoil Eagles and about a third of his men slipped away. The rest were subdued and captured.

Haslet then pushed on toward the main camp. Rogers's troops, thoroughly alarmed, had turned out. There was an exchange of fire, but the advantage of a surprise had been lost. Haslet, contenting himself with a partial success, called off his men and marched back to White Plains with thirty-six prisoners, a pair of colors, sixty muskets, and as many highly prized blankets. He had lost three killed and twelve wounded. The Rangers' loss, besides the prisoners, remains unrecorded. General Heath praised it as "a pretty affair . . . conducted with good address." [17] Like Glover's little fight, this enterprise was chiefly valuable as a stimulus to the fighting spirit of the Americans.

CHAPTER 22

White Plains

Before Howe moved in force against the American position at White Plains the American army was again reorganized. Charles Lee was again with the main army, and also Sullivan and Stirling. Sullivan had been released from captivity in exchange for General Richard Prescott, taken by Montgomery when he captured the British ships at Montreal. Stirling had also been freed, in a trade for Montfort Browne, former royal governor of West Florida. Seven divisions were formed, under the command respectively of Generals Greene, Lee, Heath, Sullivan, Putnam, Spencer, and Benjamin Lincoln. Greene, with about 3,500 men, held the fort across the Hudson from Fort Washington formerly named Constitution but now called Lee in honor of that much respected soldier. About 1,500 men under Colonel Robert Magaw occupied Fort Washington. The main army under Washington numbered about 14,500 present and fit.[1]

Washington had chosen a position on a series of hills overlooking the White Plains. Putnam's division was posted at the right on Purdy Hill, Heath's at the left on Hatfield Hill. Washington himself held the centre at White Plains village. Two lines of defensive works were thrown up, in a shallow curve from the Bronx River on the right to a millpond on the left. The ends of the lines were drawn back so as to defend the flanks.[2]

On October 19, when Howe left his camp at Eastchester, the American retreat from Harlem Heights to White Plains was only well begun. If he had seized his chance then or on the next day and sent his light infantry, grenadiers, and jägers, 4,000 strong, across by the straight road to Kingsbridge, only six miles away, in a swift attack upon the long, straggling line of Washington's army in the confusion of its movement, there could hardly have been any other result than a complete rout of the Americans. Instead he lay at New Rochelle for three days, and then only moved to Mamaroneck, two or three miles. There he encamped for four days. It was not until the 28th that he arrived before Washington's position at White Plains. He had advanced about seventeen miles in ten days.[3] Why Howe executed his flanking movement so slowly is not known.

"The sun had set and risen more than forty times," wrote Trevelyan, the English historian, in acid comment on the progress of the British army, "since General Howe broke up his Summer cantonments on Staten Island. In seven weeks—with an irresistible army and a fleet which there was nothing to resist—he had traversed, from point to point, a distance of exactly thirty-five miles." [4] Trevelyan's judgment of Howe is perhaps too harsh, on this and other occasions.

Meanwhile the British general had received reinforcements, in any event. On the day he landed at Pell's Point there came into New York harbor 120 sail bringing the second grand division of German mercenaries, 3,997 Hessians, 670 Waldeckers, and a company of jägers, all under command of Lieutenant General Wilhelm von Knyphausen, also about 3,400 British recruits. The Germans were at once dispatched by water to New Rochelle to hold that position while Howe proceeded toward White Plains.[5]

The opposing armies clashed again in the morning of the 28th. Spencer, with a half-dozen New England regiments from Lee's division, about 1,500 men, had been sent out to meet the British advance. They took a position behind stone walls about a mile and a half below the American lines and held their fire until the British van was within one hundred feet. Then they delivered a volley that halted it and threw it back. But when Colonel Rall's regiment of Hessians was about to turn their left, the Americans retreated to another wall and after that to another, holding each position until nearly outflanked. At one time a general volley delivered at close range scattered an attacking party of Hessian grenadiers "like leaves in a whirlwind; and they ran off so far that some of the Americans ran out to the ground where they were and brought off their arms and accoutrements and rum that the men who fell had with them, which we had time to drink rounds with before they came on again." So wrote one of the American officers.[6]

But the Hessians did come on again and drove Spencer's troops back across the Bronx River and to Chatterton's Hill, which two militia regiments were engaged in fortifying under the direction of Colonel Rufus Putnam. Rall's regiment, checked by the fire from that elevation, retired to a small hill just south of Chatterton's. The loss of the Americans in this series of encounters was 12 killed, 23 wounded, and 2 missing.[7]

Chatterton's Hill was about half a mile from the right of the main American lines, separated from it by the narrow valley of the Bronx River. It was a ridge three-quarters of a mile long in a north and south direction, rising one hundred eighty feet above the river, which ran along its eastern foot. That side of the hill was steep and heavily wooded. The gently rounded top was divided by stone walls into cultivated fields. Because the hill was a menace to the westerly end of the American lines a belated effort to fortify it was now being made.[8]

After the retreat of Spencer's corps Washington ordered Colonel Haslet with his Delaware regiment to reinforce the men entrenching there. Haslet took post a little below the top of the hill on its eastern side. Later General Alexander McDougall's brigade was also sent there. It was composed of McDougall's own regiment, the 1st New York, Ritzema's 3rd New York, Smallwood's regiment of Marylanders, lately strengthened after its disaster at Long Island, Webb's from Connecticut, and two fieldpieces. These, with Haslet's men, made up a force of about 1,250 rank and file. With the militia already there, the American detachment numbered about 1,600.[9] As senior officer McDougall took command.

Before he arrived several enemy fieldpieces had opened fire on the hill and had hit one of Colonel Putnam's militiamen. "The whole regiment broke and fled immediately and were not rallied without much difficulty." [10] On McDougall's arrival the two militia regiments, Brooks's from Massachusetts and Graham's from New York, were stationed on the right behind a stone wall, at Haslet's suggestion. Smallwood and Haslet held the centre, from which McDougall's, Ritzema's, and Webb's regiments extended to the left.[11]

The whole British army was now coming on in the plain below. It halted, and its general officers gathered in a wheat field for consultation. To the Americans on Chatterton's Hill and in their fortified lines, it presented a brilliant, though formidable, spectacle. "The sun shone bright, their arms glittered, and perhaps troops never were shewn to more advantage than those now appeared," wrote General Heath in his memoirs.[12] An officer in Webb's regiment even more eloquently described the scene: "Its appearance was truly magnificent. A bright autumnal sun shed its lustre on the polished arms; and the rich array of dress and military equipage gave an imposing grandeur to the scene as they advanced in all the pomp and circumstance of war." [13]

After the council in the wheat field a British detachment of eight regiments, 4,000 men, and a dozen guns drew away from the main body and marched to a hill facing Chatterton's at about a half-mile distance. It was obvious that they were to attack McDougall's force. The rest of the army "all sat down in the same order in which they stood, no one appearing to move out of his place," [14] a professional audience of 10,000 awaiting the rise of the curtain on an interesting drama.

The overture to the performance was played by the British artillery. From the high ground facing Chatterton's Hill, it began a furious cannonade against the little force of Americans awaiting the attack. General von Heister's adjutant general afterwards said that these guns made such a thunderstorm that one could neither see nor hear. Haslet wrote that the enemy's artillery "kept up a continual peal of reiterated thunder." [15] The attacking force meanwhile deployed in line of battle on the other side of the Bronx River. It was obscured from the Americans by the woods on the slope below and by the smoke of a fire among the trees, probably ignited by the artillery discharges.[16]

The Americans had two fieldpieces. Haslet urged McDougall to bring them into action. The general ordered one forward. It was "so poorly appointed," says Haslet, "that myself was forced to assist in dragging it along in the rear of the regiment. While so employed, a cannon-ball struck the carriage and scattered the shot about, a wad of blazing tow in the middle. The artillerymen fled. The few that returned made not more than two discharges when they retreated with the field-piece." [17]

As soon as the British line was formed a battalion of Hessians, supported by a British brigade and von Donop's Hessian grenadiers, started toward the river. The little Bronx was unusually high because of recent rains, and was much obstructed by an accumulation of old tree trunks and by the remains of ancient beaver-dams. The Hessians declined to try to cross it. It was therefore necessary to construct a rough bridge by felling trees and laying fence rails across them. While the bridge building was in progress, Smallwood's Marylanders and Ritzema's 3rd New York came more than halfway down the hill and opened fire, throwing the Hessians into disorder.

The British General Leslie was then informed of a ford a short distance downstream. He called on the 28th and 35th British regiments to show the Hessians what true British courage could do. Cheering lustily they followed him to the ford and across it. Immediately he ordered a charge with the bayonet; but the hill was steep, the trees thick, and the fire of the Americans heavy. The attackers were thrown back upon the 5th and 49th regiments and the Hessians, who were hurrying to their support.

The whole attacking force had now crossed the stream, either by the bridge or through the ford. It formed in column, marched north along the base of the hill, faced into line parallel with the Americans, and started up the steep slope. Ritzema and Smallwood contested the advance with great gallantry. A detachment of British light infantry tried to turn the Americans' left flank. Webb's Connecticut regiment moved to the left, met the detachment and drove it back.

The British cannonade was now imperiling the attack well advanced up the hill. It was silenced, and orders were sent for attack from another quarter.

Rall's Hessian regiment, unobserved by the defenders since it had betaken itself to the hill on their right after driving back Spencer's force, now went into action. Suddenly, it swept down the slope, across a little intervening valley, and charged up Chatterton's Hill against the New York and Massachusetts militia regiments of Brooks and Graham. They changed front to face the attack, and fired a good volley. But then Birch's British light dragoons came into view, kettledrums beating, trumpets sounding a charge. The galloping horses and the flashing sabers struck terror into the hearts of the green militiamen, who had never seen cavalry in action. They broke and fled in the utmost disorder. The horsemen pursued them, cut off their retreat to the camp, fell upon them in scattered groups, killing and wounding many. For half a mile this rout continued. Then a hundred of the fleeing men rallied and tried to resist, but in vain. Some of them escaped into the woods. The rest surrendered.

The flight of the militia had uncovered the right flank, had left the Delaware regiment unsupported on that side. Haslet drew his men back toward the north, but Rall's Hessians fell upon them in full force. A part of the first three Delaware companies broke and were driven from the field, but Haslet held the rest, lined them up behind a fence, and "twice repulsed the Light Troops and Horse of the enemy." [18]

"During the struggle thus made by the heroic Haslet," [19] the frontal attack had continued. The New York and Maryland troops were driven back. Smallwood's men fought desperately. Smallwood himself was twice wounded, and at last his regiment was thrown into confusion. Ritzema's New Yorkers made an equally gallant effort, but the weight of the onslaught was too heavy. McDougall saw that further resistance was hopeless. He retreated with the New York and Maryland troops to a road leading to the American camp and held them there to protect the withdrawal of the Delawares, standing alone on the field.

Now the dragoons were returning from their chase and forming for a charge on the Delawares, along with all the rest of the attacking force. "Seeing ourselves deserted on all hands," says Haslet, "and the continued column of the enemy advancing, we also retired." [20] "In a great body, neither running nor observing the best of order," they were the last to leave the field, and they brought off the one remaining American gun.[21]

Trevelyan says, "The Delaware regiment, which had learned at Long Island that prisoners are not easily made, unless they make themselves, brought up the rear and fought sullenly and composedly while any of the assailants followed them within shooting range." [22]

The retreating troops were met by a detachment from the main body coming too late to help them in the fight. Haslet then re-formed his men and "marched into camp in the rear of the body sent to reinforce us." "The British ascended the hill very slowly; and, when arrived at its summit, formed and dressed their line without the least attempt to pursue the Americans." [23]

The loss of the Americans is variously reported. Bancroft says fewer than a hundred killed and wounded. Irving says three to four hundred, including prisoners taken. Whitton, citing an English account, says very definitely 313. Hufeland, citing regimental returns, says 175.[24] On the other side, as officially reported, there were 28 killed, including 5 officers, and 126 wounded, also including 5 officers. Among the Hessians there were about 77 casualties.[25]

This battle, measured by the numbers engaged, was a small affair, but it had important results. The check Howe received changed the course of events, as will be seen.

CHAPTER 23

Fort Washington

The British army dug in on Chatterton's Hill, establishing in that position the left wing of a line of entrenchments that extended eastward in a curve threatening both flanks of the American lines. Anticipating further British attacks, Washington prudently had his sick and wounded removed to a safer place in the rear and, even while the battle on the hill was in progress, transferred much of his baggage and equipment to a stronger position on the heights of North Castle.

The results were uncomfortable to the Americans who had been engaged in the fight. When they got back to camp they found that their baggage had been removed. For three or four nights they slept in the woods without even blankets, covered only by the snow that fell upon them.[1] In the night of October 31 the American army slipped away to the North Castle heights, leaving Stirling's brigade to hold the old position temporarily. The garrison at Fort Washington was not moved.

Howe, reinforced by two brigades from Percy's force on Manhattan, now had about 20,000 men. He took possession of the old American lines but made no other hostile move for the next four days except a brief and unimportant artillery engagement with Heath's division on November 1.[2]

Washington busied himself with his entrenchments. Three redoubts, with a line of earthworks in front, were erected with what must have appeared to the enemy to be magical swiftness. Indeed, there was something of magic about them, that is to say of illusion, for that line of earthworks was, in fact, largely made up of cornstalks pulled from near-by fields, with lumps of earth clinging to their roots. They were piled, tops inward, clods outward, and covered with loose earth.[3]

267

Considering these apparently formidable defenses, Howe altered his plans. During the night of November 4, the sentinels at the American outposts heard sounds like the rumbling of heavy wagons in the British camp. In the morning it was seen that their advanced sentinels had been withdrawn. Some hostile movement of their army was apprehended, and the Americans were ordered under arms. But before long it appeared that the enemy forces were on the march towards the southwest. They were, in fact, on the way to Dobbs Ferry.

A cheering sight to the Americans was this withdrawal. They were again feeling satisfied, in spite of Chatterton's Hill, having "good flour, beef and pork in plenty, with grog to wash it down." They had been retreating and retreating. But now it appeared that they had balked Howe's repeated efforts to get behind them and hem them in. He had given up and was decamping. Contented with the results of the strategy of their generals, warworn and ragged though they were, soldiers and officers were "in high spirits, loath to give an inch to their enemies." [4]

But where were their enemies going right now? That was, as Washington wrote to the Congress, "a matter of much conjecture and speculation." His own belief was that Howe would "make a descent with a part of his troops into New Jersey, and with another part invest Fort Washington." [5]

A council of war was held on November 6. It was decided that, "supposing the enemy to be retreating towards New-York," it would be "proper to throw a body of troops into New Jersey immediately," and that 3,000 men should take post at Peekskill and the passes of the Highlands.[6] But no serious consideration seems to have been given to abandoning Fort Washington, against which, as soon after appeared, Howe was now actually marching.

The northernmost part of Manhattan Island, extending from Washington's old lines on Harlem Heights to Spuyten Duyvil Creek, a distance of about four miles, is a narrow tongue of high land lying between the Harlem River and the Hudson, its width about three-quarters of a mile. It is bordered on both rivers by precipitous rocky cliffs a hundred feet high. These flank a plateau which rises close to the Hudson, to a narrow hill one mile long and 230 feet high above the water. This hill, called Mount Washington in 1776, is now known as Washington Heights. On the Harlem River side was Laurel Hill, nearly as high. Between the two there was a narrow valley, a gorge through which a road led to Kingsbridge beyond the Harlem. The sides of these two eminences were steep, rocky, and rugged. They and most of the whole tongue of land were densely wooded.[7]

On Mount Washington Colonel Rufus Putnam, the American army's chief engineer, had laid out the lines of a fort which the 3rd and 5th Pennsylvania regiments had erected in July under the command of Colonels John Shee and Robert Magaw.

The fort was a pentagonal earthwork with five bastions. It covered about four acres of ground, but it was a simple, open earthwork with a surrounding abatis and no ditch worth mentioning. It had no casemates, no bomb-proofs, no barracks, no buildings of any sort except "a wooden magazine and some offices," [8] no fuel, and no water. There was no well, nor any interior water supply whatever. In case of a siege water could be got only from the Hudson, 230 feet below. It had no outworks except "an incipient one at the north, nor any of those exterior, multiplied obstacles and defences, that . . . could entitle it to the name of fortress, in any degree capable of withstanding a siege," wrote Captain Alexander Graydon in his *Memoirs*.[9]

The function of the fort, its only important function at least, was to defend the eastern end of a line of sunken hulks and a chevaux de frise stretching across the Hudson. The purpose of these was to prevent the passage of British ships up the river. The western end of the line was similarly supported by Fort Lee on the New Jersey shore. That anyone should have seriously considered trying to hold such a fort against Howe's whole army of more than 20,000 completely equipped soldiers, operating freely both by land and by water, seems incredible. That such an attempt should have been persisted in after November 7, when the passage of three British ships around those obstructions had proved them to be ineffective and, by the same token, demonstrated the uselessness of both forts, is still more unbelievable. Yet such was the case.

Israel Putnam, with his characteristic exuberant optimism, had "an overweening confidence" [10] in the impregnability of Fort Washington. Colonel Magaw, its commandant, said he could hold it "till the end of December," and that, "should matters grow desperate," [11] he could carry off the garrison and even the stores to the New Jersey side. Strangest of all, Nathanael Greene, one of the most competent general officers in the army, entertained a similar delusion. He could not "conceive the garrison to be in any great danger." He was sure that it could be "brought off at any time." [12] Washington, however, doubted.

On November 8 Washington wrote to Greene, who commanded the troops in both forts: "The late passage of the 3 Vessels up the North River . . . is so plain a Proof of the Inefficacy of all the Obstructions we have thrown into it, that I cannot but think, it will fully Justify a Change in the disposition which has been made. If we cannot prevent Vessels passing up, and the Enemy are possessed of the surrounding Country, what valuable purpose can it answer to attempt to hold a Post of which the expected Benefit cannot be had; I am therefore inclined to think it will not be prudent to hazard the men and Stores at Mount Washington, but as you are on the Spot leave it to you to give such Orders as to evacuating Mount Washington as you Judge best." [13]

Four days later the commander in chief crossed the Hudson and rode down to Greene's camp at Fort Lee. The matter was discussed, "but finally nothing concluded upon." That the failure to give Greene positive orders to evacuate the fort was an instance of the indecision that so often throughout the war beset Washington's mind is proved by his own words. Three years later he wrote to Joseph Reed that Greene's opinion, the wishes of the Congress, and various other conflicting considerations "caused that warfare in my mind, and hesitation which ended in the loss of the garrison." [14] It is somewhat difficult, however, to find fault with Congress in this connection.

Two days after his visit to Greene, Washington made another, and was rowed with Greene, Putnam, and Mercer to Fort Washington early in the morning, "to determine what was best to be done." They were just in time to hear the beginning of Howe's attack on the fort, "a severe cannonade." It was too late to determine anything, except that it was too late. They went back to Fort Lee.

The decision of the council of war to maintain the post having been left standing, the question had arisen whether the Americans should try to hold, in addition to the fort, "all the ground from King's Bridge to the lower lines," that is to say the old American lines on Harlem Heights. On October 31 Greene had asked for Washington's opinion. "If we attempt to hold the ground, the garrison must still be reinforced, but if the garrison is only to draw into Mount Washington and keep that, the number of troops is too large." [15] To this Washington's secretary, replying for him on November 5, wrote that "the holding or not holding the grounds between Kingsbridge and the lower lines depends upon so many circumstances that it is impossible for him to determine the point. He submits it entirely to your discretion." [16]

Magaw's original force in the fort was made up of his own and Shee's regiments, numbering about 700 of all ranks, including those on the sick list.[17] Various additions had been made from time to time. While waiting for Washington's reply Greene had sent Colonel Moses Rawlings from Fort Lee with his regiment of 250 Maryland and Virginia riflemen and Colonel Baxter with 200 Bucks County, Pennsylvania, militiamen. Magaw's troops had thus been raised to 2,800 or 2,900 too many, as Greene himself had said, merely to hold Fort Washington. Greene's intention, therefore, may have been to try to hold all the ground between Harlem Heights and Kingsbridge, although the council of war on September 12 had declared that 8,000 men would be needed for that task.[18]

In pursuance of this hopeless plan Magaw disposed his force. At the northern end of Mount Washington, half a mile from the fort, Rawlings and his riflemen held a small redoubt and a battery of three guns. In a couple of flèches on Laurel Hill near the Harlem River, Colonel Baxter and his militiamen were posted. Two miles to the south, Lieutenant Colonel Lambert Cadwalader had Magaw's and Shee's Pennsylvanians, a part of Miles's, the Rangers, and some others, about 800 men. They occupied the front line of the old entrenchments on Harlem Heights. Minor detachments were posted at other points, leaving Magaw himself, with a small party, in the fort.[19] It was an ambitious plan, an attempt to hold a circuit of four or five miles with such small detachments posted at such distances from each other.

Howe devoted about 8,000 of his men to simultaneous attacks upon these three points. Lord Percy was to go from New York with a brigade of Hessians and nine British battalions[20] against Cadwalader. General Matthews with two battalions of light infantry and two of the Guards, supported by two battalions of grenadiers and the 33rd Regiment under Lord Cornwallis, perhaps 3,000 men, was to cross the Harlem River and take on Baxter's militia. General Wilhelm von Knyphausen had claimed the honor of making the main attack with German troops alone. Rawlings's position was therefore assigned to him, his force to number 3,000 Hessians and Waldeckers. Besides these three real attacks there was to be a feint by the 42nd Highlanders under Colonel Sterling from the Harlem side at a point between Cadwalader's position and the fort, to confuse the Americans.[21]

Operations began on the night of November 14, when thirty British flatboats were sent up the Hudson, through Spuyten Duyvil Creek, and so into the Harlem River, entirely unobserved by the Americans. The next morning, the British Lieutenant Colonel Patterson with flag and drum approached the fort and demanded a surrender, making the usual threat that the entire garrison might be put to the sword if the fort had to be stormed. Magaw declined with the customary assurance of his determination "to defend this post to the last extremity."[22]

At a little after seven the next morning the battle began. Twenty-one guns in British batteries on the eastern side of the Harlem, and those of the frigate *Pearl,* stationed in the Hudson between the fort and Rawlings's position, opened fire on all the American positions and kept up a heavy cannonade for two hours or more. At ten o'clock, Percy advanced against Cadwalader. His field artillery having driven in a small outpost, he crossed the Hollow Way, gained the heights above it, and approached the lines marching in column. At a proper distance, his fieldpieces and a howitzer opened fire. Cadwalader replied with his lone 6-pounder. Thereupon, to the surprise of the Americans, Percy's column inclined to the left and halted behind a piece of woods, where it remained inactive for an hour and a half. The reason for this seemingly peculiar behavior was that the detachments under Matthews and Cornwallis had been delayed in crossing the Harlem by an adverse condition of the tide and by "some neglect not foreseen before," [23] and the plan for simultaneous attacks compelled Percy to wait.

About noon Matthews and his light infantry crossed the Harlem in the thirty flatboats and landed below Baxter's position. While crossing and on landing they were under a galling American fire, but they came on and, with characteristic gallantry and dash, swarmed up the steep, wooded sides of Laurel Hill. Cornwallis, with the Guards, the grenadiers, and the 33rd, crossed without injury and followed the light infantry. Colonel Baxter was shot down. Leaderless, his militia fled to the fort.

Knyphausen had started his troops from their camp on the mainland side of the Harlem early in the morning. By seven o'clock he had crossed Kingsbridge. In two columns, that on the right led by Colonel Johann Rall, the other by Major General Martin Schmidt, his troops came down into the ground below Rawlings's position; but there, because of Cornwallis's delay, they had to halt. About ten o'clock they got word to advance. They pushed forward eight or ten fieldpieces in the ground below Rawlings and opened fire. Rall led his column to the right through a break in the wooded hills along the Hudson and toward the north end of Mount Washington. Knyphausen, with Schmidt's column, kept to the left and "made a Demonstration . . . as if he intended to attack" [24] the easterly side of that elevation. His men had to wade through a swamp and break through a triple abatis of trees felled by the Americans on their retreat from Kingsbridge on November 2.

Rall's men had "an Excessive Thick Wood" to get through and "Steep Rocks to get up." Struggling up the long, steep, rugged height, grasping bushes to pull themselves up the almost precipitous slope, they came under the fire of the American guns. Grape and round shot were hurled upon them; then came a shower of bullets. The riflemen, in the redoubt and from behind rocks and trees outside, poured a well aimed and deadly fire on their foes. But the persistent Hessians pressed on with great gallantry against the unseen defenders of the height.

When Rall had come near to the top, Knyphausen "made a sudden face to the Right" against the side of the hill assigned to his force and met the same difficulties, the same fire. For nearly two hours these courageous assaults and this stubborn defense continued. But the rifles of the Americans became fouled by the frequent and long continued discharges. Man after man found that he could not drive home a bullet in the clogged barrel of his gun. The fire of the defenders waned and at last was too feeble to hold back the enemy, now nearing the top of the ascent. They had no bayonets to repel a charge with that weapon. A retreat was inevitable. Rawlings drew them back toward the fort. They gained it ahead of their pursuers. This was the hottest fight of the day and the longest.

While all this was going on Percy emerged from his cover and with his two brigades—one English, the other Hessian under Major General Johann Stirn—assailed Cadwalader's lines. An outwork fell to him. He extended his front across to the North River, temporarily desisting from further attack.

After his success against Baxter's small force Cornwallis, foreseeing a necessary retreat by Cadwalader's men, also saw that the proposed feint by the men of the 42nd could be turned into an actual participation in the fight. He ordered Sterling, their commander, to join two battalions of the 2nd Brigade with his Highlanders and come over the Harlem River so that he could strike across Manhattan Island and intercept Cadwalader's withdrawal.

Cadwalader had news of Sterling's embarkation and sent Captains David Lennox, George Tudor, and Evan Edwards of the 3rd Pennsylvania with 150 men to oppose the landing. Magaw sent one hundred men from the fort. They acted with spirit. From an 18-pounder and their rifles and muskets they poured a heavy fire on the boats. But the Highlanders and British were not to be denied. In spite of a loss of 90 men, they made their landing, clambered up the high, steep, rocky ascent from the river, and assailed the Americans with such speed and dash that they actually captured 170 of them.

Percy, hearing the fire from that quarter, pressed hard on Cadwalader. Alarmed by the sounds in his rear and fearing to be caught between two fires, Cadwalader precipitately retreated. He was closely pursued. Near the fort he halted his men in a small wood and delivered a heavy fire, which for a moment checked the enemy. But the 42nd had come across. They drove him out of the wood and took some prisoners. The rest of Cadwalader's men reached the fort just before Rall's Hessians arrived within a hundred yards of it and took a position behind a large storehouse.

Rall peremptorily demanded a surrender. Magaw demurred, asking for time to consider. Rall refused. There were more than 2,500 men in the fort, crowded within a space not adequate to receive more than a thousand. Under bombardment it would become a hideous slaughter pen. Magaw's "last extremity" had arrived long before the end of December. To Knyphausen, who came up with Schmidt's column a little after Rall, Magaw yielded his sword. Two Hessian regiments, Rall's and Lossberg's, were drawn up in lines. Between them the Americans, having laid down their arms in the fort, marched out and gave up their colors, "which were yellow, red and light blue." Knyphausen, a grim and silent man, is said to have looked on these banners "with disdain." It was one of the ironies of the war that these Hessian regiments, thus especially honored, were to surrender their flags to Washington within six weeks.

The casualties in the British army were more severe than in the American, except in the matter of prisoners taken. The defenders had 59 killed and 96 wounded. The British had 78 killed and 374 wounded. Of these the Hessian share was 58 dead and 272 wounded. But the American loss in prisoners taken and matériel captured was stupendous. Officers to the number of 230 and 2,607 private soldiers fell into the hands of the British.[25]

The amount of precious matériel lost was staggering. At Fort Washington, Fort Lee which fell a few days later without opposition, and their various small dependencies, the British took 146 iron and brass guns, ranging from the smallest to 32-pounders, 12,000 shot and shell, 2,800 muskets, and 400,000 musket cartridges, besides tents, entrenching tools, and equipment of various sorts.[26]

It was one of the greatest disasters of the war for the Americans, and the blame for it must rest upon the shoulders of Greene and Magaw for their inexplicable infatuation in attempting to hold the fort, and upon those of Washington for his vacillation and indecision when by prompt and decisive action he might have prevented his inferior officers from persisting in their suicidal folly.

CHAPTER 24

The Retreat Through the Jerseys

After the fall of Fort Washington the main American army was still divided into three parts. General Lee was in command of the position at North Castle with three divisions—his own and those of Generals Sullivan and Spencer, each composed of two brigades. His paper strength was about 10,000 rank and file, but 4,000 men were absent, either on command or sick. Of those present 1,200 were on the sick list. His effectives numbered only 5,500.[1] General Heath had four brigades at and about Peekskill. There was a similar discrepancy between his paper strength and those actually present and fit, 5,400 on paper, 3,200 effective. Washington had the rest, 5,400, including Greene's men at Fort Lee.[2]

Thus there would seem to have been 14,000 able-bodied private soldiers to be relied upon for the rest of the campaign, a substantial force. But the number was rapidly dwindling. For a time after the affair at White Plains, while they were idle at North Castle with plenty to eat and drink, the men were cheerful and hopeful. But the catastrophe at Fort Washington had been enough to chill the ardor of a far more experienced, better disciplined, and more comfortably equipped army than this one.

Winter was coming on. The nights were already frosty. November rains were frequent and chilling.[3] Tents were lacking, blankets scarce, and the men's clothing was too meager and too ragged to keep them even passably warm. An English officer noted in his diary on November 5 that "many of the Rebels who were killed in the late affairs, were without shoes or Stockings, & Several were observed to have only linen drawers on, with a Rifle or Hunting shirt, without any proper shirt or Waistcoat. They are also in great want of blankets." The weather before that, he noted, had been mild, "but in less than a month they must suffer extremely." [4]

No one knew that better than the men themselves. Their terms of enlistment were soon to expire. The time of 2,060 of Washington's own force would be up on December 1, and all the rest, not only of his contingent, but of the whole army, would be free by the 1st of January.[5]

Under these conditions it is not surprising that "the contagion of desertion, which had been epidemic in his [Washington's] cantonments, now raged after the manner of a plague." [6] On November 9 Washington wrote that many of the Connecticut militia regiments had been reduced "to little more than a large company." On November 30 he said that the Pennsylvania militia of General Ewing's brigade, though enlisted to January 1, were "deserting in great numbers." [7] The prospect of any success in the rest of the campaign of 1776 was slight.

A few days before the fall of Fort Washington the American commander in chief moved westward with the force mentioned above, leaving General Lee and his detachment to protect New England. Washington detached Stirling's brigade to find a suitable crossing over the Hudson and to act as advance guard. Stirling crossed from Peekskill to Haverstraw on the 9th, found a gap in the Palisades through which passed a road to the west, posted a hundred men to hold it, and sent scouts to spy out the country beyond.[8] Washington followed on the 10th, marched through the gap, called the Clove, and encamped at Hackensack. From that point he rode down to Fort Lee and became a spectator of the disaster at Fort Washington. The surrender completely upset his plans. Instead of detaining the British army for months in a siege, the fort had fallen in a few hours. Howe was free to move any force he pleased into the Jerseys at once.

On the day Fort Washington was surrendered, the commander in chief wrote to the Congress that he hoped to hold Fort Lee. But three days later he had convinced himself that the fort was "only necessary in conjunction with that on the other side of the river" and was now "of no importance." He proposed to evacuate it and remove his stores. He was a day too late in reaching that conclusion, for Howe had taken prompt advantage of his freedom of movement and was preparing that very night for an attack to be launched on the morrow.[9]

At nine o'clock in the "very rainy" evening of the 19th, the 1st and 2nd battalions of British light infantry, two of British and two of Hessian grenadiers, two of the Guards, two companies of Hessian jägers, and the 33rd and 42nd British regiments, about 4,000 in all, struck their tents. By daylight, under the leadership of Cornwallis, they landed on the Jersey side of the Hudson at Closter, five or six miles above Fort Lee, and marched down the river, intending to cut off its garrison from retreat to Washington's army at Hackensack and pen it up between the Hackensack River and the Hudson.[10] Fortunately an American officer on patrol discovered their advance, rode down to the fort, got Greene out of bed, and told him about it. Greene relayed the news to Washington, ordered his men under arms and out of the fort, and hurried them away, in flight rather than in retreat, to the head of a small stream in his rear, thus gaining the road to the bridge over the Hackensack. Here he assembled as many as possible of his confused and disordered men, left them in charge of Washington, and galloped back on the road to the fort to round up three hundred stragglers and bring them off. But the British force was so hot on his heels that one hundred and five Americans were captured and eight or ten were killed.[11]

When the British arrived at the fort there was no one to oppose them. Three hundred precious tents had been left standing, all the blankets were there, and the breakfast camp kettles were boiling over the fires.[12] Besides the cannon already mentioned in the account of Fort Washington, a thousand barrels of flour fell into the enemy's hands. Fortunately the store of gunpowder had been got away a day or two before.[13]

While there was still doubt as to Howe's intentions, Lee's division had been left at North Castle to oppose him if he moved north. Washington in his instructions to Lee had said that, if the enemy moved westward into New Jersey, "I have no doubt of your following with all possible dispatch." [14] There was no longer any doubt that Howe was throwing large forces into New Jersey. He had actually sent over Cornwallis. It seemed to be time for Lee with his 5,000 effectives to come to the aid of Washington "with all possible dispatch." Colonel William Grayson, one of Washington's aides-de-camp, wrote Lee on the day Fort Lee fell, "His Excellency thinks it would be advisable in you to remove the troops under your command on this side of the North River." [15] Washington wrote the next day, "I am of opinion . . . that the publick interest requires your coming over to this side." [16]

These letters were not couched in the terms of a positive order. Lee did not move immediately, suggesting that part of Howe's army might still move against New England. He wrote to Colonel Joseph Reed, Washington's adjutant general: "His Excellency recommends me to move . . . to the other side of the river . . . but we could not be there in time to answer any purpose." [17]

Lee was vain, as he himself admitted, and his vanity had been fed to bursting by the admiration and adulation which had been his from the moment he joined the army. At a time when the Congress was making generals out of blacksmiths and booksellers, farmers and lawyers, whose military knowledge and experience were of the most meager sort, the appointment of Charles Lee as second in command under Washington was hailed with enthusiasm. Here was a professional soldier who from the age of fifteen had worn a military coat and had flashed a gleaming sword on many a battlefield in Europe and America. His homespun colleagues listened with awe and with but little understanding to his talk of redans and redoubts, ravelins and counterscarps. Simple provincials as they were, they looked upon him as the very epitome of the arts of war in the grand manner and valued him accordingly.

Lee, always ambitious, tended from now on, with his own division separated from that of the commander in chief, to use his own judgment rather than follow Washington's recommendations; and at this crucial time in his career Colonel Reed, Washington's adjutant general, encouraged him to act independently.

On November 21 Reed wrote to Lee in most fulsome adulation: "I do not mean to flatter or praise you at the expense of any other, but I confess I do think it is entirely owing to you that this army, and the liberties of America . . . are not entirely cut off. You have decision, a quality often wanted in minds otherwise valuable." Washington's for one, of course. Reed wanted him to join Washington's army, where his judgment and experience were "so likely to be necessary." He assured Lee of the confidence in him of every member of Washington's staff and of the officers and soldiers generally. Of Washington's part in the retention of Fort Washington he exclaimed: "Oh! General, an indecisive mind is one of the greatest misfortunes that can befall an army; how often have I lamented it in this campaign . . . We are in a very awful and alarming situation—one that requires the utmost wisdom and firmness of mind." Lee's and Reed's to be sure.[18]

Lee answered on the 14th that he too lamented "that fatal indecision of mind which in war is a much greater disqualification than stupidity." Acknowledging that Washington had recommended his crossing over to New Jersey "in so pressing a manner as almost to amount to an order," he had various reasons for not coming at once. He would, however, soon come, "for to confess a truth, I really think our Chief will do better with me than without me."[19]

A MAP OF THE
NORTHERN PART OF NEW JERSEY

SCALE OF MILES

5 4 3 2 1 0   5   10

Washington could not hold Hackensack. Not only was his force too weak—he had, he said, "not above 3,000 men and they much broken and dispirited" [20]—but the country was, as he expressed it, "almost a dead Flat." Since the fall of Fort Washington and the consequent loss of "500 intrenching tools," he had not a pick nor a shovel with which to entrench. There was danger of his being cooped up in the narrow space between the Hackensack River and the Passaic. He left three regiments to dispute the crossing of the river by the bridge, marched westward on the 21st to Aquackanock, crossed the Passaic there, and hurried on to Newark, arriving the next day. His rear guard at Hackensack destroyed the bridge on the approach of the British and hastened to join the main body.[21] The great retreat across the Jerseys was now well under way.

Stirling's brigade of eight regiments, about 1,200 men, had been sent ahead after its crossing of the Hudson. It reached New Brunswick on the 17th and there awaited Washington. It was, like the rest of the army, in a deplorable condition. Lieutenant Enoch Anderson of Haslet's Delawares wrote: "We arrived at Brunswick broken down and fatigued—some without shoes, some had no shirts."

At that time Washington considered his army and the American cause to be in the gravest danger. The contemporary historian William Gordon relates a conversation which he describes as taking place between Washington and Reed at Newark. Whether Gordon was or was not accurate, the conversation well represents the American army's situation. According to Gordon, Washington asked Colonel Reed, "Should we retreat to the back parts of Pennsylvania, will the Pennsylvanians support us?" Reed answered, "If the lower [eastern] counties are subdued and give up, the back counties will do the same." Washington passed his hand over his throat and said: "My neck does not feel as though it was made for a halter. We must retire to Augusta County in Virginia. Numbers will be obliged to repair to us for safety and we must try what we can do in carrying on a predatory war, and, if overpowered, we must cross the Allegheny Mountains." [22]

Washington lingered at Newark for five days, calling on the governor of New Jersey for militia reinforcements.[23] He was waiting for them and for Lee, to whom he wrote again, urging him to come.[24] But Lee did not begin to cross the Hudson until early in December. He believed that the British would move against lower New England, as indeed they did, and that he might accomplish something in the way of defending that area. His men lacked blankets and shoes, and he hesitated to begin a long march. Besides, he seems to have overestimated the size of Washington's force, and to have thought that Howe intended to go into winter quarters rather than attack

Washington. Lee continued for many days to follow his own judgment rather than the recommendations of the commander in chief. Perhaps Washington did not trust *his* own judgment, since he did not send Lee explicit orders.

Dispirited by a succession of defeats, wearied with marching day after day, lacking tentage, blankets, clothing, and even shoes, Washington's force was indeed, as Reed described it, "the wretched remains of a broken army." [25] It is not surprising that British officers were writing home, "Peace must soon be the consequence of our success." Howe was so confident of his ability to finish off his staggering opponent that he divided his army and sent Clinton, with more than 6,000 men, to possess Rhode Island and winter there. Clinton took Rhode Island without opposition. His troops remained in and about Newport three years. Trevelyan says, "For any effect which they produced upon the general result of the war, they might have been as usefully, and much more agreeably, billeted in the town of the same name in the Isle of Wight." [26]

Washington had called on the Congress and on the governor of New Jersey for more men.[27] The Congress called on the Philadelphia Associators, a volunteer organization, to march. They were coming, but had not yet arrived. The New Jersey militia failed to respond to Washington's call.[28] On the 28th the van of Cornwallis's troops, in their inexorable pursuit of their quarry, marched into Newark as Washington's rear guard was marching out to join Stirling at New Brunswick.[29] November 30 came and went, and with it went the Maryland and New Jersey militia brigades of General Reazin Beall and General Nathaniel Heard, the 2,000 time-expired men: "being applied to they refused to continue longer in service." [30] "But what is still worse," Washington wrote, "Altho' most of the Pennsylvanians are inlisted till the first of January, I am informed that they are deserting in great numbers." [31]

There was a postscript to Washington's letter of December 1, from New Brunswick to the Congress: "½ after 1 o'clock P. M. The Enemy are fast advancing, some of 'em in sight now." At seven o'clock he wrote: "We had a smart cannonade [across the Raritan] whilst we were parading our Men, but without any or but little loss on either side. It being impossible to oppose them with our present force with the least prospect of success we shall retreat to the West side of Delaware [River] and have advanced about Eight miles." [32] At Princeton he did not stop. Pushing on in full flight he came to Trenton the next day. Safety was now his only aim, and the other side of the Delaware offered that.

He had hurriedly ordered the collection or destruction of all the boats on the river for a space of seventy miles above Philadelphia. In such as had arrived at Trenton he immediately began the transportation of his stores and baggage, his sick and wounded men.[33]

At New Brunswick, Stirling's brigade—five Virginia regiments and one from Delaware, about 1,200 men, "the flower of the army, though a faded flower it was" [34]—had joined in the retreat, first burning a hundred of their precious tents, which they had no wagons to carry off. "When we saw them reduced to ashes," wrote Lieutenant Enoch Anderson of Haslet's Delaware Regiment, who was detailed for that purpose, "it was night. We made a double quick-step and came up with the army about eight o'clock. We encamped in the woods, with no victuals, no tents, no blankets. The night was cold and we all suffered much, especially those who had no shoes." [35]

While the rest pushed on to Trenton, Washington left Stirling's brigade at Princeton to hold back the enemy. There it found a welcome though temporary relief from the hardship it had endured. "We had comfortable lodgings in the College," says Anderson.

But Stirling's men were not put to the expected test of holding back Cornwallis, for a most surprising thing had happened. Cornwallis was an energetic, swift-moving soldier. To overtake Washington at New Brunswick he had marched his men twenty miles through a heavy rain, over the most wretched roads deep with mud, in a single day. Washington had destroyed the bridge there, but the Raritan was easily fordable, "in a variety of places, knee deep only." [36] Cornwallis might have crossed it and caught up with the retreating army to its destruction. Instead, he halted his men, and did not move again for four days; meanwhile Washington made good his escape across the river. It was not Cornwallis's fault. He was under orders to remain there until Howe came up with the main army.

Charles, second Earl Cornwallis, was born of an ancient family on December 31, 1738. He began his military career as an ensign of the Grenadier Guards at the age of eighteen. He served in the Seven Years' War on the continent of Europe, was a captain at twenty-one, lieutenant colonel at twenty-three, a colonel of the 33rd Regiment of Foot at twenty-eight. Although he was a Whig and had stood in the House of Lords with Lord Camden and a few others in opposing the taxation of the American colonists, the King made him a major general in 1775 and sent him to America in 1776. Two years later he was made a lieutenant general. Trevelyan has described him as "an English aristocrat of the finest type . . . a man of immense and varied experience; careful and industrious; modest in success and equable in adversity; enlightened, tolerant and humane; contemptuous of money and indifferent to the outward badges of honour . . . he presented . . . a living and most attractive example of antique and single-minded patriotism."

As a soldier, Cornwallis was personally courageous; as a general, he was vigorous, active, and enterprising. Trevelyan contends that "the energy and enterprise, which . . . marked his two campaigns in the Carolinas, revived the dying credit of our natural generalship"; but this is overgenerous praise, for though his notable energy was in strong contrast to the habitual sloth of Howe, and though he is rated by Fortescue as "a good skilful and gallant soldier," it may be doubted that he was a military leader of exceptional genius. Certainly he was outgeneraled in the Carolina campaigns by Greene, who drove him to his final defeat at Yorktown.

In person, Cornwallis was a figure of distinction, thirty-eight years old, tall, erect, and handsome in the full-fed, well fleshed, portly fashion of the period. His features were bold, his nose well shaped, his full lips curved in an agreeable, rather humorous expression, his chin strong and deeply cleft, his face marred by an injured eye, the result of colliding in a hockey game with a future bishop of Durham while they were schoolboys at Eton.

He distinguished himself after the war in America by his services as Governor General of India and commander in chief of the British forces there.

By the 5th of December, Washington was strengthened by the arrival of some of the Pennsylvania Associators and part of Colonel Nicholas Haussegger's regiment of Pennsylvania and Maryland Germans.[37] Having to cross the river and lacking information as to the movements of the enemy at New Brunswick, he decided to "face about with such Troops as are here [Trenton] fit for Service and March back to Princeton and there govern myself by Circumstances and the movements of General Lee." [38] On the 7th he set out with 1,200 men. But when he was within a few miles of the college town he met Stirling in full retreat. Howe had arrived at New Brunswick the day before and had sent Cornwallis forward.[39] While Washington was marching, Cornwallis was on his way to the same destination. Washington turned back.[40]

Haslet's Delawares were the rear guards in that final retreat. Lieutenant Anderson of the regiment has left a lively picture of the commander in chief's personal activities during the withdrawal: "We continued in our retreat—our Regiment in the rear and I, with thirty men in the rear of the Regiment and General Washington in my rear with pioneers—tearing up bridges and cutting down trees to impede the march of the enemy. I was to go no faster than General Washington and his pioneers. It was dusk before we got to Trenton. Here we stayed all night." [41]

Cornwallis had marched slowly and cautiously, with flankers thrown out on both sides to scour the woodlands and look out for ambushes. The broken-down bridges and other obstacles also delayed him. His vanguard reached Trenton about two o'clock the next afternoon, just as the last of the Americans were putting off for the Pennsylvania shore. His light infantry and jägers were greeted by the fire of American batteries across the river and put to flight, with the loss of thirteen men. [42] The British responded, "but," says Anderson, "we were in the woods and bushes and none were wounded that I heard of. . . . That night we lay amongst the leaves without tents or blankets, laying down with our feet to the fire. We had nothing to cook with, but our ramrods, which we run through a piece of meat and roasted it over the fire, and to hungry soldiers it tasted sweet."

The British ranged up and down the river, looking for boats, but found none. Washington had them all on the other side.

The next morning, Washington posted Stirling's brigade in detachments at different landing places up the river to "prevent them from Stealing a March upon us from up above." [43] Howe gave up the idea of crossing and distributed his troops in various posts, at Pennington, New Brunswick, Trenton, and Bordentown. Now, for some little time, all was quiet along the Delaware. Howe seems to have assumed that the campaign of 1776 was ended, and that there would be no further major military activity until spring.

CHAPTER 25

The Crisis

"A thick cloud of darkness and gloom covered the land and despair was seen in almost every countenance," wrote one of the American officers of that period.[1] Said another, "Such is now the gloomy aspect of our affairs that . . . strong apprehensions are entertained that the British will soon have it in their power to vanquish the whole remains of the continental army."[2]

It was indeed the darkest hour of the war. Newport and New York were already held by the enemy. Philadelphia, the largest and finest American city, the seat of such government as the infant republic had, was unfortified, virtually ungarrisoned, open to attack on all sides. Only thirty miles away lay an army of 10,000 British and Hessian soldiers flushed with repeated victories, confident of their strength, and eager for rest and refreshment in such pleasant winter quarters as Philadelphia afforded. There was nothing to hinder a descent upon that apparently doomed town but the Delaware River, Washington's little force "crouching in the bushes"[3] on its western side, and possibly the weather.

The river was no substantial barrier. It could easily be crossed in boats and barges. The material to construct them was at hand in lumber yards in Trenton and, if more was needed, in the wood of its houses. Or the ice might within a few days be thick enough and strong enough to bear the weight of marching men, their horses, wagons, and artillery. The river offered little hope of enduring protection.

Nor did Washington's army seem to offer much more. It numbered no more than 5,000 men "daily decreasing by sickness and other causes," half of them militia or raw recruits, most of them clad like scarecrows in worn and ragged garments, shod like tramps, if shod at all, "many of 'em being entirely naked," said Washington, "and most so thinly clad as to be unfit for service." [4] Shivering in their unprotected posts or in their blanketless, restless sleep, these wretches were trying to cover thirty miles of the western shore of the river against an enemy that might strike at any time, at any place, or at several places at once. Washington was forced to say that he could see no means of preventing the British from passing the Delaware. "Happy should I be," he wrote to the Congress, "if I could see the means of preventing them. At present I confess I do not." [5] He told his nephew that, without reinforcements, "I think the game is pretty near up." [6]

The Howe brothers were ready to take full advantage of America's extremities. They had come to America not only as military commanders, but also as peace negotiators, bearing the King's commission "for restoring peace to his Majesty's Colonies and Plantations in North America." In New York, Admiral Lord Howe issued a proclamation, signed also by Sir William, offering "a free and general pardon" to all who would return to "their just allegiance" and take oath accordingly.[7] The effect of this announcement on the inhabitants of New Jersey was instantaneous. Already disaffected to the American cause by reason of their desire to rank as tranquil and obscure supporters of the winning side, which the American side no longer appeared to be, large numbers of them flocked to the British to take the oath and receive protection papers. Washington was disgusted by this desertion of the cause. "The Conduct of the Jerseys," he wrote, "has been most Infamous. Instead of turning out to defend the Country and affording aid to our Army, they are making their submissions as fast as they can." [8]

Philadelphia took notice. Estimating its chances of continued liberty at their apparent value—not much—its inhabitants in droves sought an asylum in the country. An observer there noted in his diary, "Numbers of families loading wagons with their furniture &c., taking them out of town. . . . Great numbers [of] people moving. . . . All shops ordered to be shut. . . . Our people in confusion, of all ranks, sending their goods out of town." The city was "amazingly depopulated." [9]

The fear of final defeat of the American cause and of the consequent ill fortune of its adherents smoked out many of the more faint-hearted Americans in high places. The wealthy and respected Allens of Philadelphia— John, a former member of the Committee on Observation, Andrew, a member of the Congress, and William, a lieutenant colonel of the 2nd Pennsylvania—went over to the enemy and joined Howe at Trenton. So did Joseph Galloway, a leader of the bar and a talented member of the First Continental Congress.[10]

Even John Dickinson, so prominent in the early efforts for liberty and whose *Letters of a Farmer in Pennsylvania* had done so much to arouse the country, now was said to have "discovered sentiments inimical to the freedom and independence of the American states." When elected a delegate from Delaware to the Congress, in January, 1777, he declined the office on the ground that he was "in a very low state of health . . . forced to attend my wife and child in the country." He retired to his farm in Kent County, whence he wrote urging George Read to exert himself for peace "before we suffer indescribable calamities." [11] Dickinson was discouraged, though hardly disloyal to the patriot cause.

In contrast with Dickinson's conduct was that of another pamphleteer, whose *Common Sense* was also a popular and potent force in the Revolution. Thomas Paine had joined Greene at Fort Lee as a volunteer aide-de-camp. Musket on shoulder, he had tramped day by day, all day long, in the weary retreat. At Newark, however, he began to fight with his proper weapon, the pen, with a drumhead for a desk.

In the middle of December, Paine published in Philadelphia a new pamphlet, *The Crisis*. It began with the eloquent words known ever since to many a schoolboy:

These are the times that try men's souls: The summer soldier and the sunshine patriot will, in this crisis, shrink from the service of his country; but he that stands it Now, deserves the love and thanks of man and woman. Tyranny, like hell, is not easily conquered; yet we have this consolation with us, that the harder the conflict, the more glorious the triumph.[12]

This little book "flew like wildfire through all the towns and villages." The privates in the army were called together in small groups to hear it read. It animated them to endure their hardships and renewed their determination to prove themselves all-season soldiers and all-weather patriots.

Apprehension of oncoming disaster induced the Congress to order the removal of all the principal military stores from Philadelphia down to Christiana Bridge in Delaware. Then, on December 12, it abandoned completely its control of the operations of the army by conferring on Washington "full power to order and direct all things relative to the [military] department and to the operations of war until otherwise ordered. Having thus prudently shifted to his shoulders additional responsibility for the conduct of a desperate war, it adjourned to Baltimore "amid the jeers of tories and the maledictions of patriots." [13] No doubt Congress was wise to remove to Baltimore and also to vest larger powers temporarily in the commander in chief.

On the very next day after this adjournment, two events occurred which later led the English historian George Trevelyan to remark that the Americans, "a people observant of anniversaries . . . might well have marked the thirteenth of December with a white stone in their calendar," and that these two events "must have presented every appearance of special providences." [14]

The first was Howe's decision, disclosed that day, to suspend military operations until spring and to retire with the greater part of his army into winter quarters in New York, leaving only a chain of military outposts to hold New Jersey. Boats were not to be built to cross the Delaware, and there was to be no crossing on the ice. The pressure on the Americans holding the river was lifted. The patriots in Philadelphia took heart; the Tories were correspondingly downcast.

The second event characterized by Trevelyan as fortunate for the Americans had to do with General Charles Lee. Washington had continued to write to him at every stage of the retreat, from Newark, from New Brunswick, urging him and almost entreating him to come over to the Jerseys. Lee was fertile in excuses for not joining his superior. He wrote Heath that he had "received a recommendation—not a positive order—from the General to move the corps under my command to the other side of the river," and asked Heath instead to send 2,000 of his men to Washington. Heath, being under orders to stay where he was, refused and stuck to his refusal, in spite of efforts to make him comply. Lee then tried to get the 2,000 men from Heath to join his own, Heath's men to be replaced from Lee's forces coming up to the Hudson. "I am going into the Jerseys," he said, "for the salvation of America." Heath again refused, and at last, on December 2, Lee started over the river with part of his original force, the remainder having served out their time, deserted, or fallen ill.[15]

But even then Lee had no intention of joining Washington and giving up his independent command. He thought it would be better for him to act in the rear of the enemy, "beating up and harassing their detached parties." To be sure, he did have an excellent chance to assail the long line of British communications across New Jersey. He was "in hopes . . . to reconquer the Jerseys" on his own hook. New Jersey, he wrote, "was really in the hands of the enemy before my arrival." [16]

Lee's progress southward seems to have been slow beyond any reason or excuse. He marched at an average rate of three miles a day. At Morristown he rested two days. The day after that rest, he made only eight miles, to Vealtown.

In the evening of the 12th he left his army at Vealtown in Sullivan's care, and with a small guard rode off about three miles to a tavern in Basking Ridge to spend the night, indulging in that "folly and imprudence . . . for the sake of a little better lodging," as Washington caustically observed.[17] He breakfasted the next morning and then employed his leisure in writing a letter to his friend General Horatio Gates, in which he characterized Washington as "most damnably deficient."[18] He had not even sent the letter when British cavalrymen surrounded the tavern.

Colonel William Harcourt, with thirty horsemen, had been scouting in the neighborhood under orders from Cornwallis to find Lee's army. He learned of Lee's presence in the tavern. His men surrounded the house and let fly a shower of bullets. Lee's guard, surprised, fled. Within a few minutes Lee was forced to surrender. He was carried off and was locked up in New Brunswick before twenty-four hours had passed. The crowning irony of his capture was that the dragoons, his captors, were of a regiment which he had led in a notable feat of his European military career, a dashing raid across the Tagus against the Spanish in Portugal in 1762.

The news of Lee's capture was a dreadful shock to the Americans; many of them had looked upon him as their most capable leader. To some his capture seemed the last straw. "His loss was almost universally bewailed as one of the greatest calamities which had befallen the American arms." Washington wrote, "Our cause has also received a severe blow in the captivity of Gen. Lee."[19]

Events were soon to prove that the American cause was not dependent upon Lee's services. General John Sullivan, Lee's second in command, promptly marched his troops into Washington's camp on December 20, though there were only 2,000 of them, instead of the 5,000 Lee had led across the Hudson. Gates came from the north with what were called seven regiments, though they numbered only 500 men. A thousand Philadelphia Associators under Colonel John Cadwalader also came in, as did the rest of the German Regiment. There were with Washington by Christmas time about 6,000 men listed as "fit for duty."[20] Something like an American counteroffensive could be undertaken, since Howe's forces were divided and going into winter quarters.

But the condition of these new recruits, except for the Associators and the Germans fresh from home, was no better than that of the men who had retreated across the Jerseys. Sullivan's 2,000 were "in a miserable plight; destitute of almost everything, many of them fit only for the hospital."

Gates's 500 were in no better shape. "Fit for duty" seems to have been a term reeking with optimism. And this army, such as it was, had only about ten days more of life. The enlistments of so many were to expire on December 31 that no more than 1,400 would be left.

To guard "every suspicious part of the river" Washington divided his force into three separate corps. The brigades of Generals Stirling, Mercer, Stephen, and Roche de Fermoy, about 2,000 men, were posted along the stretch from Yardley up to Coryell's Ferry. General Ewing had about 550 along the river from Yardley down to the ferry to Bordentown. Cadwalader, given the temporary rank of a brigadier general, with 1,800 took over the ground south of Ewing down to Dunk's Ferry, with headquarters at Bristol. There were no fewer than nine ferries to be guarded; at each of them a small earthwork was thrown up, and a few guns mounted. There being a great scarcity, almost a total lack, of tents, the men built themselves rude huts. So the army settled down, as it seemed to many, for the winter.[21]

CHAPTER 26

Trenton

"Headquarters, December 14, 1776. The Campaign having closed with the Pursuit of the Enemies Army near ninety Miles by Lieut. Gen. Cornwallis's Corps, much to the honor of his Lordship and the Officers and Soldiers under his Command, the Approach of Winter putting a Stop to any further Progress, the Troops will immediately march into Quarters and hold themselves in readiness to assemble on the shortest Notice." [1] In those words General Howe officially closed the campaign of 1776 in New Jersey —officially, but not effectively.

For "the Protection of Inhabitants and their Property," much of which had already been taken into permanent protective custody by his marauding troops, he established a chain of posts on a line from Staten Island to Princeton. There was one at Amboy, one at New Brunswick, and one at Princeton. Along the Delaware, from Bordentown to Burlington, the Hessian Colonel von Donop was in command of about 3,000 men, Hessian grenadiers, jägers, and the 42nd Highlanders. Half of these were based at Trenton and half at Bordentown, the distance between the two being six miles.

The line was eighty miles long, "rather too extensive" as Howe admitted. [2] The distances between the various posts invited trouble. But who was there to trouble them? Six thousand or so American soldiers, [3] a large part of them untried militia, the rest ragged, war-worn, discouraged Continentals, lay on the other side of the Delaware, whose ice-laden waters seemed impassable. And three-quarters of the whole force would be leaving for home in two weeks or less. Howe had good reason for his trust in "the strength of the corps placed in the advanced posts" and for his belief that "the troops will be in perfect security." [4] For himself there were the comfort and the pleasures of life at headquarters in New York. For Cornwallis there was leave to return to England for the winter. So everything was arranged to the satisfaction of everybody, including the Americans.

On no day, from the time his thin line of posts had been strung along the river, was Washington free from apprehension that an attack on that line was planned, to be carried out in boats especially built for it, or on the solid ice when it should form. He knew well enough that such an attack, properly organized and carried out, could not be effectively resisted, that it would be fatal to his army and perhaps even to his cause. And there was the 31st day of December coming so soon, when his army would practically disappear on one day; he would have left but 1,400 men, sick and well. Before he could be reinforced by newly enlisted troops even a small fraction of his foes, say the three thousand Hessians already on the other shore, might cross and march against Philadelphia.

Here was food for thought. If no adequate defense to an attack launched at some unexpected point were possible, could anything be done to forestall it? Could he possibly, with such a force as he had, reverse the situation, attack instead of being attacked? It was a desperate idea, but his situation was desperate.

Washington had begun to think as early as December 8 that audacious counterattacks upon British detachments might pay. On December 14 he expressed in three letters the same hope, that, if he were reinforced by Lee's troops, he might "under the smiles of Providence, effect an important stroke." [5] The news of the withdrawal of Howe's main force to New York and of the straggling disposition of the troops left to hold the river territory was vastly encouraging; but there was yet the fateful decision to be made, a definite plan to be evolved. One who came with Lee's troops under Sullivan on the 20th observed him in the last stages of his cogitation. "I saw him in that gloomy period," reports the erratic James Wilkinson, "and attentively marked his aspect; always grave and thoughtful, he appeared at that time pensive and solemn in the extreme." [6] And well he might, for it was no ordinary expedition that he was planning, no affair of an American detachment whose defeat would be merely a regrettable incident of the war. His whole army was to be risked. If the attempt failed, it would be cut off from retreat by the river behind it. There could be no hope of another unmolested crossing. It was, indeed, a desperate venture, and Washington knew it to be so; "but necessity, dire necessity, will, nay must, justify my attack," he wrote to Colonel Reed on the 23rd. [7] The next evening, at a meeting with

Generals Greene, Sullivan, Mercer, Stirling, Roche de Fermoy, and St. Clair and several colonels, including John Glover, the plan was discussed and adopted.

The principal objective was to be Trenton. The river was to be crossed at three places by three separate divisions. Lieutenant Colonel John Cadwalader as a temporary brigadier general was to command one, composed of about 900 men from Hitchcock's Rhode Island Continentals, 1,000 Philadelphia Associators, Captain Thomas Rodney's little Delaware militia company from Dover, and two artillery companies, each with one 6-pounder. This division was to cross the river at or near Bristol and engage Donop's forces at Mount Holly so as to divert their attention from the principal attack.

The second division, under Brigadier General James Ewing, was made up chiefly of Pennsylvania militia, with a few from New Jersey, about 700 in all. It was to cross at Trenton Ferry, take up a position south of Assunpink Creek and hold a bridge over that stream so as to close that avenue of escape of the Hessians in Trenton after the attack on the town from the north by the principal division.

The third and principal division was to be commanded by Washington. It was to be made up of about 2,400 men selected from the brigades of Stephen, Mercer, Stirling, St. Clair, Glover, Sargent, and Roche de Fermoy, each of whom was to lead his own men. It was to be divided into two corps under Greene and Sullivan respectively. Colonel Henry Knox was to be in charge of the artillery, 18 fieldpieces in all. Each man was to carry his blanket, cooked rations for three days, and forty rounds of ammunition. This division was to cross at McKonkey's Ferry, about nine miles above Trenton, and take the roads leading down to that town.

When his own and Ewing's division had converged upon and taken Trenton, and after Cadwalader had driven Donop from his cantonments, Washington planned that the three bodies should join and, if circumstances favored, should push on against the British posts at Princeton and New Brunswick.

Provided and equipped as ordered, the various elements of the main division were paraded in the valley behind the hill at McKonkey's Ferry, out of sight of the opposite shore, in the afternoon of Christmas Day. By three o'clock they were on the march toward the river, where the boats had been assembled.

These vessels were for the most part of a kind peculiar to the Delaware. They were called Durham boats from their first builder, Robert Durham, who had been turning them out since 1750. They were from forty to sixty feet long, eight feet wide, and two feet deep, and were provided with keels. Pointed at both ends, they could travel in either direction, the heavy steering sweep fitting either end. Each carried a mast with two sails, useful when the wind served. At other times its crew of four, exclusive of the steersman, used setting poles, two on each side. Thrusting them against the river bottom at the bow, the four walked aft on running boards built along each side, thus pushing the boat forward its full length, and then returned to the bow to repeat the operation. As the larger boats could carry fifteen tons while drawing only twenty inches, they could easily convey artillery, horses, and many men.[8] For this expedition these boats were manned by the amphibious Marbleheaders of Glover's regiment, the same men who had rescued the army after the defeat on Long Island.

At dark the embarkation began. The Virginia Continentals of Stephen's brigade, the advance party, were the first to enter the boats and push off for the opposite shore. The river was full of cakes of ice, so that the crossing was slow and exceedingly difficult even for those hardy and veteran crews. The second section to cross was Mercer's, composed of men from Connecticut, Maryland, and Massachusetts, chiefly Continentals. Stirling followed with his men, drawn from two regiments of Virginia Continentals, Haslet's Delawares, and a Pennsylvania rifle regiment. These three corps constituted the left wing of the expedition, under command of Greene, Stirling's forming the reserve.

Roche de Fermoy followed with men chosen from the German Regiment and from one of Pennsylvania, and then Sullivan's division, drawn from the brigades of St. Clair, Glover, and Sargent—New Hampshire, Massachusetts, Connecticut, and New York troops. This was the right wing, Sullivan commanding, Roche de Fermoy in advance, St. Clair in reserve.

The moon was full, but the sky was so shrouded by dense clouds that darkness covered everything. In this respect the night was most suitable for a secret adventure; but it was a dreadful night indeed for the men engaged. It was bitterly cold, the current was swift, and the floating ice prolonged the passage. About eleven o'clock hail and sleet, driven by a high wind, broke upon them, doubling the difficulties of the boatmen and making the soldiers in the boats or on shore acutely miserable. Captain Thomas Rodney wrote, "It was as severe a night as ever I saw . . . [with this] storm of wind, hail, rain and snow." [9]

It had been expected that the entire division would be over the river by midnight and that it would have five hours before daybreak in which to cover the nine miles to Trenton. But it was past three o'clock when the last man got ashore, and nearly four o'clock when the army formed and began to march.

None of these men were warmly clad; many of them wore threadbare summer clothing. Few were properly shod, and many were not shod at all. Slogging along on the rough, frozen road made slippery by ice and snow, buffeted now by hailstones, now by rain that froze upon their hair and their clothes, they underwent a prolonged and continuous torture. The story of ragged, shoeless men leaving bloody footprints in the snow has been told so often that it has become commonplace, and often fails to impress the reader as it should. But to one of Washington's staff, as to every other man on that march, it was sufficiently real. He made an entry in his diary before the embarkation. "Christmas, 6 p.m. . . . It is fearfully cold and raw and a snow-storm setting in. The wind is northeast and beats in the faces of the men. It will be a terrible night for the soldiers who have no shoes. Some of them have tied old rags around their feet, but I have not heard a man complain." [10]

Added to these physical tortures was the mental stress of the knowledge that they were three or four hours behind time and could not now hope to surprise the enemy at daybreak. It would be broad day before the attack could be launched, and that might make all the difference between victory and defeat, a defeat that might develop into a catastrophe fatal to the American cause.

Such forebodings were, of course, still more depressing to the officers, who were familiar with the details of the plan. Even while crossing the river many of them, well knowing what a touch-and-go affair it was, were despondent.[11] How much more so, then, were they when they realized how sadly the timing of the plan had gone awry. But Washington kept his poise and never faltered. The same officer who wrote about the shoeless soldiers also wrote: "I have never seen Washington so determined as he is now. He stands on the bank of the stream, wrapped in his cloak, superintending the landing of his troops. He is calm and collected, but very determined. The storm is changing to sleet and cuts like a knife." When on the march a man came to Washington with a message from General Sullivan that the storm was wetting the muskets and rendering them unfit for service his answer was: "Tell General Sullivan to use the bayonet. I am resolved to take Trenton." That resolve, that unbending will carried the army to Trenton in spite of everything.

At Birmingham, about four miles from the landing, the column halted for a meal of the prepared rations. When the order to march was given many of the men were found asleep by the roadside and were roused with difficulty.

Two roads led from Birmingham to Trenton. The right-hand road ran roughly parallel to the curve of the river and entered the town at its south or lower end. The other, the Pennington road, swung left in a similar shallow curve and came into Trenton at its upper end. They were about equal in length.

Stephen's advance, followed by Mercer's and Stirling's corps and a small troop of Philadelphia light horse, all under Greene, with four guns, took the Pennington road. Washington rode with this division. Roche de Fermoy followed, with orders to break off to the left and interpose his men between the Trenton garrison and the troops at Princeton. Sullivan, with St. Clair's, Glover's, and Sargent's troops and four guns, set out on the river road.

The garrison in Trenton consisted of three regiments of Hessians, known by the names of Rall, Knyphausen, and Lossberg, 50 Hessian jägers, and 20 light dragoons of the 16th British regiment, about 1,400 in all, with six 3-pounder fieldpieces. Colonel Johann Gottlieb Rall was in command, the officer who had led the flank attack against Chatterton's Hill and had summoned Fort Washington to surrender.

The town had two nearly parallel main streets, King and Queen, running in a north and south direction, but coming together at the north end so as to form a long, narrow wedge. These were crossed near their lower ends by Front, Second, and Third streets. At the south end of Queen Street a bridge crossed Assunpink Creek to the road for Bordentown. The town was largely depleted of its usual residents, whose houses, the jail, the taverns, the churches, and other buildings, mostly along the main streets, now furnished quarters for the soldiers. One company was in an outlying position north of the town, and another south of the creek. Rall had his headquarters in the middle of the town on King Street.

There were no natural defenses against attack from any quarter, except the Delaware River on the west side; the town was approachable over a flat country by many roads from every other direction. Several of Rall's officers had urged him to fortify the approaches, and Colonel von Donop, in command of the district, had actually instructed him to do so. But, although two positions for redoubts were chosen and even approved by Rall, nothing was done. He scoffed at the idea that the miserable rabble on the other side of the river, "nothing but a lot of farmers," were capable of an attack in force sufficient to endanger him. "Let them come!" he said. "We want no trenches. We'll at them with the bayonet!" In this attitude he was supported by General James Grant, who commanded all the British forces in New Jersey. Grant went even further in his contempt of the rebels. When Rall suggested that it would be well to have more troops to keep open his communications with Princton and New Brunswick, Grant is said to have replied to the messenger: "Tell the Colonel he is safe; I will undertake to keep the peace in New Jersey with a corporal's guard." This was the same Grant that had boasted before the war that he could march through all the colonies with 5,000 men.

Christmas Eve and Christmas Day were high holidays in Trenton, celebrated with much feasting and drinking in the hearty German fashion. The merrymaking and revelry were kept up all day and late into the night, interrupted only for a short time in the early evening by an attack on one of the pickets by about thirty Americans, who, without Washington's knowledge, had been scouting in the neighborhood. They had shot up the picket guard as a mere adventure. After an exchange of fire in which six Hessians were wounded the Americans quickly withdrew, carrying off six muskets as trophies. The troops in the town had been called to arms; but the affair was over in a few minutes, and they returned to their quarters.

Rall had then dropped in on a supper party in the house of a wealthy merchant of the town, who seems to have been a political trimmer. The attractions of wine and cards kept the party going all night. Near the middle of the night there came a knock at the door; a visitor wanted to see the colonel. The servant refused to let him in. The caller then wrote a note, which the servant delivered to Rall. It contained the information that the American army was on the march against the town. Rall thrust it into his pocket unread. Perhaps he never read it; it was found in his pocket after his death two days later.

The pickets had been posted as usual. On the Pennington road, by which Greene's column, with Washington, was approaching, there was an outlying post of a lieutenant, a corporal, and twenty-four men at some distance from the town. About halfway between that and the town, Captain von Altenbockum's company of the Lossberg Regiment was posted. On the river road, the route of Sullivan's division, there was a guard of a captain and fifty jägers about half a mile from the town. Other posts were at the Assunpink bridge, on the road to Maidenhead (now Lawrenceville), on the road to the ferry landing, and on the road to Crosswicks, these four being away from the direction of the American attack.

At about quarter to eight in the morning of the 26th, Lieutenant Andreas Wiederhold, in charge of the picket post on the Pennington road, stepped out of the "alarm house," the center of his guard, and saw a small body of men about two hundred yards distant coming toward him from the northwest, the advance guard of Stephen's corps. At the same time his sentinels came running toward him, shouting: "Der Feind! Heraus! Heraus!" (The enemy! Turn out! Turn out!) There was a brief exchange of fire, and the picket turned and fled to Captain von Altenbockum's post in their rear. The company there had turned out on the alarm. It fired one volley, but Stephen's men, backed by Mercer's, charged it with such spirit that the Hessians retreated in haste toward the town, the Americans following and firing as they came. At almost the same moment, the advance guard of Sullivan's division fell upon the picket of jägers on the river road and drove it pellmell back into the town. So far the plan of simultaneous attack at the two ends of the town had been perfectly executed.

Lieutenant Jacob Piel, hearing the musket shots, ran to Rall's house and aroused him by hammering on his door. Rall, in his nightclothes, appeared at an upper window. Piel asked him if he hadn't heard the firing. In a very few minutes Rall was out and on his horse. His own regiment formed in the lower part of King Street. The Lossbergs hurriedly paraded in a cross street with orders to clear Queen. Dechow's battalion of Lossbergs was in the rear at a right angle to the rest, to face Sullivan's men in the lower part of the town. The Knyphausen regiment was held in reserve at Second and King streets.

Meanwhile Stephen's and Fermoy's corps had left Greene's division, swung to the left past the upper part of the town, and drawn a line around it from the Princeton road to Assunpink Creek. Mercer's had turned to the right to the west of the town and down toward the river until it got in touch with Sullivan at the lower end. Stirling, in the rear of the column, had marched straight to the junction of King and Queen streets at the upper end. At that point, from which artillery fire could command the whole length of the town, four fieldpieces under Captain Thomas Forrest were trained down Queen Street and two under Captain Alexander Hamilton pointed down King. Both immediately opened fire.

Rall's regiment and a part of Lossberg's advanced up King Street. Hamilton's shot tore into their ranks. Mercer's corps, coming in on their left, fired upon their flank. The Hessians gave two volleys and then fell back in disorder, throwing the rest of the Lossbergs into confusion. Two Hessian guns that had been brought up opened fire, but the gunners fell under the fire of the Americans. Stirling's troops charged down both streets, Weedon's

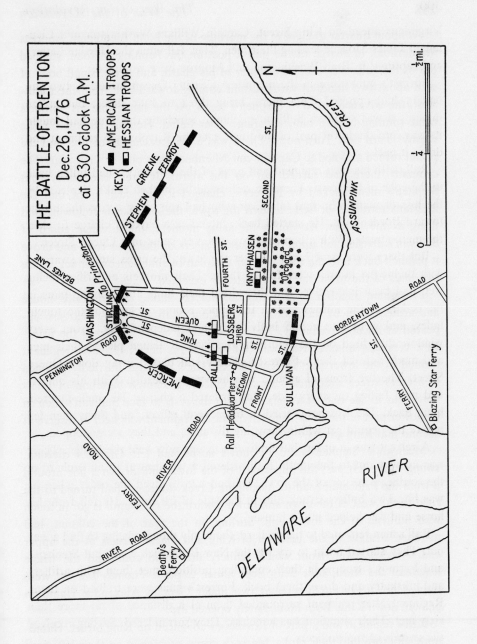

THE BATTLE OF TRENTON
Dec. 26, 1776
at 8.30 o'clock A.M.

KEY { ■ AMERICAN TROOPS
      □ HESSIAN TROOPS

Virginians ahead on King Street, Captain William Washington and Lieutenant James Monroe leading their men. They fell upon the Hessian battery and captured it. Both Washington and Monroe were wounded.

Forrest's guns were in the meantime clearing Queen Street. A two-gun battery had opposed them there, firing three or four times; but in ten minutes it was silenced. Sullivan's column, which by this time had fought its way into the lower part of the town, met the Knyphausen regiment and drove it back.

Rall, with his own regiment and most of the Lossbergs, had fallen back to the edge of the town. There he re-formed his broken ranks, depleted by the loss of many who had fallen, or who had run away across the bridge toward Bordentown. He started back, intending a bayonet charge to clear the main streets. With a band playing, his men came into Queen Street.

But there were Americans all over the town; the cross streets swarmed with them; the houses were full of them. Their muskets and rifles, being wet, had been ineffective. But they dried their flints and priming pans in the cellars of the houses and in the upper rooms, picked out the touchholes, and went into action individually and independently. From every window they fired on the returning Hessians. Riflemen picked their men and made sure of them. Forrest's battery still blazed away down Queen Street. The fire from all around was heavy and deadly. With his officers and men falling on every side, Rall ordered a charge. His men faltered, hung back. The Lossbergs tried it, but several officers and thirty men fell before they could get within thrusting distance, and they were stopped.

A retreat was in order, but Sullivan's troops now held the bridge. There was no way out to the south. Rall ordered a withdrawal to an orchard at the southeast corner of the town. He had hardly given the order when he was hit. Two bullets struck him in the side of his body. He fell from his horse and was helped into a house.

Rall's men retreated to the orchard, their only thought being to find a way out. They started north to try for the New Brunswick road; but Stephen's and Fermoy's troops, in their encircling position, met them with artillery and musketry and drove them back. Forrest's guns were trained on them. Regiment after regiment surrounded them at a distance of no more than sixty feet. Their situation was hopeless. They surrendered. Stirling received the swords of their officers.

Meanwhile Sullivan's division was taking care of the Knyphausen regiment and a battalion of the Lossbergs under Major von Dechow at the lower end of the town. Colonel John Stark of New Hampshire, shouting to his men to come on, led them in a charge that drove back the Hessians. Dechow was mortally wounded and gave himself up. His men tried to retreat by the bridge, but it was too strongly held. They tried for a ford above it, but found none. Their two guns were bogged down in a marsh. They left them and made a desperate effort to cross the creek through deep water. Some of them got through, only to meet St. Clair's corps drawn up on the other side ready to mow them down. Amid a shrieking crowd of camp followers, men and women milling about in helpless terror, they lowered their colors and grounded their muskets, while their officers raised their hats on the points of their swords in token of submission. The Americans tossed *their* hats in the air and shouted so loud that they were heard throughout the town. It was nine o'clock, and the battle was over.

That is a description of the Trenton fight in its essentials; in detail it is indescribable. From the beginning to the end, the little town was the scene of a hurly-burly of 4,000 fighting men moving here and there by regiments, by companies, and in smaller groups. Single men fired on their enemies in the streets, from inside the houses, from behind houses and fences. The usual chaos of street fighting was made worse by the fog of gunpowder smoke that hung over the town and by the hail, snow, and sleet that continued to beat upon the fighters. It was a grand mêlée, a great, informal "battle royal."

One outstanding feature of the fight was the comparative lack of musketry fire. The Americans had done the best they could to keep their flints and the pans of their flintlocks dry during that long march through the rain and sleet, by wrapping them in greased rags and covering them with their blankets and the skirts of their coats. The Hessians, emerging from their dry quarters, had their muskets in firing condition. But the rain soon drenched the weapons of both sides. The flints would not strike a spark; the priming charges would not flash; the touchholes were clogged with wet powder. Men on both sides could be seen chipping their flints, pulling their triggers again and again without effect. Those that got into the houses dried their gunlocks and could fire toward the end of the battle. Otherwise, it was mostly an affair of artillery, bayonet, sword, and spontoon.

But there was noise enough. The roar of the fieldpieces, the yells of both sides in their bayonet charges, the vociferous words of command or of encouragement of the officers, the indescribable general tumult filled the little town with a howling pandemonium of sound, even when the musketry fire slackened.

It was a great victory for the Americans, the more important because it was won at such a crucial time. But it was not so complete as Washington had planned and hoped. General Ewing's division was not in its appointed place, south of the Assunpink Bridge to cut off the fugitives. Many escaped that way—the picket of fifty jägers on the river road, the guards at the bridge, the guards at Trenton landing and other outposts, various groups from the regiments engaged and the detachment of twenty British dragoons, who galloped away soon after the first attack. In all about 500 escaped.

Nevertheless, the bag was substantial. Of the Hessians 22 were killed and 92 wounded. Prisoners were taken to the number of 948, including 32 commissioned officers. Of spoils there were six brass fieldpieces; six wagons; 40 horses; 1,000 muskets and rifles with bayonets and accouterments; 15 regimental and company colors; 14 drums; all the trumpets, clarionets, and hautboys of two bands; and 40 hogsheads of rum, which Washington ordered staved in and the liquor spilt on the ground, though perhaps not before his cold and tired men had had at least one drink. The casualties on the American side were two officers and two privates wounded.[12]

The failure of support of Ewing's and Cadwalader's divisions, neither of which had fulfilled its allotted task, made it impossible to proceed with the original plan of pushing on to attack the stations at Princeton and New Brunswick. But it is more than doubtful, considering the hardships and fatigues suffered by Washington's force and the necessity of caring for nearly a thousand prisoners, that that plan could have been carried out even if Ewing and Cadwalader had been at hand. With Donop's troops so near at Bordentown, aroused by the news of the battle brought by the escaped Hessians, it was manifestly inadvisable to linger in Trenton. Safety and rest on the other side of the river were plainly indicated.

Twenty-eight of the badly wounded Hessians were paroled to be left there, including Rall and Dechow, both of whom died of their wounds within two days. The rest of the prisoners were committed to the care of Stirling's corps, and the toilsome march back to the boats was begun soon after noon.

The storm had not abated. The northeast wind still drove the snow and hail against their faces. The road was no better than in the morning. Crossing the river proved even more difficult than before. It is said that three of the American privates were frozen to death in the boats. It was night before they all got across, and it was morning again before all got back to their huts. Some of the most remotely posted did not reach their camps before noon.

These men had marched and fought continuously for thirty-six, forty, and even fifty hours. Some of them had covered more than forty miles, in the bitterest cold and a driving storm, with no more than two or three hours' cessation of the most arduous labor. It is not surprising that more than a thousand were reported the next day as unfit for duty. "This was a long and a severe ordeal, and yet it may be doubted whether so small a number of men ever employed so short a space of time with greater or more lasting results upon the history of the world." [13]

Now it may be asked why Ewing's force was not on hand south of the bridge as ordered, and what Cadwalader's troops were about that night that they did not appear where they were expected. The answer to the first question is short. General Ewing, having seen the condition of the river, thought a crossing impossible. He did not even try it. Concerning the other, there is more to be said.

Cadwalader took a look at the floating ice above Bristol. It seemed to him too great an obstacle. He marched his men from the Neshaminy Ferry a few miles down to Dunk's Ferry. There four companies of Philadelphia militia and Captain Thomas Rodney's Dover company, acting as light infantry, embarked in five large bateaux and three scows about eight o'clock in the evening. They were to land on the Jersey shore and cover the subsequent disembarkation of the rest. They did land, "with great difficulty through the ice," having to walk on it a hundred yards before they got ashore. About two hundred yards from the river's edge, they formed and awaited the others. [14]

About nine o'clock the 1st and 3rd battalions of the Philadelphia Associators, with two fieldpieces, started across. They got no nearer to land than the advance party, but they all scrambled ashore, 600 of them. But Cadwalader did not see how he could land the fieldpieces. [15] The former colonel of the Philadelphia Silk Stocking Regiment therefore gave up and ordered his men back to the Pennsylvania side. [16] Rodney described the scene in a letter to his brother, Caesar: "We had to stand six hours under arms—first, to cover the landing, and till all the rest had retreated again; and by this time, the storm of wind, hail, rain and snow was so bad that some of the Infantry could not get back until the next day." [17] So that part of Washington's plan failed entirely of execution.

Rodney wrote in his diary that the order to retreat "greatly irritated the troops that had crossed the River and they proposed making an attack without both the Generals and the artillery"; but they were dissuaded from the attempt by the argument that, "if Gen. Washington should be unsuccessful and we also, the cause would be lost, but, if our force remained intact, it would still keep up the spirit of America." Washington's plan and his orders involved risking the whole army on the success of the combined attack, so that that reasoning seems to be altogether specious. Rodney expressed the opinion that "if our Generals had been in earnest, we could have taken Burlington with the light troops alone." He concluded that Washington meant these secondary expeditions under Ewing and Cadwalader "only as feints." [18] In this conclusion he was in error. Washington fully intended that those two forces should cooperate with his in reality, the one to hold the Assunpink against Rall's retreat, the other to attack Donop and at best defeat him, but at least to keep him from going to the aid of Rall. Even without those two little fieldpieces, a vigorous and bold commander could have done that much.

That Washington desired such an effort made, under any and all conditions, he had made plain to Cadwalader in a letter written at six o'clock that very evening: "Notwithstanding the discouraging Accounts . . . of what might be expected from the Operations below, I am determined, as the Night is favourable, to cross the River and make the attack upon Trenton in the Morning. If you can do nothing real, at least create as great a diversion as possible." [19]

Cadwalader could have put 1,900 men ashore as easily as 600. Colonel Reed and one other officer got their horses ashore. It would seem that, with the proper amount of courage and dogged determination, even the two 6-pounders could have been landed. Guns have been got over worse terrain than ice which a horse could negotiate. But, with 1,000 well clothed and equipped men, as were these Philadelphia Associators, fresh from home, and even without the guns, Cadwalader could have made "as great a diversion as possible," and held, if not actually defeated, Donop's force. If Washington's victory at Trenton had not been so swift and so complete, he might have had to fight all Donop's troops as well as Rall's to a disastrous finish. One can only conclude that it took a Washington to cross the river that night, and a Ewing and a Cadwalader to funk a crossing.

Washington's prisoners were immediately marched to Newtown in Pennsylvania and thence on December 30 to Philadelphia, where, with the captured colors, they were paraded through the streets. In their handsome uniforms, dark blue for Rall's regiment, scarlet for the Lossbergs, black for the Knyphausens, and dark blue coats with crimson lapels for the artillerymen, they made a fine show. An eyewitness gave an account of this display. "They made a long line—all fine, hearty looking men and well clad, with knapsacks, spatterdashes on legs, their looks were *satisfied*. On each side in single file, were their guards, mostly in light, summer dress and some without shoes, but stepping light and cheerful." [20] They were finally sent, by way of Lancaster, to the western counties of Pennsylvania and into Virginia, where they proved to be the most docile of prisoners.

The effect of the battle on the disposition of the enemy near the Delaware was instantaneous and drastic. Donop immediately withdrew from Mount Holly to Allentown and ordered the Hessians at Bordentown to join him at once. Burlington was evacuated, part of its garrison going to Princeton, the rest to New Brunswick. Within the shortest possible time for the movement of troops, every post in the Delaware River territory was cleared of the enemy.[21]

Howe was staggered by the news. "That three old established regiments of a people, who made war a profession, should lay down their arms to a ragged and undisciplined militia" [22] was simply stupefying. He stopped Cornwallis, who was on the point of embarking for England, and sent him to take command in New Jersey. He himself set out with reinforcements for the scene of trouble.

The effect upon the American people was as instantaneous, but different. From the depth of despair they rose to new confidence. From every direction came news of militiamen on the march to serve for two months, while the new Continental army was being organized.

Washington's reputation as a military leader had been on the wane ever since Long Island. Successive defeats and retreats had cumulatively discredited the commander in chief. But Trenton wiped out all that. "The country awakened to the belief that its general was a genius." [23] The Congress at Baltimore gave him full support. On December 27 it adopted a resolution vesting in Washington "full, ample and complete powers" to raise more battalions, infantry, light horse, artillery, and engineers, to appoint all officers under the rank of brigadier general and to displace them at will, to fix their pay, to commandeer "whatever he may want for the use of the army," and to arrest the disaffected. In short, he was to be something of a military dictator—for a period of six months.[24]

Princeton

In the morning of December 26 Cadwalader, presumably dry and un-fatigued in his quarters at Bristol, wrote a letter to Washington, telling him why he did not get his corps across the river. "I imagine the badness of the night must have prevented your passing as you intended." [1] Then he heard the thunder of the guns at Trenton, but could hardly believe his ears. The firing, he thought, must be on the west side of the river. Two or three hours later Ewing disabused his mind with news of the victory. "Such was the exhilaration produced by this intelligence" [2] that he ordered his men to be prepared to cross at sunrise the next day.

About ten o'clock Cadwalader's men began to embark at the ferry above Bristol, the exact point of departure fixed for him in Washington's orders for the night of the 25th, which he had not tried. The condition of the ice in the river could not have changed greatly, but now he was sufficiently "exhilarated" by the news of the victory to try it. He had got nearly all his men and his guns across when he received a reply from Washington to his letter. It politely regretted his failure to cross on the 25th, also Ewing's, which had prevented complete success: "The whole of the Enemy must have fallen into our hands," if Ewing had been at the bridge. Also it announced the return of the army to the west side of the river. [3]

Here was a pretty situation! Cadwalader and his 1,800 men were alone in New Jersey, facing he knew not what force of an aroused and revenge-ful enemy. There was Donop at Mount Holly, he thought, with perhaps 1,500 Hessians and the 42nd Highlanders, besides 500 of Rall's men who had escaped from Trenton. And Mount Holly was less than ten miles distant. Donop might even have advanced to Bordentown, six or seven miles away. Who could tell and what was one to do? He was "in a dilemma." [4] Among his officers there was "much perplexity and a great variety of opinions." It was urged by some that, as Washington was now back in Pennsylvania, the whole purpose of the expedition had failed. They had no support; Donop was a dangerous menace; if he came up, it would be impossible safely to retreat across the river; they had better go back at once. Cadwalader agreed with this opinion.

Colonel Reed, on the contrary, urged that the militia wanted action without any more fooling. They had crossed that damned river three times, and, if this present movement proved to be a fiasco, they would all go home in disgust. What was needed was enterprise. Follow up Washington's success by attacking a demoralized enemy. "On to glory!" was his watchword. But the majority was against him. At last, as a compromise, it was agreed to march to Burlington, where they were pretty sure no Hessians would be found. The bewildered temporary brigadier general gave orders accordingly.[5]

Cadwalader's men reached Burlington by nine o'clock in the evening and found no enemy there. Reed had been ahead, scouting. He brought word that Bordentown had been cleared of the foe. At four in the morning they marched toward that town through a "scene of devastation. Neither Hay, Straw, Grain, or any live stock or poultry to be seen." The Hessians had swept the area clean. Half a mile from the town they got word that the enemy was only five miles away and "were disposed to return." They lingered for an hour in a cornfield, then heard that "the enemy were flying with all speed." They marched in and "took possession of a large quantity of stores" left by the fleeing Hessians, whom they followed as far as Crosswicks.[6]

Colonel Reed had pursued his scouting activities to Trenton. Finding it entirely devoid of soldiers of either army, he so informed Washington and urged him to come over and follow up his victory. Washington had already planned a return to the Jerseys "for the purpose of attempting a recovery of that country from the enemy." [7] On the 29th his army started to cross the river, but it took two days to get them all across and into Trenton. There he learned that Cornwallis and Grant, with 8,000 men and a powerful train of artillery, were at Princeton, no more than a dozen miles distant, and that their advance troops were already feeling their way toward Trenton. Why Washington ventured to place the river at his back when it was likely that the British would appear in major force is not easy to explain. It would seem that prudence dictated remaining on the west side of the Delaware.

Washington's situation was critical. The hardships suffered by his men in those recent marches to and from Trenton had incapacitated many of them for immediate active service. He had left guards in the camps on the other side of the river. His present force numbered no more than 1,500. Clearly he could not hope to withstand his approaching enemy with so few. He might again retreat to Pennsylvania, but that would dash the hopes raised by his late exploit and depress the morale of his whole army. However, some reinforcements were near. General Mifflin's eloquence had raised 1,600 militia in Philadelphia. They were now at Bordentown. He sent for them and for Cadwalader's troops at Crosswicks, 2,100 men.

But there was still the fact that the enlistment of most of his Continentals would expire on the 31st. Knox and Mifflin addressed them, offering a bounty of ten dollars for six weeks' additional service, which many of the New England men accepted.[8] It was easy enough to promise a bounty, but what about paying it? The military chest was empty. Washington wrote to Robert Morris in Philadelphia: "If it be possible to give us Assistance, do it; borrow Money where it can be done, we are doing it on our private Credit; every man of Interest and every Lover of his Country must strain his Credit upon such an Occasion. No Time, my dear Sir, is to be lost." [9] Morris raised $50,000, paper money, on his own credit and sent it to him.

By the addition of the Pennsylvania militia and Cadwalader's troops, Washington had now 5,000 men and forty pieces of artillery. But many of the men were not merely militia, they were untrained, inexperienced militia, farmers, mechanics, men fresh from offices and shops who knew nothing of war, nothing whatever of the duties of a soldier. Fresh from home, they were doubtless sufficiently clad, properly shod, and in a fairly well fed condition. But the old Continentals, the backbone of the army, on whom alone the General could rely in action, were almost at the ends of their tethers. Ragged, gaunt, footsore, fatigued by their recent exertions, and worn almost to exhaustion by lack of sleep, that "flock of animated scarecrows" [10] was more fit for a hospital than for active service. It seems that they must have carried on rather by force of habit than by their own volition. Against these Cornwallis had 8,000 of the flower of the British army, presumably reasonably fresh.

Cornwallis left three regiments of the 4th Brigade, 1,200 men, under Lieutenant Colonel Charles Mawhood as a rear guard at Princeton, the 2nd Brigade, about as many, under General Leslie at Maidenhead (now Lawrenceville), and with the rest, 5,500 strong, set out for Trenton on January 2 accompanied by twenty-eight guns of various calibers up to 12-pounders.

Washington had sent forward, on January 1, General Roche de Fermoy, with his own brigade, Colonel Hand's Pennsylvania riflemen, Colonel Haussegger's new German battalion, Colonel Charles Scott's Virginia Continentals, and Captain Forrest's two-gun battery. They had taken a position a short distance south of Maidenhead.

It rained heavily that night and, the temperature being high for January, the roads were deep with mud. Cornwallis's troops in three columns had no easy going. His advance came upon the American vedettes about ten o'clock and drove them in. General Fermoy had left his troops and had returned to Trenton "in a very questionable manner." [11] Hand took charge of the detachment and ordered a slow retreat. At every point where they could find a good position, the Americans disputed the advance of the enemy. In the woods beside Shabbakonk Creek they made a stand, and there was a smart skirmish. The Americans' fire was so heavy and so well aimed that the British advance was confused, and two Hessian battalions were drawn up in battle order expecting a general engagement. For full three hours the Americans held this position. Again at the northern end of Trenton, where some little earthworks had been thrown up and four guns placed, they held off the enemy. A British battery was brought up, and an hour was consumed in forcing this point.

Following on the renewed retreat the British advance party, about 1,500 men, entered the town to meet an irregular fire from behind houses and fences and from American batteries posted on the south side of Assunpink Creek, to which the retreating Americans had retired. The main body of the British army, delayed by the condition of the roads, had not yet come up.

Washington had taken a position on a ridge along the south bank of Assunpink Creek, his line extending nearly three miles. Earthworks had been thrown up. Mercer's brigade was in the front line on the extreme left, Cadwalader's in the center, and St. Clair's next. Behind these there was a line of reserves.

It was five o'clock in the afternoon of the 2nd when the British advance neared the creek. They made three attempts to force a bridge. The failing light made the American fire uncertain, but it was heavy enough to hold the bridge. A party of Hessians tried to cross at a ford, but Hitchcock's Rhode Island Continentals dissuaded them from the attempt. For some time there was cannonading from both sides, which gradually died down.

When Cornwallis came up with his main army he consulted with his

generals. Sir William Erskine urged an immediate attack in spite of the
darkness. "If Washington is the general I take him to be," he is reported
to have said, "he will not be found there in the morning." But the others
saw the Americans caught with the Delaware River behind them and no
way out. Cornwallis decided that he had Washington in a trap, and that he
could easily "bag him" in the morning. So the British and Hessians withdrew to the upper part of the town. The Americans lighted their campfires
along the ridge, and both armies settled down for the night.

Washington's plans for the "recovery" of the Jerseys seem not to have
been disclosed to anyone. Howe's forces in that state, even after the withdrawal from the Delaware River territory, were strung out in a long line of
posts from Amboy through New Brunswick to Princeton. The line would include Trenton if and when he recovered it. The main highway from New
York to Philadelphia, the main artery of his supply line, ran through those
towns. If the Americans cut it at any point, the posts below would be left in
desperate straits. It seems probable that Washington intended to do that.
Trenton was not of first importance, since it was at the end of the string.
New Brunswick was, both because its possession by the Americans would
leave Princeton out on a limb, and because it was the principal depot of
British military stores in New Jersey. Trenton was merely the first station
on the road to New Brunswick.

But Washington had not taken into consideration certain traits absent in
Howe, but conspicuously present in Cornwallis's make-up; namely, energy
and swiftness of action. Instead of having time to go on to New Brunswick
before his foes could be got into the field to oppose him Washington found
himself at the very threshold of his adventure face to face with Cornwallis
in force. For the moment the British had been held off, or perhaps one
should say they had held off. But the morrow was on its way. In a few
hours the attack would be renewed in full strength, and Washington had
neither the strength of men nor that of position to repel his enemy
indefinitely.

His position was only apparently strong. The Assunpink was there, and
its only bridge might be held. But it was after all a very small stream, and
there were several fords a few miles above the bridge. If Cornwallis threw a
body of troops across there, he would be "bagged" indeed, with the Delaware River in his rear, and neither the time nor the means to cross it. It
was evident that some plan to extricate the army must be devised.

An American council of war was held. Should they fight it out there, or
retreat down the river and try to get across at some lower point? Both

attempts would be hazardous in the extreme—a battle because of their obvious weakness, and a retreat because the enemy hot on their heels would make it a disastrous rout and there were no boats below to rescue even a remnant. Then someone made an audacious suggestion. Who made it, no one knows; it has been claimed for several, but it is quite possible that Washington himself proposed it.[12]

The plan was to withdraw in the middle of the night, but not down the river. Instead, the army was to march around the left flank of the enemy, avoid the British post at Maidenhead, strike the British rear guard at Princeton, some twelve miles away, defeat it, and go on to New Brunswick. The very audacity of the plan seized the imagination, and it was adopted.

One obstacle in the way of success was removed while the council was in session. "A providential change of weather" occurred. A cold northwest wind sprang up, the temperature fell, and the roads froze hard.[13]

Preparations for the move began at once. The campfires were heaped high with fence rails. A party of 400 men was detailed to work on entrenchments at certain points whence the sound of pick and spade would be heard in the British camp. They were also to keep the fires going and to make a show of patrolling at the bridge and elsewhere. Finally they were to steal away at daybreak and follow the army as speedily as possible.

The baggage, stores, and three heaviest guns were started for Burlington under a strong guard. The wheels of the other gun carriages were wrapped with rags to deaden their sound on the frozen roads. At one o'clock in the morning of January 3 the march began, no one under the rank of a brigadier general having any knowledge of its destination or purpose.[14]

The Dover light infantry and the Red Feather Company of Philadelphia militia led the van, followed by Mercer's brigade. Beside Mercer's horse Colonel John Haslet, whose Delaware regiment of time-expired men had gone home, trudged along on foot. St. Clair's brigade, with Washington and his staff, came next, and then the rest of the army. Captain Henry, with the other three companies of the Philadelphia light infantry militia, brought up the rear. Orders were given in whispers; the muskets were carefully handled, and every care was taken to maintain silence. So the army passed along the front of the enemy's lines and took the road to Sandtown. That road ran through dense woods and had been lately made. It was rugged and rutted. Stumps had been left standing, which "stopped the movement of some of the guns and caused many a fall and severe bruise to some of the overweary, sleepy soldiers." [15] At Sandtown, they took the road to Quaker Bridge. At some time on this part of the march, "great confusion happened in the rear" among Henry's Philadelphia militia. "There was a cry that they were surrounded by Hessians, and several corps of Militia broke and fled towards Bordentown, but the rest of the column remained firm and pursued their march without disorder." [16]

At Quaker Bridge, the column swung toward the northwest on a road leading directly to Princeton. Two miles from that town it came to Stony Brook. It was then daylight. "The sun rose as we crossed the brook on a clear frosty morning." [17] Here the army was divided. Mercer's brigade of 350 tired, sleepy, hungry men, with Cadwalader's Associators, was split off to the left to secure a stone bridge on the direct road to Trenton, so that, if Cornwallis were pursuing, he could be held or at least delayed there. Sullivan, with three brigades, took a road to the right to enter Princeton on the east.

The British force in Princeton consisted of three regiments, the 17th, 40th, and 55th, with three troops of light dragoons. Lieutenant Colonel Charles Mawhood, the commander, was under orders to march the bulk of these, join General Leslie at Maidenhead, and then push on to Trenton that morning, leaving the 40th as a guard for the stores in Princeton. At about dawn Mawhood set out. He rode a brown pony, and his two favorite spaniels trotted by his side. The 17th, a part of the 55th, and a troop of the 16th light dragoons were with him. The rest of the 55th followed at a short distance. Mawhood had crossed Stony Brook bridge and was at the top of a small hill on the Trenton road when his eye caught the glitter of the sun's level rays reflected from bright metal at some little distance on his left. A searching look disclosed a motley band of armed men just emerging from a wood. It was the vanguard of Mercer's troops on its way to the bridge.

Having no thought of an attack in that vicinity, Mawhood supposed this was some part of the American army fleeing from a defeat by Cornwallis. He sent two mounted officers to reconnoiter the approaching body. As a measure of precaution, in order to intercept the Americans, if indeed they were bound for Princeton, he withdrew his force across the bridge to take up a position in an orchard and some farm buildings on a piece of rising ground on the other side of the stream. He led his men at the double in a dash for the orchard, but the Americans were nearer to it. With equal speed they gained it first and formed behind a hedge facing the British in an open field below.

Mawhood quickly deployed his men in line of battle at a distance of forty yards. Both sides at once opened fire, each having two fieldpieces in play. Mercer's horse was hit in one leg. He dismounted to fight on foot.

BATTLES
OF
TRENTON AND PRINCETON

SCALE OF MILES
0   1   2

Kingston

Retreat of the
remainder of the
40th and 55th
regiments to
New Brunswick Jan.3

Bridge destroyed by
Gen. Washington

PRINCETON

Nassau Hall

Mawhood

Hitchcock

Stony Brook Bridge

Mercer

Hand

Washington

Quaker Meeting House

Pennington

Flight of the 17th
regiment after
the battle Jan.3

Stony Brook

Eight Mile Creek

Bear Swamp

Leslie

Maidenhead

Five Mile Cr.

Quaker Road

The Barrens

Quaker Bridge

Assanpink Cc.

Birmingham

Shabbakonk Cr.

Cornwallis

Miller

Hand

Miry Run

Delaware River

Greene

Phillips Ford

Sandtown

Trenton Ferry

Mercer

Washington's March Jan.3

Hamilton Square

TRENTON

Cadwalader

Washington returns to
Jersey Side

St. Clair

Washington
Jan.2

Mawhood, after his first volley, called on his bayonets. The Americans fired again, but the sight of the cold steel was as usual too much for them. They broke and retreated in confusion.[18] Mercer and some of his officers tried to rally them, but Mawhood's bayonets were upon them. A blow from the butt of a gun knocked Mercer down. He got to his feet and tried to defend himself with his sword but fell again and, with seven bayonet wounds in his body, was left for dead. Captain Neil of the artillery also fell. Haslet ran to a spot where some of Mercer's men had halted and tried to bring them back to the fight. A bullet struck him in the head and killed him instantly.[19] That finished Mercer's brigade. They fled in disorder.

Mawhood pursued the Americans to the top of another ridge, but checked when he saw another American force coming out of the wood from which Mercer had emerged but a little while before. It was Cadwalader's Associators following on after Mercer. Mawhood withdrew to low ground between the two ridges and took a position behind a fence and a ditch, extending his line so that all his men could fire at once.[20]

From the ridge behind the British eight guns were keeping up a continuous fire of grape and round shot. Cadwalader came on; he led his men within fifty yards of Mawhood's line. But that was rashness. He had to fall back, leaving one of his guns. At a hundred yards from the enemy's line he tried, with some success, to form his men. A few companies did form and fired two or three volleys. But they soon gave way and the whole corps broke and ran back towards the woods.

At this moment Washington arrived on the scene. He had joined Sullivan's division when it turned to the right to attack Princeton. Hearing the firing on his left, he put spurs to his horse and, with his staff, galloped across ahead of his troops.

He came upon a scene of desperate confusion, Mercer's men and Cadwalader's in disorganized retreat. Waving his hat to the huddled groups as he passed, and calling on them to stand their ground, he dashed to the front, into the hottest fire and within thirty paces of Mawhood's line, to encourage his troops by the force of his own example.

The British soldiers were amazed at the sight of this big man on a great white horse so recklessly exposing himself. One of his aides thought to see him fall and covered his eyes to shut out the sight. A volley rang out from the enemy's line. The smoke from it shrouded Washington from all eyes. But when it blew away there he was, unhurt and still calling his men to come on.

They did not respond. It seemed that they were completely beaten. Then Hitchcock's Rhode Island Continentals, Hand's Pennsylvania riflemen, and the 7th Virginia came hurrying over from Sullivan's division. The defeated men took heart. Cadwalader's men rallied, and a part of Mercer's.

Meanwhile Captain Joseph Moulder's two-gun battery in the farmyard on the ridge, which had been first occupied by Mercer's men, had held its position and continued to pour grape on the enemy. While the Americans were re-forming for an advance Captain Thomas Rodney brought his handful of men and a few of the Philadelphia Associators to support Moulder. From behind strawstacks and buildings they kept up a good fire, deceiving the enemy as to their numbers by its continuity and rapidity.

At last the retreating troops were re-formed and, led by the Virginians yelling lustily, they came up to the battery's post, firing by platoons as they advanced.[21] Hand's riflemen went against Mawhood's right, and St. Clair's corps attacked the rest of the British 55th, now coming up to support the part of their regiment that had marched with Mawhood. They gave way and retreated across the fields and then along the road to New Brunswick. Mawhood was now almost surrounded, but his men fought on with great bravery. The action increased in intensity. The Americans' fire was hot and was delivered at such close range that they could hear the cries of its victims; they "screamed as if so many devils had got hold of them."

The 40th Regiment, cut off from the fight by St. Clair's brigade, had not come up from Princeton. But gallant Mawhood had no thought of surrender. He ordered a charge with the bayonet, broke through the swarm of Americans on the main road, crossed the bridge, and began a rapid retreat to Trenton, the dragoons covering his rear.

Washington with a troop of Philadelphia light horse led the pursuit, followed by many of his men on foot. The retreating British at first maintained good order, but finally broke and scattered away from the road with the American infantry after them. Many were shot down, 50 were captured. The fields were littered with their muskets and accouterments thrown away in their flight.[22] The pursuit continued until the British dragoons halted and made a determined stand to let such as still followed the road get away. Then it was called off.

Meanwhile the 40th Regiment and the men of the 55th who had not joined Mawhood had been driven back to Princeton. A part of them fled towards New Brunswick, the rest took refuge in Nassau Hall. It was surrounded. Captain Alexander Hamilton fired one ball from his fieldpiece into it, and a party of Jerseymen entered it. A surrender was inevitable; 194 prisoners were taken there.

The actual battle near the bridge had lasted only fifteen minutes; but it had been a very hot combat, fought at close quarters. In that short time 40 Americans were killed or wounded. Among the dead were General Mercer, who succumbed to his wounds, and Colonel Haslet—both of them officers of great merit and promise—Captain Daniel Neil of New Jersey, Captain William Shippen and Ensign Anthony Morris, Jr., of Philadelphia, and Captain John Fleming and Lieutenant Bartholomew Yeates of Virginia.

Washington estimated that the British lost 400, of whom 100 lay dead on the field; [23] but Howe's official report showed 18 killed (to which must be added 10 artillerymen not included in the return), 58 wounded, and 187 missing. As usual, the two claims cannot be reconciled. The Americans took two brass guns, which, for want of horses, could not be carried away, and some blankets and shoes, whose transportation was not difficult.

This victory, like that of Trenton, had an effect on the American cause entirely disproportionate to the number of men engaged. It heartened the people of all the states with hopes of ultimate complete success. Moreover, it strengthened Washington's military reputation at home and abroad, with a corresponding increase of his authority. "From Trenton onwards," says Trevelyan, "Washington was recognized as a far sighted and able general all Europe over—by the great military nobles in the Empress Catherine's court, by the French Marshals and Ministers, in the King's cabinet at Potsdam, at Madrid, at Vienna and in London. He had shown himself (says Horace Walpole) both a Fabius and a Camillus, and his march through the British lines was allowed to be a prodigy of leadership." [24]

A stroke at New Brunswick had been part of Washington's plan; but his men had been under arms for forty continuous hours of bitter winter weather, with no interval to rest or to cook a meal. They had made a most difficult march of sixteen miles over the roughest of roads in the darkness of night, and had then fought a hotly contested battle. They were so spent that there was hardly anything left in them. They were actually falling asleep on the frozen ground, and New Brunswick was eighteen miles away. Moreover, Cornwallis was surely now on the march against them with his much stronger army, and would be deeply interested in his stores at New Brunswick. Also, General Leslie at Maidenhead was only six miles distant.

Halting the pursuit of Mawhood's troops at Kingston after a three-mile chase, Washington held a council of war on horseback and put the question of his next move to his officers. It was agreed that they should give up New Brunswick and push off at once for the hills and the broken, heavily wooded country about Morristown, where a northern base for the army had been already established.

Washington confirmed this inevitable decision with much regret. He wrote to the Congress on January 5 that in his judgment "six or seven hundred fresh troops, upon a forced march, would have destroyed all their stores and magazines" at New Brunswick, "taken (as we have since learned) their military chest, containing seventy thousand pounds, and put an end to the war." [25] If his men had known £70,000 was to be had at New Brunswick, they might have summoned the strength to go and get it, despite their officers' judgment as to their incapability.

The army was on the move none too soon. Cornwallis, when he awoke that morning and overcame his astonishment at the discovery that the American army was not on the ridge across the Assunpink, was informed by the distant sound of guns that it was fighting elsewhere. He broke camp and marched for Princeton with haste and, coming to the bridge over Stony Brook which the Americans had broken down to delay his advance, did not pause, but drove his troops through the breast-deep stream. His speed was so great that his van, when it entered Princeton, was within sight of the American rearguard quitting the town.

Cornwallis was now convinced that Washington was headed for New Brunswick and its treasures. He followed on, but when the Americans took a left-hand road along Millstone River at Rocky Hill he took the right-hand road leading straight to New Brunswick. For how could he tell that the elusive Washington was not making a roundabout march to that valuable objective, in order to deceive his pursuers?

The van of the Americans reached Somerset Courthouse at dusk, but not all were in before eleven o'clock. There they encamped, if sleeping on the frozen ground without blankets, as many of them did, can be called "camping." "Our army was now extremely fatigued," wrote Captain Rodney, "not having any refreshment since yesterday morning." But they were up at daybreak and on the road again. At Pluckemin they halted to "await the coming up of nearly 1,000 men, who were not able through fatigue and hunger to keep up with the main body, for they had not had any refreshment for two days past" and had been "obliged to encamp on the bleak mountains, whose tops were covered with snow, without even blankets to cover them." They rested there for two days and were "pretty well supplied with provision." On the 6th the army went on to Morristown, where it was safe from sudden attack.

Meanwhile American contingents captured Hackensack and Elizabeth-Town, on January 6. Washington had swept the Jerseys clear of the enemy, except at Amboy and New Brunswick, which Howe still held with a force of 5,000 each. They were harmless posts, offering no opportunity for a blow against the Americans. This considerable feat had been accomplished by an army of fewer than 5,000 ragged, shoeless, ill fed, poorly equipped, often defeated amateur soldiers, mostly militia, operating against twice that number of veteran professionals, abundantly supplied with all martial equipment, and within a space of eleven days in the depth of winter.[26]

So ended the New Jersey campaign of 1776, which had ignored the calendar and lapped over a few days into 1777.

CHAPTER 28

Morristown

Morristown was a village of a church, a tavern, and about fifty houses of the better sort, set in an excellent defensive position on a high triangular plateau, with steep declivities on two sides and the bold ridge of Thimble Mountain at its back. It was approachable from the east only through rugged defiles in a chain of hills, while various passes to the west afforded access to a rich country for supplies, as well as ways for retreat, if necessary. For offensive operations it threatened Howe's flank if he should move either towards Philadelphia or up the Hudson.

In Freeman's Tavern on the village green Washington set up his head-quarters. The troops were lodged in log huts in and about the village and outlying posts.[1] He had come there, as he said, "to draw the force on this side of the North River together . . . watch the motions of the Enemy and avail Myself of Every favourable Circumstance," [2] expecting to remain a few days. He lay there for nearly five months.

Whatever activities Washington may have had in mind, in the event of favorable circumstances, the condition of his army enforced a winter of inactivity. Depleted by expiration of enlistments and by the usual desertions, worn down by its recent severe service, it was at its lowest ebb in numbers, in physical condition, and in equipment.

On January 29, 1777, Washington wrote to the Congress that, unless speedily reenforced, he would be reduced "to the Situation . . . of scarce having any army at all." [3] By March 14 he had fewer than 3,000 men, of whom two-thirds were militia enlisted only to the end of the month.[4] At times, he was put to it to find men to mount the ordinary guards.[5] Yet

319

with this handful he had to "keep up Appearances" before the enemy. "How I am going to oppose them, God knows," he wrote on April 3, "for except a few hundred from Jersey, Pennsylvania and Virginia I have not yet received a Man of the new Continental levies." [6]

The army was not only small; it was also destitute, "absolutely perishing for want of clothes," many of the men "quite bearfoot," so the General said. An ill organized commissariat failed to supply food. He wrote angrily to one of the commissaries: "The Cry of want of Provisions comes to me from every Quarter. . . . What, sir, is the meaning of this? . . . Consider, I beseech you, the consequences of this neglect and exert yourself to remedy this Evil." [7] He had to use the plenary powers granted him by the Congress in December, 1776, and order that "all the Beef, Pork, Flour, Spirituous Liquors &C &C, not necessary for the Subsistence of the Inhabitants" of lower East Jersey, should be commandeered.[8]

To crown the misfortunes of the army, smallpox ravaged the camp. The commander in chief took vigorous steps to combat it,[9] quartering the troops in small parties in the houses in Morristown and the near-by villages and ordering the inoculation of soldiers and citizens alike. Despite the protests of the dismayed civilians, this was done "with amazing success," [10] although at one time a third of his army was ill from the treatment.[11]

In addition to calling on the states in September, 1776, to raise eighty-eight battalions, Congress had authorized Washington on December 27 to raise sixteen Additional Battalions of infantry, 3,000 light horse, three artillery regiments, and a corps of engineers,[12] a grand total of 75,000 men —on paper, never to be realized in fact.

Recruiting lagged painfully. The soldiers of the old army were loath to reenlist. They had had enough of hardship, enough of cold and hunger, enough of barefoot marching in winter, enough of the dreadful squalor and filth of the "hospitals," where men merely lingered awhile in misery and wretchedness on their way to the grave. They told their tales of woe in the taverns and market places and so discouraged others that might have been ambitious to go a-soldiering.

The bounty system also acted against enlistment in the forces to be raised. The Congress offered $20 to each recruit enlisting for three years or the duration of the war and promised each man who served his full term a hundred acres of land.[13] In their efforts to fill their quotas of the original eighty-eight battalions, some of the New England states began to offer an additional bonus of $33.33. To the men whom Washington tried to enlist in the sixteen Additional Battalions $53.33 in hand looked better than $20 and a hundred acres, if they survived the war. He protested that the colonels appointed to raise the sixteen could not "get Men for 20 dollars when the state allows 53⅓." [14] Massachusetts answered by doubling its offer, making the total bounty $86.66; other states fell in line and went even higher.[15]

Some of the states made difficulties for themselves by raising regiments exclusively for home duty, while their quotas for the eighty-eight Continental battalions were yet unfilled, and paying these home guards £3 a month for "easy and secure duty at, or near their own firesides," against Continental wages of 40 shillings "for hard and dangerous service, far distant from home," as Washington put it in a protest to the executive officials of Massachusetts.[16]

On December 27, 1776, the Congress had called upon the new levies in the states from Pennsylvania down to Virginia "to march by companies or parts of companies, as far as they shall be raised, and join the army under General Washington with the utmost dispatch." [17] A month later Washington wrote, "They are so extremely averse to turning out of comfortable Quarters, that I cannot get a man to come near me." [18] And all through the spring and early summer, he kept repeating his call for more men.

There was a bit of good news in March; a ship from France came in with a useful cargo: nearly 12,000 muskets, 1,000 barrels of powder, 11,000 gun flints, and an assortment of clothes and incidentals, such as "1 case of needles and silk neck-cloths." [19] In its wake came another with 10,000 muskets. Guns and ammunition in plenty, but where were the men to use them?

They came at last. The thin trickle of recruits became a rivulet, then a clear stream, though never a flood. By the middle of May, forty-three of the new Continental regiments had arrived at Morristown, but not in full strength; they averaged 200 each, officers and men. Still, an army of 8,738 soldiers was something to be thankful for, even if only two-thirds of them were actually present and fit for duty. This force was organized in five divisions under Major Generals Greene, Stephen, Sullivan, Lincoln, and Stirling. Optimism returned; Congress moved back to Philadelphia.

Howe had learned the lesson of Trenton and Princeton; outlying posts, even if fairly strong, were not safe from those night-prowling Americans. By January 10 he had withdrawn all his troops to New Brunswick and Amboy. His own winter quarters were in New York, where he diverted himself in "feasting, gaming and banqueting" and in dalliance with his mistress, Mrs. Joshua Loring.[20] His troops were not so well off. Fourteen thousands of them were cantoned at Amboy and New Brunswick and the villages of that district in every sort of makeshift quarters. An entire company was crowded into two rooms; a regiment, in a church. Stables were filled with them. Open sheds were boarded up for them to freeze in. Many lay in the open. And it was not only overcrowding and the cold that made their lot hard. They were hungry, too. Food, as well as fuel and forage, was scarce, for "Amboy and Brunswick were, in a manner, besieged." [21]

The Americans were constantly on the alert to prevent the British from drawing subsistence from the countryside. No British foraging party could venture out of the lines with impunity. Attacks on such parties were frequent, and usually successful. The depredations and ravages committed, by the Hessians especially, but also by the British soldiers, had so angered the populace that they became fervent patriots, spied on the enemy, and kept Washington informed of their every move. The militia turned out in great numbers and aided the Continentals in harassing the foe. General Philemon Dickinson, with 400 militia and 50 Pennsylvania riflemen, fell upon a British foraging party of about the same strength, defeated it, and recaptured 40 wagonloads of plunder, 100 horses, and many cattle and sheep. Even 4,000 men in another party were not safe from attack. Washington kept his own men busy in such affairs and in "incessantly insulting, surprising and cutting off their pickets and advanced guards." [22]

But, except for such sporadic skirmishes, there was no military activity in the Jerseys that winter. Howe was now thinking of Philadelphia as his next major objective, but did nothing to achieve it. There is no doubt that the British army of 27,000 of the best professional soldiers, directed by Howe's military genius, led by the active and vigorous Cornwallis, and opposed only by Washington's meager 4,000, could have attained its object at any time in the first four months of 1777. Washington's position at Morristown could have been circumvented; and if he had seen fit to come down and attack the British on the march Howe would have had his opportunity for a decisive battle in the open field, in which his troops would have had every advantage.

Whether it was Howe's naturally sluggish temperament, or his adherence to the classic tradition that winter was a season for quarters and not for a campaign, or an exaggerated estimate of Washington's total strength, or an imagination of "hordes of Americans" ready to fall on his army if he advanced through the Jerseys, that caused him to waste those winter months and even the whole spring, no one can tell. But waste them he certainly did, while Washington's army grew stronger and stronger and his own job grew more and more difficult.[23]

There was, however, some activity elsewhere. It will be remembered that in November, 1776, when Washington withdrew from North Castle, he left Heath with four brigades, about 3,300 men, at Peekskill to guard the Highlands of the Hudson. Although a very large quantity of military stores had since been accumulated in magazines the troops had been drawn away for one reason or another until few remained. Washington had urged Massachusetts to send eight regiments to hold that post, but without result. In March, 1777, General Alexander McDougall, an inexperienced officer, was there, with but 250 men. The situation invited attention by the British. At midday of March 23 nine or ten British vessels arrived before Peekskill and disembarked 500 men. McDougall attempted to remove some of the stores, with little success. He then retired from the town, having first appealed for aid to Colonel Marinus Willett in Fort Montgomery on the other side of the river. Willett, a capable officer who was to prove his military efficiency a few months later at Fort Stanwix, crossed with 80 men, but the British had already been effectively busy burning the barracks and firing the magazines. He urged McDougall to attack, without avail. However, he obtained permission to try his luck. After firing one or two volleys he charged the British advance guard with the bayonet and drove it back on the main body, which at once took to its boats and withdrew to the ships.

The British had, however, accomplished their purpose, having practically destroyed the town by fire and burned great quantities of provisions, including 400 hogsheads of rum, 150 new wagons, several sloops and boats, and a quantity of entrenching tools. They carried off other stores of food, arms, artillery equipment, and munitions. They boasted that "the destruction was complete and effectual, scarce anything escaping that could be of use," which was no more than the truth. McDougall was relieved of his command and replaced by General Putnam, who held the post seven months before he too proved his incapacity and was removed.[24]

There was a similar British foray against Danbury, Connecticut, in the following month, which will be treated in connection with the northern campaign of 1777.

The Americans had their turn in May. A British foraging party was sent from New York to Sag Harbor near the eastern end of Long Island in twelve vessels protected by an armed schooner carrying 40 men and 12

guns and by a company of 70 men from Lieutenant Colonel Stephen
De Lancey's Tory battalion. Colonel Return Jonathan Meigs with one of
the Additional Battalions heard of this incursion. He embarked 170 men
in whaleboats at Guilford in Connecticut in the evening of May 23, crossed
Long Island Sound, which was "full of British cruisers," and landed at Sag
Harbor at two o'clock the next morning. Taking De Lancey's troops by
surprise, he killed six of them and captured all the rest, burnt all their
vessels, except the schooner, also a large quantity of provisions and forage,
and was back at Guilford by noon, having covered a distance of nearly 100
miles in eighteen hours. For this feat, the Congress voted him "an elegant
sword." [25]

Maneuvers in New Jersey

Winter had gone, spring had come and had nearly gone before the first move was made in the game played by Washington and Howe with Philadelphia and perhaps American independence as the stakes. On May 29 Washington made it.

Fearing that Howe might make a swift march from New Brunswick straight to Princeton and so to Trenton, passing some thirty miles below the American position, Washington marched twenty miles south to Middlebrook, near Bound Brook and about eight miles from New Brunswick. His new position, at which he hoped to intercept Howe, was in the first range of the Watchung Mountains behind certain commanding heights from which the country between Amboy and New Brunswick and the road to Philadelphia could be watched. It was strengthened by entrenchments and artillery posts.[1] At Princeton, he placed Smallwood's Maryland and Delaware brigade and Hazen's "2nd Canadian Regiment," under Sullivan.[2]

It was now Howe's turn. He wanted to get the Americans down on open ground, for a fair stand-up fight in which his trained army might beat them and so open the way to the American capital. To this end he made a series of three maneuvers.[3]

The first began on June 12. The British forces operating in New Jersey had been assembled at Amboy, 18,000 rank and file.[4] They marched to New Brunswick and thence in two columns: one, led by Cornwallis, to Somerset; the other, under von Heister, to Middlebush near Somerset.[5] They hoped not only to entice Washington down from Middlebrook, but also to cut Sullivan off from the main American army. Washington saw Sullivan's danger and ordered him to retire to Rocky Hill, where he could cover the road from that point to Pennington and also have a way of retreat open to the main army. While there he was to "harrass the Enemy by incessant parties when they attempt to march thro the country" but "by no means to risk a General Engagement." [6] A few days later Sullivan was shifted to Flemington on the enemy's right flank. Howe was also foiled in his other purpose. Washington refused to be drawn down from his stronghold.

Washington knew that Howe was "marching light," that is to say, that he had left at New Brunswick all his heavy baggage, his bateaux, and the portable bridge intended for crossing the Delaware. He knew, too, that if Howe really had intended now to march for the Delaware he would have pushed on with speed and would not have halted at Somerset or Middlebush and entrenched there.[7] As Stedman says, the American general "easily penetrated into the designs" of Howe "and eluded them by his cool and prudent conduct." [8] To strengthen his right, his most vulnerable point, Washington called on Sullivan to send him 1,000 Continentals and an equal number of the militia which had joined him and posted them at Steel's Gap in the Sourland Mountain, about two miles from Middlebrook.

Howe was now in an embarrassing position. He could not go on to the Delaware without his baggage, boats, and bridge, and, even if he brought them up, the American army still threatened his flank. Also there was a considerable force of Continentals and militia on the opposite side of the Delaware to oppose his crossing.[9] With Washington in his rear, he would be between two fires. There was, too, an ominously increasing number of Jersey militiamen hovering about his camp like a cloud of mosquitoes, picking up any men that strayed outside and promising more material aid to Washington when it was needed.[10]

But the British general had not yet exhausted his store of artful devices to lure Washington from his position. In the night of the 19th of June, he suddenly and secretly retreated from Middlebush and Somerset towards New Brunswick "with marks of seeming precipitation." [11] This time he was partially successful. Washington was deceived into thinking the movement was a final retreat. He sent Greene with his division of three brigades, reinforced by Wayne's brigade and Daniel Morgan's riflemen, to fall on the rear of the enemy. Orders were sent to Sullivan and Maxwell to cooperate with Greene.

Morgan led the advance along the right bank of the Raritan. At dawn he came upon Howe's Hessian picket guard at the New Brunswick bridge. The picket fled, hotly pursued by Morgan, until it came to the British rear guard. Greene and Wayne came up and charged upon the enemy, driving them through the town and across the bridge to their redoubts on the east side of the river. The Americans pushed them from these works and pursued them as far as Piscataway. But Sullivan had received his orders too late to come up with the pursuit, and Maxwell never got his. So Greene gave over the chase. The main body of the British went on its way towards Amboy, burning houses and barns along the road.[12] An English civilian, who accompanied the army, described this feature of the retreat: "All the Country houses were in flames as far as we could see. The Soldiers are so much enraged" at being called upon to retreat "that they will set them on fire in spite of all the Officers can do to prevent it." [13]

The Americans accomplished little by this affair, but Howe gained a point in the game. Deluded by him Washington came down from the hills to Quibbletown (now New Market) and encamped there, so as to be "nearer the enemy" and "act according to circumstances." [14] He sent Stirling with a strong detachment to the Short Hills in the neighborhood of Metuchen.

Howe's second maneuver having so far succeeded, he grasped at the chance to bring on a general engagement by a third movement. At one o'clock in the morning of the 26th his army moved out of Amboy in two columns. Cornwallis led one towards Woodbridge; Vaughan, the other towards Bonhamton. Howe accompanied Vaughan. Marching on parallel lines, they intended to pinch Stirling between them and to seize the passes back to Middlebrook, thus cutting Washington off from a retreat to the heights and compelling him to fight where he was.

They were long hours on the road. The weather was exceedingly hot. As the sun rose and climbed the sky the heat became increasingly intense. The marching men, especially the more heavily clad and equipped Hessians, suffered almost as much loss from sunstroke as from the bullets of snipers along the way.

The two columns joined before they came to Lord Stirling's camp, "strongly situated and well provided with artillery." [15] They attacked furiously. "His lordship was in no hurry to retreat, but preferred engaging for a while, wherein he made a wrong choice, for he had been nearly cut off by the right column under Lord Cornwallis." [16] He was driven from his position and pursued as far as Westfield where, "on account of the intense heat of the day," Cornwallis halted his men. The losses in this affair are impossible to reckon with certainty. The British claimed 100 Americans killed or wounded and 70 taken captive. They admitted 70 casualties on their side. These figures are all doubtful, but the Americans certainly did lose three small but valuable French brass guns.[17]

Near Woodbridge the British had fallen in with a party of American riflemen. Washington heard their fire, retired at once to the Middlebrook passes, and regained the heights before the enemy cut him off. So there the two armies were again in the same old positions.[18] Howe's third attempt had failed. "Sir William Howe," says Stedman, "being now sensible that every scheme of bringing the Americans to an engagement would be unattended by success, resolved to retire from the Jerseys." [19] He withdrew all his troops to Amboy and thence to Staten Island. By June 30 "the Province of New Jersey was entirely evacuated by the King's Troops." [20]

Now ensued a period of inactivity for both armies. For Washington, however, it was a time of increasing doubt and anxiety as to Howe's next move. General John Burgoyne had arrived in Quebec early in May, intending, as was well known, an expedition southward by way of Lake Champlain and the Hudson to Albany. He had now set out with a force of 8,000 British, Brunswickers, Canadians, and Indians. To Washington it seemed "almost certain" that Howe would go to meet him in Albany. That would mean that the great fleet, which Howe had been assembling for two months in New York waters, would sail up the Hudson.[21]

But there were other possible destinations—Philadelphia, for instance, by way of the Delaware River or Chespeake Bay, or even Charleston in South Carolina. With such a crafty strategist as Howe you never could tell. Then came news of Burgoyne's approach to Ticonderoga. Washington was surer than ever that Albany was Howe's objective.[22] In that case the American forces on the Hudson should be strengthened.

But not too indiscreetly or prematurely. If Washington's army went up there, Howe could make a swift and easy march to Philadelphia, take that city, and still have time for the Hudson River enterprise. Only Varnum's and Poor's brigades were sent to Peekskill, and Sullivan's as far as Pompton "till the intentions of the enemy are more clearly and fully known." In order to be "more conveniently situated for Succouring Peekskill," and yet "near enough to oppose any design upon Philadelphia," Washington transferred his main army to Morristown.[23]

When he received information as to the fitments of Howe's transports for carrying horses and the amount of "Provender taken in"—enough for a month's voyage—he began to doubt that the fleet would go up to Albany and to think of Charleston as its destination.[24] He was puzzled. Nevertheless, he ordered Sullivan farther north, to the Clove in the Ramapo Mountains, a rugged defile through the Highlands on the west side of the river.[25]

Howe began to embark his troops on July 8, but did not immediately sail. For nearly two weeks "both foot and Cavalry remained pent up in the hottest season of the year in the holds of the vessels." [26] The day after the embarkation, Washington learned to his "Chagrine and Surprise" that General Arthur St. Clair, with 3,500 men, had evacuated Ticonderoga, without firing a shot in its defense and that Burgoyne was rapidly advancing towards Albany.[27] He could not believe that Howe would not go up to meet him, and wrote on July 12, "His designs I think are most unquestionably against the Highlands." Washington therefore decided to march "towards the North River and cross or not as shall appear necessary from the circumstances." On his arrival in the Clove he sent Sullivan and after him Stirling across the river to a position behind Peekskill.[28]

On July 23 Howe's fleet of more than 260 warships and transports, laden with fifteen to eighteen thousand soldiers, innumerable horses, field-pieces and small arms, quantities of ammunition, provisions, and military equipment of every sort, set sail from Sandy Hook. It was an impressive armada. A little below, the transports formed in two divisions. The flagship *Eagle*, 64 guns, and the frigate *Liverpool*, 32 guns, led the convoy. After them and on both sides of the transports came the warships *Augusta*, 64 guns, and *Isis*, 50 guns. In the rear were the *Nonsuch*, 64 guns, with its "couriers" the armed schooners *Swift* and *Dispatch*, 16 guns each. Nine frigates "sailed around the fleet at some distance." So they left the Hook bound for—no one on the American side knew where.[29]

Washington, up in the Clove, got the news the next day and perceived that he had guessed wrong. He ordered Sullivan, Stirling, Stephen, and Lincoln, with their divisions, Morgan's riflemen, and the squadrons of horse led by Sheldon, Moylan, and Bland to proceed immediately to Philadelphia. He detached Wayne from his brigade and sent him to Chester in Pennsylvania to command the militia there. With the rest of his army he started southward.[30]

When he gave those orders he was sure Howe was for Philadelphia by way of the Delaware River; but by the time he himself got to that river, on the 29th, he began again to doubt. Howe had then been six days at sea, yet had not appeared at the Delaware capes. Perhaps after all his start southward from New York was merely a ruse to draw the American army away from the Hudson. That fleet might have turned about and be now on its way back to join Burgoyne. He decided to hold his troops on the Jersey side of the Delaware, at Trenton, Coryell's Ferry, and Howell's Ferry. He halted Sullivan at Morristown until further orders.[31]

But the very next day Henry Fisher, a pilot at Lewes, at the mouth of the Delaware Bay, sent an express to Philadelphia telling that the fleet was in sight. Washington got the news at Coryell's Ferry, 150 miles from Lewes, at ten o'clock in the morning of the 31st—in twenty-four hours, a creditable performance for men and horses.[32]

Washington immediately ordered his troops across the Delaware and to Philadelphia, called on Sullivan to come on, and himself took horse for Chester "to look out for a proper place to arrange the army."[33] But on August 2 Fisher wrote that the fleet had left: "A large ship which we took to be the Admiral fired a gun and immediately the whole Fleet backed and stood off . . . to the eastward . . . about four o'clock P.M. they were ought of sight; whether they were bound to New York or Virginia is not in my power to tell."[34]

Nor was it in Washington's power; but he guessed—and guessed wrong again. It seemed to him, he said, that Howe had been "practising a deep feint, merely to draw our attention and whole force to this point." "There is the strongest reason to believe that the North River is their object." "This unexpected event makes it necessary to reverse our disposition." "I shall return again with the utmost expedition to the North River." So he wrote to this and that one of his generals, with orders to hasten back to Peekskill.[35]

But on more sober thought he decided on August 3 to wait until he had sure intelligence that the fleet was back at Sandy Hook before he returned to Peekskill. So he halted Sullivan at Hanover in New Jersey and held his main army at the Falls of Schuylkill near Germantown in Pennsylvania.

Yet again, on the 8th, his fears of Howe's strategy prompted him to move back to Coryell's Ferry; and he was actually on the march when, on the 10th, another flash came from the south. The fleet had been seen off Sinepuxent Inlet in Maryland, thirty miles below the Delaware capes, and was headed south. He halted his army and went into camp beside Neshaminy Creek, thirty miles north of Philadelphia.[36]

Still, he was "puzzled . . . being unable to account upon any plausible Plan . . . why he [Howe] should go to the southward rather than co-operate with Mr. Burgoyne."[37] Even as late as the 21st of August he still thought Howe was making a feint and would return either to the Delaware or to the Hudson, for, "had Chesapeake Bay been his Object, he would have been there long since." A council of war held that day decided unanimously that Charleston in South Carolina was Howe's most probable destination. So sure were the American generals that it was decided to move "to-morrow morning towards Hudson's River," and orders were given accordingly.[38] But on the next day came an express: the fleet was in the Chesapeake, "high up in the North East part of it." [39] The orders were canceled.

Why Admiral Lord Howe, in command of the fleet, and his brother, Sir William, in command of the army, after reaching the Delaware capes, failed to attempt a landing near Philadelphia and instead made the long voyage south, around Cape Charles, and up the Chesapeake, has puzzled many able historians and they still continue to debate the question. Yet the facts seem to give a plain answer.

The fleet had sailed from Sandy Hook on July 23, 1777. Meeting variable weather and winds, it made the Delaware capes on the 29th. After tacking to and fro for a whole day, it was joined by the *Roebuck*, which had long been stationed in Delaware waters under command of Captain Sir Andrew Snape Hamond. Captain Hamond boarded the flagship and gave the Admiral such a report of conditions in the bay and river that it was decided to draw off and make for the Chesapeake.

The first question debated by the historians is whether it was General Howe's intention, when he planned the excursion, to go up the Delaware or the Chesapeake. But that question is certainly easily answered. He planned at first to enter the Chesapeake. However, he wrote to Germain July 6, 1777, "I propose going up the Delaware." The second question is why he changed his mind. That is answered in a letter to Germain dated August 30: "Arrived off the Capes of the Delaware . . . when from information, I thought it most advisable to proceed to Chesapeake Bay." Hamond gave him reasons that quite properly seemed sufficient to make him change his plans.[40] Lieutenant William John Hall of the 45th regiment makes this point clear in a letter dated December 26, 1777: "In our appearance off the capes of Delaware, the *Roebuck* came out and Capt. Hamond going on board the Admiral produced a chimerical draught of fortifications that were never erected and Chevaux de Frise that were never sunk. This intelligence caused us to bear away for the Chesapeake." [41] What was even more important in the situation was that Howe hit upon the idea of using the Delaware because he feared Washington was about to go to the assistance of the American army in northern New York and because he could follow Washington much more readily from the Delaware. When he learned that the American commander in chief was not moving northward, he was able to pursue his original plan.

One may ask two more questions: Was Hamond's advice justified by conditions in the Delaware? Was the decision unfortunate in fact?

The substance of Hamond's objections to going up the Delaware was the condition of the river itself and the condition of its defenses. Of the river itself he said that its navigation was intricate and hazardous; that large ships could pass certain places only at particular times of the tide; that its shores from Henlopen to Reedy Island were marshy and full of creeks; that from Reedy Island to Chester the channel was so narrow as to require four miles of anchorage for the fleet, which must lie within cannon-shot of the shore; that the tidal current ran at three to four miles an hour.[42]

In answer one might urge that the navigation was not too difficult, nor the tidal current too strong to prevent the flagship and twelve other ships from going up in October as far as Chester. As to anchorage, in November there were 100 vessels anchored between Reedy Island and New Castle; although much of the shore was marshy, both New Castle and Chester afforded good landing places, New Castle being a port much used by overseas vessels. On this point Hamond's advice was clearly unjustified.

Of the river's defenses, he said that the Americans had a fleet of one frigate, two xebecs, one brig, and two floating batteries, and that there were numerous channel obstructions.[43] Certainly that little American fleet could offer no substantial opposition to Howe's great warships, and there were no forts and no "channel obstructions" even as far down as Chester. Hamond's advice was bad on all those points, too.

That the decision was unfortunate in fact is equally certain. From the 31st of July, when the fleet left the Delaware capes, to the 14th of August, when it sighted Cape Charles, it fought adverse winds and endured calms. It took eleven more days to reach its landing at the Head of Elk—thirty-two days out from Sandy Hook—having sailed three hundred and fifty miles from Henlopen to land only fifteen miles from New Castle, which it might have reached in less than ninety miles from Henlopen. In all that long voyage men and horses suffered greatly from the rough sea, the heat, the shortage of fresh provisions, fresh water, and forage. Many of the horses, dead or dying, were thrown overboard; those that survived were "mere carrion."

As against Head of Elk, New Castle would have been a much more favorable landing place. From Head of Elk the army had to march fifty miles to Philadelphia. From New Castle, the distance is but thirty-three miles. Better still would have been Chester, only fifteen miles from Philadelphia with no such defensible river to cross as the Brandywine, until they came to the Schuylkill at Philadelphia itself.

As Trevelyan points out, after all that delay and all those hardships, the army at Head of Elk was ten miles farther from Philadelphia than it had been the previous December at Amboy. And it had the same army, but much larger in numbers, to contend with in August as in the previous December.

Altogether the decision to go to the Chesapeake was undeniably unfortunate. But that the fault lay with Howe, because he took advice that sounded convincing from a sea captain who should have been well informed, is probably not true. Howe chose the Chesapeake route in the beginning with a rather vague idea that he could more or less cut off communication between the middle and southern colonies and at the same time possibly force Washington to fight at a disadvantage somewhere east of the Susquehanna River. No doubt he also calculated that he could later open up the Delaware as a safe supply route.

Whatever Howe may have planned, Washington's suspense and anxiety were now at an end. Orders went to Sullivan to join the army "with all convenient speed"; to General Nash to hasten with his brigade and Proctor's artillery to Chester; and for all the troops to march "to-morrow morning very early towards Philadelphia and onwards." [44] News of the American victory at Bennington was given out and greatly cheered the soldiers.

CHAPTER 30

Head of Elk

Washington started southward from his camp on the Neshaminy on August 23, at four o'clock in the morning. That evening he camped near Germantown, and the next morning he formed his troops for the march through Philadelphia in such manner as to impress the strong Tory element there, including the Quakers. His preparations and directions for this display of strength were "pathetically minute." [1]

The army was to march in one column "First—A Sub. and twelve light horse, 200 Yards in their rear a complete troop," then a space of 100 yards, and "a company of pioneers with their axes in &c in proper order." At another hundred yards distance, a regiment of Muhlenberg's brigade, followed by field artillery, then Weedon's, Woodford's, and Scott's brigades, Lincoln's and Stirling's divisions, the artillery, and the cavalry, winding up with a troop of horse 150 yards in the rear of all the rest. The men were to be "made to appear as decent as possible" and to "carry their arms well"; any man who dared "to quit his ranks" was to receive thirty-nine lashes at the next halting place. The drums and fifes were to play "a tune for the quick step . . . but with such moderation that the men may step to it with ease; and without dancing along." To give them some appearance of uniformity in default of uniform dress, they were to wear sprigs of green leaves in their hats. [2]

So, with Washington riding at the head, the Marquis de Lafayette at his side and his mounted staff following, the long column of 16,000 men marched down Front Street and up Chestnut to the awe of the disaffected and the delight of the patriots. John Adams watched the procession. "They

334

marched twelve deep," he wrote to his wife, "and yet took up above two hours in passing by." They were "extremely well armed, pretty well clothed and tolerably disciplined," yet had not "quite the air of soldiers. They don't step exactly in time. They don't hold up their heads quite erect, nor turn out their toes exactly as they ought. They don't all of them cock their hats, and such as do, don't all wear them the same way." [3] Another observer, a military gentleman, Alexander Graydon, who was inclined to be critical, noted that "though indifferently dressed, [they] held well burnished arms and carried them like soldiers, and looked, in short, as if they might have faced an equal number with a reasonable prospect of success." [4]

They marched to Darby that day, and moved on to Naaman's Creek on the next, under orders to "encamp in the first good ground beyond it." The horsemen, however, were to keep on to Wilmington before encamping. Washington himself with his staff also kept on, entered Wilmington, and set up his headquarters in a house on Quaker Hill. Here he learned that the enemy had begun to land that morning "about Six Miles below the Head of Elk opposite to Cecil Court House." He set about gathering in all available troops, called on Armstrong to send on "every Man of the Militia under your command" at Chester and Marcus Hook "that is properly armed, as quick as possible," to march them, indeed, that very night. He called on Baylor to bring "Such Men as you have ready," on Greene's division and Stephen's, also on Sullivan's; but Sullivan was not to press his men "too hard in their march," as they "must no doubt have been greatly harassed" in a futile expedition against Staten Island he had undertaken while at Hanover.[5] Washington had already detached General Smallwood and Colonel Mordecai Gist from their commands in Sullivan's division and sent them to Maryland to take over the militia of that state, called out to the number of 2,000 in accordance with a resolution of the Congress.[6]

On the following morning Washington, accompanied by Greene, Lafayette, his aides, and a strong troop of horse, rode southward on a scouting expedition. From the summits of Iron Hill and Gray's Hill they scanned the country below. Although Gray's Hill was within two miles of the enemy's camp and they could see their tents, they could not form a satisfactory estimate of their numbers. After spending the rest of the day in surveying the surrounding country, they were overtaken by a severe storm. Having taken refuge in a farmhouse Washington showed no inclination to go out into the tempestuous night. His companions urged upon him the danger of capture, perhaps citing the fate of Charles Lee in similar circumstances, but he chose to remain until daybreak. The owner of the house was a Tory; he might have sent word to the British camp of the archrebel's presence and so led to a coup disastrous to the Americans, if Washington's escort had not surrounded the house and guarded against that danger. Washington himself afterwards acknowledged his imprudence at this time.[7]

It was on a Monday morning, August 25, "a distressingly hot, close morning," that the van of the British fleet dropped anchor in the Elk River opposite Cecil County Courthouse and the debarkation began. Two regiments of British light infantry, two of British grenadiers, and the Hessian and Anspach jägers in flat-bottomed boats were the first ashore on the courthouse side and the first to come in contact with the Americans—four companies of militia stationed there, who "fled without firing a shot." The light infantry at once advanced to a post about four miles towards the Head of Elk. The rest of the army landed that day, all except the light dragoons, who came ashore with their horses on the morrow. The troops were ordered to hut themselves with fence rails and cornstalks, which could have afforded little protection from the "heavy storm of Rain, Lightning and Thunder" that broke upon them that night.[8]

Orders were given by Howe to march at three o'clock in the morning, but were countermanded because of another heavy storm that lasted all night and part of the third day. In spite of the rain and the hanging of two soldiers and the severe whipping of five others as a punishment for plundering, the troops indulged in extensive looting of houses and farms. The inhabitants were not to be seen "having deserted their houses and drove off their stock." Not all of it, however, for "the soldiers slaughtered a great deal of cattle clandestinely." [9]

There were other reasons for the British delay than the storm; the troops were not yet sufficiently refreshed from their long confinement in the transports, and the "miserably emaciated" horses—those that had survived—were in no shape to be used. On the 28th, however, the weather being "extremely fine" and the roads somewhat dried, the van of the army marched to Elkton, a town of "about 40 well built brick and stone houses," from which "one thousand men under a Colonel Patterson and the Philadelphia Light Horse" fled to Gray's Hill. They fled again when the British advance guard came up. In Elkton the invaders found "Storehouses full, consisting of molasses, Indian Corn, Tobacco, Pitch, Tar and some Cordage and Flour," which the American troops had failed to remove.[10]

The British army was in two grand divisions. It was the one commanded by Cornwallis that had moved on Elkton; the other, under the Hessian general, Wilhelm von Knyphausen, had crossed the Elk and encamped at Cecil Courthouse. This arrangement was designed to permit an advance up

THE
PHILADELPHIA
CAMPAIGN

-------- *British Advance*

+++++++ *American Retreat*

Schuylkill R.

Valley
Forge

#Whitemarsh

Germantown

HOWE

Philadelphia

Chadd's Ford

Brandywine Creek

Chester

CORNWALLIS

Fort Mercer

Delaware River

Wilmington

Chesapeake Bay

Head
of Elk

both sides of the Elk, the two bodies to join at a point seven or eight miles south of the Christina River.[11]

They lay in those camps for the next five days. There were unimportant skirmishes with small bodies of Americans. On the 29th "the Chasseurs [jägers] encountered a body of the rebel infantry" and on the 30th "the Welch fusileers fired a few Platoons into a body of rebel cavalry of about 200." But there was organized foraging on a grand scale. On the 31st Knyphausen with a large detachment made a foray "thro Bohemiah Mannor" and rounded up "261 head of horned Cattle and 568 sheep and 100 horses." [12] Another party got 350 sheep, 55 horned cattle, and 204 horses or mules. There was great need of horses, over 300 having died on the voyage or been rendered unfit for duty.[13] There was also a great hunger for fresh meat. "Some Hessians . . . demolished a whole flock of sheep which the owners were voluntarily driving to us." [14] On September 1 Wemyss's corps of rangers attacked an American outpost and took the commanding officer, "his lieutenant and 3 privates—killed 2 and wounded 1—the rest consisting of 100 fled—this was effected without any loss on our side." [15]

While Washington was encamped on the Neshaminy and was still in doubt as to Howe's purposes he had sent Colonel Daniel Morgan and his corps of riflemen to join Putnam at Peekskill and to go thence to reenforce the Northern American army facing Burgoyne. To provide a corps of light infantry in place of Morgan's men, a hundred good soldiers were selected from each of six brigades and placed under command of Brigadier General William Maxwell of New Jersey. With two captains, six subalterns, and the appropriate number of noncommissioned officers, they numbered about 720 in all. They were to be "constantly near the Enemy and to give them every possible annoyance." Maxwell posted his corps in the neighborhood of Cooch's Bridge on the upper waters of the Christina River. On September 2 Washington warned him of the intention of the enemy to march next day and begged him "to be prepared to give them as much trouble as you possibly can." [16]

The British army had, indeed, begun its movement that very day. Knyphausen, commanding one of the two grand divisions, marched from his camp at Cecil Courthouse and encamped that night at the Buck Tavern, otherwise called Carson's, just below the present Delaware and Chesapeake Canal.[17] At daybreak on the following morning Cornwallis with the other column, Howe accompanying him, took "the lower road to Christeen by way of Rikin's [Aiken's] Tavern in order to avoid Iron Hill." They had expected to join Knyphausen at the tavern (now the town of Glasgow) "but did not perceive them." They pushed on through a "close" country, "the woods within shot of the road frequently in front and flank and in projecting points towards the Road." [18] Evidently it was the kind of country disliked by the regulars, who preferred combat in the open in regular battle formation.

Along this unpleasant road at about nine o'clock in the morning the van of the column, Hessian and Anspach jägers, under Lieutenant Colonel Ludwig von Wurmb, followed by British light infantry with two small fieldpieces, was making its way—cautiously, no doubt—when it met a sudden fire from Maxwell's men posted among the trees by the roadside. Wurmb formed his men, and there was a hot fire from both sides. The fieldpieces were brought into play; a detachment of Hessians shifted to the woods and attacked Maxwell's right flank; Wurmb charged with the bayonet. The Americans retreated up the road, took a new position under cover, and renewed their fire. Again they were driven back to another stand. The British light infantry entered the engagement; the Americans again retreated, keeping up a running fight. At one point "a body of Riflemen formed a kind of Ambuscade" and gave the British "several close, well-directed Fires." An attempt at getting into the American rear failed because "an unpassable swamp" intervened, "which prevented this spirited, little affair becoming so decisive" as it might have been. But Maxwell's men were now pretty well disorganized. Their retreat became a flight. They were pursued for some distance, but finally made their way to the main army on the White Clay Creek.[19] The casualties were perhaps thirty killed on the American side and about as many killed or wounded on the other.[20]

Knyphausen's column came up to Aiken's Tavern just after this affair, and both columns encamped between Iron Hill and the tavern. They had moved slowly, having to drive a herd of cattle with them and to keep pace with two detachments flanking Knyphausen's column sent out to comb the country for livestock. These brought in "500 Head of Horned Cattle, 1000 Sheep and 100 horses, but not above forty of these Horses were fit for draught." [21]

The next four days the British spent in reconnoitering the country, bringing up provisions from the fleet, and sending back the sick and wounded. Grant, with two brigades left at Elkton, came up on the 6th. All communication with the fleet was then abandoned, and it withdrew down the bay.

On August 28 Greene's and Stephen's divisions, mostly Virginia Continentals, under Brigadiers Muhlenberg, Weedon, Woodford, and Scott, with

Sheldon's horse, were advanced to the White Clay Creek.[22] But an American council of war decided to concentrate the army on the northerly side of the Red Clay Creek near Newport, on the main road to Philadelphia. To that position it was moved on September 6,[23] Maxwell's corps remaining in advance on the White Clay. Washington, having learned that the British had disencumbered themselves of their baggage and tents, indicating "a speedy and rapid movement," ordered his troops similarly relieved. Both officers and men were to retain only their greatcoats, if they had any, and their blankets. Everything else was to be sent north of the Brandywine.[24] Thus stripped for action they awaited the enemy's next move.

It began on the 8th two hours before daybreak when the whole British army advanced by the light of "a remarkable borealis." Washington had expected a movement against his position on the Red Clay and seems to have been desirous of bringing on an engagement there. Howe fostered this delusion by sending a detachment to a point opposite the American position [25] but marched his main army northward. This was construed by Washington as a flanking movement to carry the enemy around his right to his rear and so on to Philadelphia. To prevent this he withdrew his force at two o'clock in the morning of the 9th to Chad's Ford on the Brandywine and on the more northerly Philadelphia road. But Howe was proceeding in good faith to Kennett Square in Pennsylvania. Early in the morning of the 10th the whole British force was collected at that place on the road which Washington held at Chad's Ford.[26]

Brandywine

The Brandywine proper begins at the confluence of two streams, known as the east and west branches, which meet at a place called the Forks about six miles northwest of Chad's Ford. It flows in a valley, now very narrow and again somewhat wider, where meadows border the stream, between hills rising to a height of 200 feet or more three-quarters of a mile from the river edge. In places these hills slope gradually down to the river; in others they drop steeply, 200 feet in a half-mile or even in a quarter-mile. The uplands back of the hilltops were largely cultivated, but the slopes were densely forested. Between the Forks and the Ford the river receives little streams coming down small valleys.

Along the valley ran roads to find shallow crossings. These several roads and fords played an important part in the battle and must be distinguished by name.

The Nottingham Road (now the Baltimore Pike), running eastwards through Kennett Square on its way to Chester and Philadelphia, came to the river at Chad's Ford. Just before it reached the stream, it forked and crossed by two fords, one about 300 feet north of the present bridge, the other about 150 feet below the bridge. At this point the shallow but swift stream was about 150 feet wide.[1]

About a mile upstream, another road crossed at Brinton's Ford. Two miles above that, the Street Road ran to Painter's Ford. A branch of that road used Wistar's Ford, an equal distance farther up. Again there was a two-mile interval to Buffington's Ford, where a road running roughly parallel to the stream on its east side swung to the west to cross the East Branch a little above the Forks. A mile above that Jefferis Ford crossed the East Branch and, opposite it, Trimble's Ford crossed the West Branch. The width of the tongue of land between them was about two miles. About a mile and half below Chad's was Pyle's Ford.[2]

The American army arrived at Chad's Ford in the morning of September 9 and established its center there, Wayne's brigade of Pennsylvania Continentals being posted on the brow of an eminence near Chad's house a little above the Ford, and Weedon's and Muhlenberg's brigades of Virginia Continentals directly east of the Ford. Proctor's Pennsylvania artillery was with Wayne. Greene commanded the center. Light earthworks and a redoubt were erected for Wayne and Proctor as a front line, the Virginians being in reserve.

The right wing was composed of three divisions of two brigades each posted along the east bank of the river, covering Brinton's Ford and running up some distance below Painter's. Stirling held the extreme right; Stephen was next below him; and Sullivan was nearest the center, he being in general command of the wing.

The left wing was posted at Pyle's Ford, where the heights on the east side were steep and rugged and there was little apprehension of a crossing. Its defense was entrusted to a thousand Pennsylvania militia under Armstrong.

To guard the forces above the right wing, Sullivan detached the Delaware Regiment to Painter's Ford, one battalion from Hazen's "Canadian Regiment" to Wistar's and another to Buffington's.[3]

Maxwell's light infantry took a position west of the river on high ground on both sides of the main road. Picket guards were thrown across the upper part of the stream. Colonel Theodorick Bland with the 1st Dragoons, one of Washington's few cavalry corps, which were all commanded by Count Pulaski, was stationed about opposite Painter's Ford. Major James Spear, with a body of Pennsylvania militia, picketed the ground above the Forks near Buffington's Ford. Washington established his headquarters in a house about a mile back of Chad's Ford, and Lafayette set up his a half mile farther back.[4]

September 11, 1777, began with a foggy morning, but ripened to a noon of blazing sunshine and sweltering heat. Before daybreak Maxwell's corps, with three small detachments from the Virginia line, was sent back along the main road towards Kennett Square to feel out the enemy and delay their approach. Maxwell marched as far as Kennett meetinghouse, about three miles from the Ford, and sent a party of mounted vedettes farther forward.

They stopped at Welch's Tavern a mile or so beyond, tied their horses to a rail, and gathered at the bar, waiting for something to turn up. About nine, o'clock, one of them espied through a window uniformed men coming down the road and not more than a few rods away. It was Major Patrick Ferguson's Riflemen and the Queen's Rangers, Tory troops, the point of the vanguard of Knyphausen's columns. The vedettes fired a single harmless volley and fled through the back door, leaving their horses.[5]

The Riflemen and Rangers were followed by two British brigades under General Grant, Stirn's brigade of three Hessian regiments, half of the 16th Dragoons, and two brigades of heavy artillery. Behind them the rest of the artillery, the provision train, the baggage and cattle dragged along, followed by the rear guard of one battalion of the 71st Regiment of Highlanders, two others marching beside the train as flankers. There were about 5,000 men in all in this column.[6] They had left Kennett early in the morning and advanced so far without the Americans even knowing that they were on the march.

After dispersing the little band at Welch's Tavern, the column kept on to the Meetinghouse. There it met with a surprise. A sudden burst of fire from Maxwell's corps posted behind the graveyard wall checked the van and threw it into confusion. It rallied and returned the fire. Maxwell fell back slowly down the road, taking cover from time to time and keeping up his fire until he reached the Ford. There he was reinforced. He turned back to high ground above the road and again engaged the enemy. The vanguard was not strong enough to dislodge him, and the British deployed. Ferguson's Riflemen supported by a hundred Hessians were thrown out to the right. But in the meantime Porterfield's and Waggoner's Virginians had crossed the stream to Maxwell's aid. They drove the Riflemen and Hessians back to the shelter of a stone house. The British 49th Regiment, with two heavy guns and two three-pounders, taking a position on an elevation behind Ferguson, backed him up and opened fire on the Americans. The Queen's Rangers, led by Captain Wemyss, and the 23rd Regiment filed off to their left and flanked Maxwell, whose men "had been shouting Hurrah! and firing briskly." The 28th Regiment also went into action, and Maxwell was driven out of the woods and back across the upper branch of the Ford. The Rangers then joined the Riflemen and Hessians at the stone house, swept down on Porterfield and Waggoner and drove them back by the lower ford to the other side.[7]

While all this was going on Porter's artillery was cannonading from its position on the east side; but "though the balls and grapeshot were well aimed and fell right among us," says Captain Baurmeister of the Hessian

Regiment von Mirbach, "the cannonade had but little effect—partly because the battery was placed too low." [8]

Under the covering fire of their guns, mounted hastily in strategic places and on the high ground west of the river, the 28th, 23rd, 55th, and 40th British regiments and the Leib and Mirbach Hessian regiments formed a line on the heights overlooking the Ford; the Combined Battalion and Donop's Hessians held the road; and the 4th, 5th, 27th, and 49th British regiments took position on the slope from the heights down to the lowland along the river. The light troops and outposts were pushed forward close to the stream. The lines were straightened in formal fashion, and one battalion of the 71st, with the 16th (or Queen's Own) Regiment of light dragoons, was posted on the right flank, while two other battalions of the 71st guarded the baggage in the rear. These dispositions were completed by half-past ten. Then things quieted down; the musketry ceased; the artillery fired only occasionally, and was similarly answered by the Americans. [9]

One might suppose that this cessation of activity on the part of the enemy, this desultory firing with no attempt to advance, would have brought to Washington and his officers memories of an exactly similar situation at Long Island a year before, when Grant held Stirling by the same tactics while the main British army was about its business elsewhere; but the same bland confidence that Howe intended a frontal attack seems to have persisted in the minds of all. Washington and Greene spent most of the morning at headquarters, a mile back from the Ford. [10] At the front the hours passed in watchful waiting for the enemy to launch their attack.

This confidence was first disturbed after nine o'clock when word came to headquarters from Colonel Hazen that a body of the enemy had been seen marching up the Great Valley Road, parallel with the river on its western side and leading to Trimble's Ford on the west branch a mile above the Forks. Washington sent a note to Colonel Bland, who was on the west side of the stream opposite Painter's Ford, earnestly entreating "a continuance of your vigilant attention to the movements of the enemy" and calling for reports of such movements, of their numbers "and of the course they are pursuing." "In a particular manner," he wrote, "I wish you to gain satisfactory information of a body confidently reported to have gone up to a ford seven or eight miles above this. You will send an intelligent, sensible officer immediately with a party to find out the truth." [11] Bland reported that he had seen a body of the enemy advancing on "the valley road" towards Trimble's Ford. [12]

On top of this came a dispatch forwarded by Sullivan, from Lieutenant

THE BATTLE OF BRANDYWINE
Sept. 11, 1777
at 3.30 o'clock P.M.

KEY
■ AMERICAN TROOPS
■ BRITISH TROOPS
□ BEFORE THE BATTLE

To Chester

To Chester

N

Dilworth

Darlington Corners

Birmingham Meeting House

Widow S. Davis
Widow J. Davis

STEPHEN

SULLIVAN
STIRLING

HOWE
CORNWALLIS

WAYNE

GREENE

CHADS FORD

ARMSTRONG

PILES FORD

KNYPHAUSEN

Osborne Hill

Sconneltown

BRINTON'S FORD

DELAWARE

BRANDYWINE

HAZEN

BLAND

PAINTER'S FORD

STIRLING

STEPHEN

SULLIVAN

WISTAR'S FORD

BUFFINGTON'S FORD

HAZEN

JEFFRIES' FORD

EAST BRANCH

movement

WEST BRANCH

TRIMBLE'S FORD

Flanking

British

Route

of

Kennett Meeting House

Welch's Tavern

2 mi.

1

½

0

Colonel James Ross of the 8th Pennsylvania, who had apparently been scouting in the rear of the enemy. It was dated "Great Valley Road, Eleven o'clock A.M." and told of "a large body of the enemy, from every account five thousand with sixteen or eighteen field-pieces," which had "just now" marched along that road. Ross said that he was on their rear with 70 men, that Captain Simpson with 20 men had lain in ambush and fired on them, and that General Howe was with them.[13]

Nothing could have been clearer, more circumstantial, more convincing than that, and to Washington nothing could have been more amazing. He and his generals thought it was "a terrible blunder" on Howe's part to divide his force in the face of his enemy; they were puzzled by "the very magnitude of the blunder," [14] but not in the least hesitant about taking advantage of it. Sullivan, Stirling, and Stephen should cross the river at once and attack the rear of Howe's column. Washington himself with Greene's division would fall on Knyphausen in front, while Armstrong's militia should cross below and strike Knyphausen's right. It was a most daring and a most dangerous plan, "magnificent, if it succeeded, insane, if it failed." It was a proposal to do just what they thought a "terrible error" in the British tactics, divide their force. But the orders were given, and troop movements were soon under way. Greene's advance guard was actually across the river when another dispatch arrived.[15]

Sullivan wrote that he had seen Major James Spear, who had been on the Great Valley Road and the Kennett Road from Martin's Tavern at the Forks to Welch's Tavern and had heard nothing of the enemy "and is confident they are not in that quarter; so that Colonel Hazen's information must be wrong." [16]

That note, incredible as it may seem in the face of Bland's and Ross's specific statements, was accepted as reliable. There *was* no division of the British army, no force threatened the American right wing; all the enemy were in front. The orders to cross were canceled; Greene's advance was withdrawn. The army settled down to await a frontal attack. Time passed. Knyphausen made no move. Only his intermittent cannonading declared him an enemy. And still no one remembered Long Island. Two o'clock came; no change. Then there was a sudden commotion.

A sweating horseman, a hatless, coatless, barelegged farmer, dashed into Sullivan's lines. He must see the General—Washington—at once. Sullivan couldn't allow that; the General mustn't be disturbed by such an uncouth person. But the man *must* see him; he was Thomas Cheyney, a good patriot, one of the few about there, and he had important news. What was it? He told it. He had been watching the movement of the armies, and had got up that morning early to do a bit of scouting, dressed in a hurry without bothering to put on his stockings. He rode to the top of a hill, and there the British were, not a hundred yards away. He turned his horse and fled. They followed, fired on him, but his horse was fast. He got away, and here he was. They were across the creek and coming down this way. Wasn't that important? It seemed so. He was taken to the commander in chief.

Cheyney told his tale again. Washington was incredulous. He had had that Spear report to the contrary. Probably he thought the man was a Tory, trying to mislead him; they were all Tories, these Chester Countians. The staff smiled and shook their heads. Cheyney turned on them. "I'd have you know I have this day's work as much at heart as e'er a blood of ye!" Then to Washington: "If Anthony Wayne or Perse Frazer was here, they'd know whether I'm to be believed." He dropped on one knee, drew in the dust with his finger a map, the roads, the fords, marked the place where he had seen the enemy. Still Washington disbelieved. "You're mistaken, General," cried the exasperated man. "My life for it you're mistaken. By hell! it's so. Put me under guard till you can find out it's so!" [17]

What to do? It might be so. Those conflicting reports? Then came the thunderclap that cleared the air, banished all doubt, a courier with a dispatch enclosing another:

Dear General;
Col⁰ Bland has this moment Sent me word, that the enemy are in the Rear of my Right about two miles Coming Down, there is, he says about two Brigades of them. 2 of Clock PM he also says he Saw a Dust Rise back in the Country for above an hour.

I am &c   JOHN SULLIVAN

The enclosure read:

A quarter past One o'clock.
Sir:
I have discovered a party of the enemy on the heights, just on the right of the two Widow Davis's who live close together on the road called the Fork Road, about half a mile to the right of the [Birmingham] Meeting House. There is a higher hill in front.

THEODORICK BLAND [18]

There at last was the indubitable truth. At four o'clock that morning, a full hour before Knyphausen had started, Howe and Cornwallis had left Kennett Square with the Hessian jägers, the 1st and 2nd battalions of grenadiers, the Guards, two squadrons of light dragoons, one of dismounted dragoons, and the 3rd and 4th brigades of infantry. They had kept to the

main road until within a mile and a half of Welch's Tavern. There they
had taken a left fork and so had come into the Great Valley Road, which
led to Trimble's Ford on the west branch, crossed the two-mile interval to
Jefferis's Ford on the east branch, crossed that, turned south past Sconneltown, and come out into the open at Osborne's Hill, a mile and a half east
of the Brandywine, in the rear of the American line and within two miles of
their extreme outposts on the right.[19]

Hazen picked up his two battalions at Buffington's Ford—the outpost
nearest the enemy crossing at Jefferis's Ford—and at Wistar's, and the
Delaware Regiment at Painter's Ford, and started south towards the main
army.

The van of the British column had halted at Sconneltown, just beyond
Jefferis's Ford, to let the rear catch up and then had gone on to Osborne's
Hill. It was now half after two. The soldiers had been afoot since four in
the morning, marching fifteen miles on a swelteringly hot day. Food and
rest were needed; they took both sprawling on the grass, and the countryside turned out to see them.

Joseph Townsend, a Quaker youth of twenty who saw them first when
they came out of the woods, wrote afterward: "In a few minutes the fields
were literally covered with them. . . . Their arms and bayonets being
raised shone as bright as silver, there being a clear sky and the day exceedingly warm." He saw Cornwallis: "He was on horseback, appeared tall and
sat very erect. His rich scarlet clothing loaded with gold lace, epaulets &c.,
occasioned him to make a brilliant and martial appearance." Most of the
officers were "rather short, portly men, well dressed and of genteel appearance, and did not look as if they had ever been exposed to any hardship,
their skins being as white and delicate as is customary for females who were
brought up in large cities and towns." The Hessians interested him: "Many
of them wore their beards on their upper lips, which was a novelty in that
part of the country." General Howe was "mounted on a large English horse,
much reduced in flesh. . . . The general was a large, portly man, of coarse
features. He appeared to have lost his teeth, as his mouth had fallen in." [20]

Meanwhile, the Americans had been astir. Washington ordered the whole
right wing—Sullivan's, Stephen's, and Stirling's divisions, all under Sullivan
—to shift from their position along the river and oppose the approaching
enemy. Wayne's brigade of Pennsylvanians, Maxwell's light infantry, and
Proctor's artillery were to continue to hold the Chad's Ford position against
Knyphausen. Greene's division of two brigades—Weedon's and Muhlenberg's Virginians—was to remain in reserve to help Sullivan or Wayne as
needed. Washington remained with Greene.[21]

There was some delay in starting the march of one of Sullivan's own two brigades. Stirling's and Stephen's divisions and even one brigade of Sullivan's, under General Prudhomme de Borré, got away before Sullivan did with the other. When he moved with that other he met Hazen with the "Canadians" and the Delawares on the march down to the main army. Hazen told him that "the Enemy were Close upon his Heels." While these two were talking together, the soldiers still moving on, "the Enemy headed us [Sullivan's men] in the Road about forty Rods from our Advance Guard." This was probably one of two small detachments thrown out to the right of Cornwallis's column to cross at Wistar's Ford or Painter's. To avoid them, Sullivan swung his column to the right and got away without a fight. Soon after that he discovered Stirling's and Stephen's divisions already "Drawn up on an Eminence, both in the Rear & to the Right of the place" where his men were and facing the British force on the opposite hill to the north of them, that is to say on Osborne's Hill. Sullivan had simply overshot his mark by coming up too near the enemy and undershot it by not being near enough to his colleagues. He was separated from them by an undefended space of half a mile.[22]

Sullivan now ordered Hazen's regiment and the Delawares to pass a slight depression between two hills, "File off to the Right & face to Cover the Artillery," thus separating them from his own brigade. With the rest of his troops he fell back and formed them "on an advantageous Height, in a Line with the other divisions," but with that half-mile still open between him and the others. He then rode off to consult with Stirling and Stephen. They told him that the enemy, now advancing down the slope of Osborne's Hill, were aiming to outflank the American position on the right, wherefore his troops should be brought up to join theirs, and "that the whole Should incline further to the Right," to prevent being outflanked. Sullivan went back to his men to bring them up.

The American line was formed on the northern slope of a round hill a hundred rods southeast of Birmingham Meetinghouse and facing Osborne's, with an interval of a mile and a half between their summits. Northeasterly through this valley ran the Street Road from Painter's Ford. The line curved around the face of the hill. De Borré's brigade held the right; Stephen's division was next; and then came Stirling's, these two composing the center. Sullivan was to hold the left. The artillery, four pieces, was "judiciously placed," and several outposts were thrown out in front of the line. "This position," says Captain John Montresor, chief engineer of the British forces in America, "was remarkably strong, having a large body advanced, small bodies still further advanced and their rear covered by a wood wherein their main body was posted, with a natural glacis for ¾ of a mile." The flanks also rested on woods.[23] Cornwallis, watching from the top of Osborne's Hill the arrangement of the Americans, remarked, "The damn rebels form well." [24]

By about half-past three the British army had formed in three divisions on Osborne's Hill. On the right were the Guards; the British grenadiers composed the center; the left was made up of the light infantry and the Hessian and Anspach jägers. The support, from right to left, was the Hessian grenadiers and the 4th Brigade. The 3rd Brigade, under Major General Charles Grey, was held in reserve.[25] A little after four o'clock the advance began in style. The uniforms were gay in their various colors, the muskets and bayonets "shining like silver," the bands playing "The British Grenadiers." So the exactly formed columns marched down the slope of Osborne's Hill and across the vale. There was no irregularity, no hurry. They came on with the arrogant assurance that marked the disciplined troops of that period of formal, dress-parade warfare.

The advance guard almost reached the Street Road. No shot had yet been fired. Then suddenly the jägers, on the left of their line, met a blaze of musketry from an American outpost in an orchard beside the road. They "stepped up" the roadside bank to the orchard fence, rested their muskets on it, and fired a volley. The artillery on both sides opened up, and the battle was on.[26]

The British light infantry and the Hessian and Anspach jägers were the first up the hill. They fell upon the American right, De Borré's brigade of three Maryland regiments, and met little resistance. The brigade broke and fled into the woods behind, exposing Stephen's right flank. The British Guards and grenadiers fired no shot, but advanced up the hill, their bayonets their only weapons.[27] Sullivan's men were on the way to close the gap that separated them from Stirling's left. In a column that straggled irregularly because of excitement and lack of training, they marched right across the front of the oncoming Guards and grenadiers, both British and Hessian. They had hardly formed a ragged line facing the enemy when the bayonets were upon them. Few of the American troops in that war could ever stand against the cold steel of the bayonet. These were unready for battle; Sullivan, their leader, had left them, gone to the center to direct the artillery. They fell back in confusion. Sullivan sent his aides to rally them and re-form them in the rear. He went back himself, "but all in vain," he says; "no Sooner did I form one party than that which I had before formed would Run off." He went back to the artillery, "left them to be Rallied if possible by their own officers and my aid De Camp." It was not possible. The entire left of the American line was swept away. Shorn of its wings, the center of Stirling's and Stephen's divisions with Hazen's "Canadians" and the Delawares now held the field alone.[28]

Miles in the rear with Greene and the reserve, Washington had been awaiting news of the grand attack, either at the Ford or at Birmingham. It came at half past four, in "a sudden burst of cannon from the northwestward," so loud that it was heard in Philadelphia. The grand attack was on up there at Birmingham. It was a signal for Knyphausen; he got ready to cross the Ford. The battle was to be fought on two fronts.

There must have been some hesitation in Washington's mind about the use of the reserve, whether at the Ford or at Birmingham, for about five o'clock his aide, Lieutenant Colonel Robert H. Harrison, was writing to the Congress about the attack at the north: "The Action has been very violent ever since. . . . It still continues." Knyphausen was preparing his attack. "A very severe cannonade has begun here too and I suppose we shall have a very hot evening." [29]

But at last the decision was made. The Ford must be left to Wayne, Maxwell, and Proctor. Greene with the reserve must go north to back up the troops on the hill and hold that road to Philadelphia. Washington himself wanted to be at that scene of action, but he did not know the way to it. Among the country people standing about was an old man, Joseph Brown. Washington asked him to lead the way by the shortest road. Brown demurred; Washington insisted. One of his aides dismounted, threatened the old man with his sword, hoisted him into the saddle. Across country they went; three miles as the crow flies, Washington continually crying, "Push along, old man! Push along!" His staff trailed behind. They came out on the road leading to Philadelphia, half a mile west of Dilworth.[30] Greene was coming along, with Weedon's brigade in advance, Muhlenberg's following. They arrived with speed. Weedon covered nearly four miles in less than 45 minutes.[31]

On the hill there had been hot fighting. Sullivan, Stirling, Stephen, and Thomas Conway the French-Irishman, one of Stirling's aides, encouraged the 3,000 Americans still there to repel the repeated attacks of twice their number of the best soldiers of Britain and Germany. They were seconded by Lafayette, who, ardent for battle, had galloped to the fight ahead of Washington and Greene. On the left Hazen's men and the Delawares with Dayton and Ogden of Stirling's division stood firm, although that flank had been exposed by the flight of Sullivan's brigade.

Cornwallis was edging his troops towards the Americans' extreme right and towards Dilworth, which was the key of the situation because it was on the Philadelphia road. The Americans had to shift and shift again in order to avoid being outflanked.[32]

For an hour and forty minutes, under fire of Cornwallis's artillery, four 12-pounders, the Americans on the hill disputed the way of the enemy. For fifty minutes of that time they fought "almost Muzzle to Muzzle, in such a manner that General Conway, who has Seen much Service, says he never Saw So Close & Severe a fire." A captain of the Delawares describes it: "Cannon balls flew thick and many and small arms roared like the rolling of a drum." Five times the Americans were driven back, and five times they surged forward to their old position. But the odds against them were too great. Stephen's division on the right, upon which the fire had been especially heavy, retreated. Stirling and the rest could no longer resist. The order to withdraw was given.

They were pursued by the British and Hessians, except the British Guards and the British and Hessian Grenadiers, who when they followed Sullivan's retreating brigade had "got entangled in a very thick woods" and "were no further engaged" until near the end of the battle.[33]

The American retreat was developing into a stampede when the fugitives met the head of Greene's column. He opened his ranks, let them through to rally and re-form in his rear, closed again, and stood against the pursuers, turning his artillery upon them. But the pressure was too great. Retreating slowly and in good order, keeping up their fire, Greene's troops at last made another stand in the road from Dilworth about a mile from the Meetinghouse, in a place called Sandy Hollow, "a narrow defile flanked on both sides by woods and commanding the road."[34] Weedon's men were posted in the defile, Muhlenberg's on the side of the road.

The enemy came on and there was hot fighting. The musket fire on the Americans was heavy, and there were repeated bayonet charges. The fighting was so close that some of the Anspach jägers recognized Muhlenberg, who had served in the ranks in Germany in his youth, and greeted him with his old nickname, "Hier kommt Teufel Piet!" (Here comes Devil Pete!) Weedon's brigade, especially the 10th Virginia under Colonel Stephens and Colonel Walter Stewart's Pennsylvania state regiment, which had never before been in action, bore the brunt of the attack. For forty-five minutes, until the sun went down, they held the pass.[35]

At last, again overborne, Weedon's force retired, but in good order. They retreated to the rear of Muhlenberg's brigade, and Greene drew off his whole division. The tired British and Hessians made no attempt to follow.[36]

Meanwhile, there had been desperate fighting at the Ford. The sound of Cornwallis's gunfire was the signal to Knyphausen that his function of "amusing" the Americans, while the flanking march was made, was now fully performed. He first opened fire with all his guns, six 12-pounders, four howitzers, and the light artillery, bombarding the positions held by Wayne, Maxwell's light infantry, and Proctor's batteries, while he formed his troops. After severely blasting the American defenses he launched his attack. A battalion of the 71st Highlanders led the van; the Riflemen and Queen's Rangers with the British 4th Regiment and Knyphausen in person followed. Then came the rest, Stirn's Hessians last. In the face of the American artillery and musketry they advanced to the lower of the two fords, waded in, and gained the opposite bank. Forming again, they attacked "furiously." The American left gave back and lost the battery near the river, three field-pieces and a howitzer.

The British Guards and the grenadiers of Cornwallis's column, who had got lost in the forest while pursuing Sullivan's brigade, now "came blundering through the woods—accidentally, but most opportunely—upon the uncovered flank of the American centre," and the whole American line fell back.

The British followed, "gained one height after another as the enemy withdrew." There was a check, says Baurmeister, when the Americans or some of them made a stand "behind some houses and ditches" and for a time "withstood one more rather severe attack. Finally we saw the entire enemy line and four guns, which fired frequently, drawn up on another height in front of a dense forest, their right wing resting on the Chester road." [37] "Darkness coming on before Lieutenant General Knyphausen's corps could reach the heights, there was no further action." [38]

The battle was over except for one last flare-up. Two battalions of British grenadiers were ordered to occupy a cluster of houses beyond Dilworth. "They marched carelessly, the officers with sheathed swords. At fifty paces from the first houses, they were surprised by a deadly fire from Maxwell's corps, which lay in ambush to cover the American retreat. The British officers sent for help, but were nearly routed before General Agnew could bring relief. The Americans then withdrew, and darkness ended the contest." [39]

It had been a fierce and many-sided fight, but the losses on both sides were less than might have been supposed. Howe reported 90 killed, 480 wounded, and 6 missing. The American casualties were never definitely ascertained. Howe estimated them at 300 killed, 600 wounded, and "near 400" made prisoners.[40] But his figures are properly subject to some discount, because of his customary exaggeration of enemy losses and because the numbers of wounded and captured to a considerable extent duplicated each other. The Americans had to leave many of their wounded on the field, so that they were taken by the enemy; but not many unwounded men were taken prisoner. Among the American wounded was Lafayette, who received a bullet in his leg, but was able to escape capture. One howitzer and ten fieldpieces were lost by the Americans, among them two brass guns captured at Trenton.[41]

The whole American army was in retreat towards Chester. Except for a few regiments and companies that withdrew in good order, its units were completely disorganized. There was no coherence of divisions, of brigades, of regiments, or even of companies. Thousands of beaten men, already dispersed before the final retreat began and now uncontrolled by any sort of military discipline, thronged the road in utter confusion. Darkness added to their bewilderment. All any man knew was that he must hurry forward with the crowd before him and the crowd behind. Twelve miles of this chaos brought them to a bridge across Chester Creek and found at last someone in command of the situation. Lafayette, with an improvised bandage about his wounded leg, had set a guard there to stop the passage of the mob. Washington and Greene (with his division unbroken) soon arrived and aided in restoring order. They all encamped "behind Chester."

And yet, though they had been as badly beaten as any army could be without being entirely destroyed, there had been no panic; there was no suggestion of despair. The American Captain Anderson wrote: "I saw not a despairing look, nor did I hear a despairing word. We had our solacing words already for each other—'Come, boys, we shall do better another time'—sounded throughout our little army." That this was true of the army in general was proven by their ready reorganization the next day and by the spirit in which the campaign was so soon and so courageously resumed.

C H A P T E R   3 2

Philadelphia

Howe's army encamped on the battlefield. But first he sent the 71st Regiment, Fraser's Highlanders, to take possession of Wilmington. They also took possession of John McKinly, President and commander in chief of Delaware, and confined him on the frigate *Solebay,* lying in the river off the town.[1]

At midnight of September 11–12 Washington sent a dispatch to the Congress, informing it of the result of the battle and adding, "Notwithstanding the misfortune of the day, I am happy to find the troops in good spirits." [2] Congress was, as John Adams expressed it, "yet in Philadelphia, that mass of cowardice and Toryism." John Hancock received the dispatch at four o'clock in the morning. The delegates to the Congress were routed out of their beds to meet at six and hear the news. At ten they reassembled, called on Putnam at Peekskill to send down 1,500 Continentals at once, on Philemon Dickinson in New Jersey and on Smallwood and Gist in Maryland to send their militia, and on the Pennsylvania militia generally to join Washington. Aid from Virginia was also solicited. To the soldiers of the army, thirty hogsheads of rum were donated "in compliment . . . for their gallant behaviour," each man to receive "one gill per day, while it lasts." [3]

Washington marched from Chester in the morning of the 12th to the Falls of the Schuylkill and encamped there on the edge of Germantown. Notwithstanding his defeat at the Brandywine, his army was still between Howe and Philadelphia, and his maneuvers were directed toward holding that advantage. He guessed that the British would try to turn his right flank, cut off a retreat to the west, and force him into the pocket beween the

355

Schuylkill and the Delaware. To prevent that, he broke camp on the morning of the 14th and marched west to the neighborhood of the Warren Tavern and the White Horse Tavern, thus, "with a firm intent of giving the Enemy Battle," [4] interposing his army between the British and Swede's Ford across the Schuylkill, at which point he thought they would try to cross.

On the 16th Howe marched from Chad's Ford in two columns. Cornwallis led one towards the White Horse Tavern, Knyphausen the other towards the Boot Tavern.[5] Early in the morning Washington had news of their approach. Howe heard that the Americans were "advancing upon the Lancaster Road and were within five miles of Goshen Meeting House." He decided to "push forward the two Columns and attack them." [6] Thus, with one intention, the two armies approached each other.

Washington sent Count Casimir Pulaski, newly appointed "commander of the horse" ranking as a brigadier, with the cavalry and 300 infantry to retard the advance of the enemy; but the foot soldiers "shamefully fled at the first fire" and delayed the enemy not at all.[7]

The first real encounter came when Wayne and Maxwell, who had been detached forward to observe the enemy's movements on the Chester-Dilworth road, met Knyphausen's column near the Boot Tavern. Colonel von Donop, with a part of the Hessian jägers, was reconnoitering the road ahead of that column when Wayne and Maxwell suddenly came upon him. He "was almost cut off, but joined the vanguard again with all possible speed, after skilfully executing some manoeuvres to his left." [8] The Hessian jägers and grenadiers immediately formed and advanced in line against Wayne and Maxwell, who had taken a position "on high ground covered with a cornfield and orchards." The jägers delighted in displaying the results of their training and experience in irregular fighting; "ducking behind fences around the fields and woods, [they] had an opportunity to demonstrate to the enemy their superior marksmanship and their skill with the amusettes." There was a considerable exchange of fire before the Americans "retired to a dense forest," leaving behind a number of killed and wounded.[9]

Howe was ahead in the choice of ground; he seized an eminence near the White Horse. Washington started to form his troops in an inferior position, with "a valley of soft wet ground, impassable for artillery" behind his center and left, but was persuaded to withdraw to "high ground on the other side of the valley." [10] A real battle seemed to be in the making when Nature took a hand. The extreme heat of the day at the Brandywine had been dispelled on the 13th by "a hard North West wind," which continued to blow colder and colder. On the 15th it shifted to the northeast and increased in violence; the sky was heavily overcast with clouds. Now the gathering storm broke.

Major Baurmeister had never seen the like of that cloudburst. "I wish I could give you a description of the downpour," he wrote to the "Right Honourable Lord, Gracious and Mighty Colonel von Jungkenn" in Hesse-Kassel. "It came down so hard that in a few minutes we were drenched and sank in mud up to our calves." [11]

That deluge fell upon the two armies in line of battle and about to engage. It soaked their clothes, wet their muskets inside and out, and drenched their ammunition, ruining 400,000 of the Americans' cartridges—"a most terrible stroke to us," said Henry Knox. No flint would flash, no charge ignite.[12] So there the two armies stood, face to face and unable to fire a shot. The British might still have used a favorite weapon that worked wet or dry—the bayonet; but a wind of great force was driving the rain directly into their faces, and the low ground between the armies was a treacherous quagmire. There was simply no fighting to be done by either side.

"At first," Washington wrote to the Congress, "I expected that the loss [of ammunition] was by no means so considerable and intended [only] to file off with the Troops a few Miles to replace it and clean their arms"; but, finding it completely ruined with no other supply at hand, he had to march "as far as Reading Furnace" to refit.[13] So, under the heavy rain driven by the howling northeast wind, the blanketless men, "nearly a thousand of them actually barefooted," slogged along through the mud the rest of that day and much of the night eleven miles to Yellow Springs, and "there Stay'd all night on the Brow of a hill without tents." [14]

At Yellow Springs, Washington discovered the true state of his ammunition supply and realized that he must go at once to a more secure position at Reading (Warwick) Furnace to await a new supply from the magazines. So on the Americans went—it was still raining—nine miles and camped, again without tents. Then up at three in the morning and on, twelve miles more, to the Furnace. Presumably the new ammunition was supplied there, for the third day they were on the march back to Yellow Springs, twelve miles, crossed the Schuylkill at Parker's Ford, through rapid water breast-deep [15]—they were all night at it—marched seven miles towards Swede's Ford and then ten miles to Richardson's Ford, twenty-nine miles in all,[16] and certainly a great feat of endurance in their distressed physical condition. But they were again east of the Schuylkill and between Howe and Philadelphia, their camp being along Perkiomen Creek.

The movement of Howe's army from Goshen was a mere saunter, in comparison. It lay on the field the day after that aborted battle and "suffered much from the weather." On the 18th Knyphausen marched three miles to White Horse, where he joined Cornwallis in going eight miles to camp at Tredyffrin. At Valley Forge they found a store of the rebels' supplies: "3800 Barrels of Flour, Soap and Candles, 25 Barrels of Horse Shoes, several thousand tomahawks and Kettles and Intrenching Tools and 20 Hogsheads of Resin." On the 19th, when the rebels were making that grueling twenty-nine-mile march, the British found halting "very necessary for the men and particularly for our horses," though there was a small shift of Cornwallis's column to another camp at the Bull's Head and Mouth Tavern and a foraging party took 150 horses at New Town Square. On the 20th a post was established at Valley Forge.[17]

Before Washington's army crossed at Parker's Ford on the 19th Anthony Wayne's division, 1,500 men and four fieldpieces, was detached with orders to lie in the neighborhood of the Warren Tavern so as to be in a position to fall on the enemy's rear guard and baggage train. With every effort at secrecy he took post in a wood on a hill about a mile north of that tavern and two miles southwest of Paoli Tavern,[18] confident that his movement and his place of lodgment were unknown to the enemy; but there were too many Tories about, and some of them disclosed his secret to the British.[19] Major General Grey, with the 40th, 42nd, 44th, and 55th regiments of foot, the 2nd battalion of light infantry, and a handful of the 16th Dragoons, was sent to surprise him.[20]

Grey ordered his men to march with unloaded muskets, those that could not draw their loads to remove their flints, and set out at ten o'clock in the evening of the 20th. He advanced by the road leading to the White Horse, picking up every inhabitant as he went along to prevent an alarm. Near the Warren Tavern, he came upon Wayne's outsentries, who fired and ran off; but his van fell upon the pickets with the bayonet and killed most of them.

The reports of the sentries' muskets alarmed the camp. Wayne ordered his men formed for action, himself taking post with the artillery on the right. Unfortunately his men were drawn up in the light of their campfires and thus were clearly in view of the enemy. Grey ordered a charge with the bayonet. The Americans met it with musketry but were overwhelmed by the impetuosity of their opponents and swept into a confused retreat, followed by the stabbing bayonets. Wayne managed to draw off his guns and, at some distance in the rear, re-formed such part of his fleeing men as could be induced to stand. Satisfied with the execution effected, Grey called off his troops and returned to the British camp, taking with him seventy-one prisoners, of whom forty, badly wounded, were left at houses along the road. He also took eight or ten loaded four-horse wagons. The next day a British detachment returned to the deserted field and gathered up and destroyed a thousand muskets abandoned by the fleeing Americans.

General Smallwood and Colonel Gist, with a force of Maryland militia, had been ordered to reenforce Wayne's post; but they were still on the road at the time of the attack. Within a half-mile of the scene they met a part of Grey's troops returning from the fray. At the sight of the enemy the militia fled in a panic.

It is impossible to make a certain estimate of the Americans' loss. The British claimed 300 killed or wounded and 70 to 80 taken prisoner; but their figures are probably exaggerations. The British loss was one officer and one or two privates killed, and four or five wounded.[21]

Wayne's defeat relieved Howe of all fear of attack from the rear; he was now able to move as he would. On the morning of September 21 he set out from Tredyffrin in a northerly direction, marched to Valley Forge, and encamped along the Schuylkill from the Forge to French Creek.[22] To Washington, who had been expecting a southward march towards one of the lower fords, this was a "perplexing manoeuvre." But this northward movement meant that they might turn his right, and it was in the direction of Reading Furnace. That spelled danger for his stores. He believed they had both objects in view.[23] "To frustrate those intentions," he decided to move north, too.

He first ordered Sullivan's division to "a Line between us and the Schuylkill, leaving a small Pickett at each Fording Place as a party of Observation." Then, "two hours before day" on the 22nd, he got his men afoot and marched them ten miles up the Reading road on his side of the Schuylkill. After rest and refreshment they went five miles farther and encamped near Pott's Grove [24] (now Pottstown). They were now well ahead of Howe towards Reading Furnace and well past danger of being outflanked on the right; also they were just where Howe wanted them to be.

He had intended neither the supposed flanking movement, nor yet the capture of the stores at the Furnace. What he did intend was disclosed by what he immediately did. He countermarched swiftly southward in the night to Fatland Ford and Gordon's Ford, blasted away a slimly held American militia post at Fatland with "a few cannon-shot," and sent the Guards, a battalion of light infantry and six guns, with twenty-five dragoons, across the river to hold the opposite end of the ford. Von Donop, with sixty jägers, twenty horse, and a hundred grenadiers cleared the way at Gordon's without difficulty and crossed there. That night "at the rising of the moon" the whole British army began crossing at Fatland. By eight the next morning all except Grant's brigade of British infantry, covering the baggage, artillery, and provision train, were on the east side of the river. The others soon followed, and the road to Philadelphia was clear before them.[25] Thus again Howe, with the greatest of ease, had outwitted the American commander in chief.

Washington got the news, doubtless from some of the expelled militia, while the enemy was still in the act of crossing. Here was an opportunity for an attack while they were in such a disabling condition. But the alertness of the Americans to the danger of being outflanked, and the effort they had made to prevent it, was now their undoing. They were nearly twenty miles from Fatland. With "Troops harrassed as ours had been with constant marching since the Battle of Brandywine" it was "in vain to think" of covering that distance in time to seize the opportunity. As strong a reason "against being able to make a forced March is the want of Shoes," so Washington wrote to the Congress that day. A council of war agreed with him that the best course was to stay where they were until rested and reenforced.[26]

Unopposed and unmolested, the British army continued its march "till three o'clock in the afternoon when it arrived at Norriton" and there encamped, but seventeen miles from Philadelphia, just half the distance of the American army from it.[27]

Washington lay at Pott's Grove for four days, resting his men and awaiting reenforcements. He had called on Putnam in the north for 2,500 Continentals, including McDougall's brigade; on Smallwood and Gist to bring their Maryland militia; on Wayne for his division; on Gates at Saratoga to send back Morgan's riflemen; on Philemon Dickinson for his New Jersey militia.[28] The men he already had were in a sad condition. They had marched 140 miles in the last eleven days. "While in almost continual motion, wading deep rivers and encountering every vicissitude of the season, they were without tents, nearly without shoes or winter clothes and often without food." [29] In the heat of the day and the heat of the battle at the Brandywine thousands of them had shed their blanket rolls and left them on the field. Washington had written to the Congress on the 15th begging for blankets. The Congress had "disguised its impotence" by again making him a "dictator" for a period of sixty days, with special authority "to take wherever he may be, all such provisions and articles as may be necessary for the comfortable subsistence of the army under his command, paying or giving certificates for the same." [30]

Washington accepted the job. He sent Alexander Hamilton to Philadelphia to "procure from the inhabitants, contributions of blankets, and Clothing and materials . . . with as much delicacy and discretion as the nature of the business demands." [31] But "the canny Quakers and the sly Tories 'hid their goods the moment the thing took wind' and the Whigs had already 'parted with all they could spare.' " [32] Washington tried the country districts, ordered Colonel Clement Biddle "to impress all the Blankets, Shoes, Stockings and other Articles of Cloathing . . . that can be spared by the Inhabitants of Bucks, Philadelphia and Northampton," [33] to be paid for with cash or promises, and gave similar orders for Lancaster, with small results from any place.

On the 26th the Americans marched from Pott's Grove to encamp at Pennybacker's Mill (now Schwenksville) on the Perkiomen; and on the same day Cornwallis, with two British and two Hessian grenadier battalions, two squadrons of the 16th Dragoons, and ten guns in his train, took possession of Philadelphia, "amidst the acclamation of some thousands of the inhabitants, mostly women and children," [34] while the major part of the army encamped at Germantown. The Congress had fled to Lancaster eight days before.

C H A P T E R 3 3

Germantown

Reenforcements came to Washington—McDougall, with 900 Continentals from Peekskill, Smallwood with 1,000 Maryland militia, Forman with 600 militiamen from New Jersey, Maxwell's corps of 650 light infantry, and Wayne's division. It is hard to say how large the army then was. Washington informed the Congress on September 28 that he had 8,000 Continentals and 3,000 militia at Pennybacker's Mill,[1] yet Henry Knox declared that the army was "more numerous after the battle of Brandywine than before." [2] There was some thought of an attack on the British camp at Germantown at this time, but a council of war, voting ten to five against that, decided that it would be well to move closer, "within about 12 Miles of the Enemy," and await events.[3] On the 29th the army marched five miles to the Skippack Road, and on October 2, three miles down that road to encamp sixteen miles from Germantown.[4]

There the question of an attack was again considered. Three thousand of Howe's men had been sent down to escort supplies from Elkton, which, because of the obstructions and the forts in the Delaware River, he could not bring up by water. Cornwallis had two British and two Hessian grenadier battalions with him in Philadelphia, and he had just sent one of the British battalions and two regiments of foot across to New Jersey to capture the fort at Billingsport. Probably not more than 9,000 men were left with Howe at Germantown. A council of war decided that conditions were favorable.[5]

Germantown was a village consisting of a string of houses, each in its enclosure of rail fence, stretching for two miles along the Skippack Road, which ran northwest from Philadelphia to Reading. At its center this main street was crossed at a right angle by a road called School House Lane west of the street, Mill Street on the east. At this crossing stood the market house. The village was approachable directly from the northwest by this Skippack (Reading) Road running over Chestnut Hill and Mount Airy and so to its center. There was another avenue of approach from the north by the Limekiln Road, east of the Skippack, which swung into the east end of Mill Street. East of that road the Old York Road came down from the northeast to a crossroad running past Luken's Mill and so into Mill Street. Far to the west, on the other side of the gorge of Wissahickon Creek, the Manatawny or Ridge Road met the west end of School House Lane where the creek empties into the Schuylkill.

The British camp was a little south of the Lane, extending east and west parallel to it and across the main street from the Schuylkill on the left (west) to a point beyond the Old York Road on the right. It had no definite center. Generals Grant and Matthew lay on the right of the main street, with the Guards, six British battalions, and two squadrons of dragoons. Generals Knyphausen, Stirn, Grey, and Agnew lay on the left, with seven British and three Hessian battalions. The mounted and dismounted jägers were on the far left, beside the Schuylkill and below the mouth of the Wissahickon. On the far right and somewhat in advance were the 1st Battalion of British light infantry and the Queen's Rangers. At Mount Airy, on the Skippack Road and about two miles north of the Lane, was an outpost held by Colonel Musgrave's 40th Regiment and the 2nd Light Infantry.[6] Howe's headquarters was in the Logan House at a short distance in the rear of the camp.

The plan of attack called for a division of the American army into four columns, each one operating on one of the four approaching roads above mentioned. Sullivan was to command the first column, composed of his division and Wayne's, flanked by Conway's brigade. Stirling, with Nash's and Maxwell's men, was to follow this column as a reserve. It was to enter the town by the Skippack Road and strike the British left.

Greene was to command the second column, his own and Stephen's divisions, flanked by McDougall's brigade. He was to approach by the Limekiln Road, take care of the light infantry and Rangers advanced on the extreme British right, enter the town by the Mill Street, and attack Grant and Matthews. As this part of the British force was esteemed the strongest, Greene had the strongest column, about two-thirds of the American army.

The third column, Maryland and New Jersey militia under Smallwood and Forman, was to march by the Old York Road, a mile or more east of Greene's route, and fall on the rear of the British right.

Far to the other side, farther still from the main battle, coming down the Manatawny or Ridge Road, Armstrong and his Pennsylvania militia were to cross the mouth of the Wissahickon at Vandeering's Mill and strike the rear of the British left.

All four columns were to arrive "within two miles of the enemy's pickets on their respective routs by two oClock and there halt till four in the morning." They were to make simultaneous attacks "precisely at five oClock with charged bayonets without firing." [7] In that order for a bayonet charge no consideration was given to the fact that the terrain was crossed by many stout rail fences which would repeatedly interrupt the proposed charge and make it practically impossible.

It will be seen that that was a plan for a great pincers movement, in which, while the British main force was to be smashed by Greene and Sullivan, Armstrong and Smallwood were to close in on its right and left wings and crumple the whole line in upon itself. It was to be somewhat like the attack on Trenton, including the element of surprise, but on a grander scale. As the attack was to be made before dawn, each soldier was to have a piece of white paper fixed in his hat to identify him to his comrades.

It was "one of the most carefully elaborated designs" that Washington ever evolved,[8] and it had classical authority. Hannibal had so planned and won the battle of Cannae, nearly two thousand years before. Scipio Africanus had, in like manner, gained a victory at Ilipa in Spain, annihilating 74,000 Carthaginians with 48,000 Romans. There was, however, in both those cases, a difference. Hannibal and Scipio had put their weakest forces in the center, their strongest in the crushing pincer jaws. Washington reversed this arrangement; his two jaws were made up entirely of militia, whom he had so often found to be unreliable.

There were, too, faults inherent in the character of the troops involved and in the terrain, the like of which the Carthaginians and Romans had not confronted. Green troops—even the Continentals were largely new recruits —led by relatively amateur officers, were to march in perfect concert sixteen miles in four columns over roads separated by six or seven miles of rough, broken country, with no means of communication among their several bodies, and arrive at the scene of action at the same moment of time, ready to fall with vigor and determination upon a not much smaller, compact army of professional soldiers led by competent officers. The failure of any one of the four elements of the attack meant the failure of the whole scheme. It was typically the kind of plan easily worked out at headquarters and looking perfect on paper, yet practically impossible of execution in the field. Yet it very nearly did succeed, though not as planned.

The march from Metuchen Hill on the Skippack Road began at seven in the evening of October 3, the several columns taking their respective roads. According to the plan, Sullivan's column, with Conway in advance, followed by Sullivan, Wayne, Stirling, Maxwell, and Nash, in that order, Washington marching with it, was to reach the British outpost at Mount Airy before dawn. But it was a long march on rough roads and a hard march for men so ill equipped, especially so ill shod, and so worn down by their incessant movements to and fro for months past. The column had to stop twice to rest and to bring up its rear. The sun was coming up when it reached Chestnut Hill.

At Mount Airy, Conway's advance brigade came upon the pickets of the first British outpost. Captain Allen McLane of Delaware, with his company of light horse, charged upon this picket, killed two men and, at the loss of one of his own, drove it back, but not before it had fired two fieldpieces as a signal to its support and an alarm for the whole British army.

To the rescue of the retreating pickets came the 2nd Light Infantry, and the real fighting began. They attacked Conway so viciously that he had to throw forward his entire brigade to meet them. The rest of the outpost, Colonel Musgrave and his 40th Regiment, came up. Conway was stopped in his tracks. Sullivan deployed his men in line of battle along a lane to the west of the main road. Musgrave, a courageous man and a fine officer, refused to give way. He led his men against Sullivan's too narrow front. Sullivan called up Wayne's division from the rear to his left and part of Conway's brigade to his right. Then with the bayonet he drove against Musgrave's line. Wayne's division, smarting under the recollection of the Paoli "massacre," fought bitterly. The British fell back, charged, and charged again. The Americans answered in kind and "took Ample Vengeance for that Night's work," striking down "many of the poor wretches who were Crying for Mercy, in spite of their officers' exertions to restrain them." At last a British bugle sounded a retreat.

But the British fell back doggedly, making a stand at every fence, wall, and ditch, firing and falling back again. Sullivan's troops followed, tearing down fences as they came to keep their line. For a full mile they drove Musgrave's regiment and the light infantry before them.

Howe had hurried to the front. He cried shame on the retreating men "Form! Form! I never saw you retreat before! It's only a scouting party.

To the delight of the men he chid, a burst of grape from the American guns rattled in the leaves of a chestnut tree under which he sat on his horse, and showed it was no mere scouting party.

It had been misty at sunrise. The mist thickened into fog; the fog grew more dense, so dense that Musgrave was able to slip aside and throw six weak companies of his regiment into a great, square stone house on the east of the main road, the house of Chief Justice Benjamin Chew. He closed the thick shutters, barricaded the doors, and posted his 120 men at the windows of the second story, whence they delivered a continuous and deadly fire upon Sullivan's and Wayne's men passing on either side of the house.

Now, what to do? The reserve was held up, except Nash's North Carolinians, who pushed on after Sullivan and fought most bravely throughout the battle. Washington and his generals consulted. Some of them were for leaving a regiment to immobilize the garrison in the house and going on. But Henry Knox, deeply imbued with the lessons he had learned while studying the military classics in his bookshop, said "No!" While penetrating an enemy's country, you must not leave an occupied castle in your rear. Washington, always respectful of Knox's larger store of military science, as he was of Greene's military genius, agreed. The "castle" must be summoned in due form. An officer, sent with a flag to demand surrender, was fired upon and killed. So much for classical warfare!

Knox turned his artillery upon the stronghold. His six-pounders blew in the front door and smashed windows, but the balls rebounded from the thick, stone walls; and a barricade of furniture in the hallway, backed by bayonets, denied entry. Burn it, then. The Americans tried, but a would-be incendiary was shot down. In spite of that, two spirited young fellows, Colonel John Laurens of South Carolina and the Chevalier de Mauduit du Plessis from France, volunteered to try again. Laurens got straw from the stables. Mauduit forced the shutters of a window, mounted the sill. A single British officer, pistol in hand, demanded to know what the Frenchman was doing there. "I'm only taking a walk." "Surrender, sir!" Before Mauduit could answer, a British soldier came into the room, took a shot at him, but only hit the British officer. He escaped unharmed. Laurens got a bullet in his shoulder. The artillery resumed its futile bombardment, in which Maxwell's musketry joined uselessly.

But where was Greene, with two-thirds of the American army, all this time? He had four miles longer to march and had also been led astray by his guide, so that his column was an hour late when it drew near. Without orders from Greene, Stephen on hearing the gunfire swung his division off

CHESTNUT HILL

SKIPPACK ROAD

MOUNT AIRY

SCOTT
STEPHEN
GREENE MUHLENBERG
McDOUGALL

SMALLWOOD
FORMAN
On York Road

NASH
STIRLING MAXWELL
WASHINGTON
WAYNE
CONWAY SULLIVAN
CONWAY
LT. INFANTRY
MUSGRAVE
Chew House

ALLENS LANE

WISSAHICKON CREEK

MANATAWNEY ROAD

Meeting House

Market House

MILL

HOUSE ST.

LIMEKILN LANE

Luken's Mill

LIMEKILN ROAD

QUEEN'S RANGERS

GRANT DONOP

ARMSTRONG

SCHOOL HOUSE LANE

AGNEW GREY STIRN
KNYPHAUSEN

Howe
Headquarters

YORK ROAD

OLD

SCHUYLKILL

Van Deering's Mill

YAGERS

British Camp

N

RIVER

To Philadelphia

0   ½   1   1½ mi.

KEY
◼ AMERICAN TROOPS
◪ BRITISH TROOPS
◻ HESSIAN TROOPS

THE BATTLE OF GERMANTOWN
Oct. 4, 1777
before the halt at the Chew house.

to the right away from the column and made for the Chew House, thus departing from the plan. Woodford's artillery of Stephen's division joined in the bombardment with no more success than Knox had achieved. They fought that impregnable "castle" for a full hour.

Greene with his own division, including Muhlenberg's, Scott's, and Mc-Dougall's brigades but lacking Stephen's, kept on, met the British advance at Luken's Mill, had a hard time there but drove the enemy back, and swung into the planned attack on the British right. But that wing had been so extended that he was in danger of being outflanked. Shielded by the fog and the battle smoke, Greene countermarched to the right, avoided the British wing, bore down on the market house, and attacked the British line there with such impetuosity that it gave way. Muhlenberg led a bayonet charge that drove clear through it and the line of tents in the camp in its rear and took many prisoners. It seemed to Greene's men to be the moment of victory.

Meanwhile, Sullivan and Wayne were driving at the British center, each on his own side of the main street. They were supposed to be acting in concert, but the fog, thickened by smoke, was so dense that they could not see each other; neither knew where the other was; no one could see more than thirty or forty yards. The uproar of the artillery and the musketry, blasting away at the Chew House, convinced Wayne that his comrade in arms, Sullivan, was in trouble back there. He wheeled about, started to the rescue, and met Stephen's division coming down to the main battle. Stephen's men dimly saw an opposing force—the enemy of course. They fired on Wayne; Wayne fired on them. Suddenly, both divisions broke, each fled from the other, panic-stricken. That was the beginning of the end.

Sullivan's division was fighting on, but, though it had started with forty cartridges to each man, its ammunition was running low. General Grey, finding little pressure on his position on the left, wheeled up a brigade and threw it on Sullivan's right flank. At the same time General Grant brought up the 5th and 45th regiments from the British right center and attacked Sullivan's left, which was without support. Thus engaged on their front and on both flanks and already alarmed by the sound of fighting at the Chew House in their rear, Sullivan's troops fell into a panic on the arrival of a light horseman crying that they were surrounded. A part of them broke, and then the rest. Their officers tried in vain to rally them. "With as much precipitation as they had before advanced," they turned and ran.[9]

Greene had no support, right or left. The British and Hessians who had been fighting Sullivan let his men run without pursuit and swung to the center against Greene. He was caught on both sides. Muhlenberg was far off, more than a thousand yards in the rear of the enemy, far behind their camp. But he turned his bayonets back against the encircling British line, charged through it and joined Greene with all of his regiments but one.

Colonel Matthews, with the 9th Virginia, had been conspicuously daring and successful. He had led Greene's advance, crushed the resistance at Luken's Mill as the division swung in from the Limekiln Road, and fought all the way to the market house, driving the enemy before him and taking a hundred prisoners. He tried to draw them off by Luken's Mill, but a breastwork there had been manned again. The British right wing enveloped him. He lost his captives, and he himself, with his 400 men, was taken. That was the regiment missing from Muhlenberg's brigade.

Now Greene, with Muhlenberg, Scott, and McDougall, faced the divisions of Grey, Grant, and Agnew drawn together to oppose him. The Americans were worn out by their long march and the strain of the battle. There was little fight left in them, but they did fight as they withdrew through the village, using fences, walls, and houses in a delaying rear-guard action. Greene drew off his guns. When the wheels of one were shattered, he got it into a wagon, and it went on. Muhlenberg rode in the rear of his retiring men. His tired horse refused a fence. While his men were pulling it down, the exhausted general fell asleep in his saddle. He was awakened by the whistle of a ball past his ear and by the cries of the oncoming enemy.

Washington tried to check the retreat, to rally the fugitives, "exposing himself to the hottest fire." But his efforts could not avail. Entirely out of hand, the whole army swept on in full retreat, the men holding up their empty cartridge boxes to show him why they ran. Greene and Wayne in the rear did their best to hold back the pursuers, even bringing their artillery, all of which they kept, into play more than once. But it was no orderly withdrawal. It was a confused mass, "past the powers of description; sadness and consternation expressed in every countenance," that swarmed up the Skippack Road. Pulaski's small cavalry contingent, hovering in the rear, was attacked by British dragoons, fled, and, in their flight, rode into and through Greene's men, who thought they were British and scattered in every direction. Greene nearly had to abandon his guns, but got together enough men to save them. The celebrated Thomas Paine, who was on Greene's staff, said: "The retreat was extraordinary. Nobody hurried themselves." With good reason, it was all those tired men could do to tramp wearily onward.

Cornwallis led three fresh battalions, brought up from Philadelphia, after them for eight miles, apparently with as little haste. "The enemy kept a civil distance behind," says Paine, "sending every now and then a shot after us and receiving the same from us," then gave over the pursuit. Some of the American officers would have stopped at that distance, but Washington drove them on, not only to their last camping ground, sixteen miles from Germantown, but clear back to their former camp at Pennybacker's Mill, eight miles farther. All of them had marched that sixteen miles, some of them as much as twenty, the night before. They had fought fully two and a half hours and now they were trudging twenty-four miles more. "Here we old soldiers had marched forty miles," wrote Captain Anderson of the Delaware Regiment. "We eat nothing and drank nothing but water on the tour."

But what of Armstrong and his Pennsylvania militia, Smallwood and the militia from Maryland and New Jersey—the jaws of the pincers, the claws of the crab? Nothing had been heard or seen of them. Well, Armstrong did march his men down the Manatawny Road clear to the point where they were to cross the Wissahickon at Vandeering's Mill. There they found the Hessian jägers, the extreme left of the British line, trained their four guns on them, and drove them back from the bridge. The Hessians retired to a hill and replied with musket fire. Instead of crossing the bridge and charging on the Hessians, Armstrong continued his cannonading until nine o'clock, when the Hessians charged across the bridge and drove him from an opposite height. He and his men retreated three miles, pursued by the same Lieutenant Colonel von Wurmb who had fought Maxwell at Cooch's Bridge. This pursuit relaxing, Armstrong came on a casual detachment of the enemy, was overcome, and made a final, complete evasion. He did not even know what had happened in the main battle. When Smallwood's force, the other pincer jaw, arrived at the scene of action, it was too late for it to do anything but join in the retreat.

Yet, in spite of the failure of the pincers to operate, the battle had been nearly won by the Americans. While Sullivan and Wayne and Greene were still in the fight and Muhlenberg was piercing the enemy's line, victory was within their grasp. It is said that at that time the British were actually appointing Chester as the place of rendezvous after the expected defeat. If Stirling and Maxwell, the reserve, had not been held up at the Chew House, or if Stephen had not disobeyed orders and taken his division away from Greene, or if Wayne had not turned back thinking to help Sullivan and so collided with Stephen, or if Sullivan's ammunition had not been all shot away, or if Armstrong and Smallwood had not failed to attack the British left and right with vigor and determination—if any one or two of these miscarriages had not happened, the Americans might have won. For with all the misadventures it was a near thing, a very near thing. But they all did happen. The whole affair was a tragedy of errors.

The British losses, as officially reported, were 4 officers and 66 men killed, 30 officers and 420 men wounded. The Americans were reported by the Board of War to have lost 152 killed, 521 wounded, and upwards of 400 captured. General Nash of the Americans and General Agnew and Colonel Bird of the British were among the slain. The disastrous siege of the Chew House laid 53 Americans dead on its lawn, 4 on its very doorsteps.

A sad incident of the battle was the discovery of General Stephen, a brave and generally competent officer, helplessly intoxicated, lying in a fence corner. It resulted in his being cashiered. Lafayette, who had been appointed a major general without command, got Stephen's division. In Stephen's defense it might be urged that his condition was the result of overstimulation to combat extreme fatigue; for Conway, a magnificently brave soldier, was found asleep in a barn on the retreat, and Pulaski, whose merit is undeniable, was found asleep in a farmhouse. The exhaustion of those mounted officers casts a revealing light on the wonderful stamina of their foot soldiers, who endured far greater hardship and fatigue in that heartbreaking retreat.

It was unquestionably a defeat for the Americans; but, as has happened more than once in warfare, that fact was of small consequence in comparison with its ulterior effects. In its larger aspects it was of "great and enduring service to the American cause." Trevelyan says: "Eminent generals and statesmen of sagacity, in every European court, were profoundly impressed by learning that a new army, raised within the year, and undaunted by a series of recent disasters, had assailed a victorious enemy in its own quarters and had only been repulsed after a sharp and dubious conflict. . . . The French government, in making up its mind on the question whether the Americans would prove to be efficient allies, was influenced almost as much by the battle of Germantown as by the surrender of Burgoyne." [10] It is doubtful, however, that Germantown had so much effect at the French court.

CHAPTER 34

The Forts on the Delaware

"This morning 36 Sail of the Enemies Ships went past this Town up the Bay and this Evening 47 more were seen from the light House Standing in for the Cape." So, on October 5, 1777, William Peery, captain of the "independent company of 100 men on the Continental establishment" on guard at Cape Henlopen,[1] wrote to Caesar Rodney.

It was a part of Admiral Lord Howe's fleet, which now, more than a month out from the Head of Elk, was about to ascend the Delaware without difficulty, as it might have done two months before, except for the dissuasion of Captain Hamond of the *Roebuck*. The admiral himself, with twelve vessels, had preceded this part of his fleet by three or four days.[2]

The ships went on up the bay and the river, past Bombay Hook on the 9th, past New Castle on the 11th, where General Howe's army might have disembarked on, say, the 9th of August instead of at Head of Elk on the 25th and been nearer Philadelphia than it was on that day. On the 12th, the flagship was off Chester; but that was about as far as it dared try to go, for above that point began the obstructions of the channel and the fortifications of which Captain Hamond had warned the Howes. The main fleet was then anchored in the river from Reedy Island up to New Castle.[3] But it was necessary that the river should be opened to shipping if the British were to continue to hold Philadelphia.

While the enemy army lay in that city Washington's army was active in cutting off its supplies from the back country. The British had to be supported and supplied by the ships. The way from Head of Elk to Philadelphia by land was too difficult, too liable to interruption by the Americans. Therefore water communication was vital to the continuance of the occupation of the rebel capital.

Washington understood that. If the river's defenses, he wrote, "can be maintained General Howe's situation will not be the most agreeable; for if his supplies can be stopped by water, it may easily be done by land . . . the acquisition of Philadelphia may, instead of his good fortune, prove his ruin." [4]

The first obstacle was at Billingsport—a double line of chevaux-de-frise that extended from the Jersey shore across the channel to Billings Island. These were cratelike structures made of heavy timbers, loaded with stones and sunk in the water. They were mounted with wooden beams, shod at the upper end with iron points, slanting upwards to within four feet of the surface of the river at low tides and pointing downstream. They were capable of ripping open the bottom of any ship that tried to pass over them. This line was protected by a small redoubt on the Jersey shore. [5]

That redoubt, however, was a slight affair, unfinished and lightly held. On October 2 Howe sent against it the 42nd Regiment and part of the 71st, under Colonel Sterling. When they landed below the fort and attacked it in the rear, the garrison spiked its guns, set fire to the barracks, and fled. Captain Hamond cut through the chevaux and opened a passage through which six ships passed. [6]

The next obstacle was thirty chevaux strung in a triple line from Mud Island, a little below the mouth of the Schuylkill, across the channel to Red Bank on the Jersey side. This line was guarded by a fort at either end. [7] Above this lay the American fleet, comprising the frigate *Montgomery*, a brig, a schooner, two xebecs, thirteen row-galleys, two floating batteries, fourteen fire ships, and several fire rafts. [8] The best vessel, the frigate *Delaware* of thirty-two guns, had run aground September 7 on the Jersey shore, where it had been set on fire by shots from British batteries and had surrendered. [9]

The first attempt against the forts was made on October 21 by Colonel von Donop with three Hessian grenadier battalions, a regiment of foot, four companies of jägers, and some artillery, about 2,000 men in all. [10] It was directed against Fort Mercer at Red Bank. Washington had garrisoned it with a Rhode Island Continental regiment under Colonel Christopher Greene, and had called on New Jersey for militia to strengthen that force and to cover the rear of the works on the outside, but had met with no response. He had therefore added to the garrison another Rhode Island Continental regiment under Colonel Israel Angell, making a total force of about 400 rank and file. The Chevalier de Mauduit du Plessis, a young

French engineer, had also been sent to assist Greene in strengthening the fort. He found that the Americans, "little practised in the art of fortification," had overbuilt the works to an extent "beyond their strength" to hold. He reduced them by drawing a wall across an extension along the river side "which transformed them into a large redoubt nearly of a pentagonal form." [11] The walls were of earth, guarded without by a ditch and an abatis and mounting fourteen guns.

The attacking troops crossed the Delaware at Philadelphia and marched to Haddonfield, where they encamped for the night. They were again afoot at three o'clock in the morning, but were delayed by having to make a detour where a bridge had been taken up, so that they did not arrive at the fort until noon. Their preparations seem to have been very leisurely; it was half-past four when they made their demand for surrender.

A Hessian officer, with flag and drum, then advanced. "The King of England," said he, "orders his rebellious subjects to lay down their arms and they are warned that if they stand the battle, no quarters whatever will be given." That this summons should be made by one of the hated Hessians added insult to the arrogance of his language. "It only served to irritate the garrison and inspire them with more resolution." [12] Greene replied that he accepted the challenge, and that there would be no quarter on either side.

Von Donop opened fire from a battery he had erected in the rear of the fort. The attack was made in two columns, one against the northern wing of the works, the part that had been cut off and abandoned. The other, led by von Donop, was against the redoubt. Like a torrent the first flowed over the breastworks, the men shouting, "Vittoria!" and waving their hats in air, only to find themselves faced by the new wall forming one side of the redoubt. At the same time, with equal confidence, von Donop's column approached the redoubt. Meeting no fire, they penetrated the abatis, crossed the ditch, and reached the berm, the space between the ditch and the parapet. There they were checked; they had no scaling ladders. Then, and not until then, Greene gave the order to fire—to fire at the broad belts of the Hessians as he had before instructed his men. Such an avalanche of grapeshot and bullets fell upon the Hessians of both columns in front and in flank, from the projecting corner of the redoubt, as had been seldom heard and felt. They went down in rows and heaps. "It may well be doubted," says Trevelyan, "whether so few men in so small a space of time had ever delivered a deadlier fire." [13] The officers, von Donop conspicuous among them, tried to rally their men. Their leader was too conspicuous by his dress, as well as by his efforts. He fell, mortally wounded, and his men

OPERATIONS

ON THE

DELAWARE

OCT. & NOV. 1777

PHILADELPHIA

Coopers Ferry

DELAWARE R.

Gloucester R.

Gloucester

Point House

Hollanders Cr.

SCHUYLKILL R.

League Island

American Armed Ships

Hessians Advancing

Battery

Bridge of Boots

Red Bank Island

RED BANK

Little Mud Island

Hospital

Redoubt

Ft. Mercer Attacked Oct. 22

Redoubt Mingo Cr.

BRITISH BATTERIES

Mud Island FORT MIFFLIN

Ferry

Chevaux de Frise

American Galley

Vigilant

Augusta Wrecked

Merlin Wrecked

Kingser's Cr.

Boon's Cr.

Hog Island

Bew Cr.

British Ships

Galley

Billings Island

Billings Port

Redoubt

Passage Opened

faltered. They tried again against the redoubt on its southern side; but there they were under fire from the row-galleys in the river as well as from the fort, and suffered heavy damage. So they finally withdrew to the shelter of the woods, leaving the ground strewn with dead and disabled. After the fight, twenty of them uninjured were found on the berm, clinging to the parapet so as to be out of danger from the Americans' fire, and were captured. The loss of the Hessians in killed, wounded, and captives was 371, including 22 officers. Within the fort there were 14 dead Americans and 23 wounded.[14]

The British had another setback on the same day. The frigates *Augusta, Roebuck, Liverpool,* and *Pearl* and the sloop *Merlin* ran aground. The Americans opened fire on them from the fort, the row-galleys, and the floating batteries. The *Augusta* caught fire and blew up. The *Merlin* could not be got off; she was abandoned and burned.[15]

Fort Mifflin on Mud Island was "unskillfully constructed." One contemporary observer called it "a Burlesque upon the art of Fortification." [16] Strong in front against vessels on the river, it was weak in the rear and on the north, where only ditches and palisades with four wooden blockhouses, each mounting four guns, offered means of defense. The east or river side and the southern side, also facing the river, were high and thick stone walls pierced with loopholes for musketry. Outside this wall at its northern end were two ravelins, or earthworks forming an angle, towards the river.[17] In the middle of the main enclosure was a small redoubt. The garrison had fallen in numbers to 300 men, to which Washington had added 150 Pennsylvania troops; but it would have required nearer a thousand properly to man the works. North of Mud Island and separated from it by a channel less than 500 yards wide, was Province Island, a mud bank mostly under water at high tide, but having two small humps of dry land. Obviously that weak northern side of Mifflin was dangerously exposed to gunfire, if the enemy erected batteries on Province. They did—five, mounting ten heavy guns, 24- to 32-pounders, two howitzers, and three mortars.[18] The current of the river, deflected by the chevaux-de-frise, had swept a new channel between the Mud Island and the mainland. Into this the enemy brought a floating battery carrying twenty-two 24-pounders and stationed it within forty yards of an angle of the fort. On November 10 all these guns opened a fire on the fort that continued all day long and for five days after, the Americans replying as best they could with their few guns. The barracks were heavily battered, many of the palisades were overthrown, and some of the guns dismounted. A ball knocked down a chimney and its bricks fell on Lieutenant Colonel Samuel Smith, injuring him so severely that he had to be evacuated to Red Bank, Major Simeon Thayer of Rhode Island taking over the command. During those five days many of the garrison were killed or disabled.[19]

On the 15th, the British brought their ships into play. The ship of the line *Somerset*, 64 guns, the *Isis*, 50 guns, the *Roebuck*, 44, the *Pearl*, 32. the *Liverpool* frigate, with 32 guns, moved into position within range of the fort, while the *Vigilant*, 16 guns, and a hulk with 3 reenforced the floating battery in the new channel. The garrison had only two guns that had not been already dismounted by the cannonading of the previous days.

The rain of cannon balls from the ships and the shore batteries was terrific. It was estimated that over a thousand shot were fired every twenty minutes.[20] Within an hour the last two guns were overthrown. The ships were so near that marines in their maintops shot down every man that showed himself in the fort. By night the palisades were gone, the blockhouses destroyed, the whole parapet overthrown. Fort Mifflin was only a name. In the darkness Major Thayer and his surviving men crossed the river to Red Bank, after having set fire to whatever was inflammable.[21]

The defense of Fort Mifflin was one of the most gallant and obstinate of any in the war. Two hundred and fifty of the garrison were killed or wounded during the bombardment, their number having been made up by reliefs sent from time to time. They had had no assistance from the American fleet. Its commander, Commodore Hazelwood, having perhaps the safety of his ships too much in mind, had failed to respond to calls for assistance. The loss on the British side was but seven killed and five wounded.[22]

With the fall of Mifflin, Mercer was doomed. Cornwallis took 2,000 men across the river to storm it. Washington had sent General Greene around by Burlington to reenforce it, but Greene found himself so greatly outnumbered by the approaching force that he wisely refrained from attempting to hold it. Colonel Christopher Greene, seeing that his position was hopeless, evacuated it. The idle American fleet was abandoned and burned.[23] The Delaware from the Capes to Philadelphia was now altogether in the hands of the enemy.

For two months after the retreat from Germantown to the campground on the Perkiomen, the Americans engaged in no aggressive military operations. The time was spent in resting the men; combing the countryside for blankets, shoes, and clothing; and drawing troops from the north, from Putnam and Gates,[24] Burgoyne's surrender having permitted such withdrawals. Varnum's Rhode Island brigade, 1,200 men, came, and about a thousand others from Pennsylvania, Maryland, and Virginia. Gates sent down Patterson's and Glover's brigades and Morgan's invaluable rifle corps. By October 29 the army numbered 8,313 Continentals and 2,717 militia rank and file.[25] But the terms of enlistment of many of the Maryland and Virginia troops were about to expire.[26] The army was, as usual, in a state of incipient dissolution. The distress of the men for want of blankets, shoes, and clothing was "amazingly great."

Washington hardened his heart in his search for his army's necessities. "Buy, if you can," was his policy; if not, take, especially from the Tories. He wrote to George Read of Delaware, "You are to take care, that the unfriendly Quakers and others notoriously disaffected to the cause of American Liberty do not escape your Vigilance." "Obtaining these things from the Quakers and disaffected inhabitants is recommended, but at all events get them." [27] The returns from anywhere were never enough. To meet the appalling need for foot covering, Washington offered "a reward of *Ten Dollars*" to the person who should produce the best "substitute for shoes, made of raw hides." [28]

During those two months he was changing his camps restlessly and, except in one instance, with no apparent purpose. On October 8 he marched from the Perkiomen eight miles to a position in Towamencin Township. On the 16th the men "struck tents and marched to the Skippack Road and Encamped on the Same Ground we were at on the 3rd instant." [29] The purpose this time was "to divert the Enemy's attention and force them from the Forts," [30] but the enemy took no notice. On the 20th, the Americans again broke camp and marched to a new one in Whippany Township. On November 2 they made their last shift for the time being; "Cross'd Whissahickon Creek on Skippack Road, march'd to the left & encamped on the brow of an hill on ye North Wales Road White Marsh Township." [31] They remained there nearly six weeks.

The only bright spot in this dull period of marches to and fro was the announcement on October 18, in general orders, of Burgoyne's surrender. Washington expressed his own happiness and adjured his men, "Let every face brighten and every heart expand with grateful Joy and praise to the supreme disposer of all events who has granted us this signal success." A salute by "*Thirteen* pieces of cannon" to be followed by a "*feu-de-joy* with blank cartridges or powder by every brigade and corps of the army" was ordered. To add to the gayety of the celebration, the chaplains were directed to deliver to their several corps or brigades "short discources suited to the joyful occasion." [32]

Other than that, there is little of interest in the records of Washington's army of that period, save such as can be gleaned from the usual, dreary routine of courts-martial for various offenses. Drunkenness was common, desertion frequent. Cowardice was charged against not a few officers; most of them were acquitted, a few cashiered. On conviction of the privates, sentences of reprimand, of lashes on the bare back, of running the gantlet between files of fifty, one hundred, two hundred men, of death for desertion, were imposed. Disobedience usually drew thirty-nine lashes; drunkenness, the same. Sometimes noncommissioned officers were reduced to the ranks.

On October 19 Howe withdrew his troops from Germantown and concentrated his whole force in Philadelphia. He established a chain of fourteen redoubts, connected by a strong stockade and extending from the Upper Ferry on the Schuylkill to the shore of the Delaware above the town.[33]

Washington's army with its recent additions felt its strength. The near-success at Germantown had made it confident of its fighting ability, and Saratoga had aroused a spirit of emulation. On November 25, a council of war discussed the advisability of an attack on Philadelphia. Stirling had a prettily complicated plan for it; [34] Wayne was eager to try it. But eleven of the fifteen officers in attendance, including Greene, Knox, Sullivan, de Kalb, Smallwood, du Portail, and Maxwell, prudently voted against it. An open town, like Germantown, with only a part of the enemy's force to defend it, was one thing; a fortified city, garrisoned by such troops as held Philadelphia, was quite another thing. Disaster would certainly have resulted from such an attempt.

But the mere presence of the American army so near at hand was a continuous menace to the British. Howe decided to try once more to bring on a battle. At midnight of December 4 he set out from Philadelphia, with almost his entire force, to surprise the American camp at Whitemarsh. But that vigilant leader of American partisan troops Captain Allen McLane, who had been constantly scouting between the lines, discovered the enemy's intentions and reported them to Washington. Dispositions to receive the attack were made accordingly, one of them being the dispatch of McLane, with a hundred picked horsemen, to observe the enemy's movements.[35]

The British were advancing in two columns on the Manatawny and Skippack roads. At Three Mile Run on the Skippack Road, McLane, not content with mere observation, attacked the British van with "brilliant cavalry rushes" and with such effect that the front division was obliged "to change its line of march." [36] After that he hovered on the enemy's front and flank, "galling them severely."

At three o'clock in the morning of the 5th the British encamped on Chestnut Hill. When day dawned they "had a fine View of the Rebel Encampment about 3 miles distant on a Ridge of hills lying North of Whitemarsh," the "smoke and huts being plainly in view." [37] Before the British arrived the Americans had "increased their fires lighting many large ones in straight and deep lines, so that it looked as if fifty thousand men were encamped there. By day we could see this was merely a trick to deceive us," [38] says the Hessian Major Baurmeister.

Washington's camp was well defended. "Both wings were fortified by strong abatis; the center approaches were completely covered by several batteries; the whole position was strongly fortified by fifty-two heavy pieces." [39] There was no point in leaving such defenses and attacking the enemy in the open ground. If Howe wanted to bring on a battle, let him assault the American works.

Washington did, however, take the precaution of striking his tents in the early morning and sending his heavy baggage to the rear.[40] At eleven o'clock he sent Brigadier General James Irvine, with 600 Pennsylvania militia, to feel out the enemy. Irvine attacked an advance post held by the 2nd Battalion of British light infantry and supported by British and Hessian grenadiers. There was a heavy fire from both sides, and several men fell in either party. Irvine himself was wounded and captured. His force was driven back, broke, and ran away.[41]

The two armies held their respective positions until one o'clock in the morning of December 7, when the British marched from Chestnut Hill to Edge Hill, within a mile of the American left wing. Their line then was formed in a curve, threatening both the American wings. Washington moved Morgan's riflemen and Webb's Continental regiment, together with Brigadier General James Potter's brigade of Pennsylvania militia, all to the right.[42]

Howe then decided to try again his old Long Island and Brandywine trick. His army moved at ten o'clock that night in one column to Jenkintown. Grey was detached with the Hessian jägers, Simcoe's Tory Queen's Rangers, the light infantry, and the 3rd brigade and sent towards Tyson's Tavern on the Limekiln Road, "where he was to drive in a Post of the Enemy and draw up in view of their camp," says Major André. "While they presumed an attack impending from that quarter, Sir William Howe with the *Elite* and main army was to have made the real attack" on Washington's left.[43]

On the Limekiln Road, Grey's troops were received with a burst of fire from a woody ridge held by Morgan's riflemen and Gist's Maryland militia.

The jägers and Simcoe's Rangers advanced on the right and left, "with great activity and ardor." Outflanked on both wings, the Americans retreated. There were inconsiderable losses on both sides in this engagement, but, as usual, the account of the casualties varies with the side giving it.[44]

On the American left Potter's Pennsylvania militia and Webb's Continentals, with whom were General John Cadwalader and General Joseph Reed as observers, had taken post in a wood in Cheltenham Township. Grey's column attacked them. At the first fire Reed's horse was shot, and he fell to the ground. The British charged; the Americans gave way and fled in confusion. Some of the foe ran to bayonet Reed where he lay, but the ubiquitous McLane was at hand. He and his men charged, drove back the bayoneteers and rescued the injured general.[45] The Americans lost about 50 men.

The main body of the British army now occupied the position which had been held by Potter and Webb. But, says Major André, "the fullest information being procured of the Enemy's position, most people thought an attack upon ground of such difficult access would be a very arduous undertaking; nor was it judged that any decisive advantage could be obtained, as the Enemy had reserved the most easy and obvious retreat. Probably for these reasons the Commander in Chief determined to return to Philadelphia." [46] So both columns started back home.

Grey's column was unlucky in the weight of its artillery and the insufficiency of its horses. A body of American light infantry and some horsemen pursued it, "pressed on the rearmost parties and drove them in." The jägers were drawn up to oppose the attack. The Americans "formed at a fence and delivered a very brisk fire." The Hessians brought their field-pieces into play and finally drove off their assailants. And so ended the abortive Battle of Whitemarsh.[47]

Washington decided to move his camp again, for what purpose does not appear. Early in the morning of December 11 the Americans left Whitemarsh, intending to cross to the west side of the Schuylkill at Matson's Ford by a bridge "consisting of 36 waggons, with a bridge of Rails between each." [48] Sullivan's division and half of another were across when a body of British soldiery appeared on the opposite hill. It developed as the van of a force of 3,500 led by Cornwallis on a foraging expedition. The Americans were in an awkward position, astride the river with a rickety bridge between the two parts. Washington recalled Sullivan and the others with him and broke the bridge. The two forces were then aligned in battle formation face to face with a river between, which neither dared to cross.

But Potter and his militia, who had been operating on the other side, had not been able to get back before the bridge was broken. Cornwallis scattered them and went on with his foraging. Washington returned to Whitemarsh.[49]

It was getting cold now; snow had already fallen, "though not to lay." It was time to plan for the coming winter. Should the Americans continue their campaign, as they had done throughout the last wintry season, or go into winter quarters in the approved military manner? Washington knew the answer, knew that his worn, half-fed, half-frozen, half-naked men simply could not endure the rigors of a winter campaign. When a committee of the Congress, now a bobtail organization of a score or so of mediocre gentlemen, most of whose names have all but passed into oblivion, came to him to confer on the means of carrying on a "Winter's Campaign with vigor and success," he gave them an earful, plenty of reasons why it could not be done. The committee seemed to be convinced.[50]

Winter quarters, then, but where? Some of the officers proposed a chain of posts from Lancaster to Reading; but such a scattering of a none-too-cohesive army would only result in its disintegration. Wilmington in Delaware was proposed. Greene favored it, and so did Joseph Reed, Lafayette, Armstrong, Smallwood, Wayne, and Scott. Cadwalader urged it. If this step were not taken, he said, the enemy might take over that town and so secure "the lower counties on the Eastern Shore" of the Chesapeake. Besides, gondolas based on that "strong post" could annoy the British shipping.[51] Washington favored the idea, looking for mild weather there and facilities for securing supplies by the river. But Pennsylvania had to be heard from. It raised an outcry.

The Pennsylvania Council and Assembly drew up a hot remonstrance and sent it to the Congress at York. It cried aloud against letting the army go into winter quarters anywhere. Pennsylvania and New Jersey would be ravaged. The inhabitants would be obliged to fly or to submit to such terms as the enemy might prescribe—regardless of the fact that the Philadelphians were already submitting and having rather a better time, on the whole, than Washington's hungry and cold troops.

The Congress submissively sent the document to Washington, and the gentlemen from Pennsylvania got an answer that burned their ears. Who had told them whether he intended to hibernate or to fight all winter? Assuredly, he had not. They were reprobating the idea of winter quarters "as if they thought the Men were made of stocks and stones and equally insensible to frost and Snow," as if they thought the army, in such condition as it was in, could hold "a superior one, in all respects well appointed

. . . within the city of Philadelphia and cover from depredation and waste the States of Pennsylvania and New Jersey." It amazed him still more that these very gentlemen, who, knowing the nakedness of his soldiers, had asked him to postpone his plan of commandeering clothes "under strong assurances that an ample supply would be collected in ten days . . . not one Article of which, by the bye, is yet come to hand"—that these same gentlemen should think "a Winter's Campaign and the covering of these States from the Invasion of an Enemy, so easy and practicable a business. I can assure these Gentlemen, that it is a much easier and less distressing thing to draw remonstrances in a comfortable room by a good fireside, than to occupy a cold, bleak hill and sleep under frost and Snow without Cloaths or Blankets; however, although they seem to have little feeling for the naked and distressed Soldiers, I feel superabundantly for them and, from my Soul, I pity those miseries, which it is neither in my power to relieve or prevent." [52] If the gentlemen of the Pennsylvania Council and Assembly did not curl up under that lash, they certainly had rhinoceros skins.

Washington was already at Valley Forge when he wrote to the state Assembly. That place, selected as a compromise between campaigning and wintering in Wilmington, was suggested by Wayne, a Pennsylvanian, "to cover this Country against the Horrid rapine and Devastation of a Wanton Enemy." [53] Like most compromises, it was not a good solution of the problem—"a most unwise one," indeed. Chester County had been so stripped by both armies that it was "doubtful if any location could have been secured where supplies were more difficult to secure than Valley Forge." [54]

De Kalb expressed himself forcibly against that location for the camp, writing: "The idea of wintering in this desert can only have been put into the head of the commanding general by an interested speculator or a disaffected man." [55] Varnum was even more emphatic: "I have from the beginning viewed this situation with horror! It is unparallelled in the history of mankind to establish winter-quarters in a country wasted and without a single magazine." [56] Nevertheless, the choice was made, and on those bleak and barren hills the army settled down for a winter of torture and heroism.

With this, our narrative will turn back six months to the army on Lake Champlain.

CHAPTER 35

Valcour Island

"Our Army at Crown Point is an object of wretchedness to fill a humane mind with horrour; disgraced, defeated, discontented, diseased, naked, undisciplined, eaten up with vermin; no clothes, beds, blankets, no medicines; no victuals, but salt pork and flour." [1] In those words, which for clearness, force, and accuracy could not be bettered, John Adams described the condition of the American troops who, after the disasters at Quebec and Trois Rivières, retreated from Canada in June, 1776.

Three thousand of them, afflicted with smallpox, dysentery, malarial fevers, and all sorts of camp diseases, were in hospital; that is to say, they were lying in tents and huts with no proper care or treatment. Surgeons were few, medicines almost entirely lacking. For food they had almost rancid salt pork and flour, nothing else.[2] "I can truly say," wrote Colonel Trumbull, "that I did not look into a tent that did not contain a dead or dying man." [3] Five thousand were supposed to be fit for duty, but they seemed mere "walking apparitions." Five thousand men had been lost in the whole Canadian venture.[4]

Schuyler at Albany was in command. Sullivan, his second, was with the troops. But on June 17 the Congress, having news of the disaster at Trois Rivières and of the retreat, had resolved that "an experienced general be immediately sent into Canada" and directed Washington to order Major General Horatio Gates "to take command of the forces in that province." [5]

Washington sent Gates his orders, with the comment, "The Command is important." John Adams wrote him, "We have ordered you to the Post of Honour and made you Dictator in Canada for Six Months or at least until the first of October." [6] To Gates this naturally meant that he was to take over the chief command from Schuyler. But Schuyler thought that only Sullivan was displaced, and that he himself still held the dominant position, pointing out, with some logic, that, while the order gave Gates chief command of the troops in Canada, there were, in fact, no longer any troops whatever in Canada. On July 8 the Congress gave Schuyler support by declaring that its intention was to give Gates "command of the troops whilst in Canada," with no purpose of giving him "a superior command to General Schuyler, whilst the troops should be on this side Canada." It also recommended to both generals that they "carry on the military operations with harmony." [7] So Gates had to accept the inferior position, which, to give him due credit, he did with good grace.

Gates arrived at Crown Point along with Schuyler on July 5. A council of war was held, in which Schuyler, Gates, Sullivan, Arnold, and the Prussian general Baron de Woedtke took part. They unanimously agreed that Crown Point was not tenable, that they should retire to Ticonderoga, sending all the sick to Fort George, and that "a naval armament of gondolas, row-galleys, armed batteaus &c" should be provided. [8]

Some of the field officers were not content with this intention to retreat further. Twenty-one of them signed a remonstrance and delivered it to Schuyler. There was discontent also in higher quarters. Washington was inclined to the view of the malcontents. He wrote to Schuyler that, while he did not wish to encourage inferior officers in setting up their opinions against their superiors' decisions, yet he felt as they did and stated his reasons at length. Indeed, he said, nothing but a belief that, by the time he had news of the intended move, the works had been demolished and the withdrawal already made, plus a fear of encouraging such remonstrances, had prevented him from ordering the retention of the post at Crown Point. [9]

Schuyler defended the decision to withdraw with reasons that were cogent, [10] but not so briefly and briskly stated as were Gates's. "Your Excellency Speaks of Works to be Destroyed at Crown Point," Gates wrote to Washington on July 29. "Time & the Bad Construction of those Works had Compleatly Effected that business before General Schuyler came with me to Crown Point. The Ramparts are Tumbled down, the casements are Fallen in, the Barracks Burnt, and the whole so perfect a Ruin that it would take Five times the Number of Our Army for several Summers to put Those Works in Denfensible [*sic*] Repair." [11]

Under these conditions, no other course was possible, and so the sick were sent on to Fort George, and the rest of the army moved to Ticonderoga. The remnant of their salt pork had become utterly rancid and was thrown away. They had nothing to eat but flour, boiled to a gruel or baked into thin cakes on flat stones. They had no attention except what less than a dozen surgeons could give to 2,000 desperately sick men. Nature and Death took care of them. Some recovered, some did not. By the middle of August, they were down to a thousand.[12]

Three thousand "effectives" were now at Ticonderoga. The 6th Pennsylvania, under Lieutenant Colonel Thomas Hartley, had been left to establish an outpost at Crown Point—one not to be held against the enemy appearing in force.[13] A reenforcement, consisting of the 1st and 2nd Pennsylvania and three companies of the 4th, arrived at Ticonderoga on July 9, without shoes or stockings and almost in rags, "in miserable plight from the fatigue and sickness they had undergone," but, compared with the rest, "robust and healthy." [14]

The army was now divided into four brigades. The 1st, commanded by Arnold, comprised Bond's, Greaton's, and Porter's Massachusetts Continentals, and Burrell's Connecticut. The 2nd, under Colonel James Reed, was composed of his own, Poor's, and Bedel's from New Hampshire and Patterson's from Massachusetts. The 3rd commanded by Colonel John Stark, was made up of his own New Hampshires, Wind's and Maxwell's New Jerseymen, and Wynkoop's New Yorkers. The 4th, General Arthur St. Clair's, had his own, De Haas's, Wayne's, and Hartley's commands, all Pennsylvanians.[15]

The first three brigades were encamped on Mount Independence, on the east side of the lake, to keep them away from St. Clair's Pennsylvanians, encamped on the Ticonderoga side. The intense jealousy and ill feeling between the "southern" troops and those of New England and the consequent disorder had made this separation necessary.[16]

When Ethan Allen and Benedict Arnold took Ticonderoga from the British in May, 1775, it was well supplied with ordnance and ordnance stores; but Knox took most of the heavy cannon to the army at Boston. There were left, however, 120 guns of various sizes from 3-pounders to one 32. But there were not enough carriages to mount more than 43 of them, and there was a great lack of all their equipment, sponges, rammers, and so on. Powder was, as always, deficient, also lead, flints, and cartridge paper, for all which Gates now called on the Congress. He got them at last, on October 6.[17]

More men were needed to man these extensive works. Two emotions, prevalent throughout the northern states, affected the supply of such reenforcements. One was fear of the British invasion, which prompted the militia to come forward. The other was dread of the smallpox in the camp, which deterred them. The first was, however, the stronger. Militiamen from the neighborhood and from the New England states began to come late in July. By August they were coming in considerable numbers, though for the most part they were so ill provided and so worn down by the fatigue and hardships of their march that they were more of a burden to the garrison than a help. But three Continental regiments from Massachusetts really strengthened the army in July.[18]

By August 24 the returns showed twenty regiments in five brigades, a total of 9,157 rank and file, but only 4,899 present and fit for duty, besides 1,500 effectives at Crown Point, Fort George, and Skenesboro.[19]

The Americans had a flotilla on the lake, the schooner *Royal Savage,* captured the year before by Montgomery at St. Johns, the sloop *Enterprise,* which Arnold had taken when Ticonderoga fell, the schooner *Liberty,* taken at Skenesboro by Herrick at the same time, and the schooner *Revenge,* built at Ticonderoga. Arnold, whom Gates adjudged to be "perfectly skilled in naval affairs," had "most nobly undertaken to command" this fleet.[20] But Carleton was building boats at the other end of the lake, and Arnold wanted more than those four. He wanted auxiliary craft, gondolas, row-galleys, gunboats. They had to be built. But how could they be built?

There was plenty of standing timber, but it must first be felled, then hewn into keels and ribs and sawn into planks. Felling axes were scarce. Of broadaxes, adzes, crosscut saws, hammers, grindstones, chisels, augers, and all sorts of necessary hand tools, there were none. There were, to be sure, three sawmills in the neighborhood—one at Ticonderoga, another at Crown Point, a third near Skenesboro. Though disuse and neglect had left them in bad shape, they could be repaired. Planks could be got out in them. But how could those necessary tools be had in that wilderness? Where were bolts and nails, oakum and other naval stores, hawsers and anchors, paint, iron, ropes and blocks for rigging, canvas for sails, and all the hundred and one necessary articles and things for equipment to be procured? [21]

And, if you had all those, who was to use them? Who was to build and rig the vessels? Ship carpenters, sailmakers, and riggers were few in that army. The shipyards and sail lofts along the seacoast were humming with work for shipmasters and privateersmen. Few mechanics were fools enough to join a naked, starved, diseased army, when plenty of work with good pay was to be had at home. Nevertheless, those boats had to be built, and they were built.

Felling axes came first, in quantity, 1,500 from Schuyler at Albany, a thousand more from Governor Trumbull of Connecticut.[22] The soldiers were put to work in the forest. A few ship carpenters, so improvident as to have enlisted, were combed out of the army, a few house carpenters also. These were sent to Skenesboro, where the boatyard was established; Schuyler sent thirty more from Albany.[23] But these were not enough, not nearly enough. The coastal towns were called on.

In four companies of fifty each, bringing their own tools, ship carpenters came on from Massachusetts, Connecticut, Rhode Island, and even from far-off Philadelphia. Not for nothing, however, and not for soldiers' pay. They demanded and they got "prodegious wages," as much as five dollars a day, hard money, it was rumored. Blacksmiths also came and oarmakers and riggers and sailmakers, on similar terms.[24] Brigadier General David Waterbury, Jr., of Connecticut took charge of the work. Arnold came to Skenesboro from time to time, "to give Life & Spirit to Our Dock Yards," as Gates put it.[25] His energy and drive were contagious among the workers, and Waterbury's constant attention kept things going. Hard as it was to get them, spikes and nails being especially scarce, the necessary supplies and equipment came in.

Two types of craft were built—row-galleys and gondolas. The row-galleys were the larger, 70 to 80 feet long and 18 feet beam. They had round bottoms with keels, quarterdecks, and cabins, and were of "Spanish construction" as to their rigging; that is to say, they had two short masts, equipped with lateen sails that gave them an exotic appearance on that lake but made them easy even for landlubbers to handle.[26] Their armament was a 12- and an 18-pounder in the bow, two 9-pounders in the stern, and from four to six 6-pounders in broadside. Their complement was eighty men each.

The gondolas were flat-bottomed, but had keels. They were about forty-five feet long, rigged with one mast and two square sails and carried forty-five men each. They were slower and less handy than the galleys and could sail only before the wind while the galleys could beat to windward. Their armament was one 12-pounder and two 9-pounders.[27]

The schooner and the sloop were not so heavily armed as the galleys. The *Royal Savage* carried four 6-pounders and eight 4-pounders; the *Enterprise*, twelve 4-pounders; the *Revenge*, four 4-pounders and two 2-pounders; the *Liberty*, the same. All the craft also mounted on their bulwarks several light swivel guns. Both galleys and gondolas were equipped with oars, the galley with thirty-six.[28]

While the boats were building, the army was cheered and refreshed by the arrival of beef on the hoof, twenty head a week, and plenty of bread. To those who could afford to pay, sutlers offered vegetables, sugar, butter, cheese, chocolate, rum, and wine. The condition of the troops was much improved.[29] On July 28 General St. Clair read the Declaration of Independence to the troops. They "manifested their joy with three cheers." "It was remarkably pleasing to see the spirits of the soldiers so raised after all their calamities; the language of every man's countenance was, Now we are a people; we have a name among the States of the world." [30]

Carleton had halted his pursuit of Sullivan's retreating army at St. Johns. But he had no intention of remaining there long. He was receiving large reenforcements from Britain, and he intended, if possible, to march to Albany and cooperate with Howe. The plan to isolate New England by occupying the Lake Champlain and Hudson River passageway, attempted in 1777, was to be executed, if feasible. As indicated above, the Americans were alarmed because of the threat of Carleton's army. At St. Johns, Carleton proceeded to assemble and construct a fleet of vessels for the lake, because he could not advance without commanding its waters. There were on the St. Lawrence a three-masted ship, the *Inflexible*, and two schooners, the *Maria* and the *Carleton*; but, because of the ten-mile-long rapids between Chambly and St. Johns, they could not be brought up the Richelieu. He tried to bring them around the falls on rollers, but the ground was too soft to bear their weight; he had to take them apart and carry them up in pieces. From England a frigate had brought him ten gunboats knocked down. These were brought to St. Johns to be reconstructed. A thirty-ton gondola, thirty longboats, and four hundred bateaux were also brought up, either overland or by dragging them through the rapids. The longboats and bateaux were to transport troops and baggage up the lake.[31]

Carleton had little difficulty in securing workmen, materials, tools, and supplies. There were the fleet in the St. Lawrence and the towns along that river to furnish them to his full requirement. The work was swiftly carried on. For instance, the *Inflexible* was rebuilt and equipped within twenty-eight days of the time the keel was laid. With equal dispatch, he rebuilt the others and constructed ten more gunboats and an extraordinary thing called a *radeau*. It was a huge, flat-bottomed affair, with two masts carrying square sails, but it was more like a raft than any other sort of vessel, having very low bulwarks. It was to be manned by three hundred men, and was armed with the heaviest ordnance, six 24-pounders, six 12-pounders, and two howitzers. It was, indeed, a sort of floating fortress. Its name was *Thunderer*.[32]

By October 4 Carleton's fighting fleet was complete and ready to sail. In it were the *Inflexible*, armed with eighteen 12-pounders, the *Maria*, with fourteen 6-pounders, the *Carleton* with twelve of the same, the gondola *Loyal Convert* with seven 9-pounders, the giant *Thunderer,* and twenty gunboats having bow-guns ranging from 9-pounders to 24-pounders.[33]

The British army in Canada had been reenforced by the arrival, in June, of the Regiment Hesse Hanau, 660 in number, and in September by a second installment of Hessians and Brunswickers, making up a total force of 5,000 German mercenaries under command of Major General Baron von Riedesel. Carleton's whole army now numbered about 13,000 rank and file.[34]

On September 10 operations against the Americans on the lake began General William Philips with two regiments, part of a third, and some artillery was posted at St. Johns. Another regiment held Chambly. Lieutenant Colonel Carleton, a younger brother of the general, started up the Richelieu with 400 Indians in canoes, to be strengthened shortly afterwards by the addition of 100 Canadian volunteers under Captain Fraser. And 1,300 German troops embarked in eighty-two boats and moved up the river.[35]

General Simon Fraser with the light infantry, the grenadiers, and the 24th British regiment took post on the river about five miles above the New York State line. Burgoyne with the 9th, 21st, 31st, and 47th British regiments, the Hessian Regiment Riedesel, and the Hanau Regiment, moved up to Ile aux Noix, which had been possessed by the British in August and had been fortified and equipped as a base of supplies with magazines, blockhouses, and barracks.[36]

But it was not until October 14 that Burgoyne and Fraser, having left the 20th and 61st to hold Ile aux Noix, embarked for the final advance against the Americans. All the German troops were left in Canada, except the Hanau artillery, which was with Carleton's fleet on board the *Thunderer.*[37]

Arnold's preparations to meet the enemy had been pushed with such success that, by August 20, the schooners *Royal Savage* and *Revenge,* the sloop *Enterprise* and the gondolas *Boston, New Haven, Providence, New York, Connecticut,* and *Spitfire,* the cutter *Lee,* and the sloop *Liberty* were ready. On the 24th he set sail at Crown Point. At Willsborough, halfway down the lake, a hard storm, with heavy rain, overtook him and nearly foundered the *Spitfire.* The whole fleet had to weigh anchor and run before the wind up to Buttonmould Bay, where, for three days without intermission, it was lashed by the gale. On September 1 the anchors were again

Montreal

Chambly

La Prairie

St. Lawrence R.

Richelieu R.

C A N A D A

Cumberland H

VALCOUR I.

Lake Champlain

Split Rock Pt.

Where Arnold burned
his boats

Crown Pt.

Ticonderoga

*Lake
George*

Two Rocks

Drowned Lands

Skenesboro

South Bay

French Mt.

Fort Edward

N E W   Y O R K

Mohawk   River

Hudson R.

ACTION ON
LAKE CHAMPLAIN

0 5 10   20   30
SCALE OF MILES

Schenectady

Albany

lifted, and a fresh southerly breeze carried the fleet down to Schuyler's Island and then to Windmill Point at the northern end of the lake and within two or three miles of the Canadian border.[38]

At Windmill Point the fleet was joined by the *Lee*, which, sloop-rigged but with oars, might be called either a cutter or a row-galley, and the gondola *Jersey*. Arnold moored his vessels in a line across the lake and sent men ashore to fell spruce trees and make fascines for lining the sides of his galleys and gondolas "to prevent the enemy's boarding and to keep off small shot." [39] They were attacked by some of Carleton's Indians, who were now in the woods along the shore; three of the Americans were killed and six wounded before a few shot from the fleet drove off the assailants.

The lake is narrow at this point, and Arnold feared the erection of batteries on both sides to rake the line of his boats. He therefore retired to good anchorage in a broader part beside Ile la Motte. On the 19th he again shifted his position to a point farther south, Bay St. Amand above Cumberland Head, a long, curved promontory on the New York side of the lake about ten miles north of Valcour Island. While there he took soundings of the channel between that island and the shore. Finding it "an exceeding fine and secure harbour," he retired to it on the 23rd and remained there until the day of battle.[40]

He had been calling and continued to call on Gates to send him 200 sailors. His force was made up almost entirely of landsmen, "very indifferent men in general," he said. "Great part of those who shipped for seamen know very little of the matter." [41] "We have a wretched, motley crew in the fleet," he wrote to Gates, "the marines, the refuse of every regiment and the seamen few of them ever wet with salt water." [42] He also wanted gunners, for few of his men knew anything about laying a gun. And he wanted clothing for his men, watch coats, breeches, blankets, caps, and shoes. It was cold at night in October on Lake Champlain, and the men were scantily clad. But he got none, neither seamen nor clothing. Indeed, his last call was made on October 10, the very day before battle. He did, however, get the rest of his boats: the *Washington, Trumbull,* and *Congress,* galleys, and the *Jersey* and *Success,* gondolas, came on as they were finished.[43]

Valcour Island lies about half a mile off the New York shore. It is two miles long and half as wide, and rises steeply to heights of 120 to 180 feet. It was then heavily wooded. The vessels lying behind it were concealed from the north by a small promontory projecting from the island on its west side, and could not be discovered by a southbound fleet in the main channel until it had passed the island and opened a view of the water behind it.[44]

Arnold moored his fleet—two schooners, one sloop, eight gondolas, and four row-galleys—in a curved line, a "half-moon," between the island and the mainland, keeping the vessels as near together as practicable. He made the galley *Congress* his flagship, taking a position in the middle of the line. General Waterbury on the *Washington* galley commanded the right wing, and Colonel Edward Wigglesworth of Massachusetts on the *Trumbull* galley, the left. The entire force on the fleet was about 800 men.

Carleton sailed from St. Johns on October 4. His fleet consisted of the square-rigged ship *Inflexible*, the schooners *Maria* and *Carleton*, the great radeau *Thunderer*, the gondola *Loyal Convert*, twenty gunboats, four long-boats with fieldpieces in their bows, and twenty-four longboats for provisions and stores. The fleet was manned by 670 seamen from the British transports on the St. Lawrence, and each of the four larger vessels carried a company of the 29th Regiment acting as marines. Captain Thomas Pringle was in command.[45]

The fire power which this fleet could bring into action at one time was fifty-three guns, though in the approaching battle it was only forty-two, because neither the *Thunderer* nor the *Loyal Convert* was engaged. On the American side, the number was thirty-two.[46] The weight of metal which the British could throw in one complete discharge was perhaps 500 pounds, not counting the swivels, against the American 265.

The British fleet proceeded up the lake slowly and with apparent caution, yet really, at the last, incautiously. It first came to anchor below Ile la Motte and lay there until the 9th, while scouts went ahead looking for the Americans, without success. On the 10th it went on to an anchorage between Grand and Long islands. Here Carleton got news that the American fleet had been seen in the vicinity.

Getting under way the next morning, it stood up the lake before a strong northerly wind, rounded Cumberland Head, and passed Valcour Island. It was in mid-channel, about two miles beyond the southern end of Valcour, when the American fleet opened to its view.

Then the incaution of its proceeding was made plain. No scout boats had been sent ahead, which might have found the Americans before it had put itself to the disadvantage of having to attack from the leeward, that is to say, against the wind.

The Americans had been on the alert. The *Revenge* had been scouting to the north and had seen the British ships coming around Cumberland Head. On receiving this news Waterbury had urged Arnold "to come to sail and fight them on a retreat in [the] main lake as they were so much superior to us in number and strength and we being in such a disadvantageous harbour." But Arnold persisted in his plan to fight where he was.[47]

When the British discovered the American vessels, they hauled up for them. Arnold ordered the *Royal Savage* and the four galleys to get under way and commence the attack. He himself was on board the *Congress* galley. But when he got out into open water and saw the full strength of the enemy he signaled for a return to the line behind the island. The enemy, who by this time had made some headway in beating against the wind, opened fire at long range on the schooner and the galleys, to which the Americans replied with all the guns they could bring to bear.

The *Royal Savage*, either by misadventure or, as Arnold claimed, by mismanagement, fell to leeward while drawing under the lee of the island. Three shots in quick succession hit her, damaging one of her masts and cutting her rigging. She came up into the wind, but failed to go about on the other tack, hung in the eye of the wind for a long moment, fell off on the same tack as before, and grounded on the island shore. But her crew continued to fire her guns.

Neither the *Inflexible* nor the *Maria* had been able to beat back into close range. They anchored at long gunshot distance, and the *Inflexible* brought her heavy guns to bear on her enemy. Neither the *Thunderer* nor the *Loyal Convert* was engaged.

The schooner *Carleton*, boring into the fight, was caught by a flaw of wind and brought up opposite the middle of the American line. Lieutenant Dacres, her commander, anchored her, with a spring on her cable, broadside to the American fleet. Seventeen of the British gunboats came up into line with her. With no more than 350 yards distance between the two lines, the real battle began about noon.

"A tremendous cannonade was opened on both sides," wrote Baron von Riedesel. To the storm of shot and shell that fell upon the American fleet was added musketry from Captain Fraser's Indians and Canadians, who had landed from their canoes on the island and on the mainland west of the vessels. The crew of the *Royal Savage* was forced to abandon her. She was boarded by a boat's crew from the *Thunderer*, who turned her guns on her former friends. But they were soon driven off by the American fire. Another boat's crew, from the *Maria*, set her afire, and she blew up.

Meanwhile, the Americans' guns converged on the *Carleton*, Arnold himself sighting the guns of the *Congress*. She was hit time and again. Dacres was knocked senseless; another officer lost an arm. Edward Pellew, only a midshipman, a lad of nineteen, assumed command. After hours of fighting, the spring on her cable was shot away. Under the wind, she swung at her anchor, bows on to the enemy and, having no bow guns, hung there silenced, to be raked by every shot. Pringle on the *Maria* signaled her to withdraw, but she could not catch the wind so as to pay off on the right tack. Pellew climbed out on her bowsprit, under heavy musket fire, and tried to throw the jib over to make it draw, but without success. Two boats came to her assistance. Pellew, holding his position on the bowsprit in spite of a rain of musket-bullets, threw them a line, and the *Carleton* was towed away. She had been hulled several times, there was two feet of water in her hold, and half of her crew had been killed or wounded. Pellew further distinguished himself in later years, rising to the rank of admiral, and was honored with the title Viscount Exmouth.

Towards evening the *Inflexible* got within point-blank range and discharged five heavy broadsides against the American line, completely silencing its fire. But about five o'clock she dropped back to a distance of 700 yards from the Americans. The gunboats withdrew, and the whole British fleet anchored in a line across the southern end of the passage between Valcour and the mainland, keeping up a desultory fire until darkness fell.

The Americans took account of their injuries. The *Congress* had been hulled twelve times. She had two holes in her side between wind and water. Her mainmast was hit in two places. The *Washington* had also been severely punished and had one shot through her mainmast. The hull of the *Philadelphia* had been so damaged that she sank about an hour after the battle. All the sails of the fleet had been torn to tatters, and the rigging hung in tangles. The loss among the personnel was grievous; 60 had been either killed or wounded. Their store of ammunition was three-fourths gone. It was not possible to contemplate a renewal of the conflict on the morrow. It seemed that they were trapped and must surrender. But Arnold had another thought—to attempt an escape under the cover of night.

The night was dark. A heavy fog enshrouded the two fleets. A lantern, so hooded as to show a light only directly behind, was fixed in the stern of each vessel. At seven o'clock, the *Trumbull* galley got under way before a light northerly wind. The others fell in line at practicable intervals. The *Congress* and the *Washington* brought up the rear. And so, noiselessly, the whole line crept past the left of the British fleet, the fog so thick that none of the enemy's vessels could be seen. When they were beyond hearing distance the oars were got out, and the crews labored at them and at the pumps all through the night.

By dawn the *Trumbull* galley, with the *Revenge* and *Enterprise,* the *Lee* galley, and the gondolas *Boston, New Haven, Connecticut, Spitfire,* and *Success* had got ahead of the rest. The *Congress* and *Washington* galleys, the gondolas *Providence, New York,* and *Jersey,* which had made only eight miles, put in at Schuyler's Island. There the *New York* and *Providence* were found to be so badly damaged that their equipment was removed and they were sunk. The *Jersey* had run aground and, with the weight of water in her, could not be moved. The other two set out again early in the afternoon.

On discovering the escape of the Americans the next morning, Carleton immediately started after them. But, so upset was he by his surprise and rage, he forgot to give orders to his land forces. When within sight of Schuyler's Island he had to turn back to remedy his oversight.

The wind had shifted to the south, and, although Arnold put his men to the oars again, his battered galleys made little progress. By morning, after sixteen hours rowing, they had covered only six miles, and the pursuing British fleet, favored by a fresh northerly wind, which had not reached the Americans, was in sight in the rear. Also in sight, in front, were four American gondolas, which had been unable to keep up with the *Trumbull* and the others.

The *Inflexible,* the *Carleton,* and the *Maria* came on rapidly, the *Maria* ahead. At eleven o'clock, Arnold opened fire on her from his stern 9- and 12-pounders. But at Split Rock the pursuers caught up, and poured broadsides of grape and round shot upon the fleeing vessels. The *Washington* was overwhelmed by this fire. Waterbury struck her flag. In the course of the retreat, the *Lee,* like the *Jersey,* ran ashore and was abandoned; both were taken by the British.

But the *Congress* and the four gondolas kept on under the favoring wind, which had now caught up with them. For five glasses, two hours and a half, this unequal combat raged. The three British vessels, one on her broadside and two astern of her, concentrated their fire on the *Congress.* Her hull was shattered, her sails and rigging shot to rags, but there was no hint of surrender. Instead, Arnold signaled to the galleys to turn to windward so that the British sailing vessels could not follow, and to run for the east shore.

In Buttonmould Bay he beached his wrecks and set fire to them. He drew his men up on the shore and held them there until he was sure that his boats would blow up with their flags still flying, while the enemy stood off, keeping up a constant cannonade. The remains of his men, 200 in number—46 only of the *Congress* out of a crew of 73—started on a bridle path for Crown Point, ten miles away. They escaped an Indian ambush and reached the Point after dark, finding what was left of their fleet, the *Trumbull,* the *Enterprise,* the *Revenge,* the *Liberty,* and one gondola.

There was no stopping at Crown Point. Lieutenant Colonel Hartley and his garrison of the 6th Pennsylvania Regiment, together with Arnold's survivors, could not attempt to hold it. They burned all the buildings and retreated to Ticonderoga.[48]

A singular occurrence took place immediately upon their reaching that fort. A number of British rowboats came up under a flag of truce and delivered up General Waterbury and the entire crew of the *Washington*, 110 in number. Carleton had paroled them. This generous treatment made such an impression on the captives, and they were so loud in their praise of him, that it was thought dangerous to allow them to mingle with the others. They were immediately sent off on their way home.

Arnold had been utterly defeated, losing eleven of his sixteen vessels and 80 of his men; but his gallantry and theirs was not unrewarded. Indeed, the greatest American victories in the war thereafter were made possible by that desperate fight. The sequence of events is closely connected.

Carleton had been so delayed by the necessity of building a fleet to meet Arnold's, by his subsequent necessarily cautious maneuvering, and by the battle that he reconsidered his decision to attack Ticonderoga and withdrew all his army and his fleet from the lake to St. Johns. He felt that Ticonderoga was too strong to be carried by storm, and the season was too far advanced to allow siege operations. If he should be held up in the attack even for a short time he could not follow through to the Hudson in the winter and of course could not establish communication with Howe. If he could have reached Albany, the effect upon the American cause might have been disastrous. If he could have wintered at Ticonderoga and made it his base of supplies so as to start for the Hudson in the early spring, the British campaign might not have met with disaster in the next year at Saratoga. It was Saratoga that gave the needed encouragement to the French to send land and naval forces to aid the Americans. And those forces ensured the surrender at Yorktown and finished the war. Valcour Island was no defeat, therefore. "It was the American cause that was saved that day." [49]

Captain Alfred Thayer Mahan, the distinguished authority on naval affairs, has endorsed this view: "That the Americans were strong enough to impose the capitulation of Saratoga was due to the invaluable year of delay secured to them in 1776 by their little navy on Lake Champlain, created by the indomitable energy, and handled with the indomitable courage of the traitor, Benedict Arnold." [50]

CHAPTER 36

Burgoyne's Expedition

Canada in the winter of 1776–1777 had no attractions for Major General John Burgoyne. After the retirement of the British army in October, 1776, following the battle with Arnold at Valcour, there would be no more military operations in the North until the spring, which was not to be expected before May. A prospect of six months of idleness in Quebec or Montreal had little appeal to such a restless and ambitious spirit. He could look forward to active service at the end of that period; but the plans for that would not be made in Quebec, nor would commands be allotted there. London was headquarters.

This was his second visit to America. His first had been to Boston in 1775. There he had been subordinate to Gage, Howe, and Clinton and he had not relished that position. He wrote to Lord Rochford after Bunker Hill: "The inferiority of my station as youngest Major-General upon the staff left me almost a useless spectator. . . . My rank only serves to place me in a motionless, drowsy, irksome medium, or rather vacuum, too low for the honour of command, too high for that of execution." So he had gone home in December of that year.[1]

He came back in the spring of 1776, but again as a subordinate, second in command to Carleton. It was Carleton. not he, that had won the victory at Valcour. It might be Carleton that would lead the King's forces in Canada in the coming campaign of 1777. Plainly, something should be done about it. So he went home again.[2]

In London he found conditions favorable to his ambition. Carleton was definitely out of favor. The King had been disappointed and vexed at his failure to press on after Valcour and take Ticonderoga. So had the country in general, including Lord George Germain, colonial secretary, responsible for the conduct of the war in America.

At first Germain was inclined to couple Burgoyne with Carleton as blameworthy for that failure. But there was another element in Germain's feelings toward Carleton, a bitter personal animosity antedating Valcour. He was glad to put all the blame on him, eager, indeed, when he observed the King's attitude towards Burgoyne.[3]

The King had shown a friendly face to the general. "Yesterday morning," announced the *Morning Chronicle* early in January, "his Majesty took an outing on horseback in Hyde Park upwards of an hour, attended by General Burgoyne." [4] Indeed, his Majesty had already indicated to Lord North his pleasure that Burgoyne should command operations from Canada in the spring.

So everything was going smoothly, and Burgoyne did nothing to cause friction. He did not intrigue against Carleton, criticized him not at all—indeed he defended him—and so aroused no opposition among that general's friends. To aid his own cause, he wrote and submitted to the King a paper entitled "Thoughts for Conducting the War from the Side of Canada," which, because of its results, was a very important document of the Revolution.

Burgoyne's plan assumed a strong American force at Ticonderoga, perhaps as many as 12,000 men. It called for a British army of 8,000 regulars, with a sufficient equipment of artillery, supplemented by "a corps of watermen," 2,000 Canadians, and "1000 or more savages." Of this force, he would leave 3,000 to hold Canada. He proposed, after establishing magazines at Crown Point, to embark the rest upon Lake Champlain. Ticonderoga was to be attacked and reduced "early in the summer."

After that, the advance should proceed, preferably by way of Lake George and the Hudson, to Albany. Or, if the enemy should be found on that route in too great force, it should go to Albany by the lower end of Champlain, through Skenesboro and the Hudson. In either case, a chain of posts should be established along the route of the expedition to secure its communications. From Albany, after the end of the campaign, Burgoyne was to establish contact with Howe. He did not expect Howe to send forces northward during the campaign to support him. He would have sufficient strength to reach Albany and to maintain himself there.

Burgoyne also proposed an auxiliary expedition to the same objective, but by way of Lake Ontario, Oswego, and the Mohawk River, which empties into the Hudson near Albany. He did not enlarge upon the advantages of his scheme, nor even specifically suggest its strategic purpose; but an already prevailing idea among the British high command was that holding the Hudson, and thus separating the New England colonies from the rest, was a matter of the first importance to the success of the King's arms in America.

Burgoyne was tactfully silent as to the command of the expedition, except by an indirect reference to it. This business, he said, would depend for its success upon the cooperation of the governor of Canada; to wit, Carleton. His "peremptory powers, warm zeal and consonant opinion" must be had, else "plausible obstructions . . . will be sufficient to crush such exertions as an officer of a sanguine temper, entrusted with the future conduct of the campaign and whose personal interest and fame therefore consequently depend upon a timely out-set, would be led to make." Clearly, Carleton was not suggested for the leadership.[5]

The King liked the plan. Its outlines, he said, seemed to be "on a proper foundation." The Mohawk River diversion, he also approved. Germain issued the necessary orders in a letter to Carleton. He was to remain in Canada and guard that province with 3,770 men of specified British and German regiments, including McLean's Royal Highland Emigrants, and detach Burgoyne with the remainder of the troops, 7,173 in number, "to proceed with all possible expedition to join General Howe and put himself under his command." He was also to furnish Lieutenant Colonel Barry St. Leger with 675 men, "together with a sufficient number of Canadians and Indians," for the Mohawk expedition.[6]

"I shall write to Sir William Howe," Germain went on, "from hence by the first packet." But Carleton, Burgoyne, and St. Leger were also to inform Howe of the plan, so that they might receive instructions from him.[7]

Germain's letter to Carleton was long and insultingly specific in its details. Not only so, but it also charged Carleton with "supineness" in his failure to attack Ticonderoga, and even blamed him for the defeat of the Hessians at Trenton, because that failure had set free American troops to act with Washington against the Jersey outpost.[8]

Such a letter was enough to anger Carleton, and it did. He wrote a spirited reply, defending his actions in forcible language. But, magnanimous man that he was, he added that, in spite of the "Slight, Disregard and Censure" visited upon him, he would give Burgoyne all possible assistance.[9] And he did.

Looking backward, one observes the weaknesses, indeed the stupidity, of Burgoyne's plan. There was little to be gained by a march from Canada to Albany. The cutting of communications between New England and the other colonies, if it had been possible, could have had important results only after the passage of time. And it was necessary that the war be won before Britain's financial resources should be overstrained, and before France should take advantage of the American situation to win revenge for the many defeats Britain had inflicted upon her. The troops set aside for Burgoyne's expedition could have given Howe useful added strength, even strength perhaps sufficient for a final destruction of Washington's army. Further, Burgoyne's army under the plan was to cooperate with Howe's only *after* the end of the campaign. It was to reach Albany unsupported from the south; and Howe was authorized by Lord Germain to move against Philadelphia by sea, leaving only a garrison force in New York. Burgoyne was to travel through the woods to Albany, with an ever lengthening line of communications and with no assurance of help even at Albany, should he need it. Germain finally saw this defect in the plan, perhaps not too clearly, and got off a letter to Howe suggesting that he cooperate with Burgoyne during the campaign. But Howe received Germain's letter in August while he was en route by sea to Chesapeake Bay, and he could hardly act to help Burgoyne at such a late time—at least he could not without completely disrupting his own plan of operation. He did make a gesture toward assisting Burgoyne by asking Clinton, who was in command of the garrison at New York, to do what he could to help his fellow general.[10]

Burgoyne arrived at Quebec on May 6, 1777. Spring had just come; the ice in the river had broken up, "with a most astonishing noise," one week before. He found the troops, after a mild winter, in good condition, except their clothing. New uniforms to replace those worn in last year's campaign had not come from England. To patch the old ones, the tails of the coats of the British regiments had been cut off. They all now wore short jackets, like the regulation coats of the light infantry. Their cocked hats had been cut down into caps. But these alterations were all for the better in forest warfare.[11]

The Brunswickers, too, were far from smart in their appearance. Their duke, in his prudent care for his own purse, had sent them out in worn uniforms and old shoes, and Canada had not afforded complete replacements. But all such matters were merely surface. The substance was sound.

There was one difference in uniforms, however, between the British and German contingents that was important. While the British uniforms had been modeled after those of the army of Germany and were too heavy, too awkward, too tight, and too elaborate for rough campaigning in America, those of these Brunswickers were far worse in all of these respects. Their dragoons, who had come without horses and were to serve dismounted to the end of the campaign, were most preposterously equipped for such service. Their great cocked hats, ornamented with a long plume, their hair worn in a long, stiff queue, their tight, thick coats, their stiff leather breeches, their huge leather gauntlets almost elbow-length, their great jack boots reaching to mid-thigh, weighing twelve pounds a pair without the long brass spurs always worn even on the march, made up as unsuitable an outfit for marching and fighting in a forested wilderness in an American midsummer as could have been devised by the most ingenious. Add to that a long, straight broadsword to trail at the thigh and a short heavy carbine, and one could have no feeling but pity for a Brunswick dragoon.[12]

So much for the main force of British and German regulars; they were fit and ready to go. The same could not be said for the irregular auxiliaries included in the plan. After all, they were French; and, however willing they had been in Montcalm's time to fight for their flag, this war meant little or nothing to them. Instead of the desired 2,000, Burgoyne could round up only 150. The Tories were also backward; only 100 enlisted. With the Indians he had somewhat better luck. He got 400 of the 1,000 he wanted. They were collected and led by La Corne St. Luc and Charles de Langlade.[13]

For his navy, he had the *Inflexible,* the *Maria,* the *Carleton,* the *Loyal Convert,* and the *Thunderer* of last year's fleet. To these were added the *Washington,* the *Jersey,* and the *Lee,* taken from Arnold after Valcour, another ship-rigged vessel, built that winter at St. Johns, the *Royal George,* and twenty-eight of last year's gunboats. Of bateaux for the transport of troops, there was an ample number.[14]

In his artillery section there were 138 guns, ranging from little 4.4-inch mortars and light 3-pounders to heavy 24-pounders. But many of these were mounted in the vessels, others were to be left at St. Johns, others at Ticonderoga and Fort George after they were taken. His field train for the whole expedition was to consist of 42 guns, large and small.[15]

The British advance corps was composed of the 24th regiment, the light infantry, and the grenadiers, including not only those of the expeditionary regiments, but also the flank companies of the 29th, 31st, and 24th, whose "battalion companies" remained in Canada.[16] This corps was under Brigadier General Simon Fraser. The 1st Brigade, the 9th, 47th, and 53rd regiments, was under Brigadier General Powell; the 2nd brigade, the 20th, 21st, and 62nd regiments, under Brigadier General Hamilton. This division constituted the right wing of the army and was under command of Major General William Phillips.

The German advance corps consisted of grenadiers and light infantry, including a company of forty jägers and forty "marksmen" selected from the different British regiments. This whole corps was commanded by Lieutenant Colonel Breymann. The 1st brigade, the Riedesel, Specht, and Rhetz regiments, was under Brigadier Specht; the 2nd brigade, the Prince Frederick and Hesse Hanau regiments, was under Brigadier Gall. This division was the left wing, commanded by Major General von Riedesel.[17]

The British infantry division numbered 3,724 rank and file, the German 3,016. The guns were to be divided between the two and served by 245 regular British artillerymen, 150 men drawn from the infantry, and 78 of the Hesse Hanau artillery company. The Canadian and Tory volunteers were to cover the British right wing, the Indians to cover the German left wing. The Brunswick dismounted dragoons were to act as reserves. In all the army numbered 7,213 rank and file.[18]

It was not a large army, but it was, for its size, a strong fighting force composed of trained, disciplined, and experienced men, under capable officers. Burgoyne, though not a military leader of the first or even second class, was an active, resolute, courageous soldier, well versed in the arts of war and, what is very important in such an extensive expedition as was about to be undertaken, he had the trust and confidence of his men. General Phillips, second in command, had served for twenty years in the British army. He was a distinguished artillerist and an exceptionally able strategist. Fraser was a scion of the noble Scotch house of Lovat. He, too, had had long experience as a soldier, had served with Wolfe at Louisburg and Quebec, and had acquired a high reputation for energy, activity, and good judgment coupled with cool daring. Hamilton had attained his command solely because of his professional merits and accomplishments. Kingston, the adjutant general, had served with distinction under Burgoyne in Portugal. Major the Earl of Balcarres, commanding the light infantry, and Major Acland of the grenadiers were officers of high professional attainments and undoubted courage.[19]

Of the Germans, Baron von Riedesel was the most distinguished. He had been a soldier in the Hessian and Brunswick armies for more than twenty years. At the outbreak of the Seven Years' War he was attached to the staff of the Duke of Brunswick and was employed by him in special duties which called for the use of delicate tact, good judgment, and personal courage. His reputation for intrepidity thus established was later confirmed by his conduct in many dangerous enterprises. He possessed the essential qualities of a good soldier; he was cool and discreet in danger, swift in action. His clear understanding had been studiously applied to the principles of his profession, and now, at the age of thirty-eight, he was at the height of his mental and physical powers. He was of medium height, strongly built, vigorous and hardy. His florid face was full and round, his features regular, his blue eyes notably large and clear. His amiable disposition was displayed in his care for the comfort and well-being of his men.[20] Under his leadership, backed by such experienced professional soldiers as his subordinate officers, the German contingent in Burgoyne's army was bound to give a good account of itself.

Burgoyne's troops were first assembled at St. Johns. There, on June 13, was enacted a bit of pageantry strange to that wilderness. On the *Thunderer,* moored in the river, there was erected the royal standard of Britain, bravely displaying on its embroidered silken fabric the golden lions of England, the red lion of Scotland, the harp of Ireland and, somewhat reminiscently, the fleur-de-lis of France. This symbol of Britain's might was then saluted by a discharge of all the guns of the fleet and in the fort.[21]

Still further to impress the Americans with the majesty of the laws they flouted, Burgoyne a week later issued a proclamation, in language which, according to a contemporary pamphleteer, was characterized by "the tinsel splendor of enlightened absurdity." It was Burgoyne the dramatist at his worst, at his almost unbelievable worst. It is difficult for one reading it now to realize that it is not a parody of some less bombastic manifesto.

Among other emotional appeals, it called upon "the suffering thousands," that is to say, the Tories, in the colonies to declare whether they were not subject to "the completest system of Tyranny that ever God in his displeasure suffer'd for a time to be exercised over a froward and stubborn Generation." It declared that "persecution and torture, unprecedented in the inquisitions of the Romish Church, are among the palpable enormities that verify the affirmative." To consummate this tyranny, it said, "the profanation of Religion is added to the most profligate prostitution of common sense." And so it went on to offer encouragement and protection to all who would take part in "the glorious task of redeeming their Countrymen from dungeons" and reestablishing the rule of the King.

The writer gave warning to those who persisted in this "unnatural Rebellion," that he had but "to give stretch" to his Indian auxiliaries, "and they amount to thousands," to overtake such recalcitrants "wherever they may lurk," for which vengeance upon those persisting in "the phrenzy of hostility" he would "stand acquitted in the Eyes of God and Men." There was a final warning uttered in "Consciousness of Christianity," that "devastation, famine and every concomitant horror that a reluctant but indispensable prosecution of military duty must occasion" awaited the impenitent.[22]

Instead of frightening the rebellious Americans, it first made them angry, then made them laugh. Parodies by the dozen appeared, notably an excellent one by Francis Hopkinson.[23] In England, there was a similar reaction. Horace Walpole called its author "the vaporing Burgoyne," "Pomposo," and "Hurlothrumbo," and remarked upon one who with "consciousness of Christianity" could "reconcile the scalping knife with the Gospel." [24]

A few days after the issuance of that rodomontade, Burgoyne addressed a council of his Indian auxiliaries in equally high-flown language. "Warriors, you are free—go forth in might and valor of your cause—strike at the common enemies of Great Britain and America—disturbers of public order, peace and happiness, destroyers of commerce, parricides of state," and so on at length, an incitement to the usual methods of savage warfare, if ever there was one, it seemed. But no, not that. "I positively forbid bloodshed, when you are not opposed in arms. Aged men, women, children and prisoners must be held sacred from the knife or hatchet, even in actual conflict." After that speech, the savage instincts of the Indians were tamed and subdued, their excitable natures sobered by a distribution of rum and by a "war-dance, in which they threw themselves in various postures, every now and then making most hideous yells." [25]

Again Burgoyne, a good soldier afflicted with a mania for the pen, exposed himself to ridicule. Walpole called it "still more supernatural" than his proclamation. Edmund Burke blasted it in the House of Commons. He supposed a riot on Tower Hill, where the royal menagerie was kept. "What would the Keeper of His Majesty's lions do? Would he not fling open the dens of the wild beasts and then address them thus? 'My gentle lions—my humane bears—my tender-hearted hyenas, go forth! But I exhort you, as you are Christians and members of civilized society, to take care not to hurt any man, woman or child!' " And Lord North, who had sanctioned the employment of the Indians, laughed until the tears ran down his cheeks.[26]

Ticonderoga, familiar name to British and Americans alike by 1777, is a bold, squarish, blunt-nosed promontory a mile long and three-quarters of a mile wide, that juts out from the western side of Lake Champlain, whose waters wash its base on the north, east, and south. At the foot of its southwest shoulder a very narrow gorge extends westward a mile or more, through which the waters of Lake George are poured into Champlain. The highest elevation on the promontory is about seventy feet above the lake.

From the east side of Champlain, another headland, a rocky bluff thirty to fifty feet high called Mount Independence, is thrust out towards the southeast corner of Ticonderoga. The points of the two narrow the lake to a width of about a quarter of a mile. This is the gateway from the upper lake to the lower, also to Lake George. Having passed through it one may go on by water directly south into the narrow, upper end of Champlain, and from its extremity up Wood Creek to within a few miles of the upper reaches of the Hudson. Or one may turn aside at Ticonderoga into Lake George and follow it to a point as near the Hudson.

About two miles to the northwest of the nose of Ticonderoga, Mount Hope commands the road to Lake George. A mile to the southwest, another hill, called Sugar Loaf from its conical appearance as seen from the east— but renamed Mount Defiance by the British after its capture—rises 750 feet above the water. At this time both shores of the lake and all the mentioned heights, except where Ticonderoga had been cleared for its fortification, were densely forested.

As has been hereinbefore stated, the French had built a star-shaped stone fort, with five bastions, on Ticonderoga in 1755. When it was attacked by Jeffrey Amherst in 1759 its retreating garrison blew up a large part of it. The British rebuilt it in less substantial fashion; but after the Peace of Paris, in 1763, it was allowed to fall into decay, though a considerable part of it, facing the lake, was still in serviceable condition in 1777.

While the French held it, they had constructed lines, extending in a curve across the promontory, about three-quarters of a mile behind the fort. These were built of logs heaped upon one another to a height of eight feet, covered with earth and faced with an abatis.

After the evacuation of Crown Point in July, 1776, and the concentration of the American troops at Ticonderoga, vigorous efforts were made to strengthen its defenses. The remains of the old fort were to some extent repaired. Blockhouses were built to protect the flanks and rear of the old French lines, which had been enlarged. Other blockhouses, also breastworks and small redoubts, defended the lower slopes on the north and south and various other points.

On Mount Hope a new barbette battery was built in a position covering the slope down to the outlet of Lake George and the road which ran south along its shore.

Across the lake Mount Independence showed a high, rugged, precipitous face. Its rear was protected naturally by a creek and a wide and deep morass, artificially by batteries and a strong, stone breastwork cleverly designed to take advantage of the irregularities of the ground. On its summit, an eight-pointed star redoubt, enclosing barracks, was the citadel of that position.

To close the water gateway, a boom of heavy logs, strung together on a massive iron chain, was stretched across from the northern point of Independence to the southern corner of Ticonderoga. Behind it, for communication between the two, was a bridge.

The plan of these works was suggested by Colonel John Trumbull; they were designed by the Polish engineer, Colonel Thaddeus Kosciuszko. Trumbull had proposed fortifying Sugar Loaf, but Gates had declared that it was an entirely inaccessible height and could therefore neither be fortified by him, nor be possessed by the enemy. Although Trumbull, Wayne, and game-legged Arnold climbed its steepest face, the eastern side, to the top, and although the northwest side was much less steep and difficult, Gates adhered to his decision not to try to fortify it.

A return of the troops at this post, dated June 28, 1777, showed ten Continental and two militia regiments, but they were slim regiments, ranging in number from 45 rank and file, present and fit, to 265, the average being 160. There were also Benjamin Whitcomb's little corps of 19 scouts, Thomas Lee's Rangers numbering 23, 124 artificers, and 250 in the artillery section. In all, including officers, the garrison might be estimated at 2,500.[27] The outside lines around Mount Independence plus the old French lines behind Ticonderoga were over 2,000 yards long. Even distributed along them in one thin line, with no reserves, no allowance for a force to hold Mount Hope, the blockhouses, and other works, there would have been one man for each yard, a mere skeleton defense. To man the works properly, at least five times the number of that garrison were necessary.

In chief command was Major General Arthur St. Clair. Born in Scotland, he had served in the British army in the French and Indian War, earning distinction at the siege of Louisburg and the capture of Quebec. Having married an American lady of wealth, he left the British service and established a home in Pennsylvania. He took the side of the rebels and was commissioned colonel of the 2nd Pennsylvania battalion in January, 1776. He was creditably concerned in the retreat across the Jerseys and the battles of Trenton and Princeton, as well as in the disaster at Trois Rivières. In February, 1777, the Congress appointed him a major general. He had been selected by Gates to command at Ticonderoga and had arrived at that post on June 12, 1777.

He was now past his fortieth year, tall, well built, and handsome in figure. His features were regular, his blue-gray eyes clear and intelligent, his hair reddish brown.[28] His manners were easy and graceful. Though his service during the war was competent to a degree, it cannot be said that he showed the capacity, the military ability, that would have justified his appointment as major general. A brigadier's rank would have been more suitable to his qualifications.

Serving under St. Clair at that post were three brigadier generals, the Frenchman Matthias Alexis Roche de Fermoy, John Paterson of Massachusetts, and Enoch Poor of New Hampshire, none of whom achieved distinction in the war.

The condition of internal affairs at Ticonderoga was far from satisfactory. There were not only too few men, there was too little of everything—arms, equipment, ammunition, supplies, and even food and clothing.[29] Schuyler came up from Albany and held a council of war with the four Ticonderoga generals on June 20. They agreed that there were too few troops to hold the whole works; that, nevertheless, they should hold on as long as possible and then concentrate all their force on Independence, which they might be able to hold as long as their food lasted; that bateaux should be kept ready for a final retreat.[30]

How they expected to get the troops safely across to Independence in the face of an enemy force that had beaten them out of Ticonderoga, how they expected to preserve that fleet of bateaux and to make that retreat, after the enemy held Ticonderoga and possessed the water gate, seem not to have been considered. But those questions are, after all, merely academic. They never had to be answered.

Two days before that council was held Burgoyne's entire force had assembled at Cumberland Head. It was there that he issued his great manifesto. From that point, the progress of the fleet and army was smooth and deliberate at the rate of eighteen to twenty miles a day.

Twenty or more great canoes, each holding twenty Indians, with another fleet bearing the Canadians and Tories dressed—or undressed—like Indians, formed the vanguard. Then came the gunboats and the bateaux of the British advance, the 24th regiment, the light infantry, and the grenadiers. The fleet was next in line, the tall-masted, square-sailed *Inflexible* and *Royal George*; the two schooners *Carleton* and *Maria*; the gondola *Loyal Convert*; the huge, unwieldy, absurd radeau *Thunderer*, that would "neither row nor sail" [31] but had to be got along somehow; the captives of last year's encounter, the galley *Washington*, the cutter *Lee*, and the gondola *Jersey*; and the gunboats, twenty-four of them.

After the fleet came the bateaux of the 1st British brigade "in the greatest order and regularity," [32] and then Burgoyne and his two major generals, Riedesel and Phillips, each in his own pinnace. The British 2nd brigade was followed by the two German brigades. Ignominiously, the tail of the procession was a motley fleet of boats of all kinds carrying the sutlers, the women, and all the raggle-taggle of camp followers that hung on the rear of the armies of that day.[33]

Against a setting of the blue waters of the lake and the dark green background of its forested shores, the painted faces and bodies of hundreds of Indians and their make-believe savage companions, the masses of British scarlet and of German dark blue, the green of the jägers and the light blue of the dragoons, with their regimental facings of every hue, the shining brass of the tall hats of the Hessian grenadiers, the glinting of the sunlight upon polished musket barrels and bayonets, the flashing of thousands of wet paddles and oars made up a spectacular pageant, brilliant in its color, light, and motion, thrilling in its purpose and intention.

On the 26th General Fraser's advance corps left Crown Point, where the army had by that time been concentrated, and pushed on ahead with the Indians, Canadians, and Tories. On July 1, "the weather being fine," the main army divided, the British taking the west side of the lake, the Germans the east side. The whole expanse of the lake, a mile wide, was "cover'd with Boats or Batteaux's"; as Lieutenant Hadden wrote, "some of the Armed Vessels accompanied us, the Music and Drums of the different Regiments were continually playing and contributed to make the Scene and passage extremely pleasant." [34] Three miles above Ticonderoga, the British landed and encamped on their side, the Germans opposite them. Fraser was a mile in advance. Early the next day the operations against the forts began.[35]

General Phillips, commanding Fraser's advance strengthened by one British brigade, started for Mount Hope. Its garrison set the works on fire, ran down the steep, rear slope and fled to the old French lines, a sensible proceeding proving the folly of the occupation of that outpost so far from the main defenses. A quick movement by the British might have cut off the retreating Americans; but not until one o'clock did they occupy the abandoned position and send Captain Fraser with his Indians and British marksmen on a circuit around the hill for that purpose. Finding no one to cut off, they went on towards the old French lines, drove in a picket of sixty men, approached within less than a hundred yards of the lines, took cover in the woods, and opened fire. St. Clair, thinking that this was a prelude to an assault at that point, ordered its defenders to sit down on the fire steps, keep under cover, and hold their fire. But, when tempted by the very near approach of one of the British marksmen, Lieutenant Colonel James Wilkinson ordered a sergeant to take a shot at him.

At the sound of that single discharge, the entire force within the old

French lines jumped to their feet, mounted the fire steps, and loosed a volley, then another and another. The artillery joined in the fusillade. When at last the officers had succeeded in stopping these unauthorized pyrotechnics and the smoke had cleared away, it was seen that the enemy had retreated to 300 yards' distance, leaving but one man lying on the field, the man Wilkinson had ordered shot. But when a corporal's guard went on to fetch him in and bury him, he was found to be unhurt. He was merely drunk. At least 3,000 musket shots had been fired and eight pieces of artillery had been discharged; yet only one man of 500—all within 80 to 100 yards—had been killed and two wounded.[36]

In the meantime, Riedesel's division had advanced close to the creek behind Independence and had been fired on. But darkness fell before any nearer hostile move could be made. The next day, Mount Hope was occupied in force by the British, and there was a certain amount of cannonading of little avail to either side. But something less noisy, that was to prove immediately decisive of the contest, was on foot.

Burgyone sent Lieutenant Twiss, his chief engineer, to take a look at that neglected Sugar Loaf. Twiss climbed its northwest flank, came back, and reported that it commanded Ticonderoga at 1,400 yards and Independence at 1,500. He could open a road and have guns up there within twenty-four hours. Burgoyne gave the orders. Phillips took charge. "Where a goat can go," said he, "a man can go and where a man can go he can drag a gun." [37] On July 4 the engineers were at work on the road.

St. Clair had been strengthened by the arrival of 900 fresh militiamen. He was looking for an assault on some part of his works, but there seemed to be little enemy activity. Yet there were movements. Burgoyne took Gall's brigade from Riedesel and moved it to the Ticonderoga side, giving him in exchange Fraser's Indians, Canadians, Tories, and British "marksmen." Riedesel was to move to the south around Independence and close the way of retreat by the road on that side of the lake, the guns on Sugar Loaf being expected to prevent any embarkation for retreat by water. But Riedesel had not yet begun his circuitous move.[38]

On the morning of July 5, St. Clair took a good look at something moving on the top of Sugar Loaf. Were there men up there? There were and something else, two guns, 12-pounders, not yet mounted, but on the way to be. He turned to his adjutant, Wilkinson. "We must away from this," said he, "for our situation has become a desperate one." [39] At least, that is the way Wilkinson reports his speech. Doubtless St. Clair was more brief and less stilted.

A council of war, immediately held, promptly and unanimously voted to give up the forts and retreat. But the withdrawal could not be begun by day, in full sight of the enemy. The night promised concealment. There would be a new moon, setting early and leaving comforting darkness.[40]

The relics of Arnold's Valcour fleet, the *Trumbull* and *Gates* galleys, the schooners *Liberty* and *Revenge,* and the sloop *Enterprise,* had been anchored in line across the narrow water behind the bridge. More than two hundred bateaux and other small craft lay beyond these. It was decided to use all these vessels to transport, up the lake to Skenesboro, the invalids and as much of the artillery and stores as could be got away. The main force would march from the east side by a road that ran from behind Independence southeast to Hubbardton, thence around Lake Bomoseen to Castleton and thence west to Skenesboro.

To drown the noise of the preparations for departure and divert the enemy's attention, the heavy guns in the forts and the various batteries opened fire as darkness fell. When it was quite dark, the embarkation of the invalids and stores began. Colonel Pierce Long of New Hampshire, with four or five hundred effectives, was in charge of the boats. The work of loading them was toilsome, and its progress slow, because everything that was got away had to be carried on men's backs from the forts to the spot where the boats were moored.

The cannonade was continuous and thunderous throughout the evening. What the enemy thought of this apparently senseless waste of powder does not appear. One might have supposed that it would lead them to suspect just what was actually in progress. Another signal was a fierce burst of flame from the Independence fort. General Roche de Fermoy had adopted the "scorched earth" policy by setting his headquarters ablaze rather inopportunely. Indeed, some of the enemy were moved to speculate whether the Americans "were meditating an attack or . . . were retreating." [41] But it was not until about daybreak that General Fraser had definite information of the retreat, from three American deserters.

Fraser's headquarters were on the Ticonderoga side, a mile and a half from the bridge. Hurrying to it with his troops, he found that it was partially destroyed, also that several fieldpieces at the farther end were trained down its length. Four men had been left there to fire one blast at the enemy attempting to cross, and then to retire.

But when Fraser's men made a tentative approach nothing happened. They pushed on to find all four gunners lying dead drunk beside a cask of

Madeira. Only one of the guns was fired, by an Indian who picked up a lighted slow match and carelessly dropped a spark upon its priming. Fortunately for those on the bridge, the gun was elevated to such a degree that it fired over their heads.[42]

Burgoyne ordered Fraser's light infantry and grenadiers to pursue the main force of the Americans retreating by land, and directed Riedesel, with his own regiment and Breymann's grenadiers and light troops, to follow in support. The 62nd British regiment was put in charge of Ticonderoga, and Prince Frederick's Brunswickers of Independence. The British fleet was to go on up the lake after the American boats.[43]

It was along but a pretense of a road that St. Clair led his troops towards Hubbardton, a mere wagon track, new, rough, rutted, and spotted with stumps of trees. It ran up hill and down across a broken country, "a continuous succession of steep and woody hills," [44] interspersed with ponds, swamps, and streams. The day, July 6, became hotter and hotter as it wore on. Over that road, shut in on both sides by dense forest walls, there were no cooling breezes, and the men sweltered in the overpowering heat. But there was no stopping until they had gone twenty-four miles and, through a high notch in a line of hills, had come down into Hubbardton, a hamlet of two houses. Even then they did not rest long. Six miles more would bring them to Castleton, where they would be within thirteen or fourteen miles of Skenesboro. St. Clair pushed his men on to that point before night.

Colonel Seth Warner of Vermont was left at Hubbardton with 150 men, under orders to wait until the rear guard came up and then follow closely after the main body. But Colonel Warner, brave and patriotic though he was, lacked discipline. He had been a Green Mountain Boy, accustomed to acting on his own and taking orders from nobody. Instead of bringing on the rear guard, he and Colonel Francis, its commander, agreed to spend the night at Hubbardton. So three regiments, Warner's Vermonters, Francis's 11th Massachusetts, Colonel Hale's 2nd New Hampshires, and a number of stragglers from the main body bivouacked there.[45]

Fraser lost no more time than St. Clair. Starting at four o'clock in the morning, his men marched along the same road until one in the afternoon. Riedesel, behind them, was equally vigorous. When Fraser paused for breath at one o'clock Riedesel himself, with a company of jägers and about 80 grenadiers, came up. He and Fraser decided to go a few miles farther, rest for the night, and go on at three the next morning. They camped within a short distance at Hubbardton.[46]

The careless Americans had thrown out no pickets. They were all together around their campfires cooking breakfast when Fraser and Riedesel.

whose Indians had scouted the American camp the night before, marched unobserved through the notch north of the camp. Close to the camp, they deployed their 750 men and charged upon the nearest body, Hale's New Hampshires.

The surprise was complete. Hale and his men fled in disorder, each man for himself. Warner and Francis had but a few minutes to get into fighting order, but they stood their ground and gave the enemy a volley that struck down 21 men. Major Grant of the 24th was killed, the Earl of Balcarres wounded. This was the opening of a bitter fight.[47]

The ground was all forest, covered with standing trees, fallen trees, and underbrush. For the Americans, it was the best of cover. For the British and Germans it was a tangle in which there could be no orderly fighting. Warner's men held the left of an irregular American line, with an extremely steep hill, called Zion, on their left. Francis had the right upon a smaller rise of ground. The whole line extended about half a mile.

Fraser moved to turn the American left, drawing men from his own left to strengthen his right. When he was ready he ordered his grenadiers to go over Zion Hill. It was an almost precipitous ascent. The grenadiers had to sling their muskets, grasp tree branches, bushes, and rocks, and scramble up on all fours. They made it and took a position behind Francis and astride the road to Castleton.[48]

But Francis had adopted Fraser's tactics in reverse. He edged towards the weakened British left. Some of Hale's men were now coming back to fight. The firing was heavy. Major Acland commanding the British grenadiers had been wounded. That movement of the grenadiers around Francis had yielded no good results. The situation for the British was worse than unpromising. In his desperation Fraser was about to order a bayonet charge when there broke on the ears of all the combatants a surprising sound of fifes and hautboys, trumpets and drums playing a German hymn, and of hundreds of lusty German voices singing it. It was the equivalent of the Scottish pipes at Lucknow. The Brunswicks were coming! [49]

Riedesel had heard the firing and had come on with the same advance guard as on the day before. The rest of his troops were following. At Castleton, St. Clair also had heard it. Two of his militia regiments, with their customary freedom from restraint, had dropped away from his marching men the night before and had encamped only two miles from Hubbardton. He sent them orders to go to the aid of Warner and Francis. They refused and hurried on to Castleton.[50]

Without waiting for the rest of his men, Riedesel sent his jägers straight against the American right. The grenadiers, he ordered to try to turn that flank. The jägers, with a band ahead playing as if on parade, marched boldly forward. Francis's troops held their ground for ten minutes, firing as fast as they could in reply to the Brunswickers' volleys. But the turning movement had begun to envelop their right. Francis was shot down, and when Fraser's bayonet charge developed, the Massachusetts men broke and disappeared in the woods. Warner and his Vermonters had been doing well, but when their companions retreated, they could hold out no longer. Warner gave the order, "Scatter and meet me at Manchester." His force at once evaporated. Twelve guns were taken by the enemy.[51]

There had been sharp fighting in that little forty-minute battle. The enemy lost 15 officers and 183 men, killed or wounded.[52] The American casualties, including those captured, were 12 officers and 312 men, out of a force which after Hale's defection did not much exceed 600 fighting men. Hale and about 70 of his men were captured in their retreat. Though of miniature dimensions, that battle was, in proportion to the numbers engaged, as bloody as Waterloo.

In the meantime, the American fleet was pursuing a leisurely course up the lake for Skenesboro. There was no hurry. There was behind them that boom of great logs strung along a massive chain made of inch-and-a-half iron bars. This was backed by a bridge supported by twenty-two piers of timber. Between these piers were floats fifty feet long and thirteen feet wide made of logs "fastened together by rivetted bolts and double chains." It would take some time to cut through that. Colonel Long, in command of the boats, was sure he had a day's start, so he wasted no effort on trying to block the extremely narrow and, in places, tortuous channel.[53]

But he was mistaken in his confidence in the boom. Immediately on the discovery of the retreat from Ticonderoga, British gunboats were brought up, "a few well directed cannon-shots broke in two the collossal chain upon which so many hopes had hung." [54] The bridge piers were cut through. Within a few hours after Long's boats had started, the British fleet was running before a northerly wind up the lake after them. Long's men had landed at Skenesboro at one o'clock. At three o'clock Burgoyne was within three miles of them.

He landed three regiments with orders to get across Wood Creek, a small stream on which Skenesboro was situated and a part of the water road to the south, flowing into the extreme upper end of Champlain just above the mouth of South Bay. They were also to occupy the road to Fort Ann, the only other avenue of retreat to the south. After waiting awhile to give time for this operation, Burgoyne went on with his fleet to attack Skenesboro.

Long, however, had wisely decided that the weak stockaded fort at that place was not tenable against the strong force of the enemy and had sent his invalids and women up the creek, with enough sound men to row the boats. With the rest, he set about destroying the fort. The stockade, the barracks, and other buildings were set on fire. Burgoyne arrived in time to capture the *Trumbull* galley and the schooner *Revenge*, but the *Enterprise*, the *Liberty*, and the *Gates* and everything else combustible that had been brought from Ticonderoga went up in flames. What would not burn was abandoned, and Long, with the remains of his soldiers, about 150, hurried away down the Fort Ann road.[55]

Assuming that the three regiments already sent forward had gained their desired positions to intercept Long's retreat, Burgoyne dispatched Lieutenant Colonel Hill with the 9th Regiment after him early the next morning. But the three regiments were so delayed in getting over a thickly forested ridge that Long got to Fort Ann without interruption. Hill, however, pushed on after him.[56]

The road was in dreadful condition, and its bridges had been broken down. Hill made only ten miles that day. He lay that night within a mile of the fort. Early the next morning an American came to the camp, announced himself as a deserter, and told Hill there was a garrison of a thousand in the fort. Hill had but 190 of all ranks. He sent to Burgoyne for reinforcements.

The "deserter" got away secretly and told Long of Hill's weakness. Long had, indeed, received an addition, 400 New York militiamen under Colonel Henry Van Rensselaer. He now turned on Hill, whose force lay in a narrow, heavily wooded space between Wood Creek and a steep, almost precipitous, rugged ridge.

There was no possibility of regular battle formation on either side. Parties of the Americans crossed the creek and fired on Hill's left, crossed it again, and gained his rear. Although their voices were audible, they were invisible. All he knew was that he seemed to be surrounded. He ordered his men up the steep slope that hemmed them in. With great difficulty they got up, faced about, and held the ridge for about two hours of fairly heavy fire on both sides. Hill's ammunition was running low. Nothing had been heard from Burgoyne. He was about at the end of his tether, when from the woods to the north he heard an Indian war whoop.[57]

The Americans heard it too. It meant to them the arrival of British reinforcements from Skenesboro, and they started for Fort Edward. But they were deceived: there were no Indians behind that war whoop, and only one Englishman, Captain Money. He had been sent ahead with a party of

Indians, who "either stood still or advanced very slow." He had therefore run ahead and tried his luck with that one wild outcry.[58]

When St. Clair, with his main force at Castleton, got word of the disasters at Skenesboro and Hubbardton, there was nothing to do but try to save the remains of his army. He turned to the east and, unmolested, took a straight road to Rutland. Thence, by a circuitous route, he got to Fort Edward on the 12th.[59]

CHAPTER 37

Bennington

While his advance troops under Fraser, Riedesel, and Hill were engaged with the Americans at Hubbardton and near Fort Ann, Burgoyne at Skenesboro was preparing to continue his southward march. He had the choice of two routes. He could return to Ticonderoga, get his boats over into Lake George, and march his army to Fort George at the head of that lake. Thence he could march by a tolerable road ten miles to the Hudson at a point a little above Fort Edward. This way, in his "Thoughts" on the war delivered to the King in February, he had declared to be "the most expeditious and commodious route to Albany."

The other way was up Wood Creek from Skenesboro to Fort Ann, thence by road sixteen miles to Edward. This route he had predicted would offer "considerable difficulties, the narrow parts of the river may be easily choked up and rendered impassable; and, at best, there will be necessity for a great deal of land-carriage for the artillery, provisions &c." [1] Yet he now chose that route.

The principal reason he gave for this choice was his fear of the harmful impression which "a retrograde motion is apt to make upon the minds both of enemies and friends." [2] But it is thought that his decision may have been the result of the advice of Philip Skene.

Skene, formerly an officer in the British army, had obtained grants of 34,000 acres of land at the head of Lake Champlain, had founded a colony there, Skenesboro, and engaged in divers industries, operating limekilns, forges, sawmills, and a shipyard, with much success. In 1775, when Ticonderoga was taken by Allen and Arnold and he was dispossessed, he managed to get to Canada. Now with Burgoyne, he acted as a general adviser on the state of the country, with which he was so well acquainted. Under such conditions, coupled with his personal characteristics—he was "a large, fine-looking person, with a pleasant countenance and affable deportment" [3] —he had much influence with the general. His reason for using his influence in favor of the Skenesboro route is believed to have been the fact that it would require the cutting of a road from his colony to the Hudson, which would be of very great value in the event of the recovery of his property after the war. At all events, for this reason or another, Burgoyne so decided.

He did, however, also decide to send his gunboats, his artillery, and his heavy stores in boats by way of Lake George to its head.[4] That lake being more than 200 feet higher than Champlain, its waters descended through the narrow gorge that connected the two in a series of falls and rapids against which boats could hardly be propelled. It was necessary to carry his bateaux and barges around by land about three miles, a difficult and slow operation.

From the 9th of July until the 25th, Burgoyne's right wing, his British troops, lay on the heights at Skenesboro; his left, the Germans under Riedesel, about ten miles away at Castleton, with Fraser's corps between.[5] The disposition of the German troops was intended to confuse the Americans as to the next move, whether down the Hudson or east to the Connecticut River country. The long delay at this time was caused by the activities of the Americans on the road to Fort Ann and so to Fort Edward.

Schuyler, in general command of the American northern army, had come up from Albany to Fort Edward; and thence on the 8th, as has been said, he had sent Van Rensselaer and his 400 New York volunteers to reinforce Long at Fort Ann. He had at his own post six or seven hundred Continentals and about 1,400 militia. With this puny force, he could not hope to cope with Burgoyne's army, more than three times as large and many more times as strong in fighting quality, equipment, and supplies.

The fort itself was a miserable affair, a dilapidated relic of the French and Indian War.[6] Schuyler wrote to Washington that he had often jumped his horse over the remains of its ramparts. It had some guns, but they lay about on the ground; there were no carriages to mount them. Its garrison, 100 men, was in a sad condition. Not only small, but discouraged by defeat, it was out of hand that its members committed "the most scandalous depredations" [7] on the countryside. It was so short of ammunition that there were but five musket cartridges for each man. If Burgoyne had sent

Fraser's light troops forward, without the encumbrance of artillery or wagon trains, he could easily have taken that pretense of a fort. The Americans had only one circumstance in their favor, the character of the country through which Burgoyne had to march, between Skenesboro and Fort Edward, and through which the British supplies and stores had to be carried, between Fort George, at the head of Lake George, and Fort Edward.

The roads connecting those points were mere traces cut through a primeval forest of enormous pines and hemlocks. They seldom ran straight for any considerable distance. Innumerable huge, fallen trees, "as plenty as lamp-posts upon a highway about London," [8] interrupted their course, and the roads swung around them in a succession of zigzags. The way from Skenesboro to Fort Edward ran in the valley of Wood Creek and, for the most part, close beside the stream. It crossed no fewer than forty deep ravines over which high and long bridges had been built. There were also numerous bogs and swamps. The spring had been unusually wet, and the rains still fell, so that the soil was saturated and the morasses were deep and wide. At one place, if the artillery and wagons were to be got through, it would be necessary to build a causeway or corduroy road two miles long. Such a country afforded opportunity for the creation of almost insurmountable impediments, and Schuyler started to create them.

He put a thousand axmen to work. They destroyed every bridge and dug ditches to carry water from the bogs so as to create new swamps. They felled trees along the Skenesboro road and the creek so that the trunks crossed them both from each side, the tops coming together in a stiff entanglement. The creek itself was choked by great rocks rolled down from its bordering hillsides.[9] He sent out other men to warn the few inhabitants to drive their cattle out of reach of the invaders, to remove or conceal their foodstuffs. They were even induced to burn their unharvested grain. The whole country within reach of the roads was reduced to desolation.

Even without this extraordinary destruction, the passage of the British army, its guns, and its wagons over the roads would have been most difficult. It was sadly short of draught cattle. Of the 1,500 horses Burgoyne had asked for in Canada, no more than 500 had been furnished. On his way, he had managed to commandeer 50 teams of oxen, an insufficient supplement.[10] And the Canadian country carts which he had were ramshackle affairs built of green wood and likely to fall apart under any heavy strain. Under these conditions, the roads in their usual state, and the frail bridges, would have been bad enough to daunt an invader. Now, and until all Schuyler's work had been undone, progress was impossible. But Burgoyne was not stopped.

Into that jungle of obstructions he sent hundreds of his men, expert Canadian axmen among them. Working under the most difficult conditions, tormented by millions of "moschetoes" and gnats—"punkies," the natives call them—in the stifling, sultry heat of the close woods, they hacked away at the trees, drained the bogs, rebuilt the bridges, and made that two-mile causeway. By July 25 he was able to leave Skenesboro and advance to Fort Ann. Four days he lay there while his men worked on the road ahead of him. At last on the 29th, three weeks from the day he landed at Skenesboro twenty-three miles away, he came to Fort Edward.[11]

In the meantime, Schuyler had been reinforced. The remains of St. Clair's force had come in on July 12, as has been stated. Long's detachment, from Ticonderoga, had arrived. Brigadier General John Nixon with 600 Continentals had come on from Peekskill. There were now nearly 2,900 Continental rank and file and more than 1,600 militia, present and fit, in and about the fort.[12] To support the general, who was disliked and distrusted by the New England troops, Washington had sent two Yankee major generals, Benedict Arnold of Connecticut and Benjamin Lincoln of Massachusetts. But even with these acquisitions Schuyler and his generals knew they could not hold that dilapidated fort. Leaving a small rear guard to take care of it until the enemy came, he fell back down the Hudson, first about five miles to Moses Creek, then to Saratoga; at last, on August 3, he reached Stillwater, twelve miles farther. Here Kosciuszko laid out the works of a defensive position, and entrenchment was begun. But within a few days Schuyler again withdrew twelve miles down the river to the mouth of the Mohawk.

The morale of the Connecticut troops was now at its lowest ebb. Continued retreats in the face of a continually advancing enemy, and their sad physical condition, were enough to undermine their confidence in themselves as well as in their leaders; but more active causes of discouragement were working among them. There was a growing belief, now really a fullgrown belief, that both Schuyler and St. Clair were not merely incompetent, but actually traitorous.

The most ridiculous of the stories bandied about in the camp was that Burgoyne had bought both generals by firing into Ticonderoga "silver balls," which had been gathered up by St. Clair and sent down to Schuyler: that explained the surrender of Ticonderoga and the subsequent evacuations and retreats. Absurd as the story was, the New Englanders, in their dislike of Schuyler as a New York aristocrat, seem to have believed it, or at least affected to do so. The plague of desertion, to which the American troops, especially the militia, were so subject throughout the war, became an epidemic. Two hundred men were missing between the 20th and 24th of July. By the 4th of August as many more had gone. Of the remaining 4,000, fully a third were Negroes, boys, or old men. And at that time Burgoyne was only a long day's march, twenty-four miles, from Stillwater.

After their slow and enormously difficult march from Skenesboro, the British troops were in high spirits. That terrible wilderness was behind them. Before them the Hudson, a sweetly flowing river, led to their grand objective, Albany. "They considered their toils to be nearly at an end; Albany to be within their grasp, and the adjacent provinces certainly reduced." [13] That they had to wait at Fort Edward for the big guns, the munitions and supplies, and the boats to be brought down from the head of Lake George meant nothing. For the rank and file the delay was a welcome vacation. For Burgoyne, however, this was a period of some anxiety. He was not so certain that his troubles were over. And he knew by August 3 that he could expect no help from Howe, unless Washington attempted to help Schuyler. Howe had written to him on July 17: "My intention is for Pennsylvania, where I expect to meet Washington, but if he goes to the northward contrary to my expectations, and you can keep him at bay, be assured I shall soon be after him to relieve you. . . . Success be ever with you." [14] The day that letter was written, Howe's troops were already aboard their transports bound for the Chesapeake. By the time Burgoyne received it, the fleet was south of the Delaware capes.

Burgoyne did not know that, of course; but one thing he did know—that Howe was carrying out the original plan and that Howe was not coming up the Hudson. There would be no meeting of the two forces at Albany during the campaign. In view of the obstacles still to be faced, might it not be wise to abandon the advance, turn about, and march back to Ticonderoga? It might be done safely enough, no doubt. But no. His orders were to march to Albany, and march he would. He put Howe's letter away, told no one about it, not even Riedesel. [15]

Major General Baron von Riedesel had for a long time been worrying about his horseless dragoons. [16] They were not proper foot soldiers. Their costume was sufficient evidence of that. Yet here they were in their stiff leather breeches, [17] their enormous cocked hats, clumping along day after day in their great, clumsy boots over the miscalled roads of this God-forsaken wilderness in a hell of heat, their spurs catching in the underbrush, the

ends of their long broadswords clattering over the stones, their heavy car-
bines, that might have been slung on their saddles, borne on their shoulders.
Something had to be done about it.

All along he had been urging Burgoyne to find mounts for them. He was
sure horses were to be had over in the Connecticut River valley. At Skenesboro he had proposed an expedition into that country by the dragoons and
the Tories of the army. Burgoyne had approved the plan, but had been too
busy with his arrangements for pushing on southward to do anything about
it. Now, at Fort Edward, the matter came up again, and Burgoyne and
Riedesel drew up the orders for the expedition. These were very specific
and very elaborate.

Lieutenant Colonel Baum, who could not "utter one word of English,"
was to lead the foray—a most unsuitable leader of an enterprise that was to
penetrate enemy country and enlist the services of English-speaking people.
Its objects and purposes were manifold. Baum was "to try the affections of
the people, to disconcert the councils of the enemy, to mount Riedesel's
dragoons, to compleat Peters's corps [of Tories] and to obtain large supplies of cattle, horses and carriages," specifically 1,300 horses, besides those
for the dragoons. They were to be "tied together by strings of ten each, in
order that one man may lead ten horses." To get this loot, he was to impose
taxes in kind upon the several districts and to hold "the most respectable
people" as hostages for their delivery. He was also to make prisoners of
"all persons acting in committees, or any officers acting under the directions
of Congress, whether civil or military." [18]

The country to be subjected to this drastic treatment extended from Manchester in the north through Arlington to Bennington in the south, and as
far east as the Connecticut River. The whole process was to be effected by
a force of 650 rank and file, made up of 170 dismounted Brunswick
dragoons, 100 German grenadiers and light infantry, 300 Tories, Canadians, and Indians, 50 of Fraser's British "marksmen," and a few artillerymen with two small fieldpieces.[19] In the orders, it was called "a
secret expedition." To help to preserve its secrecy, a German band of
musicians was included in the outfit. It seems not to have occurred to Burgoyne that sending such a force upon such an expedition was likely to result
in another retreat from Concord.

To assist Baum with advice and to help him "distinguish the good subjects from the bad," [20] Burgoyne added Colonel Philip Skene to the party.
His advice, given at a crucial moment, had much to do with the outcome of
the excursion.

Burgoyne knew that the remains of Colonel Seth Warner's regiment had gathered at Manchester in obedience to their commander's last order at Hubbardton; but he thought it "highly probable" that they would retreat before Baum. If they did not, he left it to Baum's discretion whether he should fight them or not, "always bearing in mind that your corps is too valuable to let any considerable loss be hazarded." But, besides Warner's men, there were others of whom the British and German generals were ignorant.

The country lying west of New Hampshire had long been claimed by that colony and by New York. It had been settled under grants of land made by the governor of New Hampshire and was therefore called the New Hampshire Grants. Its settlers, the Green Mountain Boys, had long defended their land titles against New York's pretensions. Now, in 1777, it had declared itself the independent State of Vermont and organized a Council of Safety as a preliminary to establishing a regular government. Threatened with invasion by Burgoyne, its council called on New Hampshire and Massachusetts for help.[21]

New Hampshire had already taken notice of the impending danger to itself and had proposed to raise troops for its own defense; but it was thinly settled and poor, so that the problem of the expense of an armed force seemed difficult of solution. It was solved by John Langdon, the speaker of the General Court. "I have," said he, "three thousand dollars in hard money. I will pledge my plate for three thousand more. I have seventy hogsheads of Tobago rum, which shall be sold for the most it will bring. These are at the service of the State. If we succeed in defending our homes, I may be remunerated; if we do not, the property will be of no value to me. Our old friend Stark, who so nobly sustained the honour of our State at Bunker's Hill, may be safely entrusted with the conduct of the enterprise, and we will check the progress of Burgoyne." [22] So goes an old, if not true, story.

John Stark had served in the French and Indian War as a captain in the famous Rogers' Rangers. He had instantly responded to the Lexington alarm, raising a regiment with which he gallantly and successfully defended the American left wing at Bunker's Hill. He had led a regiment to Canada in May, 1776, as a part of the force sent by Washington to succor the defeated American army. In the battles of Trenton and Princeton, he had fought courageously and effectively. He was a brave, a gallant soldier, experienced in warfare, and a great leader of men, with a colonel's commission dated January 1, 1776. Yet, when the politicians in the Congress, in April, 1777, appointed new brigadier generals, they jumped certain junior colonels over his head, as over Arnold's. A proud man, tenacious of his rights and jealous of his honor as a soldier, Stark then resigned his commission and retired to his farm in New Hampshire. But now, at the call of his state, he came forward.

Tall, straight, and sinewy as an Indian, his figure was that of a fighting man. His strong nose, high cheekbones, weathered countenance lit up by steady and piercing light blue eyes, the straight, set line of his thin lips all indicated a character in keeping with his figure. They indicated also that unyielding spirit which in his New England is sometimes characterized as "cantankerous." [23]

Yes, he would take command of the proposed new brigade, but on one condition; it was to be a New Hampshire brigade pure and simple, independent of the Congress and of the Continental army, accountable only to the General Court of the state. The Congress he heartily disliked. Schuyler, he both disliked and distrusted. He would have nothing to do with either. Those were his terms. It was a case of take him or leave him. They took him, commissioned him a brigadier general, and gave him power to direct his operations according to his own judgment.

The response of his fellow citizens to his call was immediate and beyond expectation. On July 18, the day after his commission was signed, 221 men enlisted; the next day, although it was Sunday, the rolls bore the names of 419. Within less than a week, the brigade numbered 1,492 officers and men, 10 per cent of all the enrolled voters in the state, old and young. They had no uniforms and brought their own muskets or fowling pieces.[24]

By July 30, Stark had his command sufficiently organized and equipped to march it to Charleston on the east side of the Connecticut River. In the first week of August, he crossed the river and took post at Manchester, Vermont, where Seth Warner's scattered Vermonters had come together again. Here he had his first and his decisive clash with Schuyler, that disliked and distrusted New York general.

Schuyler was willing that Warner's regiment should remain in Vermont while it was uncertain whether Burgoyne would go south by the Hudson or turn east into the Connecticut valley. He even reinforced Warner with some New England militia and sent Major General Lincoln over there to command them, but he wanted this new brigade of Stark's to strengthen his own weak army. Through Lincoln, he directed Stark to join him.[25]

Stark's reply was prompt and definite. He was, he said, a New Hampshire brigadier, responsible only to its General Court, and by it he had been given a free hand in the conduct of his brigade. No, he would not go to the Hudson on order of Schuyler or anyone else except the General Court of New Hampshire.[26] Lincoln reported this insubordination to the Congress, and it resolved to inform New Hampshire that its orders to Stark were "destructive of military subordination" and to request it to instruct Stark "to conform himself to the same rules which other general officers of the militia are subject to, whenever they are called out at the expence of the United States." [27] But, before that resolution reached New Hampshire, certain events had occurred that caused the Congress to pass other resolutions of a different tone.

On August 8, Stark marched his men twenty miles south to Bennington, where an important depot of American military supplies was situated, leaving Warner at Manchester with the remains of his regiment and 200 rangers whom he had gathered in since Hubbardton.

Three days later Baum's expedition started from Fort Miller, seven miles down the Hudson from Fort Edward.[28] Just as he was leaving, Burgoyne changed his orders. Instead of Manchester, his first objective was to be Bennington, of whose treasures in the way of supplies, cattle, and horses, Burgoyne had just received an exaggerated report.[29] He had also heard that the place was held only by three or four hundred militia. All this was very promising for the success of the enterprise.

After a march of four miles Baum camped on the Batten Kill, a little tributary of the Hudson. There 50 Brunswick jägers came up to be added to his force. On the 13th he marched through a notch in the ridge between Batten Kill and the Hoosic River and down to the village of Cambridge on the Owl Kill.

He had much trouble with his Indians. Preceding the main body, they ran wild, looting and destroying property, killing cows for the sake of their bells and so alarming the country that the inhabitants drove off their horses and cattle instead of leaving them where Baum might have picked them up. There were several light skirmishes with small parties of the local militia, but at Sancoick's—or Van Schaick's—mill on Owl Kill he had his first contact with the American organized troops.

Stark, hearing of the Indian depredations, had sent Colonel Gregg, with 200 men, against them. Gregg was now in posession of the mill.[30] At Baum's approach, the Americans fired one volley and retreated. Baum pursued them. They broke down a bridge, delaying the Germans and ensuring their own escape. Baum had learned that a force stronger than a few militia was at Bennington. He sent a letter back to Burgoyne, announcing the capture of flour, wheat, and potash at the mill, and telling him that fifteen to eighteen hundred rebels were in Bennington, but were "supposed to leave at our approach " He would "fall on the enemy to-morrow early." [31]

Stark, in the meantime, had heard that a strong enemy force was following the Indians, and had set out to rescue Gregg, having first called on Warner at Manchester to join him. About four miles west of Bennington, the opposing forces sighted each other and halted. Between them were the Walloomsac River and a bridge.[32] Baum did not seem disposed to attack, and so Stark withdrew two or three miles towards Bennington. Baum took a position on a height above the river.[33] Both forces bivouacked on the night of the 14th.

The 15th was rainy, and no move was made by either side, except that Baum disposed his troops to meet an expected attack. Stark, however, was reinforced by 400 Vermont militia, also a party from Berkshire County, Massachusetts, and some Stockbridge Indians. He had then about 2,000 men. Baum was strengthened by the arrival of 90 Tories under "Colonel" Pfister, a retired British lieutenant.[34] His force then numbered about 800.

The German dragoons and half of Fraser's contingent were posted on the steep hill where they had encamped, which looked down from a height of 300 feet upon the bridge half a mile away. Trees were felled to make breastworks and one of the two 3-pounders was mounted there. In some log cabins on both sides of the bridge the Canadians were stationed. On the hither side of the bridge the other half of Fraser's force and about 50 German infantrymen, with the other gun, took their stand. In a field southwest of the principal position 50 German foot soldiers and some Tories were supposed to guard the rear of that group. About 250 yards to the south and beyond the bridge 150 Tories were posted and threw up a breastwork. Southeast of the hilltop the 50 jägers were placed. The Indians were grouped on a plateau behind the main position. Having thus scattered his men as effectively as possible all over the landscape—some of the little detachments more than a half-mile from the others—Baum awaited Stark's move.

That move was concerted between Stark and Warner, who had come from Manchester in advance of his regiment. They made a rather elaborate plan. It involved complete encirclement of Baum's main position and simultaneous attacks on his front, rear, and flanks. It was carried out without a flaw.

About noon on the 16th, the rain having ceased, Colonel Moses Nichols with 200 New Hampshire men started on a long circuit to get around Baum's left. Colonel Samuel Herrick led 300 men, Vermont Rangers and Bennington militia, similarly to turn the German right. Colonel David Hobart and Colonel Thomas Stickney, with 200 men, were to go against the Tory position south of the bridge. A hundred more were to demonstrate against the front of the main position to divert Baum's attention. Stark was to hold the remaining twelve or thirteen hundred for the principal frontal attack, the signal for which was to be the first fire by Nichols and Herrick.[35]

(SHAFTSBURY)   (BENNINGTON)

ROAD TO BENNINGTON

Stark's Camp

Baum Buried

VERMONT
NEW YORK   STATE BOUNDARY

Col. Hobart

Col. Stickney

FORD

Col. Nichols

Gen. Stark

Indians

Col. Baum
Surrendered about noon

Col. Herrick

Indians

Little White Creek

Breymann turned back by Warner's Reg't

Stand Attempted by Stark

Walloomsac River

St. Lukes Bridge

MAP OF THE BATTLE OF BENNINGTON

NORTH

ONE ENGLISH STATUTE MILE
0   1/4   1/2   3/4   1

(WASHINGTON)
(RENSSELAER)
COUNTY BOUNDARY

Col. Breymann's Advance Aug. 16.

Hoosic River

The two encircling detachments made their way through the thick woods without discovery until they had nearly reached Baum's rear. Then the Germans saw several small, irregular bodies of shirt-sleeved farmers, with muskets or fowling pieces on their shoulders, but with no other military appearance, coming up behind them. At once, Baum bethought himself of the valuable advice which Skene, now absent from the camp, had been delegated to give him and had given him. The inhabitants of that countryside, Skene had said, were Tories five to one. On the march to Bennington, small groups dressed like these newcomers, had sifted in among Baum's men, protesting their loyalty to the King, and had been kindly received.[36] These others now approaching must also be friends, either seeking protection in his rear or prepared to assist him. He made no effort to keep them off. On the contrary he drew in his pickets so that they should not be molested.

By three o'clock Nichols and Herrick had gained satisfactory positions. Nichols opened fire, followed by Herrick. On hearing this signal Hobart and Stickney went into action against the Tories beyond the bridge. Stark mounted his horse and gave the order for the principal frontal attack. "See there, men!" he cried. "There they are! We'll beat them before night, or Molly Stark will be a widow." [37]

The Tories beyond the river put up a fight for a few minutes. The Americans waited until one volley had been fired against them and then, before the Tories could reload, rushed the breastworks. Its defenders retreated pellmell down into the little river and across it. The Canadians in the log cabins and the Indians on the plateau, yelling and jangling their stolen cowbells, simply fled at the first sound of the musketry. St. Luc La Corne, in command of the Indians, and Charles de Lanaudière, his son-in-law, in command of the Canadians led their contingents in headlong retreat. There was nothing left but the main position on that steep and high hill.

The attack on that position was fiercely made and stoutly met. The defenders, those Brunswick dragoons with their heavy rifles, the British marksmen, and such of the fugitives from the other posts as had joined them, stood off the encircling foes in the open ground in their rear with a steady fire. In front, the assailants scrambled up that high, steep hill, taking cover behind rocks and trees and firing at will so fast that their gun barrels burned their hands. Some of the New Hampshire militia crept up to within a dozen yards of the artillery and shot down the gunners. For two hours this hot fight went on—"the hottest I ever saw in my life" said Stark, and he had been through many. Then Baum's fire began to slacken; his ammunition was running low. When what was left of it, in a wagon, took fire and blew up, the fight seemed to be over. But it was not quite ended.

Though the rest of his command broke and fled, Baum's dragoons still stood by him. He called for their swords. They drew those fearful weapons to cut their way through their enemies. The Americans had no bayonets to oppose them. The dragoons made a steady, if lumbering, progress through the swarming Americans, the shirt-sleeved farmers who circled around, closed in, fell back, and closed in again; but when Baum fell, fatally wounded, his men gave up the fight.[38]

Now it seemed that nothing remained but to comb the woods for more prisoners and loot the German camp. But there was yet other work to be done. Baum had sent Burgoyne a second note on the evening of the 14th asking for reinforcements,[39] and Burgoyne had ordered Lieutenant Colonel Breymann, with 642 men and two fieldpieces, to march to Baum's support. They set out at eight o'clock in the morning of the 15th. The roads were deep with mud, and a hard rain was falling. The heavily uniformed and equipped Germans were notoriously slow in movement. They had twenty-five miles to go. In rigid, regular formation, halting frequently to re-dress their ranks, they progressed at the rate of half a mile an hour,[40] making only eight miles that day. A courier was sent forward to tell Baum that they were coming, and they bivouacked for the night.

The next day, the day of the battle, they crawled on at the same rate, to reach Sancoick's mill at half-past four, with six miles yet to go. There Breymann received vague and confused reports of the fight. A little later, Stark had word of Breymann's coming.

He had promised his men the spoils of victory, and they were scattered widely among the various enemy positions gathering up their plunder. He rallied as many as he could and sent them back along the road to delay Breymann.

Breymann, pushing on from Sancoick's mill, met the first party of Americans within a mile. It was merely a disorganized body of shirt-sleeved men carrying guns. Skene, who had gone back to meet Breymann, assured him that they were friendly Tories. But when they took a position behind a rail fence on a height by the road and fired a ragged volley, killing Breymann's horse, he had his doubts. He sent a detachment to dislodge them.[41]

From that time on, there was a series of such skirmishes. Three times the Americans took positions on the high ground north of the road, fired into the solid German column, and retreated when hard-pushed. But the Germans moved steadily, if slowly, forward.

Stark was in a bad way. His men were still scattered, still busy looting, and he could assemble only a small part of them. It seemed that he would have to give way and leave the field to the enemy. But Warner encouraged him to hold on.[42] Help was coming from Manchester. Before sunset it arrived.

The rest of Warner's regiment, 130 men led by Lieutenant Colonel Samuel Safford, and 200 rangers, had made a long day's march until midnight. They came on the next day, but slowly, halting to dry their muskets when the rain stopped, again to draw ammunition at Bennington, again to put aside their coats and knapsacks, again to receive a ration of rum, again to quench their thirst with water. But they came to the battlefield at last and went on to meet Breymann a mile or so beyond it.

By this time Stark had collected a good number of his men. He joined Warner. At first they took an unfortunate position in low, swampy ground devoid of cover; but after a few shots they withdrew to a wooded hill north of the road. Breymann attacked. He tried a flanking movement to turn the American right and began to gain ground. But half of Warner's men outflanked and checked the flankers. Meanwhile the rest of Warner's men, with Stark's troops, stretched out to threaten the Germans' right. The fight then went on face to face.

Breymann's two 6-pounders were active. The musketry was continuous and heavy. About sunset his men, who had carried forty rounds,[43] had almost exhausted their ammunition; but the American fire was still sustained. Breymann gave up, ordered a retreat. Many of the artillery horses had been shot. The rest were exhausted. The Germans abandoned their guns, and started west along the road in good order. Those that still had cartridges answered the shots of pursuing Americans. But their pace was slow. The enemy was on their flanks and at their heels, still relentlessly firing. The ordered ranks became confused in the haste to get away, broke up into a pushing, shoving disorder. In the gathering dusk, the retreat became a rout.

Some of the Germans threw down their muskets and ran. Others held them out, as if to surrender them. They dropped out, kneeled down, and cried for mercy. Breymann's drums beat a parley, a call to a conference for a surrender. But the untutored Americans did not know its meaning. To them it was just drums beating. They kept on shooting.

Breymann had been hit in a leg, and there were five bullet holes in his coat, but he held together a small rear guard, himself the last man, and so kept his men going in the increasing darkness. When it was quite dark, Stark called off the pursuit. Breymann, with less than two-thirds of his men, got away. "Had day lasted an hour longer," said Stark, "we should have taken the whole body of them." [44]

It was a notable little battle in that a body of farmers, for the most part entirely inexperienced in warfare, had so decisively beaten two forces of trained, professional soldiers. It is true that in the first fight Stark outnumbered Baum more than two to one; but that was not an overwhelming advantage when the experience and training of the Germans is considered. In the second the preponderance of the Americans in number was much less. Their lack of organization and their fatigue after hours of fighting reduced their advantage practically to zero.

Of the Germans, 207 were left dead on the field; about 700, including 30 officers, were captured. The spoils were rich: four brass fieldpieces, twelve drums, two hundred fifty broadswords, four ammunition wagons, and several hundred muskets and rifles. The Americans lost about 30 killed and 40 wounded.[45]

On October 4 the Congress unanimously voted its thanks to Stark and his men, and appointed him a brigadier general in the Continental army.[46]

Notes

CHAPTER 1

The best general accounts of the Anglo-American crises, 1763–1775, are to be found in Channing, III, Van Tyne, *C,* and Miller, *O.* Miller, *T,* is the most recent account of the period of the Revolutionary War.

1. Belcher, I, 134.
2. Frothingham, *S,* 6.
3. *Massachusetts Spy,* May 19, 1774. Frothingham, *S,* 6. A Boston Tory wrote to a friend in London: "You nor your friends must not imagine there was any honesty in those marks of joy these Bostonians showed the General on this occasion—no sir, it was hypocrisy all" (Force, 4, I, 299 n.).
4. For Gage's personality and career see Alden, *passim.*
5. For a brief discussion of the Sugar Act see Lecky, 55–58.
6. Bancroft, III, 77.
7. For the Stamp Act see MacDonald, 122–131.
8. Bancroft, III, 245.
9. Bancroft, III, 238.
10. MacDonald, 107.
11. Fiske, I, 82.
12. Frothingham, 299.
13. Grahame, IV, 328.
14. Ramsay, I, 129.
15. Frothingham, 305.

CHAPTER 2

1. Frothingham, *S,* 37; Bancroft, IV, 19; Force, 4, I, 669.
2. Gage was astonished at the support given the Bostonians indicating the solidarity of the colonies. "I find," he wrote in September, "they have some warm friends in New York and Philadelphia . . . that the people of Charleston are as mad as they are. . . . This province is supported and abetted by others beyond the conception of most people, and foreseen by none."
3. Bancroft, IV, 95.
4. Force, 4, I, 768. Cf. Trevelyan, I, 317.

5. Frothingham, *S*, 113; Stiles, I, 510–511.
6. Adams, *J*, 31.
7. Percy, 46; Barker, 12; Stiles, I, 503; Force, 4, I, 1041–1043, 1054; Gordon, I, 422.
8. Frothingham, *S*, 48; Stiles, I, 523; Gordon, I, 470.
9. Trevelyan, I, 258.
10. Force, 4, III, 1330.

CHAPTER 3

Fortescue and Curtis are very useful upon the make-up of the British army; French, *C*, and French, *F*, upon that of the American forces.

1. Stiles, I, 515; Barker, 13; Force, 4, II, 441; Frothingham, *S*, 46, 55; Murdock, *B*, 5; French, *F*, 89. Belcher, I, 151, mentions two other regiments, the 29th and 40th, but indicates in a table of the services of the various regiments that the 29th had its first service with Burgoyne in 1777, and the 40th at Long Island in 1776.
2. The regiments so raised bore the name of the colonel up to 1751, when George II gave them numbers. In 1782 they received the names of counties. Thus one such regiment was originally Greville's, then the 10th, then the Lincolnshire Regiment.
3. Smollett in *Humphry Clinker* pictures an officer who, having purchased an ensigncy, had risen in thirty years' service only to the rank of lieutenant, because he had no money to buy promotions.
4. Frothingham, *F*, 99, 102–103; Belcher, I, 249–252, 259. Belcher states that three British regiments were made up entirely of men who had been in prison.
5. Sydney, 346.
6. Belcher, I, 251–252.
7. Belcher, I, 281–282.
8. Belcher, I, 322–325; Lefferts, 148–168. Lefferts's plates show crossbelts, but Fortescue, III, 542, says that it was not until after the return of the army from America that the waist belt was transferred to the right shoulder, thus originating the crossbelt, and Belcher, I, facing 323, shows the infantryman before 1783 with one shoulder belt and after that date the crossbelts.
9. Fortescue, III, 543; Sawyer, 93.
10. Sawyer, 100.
11. Trevelyan, I, 211.
12. Sawyer, 98–100; French, *C*, 28 n.
13. French, *C*, 32–35, citing Bland's *Treatise on Military Discipline* (London, 1753), the British manual of 1764, and Timothy Pickering's *Easy Plan of Discipline for a Militia* (Salem, 1775).
14. French, *F*, 34.
15. For the history of Massachusetts militia and the minutemen see French, *F*, 32–46, and the numerous citations; also *D.A.H.*, III, 413, and French, *C*, 17. The term "minutemen" goes back at least to 1756, when a company of Massachusetts soldiers called themselves "Minnit men." French, *F*, 33.
16. French, *F*, 41 and note, telling of the participation of the alarm companies in the fight at Concord.
17. Adams, *J*, 65–66. A recent apologist (Anderson, 76) for General Howe's conduct of the war attributes the lack of success of his frontal attack at Bunker Hill to the fact that "the men who lined the parapet . . . carried rifles, for the most part, instead of muskets . . . the rifle was vastly superior to the musket in precision. The men who used it on this occasion had acquired their proficiency in the hunting field." Which, he says, "the British command apparently failed to realize." The "fact" was not realized, because it was not a fact. There were no riflemen in the American troops in Massachusetts at that time, nor were there any until July–August, 1775, when 1,400 of them from Pennsylvania, Maryland, and Virginia, under Thompson, Cresap, and Morgan, joined Washington at Cambridge. Before that time, it is quite possible that there was not one rifle in

all Massachusetts (French, *C*, 28). The lack of rifles in New England could be deduced from the fact that, although between 1600 and 1800 many gunsmiths were making muskets in that territory, a single rifle maker is known to have been north of Pennsylvania prior to 1783 (Sawyer, 153–157, 216–219).

18. Sawyer, 132–136.

CHAPTER 4

This account of the affair at Lexington has been drawn from the many sources individually cited below. A complete reconciliation of discrepancies has been impossible—for instance, between the blindly patriotic Coburn and the more broad-minded French and Murdock, and between the monographs of Elias Phinney and Ezra Ripley, champions respectively of Lexington and Concord in the great dispute between the two towns in 1825 for the honor of having been the scene of the first "battle" of the war. In that contest the affidavits of many survivors of April 19, 1775, taken at a later time were marshaled, their recollections differing in many respects from the statements of the ninety-eight survivors of the day whose affidavits were taken by the Provincial Congress within the week following the 19th. These may be found in Force, 4, I, 486–501. The truth is often not easily found.

1. French, *C*, 39.
2. Trevelyan, I, 331–333.
3. Barker, 27–28; French, *C*, 41.
4. French, *C*, 51–52; Coburn, 15.
5. Barker, 29.
6. French, *C*, 65.
7. French, *C*, 66.
8. French, *C*, 75.
9. Coburn, 17; Stedman, I, 119; Frothingham, *S*, 59.
10. Phinney, 15; Ripley, 11; Coburn, 18.
11. Coburn, 22–24; French, *C*, 77–80. The lanterns were seen by British soldiers in Boston. They found the sexton of the church and arrested him, but let him go when he denied all knowledge as to who had displayed them. Pulling, disguised as a sailor, escaped from Boston in a fishing boat to Nantucket and was careful not to return until the British had left (Coburn).
12. French, *C*, 69–70; Murdock, 22. Why a major of marines was detailed to lead a detachment of infantry is a mystery. It is said, without definite authority, that it was because he was familiar with the roads to Concord and had studied the town in disguise. (French, *C*, 70.)
13. Stiles, I, 575, says 600 officers and men; Barker, 31, says "about 600"; Evelyn, 53, says "near 700"; Gordon, I, 477, says 800, "the flower of the army." According to French, *C*, 73, the last is generally accepted by American historians; but Murdock, 48 n., thinks 600 the proper number.
14. French, *C*, 100–101; Coburn, 19; Barker, 31–32; Force, 4, I, 360–364. It seems probable that the march from Lechmere began at one o'clock, to give time to reach Lexington at sunrise (Murdock, 50).
15. Coburn, 30–31; French, *C*, 90–91; Phinney, 16.
16. Coburn, 24–29; French, *C*, 91–94.
17. Coburn, 47–57; French, *C*, 102.
18. Coburn, 60; French, *C*, 95–96.
19. Coburn, 61; French, *C*, 97.
20. French, *C*, 107.
21. French, *C*, 95–99. Heath, 6, says: "This company standing so near to the road, after they had certain notice of the advancing of the British in force, was but a too much braving of danger; for they were sure to meet with insult, or injury which they could not repel. Bravery, when called to action, should always take the strong ground on the basis of reason."
22. Coburn, 63. As to the weather see Murdock, 55, quoting a contemporary diary.

23. Stiles, I, 604–650. Lieut. Barker, who was with Pitcairn, says (p. 32) the Americans "fired one or two shots, upon which our Men without any orders rushed in upon them, fired and put 'em to flight."
24. Barker, 32; Murdock, 24, 39.
25. Stiles, I, 604–605.
26. Murdock, 22.
27. Murdock, 37.

CHAPTER 5

In the main, the story of Lexington and Concord follows two excellently documented accounts. Coburn's *The Battle of April 19, 1775,* is an exhaustive study of both original and secondary materials. It is full of detail and is copiously annotated. French's *The Day of Concord and Lexington* is more discursive, less intimately factual, but is very valuable for its more impartial and less chauvinistic viewpoint. Besides these, the journals and letters of Stiles, Barker, Evelyn, Mackenzie, and Percy, the accounts of Ripley, Phinney, and Reynolds, Frothingham's *History of the Siege of Boston,* and the affidavits and letters, especially the letter of Rev. William Gordon, published in Force, 4, II, have been carefully studied. Murdock's *The Nineteenth of April, 1775,* is an illuminating discussion of the day's events, viewed with detachment and a healthy incredulity as to many generally accepted beliefs concerning certain aspects of the conflict, although his arguments seem at times to be rather casuistic.

1. Coburn, 32–46.
2. French, *C*, 149–151, 156. Rev. William Emerson was the grandfather of Ralph Waldo Emerson and the builder of Hawthorne's Old Manse.
3. Ripley, 21; Frothingham, *C*, 179.
4. French, *C*, 152, map.
5. French, *C*, 156–158.
6. French, *C*, 161.
7. Barker, 32; Stedman, I, 117.
8. French, *C*, 163. Emerson's diary is owned by the Emerson family. French obtained a copy of it; the quotations herein are drawn from his book.
9. French, *C*, 164; Reynolds, 17; Coburn, 75; Ripley, 16.
10. French, *C*, 164–165; Ripley, 17.
11. French, *C*, 177; Coburn, 77; Ripley, 19.
12. French, *C*, 167–182; Coburn, 77; Ripley, 19–20.
13. French, *C*, 186–187; Coburn, 81; Ripley, 18.
14. Coburn, 82–83; French, 187–190.
15. Barker, 34.
16. Barker, 34.
17. French, *C*, 191, 201 n.; Coburn, 84–85; Barker, 35.
18. French, *C*, 207–209; Coburn, 85, 88; Ripley, 28.
19. Coburn, 93; French, *C*, 217. At the bridge, after the fight, occurred one of the most lamentable incidents of the day. A half-grown boy, armed only with a hatchet, hastening after the Americans, found a severely wounded British soldier struggling to his knees. Conceiving it to be his duty to kill the enemy, the boy sank the hatchet in the skull of the wounded man. When Parsons's men came that way from Barrett's place, they found the dead man, his head covered with blood, and reported that he had been scalped and his ears cut off. The story spread; Gage published it; it got to England; and, though the true story was soon made known, the false one persisted. Stedman in his history (I, 119), published in 1794, wrote: 'Several of Smith's party were scalped by the Americans." In 1841, Adolphus in his history wrote that "several were scalped or had their ears cut off by the Americans" (French, *C*, 211–214). And even as late as 1911 Fortescue (III, 153) wrote that "a few of the dead and wounded had been scalped by some rough Americans at the bridge."

20. Coburn, 96–97, Supplement, 14–38.
21. Coburn, 98; French, *C*, 219.
22. French, *C*, 219.
23. Force, 4, II, 359.
24. Barker, 35. A British soldier wrote to his family, "They did not fight us like a regular army, only like savages" (Force, 4, I, 440).
25. French, *C*, 222; Coburn, 107. The pistols are preserved by the Lexington Historical Society.
26. Barker, 35.
27. French, *C*, 224.
28. French, *C*, 224.
29. Coburn, 114.
30. French, *C*, 226–227.
31. Percy, 49; Mackenzie, I, 19. Murdock, 47 n., thinks they were not more than 900.
32. French, *C*, 229 n. Percy had a low opinion of the colonials. He wrote home (Percy, 31, 35, 52): "The people here are a set of sly, artful, hypocritical rascalls, cruel & cowards. . . . I cannot but despise them completely. . . . Such a set of timid creatures I never did see." A similar opinion was general among the British officers in America before Bunker Hill. Captain Glanville Evelyn about this time wrote to his father that he believed "there does not exist so great a set of rascals and poltroons" (Evelyn, 27).
33. Coburn, 116–120; French, *C*, 230.
34. Percy, 50.
35. Mackenzie, I, 19.
36. Barker, 35.
37. Stedman, I, 118.
38. Mackenzie, I, 20.
39. Percy, 50.
40. Coburn, 133–134; Trevelyan, I, 335.
41. Barker, 36. On p. 39 Barker states that the British soldiers on the 19th, "tho' they shew'd no want of courage, yet were so wild and irregular, that there was no keeping 'em in order . . . the plundering was shamefull; many hardly thought of anything else; what was worse they were encouraged by some Officers." Mackenzie, I, 21–22, confirms the forcing of houses, killing, and plundering, but says the officers tried to stop the looting.
42. Heath, 7–8, says he did form one regiment in Lexington, "which had been broken by the shot from the British field-pieces"; but there seems to be little or no evidence that they continued to operate as a unit.
43. Coburn, 150–154; Mackenzie, I, 21. Lieutenant Barker, 36, says of the change in route that it threw the colonials off the scent.
44. Percy, 50; French, *C*, 255 n.; Coburn, 157–160.
45. Heath, 11.
46. Percy, 53.
47. Barker, 37.
48. Evelyn, 53.

CHAPTER 6

1. Force, 4, II, 363–370; French, *F*, 23–24; Jones, I, 39–40. Gage sent a ship to England with the news of Lexington and Concord. Within a week after the battle the Committee of Safety gathered the depositions of ninety-two Americans, one British officer, and two privates, prisoners, all of whom had taken part in the hostilities. The gist of the affidavits was that the British had fired first at both places (the officer could not say who had begun it at Lexington, but admitted the charge as to Concord). A letter was written to "The Inhabitants of Great Britain," giving the story of the day, briefly describing "the ravages of the Troops," protesting against the measures pursued by the British government, but declaring that "they have not yet detached us from our Royal Sovereign." This,

with the depositions, was dispatched in a light, fast vessel belonging to Richard Derby of Salem and commanded by his son John. Although it sailed four days after Gage's ship, it carried only ballast and it reached England twelve days sooner.

The news flew about London. The King refused to believe "an American newspaper," the *Essex Gazette*, which went along with the other papers. The ministry announced that there was no such official news. Nevertheless, the American report obtained wide credence, and though Gage's dispatches, when they arrived, minimized the affair as much as possible all England knew that a war was on, and that it would take more than Gage's little army to fight it. (Force, 4, III, 437–438; 489–501, 945; French, *F*, 131, 313–316.)

2. Bancroft, IV, 170; French, *F*, 83. Romantic though this story about Putnam be, it is generally accepted by other historians, of cooler blood than Bancroft. For the disturbance in New York, see Jones, I, 39–41.
3. Bancroft, IV, 170.
4. French, *F*, 31, 50, 52, 62; Bancroft, IV, 170; Force, 4, II, 378–379, 384, 446–447.
5. Force, 4, II, 765; Heath, 11.
6. Force, 4, II, 1145; French, *F*, 77–78.
7. Force, 4, II, 655; Bancroft, IV, 174.
8. Force, 4, II, 411; Bancroft, IV, 174–175; French, *F*, 85.
9. French, *F*, 66, 72.
10. Frothingham, *S*, 99; French, *F*, 86.
11. Gordon, I, 492; Force, 4, II, 1122, 1142.
12. Gordon, I, 492; Force, 4, II, 820; French, *F*, 179–182.
13. French, *F*, 184; Barker, 50–52.
14. Heath, 10; French, *F*, 183; Barker, 50–52.
15. Force, 4, II, 370–814. French, *F*, 123–124; Frothingham, *S*, 93–96; Barker, 38, 44; Stiles, I, 541.
16. Lushington, 50, 52; Barker, 38. Burgoyne wrote that the fresh provisions smuggled into the town "were of great consequence to the health and spirits both of army and inhabitants; the former live entirely on salt meat, and I hardly dare to guess how some of the latter live at all" (Fonblanque, 151).
17. French, *F*, 188–189; Barker, 48–49; Frothingham, *S*, 108; Barker, 49.
18. French, *F*, 190–191; Frothingham, *S*, 109.
19. Force, 4, II, 719; French, *F*, 191–193; Frothingham, *S*, 109–110; Barker, 50–53.
20. Barker, 38–41; French, *F*, 163–166; Harris, 51.
21. This enumeration of regiments may not be exactly correct. There has not been found a complete list of an official character. This one has been made up by comparing statements in Fortescue, Belcher, Murdock, *B*, Drake, Swett, Clarke, and others. Swett includes the 14th Regiment, but without support elsewhere except that Drake mentions "One officer of that regt a volunteer" as having been killed at Bunker Hill and one wounded who may have been on detached service. There were but three companies of the 18th and six companies of the 65th. These were combined into an Incorporated Corps. Careful calculations in Murdock, *B*, 7, and French, *F*, 737–739, seem to fix the number correctly between 6,340 and 6,716, not including officers.
22. Partridge, *passim*; Wilkin, 6–24; French, *F*, 195–198; Trevelyan, I, 308. Anderson, *T*, *passim*, gives a more favorable estimate of Howe's military ability.
23. Wilkin, 46–73; French, *F*, 198–199.
24. Hudleston, *passim*; French, *F*, 199–200; Fonblanque, 136–159.
25. Force, 4, II, 968–970.
26. French, *F*, 204, quoting London *Evening Post*, July 18, 1775.

CHAPTER 7

The material for a story of the capture of Ticonderoga and Crown Point is to be found mainly in original documents printed in Force's *American Archives*, 4th Series, Vol. II, and in *Conn. Hist. Soc. Colls.*, Vol. I. Allen French's *The First Year of the Revolution* and *The Taking of Ticonderoga in 1775* give well supported accounts of the expedition and its results. Arnold's *Life of Benedict Arnold* and Pell's *Ethan Allen* are valuable secondary sources.

1. Greene, FV, 101; French, *F*, 143.
2. D.A.H., V, 268; Pell, 74.
3. Force, 4, II, 243–244; French, *F*, 145–146; Pell, 72. Carleton had in Canada only two regiments of infantry and two companies of artillery; these were widely scattered. French, *F*, 147 n.
4. Pell, *passim;* D.A.B., I, 185; Lossing, I, 180; Tyler, II, 229; French, *F*, 148–149; Irving, 1, 442–443.
5. Arnold, 36.
6. French, *F*, 149–150.
7. Force, 4, II, 450.
8. Force, 4, II, 485, 750.
9. Van Doren, 145–150; Arnold, 17–29.
10. *Conn. Hist. Soc. Colls.* I, 165–169, 181; Chittenden, 100; Force, 4, II, 556, 557; Dawson, I, 32. The committee says they had 70 men from Massachusetts and 140 from the New Hampshire Grants. Other reports make the force 40–50 and 100; but Mott's letter to the Massachusetts Provincial Congress indicates that there were 170 in all.
11. Philip Skene, an officer in Amherst's army of 1759, had obtained a grant of 30,000 acres at the head of navigation of Lake Champlain and had established there a considerable settlement, with a great stone house, mills, docks, and stores (Pell, 90–91).
12. Pell, 79–80; Force, 4, II, 558; *Conn. Hist. Soc. Colls.*, I, 119, 179.
13. Dawson, I, 23; Lossing, I, 124; *Conn. Hist. Soc. Colls.*, I, 171–172.
14. Force, 4, II, 558; *Conn. Hist. Soc. Colls.*, I, 172.
15. Force, 4, II, 557, 734; *Conn. Hist. Soc. Colls.*, I, 165 ff.; Pell, 81; Gordon, II, 12. Allen French (French, I, 28), who has made a special study of this expedition, is inclined to believe that Arnold did secure joint command with Allen.
16. Pell, 82; Force, 4, II, 1086. French, *T*, 151, says there were nearly 300 men at the cove.
17. Pell, 83; Dawson, I, 34. A different report as to what happened after they landed on the beach may be found in two letters to newspapers that are reprinted in Force, 4, II, 1086–1087. James Easton in the first letter described the affair without even mentioning Arnold's name. "Veritas" wrote to another paper that, instead of two boats, there was but one, in which "Colonel Arnold with much difficulty persuaded 40 men to embark with him"; then he sent it back for "near 50" others. When they landed "some gentleman" proposed "to wait open day. This Colonel Arnold strenuously opposed and urged to storm the fort immediately, declaring he would enter it alone, if no man had courage to follow him. This had the desired effect. . . . Colonel Arnold was the first that entered the fort." Pell (p. 104) thinks "Veritas" was Benedict Arnold himself.
18. Pell, 83–84.
19. Pell, 84–85; Force, 4, II, 623, 624–625.
20. Lossing, I, 125. It is interesting to note that Allen's words have been taken as evidence of his orthodox theological beliefs, whereas, in fact, he was a confirmed deist. Did he use them?
21. Force, 4, II, 556. Pell, 90, preserves the original spelling.
22. Force, 4, II, 557.
23. Pell, 92–93; Force, 4, II, 584.
24. Force, 4, II, 584, 645, 686, 734; Pell, 95–96; French, *F*, 153.
25. Force, 4, II, 645, 693, 734, 839, 840; Pell, 96–99.
26. Force, 4, II, 693, 714–715.
27. Force, 4, II, 892.
28. *Journals*, II, 55–56.
29. Force, 4, II, 732–735. 847. 892. 1066; French, *F*, 154.

30. Force, 4, II, 605–606, 623–624, 705, 706, 711, 713, 715, 719, 720, 721, 730, 735–737, 808, 869, 944, 1382; *Journals*, II, 74.
31. Force, 4, II, 1539, 1593, 1596, 1598, 1649.
32. Force, 4, II, 646.

CHAPTER 8

1. Frothingham, *S*, 114 n. "Elbow-Room" clung to him as a nickname. When he came to Boston as a prisoner after Saratoga, it is said, an old woman in the crowd cried out: "Make way! Make way! The General's coming! Give him elbow-room!"
2. Dawson, I, 66–68.
3. Force, 4, II, 1354; Frothingham, *S*, 116.
4. Frothingham, *C*, 14–15; Frothingham, *S*, 119–120; Ellis, 12; Swett, 16.
5. Ellis, 17; Frothingham, *C*, 10; Martyn, 117–119. Swett (p. 15) gives a graphic picture of this council, which he describes as "Gen. Putnam's statement to his son." He represents Ward and Warren as objecting because "the enterprize would lead to a general engagement." To which Putnam answered that they would risk only 2,000 men and "defend ourselves as long as possible, and, if driven to retreat, . . . every stone wall shall be lined with their dead, and at the worst, suppose us surrounded and no retreat, we will set our country an example of which it shall not be ashamed." Warren, it seems, "walked the floor, leaned on his chair, 'Almost thou persuadest me, Gen. Putnam,' said he, 'but I still think the project rash.'" Pomeroy, to the objection as to the lack of powder, answered that he "would fight the enemy with but five cartridges apiece." Putnam said of him that he was used to going out with three charges of powder and bringing home "two and sometimes three deer." Putnam and Pomeroy were much alike in their disregard of all the basic rules of warfare.
6. Martyn, 91; French, *F*, 49, 83.
7. Tarbox, 320–322; Field, 221–222; *D.A.B.*, XI, 281; Humphreys, *passim*; French, *F*, 214.
8. Swett, 19; Frothingham, *S*, 167; Martyn, 119.
9. Frothingham, *W, passim*; Bancroft, IV, 230; French, *F*, 120.
10. Frothingham, *S*, 121–122; Frothingham, *C*, 16–17; Swett, 15–16; Dawson, I, 71.
11. Swett, 16; Ellis, 22; Frothingham, *S*, 122; Dawson, I, 51, 71.
12. Frederic Kidder, *The History of New Ipswich* (1852), 95.
13. Dawson, I, 52; Frothingham, *S*, 122–123; Coffin, 31.
14. Frothingham, *S*, 123, 393–395; Ellis, 23; Swett, 20. The Committee of Safety afterwards stated that Breed's Hill was fortified "by some mistake," which was certainly not the case. It was the deliberate choice of the officers.
15. Frothingham, *S*, 135; Swett, 20.
16. Swett, 21; Ellis, 26; Frothingham, *S*, 124–125.
17. Frothingham, *S*, 125; Ellis, 27–28; Heath, 12; Force, 4, II, 1093.
18. French, *F*, 216; Coffin, 9.
19. Swett, 22; Murdock, *B*, 3, 12–14.
20. Stiles, I, 595; Frothingham, *S*, 126; Ellis, 28.
21. French, *F*, 217.
22. Frothingham, *S*, 127; Swett, 23.
23. Trevelyan, I, 353; French, *F*, 219; Ellis, 23; Swett, 22.
24. Frothingham, *S*, 128; Swett, 24–25; Ellis, 31.
25. Swett, 28; French, *F*, 217–218; Ellis, 31; Heath, 11; Frothingham, *S*, 130 n.
26. Murdock, *B*, 10–11; French, *F*, 220–221; Swett, 23; Ellis, 29–30; Fortescue, III, 158; Trevelyan, I, 353.
27. Murdock, *B*, 11–12; French, *F*, 222.
28. French, *F*, 222.
29. Murdock, *B*, 15–17; French, *F*, 740. Stedman, I, 128, says they carried three days' provisions.

30. Frothingham, *S*, 131; Force, 4, II, 1093; Trevelyan, I, 352.
31. Ellis, 33; Frothingham, *S*, 131.
32. French, *F*, 225; Ellis, 34.
33. Coffin, 16; Swett, 26; Ellis, 31; Dearborn, 16.
34. French, *F*, 225–226; Frothingham, *S*, 132; Dearborn, 17; Frothingham, *C*, 33.
35. Frothingham, *S*, 134, 390; French, *F*, 219; Drake, 17; Coffin, 17; Swett, 26–27; Force, 4, II, 1094.
36. Frothingham, *S*, 134–135; Coffin, 11, 17; French, *F*, 227.
37. French, *F*, 227–228, 741–742.
38. This disposition of the forces in the various parts of the defense is made by Frothingham, *S*, 135–136. He admits that there is no certainty as to its correctness. Some of the troops mentioned may have arrived on the field after the action began. Some regiments were dispersed in companies or smaller parties in all parts of the defenses. The disposition here shown can be only a more or less close approximation of the facts.
39. Frothingham, *S*, 136.
40. Irving, I, 475; Ellis, 38; French, *F*, 225; Frothingham, *S*, 133.
41. Ellis, 37; French, *F*, 229; Frothingham, *S*, 133.
42. Murdock, *B*, 21; French, *F*, 231.
43. Murdock, *B*, 22–23; Force, 4, II, 1089; French, *F*, 231. Landing parties also set fire to some of the houses. Force, 4, II, 1376.
44. French, *F*, 234.
45. Frothingham, *S*, 137.
46. Frothingham, *S*, 138–140; French, *F*, 234; Swett, 290.
47. French, *F*, 233–234; Murdock, *B*, 24–26; Belcher, I, 196.
48. French, *F*, 234–235; Murdock, 27. Stedman, I, 128, says the British carried 125 pounds per man.
49. Murdock, *B*, 27.
50. Dawson, I, 66–67, quoting Burgoyne's letter of June 25, 1775, to Lord Stanley. Fonblanque, 155, contains a letter to Stanley much the same in substance but strikingly different throughout.
51. Force, 4, II, 1098; Belcher, I, 196–197.
52. French, *F*, 237; Coffin, 12; Drake, 32.
53. French, *F*, 238; Belcher, I, 174; Frothingham, *S*, 141.
54. Frothingham, *S*, 142–143.
55. French, *F*, 239.
56. Frothingham, *S*, 146.
57. Frothingham, *S*, 389–391.
58. Frothingham, *S*, 147; French, *F*, 244.
59. Force, 4, II, 1662.
60. French, *F*, 243.
61. French, *F*, 243.
62. French, *F*, 247.
63. Drake, 28.
64. Frothingham, *S*, 150; French, *F*, 249; Drake, 28.
65. Frothingham, *S*, 150–151.
66. French, *F*, 250.
67. Coffin, 13, 14, 19, 30.
68. French, *F*, 252; Frothingham, *S*, 152.
69. Frothingham, *S*, 153, 210; French, *F*, 255.
70. Clarke, 5 n.; Frothingham, *S*, 152; French, *F*, 261.
71. Clarke, 13; Percy, 56; Trevelyan, I, 359; Force, 4, II, 1098.
72. Frothingham, *S*, 193; French, *F*, 263.
73. Fonblanque, 157; French, *F*, 218, 240; Frothingham, *S*, 138, 146, 152, 185; Swett, 36. Reports as to the number of guns vary between two small brass and six iron fieldpieces; five cannon and six swivel guns; six fieldpieces. The last is probably correct.

74. Force, 4, II, 1097.
75. Frothingham, *S*, 154.

CHAPTER 9

1. *Journals*, II, 79, 84, 85, 89, 91.
2. Adams, *L*, 65; Adams, *J*, II, 415.
3. Fitzpatrick, III, 292–293.
4. *Journals*, II, 97, 103.
5. *Journals*, II, 100–101.
6. Adams, *L*, 59, 70.
7. Jones, I, 55–57; Force, 4, II, 1318.
8. Force, 4, II, 1084–1085; Fitzpatrick, III, 302–304.
9. Fitzpatrick, III, 320.
10. See notes of contemporaneous references to assumption of command in French, *F*, 299.
11. Force, 4, II, 1472–1473.
12. Fitzpatrick, III, 371, 374.
13. French, *F*, 300.
14. Reed, I, 243.
15. Graydon, 147–148.
16. Fitzpatrick, III, 339, 357, 362.
17. French, *F*, 300.
18. Fitzpatrick, III, 325, 387, 389, 404, 415, 422, 445, 511; Frothingham, *S*, 891; *Conn. Hist. Soc. Colls.*, II, 254.
19. Fitzpatrick, III, 308; Force, 4, II, 1625, 1629.
20. Fitzpatrick, III, 355–356.
21. French, *F*, 301.
22. This survey of the early commissariat has been derived from the study of it by Victor L. Johnson.
23. *Journals*, II, 100.
24. Fitzpatrick, III, 324, 409.
25. Fitzpatrick, V, 192.
26. *Journals*, II, 89, 104, 173; Bancroft, IV, 247–248; *Pennsylvania*, I, 3–5.
27. Thacher, 31; Gordon, II, 68; Frothingham, *S*, 228 n. Their shirts are variously described as white, ash-colored, and brown.
28. Sawyer, 34–37, 80, 144–153.
29. Fitzpatrick, III, 367; Reed, I, 117.
30. *Pennsylvania*, I, 9–10.
31. French, *F*, 472.
32. See letters to Congress and the colonies in Fitzpatrick, III and IV, especially IV, 288; Reed, I, 118, 119.
33. French, *F*, 272 n.; Trevelyan, I, 406.
34. French, *F*, 321.
35. Frothingham, *S*, 316, 331.
36. Frothingham, *S*, 224–230; *Pennsylvania*, I, 21.
37. Frothingham, *S*, 226–227, 230–231.
38. Fitzpatrick, III, 453.
39. Frothingham, *S*, 234; French, *F*, 481; *Pennsylvania*, I, 6.
40. French, *F*, 482–483; Frothingham, *S*, 265, 267; Fitzpatrick, IV, 118; Barker, 66; Evelyn, 74–75; Moore, I, 166–167.
41. Trevelyan, I, 408.
42. Sparks, *L*, I, 156.
43. Fitzpatrick, III, 483–484.
44. Fitzpatrick, III, 511; Force, 4, III, 767–768.
45. *Journals*, III, 273–274.
46. Force, 4, III, 1153; Frothingham, *S*, 257.
47. Fitzpatrick, III, 505–513.

48. *Journals*, III, 265–266.
49. *Journals*, III, 321–323.
50. French, *F*, 365–366; Force, 4, III, 263–266, 354; *Journals*, II, 189.
51. French, *F*, 364, 370; Force, 4, II, 1118.
52. Force, 4, III, 1416; Fitzpatrick, III, 467.
53. French, *F*, 371–375; *Journals*, III, 278–279, 486.
54. Frothingham, *S*, 261, 269, 272, 289, 308; French, *F*, 370–372, 497; Evelyn, 72–73. For particulars of many captures, see the index to Fitzpatrick, IV, under the names of captains.
55. Trevelyan, I, 385.
56. French, *F*, 533–534.
57. Evelyn, 67.
58. Trevelyan, I, 386.
59. Frothingham, *S*, 281–282; French, *F*, 534–535.
60. French, *F*, 533, 536; Frothingham, *S*, 280, 287.
61. Trevelyan, I, 386; Frothingham, *S*, 294.
62. French, *F*, 332.
63. Fonblanque, 148.
64. Force, 4, III, 927.
65. Force, 4, III, 7.
66. Force, 4, III, 642.
67. Force, 4, III, 642, 1671.
68. Trevelyan, I, 396–397; Frothingham, *S*, 293.
69. Frothingham, *S*, 275.
70. *Journals*, III, 321–324; Fitzpatrick, III, 390.
71. Fitzpatrick, III, 391.
72. Fitzpatrick, IV, 77; French, *F*, 510.
73. *Journals*, II, 220, III, 322, 393; Force, 4, IV, 1245.
74. Frothingham, *S*, 276.
75. Fitzpatrick, IV, 60.
76. French, *F*, 520.
77. Fitzpatrick, IV, 208.
78. Force, 4, III, 1666–1667.
79. Fitzpatrick, IV, 137, 142, 146; Sullivan, I, 29–30; Frothingham, *S*, 273.
80. *Conn. Hist. Soc. Colls.*, VII, 128.
81. Fitzpatrick, IV, 124, 240.
82. Sullivan, I, 130.
83. Fitzpatrick, IV, 156–157, 138 n.
84. Fitzpatrick, IV, 211; Heath, 28.
85. Fitzpatrick, IV, 202, 210.
86. Stephenson, I, 339.
87. French, *F*, 630.
88. Fitzpatrick, IV, 122.
89. Fitzpatrick, IV, 238, 242.
90. Fitzpatrick, IV, 241–242.
91. Force, 4, IV, 699.
92. Fitzpatrick, IV, 319, 243–244; Frothingham, *S*, 287–288 and n.
93. Duer, 124–125.
94. Brooks, *passim*; Fitzpatrick, IV, 74.
95. Fitzpatrick, IV, 93.
96. Sparks, *C*, I, 94–95; French, *F*, 525–526, 655–656; Brooks, 38–44; Heath, 30; Greene, *GW*, III, 94.

CHAPTER 10

1. Fitzpatrick, IV, 336.
2. Fitzpatrick, IV, 314; Dawson, I, 87 n.
3. Force, 4, IV, 1539, 1636.

4. Fitzpatrick, IV, 335; Frothingham, *S*, 290; Dawson, I, 86.
5. Dawson, I, 85–87.
6. Fitzpatrick, IV, 348.
7. See map in Sparks, *W*, III, facing p. 26.
8. French, *F*, 656; Heath, 32–33.
9. Fitzpatrick, IV, 373; Frothingham, *S*, 297; Greene, FV, 19; Gordon, II, 190.
10. Barker, 69.
11. Fitzpatrick, IV, 370; Gordon, II, 191–192; Frothingham, *S*, 297.
12. Gordon, II, 193; French, *F*, 660; Frothingham, *S*, 298; Heath, 32.
13. Gordon, II, 193.
14. Dawson, I, 94.
15. Robertson, 74.
16. Frothingham, *S*, 298.
17. Fitzpatrick, IV, 375; Frothingham, *S*, 298–299.
18. *Orderly Book at Charlestown, Boston, and Halifax, June 17, 1775 to 1776, 26 May* (London, 1890), 71, 313.
19. Gordon, II, 195.
20. Frothingham, *S*, 299; Heath, 33.
21. *Mass. Hist. Soc. Colls.*, 4, I, 261.
22. Heath, 33.
23. Gordon, II, 196; Fitzpatrick, IV, 380.
24. *Orderly Book at Charlestown, Boston, and Halifax, June 17, 1775 to 1776, 26 May* (London, 1890), 313; Robertson, 74.
25. Fitzpatrick, IV, 371–377; Frothingham, *S*, 303–304.
26. Frothingham, *S*, 305; Heath, 34.
27. Frothingham, *S*, 302 n.
28. Trevelyan, I, 435.
29. Fitzpatrick, IV, 444; Frothingham, *S*, 302.
30. Robertson, 79.
31. Fitzpatrick, IV, 448.
32. Robertson, 75.
33. Gordon, II, 197; Frothingham, *S*, 307 n.; French, *F*, 666–667.
34. Fitzpatrick, IV, 449.
35. French, *F*, 665.
36. Barker, 72.
37. Robertson, 79.
38. Robertson, 81; Fitzpatrick, IV, 403.
39. *Mass. Hist. Soc. Proc.*, XIV, 284.
40. Fitzpatrick, IV, 415, 430.
41. Fitzpatrick, IV, 401, 407, 410.
42. Frothingham, *S*, 311.
43. French, *F*, 345.
44. French, *F*, 356.
45. Fonblanque, 196–197.
46. French, *F*, 540. Howe wrote to Lord George Germain, secretary of state for the colonies, that the expedition "was concerted by the General and Admiral for the destruction of Cape Ann [Gloucester] and Falmouth, two seaport towns, that were distinguished for their opposition to government." But, in reply to Germain's inquiry as to the reasons for destroying Falmouth, Howe wrote some time later that Gage's orders to the soldiers were only to assist Mowat "in annoying and destroying all ships belonging to rebels on the coast and in the harbours to the eastward of Boston." Sparks, *W*, III, 520–521. It would seem that the orders of Graves to the sailors and of Gage to the soldiers differed from each other, and that Mowat acted according to the admiral's directions as to what was to be destroyed.
47. French, *F*, 539–544.

CHAPTER 11

1. Smith, JH, I, 37.
2. This description of the inhabitants of Canada and the effects upon them of the Quebec Act is derived chiefly from French, *F*, 395–399, and Metzger, *passim*. While French estimates the number of Old Subjects at "more than 600," Smith, JH, I, 48, apparently on good authority, says "some 2,000."
3. *Journals*, II, 68–70.
4. *Journals*, II, 68–70.
5. Force, 4, II, 230.
6. *Journals*, I, 82–90.
7. Force, 4, II, 231.
8. *Journals*, II, 75.
9. Force, 4, II, 734.
10. *Journals*, II, 55–56.
11. Force, 4, II, 732.
12. Force, 4, II, 892.
13. *Journals*, II, 105, 123.
14. *Journals*, II, 109–110.
15. This description of Schuyler is derived chiefly from Smith, JH, I, 244–265, and Lossing, *S, passim*. It is possibly too favorable to Schuyler. For interesting materials on Schuyler's patriotism, see Van Doren, 45–47, 51–58, 231, 239–240, 391, 394–395.
16. Smith, JH, I, 320–321, 367–370, 610; Lossing *S*, 393–394; Bancroft, IV, 292, 308. The first news Montgomery's young wife had of his commission and his acceptance of it was conveyed to her when he asked her to make a cockade for his hat. Observing that she wept while she worked on it, he tried to turn her thoughts from danger to glory by saying, "You shall never blush for your Montgomery"—a remark so exactly in accord with the manner of speech of the period that it might have appeared in the pages of Richardson's *Sir Charles Grandison* or *Pamela*. Stilted though it sounds to modern ears, it was a sincere and touching expression of his pride in himself and his affection for her. She never did have to blush for him.
17. Smith, JH, II, 112; Bancroft, IV, 308. Heitman's *Historical Register* accredits Macpherson to Delaware. He had, in fact, been appointed major in Haslet's Delaware Continental regiment in Jan., 1776, before the fact of his death on Dec. 31, 1775, was made known in the colony.
18. Fitzpatrick, III, 302–303.
19. *D.A.H.*, III, 1–4, II, 280; Bancroft, IV, 448–449.
20. *D.A.H.*, I, 1; Reed, I, 119; Smith, JH, I, 275.
21. Smith, JH, I, 177.
22. Force, 4, II, 914, 1670, III, 301.
23. Smith, JH, I, 356.
24. Force, 4, II, 661, 665, 842–843.
25. Force, 4, II, 1140, 669, 1666; Lossing, *S*, 349, 353–356.
26. Force, 4, II, 244.
27. Force, 4, II, 939.
28. Force, 4, II, 1319.
29. Force, 4, II, 1594–1595.
30. Force, 4, II, 1735.
31. Force, 4, III, 26.
32. *Journals*, II, 178–183. The Speech likened the King to a father, the ministry to his servants, and the colonies to his son, carrying a little pack. The "proud and ill-natured servants [become] displeased to see the boy so alert and walk so nimbly with his pack." They advise the father to "enlarge the child's pack." This being done, "the child takes it up again . . . speaks but few words—those very small—for he was loth to offend his father . . . but the proud and wicked

servants . . . laughed to see the boy sweat and stagger under his increased load." They prevail on the father to double the load, saying, "He is a cross child —correct him, if he complains any more." The load is doubled amid "the tears and entreaties of the child," who staggers under the weight, "ready to fall at any moment. . . . He entreats the father once more, though so faint he could only lisp out his last humble supplication—waits a while—no voice returns . . . He gives one more struggle and throws off the pack. . . . The servants are very wroth. . . . They bring a great cudgel to the father, asking him to take it in his hand and strike the child." Thus persuasively were the great issues of the American Revolution described for the Indians.

33. Force, 4, III, 473–496. At a preliminary meeting an Oneida sachem had, toward the end of the day, blandly suggested that "as this day is far spent . . . [and] we are weary from having sat long in council, we think it time for a little drink."
34. Lossing, *S*, 387.
35. Force, 4, III, 1275–1276.
36. Force 4, II, 611; French, *F*, 758.
37. Force, 4, III, 339.
38. Force, 4, II, 714.
39. Smith, JH, I, 603. Later in the war, in 1777, Captain Allen McLane had a number of Oneida Indians in his partisan corps operating between Valley Forge and Philadelphia.
40. Lossing, *S*, 345–346, 352, 358.
41. Force, 4, II, 1685–1686, 1702.
42. Lossing, *S*, 343, 358.
43. Force, 4, II, 1606.
44. Force, 4, II, 1646.
45. Force, 4, II, 1702.
46. Smith, JH, I, 190; Force, 4, II, 1685.
47. Force, 4, II, 1605–1606.
48. Heitman, 291.
49. Force, 4, II, 1667.
50. Force, 4, II, 760, III, 17–18; Pell, 112.
51. Force, 4, III, 95.
52. Force, 4, II, 1535, 1606.
53. French, *F*, 386–387
54. Force, 4, II, 1729, 1734, 1735, 1759, III, 141, 242, 243. Facing a lack of gunsmiths in New York, the Provincial Congress appointed a committee "to write to Great Britain for four complete sets of Lock-Smiths to make Gun-Locks and . . . to pay the passage of Smiths from Britain to America."
55. Force, 4, II, 1704, 1735; Smith, JH, I, 255.
56. Force, 4, III, 135.
57. Force, 4, II, 1730.
58. Force, 4, III, 447, 452; Smith, JH, I, 256.
59. *Journals*, I, 186.
60. Lossing, *S*, 332, 381, 392.
61. Force, 4, III, 18, 126.
62. Force, 4, III, 47.
63. Force, 4, III, 263.
64. Smith, JH, I, 94–103.
65. Force. 4, II, 243, 1729; Smith, JH, I, 93–96, 99–103.
66. Force, 4, III, 135–136.
67. Force, 4, III, 18–19.
68. Force, 4, III, 50, 135, 442.
69. Force, 4, III, 468.
70. Lossing, *S*, 393.
71. Force, 4, III, 442; Smith, JH, I, 317.

CHAPTER 12

1. French, *F*, 381.
2. Force, 4, III, 467; Smith, JH, I, 321.
3. Smith, JH, I, 397, 323.
4. Force, 4, III, 669, 738; Smith, JH, I, 323–324.
5. Force, 4, III, 671, 669; Smith, JH, I, 324.
6. Force, 4, III, 669; Smith, JH, I, 328.
7. Force, 4, III, 669–670, 757; Smith, JH, I, 328–329, 331.
8. Force, 4, III, 752.
9. Force, 4, III, 672.
10. Smith, JH, I, 330.
11. Force, 4, III, 767; Smith, JH, I, 332.
12. Smith, JH, I, 332; French, *F*, 418; Burnett, *L*, I, 143.
13. Force, 4, III, 738–740.
14. Force, 4, III, 738.
15. Force, 4, III, 741–742, 923–924.
16. Force, 4, III, 723–724, 741–742, 923–924; Smith, JH, I, 333–334; French, *F*, 418–419.
17. Smith, JH, I, 334.
18. Force, 4, III, 723–724, 741–742, 923–924.
19. Force, 4, III, 738, 742.
20. Smith, JH, I, 335.
21. Force, 4, III, 697, 739, 753.
22. Smith, JH, I, 345–346.
23. Fortescue, III, 155.
24. Force, 4, III, 925–926; Smith, JH, I, 343–344.
25. Force, 4, III, 726.
26. Force, 4, III, 926; Smith, JH, I, 347–352.
27. Force, 4, III, 779, 797, 923, 980; Lossing, I, 412–414.
28. Force, 4, III, 754; Lossing, I, 415.
29. Force, 4, III, 952, 799, 953; Smith, JH, I, 380–390; French, *F*, 422–424; Allen, 14.
30. Force, 4, III, 951, 963; Smith, JH, I, 410.
31. Force, 4, III, 1124.
32. Smith, JH, I, 445.
33. Force, 4, III, 954, 839, 951.
34. Smith, JH, I, 418.
35. Force, 4, III, 1097–1098.
36. Force, 4, III, 796.
37. Force, 4, III, 459.
38. Force, 4, III, 1093–1094.
39. Force, 4, III, 1107–1108.
40. Force, 4, III, 1131.
41. Force, 4, III, 1095, 1096, 1098.
42. Force, 4, III, 1133–1134.
43. Force, 4, III, 1132.
44. Force, 4, III, 1342, 1392, 1185, 1395.
45. Force, 4, III, 1344, 1391–1394.
46. Force, 4, III, 1343–1344; Smith, JH, I, 464–465; Lamb, 116.
47. Force, 4, III, 1394, for terms of capitulation.
48. Force, 4, III, 1603.
49. Force, 4, III, 1603.
50. Force, 4, III, 1597, IV, 290, V, 1234; Smith, JH, I, 475–477, 483.
51. Smith, JH, I, 490.

CHAPTER 13

The basic material for a narrative of Arnold's march is to be found in the many journals, diaries, and letters written by those who took part in it. Probably no other expedition of similar length made by so few men has produced so many contemporary records. Arnold's journal tells the tale to October 30, where it breaks off abruptly. There may have been more, but no more has been discovered. He also wrote many letters. No fewer than nineteen other accounts by participants are to be found, written by Dearborn, Senter, Meigs, Thayer, Topham, Humphrey, Wild, Ware, Henry, Stocking, Morison, Melvin, Pierce, Tolman, Kimball, Haskell, Fobes, Squier, and one anonymous person. They are of uneven value, as some were compiled from others, and some were written long after the expedition. Many of them are individually printed, but the most convenient access to them may be had in *March to Quebec*, in which Kenneth Roberts has annotated Arnold's journal and letters and twelve of the other more important accounts, as well as Montresor's journal and Enos's defense. In his novel *Arundel*, Roberts follows closely the actual events of the march and illuminates it with his remarkably vivid imagination, re-creating as truly as the novelist can its scenes and characters.

Among the strictly historical accounts, *Arnold's March from Cambridge to Quebec* and *Our Struggle for the Fourteenth Colony* both by Justin H. Smith, are complete, discriminating, and scholarly. *Arnold's Expedition to Quebec*, by John Codman, is more readable but not so accurate in detail. Allen French's account in *The First Year of the American Revolution* is not so full as Smith's, but is equally reliable. Graham's *Life of General Daniel Morgan*, Parton's *Life and Times of Aaron Burr*, Arnold's *Life of Benedict Arnold*, and Gordon's *History of the Rise, Progress and Establishment of the Independence of America* contain valuable material.

To limit the following notes to a reasonable compass, many references to Smith's and Codman's and French's books and to the journals and letters have been omitted.

1. Smith, J, 10.
2. Smith, JH, I, 498.
3. Fitzpatrick, III, 436. Montresor's journey, on which his map was based, had been made in a canoe, not in a bateau, in June and in the opposite direction from the one now proposed. Moreover, much of the most difficult part had been made at night, when he could not see difficulties which he fortunately escaped.
4. Smith, J, 75–76.
5. Fitzpatrick, III, 471.
6. Fitzpatrick, III, 472–473.
7. Parton, *passim*. French, *F*, 433, says of Burr: "Romance and tradition connect his name with that of an Indian girl, Jacataqua, who is said to have followed the expedition, but the historical foundation of the tale is so slight that the girl is not even mentioned by the best modern student of the march."
8. Greene, GW, III, 94–101; Bancroft, IV, 287–288; Henry, 12.
9. Fitzpatrick, III, 491–496.
10. Morison, 13. Humphrey, 8, says the delay was for the purpose of filling up the ranks of the companies.
11. Stocking, 10. Fobes, 10, says the vessels were "dirty schooners and fishing-boats."
12. Force, 4, III, 960.
13. Force, 4, III, 960–961. Whether Natanis was actually in Carleton's pay and inimical to the Americans, or whether he was merely trying to prevent the expedition from intruding on his hunting grounds, is uncertain. His subsequent conduct indicated no unfriendliness to the expedition. On the other hand, he may simply have inclined toward whichever party was, at the moment, the more useful to him.
14. Henry, 23.

15. Arnold had appointed Greene to lead the riflemen; but Morgan, Smith, and Hendricks, especially Morgan, refused to take orders from anyone but himself, nor would the other two willingly subordinate themselves to Morgan. Arnold yielded and gave Morgan a sort of leadership of the others, rather than official command of them. While he did lead them, Smith and Hendricks showed much independence at various times. Washington gently reproved Morgan for taking such an attitude. Fitzpatrick, IV, 2.
16. Force, 4, III, 960.
17. Smith, J, 468.
18. Dearborn, 6.
19. Senter, 8.
20. Smith, J, 469.
21. Smith, JH, I, 537.
22. Dearborn, 9.
23. Senter, 11.
24. Senter, 11–12; Force, 4, III, 1061.
25. Smith, J, 125.
26. Smith, JH, I, 547.
27. Henry, 46.
28. Smith, J, 472.
29. Smith, J, 131.
30. Smith, JH, I, 554.
31. Smith, J, 474.
32. Melvin (Roberts, 439) says that Morgan's men let Greene's division pass them so that they might have a chance to steal some of the provisions, which they succeeded in doing. Hence Greene's unexpected shortage.
33. Senter, 15. It has been said that this was a West Indian hurricane, following the the same course as that of September 22, 1938, and with similar devastating results.
34. Henry, 52.
35. Morison, 25.
36. Smith, J, 478; Force, 4, III, 1610, 1634.
37. Senter, 16–17. On his return to Cambridge, Enos was court-martialed "for quitting his commanding officer without leave." The only witnesses were his own officers, who had retreated with him. They testified that the return was necessary because of lack of provisions, and Enos was acquitted. But within a month he left the army; and he "never survived the stigma of having done a disreputable act." (Henry, 59–63; Force, 4, III, 1701–1721.)

   Yet there is something to be said for Enos. Though to the rest of the expedition, who went on in spite of hardship and starvation, his departure seemed a base and cowardly act, he had a case. One of his descendants, Rev. Horace E. Hayden, has defended him in a rather convincing manner, for which see Roberts, 631–648.
38. Senter, 18.
39. Smith, JH, I, 586. There were two women in the expedition. One was the wife of Sergeant Grier, "a large virtuous and respectable woman." The other, "beautiful though coarse in manner, was the wife of James Warner, a rifleman, young, handsome in appearance . . . athletic and . . . [such as] seemed to surpass in bodily strength." These two "appeared to be much interested in each other's welfare and unwilling to be separated." In the march up Dead River, Warner gave out, seated himself at the foot of a tree, and "said he was determined to die." His wife "attended him for several days, urging him to march forward," but he could not. Stocking says she "tarried with him until he died, while the rest of the company proceeded on their way." Being unable to bury him, "she covered him with leaves and then took his gun and other implements and left him with a heavy heart. After traveling twenty miles she came up with us." Henry says she stayed until she found her ministrations unable to save him,

then placed her own share of food and a canteen of water at his feet and left him. In either event, she survived the journey and arrived at the St. Lawrence with the others. (Henry, 61, 64–65; Stocking, 21.)

40. Smith, J, 482.
41. Smith, JH, I, 591; Morison, 28.
42. Senter, 23.
43. Henry, 73.
44. Stocking, 34.
45. Morison, 34.
46. Henry, 73–74.
47. The quotation is from Stocking, 23–24. Exactly how many men had survived that march is uncertain. With the volunteers and Colburn's artificers added to the original draft, about 1,100 started. The defection of Enos subtracted possibly 300. A considerable number of invalids were sent back, and with them went sound men to take care of them. Morison, one of the diarists, figures the total loss on this account at 200, which seems excessive. He says that 510 reached the St. Lawrence; hence he concludes that 70 or 80 had been lost on the way. His estimate has been questioned by Justin H. Smith (Smith, J, 233), who reckons the survivors at 675, that being the number of men for whom Arnold drew clothing from Montgomery on December 5. If that be correct and Enos's men are added, making a total of 975, it would appear that no more than 125 all told were lost by death, sickness, desertion, and as able-bodied caretakers of the invalids. As we know that about 70 invalids were sent back from the Dead River alone, in two parties, it seems incredible that no more than 55 were lost otherwise. It seems probable that the arrivals were not much more in number than half of the original party.
48. Joseph Warren wrote to Samuel Adams: "Arnold has made a march that may be compared to Hannibal's or Xenophon's." Thomas Jefferson also thought it equaled Xenophon's retreat. Murray, the English historian, wrote: "The march of Col. Arnold and his troops is one of the greatest exploits recorded in the annals of nations." A letter from Quebec dated November 9 states: "There are about 500 Provincials arrived at Point Levi . . . by way of Chaudiere, across the woods. Surely a miracle must have been wrought in their favour. It is an undertaking above the common race of men." (Force, 4, III, 1420.)

CHAPTER 14

1. Force, 4, III, 1633–1636.
2. Ogden, 24.
3. Morison, 26; Humphrey, 19.
4. Force, 4, III, 1635–1636; Morison, 36; Henry, 81; Senter, 27; Humphrey, 20.
5. Morison, 36; Henry, 82; Force, 4, III, 1724.
6. The estimates of Carleton's force vary slightly. See Force, 4, III, 1697, 1724–1725, IV, 175. But 1,200 seems to be a proper figure.
7. Smith, JH, II, 16 n.
8. Force, 4, III, 1697.
9. Fobes, 17.
10. Dearborn, 13.
11. Ogden, 29.
12. Fobes, 18.
13. Stocking, 26.
14. Humphrey, 24.
15. Henry, 94.
16. Stocking, 26.
17. Henry, 94.
18. Force, 4, IV, 188–193. The archaic sense of "pretty" as defined by *The Concise Oxford Dictionary of Current English*: "fine, stout, as *a pretty fellow*."

19. Justin H. Smith (Smith, JH, II, 90) seems to have supposed that the clothes brought by Montgomery were the conventional uniforms of the British army, scarlet coats and white breeches, for he describes the troops marching back to Quebec as "drawing a long red mark across the snow." Pierce in his journal (Roberts, 689) tells of drawing "red Coats." These may have been undercoats or waistcoats (Smith, JH, II, 90). However, the journal of Captain Pausch of the Brunswickers, who came with Burgoyne (Pausch, 93–94), describes in detail, as given in the text, the uniforms issued to Burgoyne's army for winter service in Canada. Lefferts, p. 160, pl. XXXIII, also describes and pictures them. Henry in his *Account of Arnold's Campaign*, p. 103, mentions his "fine white blanket coat" and his "cap or *bonnet rough*," which exactly accords with the descriptions of Pausch and Lefferts. Pausch tells of these uniforms being made in Montreal, not brought from England. So they were no new thing for Canada; indeed, they were of proper Canadian fashion. As Montgomery had captured a full year's supply of uniforms of the 7th and 26th regiments, they must have included these winter garments. The sealskin moccasins are also described by Henry. They were made "large, and according to the usage of the country, stuffed with hay or leaves to keep the feet dry and warm." These were, doubtless, also a part of the British equipment, for Burgoyne's entire army was taught how to use snowshoes" (Lefferts, 160). It would not have been possible with ordinary shoes or boots. The Americans were not all equipped with these new warm garments until Dec. 29, when final distribution—delayed perhaps by difficulties of transporting all Montgomery's supplies—was made (Humphrey, 24, 26).
20. Force, 4, III, 1595.
21. Sparks, *C*, I, 95.
22. Fitzpatrick, IV, 147.
23. Fitzpatrick, IV, 231.
24. Force, 4, III, 1638.
25. Force, 4, IV, 288.
26. Force, 4, IV, 289; Stocking, 26–27.
27. Force, 4, IV, 289.
28. Force, 4, III, 1638–1639.
29. Stocking, 27.
30. Force, 4, IV, 464.
31. Force, 4, IV, 464; Smith, JH, II, 117.
32. Dearborn, 18.
33. Stocking, 27.
34. Force, 4, IV, 289.
35. Henry, 105.
36. Leake, 127.
37. Force, 4, IV, 706.
38. Senter, 107.
39. Stocking, 29.
40. Henry, 108.
41. Graham, 102.
42. Dearborn, 21.
43. Dearborn, 23; Lossing, I, 200; Force, 4, IV, 656.
44. *Journals*, IV, 70, 78.
45. Smith, JH, II, 352.
46. Smith, JH, II, 406.
47. *Journals*, IV, 394.
48. Fitzpatrick, V, 78–79.
49. Stillé, 31.
50. Force, 4, VI, 1103–1104.
51. Arnold, 94.
52. Smith, JH, II, 434.
53. Smith, JH, II, 441.

CHAPTER 15

1. Fitzpatrick, IV, 407–408, 440, 442, 444, 462, 467; Heath, 32.
2. *Journals*, II, 207, 225.
3. *Journals*, III, 270.
4. *Journals*, III, 321–325.
5. Fitzpatrick, IV, 121.
6. Fitzpatrick, IV, 299–301.
7. Fitzpatrick, IV, 316.
8. *Journals*, III, 285.
9. *Journals*, II, 107, III, 291, 337, 418, IV, 59. These calls on the various colonies are to be found in *Journals*, III, 285, 291, 387, 418, IV, 59, 235, 237, 331, 347, 355, 357, V, 461, 466, 487, 607, 666. The call on Maryland mentions only two regiments, but four regiments and seven independent companies were actually raised. New York raised thirteen, New Jersey three, Pennsylvania twelve including the riflemen, Massachusetts eleven, Connecticut thirteen. Those mentioned in the text include only such as were specifically called for by resolutions of the Congress passed between October 9, 1775, and July 24, 1776. The absence of a call on Connecticut, except for one more regiment (*Journals*, IV, 360), is probably accounted for by the fact that the troops of that colony at Boston were taken into the army at its adoption in 1775. The text, therefore, is not to be taken as enumerating the whole number of regiments included in the army at the time of the Battle of Long Island, but rather the slow steps by which it was built up to become a real Continental army.
10. *Journals*, IV, 412; Lundin, 122–134.
11. *Journals*, III, 322.
12. *Journals*, V, 631.
13. Lefferts, 26. A Hessian officer who saw the regiment on Long Island remarked on their "most beautiful English muskets and bayonets" (Field, 438, Lowell, 67–68).
14. Johnston, *C*, Pt. I, 123.
15. Fitzpatrick, IV, 395, 397, 399, 414.
16. Sparks, *C*, I, 152.
17. Trevelyan, Pt. II, Vol. I, 179.
18. Field, 525.
19. Trevelyan, Pt. II, Vol. I, 179; Duer, *passim*
20. Johnston, *C*, Pt. I, 63; Irving, II, 300.
21. Johnston, *C*, Pt. I, 126–132.
22. Trevelyan, Pt. II, Vol. I, 32–34.
23. Lowell, 299–300. Lecky, 244, says the hiring of the German mercenaries "made reconciliation hopeless and the Declaration of Independence inevitable. It was idle for the Americans to have any further scruples about calling in foreigners [the French] to assist them when England had herself set the example."
    Before the Germans were hired the British government had tried to get Russians; but the other European governments, "which feared, or hated, or envied Britain," besieged Empress Catherine with "warnings and expostulations" and wrecked the negotiations. The smaller German states were next solicited, successfully (Trevelyan, Pt. II, Vol. I, 42–45). They were willing to furnish thousands of men, at a price. The Duke of Brunswick, for example, agreed to furnish 4,300 men. He was to receive an annual payment of £11,517 17s. 1½d., while his troops were in the British service, and twice as much each year for two years thereafter. He was also to get "head money" at the rate of £7 4s. 4½d. for each man furnished, and, for each one killed, the same sum additional. "According to custom three wounded men shall be reckoned as one killed": so ran the treaty. All this was to go into the Duke's own pocket, the wounded men and the dead men's families not receiving even the extra halfpenny (Lowell, 17–18). In all,

during the war six German states sent out to America 29,875 men, of whom 12,562 never returned to Germany, about 5,000 deserting and remaining in America. (Lowell, 20, 300.)

24. Ambrose Serle, who was aboard Lord Howe's flagship as secretary to his lordship, described their arrival in his journal (Serle, 28): "We were saluted by all the Ships of War in the Harbour, by the Cheers of the Sailors all along the Ships and by those of the Sailors on the Shore. A finer Scene could not be exhibited, both of Country, Ships and men, all heightened by one of the brightest Days that can be imagined."
25. Van Tyne, 243.
26. Stedman, I, 198; Kemble, 80; Serle, 28.
27. Fitzpatrick, V, 444.
28. Johnston, *C*, Pt. I, 99–100; Greene, FV, 34; Serle, 67.

CHAPTER 16

The most fully detailed story of the Battle of Long Island and the subsequent retreat is to be found in Henry P. Johnston's *The Campaign of 1776*. Although he fails to cite authority for most of the statements in his narrative, his sources are not hard to trace, especially as he reprints the greater part of the contemporary source material in Part II of his book. Another full account is in *The Battle of Long Island*, by T. W. Field. This also lacks specific citation in the text but has a supplement in which much of the source matter is printed. Field's text, however, is less reliable than Johnston's. His fervor, excitability, and one-sidedness, apparently due to excessive patriotism, and his superabundance of adjectives disqualify him as a reliable historian. In substance and style his account is very much like the Fourth of July orations of eighty or ninety years ago.

Force, Fitzpatrick, Kemble, Serle, Read, Reed, Robertson, Gordon, Ramsay, and the original documents printed in Johnston, Field, and Dawson form the major part of the contemporary or near contemporary authorities. They are supplemented by Carrington, Dawson, Johnston, Bancroft, Trevelyan, Anderson, and other writers.

1. Kemble, I, 84–85; Johnston, *C*, Pt. I, 139–140.
2. Kemble, I, 84–85; Serle, 71; Carrington, 200; Johnston, *C*, Pt. I, 140–141; Dawson, I, 154. A Hessian officer made the following comment in his diary (Lowell, 60): "Not a soul opposed our landing. This was the second blunder of the rebels. . . . Their first mistake was when we disembarked on Staten Island, for they might have destroyed a good many of our people with two six-pounders, and now they might have made it very nasty for us." The officer, however, seems to have forgotten the much heavier guns on the frigates covering the landing, which would have made it even more "nasty" for the Americans attempting opposition.

  Ambrose Serle in his journal (Serle, 73–74) describes the scene of the landing: "The Disembarkation of about 15,000 Troops upon a fine Beach, their forming upon the adjacent Plain, a Fleet of above 300 Ships & Vessels with their Sails spread open to dry, the Sun shining clear upon them, the green Hills and Meadows after the Rain, and the calm Surface of the Water upon the contiguous Sea and up the Sound, exhibited one of the finest & most picturesque Scenes that the Imagination can fancy or the Eye behold."
3. Lowell, 58.
4. Trevelyan, Pt. II, Vol. I, 271.
5. Serle, 71.
6. *Pennsylvania*, I, 306.
7. Lowell, 80; Dawson, I, 154; Kemble, I, 85; Johnston, *C*, Pt. I, 141.
8. Carrington, 201.
9. Johnston, *C*, Pt. I, 142–143.
10. Johnston, *C*, Pt. I, 142

11. Johnston, *C*, Pt. I, 148–150.
12. Graydon, 179, describes "the celebrated General Putnam, riding with a hanger belted across his brawny shoulders, over a waistcoat without sleeves (his summer costume) . . . much fitter to head a band of sickle-men or ditchers, than musketeers."

    Trevelyan, Pt. II, Vol. I, 275, describes him as "a shrewd, genial, New England uncle . . . well fitted for infusing an extra dose of hopefulness and enthusiasm into soldiers, who, just then, would have been better for a little self-distrust, but he did not possess either the training or the temperament indispensable for the leader of a regular army."
13. Johnston, *C*, Pt. I, 143.
14. Field, 146.
15. Fitzpatrick, V, 485.
16. Johnston, *C*, Pt. I, 148. The lack of intelligence service at this time is in strong contrast with the espionage which Washington organized after his retreat across the Jerseys, and which made possible his subsequent success at Trenton.
17. Lowell, 60–61; Johnston, *C*, Pt. I, 202; Field, 429–430.
18. Carrington, 202; Dawson, I, 153; Force, 5, I, 1255; Stedman, I, 193–194.
19. Fitzpatrick, V, 491.
20. Read, 17; Johnston, *C*, Pt. I, 154; Dawson, I, 152.
21. Johnston, *C*, Pt. I, 155–157.

CHAPTER 17

1. *Pennsylvania*, I, 307.
2. Greene, FV, 37.
3. Johnston, *C*, Pt. I, 175–176; Force, 5, I, 1256; Carrington, 202; Dawson, I, 154; Kemble, I, 85.
4. Serle, 77; Johnston, *C*, Pt. I, 176–177.
5. *Pennsylvania*, I, 310; Johnston, *C*, Pt. I, 160–161, Pt. II, 48.
6. Dawson, I, 151, 152.
7. Irving, II, 319.
8. Bancroft, V, 31.
9. Dawson, I, 151.
10. Field, 353; Johnston, *C*, Pt. II, 33.
11. Johnston, *C*, Pt. I, 164–166; Dawson, I, 151.
12. Field, 354; Johnston, *C*, Pt. I, 166.
13. Field, 488.
14. Dawson, I, 152.
15. Field, 354; Dawson, I, 151.
16. Field, 355.
17. Field, 356.
18. Duer, 162 n.
19. Dawson, I, 151; Serle, 78; Johnston, *C*, Pt. I, 167.
20. Field, 450.
21. Johnston, *C*, Pt. I, 173.
22. Johnston, *C*, Pt. II, 62.
23. Field, 159–160.
24. Read, 172; Johnston, *C*, Pt. I, 182–185; Dawson, I, 155.
25. Johnston, *C*, Pt. I, 183–184.
26. Dawson, I, 155. The Hessian jägers, also commonly called "chasseurs," were an element in the German forces in America, few in number—perhaps about 600— but active and efficient in combat. Their functions were like those of the British light infantry. Most of them had been foresters or gamekeepers in civil life and were therefore used to acting individually and thoroughly accustomed to the conditions of bush fighting. They were armed with short, heavy rifles of large bore, which carried no bayonets. These German rifles were the model from which

the early Pennsylvania gunsmiths, most of them German immigrants, had developed the American long-barreled, small-bore weapon.

27. Lowell, 62–63; Kemble, I, 85.
28. Trevelyan, Pt. II, Vol. I, 279. A Hessian officer in his diary (Lowell, 64) wrote: "Our Hessians marched like Hessians; they marched incorrigibly."
29. Field, 352.
30. Trevelyan, Pt. II, Vol. I, 280.
31. Onderdonk, 152. From a letter of Lieut. Col. Bedford (Read, 173) it appears that three Hessians had been picked up somewhere and were taken to the camp along with these British prisoners. It is amusing to note that the Delawares were accused of unmilitary duplicity in counterfeiting Hessian uniforms to deceive their foe, although, at the time the Delaware uniform was adopted, probably few of them had even heard of Hessians and certainly none had ever seen one in uniform.
32. Bancroft, V, 32.
33. *Pennsylvania*, I, 307.
34. Dawson, I, 147, 151; Johnston, *C*, Pt. I, 137–139; Greene, FV, 38–40.
35. Field, 489.
36. Moore, I, 296.
37. Field, 389, 511; Read, 175; *Archives*, III, 1341.
38. Field, 378. Kemble, I, 86, reports 349 casualties.
39. Dawson, I, 156.
40. Johnston, *C*, Pt. II, 64.
41. Johnston, *C*, Pt. I, 193.
42. Bancroft, V, 33.
43. Fitzpatrick, V, 489.
44. Greene, FV, 40.
45. Greene, FV, 41.
46. Irving, II, 327.
47. Adams, CF, 60.
48. Graydon, 156–157.
49. Fitzpatrick, V, 240.
50. Trevelyan, Pt. II, Vol. I, 203–204.
51. Frothingham, 134.
52. Van Tyne, 25.
53. Fisher, I, 493; Marshall, I, 109.
54. Fitzpatrick, VI, 4–7.
55. Van Tyne, 251.
56. Fortescue, III, 409.
57. Van Tyne, 251.
58. Fortescue, III, 409.

CHAPTER 18

1. Field, 452; Stedman, I, 193.
2. Johnston, *C*, Pt. I, 208.
3. Fitzpatrick, V, 497. Serle, 80, says that on the 28th "the Firing was very continual & very hot and lasted till dark night."
4. Trevelyan, Pt. II, Vol. I, 287.
5. Johnston, *C*, Pt. II, 43.
6. Graydon, 165, speaking for Shee's regiment. There were some tents, but not more than half enough for all.
7. Goldwin Smith, 85–94, has written, "Howe . . . though brave, was torpid; probably he was not only torpid but half-hearted. Had he followed up his victory [on Long Island] there probably would have been an end of the Continental army, whatever local resistance might have survived. . . . His subsequent conduct seems to have been marked with a sluggishness and irresolution which the

energy of his lieutenant, Cornwallis, could not redeem. Washington was allowed to pluck victory and reputation out of the jaws of defeat."

8. Trevelyan, Pt. II, Vol. I, 286.
9. Johnston. *C*, Pt. I, 218.
10. Force, 5. I. 1230, 1246.
11. Johnston. *C*, Pt. II, 30.
12. Dawson, I, 152.
13. Reed, I, 227; Johnston, *C*, Pt. I, 223. Of this premature withdrawal Graydon (167–168) wrote as follows: "We received orders to retire. We were formed without delay and had marched near halfway to the river, when it was announced that the British light horse were at our heels. Improbable as was the circumstance, it was yet so strenuously insisted upon that we halted and formed, the front rank kneeling with presented pikes . . . to receive the charge of the supposed assailants." None appearing, "we again took up the line of march and had proceeded but a short distance . . . when we were informed that we had come off too soon and were compelled to return to our post. This was a trying business for young soldiers; it was nevertheless strictly complied with."
14. Heath, 49.
15. Irving, II, 329.
16. Trevelyan, Pt. II, Vol. I, 290. Kemble (I, 86) says, "In the Morning, to our Astonishment found they had Evacuated all their Works . . . without a shot being fired at them."
17. Stedman, I, 193; Irving, II, 335; Trevelyan, Pt. II, Vol. I, 292; Frothingham, 137; Greene, FV, 44.
18. Johnston, *C*, Pt. I, 199–201.
19. Greene, GW, I, 212.
20. Fitzpatrick, VI, 4–7.
21. *Journals*, V, 762.

CHAPTER 19

1. Whitton, 143.
2. Fitzpatrick, VI, 16, 25.
3. Rodney, C, 112.
4. Johnston, *C*, Pt. I, 227 n.
5. Fitzpatrick, VI, 5.
6. Fitzpatrick, VI, 32.
7. Fitzpatrick, VI, 4; Johnston, *C*, Pt. I, 126–131.
8. Force, 5, II, 182–183.
9. Reed, I, 213, 235 n.; Force, 5, II, 120–121; Trevelyan, Pt. II, Vol. I, 294.
10. Fitzpatrick, VI, 6; *Journals*, V, 733.
11. Fitzpatrick, VI, 28–29.
12. Greene, FV, 45.
13. Fortescue, III, 189.
14. Fitzpatrick, VI, 30.
15. *Journals*, V, 749.
16. Force, 5, I, 326–327.
17. Force, 5, I, 329–330.
18. Fitzpatrick, VI, 53.
19. Mackenzie, I, 39.
20. Mackenzie, I, 37–38.
21. Heath, 50; Serle, 90–91, 99–100, 103; Mackenzie, I, 45; Robertson, 97; Force, 5, I, 443.
22. Evelyn, 84.
23. Serle, 103.
24. Johnston, *C*, Pt. II, 81.
25. Evelyn, 85. Trevelyan (Pt. II, Vol. I, 297) says: "It was an imposing spectacle.

The amazing fire from the shipping, the soldiers in scarlet clambering up the steep rocks, and the river covered with boats full of armed men . . . forming one of the grandest and most sublime stage-effects that had ever been exhibited."

26. Fitzpatrick, VI, 58.
27. Johnston, *H*, 34.
28. Johnston, *H*, 35.
29. Johnston, *C*, Pt. II, 83, Martin's narrative.
30. Heath, 52; Gordon, II, 327; Graydon, 174; Irving, II, 353; Rodney, C, 122; Force, 5, II, 1013; Johnston, *C*, Pt. II, 86.
31. Johnston, *C*, Pt. II, 83.
32. Irving, II, 343.
33. Johnston, *C*, Pt. I, 237. Trevelyan (Pt. II, Vol. I, 298) says: "Not one of the retreating battalions would ever have reached the American lines in military order, and with half its full numbers, if Howe had promptly pushed his troops athwart the peninsula [island] which here was less than 3000 yards wide."
34. Stephenson, I, 365. "The Rebels left a great quantity of Cannon, Ammunition, Stores, provisions, tents &c.&c. behind them" (Mackenzie, I, 50).
35. Johnston, *C*, Pt. I, 238–239. Colonel Humphrey (quoted in *ibid.*, 89) tells of Putnam, "for the purpose of issuing orders and encouraging the troops, flying, on his horse, covered with foam, wherever his presence was most necessary. Without his extraordinary exertions . . . it is probable the entire corps would have been cut to pieces."
36. Trevelyan, Pt. II, Vol. I, 298.
37. Van Tyne, 255 n.
38. Johnston, *C*, Pt. II, 90.

CHAPTER 20

The best account of this affair is Henry P. Johnston's *The Battle of Harlem Heights.* It is especially valuable for the considerable collection of contemporary letters, reports, and other documents to be found on pp. 125–234. E. C. Benedict's monograph of the same name is of very little value, being chiefly controversial on unimportant details and apparently generally erroneous in its conclusions. Carrington and Dawson add hardly at all to Johnston's account; nor is there much additional to be found elsewhere.

1. Johnston, *H*, 49–50, map.
2. Force, 5, II, 450–451; Johnston, *H*, 65.
3. Johnston, *H*, 65.
4. Johnston, *H*, maps facing 50, 70.
5. Johnston, *H*, 44–47; map facing 50.
6. Fitzpatrick, VI, 59.
7. Johnston, *H*, 52–55. One of the Ranger captains was Nathan Hale, but he was at this time on duty as a spy within the British lines in New York, a duty in which he risked and forfeited his life.
8. Johnston, *H*, 61–62.
9. Reed, I, 237. Johnston, *H*, 67, quotes from a favorite song of the British light infantry the following stanza:

> Hark! Hark! The bugle's lofty sound
> Which makes the woods and rocks around
>   Repeat the martial strain,
> Proclaims the British light-armed troops
> Advance. Behold! Rebellion droops.
>   She hears the sound with pain.

10. Johnston, *C*, Pt. I, 251–252; Irving, II, 359.
11. Fitzpatrick, VI, 68.

12. Johnston, *H*, 82–83, 143.
13. Lushington, 79.
14. Reed, I, 238; Johnston, *H*, 177.
15. Johnston, *H*, 204. Lieut. Col. Kemble of Howe's army said that 14 were killed, and that 11 officers, 5 sergeants, 3 drummers, and 138 privates were wounded. (Kemble, I, 89.)
16. Johnston, *H*, 226.
17. Fitzpatrick, VI, 96.
18. Johnston, *H*, 87.
19. Fitzpatrick, VI, 96.
20. Rodney, C, 129.
21. Johnston, *H*, 154, 177.
22. Reed, I, 238. Howe claimed a victory for his side in this affair. As the British held the ground and the Americans retreated, it was technically their success. But Gen. Sir Henry Clinton admitted that the British had been "in a scrape," and Col. von Donop reported that, but for the arrival of his jägers, "two regiments of Highlanders and the British infantry would have all, perhaps, been captured." The improvement in the behavior of the Americans engaged has caused some American historians to regard this little battle "as a turning point in the uphill progress of their national military efficiency." (Trevelyan, Pt. II, Vol. I, 304.)

CHAPTER 21

1. Heath, 53.
2. Fitzpatrick, VI, 96.
3. Fitzpatrick, VI, 96, 138.
4. Reed, I, 240.
5. Fitzpatrick, VI, 91. One ensign was caught leading 20 men "all loaded with plunder, such as house-furniture, tableware, linen and kitchen utensils, china and delf ware," as well as some women's clothing.
6. Fitzpatrick, VI, 117–118.
7. Fitzpatrick, VI, 112.
8. *Journals*, V, 762.
9. Heath, 62–63; Hufeland, 111–112; Force, 5, III, 471, 921–922; Rodney, C, 139; Irving, II, 377–378; Trevelyan, Pt. II, Vol. I, 312; Bancroft, V, 69.
10. *Journals*, VI, 866.
11. Sparks, *W*, IV, 155 n.; Hufeland, 114–115; Heath, 63.
12. Hufeland, 116.
13. Force, 5, II, 1188–1189; Hufeland, 118–122; Heath, 65.
14. Hufeland, 124. The Americans claimed to have shot down "140 or 150" (Stiles, II, 91). Other estimates ran as high as 800 to 1,000, absurd exaggerations, of course. The Americans lost Col. Shephard; the British lost Capt. W. G. Evelyn, a young soldier of great promise (Evelyn, 11).
15. McDonald, Part I, 21.
16. Reed, I, 245.
17. Heath, 66. The principal facts in this account of the affair at Mamaroneck have been derived from McDonald's narrative. See also *Archives*, II, 1030, for an account by Haslet.

CHAPTER 22

1. Force, 5, II, 607.
2. Hufeland, 135–136, map on 130.
3. Kemble, I, 94–95.
4. Trevelyan, Pt. II, Vol. I, 312.
5. Mackenzie, I, 82; Serle, 26; Force, 5, II, 1158; Lowell, 75.
6. Force, 5, III, 473, 725–726.

7. Force, 5, III, 725–726; Hufeland, 134–137; Johnston, *C*, Pt. II, 56; Tallmadge, 17.
8. Hufeland, 136–137.
9. Hufeland, 137.
10. Rodney, C, 142.
11. Hufeland, 137–138.
12. Heath, 70.
13. Hufeland, 140.
14. Rodney, C, 142.
15. Lowell, 77; Rodney, C, 142; Irving, II, 392.
16. Lowell, 75; Hufeland, 141–142.
17. Rodney, C, 143.
18. McDonald, I, 50.
19. McDonald, I, 53.
20. Rodney, C, 143.
21. Heath, 70.
22. Trevelyan, Pt. II, Vol. I, 314–315.
23. Heath, 7. Hufeland comments (p. 143) on the discipline the British and Hessian troops displayed at this point: "All of these men had waded through the cold waters of the Bronx and had fought a bloody battle in their wet clothing on a day late in October, in which hundreds of their comrades were left on the field and yet they formed and dressed their lines before being permitted to build fires to dry their clothing." He compares this "perfect military machine" with Washington's "poorly armed, ill-supplied and inexperienced army."
24. Bancroft, V, 74; Irving, II, 393; Whitton, 149; Hufeland, 144.
25. Greene, FV, 53.

CHAPTER 23

The most complete account of the battle at Fort Washington is to be found in Edward F. De Lancey's monograph *The Capture of Mount Washington*, a pamphlet published in a very small edition in 1877 after first appearing in the *Magazine of American History* for Feb. of that year. The author fortifies his statements by numerous references to original sources, and his story may be relied upon, in general. The best contemporary account by a witness is in the *Diary* of Lieut. Frederick Mackenzie, of the Welch Fusileers, I, 104–110. The *Memoirs* of Captain Graydon give interesting details, as also does the diary of Archibald Robertson. Vols. II and III of Force's *American Archives*, 5th Series, contain much valuable material, notably Howe's dispatches and his full return of casualties, prisoners taken, etc. Heath's *Memoirs* yield some material. From these and the other sources, such as Kemble, George W. Greene, Hufeland, Carrington, and Dawson, the account herein has been compiled. The individual references below are confined chiefly to the sources of quotations.

1. Anderson, 25; Read, 210–211.
2. Hufeland, 148; Greene, FV, 53; Heath, 72–73.
3. Heath, 75.
4. Force, 5, III, 521.
5. Fitzpatrick, VI, 248–249.
6. Force, 5, III, 543–544.
7. De Lancey, 6–7.
8. De Lancey, 9.
9. Graydon, 186.
10. Bancroft, V, 74.
11. Force, 5, III, 619. Graydon says (p. 186) of Magaw: "He had heard of sieges being protracted for months and even years . . . as the place he had to defend was called a Fort and had cannon in it, he thought the deuce was in it, if he could not hold out for a few weeks."

12. Force, 5, III, 619.
13. Fitzpatrick, VI, 257–258.
14. Fitzpatrick, XVI, 150–152.
15. Force, 5, III, 1294.
16. Force, 5, III, 519.
17. *Pennsylvania*, I, 106.
18. Force, 5, II, 330.
19. Graydon, 94–95; Dawson, I, 89; Johnston, *C*, Pt. I, 277.
20. Fortescue, III, 194 n.
21. Force, 5, III, 921–925.
22. Sparks, *W*, IV, 179 n.
23. Kemble, I, 99.
24. Robertson, 111.
25. Force, 5, III, 1058.
26. Force, 5, III, 1059.

CHAPTER 24

1. Force, 5, III, 831.
2. Force, 5, III, 822, 833.
3. Mackenzie, I, 114.
4. Mackenzie, I, 97–98.
5. Force, 5, III, 822.
6. Trevelyan, Pt. II, Vol. II, 18–19.
7. Fitzpatrick, VI, 265.
8. Force, 5, III, 634, 639.
9. Force, 5, III, 708, 764; Fitzpatrick, VI, 287, 293.
10. Mackenzie, I, 112; Gordon, II, 352; Greene, GW, I, 276.
11. Force, 5, III, 861, 1058; Greene, GW, I, 276–278; Serle, 144.
12. Kemble, I, 101.
13. Force, 5, III, 828; Greene, GW, I, 277.
14. Fitzpatrick, VI, 266.
15. Force, 5, III, 779; Fitzpatrick, VI, 295 n.
16. Fitzpatrick, VI, 298.
17. Force, 5, III, 792.
18. Reed, I, 255–257.
19. Reed, I, 257–258
20. Fitzpatrick, VI, 298.
21. Force, 5, III, 790.
22. Gordon, II, 354.
23. Fitzpatrick, VI, 303.
24. Fitzpatrick, VI, 305–306.
25. Bancroft, V, 82.
26. Force, 5, III, 926; Trevelyan, Pt. II, Vol. II, 20.
27. Fitzpatrick, VI, 303.
28. Force, 5, III, 1082.
29. Fitzpatrick, VI, 314.
30. Fitzpatrick, VI, 320.
31. Fitzpatrick, VI, 313.
32. Fitzpatrick, VI, 320–322.
33. Fitzpatrick, VI, 325, 397.
34. Trevelyan, Pt. II, Vol. II, 20.
35. Anderson, 27.
36. Fitzpatrick, VI, 33; Stryker, *TP*, 20.
37. Fitzpatrick, VI, 333.
38. Fitpatrick, VI, 331.
39. Force, 5, III, 1316.

40. Fitzpatrick, VI, 336.
41. Anderson, 28.
42. Lundin, 147.
43. Fitzpatrick, VI, 339.

CHAPTER 25

1. *Archives,* III, 1358.
2. Thacher, 67
3. Anderson, 28.
4. Fitzpatrick, VI, 346, 355, 381.
5. Fitzpatrick, VI, 355.
6. Fitzpatrick, VI, 398.
7. Force, 5, III, 927–928.
8. Fitzpatrick, VI, 397–398.
9. Force, 5, III, 1199, 1434; Marshall, C, 105–107.
10. Force, 5, III, 1434.
11. Read, 253–254.
12. Force, 5, III, 1290.
13. Force, 5, III, 1180; *Journals,* VI, 1027; Bancroft, V, 89.
14. Trevelyan, Pt. II, Vol. II, 63, 67–69.
15. Force, 5, III, 794, 795, 834; Heath, 79–86.
16. Force, 5, III, 1121, 1138.
17. Fitzpatrick, VI, 398.
18. Force, 5, III, 1201.
19. Fitzpatrick, VI, 347.
20. Stryker, *TP,* 59–60.
21. Force, 5, III, 1201.

CHAPTER 26

William S. Stryker's book, *The Battles of Trenton and Princeton,* contains the fullest account of the campaign in the Jerseys from Dec. 26, 1776, to Jan. 5, 1777. It is supported by the inclusion, in Part II, of more than a hundred contemporaneous letters and other documents, many of them otherwise not readily accessible. It has not been thought necessary to refer to this material in the footnotes, except in a few instances. Capt. Thomas Rodney's diary is of great value in its full details and in the sidelights it throws on the activities of the army. Force, 5, III, contains much relevant material, as also does Fitzpatrick. Lundin's *Cockpit of the Revolution* covers all the operations of the war in New Jersey in a comprehensive manner. Carrington's and Dawson's accounts are helpful.

1. Stryker, *TP,* 48 n.
2. Force, 5, III, 1317.
3. Force, 5, III, 1401–1402.
4. Force, 5, III, 1317.
5. Fitzpatrick, VI, 366, 372, 373.
6. Irving, II, 469.
7. Force, 5, III, 1376. Fitzpatrick, VII, 427 n., doubts the authenticity of this letter and does not include it in his collection. Whether authentic or not, it well describes the situation.
8. Dunbar, I, 282.
9. Rodney, C, 150–151.
10. Stryker, *TP,* 362.
11. Stryker, *TP,* 137.
12. Force, 5, III, 1443, 1445–1446.
13. Trevelyan, Pt. II, Vol. II, 113.

14. Rodney, T, 23.
15. Force, 5, III, 1441.
16. Force, 5, III, 1429.
17. Rodney, C, 150.
18. Rodney, T, 24.
19. Fitzpatrick, VI, 440.
20. Stryker, *TP*, 213.
21. Force, 5, III, 1462.
22. Irving, II, 500.
23. Stephenson, I, 383.
24. *Journals*, VI, 1045.

CHAPTER 27

The most recent account of events before and after the battle of Princeton is to be found in Alfred H. Bill, *The Campaign of Princeton, 1776–1777* (Princeton, N. J., 1948).

1. Force, 5, III, 1429.
2. Reed, I, 278.
3. Fitzpatrick, VI, 445–446.
4. Irving, II, 494.
5. Reed, I, 278–280.
6. Rodney, T, 25.
7. Reed, I, 281; Fitzpatrick, VI, 447–450.
8. It is usually stated that the extension of time was for six weeks, though Washington wrote to the Congress that it was a month (Fitzpatrick, VI, 45).
9. Fitzpatrick, VI, 457–458. Besides this call for bounty money, Washington asked Morris for more the next day. "We have the greatest occasion at present for hard money to pay a certain set of people, who are of particular use to us. If you could possibly collect a sum, if it were but one hundred or one hundred and fifty pounds, it would be of great service." These people were his spies in New Jersey. His intelligence service was very good at this time, in strong contrast to the lack of it at Long Island and in the Pennsylvania campaign of 1777. Paper money might do for the bounty to the troops, but these gentlemen required real money.
   No more revealing light could be thrown on the financial condition of the time than that of the list of hard moneys collected by Morris by scraping Philadelphia: "410 Spanish milled dollars @ 7s. 6d., 2 English crowns, 72 French crowns, 1072 English shillings" (Force, 5, III, 1486).
10. Stephenson, I, 386.
11. Stryker, *TP*, 259.
12. Stryker, *TP*, 271–272; Fischer, I, 566; Bancroft, V, 105; Irving, II, 504; Frothingham, 173; Lundin, 206; Carrington, 286. G. W. Greene, in *The Life of Nathanael Greene*, says: "Each course had its advocates, when a voice was heard, saying, "Better than either of these, let us take the new road through the woods, and get in the enemy's rear by a march upon Princetown, and, if possible, on Brunswick even.' From whom did this bold suggestion come? St. Clair claimed it as his, and why should the positive assertion of an honorable man be lightly called in question?" But it has been questioned, by Bancroft elaborately, as a tale "written in extreme old age . . . self-laudatory." He gives the credit to Washington, as do Irving, Frothingham, Lundin, Carrington, and Trevelyan. Stryker thinks it more probably originated with General Philemon Dickinson of the New Jersey militia or Reed, because thev knew the country.
13. Reed, I, 288.
14. Rodney, T, 32–33.
15. Stryker, *TP*, 276.
16. Rodney, T, 32.

17. Rodney, T, 33.
18. Rodney, T, 34.
19. Trevelyan, Pt. II, Vol. II, 135: "Colonel Haslet dropped with a bullet through his brain. In his pocket was an order directing him to go home on recruiting service, which he had divulged to no one and had silently disobeyed."
20. Rodney, T, 34.
21. Rodney, T, 36.
22. Rodney, T, 36.
23. Fitzpatrick, VI, 469.
24. Fortescue, III, 205, says, "The whole cause of the rebellion in America was saved by Washington's very bold and skilful action." Nicholas Cresswell, a young Englishman adrift in America, wrote in his *Journal* (pp. 179–180) that the news of Trenton and Princeton "is confirmed. The minds of the people are much altered. A few days ago they had given up the cause for lost. Their late successes have turned the scale and now they are all liberty mad again. Their Recruiting Parties could not get a man (except he bought him from his master) no longer since than last week, and now the men are coming in by companies. . . . They have recovered their panic and it will not be an easy matter to throw them into confusion again."
25. Fitzpatrick, VI, 470.
26. The details of the operations after Princeton have been derived chiefly from Thomas Rodney's *Diary*.

CHAPTER 28

1. Irving, III, 4–5; Lundin, 20; Stephenson, I, 394; Stedman, I, 239; Greene, GW, I, 309; Greene, FV, 75.
2. Fitzpatrick, VI, 472; Irving, II, 4.
3. Fitzpatrick, VII, 29.
4. Fitzpatrick, VII, 288.
5. Gordon, II, 422.
6. Fitzpatrick, VII, 350. Alexander Graydon, a visitor at the camp, wrote in his *Memoirs* (p. 277): "I had been extremely anxious to see the army. Here it was, but I could see nothing which deserved the name . . . the motley, shabby covering of the men."
7. Fitzpatrick, VII, 189.
8. Fitzpatrick, VI, 496–497.
9. Fitzpatrick, VII, 38.
10. Fitzpatrick, VI, 473, and VII, 128, 129, 230; Lundin, 234–235; Trevelyan, III, 56–57.
11. Fitzpatrick, VII, 288. Inoculation, at that time "rarely practised" in America, was the forerunner of vaccination. The patient was infected in such a way that a mild form of the disease was induced. Trevelyan, III, 80–82, gives a full account of the process.
12. *Journals,* VI, 1045. The Additional Battalions were not allotted among the states as the original eighty-eight battalions had been. They could be recruited anywhere, and officers could be appointed without regard to state lines.
13. *Journals,* V, 763.
14. Fitzpatrick, VII, 86.
15. Fitzpatrick, VII, 139 n.
16. *Journals,* VI, 1093.
17. Fitzpatrick, VII, 89; also 91, 120, 133, 138, and especially 349.
18. Fitzpatrick, VII, 66. Washington repeated his call for "companies or half Companies" on Feb. 23 and again on Mar. 6 (*ibid.,* 194, 254).
19. *Journals,* VII, 211. Washington (see Fitzpatrick, VII, 208) had written on Feb. 28, "Nothing distresses me more than the Universal Call . . . from all Quarters for fire Arms. which I am totally unable to supply." Trevelyan (III, 39) says

that the manufacturing capabilities of America were so limited that contracts could seldom be made for more than 100 muskets at a time.

20. Jones, I, 71; Trevelyan, Pt. II, Vol. II, 153; Lundin, 221; Kemble, I, 107.
21. Lundin, 222; Sullivan, I, 310; Stedman, I, 240.
22. Stedman, I, 240.
23. Frothingham, 189. Thomas Jones, a judge of the Supreme Court of New York and an ardent Loyalist, in his *History of New York During the Revolutionary War* caustically comments on a New York incident of March, 1777: "This month was remarkable for the investiture of General Howe with the Order of the Bath; a reward for *Evacuating* Boston, for *lying indolent* upon Staten Island for near two months, for *suffering* the whole rebel army to escape him upon Long Island, and *again* at the White Plains, *for not putting an end to rebellion* in 1776, when so often in his power, for making such *injudicious cantonments* of his troops in Jersey as he did, for *suffering* 10,000 veterans under experienced generals to be cooped up in Brunswick and Amboy by about 6,000 militia under the command of an inexperienced general." Of Howe's "cooped up" condition in Amboy and New Brunswick he says, "Not a stick of wood, a spear of grass or a kernel of corn could the troops in New Jersey procure without fighting for it." (Jones, I, 177, 171.)
24. Hufeland, 209–213; Fitzpatrick, VII, 328 n.; Stedman, I, 278; Jones, I, 177.
25. Jones, I, 180–181; Gordon, II, 468; *Journals*, VII, 579.

CHAPTER 29

The most useful account of Howe's maneuvers described in this chapter is to be found in Troyer S. Anderson, *The Command of the Howe Brothers During the American Revolution*. Anderson is always helpful on the plans and thought of the Howes. He is perhaps too gentle in his treatment of them.

1. Marshall, I, 170; Stedman, I, 283; Irving, III, 73; Lundin, 313; Greene, FV, 80.
2. Sullivan, I, 354.
3. Greene, FV, 81.
4. Montresor, 421; Frothingham, 193.
5. Montresor, 421–422; Marshall, I, 173.
6. Sullivan, I, 383.
7. Trevelyan, III, 61, writes: "To the surprise and amusement of the American officers . . . [Howe] placidly and deliberately began to entrench his camp, as if he had come into their neighborhood to spend a quiet Summer."
8. Stedman, I, 284; Lundin, 317; Sullivan, I, 393; Gordon, II, 470; Fitzpatrick, VIII, 261.
9. Fitzpatrick, VIII, 353; Lundin, 317–318.
10. Lundin, 319.
11. Stedman, I, 284; Montresor, 123; Kemble, I, 121; Fitzpatrick, VIII, 270, 276; Irving, III, 81.
12. Greene, GW, I, 394; Fitzpatrick, VIII, 281–282; Gordon, II, 471.
13. Cresswell, 242.
14. Fitzpatrick, VIII, 298.
15. Stedman, I, 285.
16. Gordon, II, 474.
17. Kemble, I, 123; Lundin, 323–324; André, 34. Trevelyan, III, 63, writes: "Stirling, who was still something of a military pedant, neglected the rare advantages which the locality presented, and drew up his command in parade-ground order; while Cornwallis made no mistakes and gave full play to the indignant valour of his followers."
18. Fitzpatrick, VIII, 307; Montresor, 429; Lundin, 323; Marshall, I, 175–176; Gordon, II, 473–474; André, 33.
19. Stedman, I, 286.

20. Montresor, 426.
21. Irving, III, 74, 85; Lundin, 312; Marshall, I, 176.
22. Fitzpatrick, VIII, 355; Whitton, 179–180.
23. Fitzpatrick, VIII, 336.
24. Fitzpatrick, VIII, 364, 365, 366.
25. Irving, III, 104; Fitzpatrick, VIII, 365; Kirkwood, 104.
26. Stedman, I, 289; André, 34; Serle, 239.
27. Fitzpatrick, VIII, 376, 407.
28. Fitzpatrick, VIII, 386, 414, 454.
29. Montresor, 429; Serle, 241; Baurmeister, 2.
30. Fitzpatrick, VIII, 460–468.
31. Fitzpatrick, VIII, 496, 497, 499. On July 30 Washington wrote to Gates: "Gen'l. Howe's in a manner abandoning Genl. Burgoyne is so unaccountable a matter, that till I am fully assured it is so, I cannot help casting my Eyes continually behind me."
32. *Pennsylvania Archives,* V, 415.
33. Fitzpatrick, VIII, 503, 505, and IX, 5.
34. *Archives,* III, 1380–1381.
35. Fitzpatrick, VIII, 1–5.
36. Fitzpatrick, IX, 37, 45; Kirkwood, 130.
37. Fitzpatrick, IX, 57.
38. Fitzpatrick, IX, 107, 110 n., 113, 114.
39. Fitzpatrick, IX, 115–116.
40. Stedman, I, 290; Fortescue, III, 214.
41. Wilkin, 238.
42. Carrington, 364.
43. Carrington, 364.
44. Fitzpatrick, IX, 119.

CHAPTER 30

There is a wealth of information concerning the movements of the British army on the way to the Brandywine in the journals of Captain John Montresor, Archibald Robertson (an engineer), Ambrose Serle (secretary to Admiral Howe), Major John André, and the letters of the Hessian Major Baurmeister. On the American side, Washington's letters and orders are the chief sources. Edward W. Cooch's *Battle of Cooch's Bridge* is very helpful.

1. Hughes, III, 149.
2. Fitzpatrick, IX, 125–127.
3. Adams, J, 298. The number of men in Washington's army is in doubt. A committee of the Congress, which visited the camp about August 1, reported 17,949 privates, exclusive of certain contingents; including officers, 16,920 were fit for duty, of whom 14,089 were privates. The number of men in September is more generally reckoned at 11,000. See Greene, GW, I, 443; Irving, III, 148, writes: "The disaffected, who had been taught to believe the American forces much less than they were in reality, were astonished as they gazed on the lengthening procession of a host, which to their unpractised eyes, appeared innumerable; while the Whigs, gaining fresh hope and animation from the sight, cheered the patriot squadrons as they passed." See also Fitzpatrick, IX, 127–128.
4. Graydon, 291.
5. Fitzpatrick, IX, 129, 130–135.
6. Fitzpatrick, IX, 128, 147; *Journals,* VIII, 667.
7. Irving, III, 194; Fitzpatrick, IX, 451–452; Stephenson, II, 20; Greene, GW, I, 444; Hughes, II, 150.
8. Montresor, 442; André, 36; Serle, 245; Robertson, 142.
9. André, 37; Serle, 245; Montresor, 442; Baurmeister, 3–4; Robertson, 143.

10. Montresor, 443; André, 38; Robertson, 143; Baurmeister, 4. Lieut. William J. Hale of the 45th British regiment wrote: "We found a great part of the stores remaining in the Town, though they had employed several of the preceding days in removing them to Wilmington. 100 butts of Porter were left in one cellar, Madeira, Rum, Melasses, Tobacco, Yams, Flower etc; a number of Sloops loaded with shoes, stockings and rum . . . fell into our hands."
11. Marshall, I, 182; Irving, III, 198; Montresor, 444; Baurmeister, 7; André, 38.
12. Montresor, 444; Baurmeister, 8; André, 41.
13. Baurmeister, 6; André, 41; Robertson, 144.
14. André, 41–42.
15. Montresor, 443.
16. Fitzpatrick, IX, 146–147, 148.
17. Baurmeister, 8–9, notes that the army's wagon train "consisted of 276 waggons loaded with rum, flour and salt-meat."
18. Montresor, 445.
19. This account of the affair at Cooch's Bridge is based on the accounts of Montresor, 445–446; André, 42–43; Baurmeister, 9; Robertson, 144–145; Irving, III, 198–199; and Cooch, *passim*.
20. Montresor says the Americans left 20 dead on the field. Baurmeister says 30, including five officers. Marshall reckons 40 killed and wounded in Maxwell's corps. On the other side Montresor admits only 3 killed and 20 wounded. Robertson says 30 killed and wounded. Washington wrote to the Congress that a woman said she had seen nine wagonloads of British wounded.

    Montresor says that Maxwell's force consisted of 720 Continentals, "together with 1,000 militia and Philadelphia Light Horse." No other account mentions any horsemen. Marshall says that there were 900 cavalry with Washington's army, who were "employed principally on the lines in watching the enemy, gaining intelligence and picking up stragglers." It is pretty safe to say that there were none at Cooch's Bridge. It is also very improbable that there were any militia in important numbers with Maxwell. They were concentrated elsewhere. Sergeant Thomas Sullivan of the British 49th regiment in an account of the fight (*Pa. Mag. of Hist.*, XXXI, 410) calls Maxwell's men "a chosen corps of 1000 men." He says the British had "3 men killed; 2 officers and 19 men wounded," and claims Maxwell's loss was "the commanding officer . . . and other officers killed and wounded, besides 50 men killed and many more wounded." Maxwell was certainly not killed.
21. Montresor, 446; Robertson, 145.
22. André, 43; Montresor, 446–448.
23. Fitzpatrick, IX, 140.
24. Fitzpatrick, IX, 179.
25. Montresor, 448.
26. Fitzpatrick, IX, 197. Montresor, 449, says: "The Army moved . . . through an amazingly strong country, being a succession of large hills, rather sudden with narrow vales . . . not a shot fired. . . . Rebel Light Horse about, but fled."

CHAPTER 31

1. MacElree, 132–133.
2. Bowen, 7–8; MacElree, 131–133; Lossing, II, 171 n. Some confusion as to these fords has arisen from the fact that change of ownership of the adjacent farms resulted in change of name of some of the fords. Painter's was also known as Jones's, Wistar's as Shunk's, Buffington's as Brinton's, confusing it with the truce Brinton's next above Chad's. To make matters worse some of the actors in the drama miscalled certain fords. Washington called Jefferis's Ford Jones's; and, as if that common name stuck in everybody's mind, Sullivan gave it to Wistar's Ford. In this narrative "Jones's" has been voided, the distinctive alternative name being used in each case.

3. Carrington, 368; Bowen, 10; Fitzpatrick, IX, 425 n.
4. Carrington, 368; Bowen, 7; MacElree, 134.
5. Bowen, 8; Hughes, III, 157–158; MacElree, 136; Lee, 89.
6. Baurmeister, 12. One of the many anecdotes clustering about this battle tells of an English Quakeress, who ran out of her house and implored Knyphausen not to go on to the Ford. "Dear man," she cried, "George Washington is on the other side and he has all the men in this world with him. To which the General replied: "Never mind, madam. I have all the men in the other world with me."
7. Baurmeister, 13; Carrington, 369–370; Bowen, 9.
8. Baurmeister, 13.
9. Baurmeister, 13.
10. Greene, GW, I, 447.
11. Fitzpatrick, IX, 205.
12. Bowen, 10; Carrington, 370; Lossing, II, 174.
13. Sparks, *W*, V, 459.
14. Muhlenberg, 492. It seems strange that Washington should have regarded Howe's division of the British army as "a terrible blunder" after his own action at the Battle of Trenton.
15. Hughes, III, 159; Lossing, II, 174; Bowen, 10, 30. Fortescue (III, 216) regards it as fortunate for Washington that he did not persist in his plan to cross and attack Knyphausen. "For Knyphausen was an able commander, his troops were far superior to Washington's in training and discipline, and, by Howe's forethought, he had been supplied with plenty of guns, so that he would certainly have held his own until Cornwallis came up in the enemy's rear and destroyed the Americans utterly."
16. Sparks, *W*, V, 459.
17. Hughes, III, 161–162; Bowen, 10.
18. Carrington, 342; MacElree, 141. It is impossible to be certain as to the order in which the conflicting messages were sent and received, and the authorities differ. Marshall mentions only Ross's dispatch received at eleven o'clock. Irving speaks only of "an express from Sullivan," giving no time, but states that Washington immediately sent Bland to reconnoiter and then resolved to cross and attack Knyphausen. Bowen sends Bland out first and states that he reported the enemy on the Valley Road and the dust arising there, which was afterwards confirmed by Ross, yet it appears that Bland's dispatch about the dust was dated 2 P.M., while Ross reported at 11 A.M. Carrington puts Bland's message at "between nine and ten o'clock," states that similar news came from Hazen, fixes Ross's dispatch at 11 A.M. and omits reference to Washington's order to Bland. Lossing puts Bland's message first and has it confirmed by Ross and by Hazen. Greene, GW, mentions only a message from Sullivan that the enemy was marching to the upper fords, follows this by Washington's order to cross, then Sullivan's contradicting message and finally Cheyney's arrival. Hughes gives Ross first place, with news of the enemy on the road, makes Washington then order the attack, but send Bland out to scout; after that he brings in the Ross message and then Spear's contradiction. Unfortunately, Washington's order to Bland was dated "11 September, 1777, 20 minutes after   o'clock," so that it cannot be placed in time.

   In the text an effort has been made to sort out the times of the messages and arrange them in their proper order. The result may not be in accord with the facts, but it certainly seems to fit in with the known circumstances and the apparently proper relations between the several messages. The questions raised may not be of the first importance, but it is annoying not to be able to be sure of their answers.
19. Montresor, 449; Dawson, I, 281. There is some uncertainty as to the strength of Cornwallis's column. In the American histories it is usually reckoned at 10,000 men. Montresor puts it at "about 7,000." Howe had reported 13,799 privates on embarkation. He had lost some through sickness, a few by capture, but pretty

certainly still had twelve to thirteen thousand. Of these there were about 5,000 with Knyphausen. That would leave Cornwallis perhaps 8,000 rank and file, which is the way an army's strength is usually computed.

20. Townsend, 21–25.
21. Carrington, 376; Marshall, I, 185; Irving, III, 204; Sullivan, I, 463, 472; Greene, GW, I, 418.
22. Sullivan, I, 463, 472–473.
23. Montresor, 449; Lossing, II, 175; MacElree, 144; Irving, III, 185.
24. Bowen, 11.
25. Montresor, 450; André, 46; Dawson, I, 282.
26. Bowen, 11; MacElree, 144; Townsend, 24; Lossing, II, 175; Dawson, I, 276.
27. Montresor, 450.
28. Sullivan, I, 463–464, 476, 555.
29. Fitzpatrick, IX, 206–207.
30. Hughes, III, 164; Greene, GW, I, 449.
31. Greene, GW, I, 449; Gordon, II, 511; Hughes, III, 163–164.
32. Anderson, 36–37.
33. Dawson, I, 282.
34. Bowen, 12.
35. Greene, GW, I, 451–453; Irving, III, 207–208; Montresor, 450.
36. Dawson, I, 282.
37. Baurmeister, 14–15.
38. Dawson, I, 282. Most histories dismiss the fight at the Ford in a paragraph or two, as if there were only a brief resistance by the troops under Wayne, Maxwell, and Proctor, followed by a quick retreat. The account sent by Major Baurmeister of the Regiment von Mirbach, a participant in the action, to his superior officer in Hesse-Kassel, on which the description in the text is based, shows clearly that the Americans put up a stiff and prolonged defense. This may be accepted, if for no other reason, because it began at half past four o'clock and lasted until dark.
39. Bancroft, V, 179.
40. Dawson, I, 282.
41. Montresor, 451; Bancroft, V, 179.

CHAPTER 32

1. Stedman, I, 293; Gordon, II, 513.
2. Fitzpatrick, IX, 207–208.
3. *Journals*, VIII, 735–738; Fitzpatrick, IX, 212.
4. Fitzpatrick, IX, 229, 215, 258.
5. Montresor, 452–453; Baurmeister, 18.
6. Marshall, I, 188.
7. Hughes, III, 181.
8. Baurmeister, 18.
9. Baurmeister, 18; Montresor, 453.
10. Greene, GW, I, 462, gives Pickering credit, on his own statement, for suggesting this move.
11. Baurmeister, 18–19; Montresor, 451–453.
12. Marshall, I, 188; Greene, GW, I, 462; Irving, III, 212; Belcher, II, 269; Brooks, 105.
13. Fitzpatrick, IX, 238–239.
14. Kirkwood, 175; Greene, GW, I, 462; Irving, III, 214.
15. Fitzpatrick, IX, 238.
16. Kirkwood, 175.
17. Montresor, 454–456.
18. Lossing, II, 163.
19. Marshall, I, 189.

20. Montresor, 455; André, 49; Baurmeister, 19.
21. Gordon, II, 516–517; Montresor, 455; Marshall, I, 89; Irving, III, 215; Stedman, I, 294; Lossing, II, 163; Baurmeister, 19; André, 49. This was the celebrated "Paoli Massacre," commonly described as a butchery of defenseless men, fleeing from the dreaded bayonet and stabbed to death while crying for mercy. The commander of the British troops was dubbed "No-Flint Grey" and execrated as a brutal murderer. Lossing says that he "marched stealthily" (an infamous practice in surprise attacks, of course), that he gave "his usual order to rush upon the patriots with fixed bayonets without firing a shot" (another indefensible proceeding), and that his men were *"to give no quarters"*—a statement for which there seems to be no basis in fact. Trevelyan (III, 234) attributes the infamy heaped upon Grey to the dread of the bayonet, which was undoubtedly prevalent among the Americans: "Men always attach the idea of cruelty to modes of warfare in which they are not proficient; and Americans liked the bayonet as little as Englishmen approved of taking deliberate aim at individual officers," against which American practice there was frequent outcry from the British, especially the officers. The dread of unaccustomed weapons and the horror of them as brutal appears also in the white man's objections to the Indian tomahawk, which is certainly, in itself, no more cruel or barbarous than the sword or the bayonet.

Against the charge that "quarter had been refused and that the wounded were stabbed to death where they lay," Trevelyan urges the fact that only 53 dead were found on the ground the next day—a statement supported by Lossing, II, 164. It should be noted, also, that many wounded, including 40 badly injured, were actually carried away by the British.

The fact seems to be that the ascription of brutal slaughter to the British was based upon a published letter, said to have been written by a Hessian participant, in which the Americans were described as "running about barefoot and half clothed," while "we killed three hundred" of them with the bayonet. "I struck them myself like so many pigs, one after another, until the blood ran out of the touch-hole of my musket." A sufficient answer to this sanguinary narration is the fact that there were no Hessians in Grey's force. That letter was probably American propaganda.

Wayne was ordered before a court-martial on a charge of having had notice of the enemy's intention to attack and failing to make "a Disposition till it was too late." He was acquitted "with the highest honor."
22. Montresor, 356; André, 51; Baurmeister, 20–21; Robertson, 149–150; Gordon, II, 517.
23. Fitzpatrick, IX, 257, 259.
24. Kirkwood, 177.
25. Montresor, 456–457; André, 31–32; Baurmeister, 20–21; Robertson, 149–151; Gordon, II, 517.
26. Fitzpatrick, IX, 257–259, 262.
27. Baurmeister, 21; Montresor, 457; André, 52; Robertson, 149–150; Gordon, II, 517.
28. Fitzpatrick, IX, 232–253.
29. Marshall, I, 191.
30. *Journals*, VIII, 752; Bancroft, V, 181.
31. Fitzpatrick, IX, 248–249.
32. Stephenson, II, 31; Fitzpatrick, IX, 275.
33. Fitzpatrick, IX, 269, 270.
34. Montresor, 458; André, 26; Baurmeister, 21.

CHAPTER 33

This account of the Battle of Germantown has been drawn from so many sources that it would unduly laden the notes to assign particular authority to each of its several elements. General reference is made to Fitzpatrick, IX, *passim*; Gordon, II, 522;

Stedman, I, 291; Ramsay, II, 15; Kemble, I, 137; Baurmeister, 24–25; Greene, GW, I, 474–481; Marshall, I, 197; Lossing, II, 110–111; Hughes, III, 187–206; Bancroft, V, 193–195; Greene, FV, 91–92; Sullivan, I, 542–547; Anderson, 44–46; Carrington, 382–391; Dawson, 318–331; André, 54–57; Irving, III, 280–287; Lee, 95; Lowell, 201–203; Trevelyan, III, 237–251.

1. Fitzpatrick, IX, 278.
2. Hughes, III, 185.
3. Fitzpatrick, IX, 279.
4. Kirkwood, 188.
5. Fitzpatrick, IX, 308.
6. Carrington, 384; Greene, FV, 92, map; Dawson, I, 330.
7. Fitzpatrick, IX, 309; Greene, FV, 90; Greene, GW, I, 473; Sullivan, I, 542–543.
8. Dawson, I, 324. Fortescue, III, 223, justly criticizes the plan as "too intricate for inexperienced officers and imperfectly disciplined troops." Chastellux, 106, calls it "absolutely chimerical" and criticizes it in detail.
9. Trevelyan, III, 245, has this to say about the break-up of Sullivan's division: "They had travelled through the night. They had been fighting for nearly three hours. They had fired away all their ammunition. Their flank was unprotected. Their reserves stopped behind to help, or to hinder, the attack upon Musgrave's garrison. . . . The roar of the American batteries around the Chew mansion told upon the nerves of Sullivan's exhausted soldiers. A rumor arose and spread that they were being assailed in the rear by a hostile force; and, to the surprise of the officers who commanded them, they broke their ranks and retired from the field in hurry and confusion."
10. Trevelyan, III, 249.

CHAPTER 34

1. Rodney, C, 240.
2. Serle, 253–256.
3. Gordon, II, 519; Stedman, I, 297.
4. Fitzpatrick, IX, 259.
5. Stedman, I, 296; Ramsay, II, 17; Lossing, II, 86.
6. Robertson, 151.
7. Stedman, I, 296.
8. Lossing, II, 293.
9. Montresor, 459.
10. Eelking, 117; Dawson, I, 356.
11. Chastellux, 124.
12. Chastellux, 125.
13. Trevelyan, III, 258.
14. Dawson, I, 355; Stedman, I, 302; Lossing, II, 87–88, 208.
15. Stedman, I, 303–304; Trevelyan, III, 256–260.
16. Waldo, 301.
17. Lossing, II, 90.
18. Lossing, II, 91.
19. Montresor, 474–476.
20. Fisher, II, 50.
21. Montresor, 474–476.
22. Dawson, I, 336.
23. Lossing, II, 93.
24. Fitzpatrick, IX, 266–268.
25. Carrington, 296; Frothingham, 330–331.
26. Fitzpatrick, IX, 462.
27. Fitzpatrick, IX, 318, and X, 19, 20.
28. Fitzpatrick, IX, 318, 319, 351, 358, 375, and X, 19, 24.

29. Kirkwood, 211.
30. Fitzpatrick, IX, 382.
31. Kirkwood, 226.
32. Fitzpatrick, IX, 390–391.
33. Stedman, I, 302; Trevelyan, III, 266.
34. Sparks, *W*, V, 168 n.
35. Marshall, I, 215; Irving, III, 328.
36. Marshall, I, 215.
37. Robertson, 159; André, 57.
38. Baurmeister, 36.
39. Baurmeister, 36.
40. Kirkwood, 265.
41. André, 67; Robertson, 159–160.
42. André, 68.
43. André, 68.
44. André, 69; Robertson, 160; Simcoe, 31; Marshall, I, 215–216. André says one of Simcoe's men was killed and 9 chasseurs killed or wounded, while 20 to 30 Americans fell and 15 were taken. Robertson says a single British officer was killed, 2 were wounded, and about 40 rank and file were killed or wounded. Simcoe, a rather boastful person, claims "near a hundred" American casualties, " little or none" among the King's troops. Marshall admits one officer of Morgan's corps killed and 27 of his men killed or wounded, besides "a small loss" among the militia.
45. Reed, I, 351 n.
46. André, 70.
47. Marshall, I, 217–218; Reed, I, 354; Fitzpatrick, X, 156; Baurmeister, 39; Robertson, 161.
48. Waldo, 305.
49. Marshall, I, 217–218; Reed, I, 354; Fitzpatrick, X, 156; Baurmeister, 39; Robertson, 161.
50. *Journals,* IX, 1029–1030.
51. Fitzpatrick, X, 133 n., 134 n.; Reed, I, 348 n.
52. Fitzpatrick, X, 195–196.
53. Stillé, 112.
54. Hughes, III, 231.
55. Kapp, 137.
56. Sparks, *W*, V, 241 n.

CHAPTER 35

Original sources of information as to Arnold's Champlain battle are to be found in Force's *American Archives,* 4th Series, Vol. IV, and 5th Series, where many letters from and to Arnold, Schuyler, Gates, Hartley, and others appear. Other contemporary sources are Riedesel's and Wilkinson's memoirs, the journals of Wells, Hadden, and Pausch. Secondary sources of much value are Mahan's *Major Operations,* Jones's *Conquest of Canada,* Allen's *Naval History,* Lowell's *Hessians,* and Patterson's *Horatio Gates.* Kenneth Roberts has told the story, in great detail and with historical accuracy, in his novel *Rabble in Arms.*

1. Force, 5, I, 103.
2. Force, 5, I, 232, 238.
3. Jones, CH, 97.
4. Force, 5, I, 339, 376.
5. *Journals,* V, 448; Force, 5, II, 637.
6. Patterson, 69.
7. *Journals,* V, 526.
8. Force, 5, I, 233, 238.

 9. Force, 5, 1, 390, 445, 450, 650.
10. Force, 5, I, 559, 794.
11. Patterson, 85.
12. Jones, CH, 105–106.
13. Force, 5, I, 474, and II, 204. Hartley commanded the 6th Pennsylvania after Col. Irvine's capture at Trois Rivières.
14. Jones, CH, 107.
15. Jones, CH, 111–112.
16. Force, 5, I, 390; Jones, CH, 112.
17. Jones, CH, 125.
18. Force, 5, I, 125, 512, 582, 797, 826, 872, 987.
19. Force, 5, I, 1199.
20. Force, 5, I, 649.
21. Force, 5, I, 745–746.
22. Force, 5, I, 350, 399, 400, 620, 623, 624, 932.
23. Force, 5, I, 209.
24. Force, 5, I, 145, 163, 194, 303, 474, 549, 563, 630, 649, 682.
25. Force, 5, I, 340, 512, 649.
26. This description was supplied by Kenneth Roberts, who secured from the British Admiralty drawings of the *Washington* galley made by a British naval officer after her capture. Before this discovery, no description of the galleys had been obtainable, except the meager account in "a letter from Skenesborough, dated August 16, 1776," printed in Force, 5, I, 988, which merely noted that they were "from sixty to seventy feet in keel and eighteen feet in beam" and gave no description of their shape or their rigging.
27. Force, 5, I, 1123, 1201, and II, 1039.
28. Force, 5, I, 988, and II, 1039.
29. Force, 5, I, 969; Jones, CH, 116.
30. Force, 5, I, 630.
31. Force, 5, II, 1179.
32. Force, 5, II, 1178–1179; Pausch, 75 n.
33. Force, 5, II, 1178. The gondola had been taken from the Americans the day the siege of Quebec was raised. Hence its new name, *Loyal Convert.*
34. Lowell, 109.
35. Riedesel, I, 65.
36. Force, 5, I, 626, 799.
37. Pausch, 74–76; Riedesel, I, 59; Jones, CH, 144, 157–159.
38. Force, 5, I, 1266, and II, 969, 1166, 1201, 1266; Jones, CH, 143–144.
39. Force, 5, II, 223. Kenneth Roberts states that these fascines were made by tying small hemlock trees, each into a bundle, and that they were fixed, butts upward, along the bulwarks of the gondolas and galleys.
40. Force, 5, II, 251, 265, 440, 933.
41. Force, 5, II, 224.
42. Force, 5, II, 481.
43. Force, 5, II, 982. The usual lists of Arnold's fleet in the battle total 15, omitting the *Success;* but Wells notes its arrival on September 11, making 16. It may be noted that Riedesel (I, 73) lists 16 vessels in the American fleet, but does not name them all. The *Liberty* galley was away from the fleet, on command, on the day of the battle. The *Gates* galley had not been finished.
44. Force, 5, II, 591.
45. Force, 5, II, 1179. The description there of the longboats puts one gun in each bow. Riedesel, I, 70, gives them "three cannons each," but Hadden, 23, says one.
46. Mahan, 17–18.
47. Force, 5, II, 224. Mahan, 19, emphasized Arnold's "sounder judgment": "A retreat before square-rigged sailing vessels having a fair wind, by a heterogeneous force like his own, of unequal speeds and batteries, could result only in disaster. . . . Better trust to a steady, well-ordered position, developing the utmost

fire . . . The correctness of Arnold's decision not to chance a retreat was shown in the [results of his] retreat of two days later."

48. Force, 5, II, 1040.
49. Van Tyne, 373–374. Riedesel, I, 83, wrote, "If we could have begun our last expedition four weeks earlier, I am satisfied that everything would have ended this year." Four weeks was exactly the time consumed in building the *Inflexible*. That it was the intention of the British command, if feasible, to join Howe on the Hudson that year is indicated by an extract from a contemporary English paper (Almon, IV, 291) of Sept. 6, 1776: "The design was that the two armies commanded by Generals Howe and Burgoyne should cooperate; that they should both be on the Hudson River at the same time; that they should join about Albany, and thereby cut off all communication between the northern and southern Colonies."
50. Mahan, 25.

CHAPTER 36

1. Hudleston, 69.
2. Fonblanque, 226.
3. Fonblanque, 227; Hudleston, 110; Nickerson, 8.
4. Nickerson, 81.
5. Burgoyne, Appendix, iii; Fonblanque, Appendix C; Nickerson, 83–89. Trevelyan III, 71, attributed the conception of this plan to Germain, but every indication seems to point to Burgoyne's authorship of it. He certainly wrote the paper that the King read and approved.
6. Nickerson, 89–90.
7. Nickerson, 91–94.
8. Nickerson, 94.
9. Hudleston, 114.
10. The best analysis of the plan, and of all others in which Howe was concerned, is in Anderson, *passim*.
11. Hadden, 43; Burgoyne, 9; Anburey, I, 121.
12. Nickerson, 110.
13. Burgoyne, 10. Luc de Chapt de la Corne Saint-Luc, commonly called La Corne St. Luc or even La Corne or St. Luc, was a Frenchman who had seen much service as a leader of Indian bands in King George's War and the French and Indian War. He had entered into the spirit and adopted the methods of Indian warfare with so little compunction and with such great success as to evidence an identity of taste and temperament with his savage followers. He had, consequently, great influence among them. Though past sixty-five at the expulsion of the Americans from Canada, he had been active in raising Indian recruits for Burgoyne and, with physical stamina and hardihood unimpaired, had undertaken their leadership in active service. The Americans feared him even more than they hated him. One described him as "that arch devil incarnate, who has butchered hundreds, men, women and children of our colonies . . . in the most inhuman manner." There seems to be no doubt that he was of a brutal, bloody and pitiless nature, cruel and remorseless in his methods of warfare. Charles de Langlade, a French officer associated with him in command of the Indians, had seen service in the French and Indian War. He is sometimes said to have planned and executed the ambush which resulted in Braddock's defeat.
14. Hadden, 34, 44, 53.
15. Burgoyne, 13.
16. Hadden, 49.
17. Hadden, 44–45; Riedesel, 105–107.
18. Burgoyne, 10–17. Fonblanque, 488, gives the total force as 7,902, presumably including officers.
19. Fonblanque, 240–241; Jones, CH, 158, 181; Nickerson, 116.

20. Riedesel, I, 2–17; Nickerson, 117–118.
21. Hadden, 52; Nickerson, 104–105.
22. Nickerson, 120–122; Anburey, I, 184.
23. Hudleston, 148–151.
24. Walpole, X, 188.
25. Burgoyne, Appendix, xxi; Anburey, I, 168, 174.
26. Walpole, X, 188.
27. Wilkinson, I, 155 ff.
28. Nickerson, 182–183.
29. Wilkinson, I, 169 n.
30. Wilkinson, I, 174–176.
31. Hadden, 54.
32. Lamb, 135.
33. Anburey, I, 182.
34. Hadden, 82.
35. Wilkinson, I, 181.
36. Hadden, 82; Wilkinson, I, 180; Nickerson, 41–42.
37. Burgoyne, Appendix, xxviii, xxxix; Anburey, I, 190.
38. Hadden, 84.
39. Wilkinson, I, 184.
40. Wilkinson, I, 184–185 n.; *The Royal Kalendar* for 1777.
41. Anburey, I, 192.
42. Anburey, I, 193.
43. Burgoyne, Appendix, xxi; Riedesel, I, 113–114.
44. Anburey, I, 194.
45. Wilkinson, I, 186–187.
46. Hadden, 92; Wilkinson, I, 186.
47. Wilkinson, I, 188.
48. Anburey, I, 195.
49. Anburey, I, 196.
50. Wilkinson, I, 187.
51. Riedesel, I, 115–116; Hadden, 85–86; Burgoyne, Appendix, xxxii.
52. Wilkinson, I, 187–188 n.; Hadden, Appendix 15. Hadden, 88, gives the enemy losses as 17 officers and 109 men killed or wounded.
53. Burgoyne, Appendix, xxv; Lamb, 146. Hadden, 89, says the lake was "so narrow that the Ships Yards almost touched the Precipes which overhung them."
54. Riedesel, I, 117.
55. Wilkinson, I, 186, 190.
56. Burgoyne, Appendix, xxxi.
57. Burgoyne, Appendix, xxxiv.
58. Lamb, 142.
59. Wilkinson, I, 189.

CHAPTER 37

Among the original sources of information for this chapter and the next following are Burgoyne's *State of the Expedition,* Hadden's *Journal,* Anburey's *Travels,* Wilkinson's *Memoirs,* Riedesel's *Memoirs,* Lamb's *Memoirs,* Digby's journal, and the letters of Schuyler. Secondary sources of value are Coburn's *Centennial History,* Hall's *Battle of Bennington,* Dawson's *Battles,* Lowell's *Hessians,* Lossing's *Pictorial Field Book,* Fonblanque's *Political and Military Episodes,* Hudleston's *Gentleman Johnny Burgoyne,* Patterson's *Horatio Gates,* Neilson's *Original Account of Burgoyne's Campaign,* Stone's *Campaign of Lieut. Gen. John Burgoyne,* Gordon's *History* and Stedman's. Nickerson's *Turning Point of the Revolution,* a large book devoted entirely to Burgoyne's campaign, is the fullest account. Its value to succeeding historians is definitely and considerably less than it might be, because the author has not provided a single footnote or specific reference by which the verity of any statement in it or the validity of any of his conclusions or opinions may be tested.

1. Burgoyne, Appendix, vi.
2. Burgoyne, 17.
3. Hadden, Appendix I.
4. Hadden, 100; Burgoyne, Appendix, xxxvi.
5. Hadden, 91–96; Burgoyne, Appendix, xxxv.
6. Hadden, 109.
7. Nickerson, 186; Wilkinson, I, 192, 200; Sparks, *C*, I, 397–399.
8. Trevelyan, III, 120.
9. Stedman, I, 327; Hadden, 94.
10. Burgoyne, Appendix, xi, xxxvi.
11. Hadden, 95, 97.
12. Wilkinson, Appendix B.
13. Nickerson, 18, gives this quotation with no indication of its source.
14. Burgoyne, Appendix, xii, xlvi, xlix.
15. Riedesel, I, 125–126; Burgoyne, 51.
16. Burgoyne, 137, Appendix, xiv.
17. Riedesel, I, 101, states that, before the southward march of Burgoyne's force began, in June, 1777, he had ordered for the dragoons "long linen trousers, striped with white and blue, and similar to those worn by the inhabitants during summer." That these were actually provided and displaced the leather breeches does not appear.
18. Burgoyne, Appendix, lxiii; Hadden, 111–117.
19. Burgoyne, Appendix, xii; Lamb, 151.
20. Burgoyne, Appendix, lxiii.
21. Coburn, B, 22–23.
22. Lossing, I, 393.
23. Stryker, *TP*, 350.
24. Coburn, B, 31.
25. Lossing, I, 394; Sparks, *C*, I, 397, 423.
26. Lossing, I, 394.
27. *Journals*, VIII, 656–657.
28. Riedesel, I, 128.
29. Burgoyne, Appendix, xi.
30. Dawson, I, 260.
31. Burgoyne, Appendix, lxx.
32. Lossing, I, 395, says there was no bridge there at that time, but only a ford. He calls the river Walloomscoick.
33. Dawson, I, 260.
34. Coburn, B, 40.
35. Dawson, I, 260.
36. Riedesel, I, 130; Lamb, I, 153. Burgoyne, Appendix, xiii, says many of these Americans took the oath of allegiance and were afterwards the first to fire on Baum.
37. Lossing, I, 397 n. This historic order is reported by the historians generally, with slight differences in verbiage.
38. Riedesel, I, 131.
39. Hadden, 118; Riedesel, I, 129–130.
40. Dawson, I, 264; Anburey, I, 233. Burgoyne (Appendix, xiv) wrote to Germain on August 20: "Could Mr. Breyman have marched at the rate of two miles an hour, any given twelve hours out of the two and thirty, success would probably have ensued."
41. Dawson, I, 264; Riedesel, I, 131.
42. Coburn, B, 55.
43. Dawson, I, 264.
44. Dawson, I, 260.
45. The various estimates of losses on both sides differ, as usual. The statement in the text seems to be approximately correct.
46. *Journals*, IX, 770.